DYNAMIC HTML

Natanya Pitts-Moultis,
C.C. Sanders, and Ramesh Chandak

Publisher
Keith Weiskamp

Acquisitions Editor
Shari Jo Hehr

Project Editor
Toni Zuccarini

Production Coordinators
Wendy Littley
Kim Eoff

Cover Design
Anthony Stock

Layout Design
April Nielsen

CD-ROM Development
Robert Clarfield

Dynamic HTML Black Book

Limits of Liability and Disclaimer of Warranty

Trademarks

The Coriolis Group, Inc.
An International Thomson Publishing Company
14455 N. Hayden Road, Suite 220
Scottsdale, Arizona 85260

602.483.0192
FAX 602.483.0193
http://www.coriolis.com

Library of Congress Cataloging-In-Publication Data
Pitts, Natanya.
Dynamic HTML black book / by Natanya Pitts, C.C. Sanders, and Ramesh Chandak
p. cm.
Includes index.
ISBN 1-57610-188-6
1. DHTML (Document markup language) I. Sanders, C. C. (Claire C.), 1971-
II. Chandak, Ramesh. III. Title.
QA76.76.H94P58 1998
005.7'2—dc21 98-10578
CIP

Albany, NY • Belmont, CA • Bonn • Boston • Cincinnati • Detroit • Johannesburg • London
Madrid • Melbourne • Mexico City • New York • Paris • Singapore • Tokyo • Toronto • Washington

Printed in the United States of America
10 9 8 7 6 5 4 3 2 1

Acknowledgments

Before the authors express their individual notes of thanks and appreciation, we'd like to start by thanking two wonderful and talented teams of individuals who helped to bring this project to its fruition: the talented gang at LANWrights, which includes Mary Burmeister, Our Lady of the Glossaries; David (DJ) Johnson, our General Manager and Project Leader extraordinaire; and especially Dawn Rader, the Queen of Editors in our local universe; plus, the equally talented bunch at the Coriolis Group, which includes Keith Weiskamp, our peerless Publisher; Shari Jo Hehr, Empress of Acquisitions; Toni Zuccarini, our editor (and now an author in her own right); plus Sandra Lassiter's immensely talented production forces, including Tony Stock, Wendy Littley, and Kim Eoff. To one and all, our profound thanks and heartfelt appreciation for your many contributions, both large and small.

Natanya Pitts-Moultis

There is a large crowd of people who made this book, and its author's continued sanity, possible. First, my loving thanks to my husband Colin, who withstood every storm and stood by me every step of the way, even as we advanced to our "Big Day." A giant thank you to my bosses, DJ and Ed Tittel, for giving me opportunities, wisdom, and guidance I couldn't find anywhere else. Also, thanks to C.C. Sanders and Ramesh Chandak, my co-authors, for providing strong content and good writing and for helping us make those deadlines!

I also have special thanks for certain staff at LANWrights. Dawn: What a nice job you did of adding a final polish to each and every page; plus, thanks for being such a great friend. Mary: Not only did you handle the Glossary and other petty details, you oversaw software and screen shot permissions; anyway, how could I be ungrateful to a fellow "Days" fan? Michael: Thanks for listening to me rant when things got tough, and for always providing a level-headed perspective on any problem, no matter how big or how small.

To my parents, Charles and Swanya, for believing in me for all these years. To DJ, who's been there, in so many ways, for the last ten years. To Jim, who taught me how to fly on my own. Even though we're not in the same place anymore, we're still somehow always together. And finally, to my two feline familiars, Gandalf and Nada, who always seem to know exactly when to sit on my keyboard and offer a warm purr.

C.C. Sanders

Thanks to Coriolis Group Books, particularly to Toni Zuccarini for her foresight and patience. Thanks also to everyone at LANWrights, especially my co-authors, Natanya Pitts-Moultis and Ramesh Chandak, as well as to David Johnson, Dawn Rader, and Mary Burmeister for their invaluable work. As always, thanks to Ed Tittel for making the project a reality.

This book was infinitely expanded through Chris Brown's kind skill and wizardry; many thanks to him, as well as to Virginia Brown of VCommunications, for their wonderful CD-ROM contributions. The DHTML creations and insight from Olivia Ongpin and Jeff Rule were also extremely valuable. Finally, thanks to my parents, George Sanders and Karen Larvick, and to my sisters, Camille and Christine Sanders, for their support over the years, and to Gina Lalli for her teachings and friendship during the writing of this book.

Ramesh Chandak

Publishing a book is the result of the combined effort of a number of different people. I would like to thank Ed Tittel and David (DJ) Johnson at LANWrights, Inc. for giving me the opportunity to be part of this book. I would also like to thank my wife, Kavita, for her endless patience and understanding in keeping me focused and supporting my writing efforts. Finally, I would like to thank my parents, Manoharlal and Padmavati Chandak, my brother and sister-in-law, Purshottam and Padmini Chandak, my Masi-Masaji, Shriniwas and Leelavati Chandak, and my Jiji-Jijaji, Shriniwas and Pramodini Soni and Satyanarayan and Prafulla Bihani, for their never-ending love, support, and patience.

Table Of Contents

Introduction

Welcome to the *Dynamic HTML Black Book*! This book is designed to help you understand and master the terminology and notation that underlies what is called Dynamic HTML (usually referred to as DHTML in Web designer's lingo). DHTML offers an amazing opportunity for page designers to create and manage interactive, dynamic content and behavior on their Web pages, and to endow them with unique capabilities and self-modifying characteristics. DHTML makes it much easier for Web designers to customize pages for a particular look and feel, and to create attractive, customized navigation and display elements.

That's why we've aimed this book not just at explaining and exploring the structure, syntax, and capabilities of DHTML, but also at describing best practices and efficient uses. We've included plenty of dos and don'ts related to the everyday use of DHTML. We've also built a set of ready reference materials at the end of the book, and have incorporated in-depth case studies and real-world implementation details wherever possible. This book also explores differing versions of DHTML in detail, and includes "guided tours" of some pretty cool sites to boot. In other words, we've tried to leaven the concepts and theories that drive and inform how DHTML behaves with plenty of practice and examples to give those ideas form and substance!

Nevertheless, to completely master this method for controlling the look and feel of Web pages, you must build some DHTML documents of your own. Nothing will help you appreciate their capabilities—and their shortcomings—like modifying existing DHTML documents for your own purposes or building your own style sheets from scratch. For that reason, we've built a Web page that you can access at **www.lanw.com/DHTMLBB.htm** that includes examples and source code from the book. These ready-made examples can be a source of raw material for your own experiments, and might help save time and energy in bringing the value and control that DHTML offers to your own Web site.

Just remember: When it comes to new tools and technologies, a book like ours can be an essential part of the learning process; but hands-on experience remains the best teacher.

What's DHTML All About?

With the release of the HTML 4.0 standard in "Recommended" form on December 18, 1997, there's no topic that falls under its broad and all-encompassing umbrella that's attracted as much furor as Dynamic HTML. Although this controversy and excitement make a book on Dynamic HTML quite interesting, it also introduces a certain element of risk to our endeavor. In fact, much of what we write about herein is subject to change, and many of the final details that will ultimately define DHTML have yet to be resolved, if only from the standpoint of what the World Wide Web Consortium (W3C) considers to represent a "standard" version of DHTML. Nevertheless, we feel strongly that there's enough interesting and useful terminology, tools, and technology in place around this subject to make this book quite worthwhile. Starting with dueling proposals from Microsoft and Netscape, and continuing with some radically different ideas about what the "dynamic" part of Dynamic HTML really means, this topic has been a bone of contention since it was initially introduced.

The basic notion behind Dynamic HTML is fairly straightforward, no matter which interpretation you might be inclined to follow: The idea is that making existing page content mutable, so that its appearance can change after it has been downloaded, relieves Web servers of the burden of having to generate and deliver new versions of a document every time some minor change occurs. This lets the client handle making such changes (as long as it knows how) and relieves the server of carrying the burden of dynamism, on top of everything else it has to do.

Of course, the details are considerably more complex than this brief overview might suggest. In the chapters that follow, you'll learn more about those details, and the competing points of view that drive them, along with where emerging standards for Dynamic HTML are headed. Better yet, you'll be able to understand the true value of Dynamic HTML to Web page authors and users alike, and why this capability may be one of the most interesting innovations to hit HTML since interactive forms in HTML 2.0.

When taken in tandem with Cascading Style Sheets (CSS), Dynamic HTML offers capabilities that permit Web documents to display the kind of interactive behavior that has heretofore been limited to those with the time and money to spend buying and learning Java-based, object-oriented Web authoring environments. By the time you finish reading this book, you should have a pretty good idea of what this nascent technology might mean to your own Web pages.

How This Book Is Organized

We've broken this book into five parts, to cover the subject of DHTML as thoroughly and completely as current circumstances—and the state of the existing technology and terminology—will permit. In Part 1 we lay the basic groundwork for DHTML. Chapter 1 describes and explains the current state of HTML and how things got to where they stood as of December 18, 1997 (when the HTML 4.0 specification attained recommended status at the W3C). We then continue on in Chapter 2 to describe HTML's limitations and capabilities, before moving into Chapter 3, an overview of DHTML as a conceptual framework, independent of contrasting notions as to how it might be explained or implemented. In the following chapter, we position our more or less abstract depiction of DHTML to this point within its present-day context, and discuss differing versions of this technology, as viewed by Microsoft, Netscape, and the W3C itself.

In Part 2, we tackle Microsoft's view of DHTML and begin our first serious foray into the Document Object Model (DOM), upon which so much of the most important thinking and work related to DHTML rest. In Chapter 5, the DOM is explored and explained in detail, followed in Chapter 6 by an explanation and exploration of the capabilities and roles that Cascading Style Sheets (CSS) can play in DHTML documents. Chapter 7 concludes Part 2 with a description of the changes and enhancements introduced into HTML 4.0 to make DHTML possible, while also covering certain proprietary terms and tags present in Internet Explorer and Netscape Navigator.

In Part 3 of the book, we switch gears a bit to explore how you might use DHTML and its components and capabilities in your own Web pages. Each chapter provides a separate focus and is intended to empower its readers to enact what they read about. The majority of these chapters focuses on task-oriented "how-to" information, beginning with Chapter 8, which explains the features of HTML 4.0 that address or interact with the DOM, and also covers how the DOM relates to HTML extensions and proprietary tags from Netscape and Microsoft. In Chapter 9, we explore DHTML's event model and list the categories and types of events that DHTML supports. This chapter also explains how events are treated in DHTML and which elements of HTML 4.0 and DHTML are involved in manipulating or delivering content in event-driven situations. Chapter 10 covers how DHTML permits connections to external data sources and databases to be established, and covers the methods that apply to creating and managing external data sources within the DHTML environment. Chapters 11 and 12 cover sound and graphics respectively, including how to work with appropriate data formats and resources, and how to most effectively use the many special-purpose tags and attributes related to these types of data. Chapter 13 concludes Part 4 with an explanation of how to lay out and structure data using various DHTML methods and techniques, and how to arrange such information to support the broadest possible audiences.

Part 4 shifts its focus to concentrate on the Netscape version of DHTML, and explains what layers are good for, and how they may best be used. This part of the book covers how Netscape's **LAYER** tags and related markup works, provides detailed hands-on instructions, and presents and analyzes numerous examples that show how layers can be used in a variety of different situations. Chapter 14 begins this adventure by explaining Netscape's layer model in detail, followed by a discussion of event-handling in Chapter 15. Chapter 16 covers data sources and layers, and describes how external sources of data may be addressed and manipulated. External data sources are explored and explained, linkages discussed, and typical data management tasks covered on a step-by-step basis. Chapter 17 concludes this part of the book with coverage of how sound and graphics files operate within the Netscape framework.

Part 5 concludes the book by addressing the interesting, but sometimes somber, realities that Web authors must confront when seeking to implement DHTML on their own Web sites. Most important, these chapters describe how to create DHTML that works equally well for both Netscape and Microsoft environments. In fact, Chapter 18 devotes itself entirely to this subject, as it explores how objects are positioned, moved, and addressed within the Netscape model and how that differs from Microsoft's approach. This chapter explores those differences, while also providing some tips on how to minimize them and build documents that support both DHTML models. Chapter 19 concludes the book with a series of case studies of actual Web sites based on DHTML; we'll explore their capabilities and explain their strengths and weaknesses.

Following the main body of the book, you'll find a set of supplementary appendices. Starting with a glossary of technical terms, you'll find a list of related resources, both on- and offline, an alphabetized list of DHTML tags and markup, and pointers to the HTML, DHTML, and related specification documents. These materials should help you to further develop your knowledge and appreciation of DHTML and should provide pointers to help you keep tabs on this emerging technology. Finally, the back matter to this book concludes with an index that you can use to search for specific terms or topics, should you decide to use our book as a reference tool.

How To Use This Book

If you're a newcomer to DHTML, we've structured the topics in this book to build upon themselves, so that some topics in later chapters will make more sense if you read the earlier chapters first. That's why we suggest you read it from front to back for your initial pass. If you need to brush up on a topic, or you have to refresh your memory after errors in your work indicate something's missing in your knowledge of syntax or structure there are several areas to examine. If your problem's tag-related, consult Appendix C. If it's a matter of terminology, please try the Glossary in Appendix A. Otherwise, use the Index or Table of Contents to go straight to the topics and markup that you need to review. We hope you find the book useful as a reference to all the important aspects of DHTML and their use alongside HTML documents, or in separate documents or sites by themselves.

Given all the book's elements, and its focus, we've tried to create a tool that you can use to learn about—and build—DHTML of your own (or perhaps just DHTML elements for an existing Web site). Please do share your feedback on the book with us, especially if you have ideas about how we could improve it for future readers. We'll consider everything you say carefully, and respond to all suggestions (if only with a thank-you email). The authors are all available via email at **natanya@lanw.com** (Natanya Pitts-Moultis), **hoyden@outer.net** (C.C. Sanders), or **rksoftware@worldnet.att.net** (Ramesh Chandak). Please remember to include the title of this book in your message.

Thanks, and enjoy the book!

PART 1

INTRODUCTION

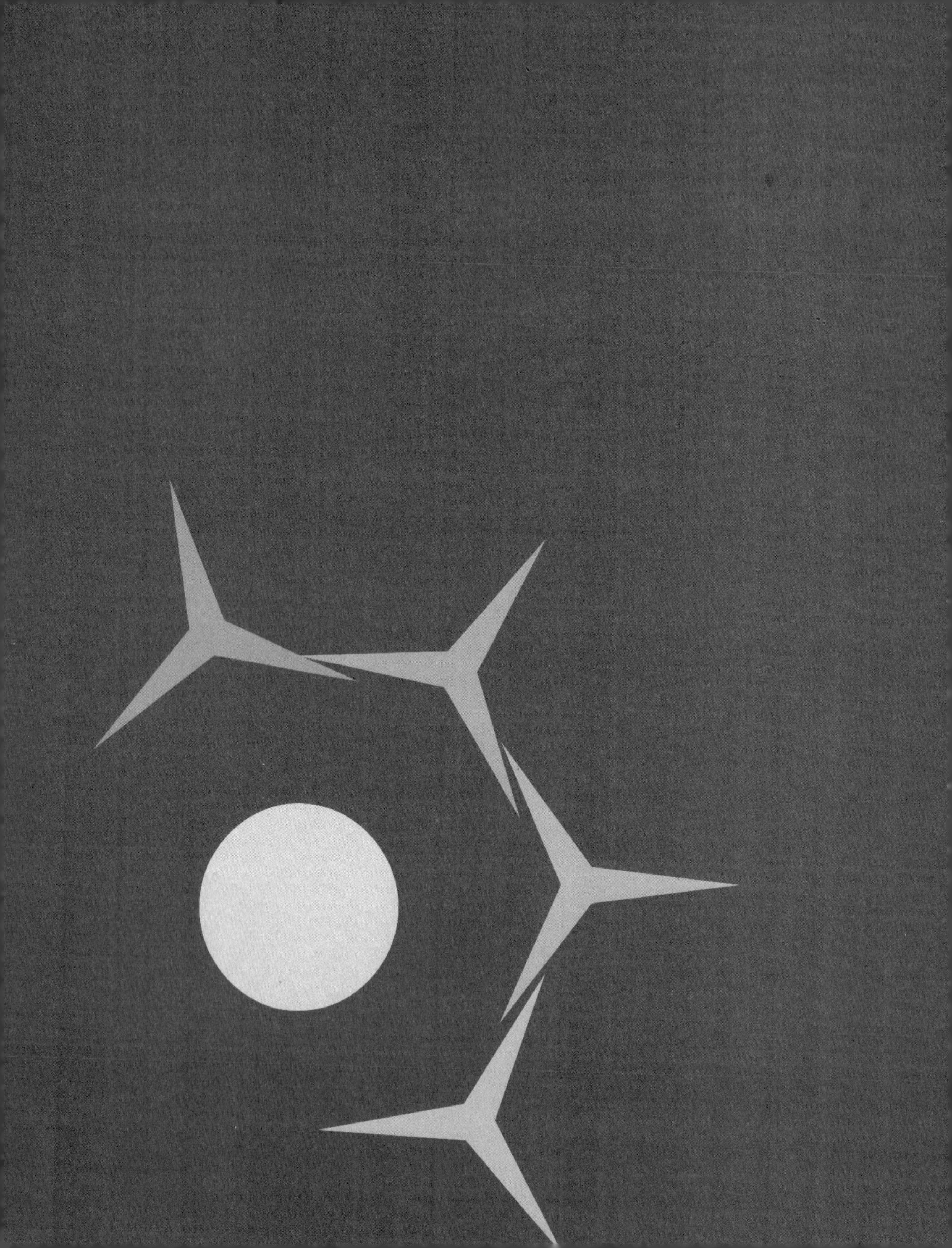

Chapter 1

How We Arrived Here: A Brief History Of The Web And HTML

To fully understand how we've gotten where we are, we must take a good look at the road we've traveled. Chapter 1 recounts the history of HTML up to the current 4.0 proposal and lays the groundwork for the explanation of why there is a need for Dynamic HTML.

Notes...

Chapter 1

With much hype and commercialism, the World Wide Web (WWW or Web) has become the latest and greatest societal trend. Hypertext Markup Language (HTML) provides the foundation for the Web and makes all Web things possible. Because its popularity has grown at such an amazing rate, few have taken the time to investigate the origins of the Web. As Cicero wrote: "Not to know what happened before you were born is to always remain a child."

Granted, not having a thorough understanding of the origins of HTML probably won't cause you to revert spontaneously to childhood. However, a broad knowledge of how HTML and the Web came to be will provide you with insight into the current status of the Web and its future. With this in mind, and because Dynamic HTML is the future of the Web, it seems appropriate to begin the book with a brief look at the history of the Web and HTML, and then to chart its growth to the current state, HTML 4.0.

How The Web And HTML Came To Be

HTML as we know it was created by Tim Berners-Lee at the European Laboratory for Particle Physics (CERN) during the early 1990s. While Berners-Lee's efforts resulted in the creation of the Web and ultimately HTML, he was not the first to attempt to create a nonlinear hypertext model. Berners-Lee's work gathered many scattered pieces, put them into place as part of a whole, and created a glue that would keep them all together and allow them to run on any platform with any software. Before we look at Berners-Lee's final steps toward the creation of a functioning hypertext system, we should tip our hats to a couple of hypertext pioneers: Ted Nelson and Bill Atkinson.

Ted Nelson's Xanadu

Although Tim Berners-Lee is credited with the creation of HTML, Ted Nelson deserves full kudos for the invention of the term *hypertext.* Nelson's adventures in the computing world began in the early 1960s when he was a student at Swarthmore College studying for a master's degree in sociology. A computer science course created for humanities students introduced him to the potential roles of computers in the world of writing and human thought. Even though the only computers available at the time were mainframes—large, expensive, clunky, and altogether unsuitable for regular use by regular people—Nelson spent a great deal of time working on theories of how computers could be used for more than just number crunching.

In a paper presented to the Association of Computer Machinery in 1965, Nelson first used the word hypertext. His vision of hypertext included linked images and moving video, detailed hypermaps, and other forms of links to resources on any computer. Nelson called his vision Xanadu, after the mythical city in Samuel Taylor Coleridge's *Kubla Khan.* Although Nelson's vision of hypertext was remarkably clairvoyant, his Xanadu has become as mythical as its namesake. Nelson announced that Xanadu would be released in 1976, 1988, 1991, and again in 1995. In 1998, some 30-odd years after Nelson first coined the term hypertext, Xanadu is still a vision in one man's mind (or two, if you count Coleridge).

Bill Atkinson's HyperCard

Bill Atkinson, the creator of such great software as MultiFinder and MacPaint and a friend to Macintosh users everywhere, is responsible for the first practical and usable implementation of hypertechnology. HyperCard, released by Apple in 1987, utilized the Macintosh graphical user interface (GUI) to create a virtual stack of cards on the computer screen. HyperCard users could include text, multimedia, graphics, navigation, and buttons on respective cards. Using HyperTalk, an interpreted programming language that was easy to learn and use, cards in a stack could be programmed to accept and respond to keyboard and mouse input. Complex games and information packages were created using HyperCard.

Although the basic concept behind HyperCard is sound, the actual implementation of the software is severely limited. The most notable omission was (and still is) the ability to create hyperlinks in text. The only way to move from one card to the other is via a programmable button. In addition, cards in a stack were limited to one size and could be viewed only in black-and-white. Regardless of these limitations, HyperCard quickly became a popular product, and, as competitive products were released, the original HyperCard was improved to support colors, multiple card sizes, scripting, and more. However, the ability to create hyperlinks was never added. HyperCard's ultimate limitation lies in its standalone status. There is no convention built into HyperCard that allows it to connect to other computers or data sources, limiting it to the resources on its host computer. Still, the idea behind HyperCard—the ability to combine and link to a wide collection of resources in a nonlinear fashion—along with Nelson's hypertext laid the groundwork for Berners-Lee and the Web.

Tim Berners-Lee's World Wide Web

When Tim Berners-Lee first joined CERN, he was working on a high-energy particle accelerator. Soon he became involved in solving a major problem plaguing the scientists at CERN and other research institutions: how to communicate and share data while using disparate computer platforms and software. This seemingly small problem prevented scientists from sharing their findings and inhibited collaboration. Working from Enquire, a program he had written for himself to make note taking and note keeping more closely resemble the human thought process, Berners-Lee created a plan for a large, shared database of information. This database was not like other databases, though. It was spread out over as many computers as necessary, and no one was in charge of it. Hypertext would be used to query the database and could create relationships between the data with hyperlinks. Berners-Lee called his concept the *World Wide Web.*

Although the concept was great, it was still just a concept. Issues of platform and software incompatibility were just the first to be considered, and even before that CERN had to approve the idea. In 1989, CERN gave Berners-Lee the go-ahead to work on his Web, and he began work in 1990. Among the problems Berners-Lee had to overcome were:

- How to avoid the loss of information if databases created by Web participants were erased or shut down as participants left.

- How to incorporate incompatible platforms, operating systems, and software into a single system.

- How to create a robust hierarchical system that would stand the test of time.
- How to deal with nontextual information.
- How to organize information without limiting the indexing to one particular format or perspective.

The ultimate solution to all of these problems was a distributed hypertext system. Participants kept data on their own computers, which were connected to a publicly available network to facilitate access. Once the ultimate public network, the Internet, was incorporated into the system it truly would become a World Wide Web. Making the solution a reality involved creating client and server software; generating appropriate protocols such as Hypertext Transfer Protocol (HTTP); and, of course, creating HTML as the universal language of the Web.

What we've described in a few sentences took many years to make a reality, and that reality is constantly evolving to accommodate the demands of science, education, government, business, and everyday people. Just as the data of the Web is dynamic, so are its foundations and practices. It only makes sense that its ultimate facilitator, HTML, should also be dynamic.

What We Can Learn From The History Of HTML

When looked at in the right (or a different) light, the history of the Web and HTML can teach us much about its founders' intentions, as well as the mechanisms built into it. Nelson saw computers and hypertext as a way to facilitate writing and thought; Atkinson created a visual card stack to communicate with pictures, text, sounds, and scripting; and Berners-Lee was solving a communications problem when he created the World Wide Web. This shows that the Web and HTML were founded in human thought and communication—from the very beginning the goal of hypertext has been to use technology to facilitate human interaction. Even the briefest look at the mechanisms of the Web reflect this theory:

- Basic HTML is straightforward and easy to learn.
- HTML files are plain-text files that can run on any computer system.
- HTML, created from SGML, was developed to describe a document's structure and make it easier to communicate regardless of formatting (see the SGML section later in the chapter).

- HTTP functions as part of the standardized, noncommercial TCP/IP protocol suite, which all major networking systems support.

These points cover the basic Web and HTML implementations, but do not address (for obvious reasons) the newer, more glamourous technologies, such as animation and advanced multimedia demanded by the commercialization of the Web. At their roots, the Web and HTML are part of an advanced communication system that allows people all around the world to share any kind of information. Complications such as browser incompatibilities and proprietary technologies are not part of the original intent of hypertext and the Web, so they aren't relevant to this discussion.

The goal of this look at the history of the Web and HTML is to remind you that, as Web developers, we are working within a vast communications system (a fact that too often gets obscured by graphics and color) and are (in theory) attempting to share information with others in the best possible way. When you take away the sound, colors, glitz, and glitter, all that's left is content, so content is where we should start. To that end, we continue our look at the history of the Web and HTML with an overview of SGML and then continue with a discussion of its relationship to HTML. When we're finished, we bet you'll see your Web pages in a whole new light.

The SGML/HTML Link

HTML is a subset of the Standard Generalized Markup Language (SGML). What does this mean in plain English? More importantly, what does this mean to you as a Web author? Both of these questions are best answered by taking a side trip into the world of SGML.

A Brief History Of SGML

Since the dawn of computing, a variety of computer platforms has been the norm. It seems that no one has ever been able to agree on how a computer should work, so multiple platforms and operating systems have emerged over time. Along with these disparate platforms and systems comes the problem of porting documents from one kind of computer to another. SGML was developed in the 1960s as a possible solution to this problem.

SGML was created by Charles Goldfarb, Ed Mosher, and Ray Lorie (the original G, M, and L) as a proprietary file format for document interchange at IBM. Their work for IBM was eventually made into a publicly available system in the 1980s and is now governed by ISO standard 8879.

SGML Primer

Basically, SGML provides a formal way to describe all of the parts—headings, styles, paragraphs, and so on—that make up a document. Every part of a document must be defined; definitions are created so that they can be consistently rendered regardless of the platform on which they are displayed. SGML can describe any kind of document ranging from government and airplane specifications to cookbooks and works of fiction. SGML uses markup, formatting, and other processing commands added to a document's text to describe the parts of an SGML document.

The description of an SGML document focuses solely on structure and is not related to any visual formatting. For example, SGML recognizes a first-level heading not as a bit of text rendered in 36-point Times, but as a top-level head in a hierarchical structure of information. Because the way a document is displayed is determined entirely by software and computer platform, SGML separates a document's structure from its physical appearance, thereby removing all dependency on platform, operating systems, and software. No one vendor has proprietary control of SGML because it is controlled by the ISO, so it will always be an open and stable standard of document formatting and communication.

An SGML document is made up of three different parts:

- *Declaration*—An SGML declaration specifies which characters and delimiters are legal to use within a particular document.
- *Document Type Definition*—An SGML DTD is a list of rules to which an SGML document must conform, including information about what markup is valid in the document and the document's structure.
- *Document Instance*—This is the actual document that contains the content and markup to be rendered by an SGML system. Many SGML documents may reference the same declaration and DTD.

HTML's Piece Of The SGML World

As we mentioned earlier, HTML is a subset of SGML, and after our short introduction to SGML anyone familiar with HTML will begin to see how they're related. All HTML documents are, in reality, SGML documents. HTML's declaration says that the ISO-Latin-1 character set is the one used to create HTML documents, and the less-than, greater-than, slash, ampersand, and semicolon are all markup delimiters. The HTML DTD is really the current version of the standard, 4.0 for now. Finally, every Web page is an HTML document instance.

SGML describes structure and not visible layout, but we all know that Web pages are very visual (isn't that why we're here now?). Although HTML is standard and part of SGML, it describes formatting rather than structure. The ultimate on-screen display is not related to the markup language at all. So who decides how structural elements should be translated into visible layout? The browsers, of course. This accounts for different browser interpretations of HTML markup. Each browser supports its own version of the HTML DTD as well as its interpretation of how elements should be displayed on screen. These different DTDs usually begin with a core based on the current HTML standard, and then proprietary tags are added in response to user demands to give the browser an edge in the market. The result of this process is that Web developers try to write a single instance of HTML that will work with a collection of DTDs. And all along you thought you were just working with one markup language. Fooled ya.

The Truth About HTML: Defining Structures, Not Format

Knowing that HTML describes structure and not formatting and that browser manufacturers decide how HTML should be interpreted visually might make you rethink your approach to Web page design. If you remember that you're describing a document's structure rather than just laying elements out on a page to create a visual effect you will actually create better Web pages that are easier for users to view. By conforming to the rules of the HTML DTD and avoiding odd workarounds, like using **<BLOCKQUOTE>** to create page indentations, you'll come closer to creating pages that are displayed consistently from browser to browser.

But wait; isn't that a contradiction? Each browser interprets the HTML DTD differently, so how can conforming to the DTD guarantee more consistent display from browser to browser? The browser manufacturers really do understand that HTML describes document structure, and their rendering of HTML elements is built on that understanding. It's when you try to force HTML to do something that violates the document structure rule—such as the aforementioned **<BLOCKQUOTE>** trick—that you're asking the browser to go against its nature.

Creative use of tables is an example of working within HTML's structural conventions to push Web page design to its very limits. Have you ever wondered why complex tables created to specify margins and exact element placement are inconsistently displayed from one browser to the other? Once you realize that table markup was not created to define document structure, you're wondering should be over. Does this mean you should create only plain, horizontally designed pages? Not at all; we're just saying you should work within the bounds of the HTML markup language and always concentrate on describing document structure rather than layout. A document's layout is intended to reflect and enhance its structure. If you concentrate on structure, layout will follow.

HTML is profoundly affected by its affiliation with SGML. New technologies such as DHTML draw on HTML's SGML ancestry to create more-advanced Web pages. However, without an understanding of this relationship it can be very difficult to comprehend and implement the new technologies. As we said earlier, we hope you see your HTML pages in an entirely new light. Now let's take a look at the history of HTML.

A Brief History Of HTML

Just as software and operating systems have versions, so does HTML. The theory is that each new version improves on the previous version. (That theory is debatable for some software packages, but that's another book.) The theory holds true for HTML. As the HTML DTD has moved from one version to the next, it has expanded and improved by responding to both users' and developers' demands for extended capabilities. Unfortunately, the standard DTD rarely reflects the different browser DTDs put into place by browser developers.

The World Wide Web Consortium (W3C), the standards body responsible for maintaining and standardizing HTML, is made up of committees with representatives from the industry and research and educational institutions. The job of the committees is to create a standard version of HTML that is vendor-neutral so that one developer is not favored over another. Originally, browser development was driven by the current standard. However, because committees take much longer to update a standard than developers' research and development departments do, the browsers quickly began to outpace the standard in support of new HTML features.

A perfect example of this is table markup. HTML 2.0 does not include any mechanism—other than preformatted text—for creating tables. Netscape was the first to create table tags, and Microsoft soon followed. By the time the HTML 3.2 standard that supports tables was introduced, table markup had been part of Navigator and Internet Explorer for over a year. Instead of the developers being guided by the standard, the standard is very much guided by developers. Users clamor for new tags, and developers deliver. Because people have become accustomed to using the tags and are oblivious to the truth about the multiple HTML DTDs, they assume the tags are here to stay. At that point, the standards committee has its hands tied. It can't very well call the tags back, and even if it did, the chances of a browser developer removing the tags from its own proprietary DTDs are slim to none.

The W3C HTML standards committee is attempting to change this current trend in developer control of HTML by moving much more quickly to improve the HTML standards. Developers have also pledged (in theory) to be guided by the work of the standards committee. Market share and user demands make it hard to keep this pledge.

As with the history of hypertext, the following coverage of the evolution of HTML should shed some light on how it has grown to encompass user demands:

- *HTML 0*—HTML 0 was the original prototype of HTML, as developed on the CERN servers. It was never released to the public, and you'd be hard-pressed to find a tool that actually functions at this level of HTML.
- *HTML 1.0*—HTML 1.0 was the first public release of HTML that included basic document structure elements (headings, paragraphs, line breaks, etc.) as well as the ability to link to other documents and graphical elements. There are still some Web browsers, such as early versions of Lynx, that support only HTML 1.0.
- *HTML 2.0*—HTML 2.0 was the first version of HTML to be widely used by the public. Netscape 2.0 and Mosaic 2.0 both supported this DTD, which included all the elements from HTML 1.0 as well as additional formatting tags. This release saw the introduction of forms as a way to solicit user input and create some semblance of interactivity on Web pages. It was the standard for quite a lot longer than previous versions of HTML.
- *HTML 3.2 (a.k.a. Wilbur)*—HTML 3.2 is the current "official" version. It includes table support, even more formatting tags, and a wider selection of attributes for more closely controlling content display. HTML 3.2 saw the explosion of color on Web pages for everything ranging from fonts to backgrounds. The **<EMBED>** and **<APPLET>** tags brought non-HTTP objects, such as sound, video, and Java applets, to Web pages. All the current full release versions of the standard Web browsers support HTML 3.2.

- *HTML 4.0 (a.k.a. Cougar)*—HTML 4.0 is quickly on its way to official status and should supplant 3.2 by the end of 1998. It is technically a proposal; that is, it's nearing the final stages of becoming a standard but is still open for suggestions and discussion. Cougar implements full support of the Cascading Style Sheets Level 1 (CSS1) standard for controlling page elements. This version of HTML also offers scripting support and advanced form markup that is geared toward making Web pages more interactive and more dynamic. Both Navigator 4.0 and Internet Explorer 4.0 fully support HTML 4.0.

HTML is growing in leaps and bounds, and there is no indication that it is going to stop any time soon. In HTML 4.0, we see the direct influence of another W3C standard—CSS1—on the HTML standard; without using style sheets you can't take full advantage of HTML 4.0. We predict that when HTML 5.0 is released, the same will be true of the Dynamic HTML standard (whatever it may turn out to be).

Now What?

Now that you're up to speed on the past and present of HTML, we need to take an objective look at its strengths and weaknesses. Obviously, HTML does something right since the Web is such a popular place, but let's be frank: If HTML did everything we needed it to do, DHTML wouldn't exist and we wouldn't be here. Chapter 2 provides an in-depth discussion of the features and limits of HTML. This sets the stage for the introduction of DHTML in Chapter 4. Now that you know how we got here, it's time to see where we're going.

Chapter 2

Features And Limits Of HTML 4.0

Picking up where Chapter 1 left off, Chapter 2 turns an investigative and critical eye to the newest features of HTML 4.0, as well as the inherent limitations that make it difficult for such a simple mechanism to perform all the duties it has been called on to fulfill.

Notes...

Chapter 2

When the World Wide Web Consortium (W3C) formally publishes the official HTML 4.0 specification, it will be over 300 pages of HTML and notes. This powerful, highly detailed version of the language reestablishes the W3C's influence over HTML developments. In recent years, the exceptional commercial competition in the computer market has added such dramatic proprietary enhancements to the official W3C version of HTML that the consortium has been in danger of losing touch with HTML development. However, by embracing popular and useful proprietary developments and meshing them with the HTML 3.2 grounding, the HTML 4.0 specification bodes well for the future of the W3C and for Web development at large. Developers no longer need to ignore the official specification to create exciting Web content; the HTML 4.0 specification arms them with the tools as well as the handbook.

The features contained in HTML 4.0 push the language into an entirely new realm. This is a radical HTML specification; by adding features that allow Web pages to change after they've been downloaded, it opens fresh avenues for Web development and creative ventures. The redefinition and restructuring of the language with HTML 4.0 changes the entire Web navigation experience. Its additions that allow content to change within a page translate into incredibly rapid user feedback; these changes suddenly shorten the loop between what we do and what we see.

The 4.0 specification's incorporation of scripting provides the opportunity for stellar multimedia productions, full of animation and streaming multimedia content.

Teamed with the control that HTML 4.0 grants to both end user and developer, this specification essentially ushers in a new age of Web development in both technological and aesthetic terms. No longer dependent on server response to provide interactivity, a Web page written in HTML 4.0 can supply Web users with information at the highest speed ever. In a period when push technology seems to be reducing Web adventurers to an unprecedented (but familiar) state of passivity, HTML 4.0 and Dynamic HTML (DHTML) infuse the Web with the possibility for new activity. In fact, one of the most striking things about DHTML is how fast it seems—and is. Given the Net's increasingly clogged arteries, an ISDN line and a 250 MHz processor don't guarantee a speedy, or even tolerable, Web experience. But DHTML—and the foundation laid down by the HTML 4.0 specification—can reclaim some of that speed and rapid response time.

There are extensive differences between HTML 3.2 and HTML 4.0. Many of them are so specific that professional developers—not to mention end users—won't notice them. But everyone on the Web will be affected by the changes that HTML 4.0 brings. In this chapter's following sections, we detail the changes in the HTML 4.0 specification and take an initial look at where they will lead Web development and use.

The Difference Between DHTML And HTML 4.0

The W3C defines Dynamic HTML as "a term used by some vendors to describe the combination of HTML, style sheets, and scripts that allows documents to be animated." So Dynamic HTML isn't a specification; rather, it is an implementation of HTML that uses the language in combination with other things, such as the document object model (DOM), a scripting language like JavaScript, cascading style sheets, absolute positioning, and ActiveX controls. HTML 4.0, therefore, is not the same as Dynamic HTML; it is the official language that's combined with other ingredients to produce DHTML.

HTML 4.0 alone can't enable the type of page movement and activity that's associated with DHTML; rather, HTML 4.0 defines the method that's used to place objects on a Web page. The movement that characterizes dynamic Web pages can't be activated unless HTML 4.0 is combined with a scripting language and other dynamic elements.

HTML 4.0's Array Of Features

Briefly, here are some of HTML 4.0's most important advancements:

- HTML markup separate from style through the introduction of style sheets
- Added flexibility with forms and tables
- Formal adoption of tags that are crucial to DHTML
- Incorporation of scripting language capabilities
- Better printing capabilities
- Ability to respond to or ignore specific media types
- Improved sensitivity to different language types
- Greater accessibility for those who use audio or Braille interfaces to access Web data
- End users may choose between styles for viewing a document, or turn off style sheets altogether

Despite these enhancements, browsers that don't implement all of HTML 4.0's attributes will just ignore them, so problems shouldn't occur no matter how archaic your browser is.

In the following sections, we examine the basics of HTML 4.0.

Changes In HTML 4.0's Elements

HTML 4.0 contains several new elements, while removing others from the specification. We'll examine many of these changes in detail in Chapter 7, but here's a brief overview for now.

New Elements In HTML 4.0

The following elements are new in HTML 4.0:

- **ACRONYM**—By using the **ACRONYM** element, Web developers can indicate a sequence of characters that compose an acronym, such as DHTML. Acronyms are handy for use with spellcheckers and speech synthesizers, as well as other Web tools that classify textual data. The acronym itself is specified by the content of the **ACRONYM** element;

the **TITLE** attribute can be used to provide the acronym's expanded definition.

- **Q**—This is intended for short quotations that don't require paragraph breaks. When you're including a long quotation with paragraph breaks, use **BLOCKQUOTE** instead.
- **INS/DEL**—These tags permit document changes to be highlighted. Viewers can look over a document they've previously visited and immediately recognize if content has been inserted or removed. The **INS** and **DEL** tags may surround words, paragraphs, sets of words, entire blocks of content, or specific letters.
- **FIELDSET/LEGEND**—HTML 4.0's new **FIELDSET** tag permits grouping of related controls on a form in a way that makes their connection clearer to people who use the form. When a form has separate sections—for demographic information such as geographical location, age, and gender—the **FIELDSET** tag can be used to indicate which part of the form holds the field-specific data. The **LEGEND** tag works in conjunction with the **FIELDSET** tag; **LEGEND** allows you to define a label for the group, as well as put the label in the position of your choice.
- **BUTTON**—HTML 3.2 actually contained the **BUTTON** tag, but essentially confined its use to forms. HTML 4.0's novel implementation of buttons doesn't require them to be to be contained within forms. The new specification also allows you to trigger scripts with buttons, with the script-triggering button controls located anywhere on an HTML page.
- **COLGROUP**—The new **COLGROUP** element has been introduced to enable you to define any number of adjacent columns in a table as a group of columns and treat that group as a unit. These sets of columns can be grouped with different alignment and width properties; **COLGROUP** facilitates their handling by letting you apply attribute-value pairs to all of a group's columns at the same time.

Deprecated Elements In HTML 4.0

You'll see references to "deprecated elements" throughout this chapter and the book. These elements are ones that the World Wide Web Consortium plans to eventually phase out. The effects of many of the deprecated elements that we discuss in this chapter, such as **APPLET** and **IMG**, can now be achieved through style-sheet usage.

The following elements have been deprecated and replaced:

- **APPLET**—Used to embed Java applets in HTML documents, **APPLET** is replaced by **OBJECT**.
- **CENTER**—Used to "float" an object in the center of a page. Replaced by the **DIV** tag with the **ALIGN** attribute set to center.
- **FONT**—Used, along with its attributes, to determine text size, typeface, and color. Replaced by style sheets and font properties.
- **BASEFONT**—Used to set base font sizes using the **SIZE** attribute. Replaced by style sheets.
- **ISINDEX**—Used to prompt users for a single line of input and would add a search interface to the document. Use the **INPUT** tag instead.
- **STRIKE** and **S**—Used to strike through text. Replaced by style sheets and the text-decoration property
- **U**—Used to underline text. Replaced by style sheets.
- **DIR**—Used to make multicolumn directory lists. Use the **UL** (unordered list) tag instead.
- **MENU**—Used to make single-column menu lists. Use **UL** instead.

Obsolete Elements in HTML 4.0

There are a few elements that have simply become obsolete and have been removed from the HTML 4.0 specification:

- **LISTING**
- **XMP**
- **PLAINTEXT**

These tags have been eliminated because they were used infrequently and might result in problematic browser performance if new browsers follow the 4.0 specification strictly. All of these tags that indicate aspects of text placement have been superseded by the **PRE** tag, which refers to preformatted text.

Common Attributes

There are six attributes, a couple of which have been around for a while, that affect over 85 percent of the tags in the HTML 4.0 DTD. It is important that you know they exist, particularly because three of them are going to be directly involved in assigning style rules to page elements and in creating DHTML. We'll list those three first. Another allows you to provide additional information about an HTML element. The other two you probably won't have the opportunity to work with much, but since they fall into this category we'd be remiss not to include them. The six common attributes are:

- **ID=*name***—The **ID** attribute assigns a specific identification name to either a style rule, so it can be used with several different HTML elements, or to an individual HTML tag so it can be referred to by an inline script.
- **CLASS=*text***—The **CLASS** attribute indicates that the element belongs to a specific class of style rule as defined in the style sheet.
- **STYLE=*text***—The **STYLE** attribute assigns a style rule to a single instance of an HTML element within a page without otherwise having to create an actual style sheet for the page.
- **TITLE=*text***—The value of the **TITLE** attribute is additional information that will be displayed—probably as balloon text—around the HTML tag to which it is tied.
- **DIR=(LTR|RTL)**—The **DIR** attribute specifies the direction the text will be read: left-to-right or right-to-left.
- **LANG=*name***—The **LANG** attribute defines the language in which an element's contents are written.

Style Sheets

One of HTML 4.0's biggest advancements comes in the realm of style sheets. Style sheets give HTML programmers the most refined control over layout and design ever. We cover style sheets in detail in Chapter 6 and also talk about the complexities of style sheets versus Netscape's layer implementation throughout Part 4 of this book.

The inclusion of style sheets in the HTML 4.0 specification—and the power they bring to Web designers—is a crucial step in HTML's development. Because the Web was initially created for the exchange of scientific data, the content of a Web page originally mattered far more than the appearance. However, once the Web's multimedia potential began to surface, developers were quick to implement whatever techniques they could to unleash scintillating Web content, and adherence to "proper" HTML was frequently ignored.

Style sheets reduce the need to resort to these types of proprietary enhancements to control Web page appearance. While acquiring the advantages once offered only by proprietary extensions, developers who use HTML 4.0-approved style sheets simultaneously resolve incompatibilities and gain excellent control over presentation.

Style sheets considerably simplify HTML markup; they add a level of control over document presentation for site designers and end users. There are two kinds of style sheets: persistent, which are applied without user input, and alternate, which users can customize. Even if a default style sheet is loaded with the page, the viewer can disable it and use an alternate style sheet instead. Style sheets also allow page content to be automatically adjusted according to the viewer's computer environment.

Designers can use style sheets to indicate a variety of styles, including:

- Fonts
- Colors
- Weights
- Margins
- Leading
- Alignment

An HTML 4.0 style sheet isn't difficult for designers to understand, because parameters are expressed in units such as ems and points (inches, percentages, pixels, and other forms of measurement can be assigned as well).

The HTML 4.0 specification doesn't require a specific style sheet language to be used for HTML, although cascading style sheets (CSS) is the dominant style-sheet language in use at this time. Both Microsoft and Netscape support style sheets with their 4.0 browsers, although the two browsers also suffer from some proprietary style quirks.

HTML 4.0 ≠ Content + Style

Through style sheets, the burden of determining how a page should appear is removed from the HTML code and lies instead within the style sheet itself. Although this separation of content from presentation is a key concept in SGML, and therefore with HTML as well, the need to control style with HTML 3.2 and earlier versions led to the nonstandard inclusion of tags such as **FONT** and **B** within the HTML code. Many of the attributes and elements that lent control over alignment, font size, and text color for HTML 3.2 were created in response to demand for exciting multimedia content. However, the introduction of these elements into HTML was a short-term solution, as it was essentially an HTML infraction. HTML 4.0 remedies this violation.

No More Tables And Huge GIFs

Using style sheets also frees Web designers from relying on tables to achieve control over layout, or using enormous GIFs to display stylized content. Developers often resort to tables and GIF images to achieve a certain look or appearance; HTML 4.0's powerful style sheets mean that use of tables and content-laden GIFs will no longer be as pervasive. This change is good for the Web and its users, because information contained within tables and images isn't automatically picked up by search engines or audio browsers. Avoiding the tedious download times that accompany large GIFs will also accelerate the Web experience.

Information expressed through style sheets can be implemented in a variety of ways. There are three fundamental levels at which Web developers add style sheets to documents. We list them here from least complex to most complex:

1. With an inline style sheet, which defines the style directly on the element
2. With a global style sheet that defines a document's style at the beginning of the document
3. With a style sheet that links to another document, thereby defining the style separately in the linked document

Inline Style Sheets

Inline style sheets are the least complex—and least abstract—type of style sheets. They're pretty similar to normal HTML. Styles within these sheets associate directly with an element, such as the font or color, and, as with regular HTML, a document's appearance can't be easily altered. However, inline style sheets differ from HTML in the amount of markup that they employ, as an inline style sheet will almost always use less markup than would its HTML counterpart.

Global Style Sheets

When global style sheets are included at the beginning of a document, they provide a clear separation of content from presentation. This separation allows a Web page's style to be rendered at a quick pace independent of the rate at which the content emerges.

Linked Style Sheets

Although linked (or external) style sheets are the most abstract and complex types of style sheets, they also take fullest advantage of style-sheet capabilities. With a linked style sheet, a page's style is defined completely separate from the page itself; the style sheet is linked to the page and exists as a separate, external document. Because of this separation, the styles that are defined in a linked style sheet can be applied to an entire range of pages and easily reused. When it's time to change a Web site's appearance, a linked style sheet eases the process of modification because rather than changing the actual site content, it's necessary to alter the style indications only within the linked style sheet.

What About Cascading Style Sheets?

The complexities of cascading style sheets are discussed in Chapter 6. Briefly, cascading style sheets allow you to combine multiple style sheets so that they create a single style definition for an entire document. Therefore, it's possible to merge an inline style sheet with a style sheet contained within a document.

For example, if you wanted to combine a variety of styles and apply them to a site, you could do so through cascading style sheets. It's possible to blend styles that apply to a set of Web resources with intranet-specific guidelines, and then apply on top of these styles that are specific to a single document. All of these styles can be stored separately and applied according to rules that determine which sheet's styles have the highest priority.

Additionally, a cascade of style sheets may include sheets that apply to different media (see the section that follows on the new **MEDIA** element for illumination). When a variety of media are invoked through the style sheets, it's up to the user agent, usually a browser, to determine which style sheets should be used.

A caveat, though: Not all style-sheet languages support cascading. Even though HTML 4.0 doesn't require adherence to a specific style-sheet language, unless your audience has highly specific needs, you're probably safest sticking to CSS, which is simple and widely used.

DOM Definition

Throughout this chapter, and this book, we'll refer to the document object model (DOM). The W3C is still in the early stages of working with the DOM, which it defines as "a platform- and language-neutral interface that will allow programs and scripts to dynamically access and update the content, structure, and style of documents. The document can be further processed and the results of that processing can be incorporated back into the presented page."

It's the DOM that grants developers the power to change a document's content. DHTML opens the DOM to scripting languages, through which developers can define and organize a document, enhancing control over every aspect of an HTML document. The DOM lets a Web document's content be defined in great detail. This elevated level of definition can be used to indicate how specific objects—such as tables, links, forms, text, and images—should appear and how they should be positioned. The movement of these objects, which can be affected either as a group or individually, can unfold in conjunction with an event schedule. For example, you could have a portion of text fly from the upper-left corner off the right side of the browser, and then have a table appear the minute the text disappears.

The **OBJECT** Element

HTML 4.0 is the first incarnation of HTML with a standard mechanism that indicates how generic media objects and applications are to be embedded in HTML documents. The past, present, and forthcoming onslaught of Web multimedia makes the simplicity of the **OBJECT** element especially attractive.

The **OBJECT** element allows objects such as video, images, sound, specialized applications, mathematics, and other objects to be wholly contained within an HTML document. This ability to contain multimedia content within the document improves the speed at which a page's multimedia transpires, and also reduces bandwidth drain. By employing the **OBJECT** element, site designers can also indicate a hierarchy of alternate renderings for user agents that don't support a specific rendering.

The **IMG** and **APPLET** tags are predecessors of **OBJECT**, and both of these tags have been deprecated in favor of **OBJECT**. Examples demonstrating how **OBJECT** can be substituted for **APPLET** and **IMG** follow.

*Using **OBJECT** Instead Of **APPLET***

Because **APPLET** has been deprecated, it's now recommended that you use **OBJECT** where you once used **APPLET** to refer to a Java applet. Applets themselves can still be used, of course, but specifying them through **OBJECT** standardizes a page's content structure.

While an applet may have been specified in this way with HTML 3.2:

```
<APPLET code="spirals.class" width="300" height="300">
Java applet that creates a gyrating spiral.
</APPLET>
```

HTML 4.0 would allow it to be rewritten with **OBJECT** in this way:

```
<OBJECT codetype="application/octet-stream"
        classid="java:spirals.class"
        width="300" height="300">
Java applet that creates a gyrating spiral.
</OBJECT>
```

*Using **OBJECT** Instead Of **IMG***

You can use **OBJECT** rather than **IMG** to insert a graphic directly into a page. This is how HTML 3.2 might be used to indicate a graphic through the **IMG** tag, with **ALT** providing alternate text:

```
As you can see, the green stone bears flecks of gold.
<IMG src="http://www.wherever.com/stones/greenstone.gif"
alt="The green stone">
```

With HTML 4.0, you would employ the **OBJECT** element in this way:

```
As you can see, the green stone bears flecks of gold.
<OBJECT data="http://www.wherever.com/stones/greenstone.gif"
type="image/gif">
The green stone.
</OBJECT>
```

The New **MEDIA** Attribute

HTML 4.0 includes a new **MEDIA** attribute that lets Web designers make documents that can be rendered on a variety of media. The 4.0 specification includes the following media descriptors:

- **all**—Suitable for all media devices.
- **screen**—Used primarily for non-paged computer screens; **screen** can also be applied to printed and projected presentations. **Screen** is the default value.

- **print**—Used for paged, opaque material, as well as for documents that are viewed on the screen in print preview mode.
- **projection**—Used for projectors.
- **aural**—Used for speech synthesizers.
- **braille**—Used for Braille tactile feedback devices.

Use the **MEDIA** attribute to indicate which type of media a page's content is intended for, or what media-type rules apply. The **MEDIA** attribute is one that has been added to HTML 4.0 with an eye toward the future: The inclusion of the **MEDIA** attribute takes set-top boxes for televisions into account, for example, as well as handheld wireless/PDA devices. The **MEDIA** attribute opens a new avenue for telephones adapted for Web data, Braille-based devices, and speech-based browsers as well.

Here's an example of how the sound effect of a barking dog could be added to anchors for use with a speech-based Web browser:

```
<HEAD>
<STYLE type="text/acss" media="aural">
   A { cue-before: url(bark.aiff); cue-after: url(yip.wav)}
</STYLE>
</HEAD>
```

Media declarations work effectively in conjunction with style sheets, especially external style sheets. Using external style sheets with the **MEDIA** attribute saves download time because when you want to examine or alter specific media-based style sheets, you have to obtain only the ones that apply to the media device. For example, if you're using a browser that renders Web content into tactile Braille data, there's no need for you to download the style sheets that correspond to visual rendering.

Here's an example of HTML 4.0 that you could use to create a Web page with headers. As you can see from the use of the "screen" media type, they would appear green when loaded on a screen, but appear as centered content when projected for a presentation:

```
<HEAD>
 <STYLE type="text/css" media="screen">
    H1 { color: green}
 </STYLE>
```

```
 <STYLE type="text/css" media="projection">
    H1 { text-align: center }
 </STYLE>
</HEAD>
```

Scripting

HTML 4.0's ability to work with scripting languages is one of the innovations that "makes" DHTML. The HTML specification gives developers the means of building dynamic networked applications, and scripting provides the mechanisms. For example, scripts allow Web designers to create smart forms that react and provide responses within a page as users fill them out. HTML 4.0 doesn't require any specific scripting language to accomplish such feats, although JavaScript and VBScript have both been primed to operate with HTML 4.0.

By working in conjunction with HTML 4.0's event model, scripting languages become more aware of user actions. Scripting languages can interpret mouse actions, such as the mouse passing over a specified area of the page through the event model, which also allows scripting languages to interpret keyboard strokes. Table 2.1 includes a description of each event and its related tags.

Table 2.1 Intrinsic events.

Event	Description	Related Tags
onload=script	Occurs when a window or all the frames within a **<FRAMESET>** tag have completely loaded.	Associated with **<BODY>** and **<FRAMESET>** tags.
onunload=script	Occurs when a document is removed from a frame or window.	Associated with **<BODY>** and **<FRAMESET>** tags.
onclick=script	Occurs when a pointing device is clicked over an element.	Associated with most tags.
ondblclick=script	Occurs when a pointing device is double-clicked over an element.	Associated with most tags.
onmousedown=script	Occurs when a pointing device's button is pressed over an element.	Associated with most tags.
onmouseup=script	Occurs when a pointing device's button is released over an element.	Associated with most tags.

(continued)

Table 2.1 Intrinsic events (*continued*).

Event	Description	Related Tags
onmouseover=script	Occurs when a pointing device is placed over an element.	Associated with most tags.
onmousemove=script	Occurs when a pointing device is moved across an element.	Associated with most tags.
onmouseout=script	Occurs when a pointing device is moved off an element.	Associated with most tags.
onfocus=script	Occurs when an element becomes the focus of the control device (the mouse or the Tab button on the keyboard).	Associated with **<LABEL>**, **<INPUT>**, **<SELECT>**, **<TEXTAREA>**, and **<BUTTON>** tags.
onblur=script	Occurs when an element is no longer the focus of the control device.	Associated with **<LABEL>**, **<INPUT>**, **<SELECT>**, **<TEXTAREA>**, and **<BUTTON>** tags.
onkeypress=script	Occurs when a key is pressed and released on an element.	Associated with most tags.
onkeydown=script	Occurs when a key is pressed down on an element.	Associated with most tags.
onkeyup=script	Occurs when a key is released on an element.	Associated with most tags.
onsubmit=script	Occurs when a form is submitted.	Associated with the **<FORM>** tag.
onreset=script	Occurs when a form is reset.	Associated with the **<FORM>** tag.
onselect=script	Occurs when some text is selected in a text field.	Associated with **<INPUT>** and **<TEXTAREA>** tags.
onchange=script	Occurs when a control loses the control device's focus and its value has changed since gaining focus.	Associated with **<INPUT>**, **<SELECT>**, and **<TEXTAREA>** tags.

Improved Tables

In prior versions of HTML, the borders of a table were treated as a single unit, which meant that they could be either on or off, and that every line around every cell adhered to the same stylistic choice; only the size of the lines could be adjusted. With HTML 4.0, using the **STYLE** attribute with tables lets you add more complex features, including dotted lines and double lines.

HTML 4.0 allows the **FRAME** and **RULES** attributes to be used with the **TABLE** tag so that you can specify what part of the table border viewers can see. This new table model provides designers with better control over structure and layout. Although previous versions of HTML required the entire table to download before it could be rendered, HTML 4.0's ability to recommend column widths lets browsers display table data in increments, as data comes through the wires. HTML 4.0 also has improved support for tables that break across pages when you're printing; scrollable tables with fixed headers and footers are also introduced in HTML 4.0.

Improved Forms

Because you can use style sheets anywhere within a form, HTML 4.0 brings a great deal more control over how forms are displayed and used. HTML 4.0 can attach active labels to form fields, as well as give labeled hierarchical groupings for form fields. In addition to text fields that permit user input, HTML 4.0 forms can also feature buttons that change values according to user actions, such as Submit buttons that change color when a selected key is pushed.

HTML 3.2 didn't allow form controls such as form fields to be made "read only," however, such restrictions are possible with HTML 4.0's new **READONLY** attribute, which lets you indicate that changes can't be made to a form field. Additionally, HTML 4.0, unlike HTML 3.2, includes the attribute **ACCEPT-CHARSET**, which specifies which character sets are acceptable to the server issuing a form.

The action that transpires when an element receives focus depends on the element. In the following example, we've mapped the access key "K" to a label that's assigned to an **INPUT** control. When you type "K", it gives focus to the label, which subsequently gives focus to the associated control. After these focuses are transferred, the user can enter text into the **INPUT** area:

```
<FORM   Action="..." method="post">
<LABEL for="name" accesskey="K">
User Name Here </LABEL>
<INPUT type="text" name="name">
</FORM>
```

Better Forms Through ***BUTTONs***

Although HTML 3.2 forms allowed only two buttons, Submit and Reset, HTML 4.0 features a new **BUTTON** element that lets you make more-complex forms. There's not a great difference between **BUTTONs** whose type is submit and the current Submit buttons (**INPUT** elements whose type is submit). Both of these allow users to submit form data. However, the new **BUTTON** element lets you use HTML directly on the button. This ability is useful if you want to put an image on the button, for example, or include character formatting within the button.

Improved Frames

HTML 4.0's advanced frame features include inline frames, which permit the inclusion of compound documents. These compound documents are created through frames placed in HTML documents.

Better Printing Options

The control that HTML 4.0 brings with the **LINK** element allows documents to be printed more efficiently and accurately. Using the **LINK** element allows you to print a specific subset of files or print files according to their unique attributes.

Internationalization Through The ISO/IEC:10646 Standard

Although the Internet's structure makes it the most powerful global information tool ever invented, non-English speakers often have trouble with the way that HTML handles characters. HTML 4.0, however, addresses many of the issues that were once barriers between non-English speakers and the Web. These changes allow authors to manage differences in language, text direction, and character-encoding schemes to make documents accessible to users regardless of language. HTML 4.0's increased sensitivity to worldwide languages also results in better text-to-speech conversion, higher-quality typography, and correct hyphenation, and makes it possible for authors to use right-to-left or mixed text. The improved support that HTML 4.0 registers for a variety of human languages within a document means that Web data can be more efficiently and accurately registered for search engines, thereby resulting in a more complete overview of the Web's information repository.

A bevy of experts from the internationalization field have been consulted regarding the process of making HTML 4.0 viable for every language. The adoption of the ISO/IEC:10646 standard as the document character set for HTML has been an important step toward internationalization. This standard is the world's most inclusive to date; it addresses how international characters should be depicted, text direction, punctuation, and similar world-language issues. Through this standard's internationalization features (such as the **LANG** tag and **CHARSET** parameter, which specify the language and character set used within a document, respectively), authoring mixed-language Web documents will become feasible. The ramifications for global exchange of data—and the increased opportunities for collaboration—are powerfully apparent.

Accessibility Features

One of the most important aspects of any graphical interface is providing an easy means of moving from one element to another. Most software packages available today include keyboard shortcuts for common tasks—such as Command-P or Ctrl-P for print—and tabs allow you to move quickly from one element in a dialog box to another. Although Web browser software incorporates these features, easy movement has been missing from Web pages themselves.

Three new attributes have been included in HTML 4.0 to provide quick accessibility to certain elements on an HTML page using the traditional shortcut and tab mechanisms: **ACCESSKEY**, **TABINDEX**, and **NOTAB**.

ACCESSKEY=*letter* assigns a single-letter access key to the **<A>**, **<LEGEND>**, **<LABEL>**, or **<CAPTION>** tags. When the assigned key is pressed in combination with an operating system's primary shortcut key—Ctrl in Windows and Command in the Mac OS—the element is brought into focus. What happens when an element is in focus depends entirely on the element's inherent functionality. Following are two examples of the **ACCESSKEY** attribute in action.

```
<A HREF="http://www.w3.org/MarkUp/ ACCESSKEY="W">The World Wide Web
  Consortium's HTML Page</A>

<FORM ACTION="/cgi-gin/form.pl" METHOD="POST">
<LABEL FOR="name" ACCESSKEY="N">
Enter your user name
</LABEL>
<INPUT TYPE="TEXT" NAME="name"
</FORM>
```

In the preceding example, adding the **ACCESSKEY** attribute to the anchor tag will cause the hyperlink to the W3C's HTML page to be activated when the access key is invoked. However, the access key assigned to the form input label will move the cursor to the user name input widget so the user can type in data.

For obvious reasons, the number of access keys per page is limited to 26 because there are only 26 letters in the LATIN-1 character set, and each access key assignment must be unique or the browser will be confused. At this time, it's unclear how the different browsers will graphically display elements with associated access keys.

Assigning the **TABINDEX** attribute to elements within an HTML document creates a tabbing order for the document. Whenever the user hits the Tab key, the next element in the tabbing order is brought into focus. When we add **TABINDEX** attributes to the code from the previous code example, the new HTML looks like this:

```
<A HREF="http://www.w3.org/MarkUp/ ACCESSKEY="W" TABINDEX=2>
     The World Wide Web Consortium's HTML Page</A>

<FORM ACTION="/cgi-gin/form.pl" METHOD="POST" TABINDEX=1>
<LABEL FOR="name" ACCESSKEY="N">
Enter your user name
</LABEL>
<INPUT TYPE="TEXT" NAME="name">
</FORM>
```

Although the anchor element is listed first in the document's source, it is made second in the tabbing order, while the user name input widget is made first. If a user were to hit Tab, the input widget would be brought into focus first. Currently, a tabbing order based on location in the HTML source code is built into form widgets to allow users to jump easily from input item to input item. The **TABINDEX** attribute extends this functionality to the **<A>**, **<AREA>**, **<BUTTON>**, **<INPUT>**, **<SELECT>**, **<TEXTAREA>**, and **<OBJECT>** tags.

The **NOTAB** attribute removes an item, such as a form input widget, from the document's natural tabbing order.

Client-Side Image Maps

HTML 4.0 sees the official inclusion of client-side image map mechanisms. These mechanisms began as proprietary markup and have been around for a while now. The **COORDS** and **SHAPE** attributes work with the **<AREA>** tags within **<MAP>...</MAP>** markup to create a hyperlinked image map defined using the **<IMG>** tag. **COORDS** and **SHAPE** may also be used with **<A>...</A>** tags within **<OBJECT>...</OBJECT>** tags that call an image as an alternative means of creating image maps.

Expanded Web Access For Nonvisual Users

It's somewhat ironic that this generation of HTML brings both the best possibilities for visual effects and the best level of Web access for those who don't visually connect with the Web. Nonvisual Web users had problems receiving consistent content with previous versions of HTML; data contained in tables was inaccessible to users with speech-based browsers, for example. However, HTML 4.0's table model now includes attributes for labeling each cell, which supports high-quality text-to-speech conversion. With the increased use of style sheets, the popularity of stuffing large GIFs full of page content will wane, thereby allowing that content to be processed by search engines and audio/Braille browsers.

Much of this increased accessibility derives from HTML 4.0's forms enhancements, which support groupings, keyboard shortcuts, labels, and titles. Although people using speech-based or Braille browsers worldwide can benefit from these additions, the visually impaired will not be the only ones using such extended features. The mounting numbers of computer users suffering from repetitive stress injuries will make audio-based navigation increasingly popular in the future.

The W3C is now working with a Web Accessibility Initiative (WAI) that compels it to create features to improve Web accessibility for users who use audio navigation or who render Web content into Braille. The WAI can be read at **www.w3.org/WAI/**.

Interoperability

HTML 4.0 has been created with interoperability in mind. Given the pace at which the W3C operates compared with the pace of the marketplace, there has traditionally been a sizable gap between the cutting edge of HTML and what's officially recognized as correct HTML. Web users often bear the brunt of this disparity and with all the proprietary bells and whistles being used, many online would say that interoperability has gotten worse in recent months rather than better. However, HTML 4.0 endeavors to close this gap. Although Netscape and Microsoft currently use two different DHTML implementations, they've both agreed to adhere to the final HTML 4.0 specification; of course, in the meantime each company promulgates its DHTML solutions as the better of the two.

The quest for interoperability has prompted the W3C to formulate a "Web Interoperability Pledge." This 1997 pledge, created by the W3C in tandem with ZDNet's Anchordesk, can be viewed (and taken) at **www4.zdnet.com/anchordesk/wip/pledge.html**.

Limits Of HTML 4.0

HTML 4.0 is, overall, an impressively thorough and viable version of the language. Of course, it's not wholly perfect. Some users might complain that by encouraging use of external style sheets, Web page presentation is delayed at the user end. However, this problem is minor, especially since it's not too different from what happens if a document head includes a lengthy set of style rules. A few other things could be more clearly perceived as drawbacks.

The Persistent Proprietary Problem

Is it really possible that the official version of HTML will be honored and that Netscape and Microsoft won't feed their competition through proprietary advancements? Probably not, despite their assurances that they'll both adhere to the final specification.

However, the quality of this gap is not as serious as it was with HTML 3.2 and earlier versions. By incorporating so many of the proprietary extensions that Netscape and Microsoft have created around official HTML, the HTML 4.0 specification is less apt to provoke proprietary development.

It's Not XML

HTML 4.0 may be a respectably mature version of the HTML specification, but the language that the W3C has its eye on for the Web's future is XML (Extensible Markup Language). XML proposes a completely new set of markup tags and allows you to both create and define your own elements. In that way, it's like SGML (Standard Generalized Markup Language), the language that has long been used for print layout and that also permits element creation. XML is a simplified version of SGML. The W3C is developing XML so that it will enable generic SGML to be served, received, and processed on the Web in the way that HTML is now. Even though there are separate W3C committees working on HTML 4.0 and XML, XML is definitely being designed with interoperability for both HTML and SGML in mind. For more information on XML, see the W3C's XML draft at **www.w3.org/TR/WD-xml-lang.html**.

It's Not 3D

We've all heard the hype about the Web going 3D; development in this arena with technologies such as VRML (Virtual Reality Modeling Language) may simply take the Web into a dimension where HTML no longer applies, no matter how brilliant the specification.

Onward To The Next Level

The new additions to HTML 4.0 reflect the growing demands placed on Web page designers. Increased user interaction, event handling, and advanced non-HTTP object support are just a few of the advanced capabilities included in HTML to make it more flexible. However, HTML is still limited in its size and scope simply because it wasn't meant to do all that we've asked it to do. Enter Dynamic HTML. It picks up where regular HTML leaves off, linking user actions with events, providing access to all of a page's elements by any script—just to name a few benefits—and all on the client side. HTML will always be needed because it defines the framework for all Web documents, but now it's time to leave the basics and move on to the next level: DHTML.

Chapter 3

Dynamic HTML

In this chapter, we move away from the historical perspectives and examine the basics and application of Dynamic HTML. In addition, we explore what this technology can do for the future of the Web.

Notes...

Chapter 3

The impact of DHTML's implementation and use goes far beyond the confines of the Web. The way today's DHTML is integrated into computers affects tomorrow's desktop computing; the megabillion entertainment industry; and how Web content will be shown through the more popular screen, the television. DHTML visions now being put into action will shape the future ways that we receive information, as well as the pathways that data uses to travel through our minds. If video killed the radio star (and MTV established the first channel that succeeded at entertaining viewers through thinly veiled advertisements), where will the powers of DHTML take the world's most revolutionary communication device?

DHTML: The Basics

At the most fundamental level, DHTML is simply HTML that has the ability to change after the browser has loaded a Web page. With DHTML, sometimes called "animated HTML," anything that can be written in HTML can be redone after the page loads. This gives Web pages an unprecedented power to receive—and respond to—user input. This dynamic capability is achieved through a combination of several key DHTML components that work in conjunction with HTML, namely:

- *Style sheets*—Instruct how the content is to change; these sheets are stored separately from the content itself.

- *Scripting languages*—Provide the juice to make the changes (and therefore enact client-side changes).
- *DOM (Document Object Model)*—Outlines Web page content in a way that makes it accessible for the style sheets and scripting languages to affect.

These components work in tandem with DHTML technologies such as *event models* (examined in Chapter 9), which indicate how user actions can set off dynamic strings of events. For example, loading a page can cause an animation to speed from corner to corner of the Web browser and then make spiral circles in the middle of the page. Similarly, the event invoked when a user runs a mouse over a block of text might cause the text to be rendered instantaneously as pink.

You can think of Dynamic HTML as a group of technologies that are intended to create and display interactive Web pages. The technologies that fall under this grouping—at least in Microsoft's DHTML implementation—include:

- Dynamic content
- Dynamic styles
- 2D layout
- Data binding
- Multimedia effects

It's through the DOM that you can program these technologies.

Harnessing Dynamic HTML's power enables you to create Web pages that possess the power of both a word-processing application and an Internet application. By removing the need to constantly return to the server to obtain updated content, performance is improved for both the client and the server, as well as made more interactive.

DHTML gives you the power to alter Web content instantly, which dramatically changes Web users' relationship to information and Web pages. For a seasoned Web user, being able to manipulate Web page content and see content reassemble on the fly without needing to refresh from the server is a radical breakthrough.

DHTML plays a crucial role in both Microsoft's and Netscape's long-term strategies. Microsoft heralds DHTML as a Java replacement, and, as we examine later in this chapter, is exploiting DHTML's ability to perform client-side processing in a variety of revamped and forthcoming products. DHTML drives the Active Desktop and Active Channels with IE 4, and forms a key component of Microsoft products, including Windows DNA, NT 5.0, and Windows 98 (Memphis). DHTML content—with some ActiveX bells and whistles thrown in for effect—is also what Microsoft wants to stream down the push channels and entertainment sites it has readied. Netscape, too, groks DHTML's portable appeal and has incorporated DHTML into its ONE (Open Network Environment) crossware initiative, which will ensure that DHTML appears in Netscape products on Unix, Macintosh, and Windows platforms.

Defining DHTML

We've explained the difference between DHTML and HTML 4.0 in Chapter 2, which also outlines the most important HTML advancements. Chapter 7 delineates many of the proprietary additions that Microsoft and Netscape include in their versions of DHTML. In this chapter, we look at the DHTML area beyond its technical capabilities and innovative extensions; here we examine the effect that DHTML will have for the meta-level of tomorrow's Web, and the way that computers and television are being primed to work with DHTML.

As we've mentioned in the previous chapters, and will continue to explore in this chapter, Microsoft and Netscape espouse dramatically different versions of DHTML. Although both companies have pledged support for the final HTML 4.0 specification, which will ultimately become the official version of DHTML, that version isn't due until the end of 1998 at the earliest. It's unfortunate that the different approaches to DHTML have resulted in the Web's most proprietary content to date. DHTML created according to Netscape's DHTML is often impossible to view with Internet Explorer, and vice versa. (There are ways to create content that works in both browsers, as we explain in several chapters, including Chapter 18, but it's not absolutely guaranteed that the pages you develop for Internet Explorer will even be accessible by Navigator users.)

DHTML And The DOM

The DOM forms the essential core of DHTML; through the hierarchy of Web page elements that this model delineates, it's possible to take Web page content into the dynamic realm by applying a scripting language. Without the DOM, the essence of DHTML wouldn't exist, as there would be no clearly elucidated structure to which you would apply JavaScript.

Microsoft has featured a DOM since IE's 3.0 incarnation, although the IE 4.0 DOM is significantly more sophisticated. Netscape and Microsoft both submitted proposals for their ideal DOMs to the W3C in the fall of 1996. Although Microsoft's version of the DOM seems to be more solid than Netscape's (and is much closer to the W3C's DOM definition), Netscape's version doesn't rely on proprietary ActiveX as Microsoft's does. However, Netscape's DOM is available for interaction only with JavaScript (EMCAScript), unlike Microsoft's, which works with JavaScript as well as JScript and VBScript. In addition to the fact that Microsoft's DOM runs with any scripting language, its DOM also allows you to manipulate *any* part of a page's HTML. Netscape's DOM is currently based on the Netscape layer model and restricts access to page elements that are placed within the layer container. Again, both Microsoft and Netscape have pledged support for whatever DOM the W3C ultimately approves.

What's In The DOM

The DOM defines a document as an object that possesses properties. These properties can in turn be objects with additional properties, and so on. The DOM includes information such as:

- Browser properties (i.e., the browser's version number)
- Information such as the page's URL and the current time and date
- HTML tags (**<DIV>**, **<SPAN>**, etc.)

Because the DOM is open to scripting languages, you can access and often modify these elements through scripting languages.

The W3C And The DOM

As the DOM is at the heart of HTML 4.0/DHTML, the W3C is intensely interested in how the DOM evolves and in the way that Microsoft and Netscape implement their respective DOMs. The W3C is looking beyond HTML in the process of pondering the DOM; it's also targeting the DOM as an underlying component of XML (Extensible Markup Language), which, for certain applications, will serve as HTML's successor.

For a full explanation of the DOM, and more specific information about how Netscape's and Microsoft's DOMs differ, see Chapter 5.

What DHTML Does

In addition to some of the specific functions that DHTML accomplishes—such as animation, generation of dynamic fonts, and style applications—it also performs more far-reaching tasks:

- Removes server/client bandwidth loop for Web feedback
- Lets the Web "show" streaming content that TV watchers understand
- Offers new possibilities for the speed and rhythm at which Web sites display themselves
- Provides artistic creators with a newly powerful set of tools to present artwork on the Web—the globe's biggest, most international, and least restricted gallery space
- Increases accessibility to Web documents for users with hearing or seeing disabilities
- Allows documents to be accurately translated into the widest range of languages, including Asian languages containing characters that earlier versions of HTML couldn't handle
- Creates the velocity for commercially persuasive, even subliminal, messages to be inserted into streamed content
- Takes HTML into a development realm formerly occupied solely by CD-ROM multimedia authoring applications
- Makes the Web more appealing to those with short attention spans, or who crave instant gratification and immediate feedback
- Integrates novel multimedia powers directly into HTML rather than relying on plug-ins

DHTML: CD-ROM Authoring Language?

Computer users experiencing multimedia through CD-ROMs often find Web content to be slow and rough. DHTML, however, pulls Web works to a level where they can compcte with CD-ROM material. In fact, DHTML is the first incarnation of HTML that prescient CD-ROM developers will be able to use as a substitute for applications such as Director or mTropolis. The benefits of this change toward embracing a version of HTML to create multimedia programming are clear. Software such as Director has prescribed limits that inevitably restrain multimedia productions, such as the 120 channels of content that Director 6 allows its movies to contain (previous versions were limited to 48 channels). DHTML has no parallel restrictions.

Because multimedia elements can be directly embedded within the HTML markup, DHTML lessens the need for plug-ins (which may worry companies such as Macromedia and make them scramble to imbue plug-ins with features that DHTML doesn't yet offer). A browser and a plug-in essentially function as two disparate applications, making HTML generally lose access to the plug-in content, which often results in choppy or awkward integration between the entities. Content that can be experienced only through plug-ins is also unavailable to search engines and Web index searches, resulting in incomplete overviews of Web content.

DHTML's Drag-And-Drop Capabilities

The ability to drag and drop—lift a Web page graphic or object with your mouse and place it somewhere else—within Web pages is a feat that wasn't possible with HTML until it became dynamic. Both Navigator 4 and Explorer 4 have drag-and-drop capabilities, which are extremely useful in applications such as games, educational situations, creating a variety of models, and artistic oeuvres. Electronic commerce investors have been rabidly anticipating HTML drag and drop, as it brings instant gratification to Web customers by allowing them to easily and instantaneously place a desired item into the virtual version of a shopping cart or bag.

Figures 3.1 through 3.4 exemplify how DHTML can be used to perform drag-and-drop actions. After the page containing the skeleton has initially loaded (a process requiring less than 20 seconds), it never needs to query the server to change the page's content. All of the skeleton's parts can be limitlessly repositioned after the page loads. The skeleton's ability to be dynamically manipulated outside of the bandwidth loop is enabled by the basic combination of a scripting language and Navigator's layers or Explorer's **IFRAME** tag.

DHTML's Intuitive Navigation

By incorporating event models such as **MouseOver** (explained in Chapter 9) that respond according to user mouse movement, DHTML ventures into more intuitive territory than its predecessors. Action can transpire in DHTML pages based on more subtle input than in previous versions of HTML.

JavaScript 1.2 also offers a "canvas mode" of viewing that puts users into a full-screen interface without navigation controls (such as a scroll-down arrow on the side of the

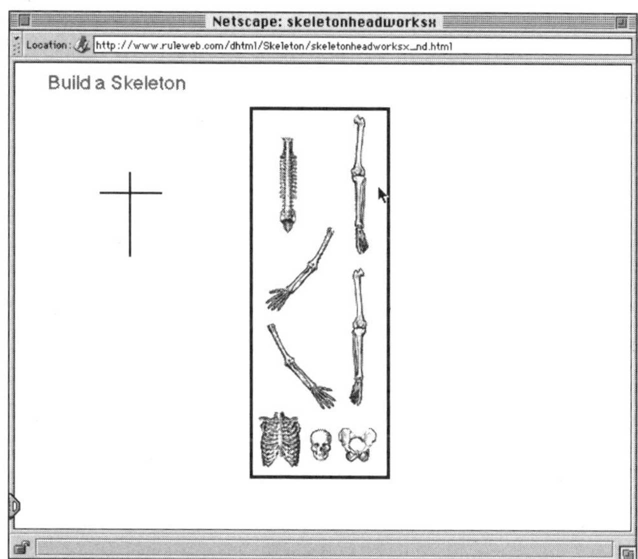

Figure 3.1

The initial appearance of Jeff Rule's Build a Skeleton.

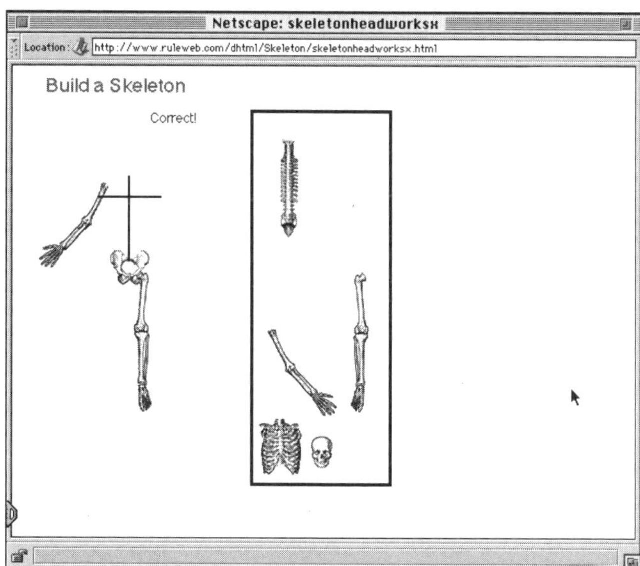

Figure 3.2

When you assemble the skeleton's bones in the right order, the page gives you a "Correct!" message.

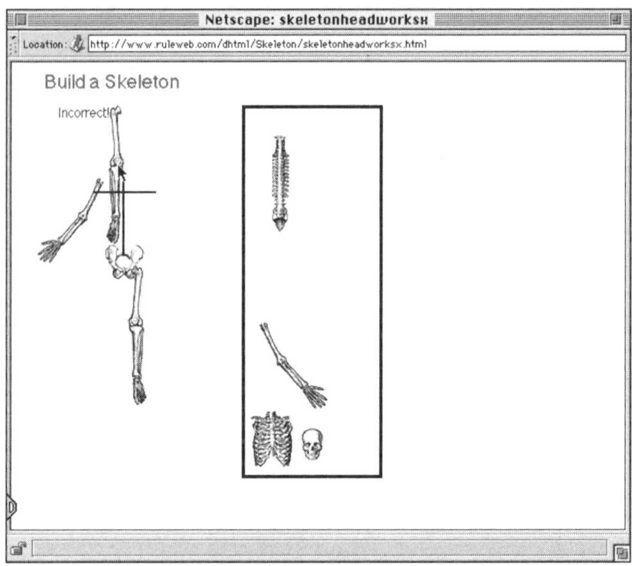

Figure 3.3

When you assemble the skeleton's bones in the wrong order, the page gives you an "Incorrect!" message.

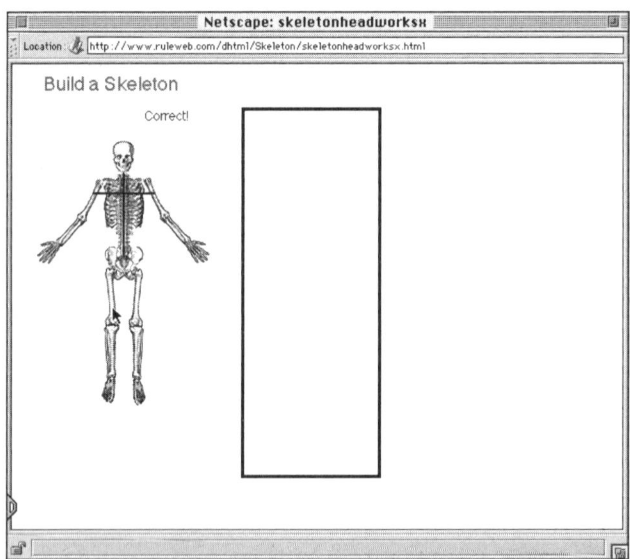

Figure 3.4

The correctly assembled skeleton, fully accomplished without a trip to the server.

browser). Canvas mode takes advantage of DHTML's intuitive navigation capacities by allowing users to change the page content through mouse actions within the actual content, not buttons on the browser's toolbar. The pop-up menu that currently appears in browsers when you right-click the mouse also shows up in canvas mode, and features options such as Save This Image and Copy This Link Location.

Figure 3.5 shows how the Freefall site, located at **www.eglobe.com/~rouyer/**, makes good use of the canvas mode; to scroll down the page, you just click at the bottom of the text, and it automatically inches down the page (or vice versa to scroll up the page).

Canvas mode drawbacks include the fact that you can't run your mouse over a hyperlink and see the URL at the bottom of the page, and you can't use the keyboard's arrows to scroll up and down the screen. Additionally, canvas mode's watching space is ideal for passive consumption of Web entertainment, and that may disconcert die-hard Webheads who feel lost without numerous navigation options at their fingertips. Web developers will have to adjust the way they structure canvas-mode Web sites so that users feel comfortable and aware of their movement options within the buttonless page. Getting "stuck" in canvas mode, through JavaScript glitches or poor navigation programming, also seems to be a problem with this incarnation of DHTML.

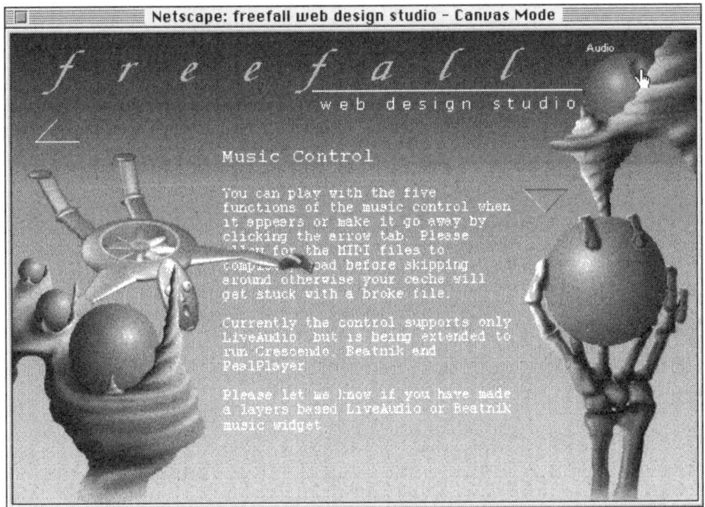

Figure 3.5

The Freefall site's canvas mode, implemented through JavaScript 1.2.

Style Sheets: Separating Content And Style

Style sheets are a crucial component of DHTML, and one that we explore in detail in Chapter 6. At the most basic level, style sheets exist to instruct a Web site about its stylistic rendering, including color, text, font control, and positioning. It's through style sheets that you can arm your Web pages with an arsenal of design information that applies no matter who loads it in what browser (well, that's the dream, at least). Style sheets bring much more precise control over the position that Web documents assume when they appear.

The W3C has avidly promoted style sheets as a means of purging HTML of the proprietary extensions that have entered into the language; these proprietary features that have cluttered HTML—such as **<BLINK>**—have largely focused on Web page style. However, these style extensions have been incorporated directly into the HTML markup, which directly violates the ideal of HTML's predecessor, SGML. SGML says that content should be separate from style, and HTML 4.0 (and DHTML) seek to reestablish this ideal.

At this point, one of the most marked differences between Netscape's and Microsoft's versions of DHTML is the style sheets they use. Microsoft's DHTML proposal interoperates with Cascading Style Sheets 1 (CSS1), which is the W3C's current style sheet standard. Netscape, however, goes down the JavaScript path once more with its DHTML implementation and uses JavaScript Style Sheets (JSSS, or JASS, JavaScript Accessible Style Sheets). Netscape can also use CSS, although at the time of writing, Netscape's actual CSS support was spotty.

Scripting Language Integration

Although HTML 4.0 is taking a welcome leap by officially incorporating scripting languages into its structure, using scripting languages is certainly nothing new for the Web. Client-side scripting languages, such as JavaScript and VBScript in particular, have long been affecting the way that HTML appears on a Web page. However, DHTML and HTML 4.0 both endow scripting languages with more power, and promote them to a much more prominent station.

The release of the 4.0 browsers witnessed a shift in the variety of HTML elements that are accessible to a scripting language from within a Web page. The mechanism through which page elements are exposed to scripting is the DOM; although Netscape's DOM is limited by its layer model in the number of elements it can expose, both Netscape's and Microsoft's version of DHTML offer scripting languages far more access to HTML than was previously possible.

It's through scripting—in conjunction with the **LAYER** tag—that Netscape's DHTML model can animate objects. However, Microsoft's DHTML animates by altering CSS position attributes at any time.

Microsoft's DHTML Strategy

As Mark Andreessen was pumping Mosaic into the hearts and minds of early tech adopters, Microsoft was, quite simply, devoting attention to other matters, suffering from the same tunnel vision that Sun was applying to Java development. Both Sun and Microsoft were initially tardy in recognizing the Internet's potential. However, once the blinds were lifted, Microsoft launched into full assault mode and devised an Internet strategy so pervasive that even if entire chunks of it are inadequate, it ensures a modicum of success. Having once failed to see the Internet as the crucial medium that it has become, Microsoft's Net strategy extends forcefully beyond mere software, into the realms of push content and Internet standards, and ensures that a weakness on the Internet front will never again threaten its position in the computing world.

DHTML is a key factor in this strategy. Overtly desirous of more than 50 percent of the Web browser market, Microsoft's strategy is to make DHTML so ubiquitous and integrated into its applications and content venues that not using it will become a disability. Microsoft craves ownership of Web software's next generation and has hatched an impressively far-reaching plan to nab this goal. If Microsoft's plans proceed as cast, the DHTML that it has primed to work with its software and "solutions" will be used not only by Internet developers and users, but by everyone sitting in front of a screen. The combination of Microsoft's WebTV investment, its foray into content with the launch of MSNBC, its attempt to imbue virtually all of its software with ActiveX components that are designed to be used everywhere and in everything (including Netscape Navigator), and its Active Desktop strategy, make the possibility of NT/TV boxes jumping with ActiveX components seem very real. NT 5.0's Management Console component is an ActiveX container that allows add-in components—called "snap-ins"—to be written in a way that permits various management tasks to be overseen from a single point.

DHTML is at the heart of a great deal of this development, particularly with Microsoft's upcoming releases of Windows 98 (Memphis) and NT 5.0. The crossover of DHTML into these traditional software products is a major occurrence, and one that is directly related to Microsoft's desire to wash Java out of its system. Microsoft has essentially realized that it can employ DHTML to accomplish the bulk of what once required Java. By incorporating DHTML, not Java, into its products, Microsoft craftily "embraces" an open standard (souped up with plenty of Microsoft add-ons) while undermining Java creator and Microsoft rival, Sun. By the time the W3C gets around to stamping HTML 4.0's final version, and thereby calling into question Microsoft's promised adherence to the final specification, Microsoft will already have made millions of dollars on the DHTML-brewed software and content it's currently dishing out. Still, Bill Gates' October 1, 1997, keynote address at the Seybold Seminars San Francisco publishing conference included the following revelatory statement: "We are putting a lot of investment into these standards groups. We have more people involved in the W3C and IETF than anybody else because we think that will drive market growth."

Microsoft's plan to incorporate DHTML across its incredibly vast selection of products means that it will trickle down into users not just of the Web, but of all Microsoft computing products. DHTML syncs perfectly with the modular component-based approach that Microsoft and other dominant players recognize as the most pragmatic investment for future success. To date, though, Microsoft is DHTML's most fervent advocate (of the DHTML version loaded with Microsoft technologies such as ActiveX, that is).

The Recombinant Coupling Of DHTML And Windows DNA

Windows DNA bridges the murky and irresolute territory between desktop applications and Web applications; its main point is to facilitate the act of building applications, which it seeks to make an easier, more casual task through DHTML's on-the-fly assembly. The hubristically named Windows DNA is positioned as the underlying genetic blueprint that serves as the model from which all ensuing creations emanate. Every piece of software that DNA spawns will contain some DNA marking its origin; DNA's component-based architecture is designed for cross-platform travel and interoperability down the line. Because object reuse is critical within DNA's plan, DHTML is perfectly suited for the architecture.

Microsoft is pumping DHTML as a core DNA technology, and one that is slated to fulfill dynamic roles that once required Java. At a Professional Developers Conference held in September 1997 in San Diego, Paul Maritz, Microsoft's group vice president for platforms and applications, said: "Java just doesn't work well on all platforms. If broad reach is the issue, then DHTML and scripting is the answer." Maritz also claims that "DHTML is the answer to what has become known as the World Wide Wait." For Microsoft to make such claims attests to its fervent interest in DHTML.

DHTML Makes Appearances With RAD, Aspen, Memphis, NT 5.0...

Once you begin to understand how Microsoft has positioned DHTML with Windows DNA, it won't be a surprise to hear that, in addition to IE 4, DHTML also appears in Microsoft's Active Directory, ActiveDesktop, ActiveX, OLE (Object Linking and Embedding), Visual Studio, Windows NT 5.0, and Windows 98 (code-named Memphis). DHTML's modularity and its ability to work with any language—including C++, Visual Basic, and Java—makes it Microsoft's logical choice for spanning the range of these applications.

DHTML's Position In The ActiveX Equation

ActiveX is a Microsoft technology that's actually a revamped version of OLE. At a very simple level, ActiveX/OLE lets you use small software components to build larger software components. ActiveX is a key part of Microsoft's ActiveDesktop plans; ActiveX controls also feature prominently in Microsoft's DHTML.

ActiveX controls are inserted into Web pages in the same way as applets, so if you encounter one at a site it is automatically downloaded. ActiveX components are neither applets nor plug-ins—they actually fall nebulously between the two. Like a plug-in, once an ActiveX control is downloaded, a local copy permanently remains on your hard disk and is used whenever the Web browser needs that control.

Although Microsoft is substituting ActiveX in many places where it once used Java, one of the problems with this switch is that ActiveX lacks the level of security that Java rides on. Microsoft is planning to address ActiveX's security weaknesses by attaching digital signatures, a decidedly less reliable security measure than Java provides.

Active Desktop And DHTML

Microsoft's Active Desktop is a full-screen HTML page that can contain other Web pages; Dynamic HTML; ActiveX controls, such as image transitions; Java components, such as stock tickers; and so on. It's the Active Desktop that ties IE 4 directly into the operating system (a unity that Microsoft terms "Complete Web Integration"). This tie-in makes IE 4 able to access folders and files from inside IE, even to the point where IE is running complete applications on your hard disk.

Active Desktop works in two layers:

1. A transparent icon layer that shows all of the desktop shortcuts that have been made

2. A customizable background HTML layer that includes all HTML-based items, such as scripts and ActiveX controls

This background HTML layer functions as a space where you can include links to oft-visited Web content; it's also possible to add HTML-based desktop items to this layer.

Data Binding

Database integration is a key part of Microsoft's DHTML strategy, and one that Netscape has yet to fully broach with its version of DHTML. Microsoft's "data-aware" Web pages all contain invisible ActiveX controls that act as data source controls. Because these controls are created to communicate with databases, HTML elements can automatically bind with fields, greatly facilitating data exchange between Web documents and databases. DHTML comes primed for database work, as it intrinsically understands how to bind HTML elements to fields in the data source control.

Microsoft uses an "open architecture" to invoke DHTML data awareness. To accomplish data control, each page contains a *data source control*, an invisible ActiveX control that is created to exchange information with a database. Because data binding lets you embed the data source on a page, it's possible to filter and sort pages in the same way as a database without requiring the actual server to be involved. Data binding supports JavaBeans as well as ActiveX interfaces; data source objects can be either ActiveX controls or Java applets.

Netscape's DHTML Vision

Like Microsoft, Netscape is interweaving DHTML components throughout its intranet/Internet/extranet applications. Netscape's ONE (Open Network Environment), a unifier for Netscape's crossware strategy, is being revamped to take full advantage of DHTML. Although Netscape lacks the extensive product base that will allow its DHTML strategy to truly challenge the scope of Microsoft's, Netscape's battle right now is to retain its majority market share of the Web browser.

DHTML In Netcaster

Netscape sees channel-oriented push as the next frontier, and Netscape's Marimba-based push client, Netscape Netcaster, was released prior to Microsoft's push client. Netcaster's 20 "premier" push channels, divided evenly between a "Business" list and a "General Interest" list, are permanently included in its main interface. Although you don't have to subscribe to the premier channels, their icons are a permanent part of the Channel Finder menu used to select channels on the right of the screen.

"Netscape Everywhere" = "DHTML Everywhere"

The "Netscape Everywhere" campaign has considerable implications for DHTML. Because intranet development is so important to Netscape—it is much more focused on the intranet/extranet, whereas Microsoft is now targeting more of the Web development market—expect to see DHTML components being used in Netscape's SuiteSpot.

A great deal of Netscape's energy must be spent defending itself against Microsoft's strategies (and negative, often inaccurate reports about Netscape products' technological shortcomings). The company has adopted the tactic of going after markets that Microsoft hasn't fully infiltrated, including the publishing industry. Netscape plans to bundle its client software with books and explanatory Net/computing guides from over 20 publishers, thereby tapping a different market—one in which it will explore DHTML development.

Another part of the "Netscape Everywhere" campaign has involved signing over 100 Internet service providers (ISPs) and telecommunications companies to distribute and bundle Netscape client software with networking products, Internet services, and communications software. Look for DHTML to appear in these packages.

Pondering DHTML

The extreme level of activity and interactivity that DHTML offers is what many Web developers and users have been waiting for since the Web's inception. The ability to manipulate Web pages through DHTML is a radical one. Although similarly interactive multimedia has been done for years on CD-ROM, when it comes to actual Web content, the type of client-based interactivity that DHTML brings is wholly unprecedented. In a few years, it will be almost incomprehensible that we ever used a Web lacking the type of interactive dynamic ability that characterizes DHTML; we'll wonder how we ever sat at the other end of a modem that was required to do so much more work for so much less streaming content.

DHTML represents an intriguing melange of push and pull technologies. Interestingly, a significant portion of early DHTML development looks like the PointCast push model that many find irritating and intrusive. DHTML can be used for so many types of content that it makes the mind swim. The ability to layer content within a page means that a great deal of textual and visual information can be stacked on each other, and then revealed according to how and where the user moves the mouse. An educational use of DHTML might include having children drag and drop visual icons to nouns and adjectives, and audio clips to words, and then receiving instantaneous feedback. Online games have been enthusiastic adopters of DHTML because it allows players to engage in the game without suffering from the old type of server lag (the ongoing game results might be surreptitiously sent to the server every few minutes and the player's score updated accordingly at a Web site).

DHTML And Download Time

Web traffic has become a serious impediment to enjoying the Web, particularly during business hours; DHTML can help or hurt this situation, depending on how DHTML sites are constructed. Many Web sites, particularly corporate ones with hefty budgets, make the classic mistake of trying to over-impress visitors with their initial page. However, keep in mind that when you're visiting a site for the first time—brainwaves throbbing in surf mode—and you encounter a two-minute download for dynamic content, there has to be a good reason to wait. At the very minimum, this first page needs to give a sort of preview and overview of what the site contains; ideally, it should convince viewers of the content feast to come.

DHTML And The Question Of Speed

The potential for animation and streaming content that DHTML brings to the Web—through a markup language, not a plug-in or separate player—is also accompanied with questions of how these freshly minted powers should be used. Although many computer professionals conceive of an ideal of brash, speedy content that engages users to the point of addiction, this perception is influenced by a variety of interests, including software and hardware manufacturers, who benefit from a high rate of obsolescence and the necessity of frequent upgrades.

Despite the speed and glitz that today's 200+ MHz processors and software developments enable, being inundated with information and visual stimulation is not the most effective way to process information. We've witnessed television advertisements becoming increasingly invasive, shocking, and high-impact because watchers are jaded and prone to hitting the remote during commercials. Attempting to apply the same content strategy to development with DHTML will have the same effect: Viewers will tune out.

The Danger Of DHTML Overstimulation

Many designers seek to imbue Web sites with extreme stimulation—loud flashing colors, relentlessly beating music, objects flying in from various locations on the page—rather than to present information in the way that users will be able to best process and remember it. In the long run, this approach is clearly not the best for business, even if the "coolness factor" seems initially high. The pace and style at which a Web site unfolds affects the way it will enter the brain. Although a television show pushes your consciousness through whatever range of ideas, audio, images, and visual data stream it deems most suitable, this push approach requires viewers to shield themselves from unwanted content as it unfolds. Pulled content, on the other hand, is much more respectful of what the user desires, and the content that it unleashes is user-driven.

The Rhythm Of Learning

The book *Superlearning*, by Sheila Ostrander and Lynn Schroeder, published in 1979, documents the relationship between rhythm and learning. If material to be remembered was presented rapid-fire at one-second intervals, people learned only about 20 percent of it. At 5 second intervals, people learned about 30 percent of it. When there was a 10-second interval between each item, the amount of material memorized was over 40 percent.

As this research indicates, out-of-sync, distracting rhythms definitely hamper the learning process. When you're adding script to your pages—sending out ideas in a stream of colors and graphics—the time you spend thinking about the best way to express your content may prove to be invaluable.

DHTML And The Feedback Loop

Demographic information is one of the most valuable—and most nebulous—quantities that the online realm offers. Tantalizingly detailed statistics on where and how people spend their time can be gleaned from their online travels and the choices they make therein. There may not be a reason for you to return a page you've altered through the dynamic movement that DHTML enables back to the server, except for the fact that the data it contains may reveal information about you that has extreme commercial value. Although you can look at an advertisement and play with the word game it streams across your screen, if there's no provision to give advertisers feedback about your interaction, how can they know they've made a worthwhile investment? Seeing the lack of economic reward offline surfing might engender, both Microsoft and Netscape have applied foresight to this situation, and their push strategies provide a way to monitor offline browsing of Web sites.

Deciding How To Use DHTML

The powerful multimedia content that DHTML can unleash on viewers makes sensitivity to issues such as the relationship between a page's color, sound, and rhythm more crucial. In fact, DHTML extends Web pages into the realm of synesthesia, the cross-experiencing of the senses. The more complex visual options DHTML brings must be carefully considered; for example, mapping colors to information is subtle yet crucial, as color can influence the speed and quality at which people consume data. Similarly, because music and sound affect brain wave patterns, the enhanced audio capabilities that accompany DHTML shouldn't be regarded as a fluffy enhancement.

Speed is not the most important thing for a Web site. A faster Web page is not necessarily a better Web page, nor is it one that users will want to spend more time visiting or return to more frequently. It's now the time to decide: Do we want to turn the Web into a channel-defined bloated medium of content that's engineered to be slowed by unavoidable commercials and unnecessary middlemen directing our voyages at every turn?

Creating (Quality) DHTML Content

DHTML can make Web pages easier to read; however, if inappropriately applied, it can (and will) also make content more difficult to read. DHTML clearly has the ability to fill the Web with vacuous yet highly active and distracting content. The new powers that DHTML brings to Web design are making many shudder; past fads of **<BLINK>**-tag abuses pale in comparison to the time that bad DHTML content can waste.

DHTML makes it possible to *condense* content, to present it in a newly efficient way. Coupled with the variety that streaming multimedia can give to an information-oriented site, the combination of densely packaged Web data is highly appealing. Waiting for a DHTML page to load is not.

DHTML And The Push/Channel Metaphor

Push technology and building channels to speed push content through is crucial to both Netscape's and Microsoft's DHTML strategies. To understand the strategies that Microsoft and Netscape are applying to Internet development—and the variety of uses they both envision for DHTML—it's useful to examine their intranet/ Internet/push approaches, all of which increasingly revolve around the same technologies. There's been a great deal of territory charted between the Mosaic browser that provided the basis of Netscape's first incarnation and the intense focus on intranet and push/channel development that characterizes Netscape's current strategy.

Channels And CDF

A channel establishes a link between users and Web content; unlike a bookmark that you add to your Web browser, the channel functions in a way that guarantees a return visit to the site.

As with Netscape Netcaster, you can access IE 4 push channels through a channel guide that sits on your desktop. The Channel Definition Format (CDF) is a file format that Microsoft created to control its channel structure. CDF essentially provides a Web site with a logical, hierarchical index or map that describes what type of information the site contains and the categories to which its content belongs. When a CDF file is on a Web site server, a Web site can build more traditional push channels that specify exactly what information should be delivered to subscribers and on what schedule. Users can place these channels on their Active Desktops by simply clicking a link to the CDF file. CDF is an application of Extensible Markup Language (XML), so its specification relies heavily on the definition of XML.

Through the CDF, Web authors can exert detailed control over how a site is "Webcast"; creating a CDF file is the only action required for a regular Web site to evolve into a push mechanism. The CDF acts as a single file that indexes a site's content. At the most basic level, a CDF file contains little more than a list of URLs pointing to Web sites. Advanced CDF files might include, in addition to directive URLs, title/abstract information that describes individual items of content, a schedule indicating when content is to be updated, and a hierarchical organization of the URLs that explain how the Web site is structured.

The information used with CDF-based channels is completely independent of content format and can, therefore, include a range of Web applications and content built on HTML, Java, JavaScript, and ActiveX technologies.

DHTML And The Net's Future

The Web will never be as homogeneous as it was a few years ago, no matter how much desktop Microsoft seizes or how widely the W3C spec is given lip service. The Net's fascinating exponential growth is still in its earliest stages, with Internet-access rates in some other countries far from what they are in the United States. Because the vast majority of humans have yet to experience the Web first-hand, the steps that DHTML takes at this juncture, particularly toward the television model, are extremely significant.

It's interesting to wonder what artists such as Leonardo da Vinci or French Futurist painters and sculptors would have done with the creative options that DHTML presents, coupled with the Net's global and inexpensive distribution network. There's little doubt that DHTML arms Web designers and developers with more creative power than has ever existed in the medium. For that reason, designers must seriously consider the process of crafting Web content, how they want viewers to take in the information and visual stimulation they provide, and what kind of relationship commercial and noncommercial content will enjoy within their pages. This is a heady time to be a Web developer—although there's still a trade-off involved at a level of visual quality, DHTML is a giant step toward putting the Web on more equal footing with television. The questions are whether users (particularly new users) will have the opportunity to explore the Web in a nonpush format, and whether the Web will transcend the killer entertainment apps that threaten to clog its wires. Only time will reveal the answer.

Chapter 4

Dueling DHTML Proposals

This chapter provides an in-depth explanation of Dynamic HTML and includes a discussion of the battle between Netscape and Microsoft regarding the proposed DHTML standard.

Notes...

Chapter 4

Nothing on the Web is simple anymore, including DHTML, because each vendor insists its way is the best to the exclusion of every other vendor's solution. Granted, protocols are standard—that's why they exist—and HTML is sort of settled down. On the other hand, both Netscape and Microsoft still have their own extended HTML DTDs, and it doesn't look like that's going to change any time soon. In theory, this is all part of the competition that makes capitalism function, but from a Web design perspective it gets very old, very fast. Still, disparate proposals are not a new phenomenon, and designers have learned to live with the situation and to create pages in this ever-changing, ever-different Web world.

There are three major players in the DHTML game: The World Wide Web Consortium (W3C), Microsoft, and Netscape. The W3C is, as always, trying to create a standard that is best for everyone; platform- and operating-system independent; and, in this case, also scripting-language neutral. Both Microsoft and Netscape are trying to create solutions that meet customer requests for dynamic Web pages and that integrate easily within existing Web infrastructures. The problem with this is that the existing Web infrastructures are growing farther and farther apart with each passing quarter, so the DHTML solutions are far from similar.

In this chapter, we'll take a good look the basic foundations of both Microsoft's and Netscape's approaches to DHTML. You'll soon see that each claims to support the

W3C's DOM, but they do so in two very different ways that are going to make it difficult for Web designers to create a single dynamic page that looks good in both browsers. We're not doing this to scare you or make you believe you'll have to design pages for an individual browser, but to arm you with the knowledge of how these two players in the DHTML game do things. You'll see similarities as well as differences in each proposal. This knowledge, combined with what you will learn in Chapter 5 about the DOM in general and the W3C's plans for DHTML, should help you pick out the portions of each proposal that will eventually become standard and those that will fall by the wayside. If you concentrate on the mechanisms that stand a good chance of surviving the standards process and don't become dependent on those that will probably disappear in the next year or so, you'll be better able to create pages that will come close to meeting the standard.

The W3C's DHTML Wish List

The W3C's only current contribution to DHTML is the specification of how a Document Object Model should look and act, and a few new additions to HTML 4.0 that make integrating scripting into Web pages easier. A full DHTML standard will eventually emerge from the W3C, but don't bother to start looking for it until sometime in 1999. Remember, the W3C creates proposals via committees that have to answer to a great many people, and that takes time. Microsoft and Netscape have to answer only to themselves, their stockholders, and their users. If they took as long to develop products and solutions as the W3C does they would be out of business in a heartbeat. Currently, the W3C's DOM and HTML 4.0 are the only standards developers have to work with; how they implement the standards and use them to create dynamic Web pages in the real world is entirely up to them.

A standard DOM must meet these 10 basic requirements:

- It should be platform independent and scripting-language neutral.
- It should be able to be used to construct and deconstruct a document.
- It should allow other mechanisms such as scripts, applets, plug-ins, and ActiveX controls to be integrated into the document.
- Other mechanisms must be able to affect and manipulate the document.
- It must work within HTML, CSS, and XML.

- HTML, CSS, and XML DOMs must be created and implemented using the basic foundations of these languages.
- It should make use of a consistent naming convention.
- A GUI should not be required to implement changes to it.
- You should able to be save to a disk an identical copy of a document.
- It should be secure and ensure validity and privacy for the user.

In a nutshell, these 10 requirements say that the DOM must provide a way for the document to be put together, taken apart, and put back together again an infinite number of times, even after it's been downloaded by the browser. The requirements are part of the W3C's continuing effort to make Web information 100 percent accessible to anyone. The W3C has definitely covered all the bases, but it has also set a complex course for anyone who wants to create a DOM that conforms to the standard.

In addition to these 10 general requirements, there are requirements in the following 10 major areas that must also be met by a standard DOM:

- Structure navigation
- Document manipulation
- Content manipulation
- Event model
- Style sheet object model
- DTD manipulation
- Error reporting
- Security, validity, and privacy
- Document meta-information
- User Accessibility (UA) information

This brief introduction to the W3C's DOM requirements is to focus your thinking on the requirements of a DOM as we discuss how Microsoft and Netscape are attempting to meet the requirements and create functioning, viable DHTML solutions that work for real users in the real world. (Chapter 5 covers the DOM and its requirements in each of these areas in detail.)

Microsoft's Dynamic HTML

The developers at Microsoft have taken Web design to a brand-new level with their DHTML implementation in Internet Explorer 4.0. To facilitate this step up, Microsoft had to completely rewrite the HTML parsing engine. (The parsing engine's job is to read an entire Web document, break it down into its component parts like tags and text, and then format the content for display on the screen based on the tags and text.) The new parsing engine takes the standard HTML tags and document elements and integrates them with the new Scripting Object Model to give designers complete scripting control over every element in an HTML page. The Scripting Object Model is designed to work with any scripting language—it's scripting-language neutral, as prescribed by the W3C's DOM—but is best used with Microsoft's own VBScript or Netscape's JavaScript.

Microsoft's DHTML has four components:

- The Microsoft DOM
- The use of scripting to control page elements
- A set of multimedia controls for including animation, filters, and other media effects
- Data binding that links live database records for a page without requiring complex CGI scripting

We'll take a brief look at the concepts and mechanisms behind each of these four components, and we'll uncover the realities of *graceful degradation*, Microsoft's name for its attempts to make its version of DHTML compatible with other browsers.

The Microsoft DOM

DOMs are not new to browsers by any stretch of the imagination. We can credit Netscape for including the first DOM as part of the Navigator 2.0 release; Microsoft soon followed suit in IE 3.0. However, all past versions of the DOM have extended limited control over anchors, forms, and a few other HTML elements. The IE 4.0 DOM changes everything by extending the DOM to provide full scripting control over every element in an HTML document. Microsoft officially calls its DOM the Dynamic HTML Document Object Model; we'll call it the Microsoft DOM for short. Notice the capital "D" in Dynamic; Microsoft actually owns the trademark for the Dynamic HTML name.

The Microsoft DOM includes four new mechanisms for creating dynamic Web pages:

- Complete access to, and control over, all page elements
- The ability to update a page instantly
- A full event model
- The ability to change the text on a page

In keeping with one of the major ideas behind DHTML, changes can be made to any page governed by the Microsoft DOM at any time, including after the page has been downloaded.

Complete Access To, And Control Over, All Page Elements

As we mentioned previously, the limited DOMs included in earlier browser versions provided control over some HTML elements such as anchors, forms, applets, and images. However, suppose you wanted to build a dynamic bulleted summary for a page based on the document's headings, so the summary would change as the document changed, without any extra work on your part. With the limited DOMs of the past this couldn't be done, because headings weren't accessible. The new Microsoft DOM makes every component of an HTML document accessible via the DOM and allows components to be manipulated via scripting in many different ways. The Microsoft DOM uses the element's name and a unique ID assigned with the **ID=** attribute as a way of indexing all the elements on an HTML page.

To collect all the heading levels on a page and create the bulleted summary, you can write a script to identify each heading and the content between the heading tags. You can then create a new group of text and tags at the bottom of the HTML page under the Summary heading that lists the collected content in one or more unordered lists. This is easily accomplished with just a little planning and some basic scripting knowledge.

The Ability To Update A Page Instantly

What good is access to all of the elements in an HTML page if you can't do something with them? The Microsoft DOM makes it possible to update a page instantly by changing an element's styles or attributes. This process works hand-in-hand with the Cascading Style Sheets (CSS) standard described in detail in Chapter 6.

The following short JavaScript changes the color of an HTML paragraph called "WhatNew" from the default to navy blue:

```
<script language=JavaScript>
function changeWhatNew() {
   WhatNew.style.color = "navy";
}
</script>

<P ID=WhatNew>This paragraph's text will now be navy blue
thanks to a bit of scripting</P>
```

The paragraph's text becomes blue as soon as the script is executed; the page doesn't even have to be reloaded. What forces the script to execute? An event, of course.

A Full Event Model

An inherent part of any graphical interface is its event model. A user clicking a hyperlink is an event that causes a new page to load. In previous HTML and browser versions, the supported events were few and far between, and there was little control over those events that did exist. Microsoft's DOM includes what the company dubs a *Full Event Model.* This means that a new variety of events is recognized by the browser and can be tied to scripts, causing the scripts to execute when a specific event occurs. These events include:

- **onload=*script***
- **onunload=*script***
- **onclick=*script***
- **ondblclick=*script***
- **onmousedown=*script***
- **onmouseup=*script***
- **onmouseover=*script***
- **onmousemove=*script***
- **onmouseout=*script***
- **onfocus=*script***
- **onblur=*script***

- **onkeypress=*script***
- **onkeydown=*script***
- **onkeyup=*script***
- **onsubmit=*script***
- **onreset=*script***
- **onselect=*script***
- **onchange=*script***

Each event works with a select group of HTML tags and requires a specific action by the user. **Onmouseover** occurs when the user moves his or her mouse over an area, whereas **onmouseout** occurs when the user moves the mouse out of an area. For a complete definition of each event and the tags with which it works, please see Table 2.1 in Chapter 2.

Events invoke script pages and are instantly updated. To continue with the blue text example from the previous section, let's create a graphic linked to an **onmouseover** event that causes the WhatNew text to turn navy when the user moves a mouse over the image:

```
<script language=JavaScript>
function makeBlue() {
   WhatNew.style.color = "navy";
}
function makeNormal() {
   WhatNew.style.color = "black";
}
</script>

<H1>Document Title</H1>
<IMG ID=imgnew SRC="/graphics/new.gif"
   ALT="What's New"
   onmouseover="makeBlue();"
   onmouseout="makeNormal();">

<P ID=WhatNew>This paragraph's text will turn navy blue when
a mouse is run over the image thanks to a bit of scripting</P>
```

When the user runs a mouse over the What's New image, the information in the WhatNew paragraph will change from black to navy. When the mouse is moved off the image, the paragraph's text will return to black. For a complete explanation of integrating events into Microsoft DHTML pages, and to learn about event bubbling, read the Microsoft Bubble Power article at **www.microsoft.com/sitebuilder/features/ie4event.asp**.

The Ability To Change The Text On A Page

In addition to being able to change the attributes and styles of text and elements in a Web page, Microsoft's DOM provides a way to change the text and elements themselves. This allows for entire groups of text, markup and all, to be replaced by new ones as designed by the Webmaster and invoked by user actions. Four properties make this possible:

- **innerHTML**—Defines the contents of an HTML element that includes HTML tags; when changes or replacements are made the content is changed, but the outer HTML tags remain.
- **innerText**—Specifies the new contents of an HTML element; this property treats the contents as a text string and does not replace an element's HTML tags.
- **outerHTML**—Defines the contents of an HTML element, including the HTML tags; both the content and tags change when changes or replacements are made.
- **outerText**—Specifies the new contents of an HTML element, but replaces the entire element, tags and all.

The **innerText** and **outerText** properties focus on the text itself and ask the browser to treat any character strings as plain text. The **innerHTML** and **outerHTML** properties ask the browser to treat character strings as a combination of text and markup, and parse it accordingly.

Scripting

Our look at the Microsoft DOM has already introduced you to the use of scripting to control page elements. We showed you how scripting, combined with an intrinsic event, can cause an element to change color when a user runs a mouse over a related graphic. In general, scripting is the key to making HTML pages dynamic. The DOM describes the document and gives you access to all of its parts, whereas scripts provide the instructions for how those parts should be manipulated, changed, replaced, and created.

Scripting allows you to set variables, store them, and later include them in your HTML code. This allows you to directly manipulate the data in your HTML code. Even before HTML 4.0, scripting was becoming more and more common as a tool for Web designers. Because earlier versions of HTML were not as scripting-friendly as 4.0, this required some creative Web authoring and HTML scripting, often to the exclusion of users with certain browsers. The new events, form controls, and a general scripting-friendly attitude in HTML 4.0 make implementing scripts as page-control devices much easier than in the past.

You can use scripts to validate user input and control applets, among other things. For example, if you create an online survey that rewards users with a free mouse pad for completing the survey, you will want to ensure that they both complete the survey in its entirety and provide you with complete mailing information so you can zip their well-deserved mouse pad off to them in a timely manner. A script embedded in the document can check to see if all the required portions of the survey have been filled out and valid input entered. If a user forgets to answer a question or responds with an invalid response, the script can bring up an alert box and reformat the text onscreen so the unanswered or incorrect questions are highlighted with a different color background. Once a user has completed the survey to the script's satisfaction, another script will check to see if the user supplied you with complete mailing information (prompting for additional information if they did not), send the survey information to the R&D folks, and forward the mailing information to the shipping department.

These types of interaction with data are not new to the Web, but before Web programming (scripting) they were all accomplished using CGI scripts that required trips to the server and back again. Now, scripts are embedded directly within the page so they are downloaded as part of the page and run on the client side. This reduces the number of times a server is hit as well as the time a user has to wait for a response, which in turn reduces stress on the server. In many cases, the scripting languages are even easier to write with than CGI. Everyone wins.

Generally, Web scripts can be written in one of two languages, JavaScript or VBScript. Microsoft calls its version of JavaScript, JScript. VBScript is Microsoft's own scripting language, adapted from its larger object-oriented programming language, Visual Basic. Although you can use either scripting language when creating pages, according to the Microsoft Dynamic HTML proposal, if you opt for VBScript, Netscape users will not be able to access your pages. Because both browsers support JScript, we suggest using it as a learning and design tool to make your pages accessible to as many users as possible.

Both VBScript and JScript support three separate classes of objects.

VBScripts support objects provided by:

- The VBScript engine
- Internet Explorer
- The Web page author via the HTML **<OBJECT>** tag

JScripts support objects provided by:

- The JScript engine
- Internet Explorer
- The Web page author via the HTML **<OBJECT>** tag

As you can see, the only difference between the objects supported by VBScript and JScript are those directly related to the scripting languages themselves. Internet Explorer has its own set of objects. As a Web designer, you can include as many objects as you want of any type using the **<OBJECT>** tag.

As a small sampling of what these two languages look like and how they function, let's examine the code used by each to create the infamous "Hello, world" dialog box.

First, VBScript:

```
<CENTER>
 <P>
 <H2>Hello, world sample</H2>

<INPUT TYPE=BUTTON VALUE="Click me" NAME="BtnHello">
</CENTER>

<SCRIPT LANGUAGE="VBScript">
<!--
 Sub BtnHello_OnClick
  MsgBox "Hello, world!", 0, "My first active document"
 End Sub
-->
</SCRIPT>
```

Now, JScript:

```
<CENTER>
 <P>
 <H2>Hello, world sample</H2>

 <FORM Name="Form1" ACTION="">
 <INPUT TYPE=BUTTON VALUE="Click me"
  NAME="BtnHello"
  OnClick="sayhello()"
 >
 </FORM>

</CENTER>

<SCRIPT LANGUAGE="JavaScript">
<!--

    function sayhello ()
    {
        alert("Hello, world!")
    }

//-->
</SCRIPT>
```

Both examples use a button to activate; it's only the actual scripting language that is different. You can always include both VBScript and JScript on your pages, writing each script in both languages for maximum browser compatibility. For an example of this, visit the Microsoft Internet Client SDK Setup page at **www.microsoft.com/msdn/sdk/inetsdk/asetup/default.htm**.

For more information on using scripting in the Microsoft environment, visit the Microsoft Scripting Site at **www.microsoft.com/scripting/**.

Multimedia Controls

Transitions, filters, drop shadows, animation, and other multimedia effects are commonplace in documents created using tools such as Macromedia Director and Authorware. To bring similar effects to Web pages, Microsoft has added a new set of style-sheet properties and multimedia controls to its Dynamic HTML arsenal. These effects work well with images, but can also be applied to page text to create unique effects that would otherwise require a graphic. The available filters include:

- Glow
- Blur

- Invert
- Shadow
- Drop Shadow
- Gray
- Wave
- Mask
- Chroma
- X-Ray
- Light

For a complete tutorial on how to add and combine these effects to your HTML pages, see the Microsoft Site Lights article at **www.microsoft.com/sitebuilder/archive/site/site0915.htm**. Keep in mind that these techniques are created using proprietary style-sheet properties and will not be displayed by browsers that don't support CSS or that support only strict CSS.

Data Binding

Until the advent of DHTML, including information from a database in an HTML document involved at least one CGI script to act as an intermediary between the Web page and the database. Pages that include CGI links to databases rely heavily on a server and can take a while to download. Data binding is a unique feature of Microsoft's DHTML that allows you to link individual elements in an HTML page to other data sources. These data sources can include traditional databases and tab delimited text files, among others. When the page is loaded, the information is retrieved from the data source and formatted to fit the page, based on the element's style and attributes. Data binding removes the CGI script from the picture entirely, speeding download time and making linking Web pages to databases much easier.

Data binding is limited only by the imagination of the Web developer and the data source itself. Tables can be automatically generated from data sources, and when the data source is updated, the page will be as well. Form fields can be tied to database fields so users can automatically enter and update database information.

A data source object is required to communicate with the database and create a successful data bind. To make your life easier, two of these are included in Internet

Explorer 4.0. One recognizes comma-delimited records in a text file and the other works with a Microsoft SQL database. Look for other data source objects to be available soon from Microsoft and third-party vendors that will make it easier for all types of database information to be tied to Web pages via data binding.

Keep in mind that data binding is Microsoft's own creation and is not in any way related to the W3C's DOM or future DHTML plans. The data source objects are created to work with other Microsoft or Windows-based products, so you'll have to do things the Microsoft way to use this technology. For more information about data binding visit **www.microsoft.com/msdn/sdk/inetsdk/help/dhtml/databind.htm #dhtml_databind**.

Graceful Degradation

The developers at Microsoft insist that they've created their Dynamic HTML solution in such a way that it gracefully degrades. In English, this means pages built using Microsoft's DHTML can be successfully viewed by other browsers—most notably Navigator and early versions of IE—even though they might not look as nice as they do when viewed with Internet Explorer 4.0. The theory is that developers can count on graceful degradation to make their pages accessible to everyone and won't have to create multiple versions of a page. It's a nice theory, but in practice it doesn't always work.

For example, let's look at Microsoft's own Dynamic HTML overview at **www.microsoft.com/workshop/author/dhtml/dhtmlovw.htm**. This page takes advantage of Dynamic HTML to hide the contents of each section until the reader clicks on the heading, causing the contents to be revealed. Figure 4.1 shows the page as viewed in Internet Explorer 4.0 on a PC, before a heading is clicked. Figure 4.2 shows the page after a heading is clicked.

It's no surprise that the page works exactly as it should for IE 4.0 on a PC running Windows NT. But what happens on a Macintosh or with Netscape Navigator? Figure 4.3 shows that we clicked in vain on a heading using IE 4.0 Preview 1 for the Macintosh; the hidden information wouldn't show. Figure 4.4 shows *all* hidden text revealed because Netscape Navigator 3.0 doesn't support style sheets or JavaScript modifications. Netscape Navigator 4.0 on the Mac fares no better than IE 4.0. Figure 4.5 shows that once again, no matter how many times we clicked a heading, no text appeared.

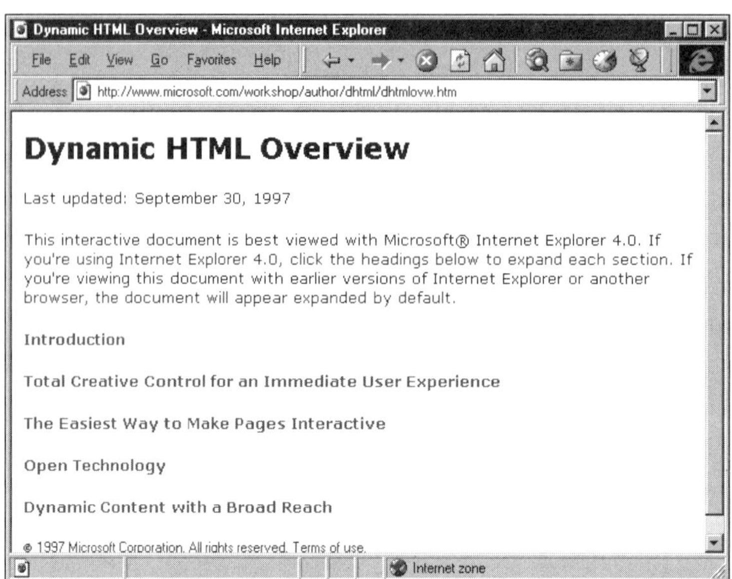

Figure 4.1

Click on a heading and text should appear below it.

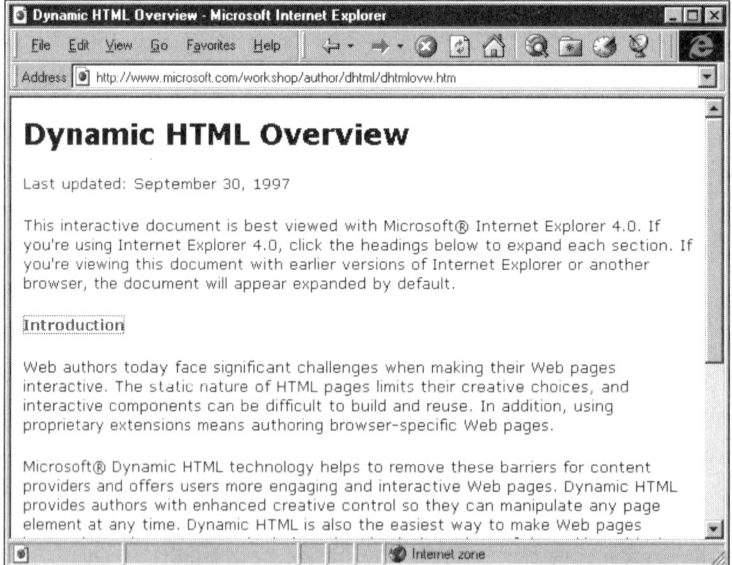

Figure 4.2

The hidden text is revealed.

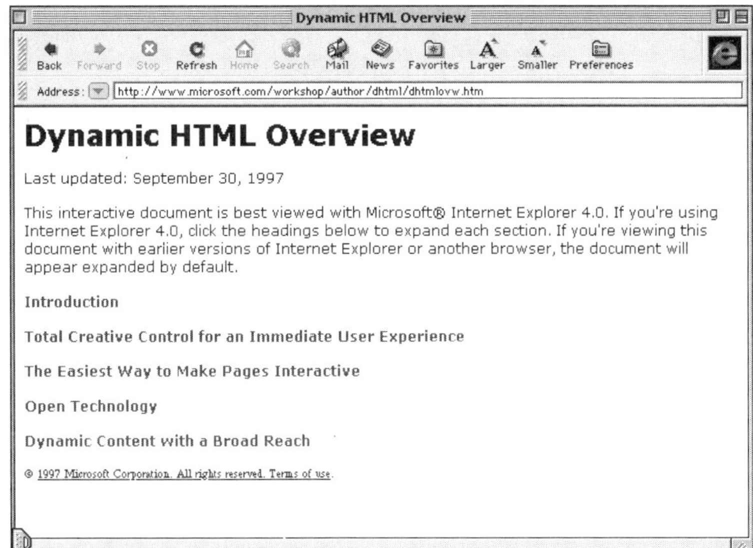

Figure 4.3

IE 4.0 Preview 1 for the Macintosh won't show the hidden text.

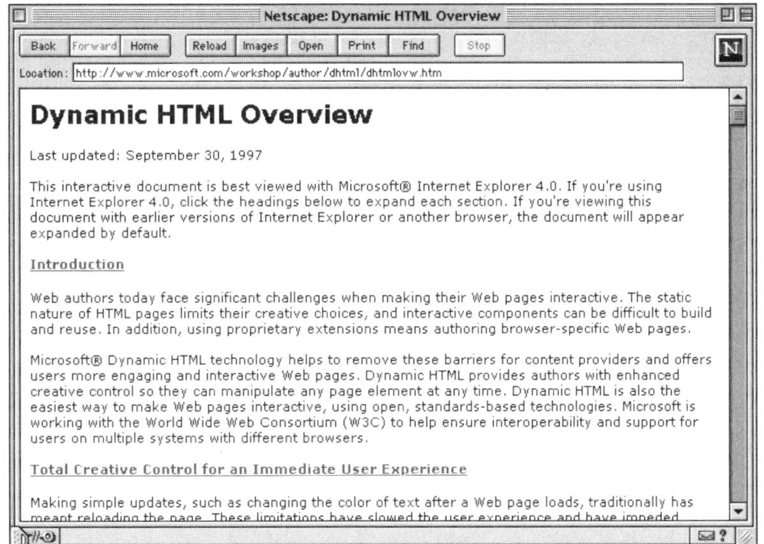

Figure 4.4

Navigator 3.0 bares all; headings and text alike.

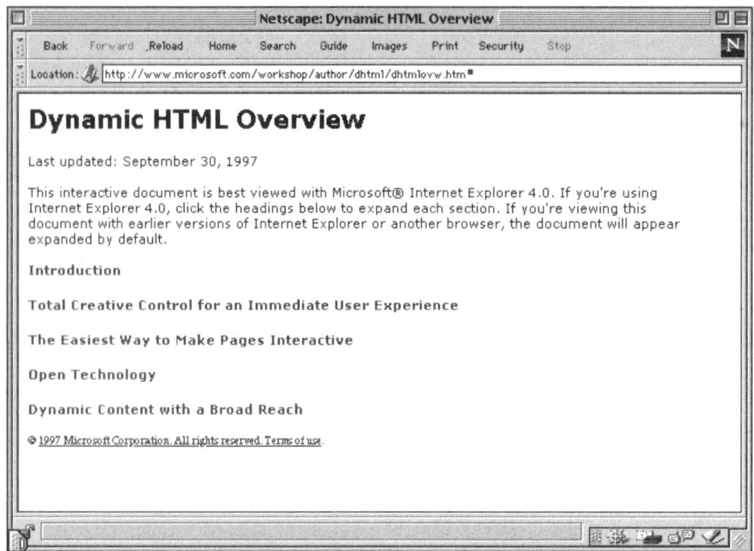

Figure 4.5

The hidden text is just as elusive when the page is viewed with Navigator 4.0 on a Mac.

As the examples show, pages created using Microsoft's DHTML don't degrade very gracefully at all. For this reason, we encourage you to let readers know you're using a new technology and what browsers work best with that technology. We also encourage you to check your pages with as many browsers and on as many platforms as possible so as not to ungracefully alienate users with browsers unfriendly to your bleeding-edge technology.

Netscape's Layers

As we mentioned, Netscape can be credited with the invention and first implementation of the DOM in Navigator 2.0. That release of Navigator also saw the advent of JavaScript, a scripting language based on Java but much easier to learn and implement. However, that first DOM provided access to a limited group of page elements that included hyperlinks, forms, colors, and a few other browser attributes.

Netscape's DOM relied on an *instance hierarchy* that was created for every individual hierarchy. An instance hierarchy describes, in a hierarchical order, the actual elements present in an HTML page. If only **H1** and **H2** are used in the page, they are the only heading elements included in the instance hierarchy, even though **H3**, **H4**, **H5**, and **H6** are all available to be used in page design. This instance method keeps the DOM small and efficient, describing only the elements being used rather than all the elements that can possibly be used.

In Navigator 3.0, the DOM extended its limited control to embedded objects such as applets. Still, although the DOM described all of the elements used in a page, a Web designer could control only a few of them without having to re-access the server. A JavaScript protocol could be used to modify the remaining page contents without accessing the server again, but the original page was wiped out and a new one loaded from scratch. Not graceful at all, but at the time it was the only option designers had.

Surprisingly enough, Netscape did not extend the DOM very much at all in its Navigator 4.0 release. Instead, Netscape has developed its own method for creating dynamic HTML pages. The three components of Netscape's DHTML are:

- Using layers to manipulate blocks of HTML on a Web page
- Tight control over positioning, colors, fonts, layout, and more using style sheets
- Attaching dynamic fonts directly to a Web page

As you can see, about the only thing the Netscape and Microsoft DHTML proposals have in common is their reliance on style sheets to control page layout, and even that varies greatly in implementation. We'll take a look at Netscape's three DHTML components to show you how the two proposals differ conceptually and in practice.

Layers

A *layer* is a block of HTML that can be hidden, displayed, moved, and manipulated. A single HTML page can have several different layers, all working together to create a single display but able to be manipulated as individual units. Think of a set of HTML layers as a set of slides you can move around on a screen and display in any combination. To create and work with layers Netscape developed the **<LAYER>** tag. This tag is strictly proprietary markup; Microsoft does not support it in IE 4.0 and shows no sign of including it in future browsers, either. The W3C has also declined to include the **<LAYER>** tag as part of the HTML standard. Because of the lack of support from both the W3C and Microsoft, it looks as if the layer method of page design will eventually disappear. Even Netscape is dropping its layer push in favor of other ways to implement DHTML that aren't platform- or browser-specific. However, for now, layers can't be ignored; they are the way of creating DHTML for Netscape.

As an introduction to layers, we'll take a look at some of the cool things they can be used for. Figure 4.6 shows three stages in the Stella Chelsea demo included on the Netscape site. The Web page grows right before your eyes, with no input from the user at all.

Figure 4.6

Three stages of the Stella Chelsea layers demo from Netscape.

To see this demo "in person," point Netscape Navigator at **search.netscape.com/comprod/products/communicator/beta_features.html** and choose the demo from the "Dynamic HTML: Layers and Positioning" section. Be sure to select the correct monitor size for best viewing. To see what the code behind this cool demo looks like, click the View Source button in the bottom left corner and you're presented with easily five screens' worth of scripting and HTML. Suffice it to say this is not your mother's HTML.

In general, the demo creates several different groups of images and text and then drops or slides them in to create effects we're more accustomed to seeing on multimedia CD-ROMs. Although this is a very simplistic description of the concept behind layers, it serves our present purpose as we discuss different ways to create dynamic pages.

Now for a reality check. Although the effects created by layers are great when viewed with Navigator 4.0, Figure 4.7 shows the results of looking at the same demo in either Navigator 3.0 or Internet Explorer 4.0, where the effects are not nearly as exciting.

An on-screen message that you need to upgrade or change your browser isn't what most users want to see. As browser installation packages get bigger and the browsers themselves require more system resources, people are reluctant to commit download

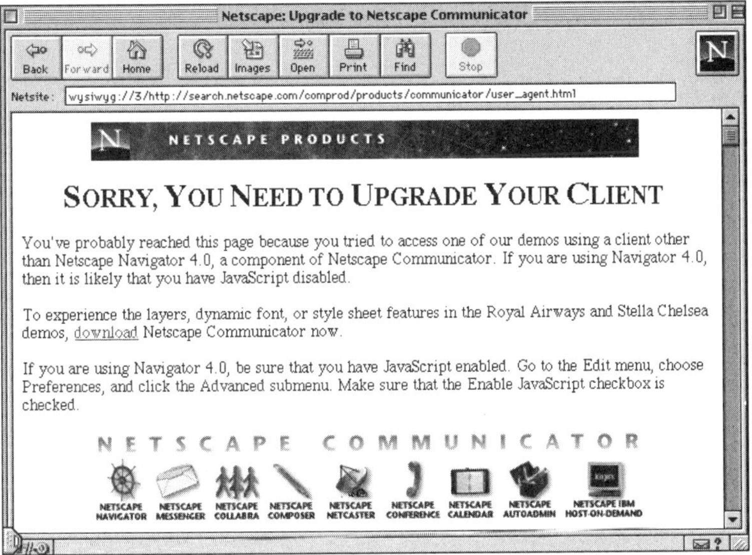

Figure 4.7

The Stella Chelsea layers demo when viewed through Navigator 3.0 or Internet Explorer 4.0.

time and disk space to a new browser. All in all, though, we must admit that the effects are pretty spectacular when viewed through the correct browser.

The possibilities of layers are almost endless. Look at the Netscape home page: A site navigation bar that is expandable and retractable is created using JavaScript and layers. Boxes of information about Netcenter, an inexpensive domain-name registration site, slide in and out from the right-hand side. To see these unique effects for yourself, visit Netscape's home page at **www.netscape.com** (with Navigator 4.0, of course).

Netscape And Style Sheets

To maintain the claim that Navigator is W3C-compliant, Netscape has integrated support for Cascading Style Sheets (CSS) in Navigator 4.0. However, true to form, they also support their own style-sheet implementation known as *JavaScript Style Sheets* (JSS). Chapter 6 describes style sheets in detail, so we're dealing only with the concepts in this section. In general, both CSS and JSS associate style attributes with properties that take values. For example, you can specify **margin-top** in CSS and **marginTop** in JSS to specify a top margin for a document. The CSS syntax for creating a style rule that makes all first-level headings teal is:

```
<STYLE TYPE="text/css">
H1 {color:teal}
</STYLE>
```

The JSS syntax for the same rule is:

```
<STYLE TYPE="text/javascript">
tags.H1.color = "teal"
</STYLE>
```

The differences in syntax and naming scheme really aren't that different, so what's the big deal? The big deal is that JSS isn't standard, so Internet Explorer doesn't recognize it. On the other hand, Netscape doesn't recognize Microsoft's manipulation of CSS styles via scripting, but uses JSS mechanisms to accomplish the same effects. So if you just want to include style sheets in your documents, use CSS and all will be well. If you want to manipulate an element's styles dynamically, you'll have to choose sides. Not very pretty, is it?

Style sheets work hand-in-hand with the Netscape layers technology to define the absolute position of a layer on the page. This works with both CSS and JSS, although manipulating layers through scripting requires JSS in combination with JavaScript.

Style sheets and scripting seem to be foundations of every variety of DHTML. The only problem is deciding which combination of style sheets and layers you should use. Right now, we simply can't say because there is no one combination that will work for all browsers. We suspect that in the future JavaScript manipulation of CSS will be the standard, but don't put your money on that just yet—the standards process has just begun.

Dynamic Fonts

One of the biggest hurdles to including font information via the **<FONT>** tag or style sheets is the lack of a way to embed fonts within Web pages. If a font element or style-sheet property calls for a font that isn't installed on the user's machine, the page will display an alternate font as specified by the designer or the default font set by users in their browser preferences.

Font selection is an important part of a page's look and feel, and Web designers who spend a great deal of time selecting and implementing just the right fonts are often disappointed when they view their pages on computers without the correct fonts installed. Netscape believes it has found a solution to the font problem: dynamic fonts.

The idea behind dynamic fonts is that the font literally will be embedded in the HTML document and sent with it as it is transferred from the server to the user's computer. This is similar to the way images, applets, and other objects can be embedded in an HTML document. The **<LINK>** tag is used to reference a specific font definition file:

```
<LINK REL=fontdef SRC="http://www.mysite.com/fonts/home.pfr">
```

Using proprietary syntax added to Netscape's own implementation of CSS, the font definition file can also be included within the **<STYLE>...</STYLE>** tags:

```
<STYLE TYPE="text/css">
@fontdef url(http://www.mysite.com/fonts/home.pfr);
</STYLE>
```

Once a font definition file is linked to a Web page, the definition file is downloaded to the user's computer along with the HTML file.

The question now is where to get or how to make the font definition files. It's much easier to get them than make them, so visit either of these two Web sites to choose from a nice collection of font definition files: **home.netscape.com/comprod/products/communicator/fonts/index.html** or **www.bitstream.com/world/**.

If the idea of dynamic fonts catches on, expect to see the big font players like Adobe quickly jump into the fray and begin providing their own font definition files. We're almost certain they won't be free.

Microsoft doesn't recognize dynamic fonts, so the only damage that will be done is that users with Internet Explorer won't get to see your amazing gallery of fonts; the information will still be there.

As you can see, Netscape's current implementation of dynamic HTML doesn't rely as much on the DOM as Microsoft's does. However, because the DOM is going to be central to the final DHTML standard from the W3C, look for Netscape to shift its focus away from the layers approach to a more DOM-centered approach. This will also mean that Netscape will need to expand the DOM (as Microsoft has) to include full access to all of the elements on a page, not to just the limited collection available now. Layers aren't all bad either, and we suspect that a modified version of layers will be part of the final DHTML specification; but, again, only time will tell.

Dueling DHTML Proposals And This Book

As you can see from our discussion, Microsoft and Netscape DHTML methods have very little in common. These disparate proposals have determined the way we've written the rest of the book. Part 2 is devoted to an in-depth look at what a DOM is and how it works, a full discussion of Cascading Style Sheets, and the enhancements in HTML 4.0 that will help make DHTML a reality. The information in these chapters will be relevant regardless of whose method of DHTML you're using. Part 3 focuses entirely on Microsoft's Dynamic HTML model, including detailed discussion of mechanisms we've only outlined in this chapter and Practical Guide sections that show you exactly what you have to do to integrate Microsoft's DHTML into your own Web pages. Part 4 takes the same sort of approach for Netscape's layer model. Once again, you'll find in-depth discussions and detailed Practical Guides to help you create dynamic, layered HTML pages. And because we're sure you're wondering if there's any way to create a dynamic page that makes both Microsoft's and Netscape's browsers happy, Chapter 18 in Part 5 is devoted entirely to that subject.

PART 2

DOM, CSS, AND PROPRIETARY ENHANCEMENTS

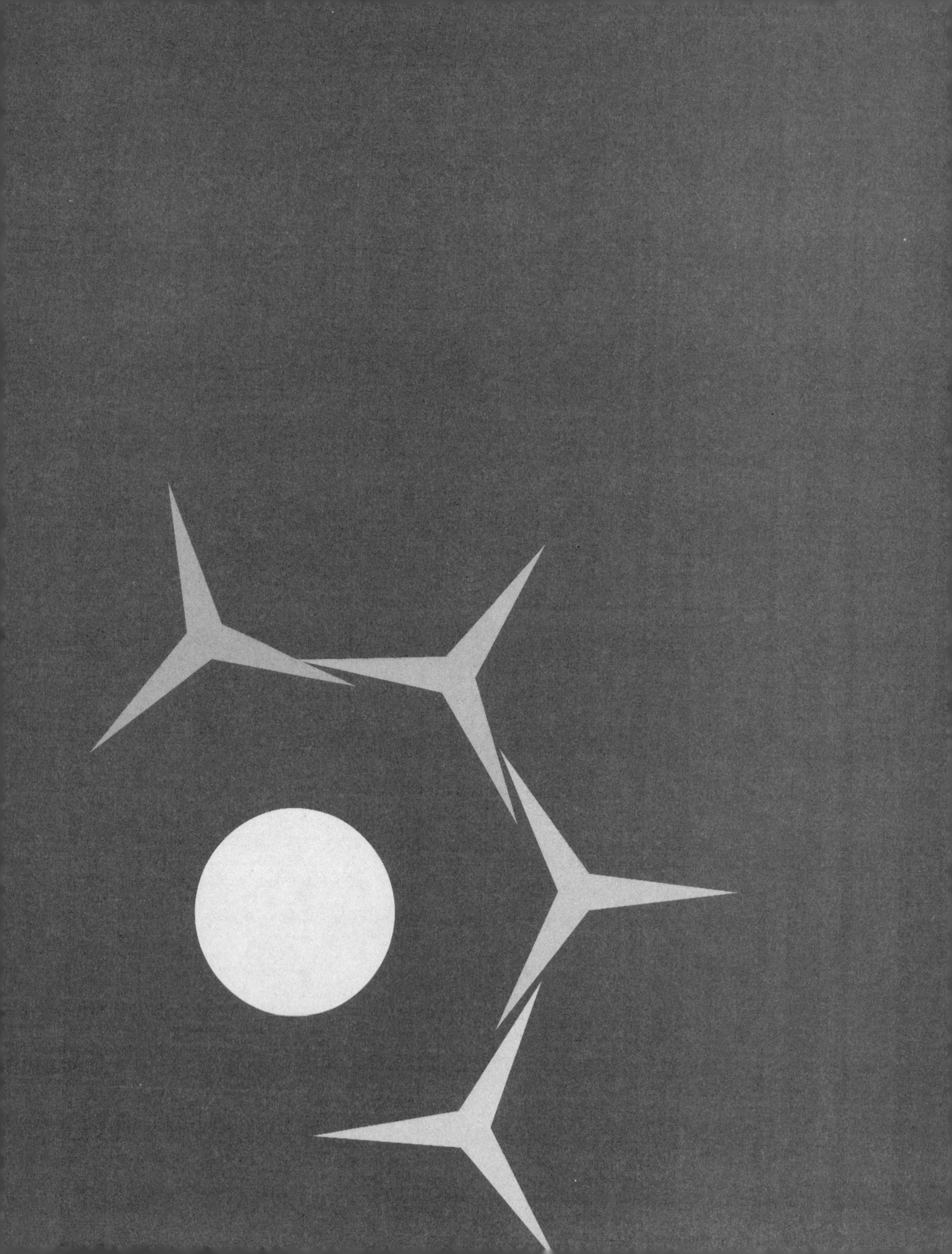

Chapter 5

Document Object Model Overview

The DOM is the heart—or the guts—of Dynamic HTML.

Notes...

Chapter 5

In this chapter, we delve into DHTML's DOM, the Document Object Model that allows developers to update a Web document's content, style, and structure dynamically.

Defining The DOM

The DOM can be identified as the heart—or the guts—of Dynamic HTML. DHTML's DOM allows a Web page's elements to be manipulated as objects, taking HTML into a more object-oriented realm. The DOM that both the W3C and Microsoft are promoting exposes all of a Web page's elements and provides full access to all the page's attributes. As we'll see later in the chapter, Netscape's DOM relies on a JavaScript Object Model that falls short of Microsoft's DOM in power and control.

Microsoft's version of the DOM enables the following:

- Dynamic content
- Dynamic style effects
- Precise positioning
- Scriptlets
- Data binding

A Brief History Of The DOM

Netscape 2.0 was the first browser to provide a document object model. Microsoft advanced on Netscape's lead by featuring a basic DOM in Internet Explorer 3.0, and an extremely strong and well-specified DOM in IE 4.0. The W3C's work on the DOM demonstrates considerable interest in Microsoft's DOM, and HTML 4.0's DOM reflects a great deal of Microsoft influence. For this reason, this chapter's coverage of the DOM will concentrate on the work that both Microsoft and the W3C have undertaken.

Compared to the latest DOMs, earlier DOMs, including the pre-DHTML JavaScript Object Models that Netscape is still using, provided extremely limited access to a page's objects. Although Netscape 2.0's object model made it feasible to employ scripting code within a Web page to access both the browser environment and the page itself, many elements remained untouchable. For example, early DOMs made it possible to access ActiveX controls, HTML text boxes, and Java applets, but impossible to manipulate essentials such as graphics and text. Within the limited number of elements that could be accessed, an even smaller number of their attributes could be modified. JavaScript Object Models also have a limited set of events that can be accessed for each object, and the events that can be triggered from within them is restricted.

Today's DOM

The W3C's DOM is being determined by a working group that consists of members from a number of companies, including Hewlett-Packard, IBM, Microsoft, Netscape, Novell, SoftQuad, and Sun Microsystems. As the DOM's language- and platform-neutral interface essentially permits scripts and programs to update Web documents on the fly, it plays a major role in advancing Web multimedia, and therefore is of major interest to the companies involved in determining its evolution.

The DOM that Microsoft and the W3C are promoting exposes Web page elements consistently, making them more transparent than ever before and bringing enhanced control and a novel level of positioning specificity to Web design. Although Netscape's layers implementation and JavaScript capabilities offer some of this advanced control, Netscape's DOM is anemic compared to Microsoft's much more clearly elucidated DOM, which is carefully crafted to exploit DHTML in conjunction with DirectX across multiple Microsoft applications.

The new level of access that the DOM brings to Web documents is powerful because it lets a Web page's structure, content, and style be altered after its initial download.

The DOM therefore makes Web multimedia much more exciting, as users can determine the speed at which multimedia unfolds on a Web page, rather than having to wait for a Web server to send responses over the Net's clogged arteries. The DHTML/HTML 4.0 DOM implementation provides a much-needed standard that specifies how HTML and scripting languages should interact.

Through its provision of a set of standard references, HTML 4.0's DOM gives HTML authors more interoperability; any scripting language can theoretically be used in conjunction with HTML 4.0, lessening the proprietary strangleholds that often threaten Web development. HTML's goal of interoperability also facilitates the reuse of objects and modules, which is of great benefit with complex programming projects. Rather than defining a new set of HTML tags or attributes, the DOM itself extends pre-existing ones, thereby bringing additional programming power to familiar attributes and tags.

Tomorrow's DOM: An Eye On XML

The W3C's work with the DOM is focused beyond HTML—even beyond DHTML/HTML 4.0. The W3C is intent on creating an object model that will function not only for HTML, but also for XML (Extensible Markup Language). The extensibility that is the essence of XML requires standardization to function smoothly. Because XML focuses on the creation of HTML tags to provide certain functions, it will greatly benefit from a standard API (application programming interface). The structure set forth by today's incarnation of the DOM provides a crucial foundation for future work in this area.

What The DOM Does

Through the DOM, every element that a Web page contains is regarded as an object, including elements such as:

- Section
- Heading
- Image
- List
- Paragraph

The DOM makes it possible to delete, add, or change an element; the content of elements can be easily changed through the DOM; and element attributes can be added, deleted, or changed as well. Naming these elements through the DOM means that they can be easily identified and affected by scripts.

DHTML's heralded on-the-fly abilities are directly related to the combination of the DOM and a scripting language that allows you to program elements to instantaneously change their appearance based on page events. The changes enacted through the DOM/scripting are instantaneous because dynamic pages download in one fell swoop. For example, you can script an event to be carried out when the user's mouse travels over a specific area of the page—a chunk of text might morph into another style or color, or components of a graphic might be dragged and dropped into a new orientation. This type of change is one of the hallmarks of DHTML and is directly enabled by the way that the DOM exposes page elements.

The DOM essentially serves as an interface between a page's DHTML source code and the browser software routines that create the window and fill it with the elements defined in the page. Rather than concerning itself with how the processes should be implemented, DHTML simply defines the results. Therefore, the DOM can be conceived of as a way of connecting Web pages to the browser. The object model exposes a range of objects, methods, properties, and events that are present and active within the browser's software to the HTML and scripting code in the page. These exposed elements can be used to communicate with the browser, which executes the indicated commands and updates pages accordingly.

You can think of the DOM as a broker between scripts and a document. By allowing you to modify existing pages, the DOM also permits you to include interaction that operates independently of a page's content and structure.

The DOM functions by creating objects. DOM objects possess child objects and properties, and the child objects, in turn, possess other child objects and properties, and so on. Through the DOM, you reference objects either by moving down the object hierarchy or by providing an HTML element with an **ID** attribute (e.g., **<IMG SRC="greenstone.jpg" ID="greenStone">**).

The following objects fall into the DOM's top level:

- All
- Anchors

- Applets
- Body
- Document
- Embeds
- Event
- Filters
- Forms
- Frames
- History
- Images
- Links
- Location
- Navigator
- Plug-ins
- Screen
- Scripts
- Selection
- Style sheets
- Window

DOM Event Models

Event models are the area of the DOM that indicate how elements can trigger changes. Events include **onMouseOver** (passing the mouse over an element), **onSubmit** (submitting a form), and **onLoad** (loading a page).

The event model ties together GUI applications. Microsoft and the W3C have embraced event bubbling, a process that permits objects to handle events by letting events "bubble up" to the parent object. Event bubbling makes coding more efficient;

you don't have to write code for each event, only code that will rise to the top. Because parent objects can take care of generic events, each object isn't required to perform. For more information on the event models, see Chapter 9.

W3C's DOM

According to the W3C, the DOM is "a platform- and language-neutral interface that will allow programs and scripts to dynamically access and update the content, structure, and style of documents. The document can be further processed and the results of that processing can be incorporated back into the presented page."

Levels Of The DOM

As we write, the W3C is in the process of defining Level 1 of the DOM. Whereas Level Zero functionality refers to Navigator 3.0/Internet Explorer 3.0 functionality, Level 1 concentrates on "the actual core, HTML, and XML document models." Level 1 addresses issues of style manipulation and document navigation and manipulation. Because it defines document structure and the way that documents are accessed and manipulated, it is regarded as the foundation of the DOM.

Subsequent levels of the DOM will specify functions to manipulate a document's DTD (Document Type Definition), as well as a model for interaction events and security. Level 2's components remain unspecified as we write, so for the latest information on where the DOM stands, see the W3C's DOM page at **www.w3.org/pub/WWW/TR/WD-dom**.

W3C's DOM Requirements

The W3C is responsible for creating a set of required DOM characteristics and components that will allow the DOM to function smoothly across the Web. For example, HTML 4.0's DOM requirements delineate not only what the DOM must contain, but also how a Web document will handle "meta information," such as source location, creation date, and associated cookies. The information in the following sections is taken from the W3C's draft and, therefore, does not represent a final and permanent reference, but a work in progress.

W3C's General Requirements For The DOM

These are the general requirements that the W3C proposes for the Document Object Model:

- The DOM is language-neutral and platform-independent.
- There will be a core DOM that is applicable to HTML, CSS, and XML documents.
- The DOM can be used to construct and deconstruct the document.
- The DOM will not preclude use by either agents external to the document content or scripts embedded within the document.
- Consistent naming conventions must be used through all levels of the DOM.
- A visual UI component will not be required for a conforming implementation of the DOM.
- The specific HTML, CSS, or XML DOMs will be driven by the underlying constructs of those languages.
- It must be possible to read in a document and write out a structurally identical document to disk (both documents can be represented by the same raw structural model).
- The DOM will not expose the user to problems with security, validity, or privacy.
- The DOM will not preclude other mechanisms for manipulating documents.

The DOM's Structure Navigation

The DOM's structure navigation refers to the way a document is navigated and determines the ways in which parent and child elements are manipulated and defined. The W3C's general requirements for a document's structure navigation are:

- All document content, including elements and attributes, can be accessed and manipulated programmatically.
- Navigation from any element to any other element will be possible, except where such navigation would compromise security.
- There will be a way to uniquely and reproducibly enumerate the structure of static documents.
- There will be a way to query for elements and attributes, subject to security and privacy considerations.

- Basic low-level functions (get first, get next, etc.) will be provided, along with convenience functions that build upon them, but have a consistent access method.

When addressing HTML documents, the W3C also sets forth these specific requirements:

- All elements known to the user agent are exposed.
- Unknown tags and attributes are exposed.
- Implied elements are exposed, even if not explicitly defined in the document (e.g., **HTML**, **HEAD**, **BODY**).
- There will be guidelines for the inclusion of new elements and attributes in the DOM.

Requirements For The DOM's Document Manipulation

The following requirements are recommended by the W3C to aid in standardizing the manner in which Web browsers manipulate documents:

- There will be a way to add, remove, and change elements and/or tags in the document structure (if permitted by the DTD and not precluded by security or validity considerations).
- There will be a way to add, remove, and change attributes in the document structure (if permitted by the DTD and not precluded by security or validity considerations).
- Operations must restore consistency before they return.
- A valid static document acted on by the DOM will deliver a consistent reproducible document structure.

Requirements For The DOM's Content Manipulation

The following items address how the DOM will affect the way Web content is manipulated:

- There will be a way to determine the containing element from any text part of the document (subject to security considerations).
- There will be a way to manipulate (add, change, delete) content.
- There will be a way to navigate content.

Requirements For The DOM's Event Model

The DOM's event model exerts a crucial influence over the way DHTML unfolds, as a great deal of DHTML's dynamism relies on the manner in which events occur on a Web page. Whether a page is successful at being fully interactive hinges on the event model, which determines how a page responds to user actions. These are the W3C's requirements for the DOM's event model (after Level 1):

- All elements will be capable of generating events.
- There will be interaction events, update events, and change events.
- The event model will allow responses to user interactions.
- The event delivery mechanism will allow for overriding default behavior.
- Events will bubble through the structural hierarchy of the document.
- Events will be synchronous.
- Events will be defined in a platform-independent and language-neutral way.
- There will be an interface for binding to events.

Requirements For The Stylesheet Object Model

As we explain in Chapter 6, Cascading Style Sheets (CSS) can be used to manipulate a document's style. The W3C is in the process of defining a Stylesheet Object Model that will allow Web authors to create, modify, and associate CSS with a Web document. This style-sheet model will be extensible to other style-sheet formats in the future. The W3C says the following about style sheets:

- All style sheets will be represented in the DOM.
- Selectors, rules, and properties of individual style sheets can be added, removed, and changed.

Through the DOM, it's possible to add, remove, and change all CSS elements. This includes, but is not limited to:

- Linked style sheets
- Imported style sheets

- Alternative style sheets
- CSS pseudo-classes and CSS pseudo-elements
- Contextual selectors
- Inline styles
- All properties as defined in the CSS specification, including font properties, colors, backgrounds, and box properties

Requirements For The DOM's DTD Manipulation

The W3C requires that the DOM contains the following information about the DTD:

- There will be a way to determine the presence of a DTD.
- There will be a way to query declarations in the underlying DTD (if available).
- There will be a way to add, remove, and change declarations in the underlying DTD (if available).
- There will be a way to test conformance of all or part of the given document against a DTD (if available).

Requirements For The DOM's Error Reporting

Because the DOM changes the entire structure of Web pages, the way error reporting is handled is also affected by the DOM. The W3C recommends the following error handling for HTML 4.0:

- The DOM will provide a documentwide error logging and reporting mechanism.
- Error reporting will occur primarily through exceptions.
- The DOM error state can be queried.

Requirements For The DOM's Security, Validity, And Privacy

Security is always an essential consideration on the Web and carries with it privacy and questions of validity. The increased use of scripting and object manipulation brought about by DHTML invokes new security issues for the W3C to address. Although the Level 1 DOM provides a simple form of security, future levels will have better security technologies. These are the W3C's recommendations for DOM security:

- Each object must be responsible for maintaining its own internal consistency.
- It must be safe to have multiple threads operating on the same object.
- Object locking must be incorporated to ensure consistent results.
- It must be possible to prevent scripts on one page from accessing another page.
- Firewall boundaries must be respected.
- It must be possible to restrict access and navigation to specific elements.
- An external security API will be provided (after Level 1).

Requirements For Information About The User Agent Environment

These are the W3C recommendations for the information that a user agent (i.e., a Web browser or user agent) can glean about the user's environment:

- There will be a way of obtaining relevant information about the display environment, including the user agent (UA) brand information and version number, and, where appropriate, the HTTP header.
- A way of determining support for a MIME type will be available (after Level 1).

The W3C's Core DOM

Now that we've examined the W3C's requirements for the DOM, let's take a look at the DOM functionality, as expressed through the W3C's core Level 1 DOM. The W3C has proposed this functionality based on HTML 4.0 and XML 1.0, with a goal of creating a simple, flexible, and extensible DOM.

Overall Type Hierarchy

The W3C's DOM exists to define the hierarchy of Web page objects (i.e., a tree or "structure model"). These objects are called *nodes* and the object hierarchy is typically created from a source representation such as HTML or XML. Here are the primary object model types, listed according to their place in the hierarchy:

- **Node**
- **Document**

- **Element**
- **Attribute**
- **Text**
- **Comment**
- **PI (processing instruction)**

Document Object Model APIs

APIs are a set of functions or methods used to access some functionality. Node, Document, and Element are the primary API types and those that developers most frequently employ.

Most objects in the DOM have the base type of Node. The Node object is regarded as the primary datatype for the entire DOM and represents a single node in the document tree. A Node object may have an arbitrary number (including zero) of sequentially ordered child nodes; however, child nodes are not required. Although the Node type usually has a parent node, the root node in a document hierarchy has no parent. Expect to see a more generalized querying mechanism for Node types in a later level of the DOM. For example, a generalized query could fetch all of the Elements in a subtree with a given **tagName**.

Node

The following are the Node object's methods:

- **NodeType getNodeType()**—Returns an indication of the underlying Node object's type. The actual type of the returned data is language-binding dependent. The W3C's Interface Definition Language (IDL) specification uses an enum. It is expected that most language bindings will represent this Node type, which can be queried during runtime, using an integral data type. The names of the Node type enumeration literals are derived directly from the names of the actual Node subtypes.
- **Node getParentNode()**—Returns the parent of the given Node instance. If this node is the root of the document object tree, null is returned.
- **Node getFirstChild()**—Returns the first child of a node. If there is no such node, null is returned.

- **NodeList getChildren()**—Returns a **NodeList** object containing the children of this node. If there are no children, null is returned. The content of the returned **NodeList** is "live" in the sense that changes to the children of the Node object from which it was created will be immediately reflected in the set of nodes the **NodeList** contains; it is not a static snapshot of the content of the Node. Similarly, changes made to the **NodeList** will be immediately reflected in the set of children of the node from which the **NodeList** was created.

- **boolean hasChildren()**—Returns true if the node has any children, false if the node has no children. This method exists both for convenience and to allow implementations to bypass object allocation, which may be required for implementing **getChildren()**.

- **Node getPreviousSibling()**—Returns the node immediately preceding the current node in a breadth-first traversal of the tree. If there is no such node, null is returned.

- **Node getNextSibling()**—Returns the node immediately following the current node in a breadth-first traversal of the tree. If there is no such node, null is returned.

- **Node insertChild(in unsigned long index, in Node newChild)**—Inserts a child node into the list of children before zero-based location index. Nodes from index to the end of list are moved up by one. If index is zero, the node is added as the first child; if index is greater than or equal to the number of children, the node is added as the last child.

- **Node replaceChild(in unsigned long index, in Node newChild)**—Replaces the child node at location index and returns the node that previously occupied that position. If the index provided is larger than the number of nodes in the list, a **NoSuchNodeException** is thrown.

- **Node removeChild(in unsigned long index)**—Removes the child node at location index and returns the node that previously occupied that position. If the index provided is larger than the number of nodes in the list, a **NoSuchNodeException** is thrown.

- **NodeEnumerator getElementsByTagName(wstring name)**—Produces an enumerator that iterates over all the Element nodes that are descendants of the current node whose **tagName** matches the given name. The iteration order is a depth-first enumeration of the elements as they occurred in the original document.

Document

The Document object is the conceptual root of the document tree and represents the entirety of an HTML or XML document. It is through the Document object that primary access to the document's data is obtained. The following list describes the Document object's methods:

- **Node documentType**—For XML, this provides access to the DTD associated with this XML document. For HTML documents and XML documents without a DTD, this returns the value null.
- **Element documentElement**—This is the root element for the given document. For HTML, this will be an Element instance whose **tagName** is "HTML."
- **DocumentContext**—The **DocumentContext** object represents information that is not strictly related to a document's content; it provides the information about where the document came from and any additional meta-data about the document. For example, the **DocumentContext** for a document retrieved using HTTP would provide access to the HTTP headers that were retrieved with the document, the URL that the document came from, and so on. The **DocumentContext** may not exist for documents that were not retrieved via HTTP or for those that were created directly in memory. Expect to see the **DocumentContext** interface described here to be significantly expanded in the DOM's Level 2 specification.
- **Document document**—This is the root node of a DOM. Any iteration, enumeration, or other traversal of the entire document's content should begin with this node.

Element

Apart from the text node, most node types that Web developers encounter are Element nodes. These objects represent the element itself, as well as any contained nodes:

- **NamedNodeList attributes**—Defines the attributes for this element. In the **elementExample** sample above, the attributes list would consist of the **id** attribute, as well as any attributes that were defined by the DTD for this element and that have default values.

- **void setAttribute(in Attribute newAttr)**—Adds a new attribute/value pair to an Element Node object. If an attribute by that name is already present in the element, its value is changed to that of the Attribute instance.

Attribute

The Attribute object represents an attribute in an Element object. The allowable values for the attribute typically defined in a DTD are:

- **wstring name**—Defines the name of this attribute. Note that this name is case-sensitive and is not changed or authorized by the DOM.
- **NodeList value**—This is the effective value of this attribute. The attribute's effective value is determined as follows: If this attribute has been explicitly assigned any value, that value is the attribute's effective value; otherwise, if there is a declaration for this attribute, and that declaration includes a default value, then that default value is the attribute's effective value; otherwise, the attribute has no effective value.

Comment

Comment represents the content of a comment, i.e., all the characters between the starting **<!--** and ending **-->**. The definition that follows refers to a comment in XML, and, in practice, HTML, although some HTML tools may implement the full SGML comment structure:

- **wstring data**—Defines the content of the comment, exclusive of the comment begin and end sequence.

PI

A PI node is a processing instruction. The content of a PI node is defined as all of the content that falls between the delimiters of the processing instruction. PI content, which plays an important role in XML, can include the following:

- **wstring name**—XML defines a name as the first token following the markup that begins the processing instruction; this attribute returns that name. For HTML, the returned value is null.

- **wstring data**—The content of the processing instruction, from the character immediately after the **<?** (after the name in XML) to the character immediately preceding the **?>**.

Reference

Reference is the base type for named entities, including parameter entities, but not numeric character entities. It is used to specify the name of the reference and contains a pointer to the object that defines the value of the entity.

- **wstring name**—Defines the name of the entity being referred to.

NamedCharacterReference

NamedCharacterReference is a subtype of Reference, used for representing named references to characters, such as **<** or **&**.

- **wstring getReplacementText()**—Returns the string that consists of the actual character that the NamedCharacterReference refers to. For example, for **<**, the returned string would be "<".

NumericCharacterReference

NumericCharacterReference objects are used to represent explicit references to characters via numeric literals, such as **<** or **H**. Applications may retrieve both the actual Character object corresponding to this numeric value and the actual digits (and any associated radix-indicating prefix) of the original reference.

- **wchar character**—The Character instance that this character reference indicated.

- **wstring original**—This is the original string representing the numeric character reference, without the introducing markup. For example, given **<** this attribute would be 60 (sans the &# and ;), and for **H**, this attribute would have x48 for its value.

Text

The Text object contains the nonmarkup portion of a document. In XML documents, all white space between markup results in Text nodes being created. The Text object can contain the following:

- **wstring data**—This holds the actual content of the text node. Text nodes contain just plain text, without markup and without entities, both of which are manifest as separate objects in the DOM.

- **boolean isIgnorableWhitespace**—This is true if the Text node contains only white space, and if the white space can be ignored by the application. Only XML processors will make use of this, as HTML abides by SGML's rules for white-space handling.

Microsoft's DOM

The DOM that Microsoft employs in Internet Explorer 4 removes the object model from language and places it into the browser. Therefore, it is the browser that stores a page's structure and presentation, which makes the data accessible for manipulation by a scripting language or compiled component. Because this DOM puts all scripting language into a consistent format, a tag's position will appear identical in VBScript, JavaScript, and JScript.

One of the impressive aspects of Microsoft's DOM is its comprehensive spectrum. It deals with a page's entire structure, not just with restricted elements, so it works well with Microsoft's ideal of applications that communicate easily with each other across a variety of platforms.

Microsoft identifies its DOM as enabling four functions:

- Access to all page elements
- Instant page update
- Full event model
- Ability to change the text on the page

With the Netscape DOM, you can access anchors, forms, applets, form elements, and images through script. You are unable to create content such as a dynamic index of site content, though, because a page's headings aren't accessible. Microsoft makes headings accessible, along with everything else (literally).

In addition to developing a DOM that embraces the W3C's vision, Microsoft also supports a Scripting Object Model (SOM) in Internet Explorer; the SOM lets site designers use their scripting language of choice to control page objects.

For extensive listings of the objects, properties, methods, events, and collections contained in Microsoft's DOM, refer to the Internet SDK at **www.microsoft.com/msdn/sdk/inetsdk/help/dhtml/references/domrefs.htm**.

Netscape's DOM

As we mentioned earlier, Netscape's DOM still relies on the JavaScript Object Model, which obscures many elements in a page. Netscape's current DOM therefore seems to be at a distinct disadvantage, especially because the W3C has clearly embraced the path that Microsoft's DOM has taken. However, Netscape says that it will conform to the DOM that the W3C ultimately approves.

Netscape's DOM relies heavily on JavaScript; it makes the formatting and positioning properties of style sheets accessible from JavaScript, therefore enabling you to define style sheets that use the DOM. In Netscape 3's Document Object Model you can read and write the attributes of image and anchor tags, as well as query some information about the browser, such as its plug-ins, accepted MIME-types, and location.

In Navigator 4, the layer tags create a tree of hierarchies; its DOM lets you query things such as the width and height of the window and of layers and **DIV** tags. With this JavaScript Object Model, when you want elements such as plug-ins and Java applets to manipulate any of the model, they have to operate through the JavaScript scripting engine (i.e., LiveConnect).

At the Netscape site, the DHTML glossary entry on "document object model" leads only to several paragraphs called "Using JavaScript and the Document Object Model to Define Styles" under the CSS chapter. Netscape's lack of detailed information about the DOM is especially remarkable considering the amount of information that Microsoft's site includes about the DOM.

The online publication Web Review interviewed Vidur Apparao, Netscape's representative on the W3C DOM Working Group, and Eckhart Walther, product manager for Gemini, Netscape's forthcoming layout engine, about Netscape's use of the DOM. That interview, in which both men express Netscape's readiness to accept the W3C's DOM, is found at **www.webreview.com/97/12/05/dom/index.html**. Also refer to **developer.netscape.com/library/documentation/htmlguid/dynamic_resources.html** to investigate Netscape's latest DHTML technical information and sample sites.

Practical Guide To Using The DOM

- Accessing Elements On A Web Page
- Triggering Events In Internet Explorer
- Triggering Events In Netscape Navigator
- DOMFactory

The most essential thing to remember about the DOM is that it can be used to both construct and deconstruct a document. Much of this book focuses on specific DHTML techniques that rely upon the DOM to achieve their effects. Event handling and tricks such as **mouseover**, for example, simply don't fly without the specificity that the DOM brings to DHTML. Let's take a brief tour through the key knowledge that's necessary to make the most effective use of the DOM.

Accessing Elements On A Web Page

As we've said throughout this chapter, the DOM makes it possible to access every element on a Web page. This is how Microsoft's DOM could be used to index a collection called the "all collection" by ID and name:

```
<H1 id=FirstH1 style="font-weight: normal">Dynamic HTML</H1>
<script language=JavaScript>
function findFirstH1() {
var e;
e = document.all("FirstH1");
}
</script>
```

The preceding code would produce an H1 heading with the ID FirstH1. To access elements directly, you could use their name or ID directly, in this way:

```
<script language=JavaScript>
            function findFirstH1() {
                 var e;
                 e = document.all("FirstH1");
                 if (e == FirstH1) {
                 alert("Enjoy unrestricted access to all elements");
                 }
            }
</script>
```

This type of unrestricted access to page elements makes it simple to instantly update a page so that its font becomes bold on the fly:

```
<script language=JavaScript>
           function changeFirstH1() {
           FirstH1.style.fontStyle = "Bold";
           }
</script>
```

Triggering Events In Internet Explorer

The DOM is also used to trigger events with the event model. DHTML's DOM makes all elements able to exploit a full set of events such as mouse and keyboard actions. For example, if you wanted to make the FirstH1 example change to bold as the user's mouse traveled over it, you could write the following:

```
<H1 id=FirstH1 style="font-weight: normal"
              onmouseover="makeBold();"
              onmouseout="makeNormal();">
              Dynamic HTML</H1>

<script language=JavaScript>
        function makeBold() {
          FirstH1.style.fontStyle = "Bold";
        }
        function makeNormal() {
          FirstH1.style.fontStyle = "Normal";
        }
</script>
```

As the mouse leaves the H1 heading, the font will return to its original, non-bold appearance. Because of the combination of the DOM and the event model used in this example, the page never needs to return to the server to activate these actions, thereby producing a faster experience for the end user.

Triggering Events In Netscape Navigator

Netscape's syntax for the DOM is slightly different (although the differences could be ironed out if both Netscape and Microsoft honor their commitment to accept the W3C's standard). Netscape defines the page as a meta-object (called "Document") that contains objects such as paragraphs and images. The following naming scheme is used to change the Document's named objects:

```
<P>
Document.ObjectType.ObjectName.SpecificProperty = "value";
<P>
```

To change an object you can affect its properties. If you wanted to change an image's height, for example, you can declare a different pixel value for it. For example, if greenstone.gif were tagged like this

```
<IMG SRC="greenstone.gif" WIDTH=100 HEIGHT=100 NAME="greenstone">
```

and you wanted to change it to eight times its original height, you could use the following:

```
<P>
document.image.greenstone.height = "800";
<P>
```

If you wanted to move the same image over to the left edge of the screen, you could write:

```
<P>
document.P.greenstone.align = "left";
<P>
```

DOMFactory

DOM clients can create new DOM objects through methods in the DOMFactory interface. For example, if you needed to create an entire document object model programmatically, you could use the methods on a DOMFactory object to build the individual objects that would comprise the object model, and then use the operations on the objects themselves to connect the objects into an overall document object model. The following would be used for such a task:

- **Document createDocument()**—Create and return a new empty Document object.
- **DocumentContext createDocumentContext()**—Create and return a new DocumentContext.
- **Element createElement(in wstring tagName, in AttributeList attributes)**—Create an element based on the tagName.
- **Text createTextNode(in wstring data)**—Create a Text node given the specified string.
- **Comment createComment(in wstring data)**—Create a Comment node given the specified string.
- **PI createPI(in wstring name, in wstring data)**—Create a PI node with the specified name and data string.
- **Attribute createAttribute(in wstring name, in NodeList value)**—Create an Attribute of the given name and specified value.

Chapter 6

Cascading Style Sheets

This chapter provides an in-depth explanation of Web style sheets and includes a step-by-step discussion of how to create style rules and link style sheets to your Web pages.

Notes...

Chapter 6

The Web before style was not very pretty. Only a few select HTML tags provided designers with some control over colors, font type and style, or text decoration. Margins were out of the question (unless you cheated and used **<BLOCKQUOTE>**); creating style templates was next to impossible. With the advent of Web style sheets everything has changed. Word and letter spacing, margins, borders, multicolored backgrounds, and nonscrolling background images are only some of the elements that are quickly becoming standard fare.

In a nutshell, style sheets provide a Web designer with tight control over how HTML elements are displayed. If it can be tagged with HTML, it can be controlled with style sheets. In fact, you can't include or invoke style-sheet rules in your Web pages without using HTML, so the two go hand in hand. You don't have to learn a new markup language, you just have to learn how to extend the one you already know.

Style sheet information is going to be part of the DOM, so it's important to learn what style sheets are, how to write style rules, and how to implement them into your Web pages. In this chapter we look at Cascading Style Sheets Level 1 (CSS1), the current style-sheet standard that works closely with Microsoft's version of Dynamic HTML to create dynamic Web pages. The good news is that CSS1 has already become a standard and is supported by both Netscape and Microsoft browsers. It's always nice to have a little firm ground to stand on when you're walking on the bleeding edge.

Introduction To Cascading Style Sheets

Cascading Style Sheets Level 1 became the official W3C standard for Web style sheets only a few months ago. As you begin to work with CSS1, you'll soon discover that it was well thought-out and carefully designed to work with the existing HTML mechanisms to bring style to the Web. As we discussed in Chapter 1, HTML is a child of SGML and as such was designed to describe a document's structure without concern for its final visual display. This accounts for the absence of visual display mechanisms in HTML. However, as the Web has become more and more a mechanism for conveying business information, the way Web pages look and are laid out has become increasingly important. The demand for more layout tools was not, and could not be, met by the conventions of HTML.

In creating Web style sheets, the W3C's goal was to find a way of providing style information for Web pages that worked within the confines of HTML, was platform- and operating-system-independent, and was as straightforward and easy-to-use as HTML.

CSS1 easily meets all these criteria.

In reality, a style sheet is a collection of style rules that describe how certain HTML elements should be rendered by the browser. No two style sheets are ever alike because the documents they affect are different. A single style sheet can be written and applied to hundreds or thousands of documents. When a change is made to the style sheet, it is automatically reflected in all of the pages to which it is linked. If you decide one day that all the first-level headings on all 2,000 of your company's HTML pages should be teal instead of red, a single change to a single style sheet will make the global change instantaneously. If you haven't used style sheets, you'll have to make the change manually on every page, and even a batch search-and-replace utility won't catch them all.

In another scenario, imagine that you have two kinds of second-level headings: titles and author names. The only way to tell them apart is to read the tag content. You want to make all the title headings blue, Arial, 24 points, and the author headings teal, Garamond, 22 points. To do this using conventional style sheet scenarios would require these two sets of tags:

```
<H2><FONT FACE=ARIAL COLOR=blue SIZE=+4>Title</FONT></H2>
<H2><FONT FACE=GARAMOND COLOR=teal SIZE=+3>Author</FONT></H2>
```

You'd have to apply each set to every title and author combination in your document collection; even with a good editor this would take time. However, if you used style sheets to create the pages, you could create two instances of the second-level heading:

```
<STYLE>
H2.title {font: arial blue 24pt}
H2.author {font: garamond teal 22pt}
</STYLE>
```

Then you can use the **CLASS=** attribute to invoke each style rule as needed, as shown here:

```
<H2 CLASS=title>Title</H2>
<H2 CLASS=author>Author</H2>
```

You may have noticed that we tricked you and threw in a little style sheet code while you weren't looking. That wasn't too difficult now was it? The nice thing is it really doesn't get any harder. We'll explain it all in detail a little later on, so don't worry.

Before we move on to the nuts and bolts of CSS1, let's take a look at what the same style-sheet-enhanced HTML page looks like in two different browsers—one that supports CSS1 and one that's style-sheet challenged. This will give you a good idea of the kind of difference style sheets can make in the final display of your Web pages.

Figures 6.1 and 6.2 show the About page at the Virtually Boston site (**www.vboston.com**), which makes use of style sheets in its Web design. The differences are easy to see between the page display of a browser that supports style sheets (Figure 6.1) and one that doesn't (Figure 6.2). The most immediately recognizable difference is the page's display font. Comic Sans, a new font created by Microsoft specifically for Web design, is the font specified by the site's style sheet (shown in the code sample following). The style-sheet-savvy browser (Internet Explorer 4.0) displays the page using the specified font, but the style-sheet-challenged browser (Netscape Navigator 3.02) does not. Notice the margin differences between the two displays; additional top and left margin space is shown in IE's version of the page. Notice also that in the first figure the descriptive text has a white semitransparent background, whereas the descriptive text in the second figure does not.

These versions of the same page also demonstrate that a page with style sheets is not a total loss or unreadable when displayed by a browser that does not support style sheets. Although the Navigator version of the Virtually Boston page is not quite as

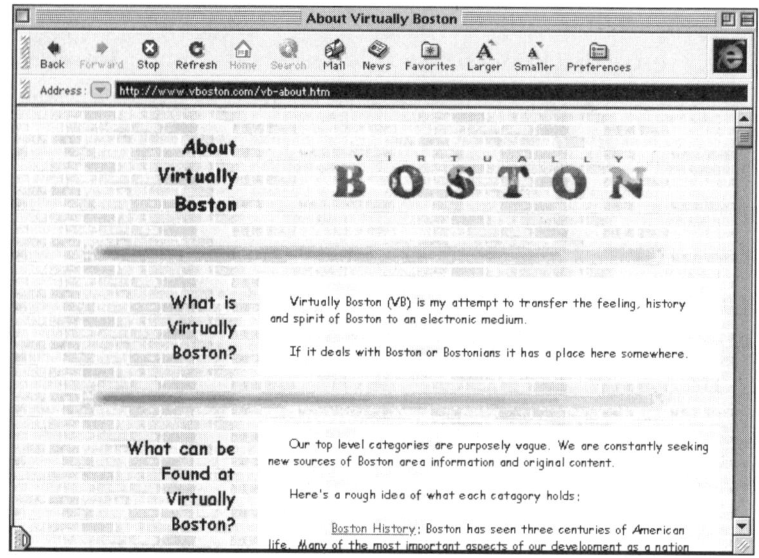

Figure 6.1

The About Virtually Boston page as seen with Internet Explorer 4.0.

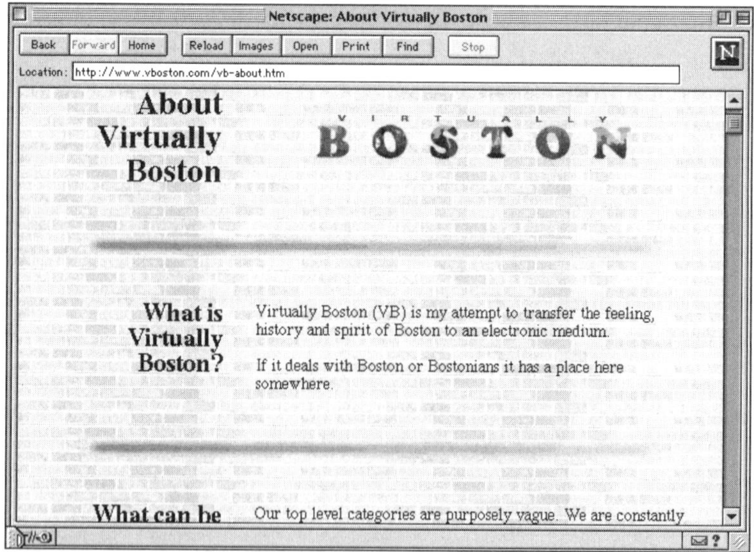

Figure 6.2

The About Virtually Boston page as seen with Netscape Navigator 3.02.

spiffy as the IE version, it still looks nice because the Web designer used the HTML **<BODY>** tag with the **BACKGROUND=** attribute to include a background for the document and table markup to create the basic page layout. This page combines solid HTML design with style sheets to create a page that looks good in any browser. FYI, the style sheet linked to this page looks like this (it may be Geek to you now, but it will make sense soon enough):

```
body      {font: 10pt Comic Sans MS; font-weight: normal;
           text-decoration: none}
p           {font-size: 10pt}
p.indent  {font-size: 10pt; text-indent: 0.25in}
p.bold     {font-size: 10pt; font-weight: bold}
p.boldindent     {font-size: 10pt; font-weight: bold; text-indent: 0.25in}
p.quote     {font-size: 12pt}
p.quoteindent     {font-size: 12pt; text-indent: 0.25in}
dt     {font-size: 12pt}
dd     {font-size: 10pt}
dt.small     {font-size: 10pt}
dd.small     {font-size: 9pt}
h1     {font-size: 17pt}
h2     {font-size: 15pt}
h3     {font-size: 12pt}
h4     {font-size: 10pt}
li     {font-size: 10pt}
```

Writing Style-Sheet Rules

As we said earlier, a style sheet is just a collection of rules that govern how HTML elements should be displayed by a browser. These rules govern everything from margins to colors to whether backgrounds scroll off the page, so the first key to a functioning style sheet is a set of functioning rules. Since you've already seen a functioning style sheet—the Virtually Boston style sheet we listed the code for earlier—you probably already have a good idea of how style rules are created. Even so, we'll start from the beginning and describe how rules are created and combined to form a style sheet.

Basic Style-Rule Syntax

A style rule is made up of a selector and a declaration, and looks something like this:

```
selector {declaration}
```

We can further break the declaration down into a property-value pair. This pair indicates which property of the HTML element—color, for example—is going to be affected by the style rule that describes how it should be affected—by being teal, for example. The final formal syntax for a style rule is this:

```
selector {property: value}
```

Using real selectors, properties, and values we can create this style rule:

```
H1 {color: teal}
```

The selector is the HTML first-level heading element, the property is color, and the value is teal. This rule specifies that all instances of first-level headings within a document linked to the style rule should be teal. Wasn't that easy?

Syntax in style rules is just as important as syntax in HTML tags. The selector is always followed by a space, then a left curly brace. Properties and values are always separated by a colon and a space, then followed by a right curly brace. If you use a semicolon instead of a colon, your style rule will be invalid and ignored by the browser. Periods, commas, and semicolons also have their places in style sheet syntax. When we're finished with our discussion of syntax, we'll put them all together for you in Table 6.1 as a handy guide for which punctuation mark to use when.

Specifying HTML Elements By Class

Here's a new scenario for you to think about: Imagine that you have three different types of paragraphs on one Web page. The first is a standard body paragraph, the second identifies information new to the page, and the third provides date information to let users know how fresh your page's content is. You want each of these paragraphs to have a distinct look. However, each paragraph uses the **<P>** element to mark them as paragraphs in the HTML document. How do you specify which **<P>** is which? You use the element class specification.

Using class as part of a selector makes it possible to create different style rules for different instances of the same HTML element. Using our scenario above, we'll create rules for paragraphs of class **body**, **new**, and **date**:

```
P.body {font:14pt Comic Sans MS;
          margin-left: .5in;
          margin-right: .5in;
         }
```

```
P.new {font: 15pt Times;
          margin-left: .5in;
          margin-right: .5in;
          }

P.date {font: 12pt Arial;
         text-align: right;
         }
```

Notice that our selectors and declarations have grown and new punctuation has been introduced. We used the period and a text string to create three different instances of the paragraph tag, each with its unique identifier. We also listed two or three separate property-value combinations for each selector and separated them with semicolons. This is called *combining declarations* and will be addressed further later on.

To invoke any one of these style rules, we simply use the **CLASS=*"text string"*** attribute with the **<P>** tag:

```
<P CLASS=body>
Body text Body text Body text Body text Body text Body text
Body text Body text Body text Body text Body text Body text
</P>

<P CLASS=date>
date
</P>

<P CLASS=new>
New text New text New text New text New text New text New text
New text New text New text New text New text New text New text
</P>

<P CLASS=date>
date
</P>
```

Figure 6.3 shows the results when these style rules and HTML are put together in a Web page and displayed by a style-sheet-savvy browser. We've used style rules to create a body paragraph style that has left and right margins of half an inch and is displayed in 14-point Comic Sans MS. The new paragraph style is slightly larger at 15 points and is displayed in Times, but maintains the same right and left margins as the regular body text. Finally, the date style is right justified and in 12-point Arial, so its effect is reduced but not totally erased, and it sits consistently to the right side of each body or new paragraph.

Body text Body text Body text Body text Body text Body text
Body text Body text Body text Body text Body text Body text

date

New text New text New text New text New text New text New text
New text New text New text New text New text New text New text

date

Figure 6.3

Multiple instances of the same HTML tag can be defined using class as a selector.

Combining Selectors And Declarations

CSS1 was developed with an eye toward brevity and efficiency. To that end, both selectors and declarations can be combined as needed to create multifaceted style rules for a single HTML element. Take the body paragraph style from the previous section's example:

```
P.body {font:14pt Comic Sans MS;
          margin-left: .5in;
          margin-right: .5in;
         }
```

This particular rule can be broken down into three separate style rules and still function in the same way:

```
P.body {font:14pt "Comic Sans MS"}

P.body {margin-left: .5in}

P.body {margin-right: .5in}
```

However, there's no need to break it down when it is faster and easier to combine all the declarations for one selector into one style rule. It's also easier to see which property-value combinations have been assigned to a particular element if they are all grouped together. Semicolons are used to separate different property-value pairs within the same style rule. What could be simpler?

There will also be times when you'll want to group selectors. For example, without grouping selectors you'll need six different style rules to make all your heading's the same font face:

```
H1 {font: Arial}
H2 {font: Arial}
```

```
H3 {font: Arial}
H4 {font: Arial}
H5 {font: Arial}
H6 {font: Arial}
```

To change the style of all six heading levels you'll also have to alter six different rules, increasing the chance you'll make a mistake. To make things faster, easier, and more accurate, these style rules can be combined into a single style rule using commas to separate the selectors:

```
H1, H2, H3, H4, H5, H6 {font. Arial}:
```

Class-based selectors can be combined with regular selectors using this method as well:

```
H1, H2, H3, H4, H5, H6, P.date {font. Arial}
```

By combining both selectors and declarations on a case-by-case basis, you can create a succinct and easy-to-manage style sheet for a single page or a group of pages. Before we move on to the specific properties and values used to create style rules, we've put together Table 6.1 as a quick style-rule syntax reference. It includes each syntax element, its formal name, and a brief description of its role in a style rule.

The Property And Value Parade

As with HTML tags, you can't just make up your own DHTML element properties and assign them the values of your choice. To make style sheets standard and accessible by

Table 6.1 Style-rule syntax elements.

Element	Name	Description
{	left curly brace	Begins a declaration
}	right curly brace	Ends a declaration
:	colon	Separates properties and values
.	period	Separates an HTML element and its class specifier
;	semicolon	Separates multiple declarations
,	comma	Separates multiple selectors

Webmasters and browsers, a specific set of properties and their associated values have been created for you to work with. The properties are grouped by type, and the groups are called *families*. In this section we'll look at each property family in turn and provide you with a complete description of each property and its associated values. That said, let the parade begin.

Background Properties

Background properties allow you to link background colors and images to a specific HTML element and to specify how the images should be tiled. Using these properties, you can assign different background colors and images to different HTML elements, and more than one of each may be included on any given page. The background properties are:

- **background-color: transparent|<*color*>**—Specifies an HTML background element as transparent or as a color using one of the accepted color names or RGB hexadecimal color notation. A transparent value allows the element's parent background to show through as the background for the element.

- **background-image: none|<*url*>**—Defines the background image to be attached to a specific HTML element. The correct notation for specifying a URL is **url(image.gif)**.

- **background-repeat: repeat|repeat-x|repeat-y|no-repeat**—Defines how a background image should be tiled. The effects produced by each value are:

    - **repeat**—Tiles the image.
    - **repeat-x**—Duplicates the image in a horizontal line across the page.
    - **repeat-y**— Duplicates the image in a vertical line down the page.
    - **no repeat**—Displays the background once and does not repeat it at all.

- **background-attachment: scroll|fixed**—Defines how a background image should act. Options include:

    - **scroll**—The image moves with the element as it scrolls up or down on the page.
    - **fixed**—The image stays in place on the screen even though its associated element may scroll away.

- **background-position: <*percentage*>|<*length*>|top|center|bottom**—Defines the position of a background image relative to the element (if **background-attachment** is set to **scroll**) and relative to the page (if **background-attachment** is set to **fixed**).

Box Properties

Box properties are used to specify border, margin, white space, height, and width information for HTML elements. To use these properties correctly, imagine that your text blocks, images, and even the page itself are "boxes" of information that are arranged together and in relation to each other:

- **margin-top: <*length*>|<*percentage*>|auto**—Defines the top margin of an element.
- **margin-bottom: <*length*>|<*percentage*>|auto**—Defines the bottom margin of an element.
- **margin-left: <*length*>|<*percentage*>|auto**—Defines the left margin of an element.
- **margin-right: <*length*>|<*percentage*>|auto**—Defines the right bottom margin of an element.
- **margin: [<*length*>|<*percentage*>|auto] {1, 4}**—Defines all of the margins for an element; the {1, 4} notation indicates that up to four numbers can be used as shorthand to describe an element's borders, as shown below:
  - *One number*—A single number defines the margins for all four sides; for example, **margin: .5** creates a half-inch margin on all four sides.
  - *Two numbers*—The first number defines the top and bottom margins, the second the left and right; for example, **margin: .5 .25** creates a half-inch margin on the top and bottom and a quarter-inch margin on the left and right.
  - *Three numbers*—The first number defines the top margin, the second the bottom, and the third the left and right.
  - *Four numbers*—Each number defines the margin for each side of the element in the order top, bottom, left, right. This notation is used in the same manner with several other box properties.

- **padding-top:** *<length>*|*<percentage>*—Specifies how much white space should be included between the top border of an element and its contents.
- **padding-bottom:** *<length>*|*<percentage>*—Specifies how much white space should be included between the bottom border of an element and its contents.
- **padding-left:** *<length>*|*<percentage>*—Specifies how much white space should be included between the left border of an element and its contents.
- **padding-right:** *<length>*|*<percentage>*—Specifies how much white space should be included between the right border of an element and its contents.
- **padding:** [*<length>*|*<percentage>*|**auto**] {1, 4}—Shorthand notation that specifies the padding for an element.
- **border-top-width:** *<length>*|**thin**|**medium**|**thick**—Defines the thickness of an element's top border.
- **border-bottom-width:** *<length>*|**thin**|**medium**|**thick**—Defines the thickness of an element's bottom border.
- **border-right-width:** *<length>*|**thin**|**medium**|**thick**—Defines the thickness of an element's right border.
- **border-left-width:** *<length>*|**thin**|**medium**|**thick**—Defines the thickness of an element's left border.
- **border-width:** [*<length>*|**thin**|**medium**|**thick**] {1,4}—Shorthand notation that defines the thickness of an element's border.
- **border-color:** *<color/#RRGGBB>*—Specifies the color of an element's border.
- **border-style:none|dotted|dashed|solid|double|groove|ridge|inset|outset**—Specifies the style of an element's border.
- **border-top: <border-width> || <border-style> || <color>**—Shorthand notation that specifies the width, style, and color of an element's top border.

- **border-bottom: <border-width> || <border-style> || <color>**—Shorthand notation that specifies the width, style, and color of an element's bottom border.
- **border-left: <border-width> || <border-style> || <color>**—Shorthand notation that specifies the width, style, and color of an element's left border.
- **border-right: <border-width> || <border-style> || <color>**—Shorthand notation that specifies the width, style, and color of an element's right border.
- **border: <border-width> || <border-style> || <color>**—Shorthand notation that specifies the width, style, and color of an element's entire border.
- **width:** ***<length>*|*<percentage>*|auto**—Specifies an element's width.
- **height:** ***<length>*|*<percentage>*|auto**—Specifies an element's height.
- **clear: none|left|right|both**—Determines whether other elements may be wrapped around the element and, if so, to which side.
- **float: left|right|none|both**—Specifies which direction text and other elements may float around an element.

Classification Properties

The classification properties define how white space, list numbers, and list bullets should be displayed by the browser.

- **display: block|inline|list-item|none**—Defines how an element should be displayed:
  - **block**—Adds a line break and space both before and after the element.
  - **inline**—Removes all line breaks.
  - **list-item**—Adds a bullet to the item but doesn't require an actual list.
  - **none**—Turns off any display associated with the element, such as a number or bullet in a true list.
- **white-space: normal|pre|nowrap**—Specifies how white space within an element should be treated:
  - **normal**—Follows the browser's standard rendering mechanisms.

- **pre**—Literally interprets every space and hard return (like the **<PRE> ...</PRE>** tag).
- **nowrap**—Prevents lines from breaking until a **
** tag is inserted.

- **list-style-type: disc|circle|square|decimal|lower-roman|upper-roman |lower-alpha|upper-alpha|none**—Defines which type of bullet should be used with list items.
- **list-style-image:** ***URL***—Specifies the URL for a graphic to be used in place of a standard bullet in a list.
- **list-style-position: inside|outside**—Defines how a list marker (bullet, image, or number) is placed relative to the text in the list.
    - **inside**—Wraps text under the marker.
    - **outside**—Indents the text so the marker stands alone to the left.
- **list-style: <list-style-type> || <list-style-position> || <list-style-image>**—Shorthand that defines the style or image and position of a list marker.

Font Properties

The font properties provide font-specific information—face, color, and size—for HTML elements:

- **font-family:** ***<family-name>*** || ***<generic family>***—Defines the font face in which text should be rendered. Examples of family names are Times, Garamond, and Helvetica. A generic family is not specific to the family, but rather describes the type of font, i.e., serif, sans-serif, cursive, fantasy, or monospace.
- **font-size: [xx-small|x-small|small|medium|large|x-large|xx-large]|*<length>*| *<percentage>*|[larger|smaller|*<relative-size>*]**—Specifies the font size in one of four ways:
    - **absolute size**—Defined by the browser and is relative to the actual size of the text; examples are **small** and **x-large**.
    - **length**—Defines the size of the font in pixels or any other valid unit of measurement.

- **percentage**—Defines the size of the current font as a percentage of the document's base font.
- **relative-size**—Makes the text larger or smaller in relation to the document's base font size.

- **font-style: normal|italic|oblique**—Defines the style in which text should be rendered.
- **font-variant: normal|small-caps**—Defines whether the font should be displayed in regular or small-caps text.
- **font-weight: normal|bold|100|200|300|400|500|600|700|800|900|lighter|bolder**—Defines the weight, or thickness, of the font using an absolute size (number measurements) or a relative size (lighter or bolder); the weight 400 represents normal text, while 700 is boldface text.
- **line-height: normal|<number>|<length>|<percentage>**—Defines the height of a line or the amount of space between text.
- **font: <font-weight> || <font-style> || <font-variant> || <font-size> || <line-height> || <font-family>**—Shorthand notation used to define all font properties at once.

Text Properties

The text properties describe how text should be rendered by the browser. Color, spacing, case, decoration, and alignment are all regulated by the text properties and values:

- **Color:** ***<color|#RRGGBB>***—Defines the color of the text using a color name or RGB hexadecimal color value.
- **text-align: left|right|center|justify**—Specifies how the text should be aligned: to the left, right, center, or both sides of the page.
- **text-indent:** ***<length>|<percentage>***—Specifies an indentation for all the contained text as an absolute length or a percentage of the parent element.
- **word-spacing: normal|*<length>***—Defines how much space should be included between words; **normal** is the browser's default spacing, while ***length*** provides an actual measurement.

- **letter-spacing: normal|<*length*>**—Defines how much space should be included between letters; **normal** is the browser's default spacing, while ***length*** provides an actual measurement.
- **text-transform: capitalize|uppercase|lowercase|none**—Specifies that the browser is to render all the enclosed text in uppercase, lowercase, or with all initial letters capitalized, regardless of how the text is typed.
- **text-decoration: none|underline|overline|line-through|blink**—Specifies how text should be decorated when displayed by the browser.
- **vertical-align: base-line|sub|super|top|text-top|middle|bottom|text-bottom|<*percentage*>**—Defines how text should be aligned relative to the surrounding text and to the page.

That's it for the parade of properties. As you can see, there are plenty to choose from, and every aspect of a page's display is addressed. We've been working with style sheets for a while now and haven't had to even think about a wish list for properties we don't have, and that's always a good sign.

Planning For An HTML Style Sheet

As with HTML pages, you need to plan and think through style sheets before actually creating them and putting them into place. Remember that the style sheet is going to affect your Web page or pages in many ways, so it should be carefully considered before any coding is done. Before you write your first style rule be sure to consider two very important questions:

- Who is your audience?
- What are your objectives?

Audience and objectives will drive much about your Web page, including the colors, fonts, figures, and overall styles used. A presentation for prospective clients on the use of the Web for their business will have a very different look from training materials describing the Web in general and how to make Web pages.

When you've considered your audience and objectives, collect the pieces of your Web document or document collection, including:

- Page content

- A basic outline
- A basic page layout

You'll find that style sheet creation will be much easier once you have all these pieces in place because you'll already have a good idea of how you want the final product to look. All that is left to write is the necessary style rules. Again, we stress how important it is to view any HTML page in progress with a variety of browsers on a variety of platforms. As Figures 6.4 through 6.6 in the next section show, no two browsers render the same HTML page alike, especially pages affected by style sheets.

Although the steps we've outlined take time to complete, we're sure you'll be happier with the results in the long run. Well-planned style sheets and HTML pages flow better, are easier to create and maintain, and require the least amount of troubleshooting.

Browser (In)Compatibility

As with all things Web, the question of browser support and compatibility must eventually be raised in reference to style sheets. The answer for style sheets is fairly straightforward, although it does have a few subclauses and dependencies. Table 6.2 represents current browser support for style sheets.

Table 6.2 may seem easy enough to understand, but it's not that easy in practice. Although Internet Explorer 4.0 and Netscape Navigator 4.0 both fully support the CSS1 specification, they each do it in a different way. Style-sheet rules are descriptive, and it's ultimately up to the browser to determine the final display of the page.

Table 6.2 Browsers that support Cascading Style Sheets.

Browser	Version	Level of Support
Microsoft Internet Explorer	3.0	Partial support; covers most font and text properties
Microsoft Internet Explorer	4.0	Full support for almost all properties
Netscape Communicator	4.0	Full support for almost all properties; also supports Netscape's own nonstandard JavaScript Style Sheets

As an experiment, let's use both IE 4.0 and Navigator 4.0 to look at the same Web page (with style sheets) for similarities and differences. The page in question is the World Wide Web Consortium's Web Style Sheets page found at **www.w3.org/Style/**. Figure 6.4 shows IE's interpretation of the page, and Figure 6.5 shows Navigator's.

Even though the same page is displayed in each figure, differences in the display are immediately noticeable. For example, the words are closer together in Netscape's view than they are in Microsoft's. However, the colors are approximately the same, as are the fonts, so some aspects of the pages are alike.

This difference in final display among browsers is not reserved just for style sheets; it affects all Web technologies, especially advanced HTML markup such as tables and forms. There is no remedy because it's doubtful that Netscape and Microsoft will join forces any time soon. Instead, it's important to look at your pages with multiple browsers and on multiple platforms to see what all the final display results will be. Incidentally, Figure 6.6 shows what this page looks like when viewed by Navigator 3.0, a style-sheet-challenged browser.

A resource to help you figure out which style-sheet properties are supported by which browsers is already online and kicking. The Browser Compatibility Chart, maintained

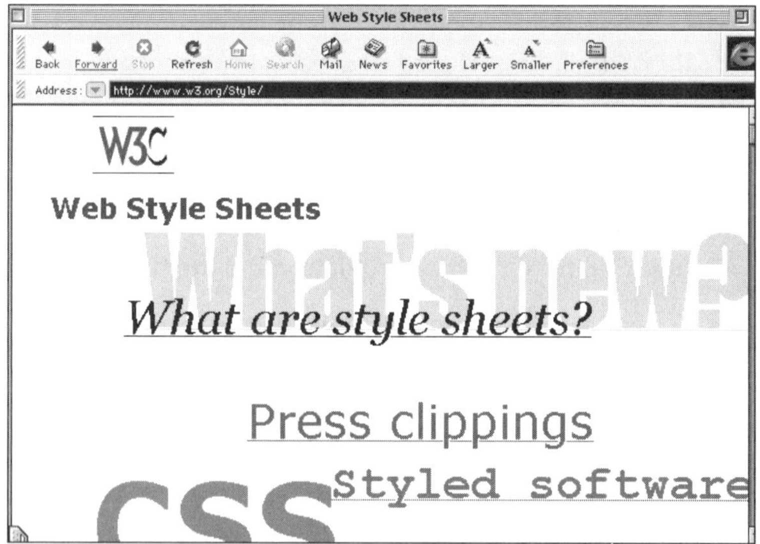

Figure 6.4

Internet Explorer 4.0's view of the W3C's Web Style Sheets page.

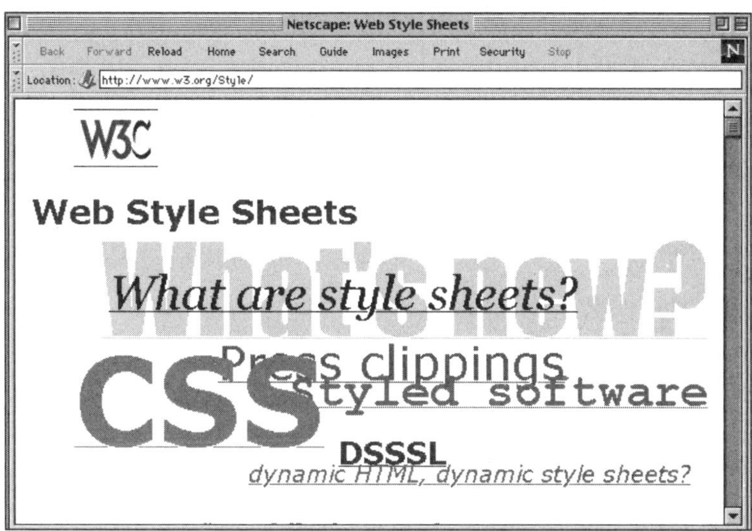

Figure 6.5

Netscape Navigator 4.0's view of the W3C's Web Style Sheets page.

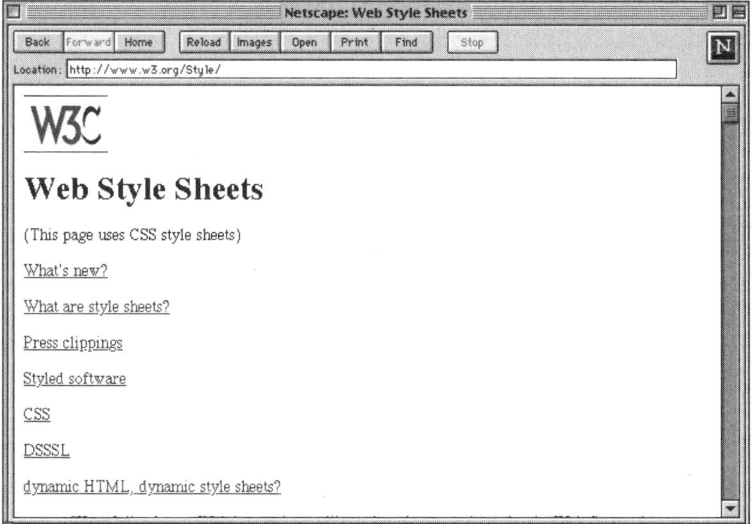

Figure 6.6

Netscape Navigator 3.0's view of the W3C's Web Style Sheets page.

by Web Review, is a comprehensive listing of which elements work with which versions of each browser. This comparison is entirely graphical in nature and may take some time to load. The properties are divided by types rather than families, and a full-color comparison chart—like the one shown in Figure 6.7—is provided for each. To see the entire listing visit Web Review online at **www.webreview.com/guides/style/mastergrid.html**.

Other Resources

This chapter serves as only a short introduction to style sheets and there are other, more comprehensive resources available. We would like to recommend the *HTML Style Sheets Design Guide*, another Coriolis Group book, featuring one of this book's authors, Natanya Pitts (with Steven N. James and Ed Tittel). The book was written for Web designers by Web designers and leaves no stone unturned in the discussion of style sheets and the Web—and it's in color so you can see style sheets come alive right on the page. Another resource is *Web Design and Development Black Book*, another Coriolis Group offering, written by Scott Jarol and Marisa Peña.

As with most Web-related topics, the best place to go for the most up-to-date information is the Web itself. To help you with your search we offer this list of Web resources:

Basic Concepts							
	Property or Value	Windows95			Macintosh		
		Nav4	IE3	IE4	Nav4	IE3	IE4
1.1	Containment in HTML						
	LINK	Y	Y	Y	Y	Y	Y
	<STYLE type="text/css">...</STYLE>	Y	Y	Y	Y	Y	Y
	@import	N	N	Y	N	N	N
	<x STYLE="dec;">	Y	Y	Y	Y	Y	Y
1.2	Grouping						
	x, y, z {dec;}	Y	N	Y	Y	Y	Y
1.3	Inheritance						
	(inherited values)	P	Y	P	B	B	B
1.4	Class as selector						
	.class	B	B	Y	B	Y	Y
1.5	ID as selector						
	#ID	B	B	Y	B	Y	B
1.6	Contextual selectors						
	x y z {dec;}	B	Y	Y	P	Y	Y
1.7	Comments						
	/* comment */	Y	B	Y	Y	Y	Y

Figure 6.7

A sample from Web Review's Browser Compatibility Chart.

- www.w3.org/Style
- www.htmlhelp.com/reference/css/
- www.microsoft.com/workshop/author/css/css-f.htm
- www.microsoft.com/workshop/design/des-gen/ss/css-des-f.htm
- www.microsoft.com/gallery/files/styles/
- www.alfaskop.net/~Egriffon/web/writing_stylesheets.html
- webreview.com/97/05/30/feature/tutorial.html
- www.netscapeworld.com/netscapeworld/nw-07-1997/nw-07-css.html#CSS
- www.windows.com/workshop/design/des-gen/ss/css-des.htm
- iwb.uni-stuttgart.de/~schwarte/cssjs.htm
- www.cwi.nl/~Esteven/www/css1-qr.html
- www.ssc.com/websmith/issues/i3/ws51.html
- www.w3.org/TR/WD-style
- ds.dial.pipex.com/pixelp/wpdesign/wpdintro.htm
- www.w3.org/Style/css/#browsers

Practical Guide To

Linking Style Sheets To Web Pages

- Inline Style Sheets
  - External Style Sheets
  - Imported Style Sheets

Inline Style Sheets

Inline style information is stored directly within an HTML document and affects that document alone. To include a style sheet in an HTML page, simply write the style rules between **<STYLE>...</STYLE>** tags within the document's header. Using our paragraph styles and HTML examples from the "Writing Rules For Style Sheets" section, the HTML page with the style information included looks like this:

```
<HTML>

<HEAD>
     <TITLE>HTML Style Sheet Sample</TITLE>

     <STYLE>
     P.body {font:14pt Comic Sans MS;
                  margin-left: .5in;
                  margin-right: .5in;
                 }

     P.new {font: 15pt Times;
                 margin-left: .5in;
                 margin-right: .5in;
                 }

     P.date {font: 12pt Arial;
                text-align: right;
                }
     </STYLE>

</HEAD>

<BODY>

<P CLASS=body>
Body text Body text Body text Body text Body text Body text
Body text Body text Body text Body text Body text Body text
</P>

<P CLASS=date>
date
</P>

<P CLASS=new>
New text New text New text New text New text New text New text
New text New text New text New text New text New text New text
</P>
```

```
<P CLASS=date>
date
</P>

</BODY>

</HTML>
```

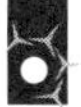

External Style Sheets

External style information is stored in a separate text file and can be linked to a large collection of HTML pages using the **<LINK>** tag. To convert the inline style sheet from the previous example into an external style sheet to be linked to many different Web pages, we would simply cut the style rules from the page and save them as a separate text file named style.css. Your external file name can be anything you like, and it doesn't have to end in .css, but we use this file naming convention to help us with file management. With the style information stored externally, the HTML page now looks like this:

```
<HTML>

<HEAD>
     <TITLE>HTML Style Sheet Sample</TITLE>

     <LINK REL=STYLESHEET HREF="style.css" TYPE="text/css">

</HEAD>

<BODY>

<P CLASS=body>
Body text Body text Body text Body text Body text Body text
Body text Body text Body text Body text Body text Body text
</P>

<P CLASS=date>
date
</P>

<P CLASS=new>
New text New text New text New text New text New text New text
New text New text New text New text New text New text New text
</P>
```

```
<P CLASS=date>
date
</P>

</BODY>

</HTML>
```

You will most often use inline or external style sheets in your pages. If you combine the two so that a page is governed by both an external style sheet and inline style rules, the inline style rules take precedence over the linked external style sheet when conflicting rules are present. For example, if the external style rule says all headings should be red, and the inline style rule says they should be blue, they will be blue. Any rules that don't conflict will be combined to create an overall style sheet for the page. An external style sheet that creates teal second-level headings and an inline style sheet that creates red first-level headings are combined to create a single style sheet for the page with red first-level headings and teal second-level headings.

The ability to include more than one source of style information for a given HTML page allows you to create a general external style sheet that governs all the pages in a collection as well as to create page-specific style rules as they are needed. Remember that when you combine style sheets, all of the elements in an HTML file work together to create the final look of a Web page, so think carefully before you create the style sheets.

Imported Style Sheets

The only difference between external style sheets and imported style sheets is the notation used to reference an externally stored style sheet. Importing a style sheet combines the inline and external style linking mechanisms, as shown in this code:

```
<HTML>

<HEAD>
     <TITLE>HTML Style Sheet Sample</TITLE>

     <STYLE>
     @import "style.css";

</HEAD>

<BODY>
```

```
<P CLASS=body>
Body text Body text Body text Body text Body text Body text
Body text Body text Body text Body text Body text Body text
</P>

<P CLASS=date>
date
</P>

<P CLASS=new>
New text New text New text New text New text New text New text
New text New text New text New text New text New text New text
</P>

<P CLASS=date>
date
</P>

</BODY>

</HTML>
```

Chapter 7

HTML 4.0 And Proprietary Enhancements For DHTML

This chapter provides an in-depth explanation of the HTML 4.0 specification and discusses additional proprietary Dynamic HTML tags from Microsoft and Netscape.

Notes...

Chapter 7

As we've said throughout this book, several definitions are applied to the language known as Dynamic HTML. While the W3C continues its process of finalizing the HTML 4.0 specification, Microsoft and Netscape carry on their proprietary developments. Although both companies keep a close watch on the W3C's actions, each is hoping that its particular extensions to the HTML language will become—either officially or in practice—the preferred implementation of DHTML.

In this chapter, we examine the extensions and additions that Netscape and Microsoft have incorporated into their versions of Dynamic HTML and will explore some implementations of HTML 4.0's new tags in this chapter's Practical Guide. The following is a brief overview of some additions that the proprietary players, Microsoft and Netscape, are including in their versions of DHTML.

Beware The Draft

As we write this chapter, HTML 4.0 is still a working draft that, unlike the stable HTML 3.2 standard, can technically be updated, replaced, or made obsolete by other documents at any time. Some Web developers were seriously disgruntled by the number of changes that HTML 3.2 underwent while in final draft stage. The INvalidated HTML Home Page was formed by designers who had adapted their work to the August 1996 draft, only to find that it was invalid once the January

1997 final recommendation kicked in. Don't say the W3C didn't warn you. If you want to commiserate with other developers over the hardships of creating content to the rhythm of morphing standards, see the INvalidated HTML Home Page at **www.pantos.org/invalid/**.

New HTML 4.0 Enhancements

HTML 4.0 contains the following new elements:

- **Q**
- **INS**
- **DEL**
- **ACRONYM**
- **LEGEND**
- **COLGROUP**
- **BUTTON**
- **FIELDSET**

We discuss how HTML 4.0 is affected by these and other changes in Chapter 2; this chapter's Practical Guide also provides examples of how these new elements can be used with DHTML.

Netscape's Idea Of DHTML

Netscape defines DHTML as a combination of HTML (including Netscape's proprietary extensions), JavaScript, and Java, in addition to an object model for HTML documents. As we discussed in Chapter 5, Netscape's DOM doesn't adhere to the W3C Requirements document. One of the reasons for this is that Netscape's DOM doesn't expose elements in the way that Microsoft's does. The JavaScript object model puts elements such as links, images, and applets into a collection of objects or arrays that allow them to be manipulated through client-side scripting. However, unlike the Microsoft implementation, this model doesn't include all HTML elements in these collections.

Netscape's DHTML **<LAYER>** tag uses a combination of content and style markup that is directly contrary to the separation between style and content that the W3C is attempting to achieve with HTML 4.0. Fonts that can load and change dynamically are another feature of Netscape's DHTML, and one that we examine in this chapter's Practical Guide.

Netscape's multimedia and image filtering DHTML extensions are much less developed than Microsoft's. Both Netscape and Microsoft are incorporating DHTML into their push/channel content strategies and exploiting DHTML's powers in their intranet offerings, but Microsoft's marriage of DHTML, DirectX, and ActiveX demonstrates a vision that Netscape currently lacks. Note also that Microsoft's long-term planning has led to the incorporation of data binding into its DHTML, whereas Netscape has no such provision.

Microsoftian DHTML

As we said earlier in Chapter 4, Microsoft defines DHTML as four things:

- The HTML document object model
- A way to control the positioning of elements on a page
- A set of multimedia controls for animation, alpha-channel filtering, and other effects
- A way to bind sets of data to an HTML page

Through Microsoft's Dynamic HTML Object Model (discussed extensively in Chapter 5), each HTML element is exposed in a Web page, attributes, and Cascading Style Sheets (CSS1) properties. This exposure is one of the crucial differences between Microsoft's and Netscape's DOM. Microsoft's exposure of all elements simplifies the process of accessing and altering a Web page's elements, including attributes, images, text, objects, and tags. Because all of these elements are visible, it's possible to navigate visually through the object hierarchy to find specific elements. This exposure of elements is in accordance with the W3C's ideals; however, the dependence of Microsoft's Dynamic HTML on Internet Explorer 4.0, the ActiveX component model, and Windows distances it from the W3C's vision.

The Pain Of (DHTML) Differences

There are obviously many differences between the ways Microsoft and Netscape view and use dynamic HTML—they even refer to DHTML with slightly different names. Netscape's version is called dynamic HTML with a lower-case "d," whereas

Microsoft implies quasi-ownership by giving its version a capital "D," Dynamic HTML.

These disparate approaches to HTML can translate into serious problems for people attempting to view proprietary comments. When we used Netscape Navigator 4.01 at the Microsoft site to research this chapter, we got back over 50 error messages within an hour, including multiple occurrences of JavaScript errors such as these:

```
JavaScript Error: http://www.microsoft.com/msdn/sdk/inetsdk/help/dhtml/
ref_collect/collections.htm, line 27: TOC is not defined.
JavaScript Error: http://www.microsoft.com/msdn/sdk/inetsdk/samples/databind/
dbsingle.htm, line 14: scrNavBtns is not defined.
JavaScript Error: http://www.microsoft.com/msdn/sdk/inetsdk/help/dhtml/
databind.htm, line 405: window.event has no properties.
```

When you're using Navigator to view Microsoft-created DHTML, also be prepared to be deprived of some multimedia bells and whistles. Microsoft's aggressive combination of DHTML and Active X/DirectX gives designers creating DHTML content with Microsoft products some significantly enhanced multimedia controls and avenues of expression. For example, in order to create fades with Netscape's DHTML, designers usually resort to straight Java, whereas Microsoft provides designers with easy multimedia fade—and swipe, and blur, and invert—tools.

Even using a version of Navigator before the 4.0 browser will prohibit you from seeing some Netscape DHTML content, and you'll encounter some similar error messages. Attempting to view Netscape's layers with Internet Explorer can be disastrous as well, although, as with the reverse proprietary browser problems, there are ways of designing DHTML pages that ensure they can be viewed by both browsers.

Netscape's Proprietary Additions To DHTML

We've devoted Part 4 of this book to discussing and documenting the critical element of Netscape's DHTML, the **LAYER** tag. Here we examine two of Netscape's other DHTML additions, Dynamic Fonts and JavaScript Style Sheets (JSSS). Examples of their use follow in this chapter's Practical Guide.

Dynamic Fonts

Creating pages with specific fonts can be difficult when you don't know what fonts are available on the user's computer—Netscape's version of DHTML attempts to solve this problem. CSS1 approaches this dilemma by giving a list of alternative fonts to use when the preferred font can't be found. For example, you can select the Geneva font and indicate that Chicago should be used if Geneva isn't available.

Netscape's font enhancements let you dynamically incorporate fonts into a document and send the font along with the document the same way you send an image. When users read a Web page that uses linked fonts, the font is downloaded to their system automatically.

Dynamic Fonts Through TrueDoc

Netscape's dynamic font technology works in conjunction with a technology from Bitstream called TrueDoc, which is built into authoring tools and Web browsers to provide a seamless—and secure—transfer of font data between the Web server housing the requested pages and the end user's system. Through TrueDoc, highly compressed versions of new fonts (like the ones shown in Figure 7.1) are downloaded by the client's machine. The fonts are mapped as a set of glyphs (shapes found in type) and use a library that already exists on the user's computer to assemble the type on the fly. While the fonts are loading, you might see a page that looks like the one shown in Figure 7.2.

Figure 7.1

The Eyeball Font is an example of a dynamic font developed by Bitstream.

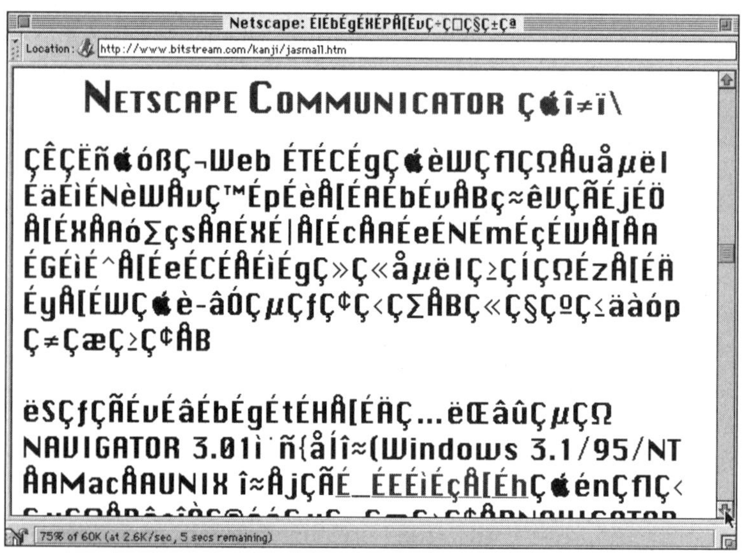

Figure 7.2

The Kanji Font, unloaded.

After the font download is complete (a process that might take 45 seconds or so), the page will render itself again with the font, as shown in Figure 7.3.

TrueDoc works through two main components:

- The Character Shape Recorder (CSR)
- The Character Shape Player (CSP)

The CSR

The CSR is the component that's included in authoring tools such as HexWeb Typograph from HexMac and Netscape Composer. If you want to create dynamic fonts for Web documents, you must use a TrueDoc-enabled authoring tool. Some of the other companies adding the CSR to their authoring tools include:

- Astrobyte
- Boomerang Software
- Corel Corp.
- Digiflyer

- FutureTense
- InfoAccess Inc.
- Macromedia Inc.
- MySoftware Company
- Network Computer Inc.
- Pacifica Internet Authoring Tools
- RMX Technologies Inc.
- SoftQuad

The CSR works by recording characters from the fonts that Web developers use in their documents, then storing them in a compact data type called Portable Font Resource (PFR). The PFR is posted for your Web site in the same way as an HTML file. PFR files can be much more economical to use than GIFs or JPEGs; the Kanji font shown in Figure 7.3 is 61K.

Another advantage of using PFR is that search engines and audio browsers treat PFR text exactly as they do regular HTML—unlike text contained in purely graphical

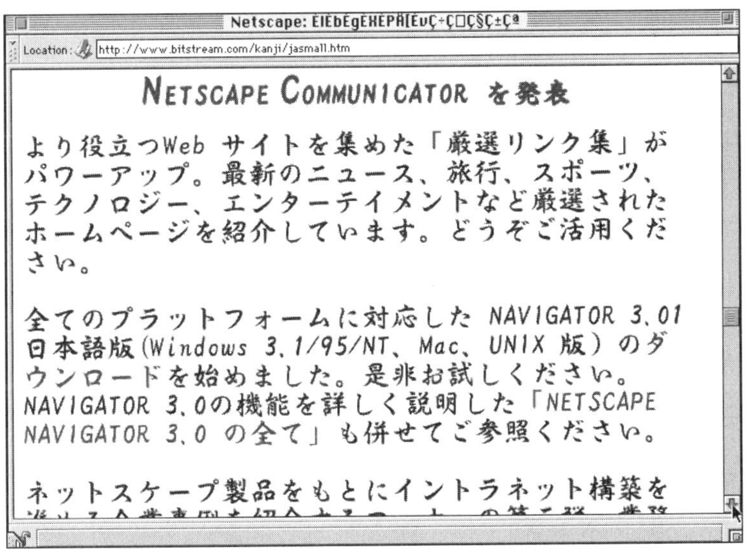

Figure 7.3

The Kanji Font, rendered after several seconds.

formats. Font definition files can contain more than one font and they're especially useful for writing foreign languages such as Kanji (a Japanese dialect) and Cyrillic.

The CSP

The CSP is a component that's included in browsers such as Navigator/Communicator 4.01 (and later). To view dynamic fonts, your browser must be TrueDoc-enabled through the CSP.

Dynamic Font Syntax

Dynamic fonts are implemented through existing HTML. To write a document that uses dynamic fonts, you specify the source for the font definition at the top of the document. This source can be indicated through either a style sheet or by the **LINK** tag. After you've specified the source, you can use fonts in that file for the value of the **FACE** attribute in the **FONT** tag.

This is the syntax for referencing a style sheet through a link (with fonts.pfr as the font definition file):

```
<LINK REL=fontdef SRC="http://www.mycomputer.org/fonts/fonts.pfr">
```

This would be the syntax for referencing a style sheet in CSS1 syntax:

```
<STYLE TYPE="text/css"><!--
@fontdef url(http://www.mycomputer.org/fonts/fonts.pfr);
--></STYLE>
```

Declaring The TrueDoc PFR MIME Type

For users to download and view TrueDoc PFRs from their TrueDoc-enabled Web browsers, system administrators have to make sure that their Web servers recognize the PFR MIME type. TrueDoc PFRs have a file extension of .pfr, and their MIME type is:

```
application/font-tdpfr
```

With Windows NT servers, the gopher type is "5:REG_SZ:" so the entire key looks like this:

```
application/font-tdpfr,pfr,,5:REG_SZ:
```

Depending on the demands of your Web server, it may be necessary to enter the extension in either uppercase or lowercase letters (or both) and add a period before the extension. It's a pending question whether an additional MIME type such as "**/font/truedoc**" will have to be specified in the future; refer to the Bitstream Dynamic Font page for up-to-date information at **www.bitstream.com/world/index.html**.

JavaScript Style Sheets

JavaScript Style Sheets (JSSS), sometimes called JavaScript-Accessible Style Sheets (JASS), are an alternative that Netscape is offering to CSS1. Like CSS1, JSSS function as a means of changing type element properties. CSS1 and JSSS have similar features, but the two use completely different command and markup syntax.

One of the biggest differences between JSSS and CSS1 is the more dynamic orientation of JSSS. Because the browser interprets JavaScript as Web pages are loaded, it's possible to modify and update the styles that are defined through JSSS. You can exploit the dynamic capabilities of JSSS to customize the way Web pages are rendered according to end-user variables, such as browser window dimensions and monitor settings.

JSSS styles and CSS1 are associated with documents in exactly the same way: as document-level styles, external style sheets, and inline styles within a tag. For example, you can use JSSS to refer to an external style sheet with a **LINK** tag in the document's head:

```
<LINK REL=stylesheet type="text/Javascript" HREF="funstyles.jss">
```

Note the similarity to a cascading style sheet reference; the difference is that the **TYPE** attribute is set to text/Javascript, not text/CSS. See the Practical Guide for an example of JSSS implementation.

Microsoft's Proprietary Additions To DHTML

Microsoft has made some significant additions to DHTML, although, like Netscape, many of the "new" developments are simply slightly reworked versions of former technologies (topped with some spin). In the following sections, we examine some of the more important additions to Microsoft's DHTML.

Data Binding

Data binding is a unique feature of Microsoft's Dynamic HTML, and one that works extremely well with Microsoft's grand networking strategies. Data binding allows you to bind individual elements in your Web document to data from another source, such as a database or a text file. When the Web document is loaded, data is automatically retrieved from the source, formatted, and displayed within the element. To bind data to the elements of an Internet Explorer 4 HTML page, a data source object (DSO) has to be present on that page.

The goal of data binding is connecting a data source object to a data consumer. To do this, Microsoft has added several new attributes to its DHTML:

- **DATASRC**—Specifies the identification of the DSO to which a recipient is bound.
- **DATAFLD**—Identifies the column exposed by the DSO to which the element is bound.
- **DATAFORMATAS**—Tells how the data in the specified column is to be rendered.
- **DATAPAGESIZE**—Tells how many records are simultaneously displayed in a table.

We include more in-depth coverage of Microsoft's data binding in Chapter 10.

Direct Animation Controls

The activity tied to Microsoft's DirectAnimation controls is important to Microsoft's DHTML. With DirectAnimation and a scripting language, you can add and integrate sound, 3D content, movies, and the like to your Web pages.

The two main concepts behind DirectAnimation are continuous behaviors and events. These concepts meld into "reactive behaviors," which shift continuously according to time, reacting to certain events by changing behaviors.

We'll explore DirectAnimation in greater detail in Chapters 11 and 12, which cover graphics and sound with DHTML. For now, here are the DirectAnimation controls that Microsoft's DHTML uses:

- *Sequencer Control*—Lets you make complex sequences of action through scripting, ActiveX controls, or DHTML elements.
- *Path Control*—Lets you move objects around a Web page using splines, geometric primitives, text outlines, or shapes. This control lets you determine speed of motion, looping, forward or reverse playback, and bouncing behavior.

- *Sprite Control*—Gives you control over playback speed, forward/reverse playback, and user interactivity on a frame-by-frame basis with still and animated images.
- *Structured Graphics Control*—Allows you to put lightweight vector graphics in your Web page that can be scaled or rotated in three dimensions. You can apply solid colors, patterns, bitmap textures, or gradient fills to these graphics.

VBScript And JScript

The release of Internet Explorer 4 includes JScript 3.0, Microsoft's object-oriented implementation of JavaScript/ECMAScript. One of JScript 3.0's most important features is its *conditional compilation,* which lets developers write scripts targeted to specific client platforms and browsers. Because JScript is an interpreted language—that is, it is compiled after the code has been interpreted by the Web server or browser—conditional compilation means that it can adopt different code paths depending on runtime variables.

Rather than creating scripts to determine the end user's platform and browser version, you can just put the JScript 3.0 features in a conditional compile section. The script placed in this section will run only if the user is running a version of JScript 3.0. People using other browsers won't see the 3.0 code; another script will run for them.

Microsoft's VBScript (Visual Basic Scripting Edition) is a subset of Microsoft's Visual Basic language. It's used as an interpreter in Web browsers and other applications that use OLE (Object Linking and Embedding) automation servers, ActiveX controls, and Java applets (when Microsoft feels like permitting them). VBScript's role in IE mirrors JavaScript's—they're both "pure interpreters" that process source code directly embedded in HTML. VBScript is a key component in Microsoft's DHTML implementation because of the interactivity it brings to Web pages.

For more information on Microsoft's scripting languages, see **www.microsoft.com/scripting/**.

Scriptlets

Curious about Microsoft's anti-applet stance? A one-word response may enlighten you: scriptlets.

Microsoft defines *scriptlets* as Web pages that can be used as components in Web applications. Scriptlets are Microsoft's answer to applets—they harness DHTML's power by combining a scripting language such as, say, Microsoft's JScript or VBScript, with HTML to create reusable objects. All platforms can run scriptlets—as long as you're using IE 4.

Scriptlets are created by inserting an **OBJECT** tag into another Web page. IE 4 recognizes a scriptlet by marking the tag with a MIME type of "text/x-scriptlet". Here's an example of how a scriptlet combines with the **OBJECT** tag:

```
<OBJECT width=100 height=200
TYPE="text/x-scriptlet"  DATA="Calendar.htm">
</OBJECT>
```

For additional information on scriptlets, see Microsoft's Scriptlet pages at **www.micro soft.com/scripting/scriptlets/**.

Practical Guide To

Implementing DHTML Enhancements

- Using HTML 4.0 Elements
  - **INS/DEL**
  - **COLGROUP**
  - **BUTTON**
  - **FIELDSET/LEGEND**
- Using JavaScript Style Sheets
- The VBScript Way
- Netscape TrueDoc Fonts

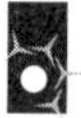

Using HTML 4.0 Elements

In this section, we take a look at different ways to use some of the most important tags that have been added or emphasized in HTML 4.0, as well as the proprietary extensions that Netscape and Microsoft have added to their versions of DHTML.

INS/DEL

INS and **DEL** are interesting new HTML 4.0 elements; unlike most other elements, they can work as either block-level or inline elements (but not both). **INS** and **DEL** are employed in places where you want to mark sections of a document that have been inserted or deleted. They are often used to indicate different versions of a document, such as a draft number for a business proposal. **INS** and **DEL** can contain one or more words within a paragraph; they can also contain one or more block-level elements, including paragraphs, tables, and lists.

In the following example, **INS** and **DEL** are used to update a number.

```
<P>
The Internet is estimated to contain <DEL>750,000</DEL>
<INS>100,000,000</INS> sites.
</P>
```

*The **INS** and **DEL** elements must not contain block-level content when these elements behave as inline elements.*

COLGROUP

Through the new **COLGROUP** tag, you can define any number of adjacent columns in a table as a group of columns and treat that group as a unit. **COLGROUP** lets you apply attribute-value pairs to all of a group's columns simultaneously.

The **COLGROUP** element creates an explicit column group. There are two different ways to indicate how many columns a column group should contain:

- Through the **SPAN** attribute (default value 1), which specifies the number of columns in the group.
- Through the **COL** element—each **COL** element in the **COLGROUP** represents one column in the group.

When you use the **SPAN** attribute, you have the advantage of being able to combine information about column widths. A table with 30 columns, each containing 16 pixels, can therefore be expressed as:

```
<COLGROUP span="30" width="16">
</COLGROUP>
```

Rather than:

```
<COLGROUP>
<COL width="16">
<COL width="16">
...a total of thirty COL elements...
</COLGROUP>
```

The **COL** elements must be used when you need to specify a certain column within a group—for example, to apply style information. If you want to single out the last column from the preceding code, you could write:

```
<COLGROUP width="16">
<COL repeat="29">
<COL id="individual-format">
</COLGROUP>
```

Through the "individual-format," an **ID** value is assigned to the thirtieth column, so style sheets can now refer to it.

In the following example, the **SPAN** attribute indicates how many columns are spanned by the column group, while the **WIDTH** attribute defines the default width for each column. The example's table features two groups of columns, with the first spanning five columns, with a width of 60 pixels each, and the second spanning three columns, each designated by the symbol "0*", which indicates that they're the minimum width necessary to hold the column's contents:

```
<TABLE>
<COLGROUP span="5" width="60">
<COLGROUP span="3" width="0*">
<TR>
...table contents here...
</TR>
</TABLE>
```

One of **COLGROUP**'s other important attributes is **ALIGN**, which can be used for precise alignments such as lining up numeric values on the decimal point. Now in addition to the pre-existing values of **left**, **center**, and **right**, you use either **justify** (which justifies left and right margins) or **char** (character) as **ALIGN** values. When you use the **char** value of the **ALIGN** attribute along with the **CHAR** attribute, you can specify a character with which to align the column's contents. To create a column group in which the contents of each column align to the decimal point, use the following syntax:

```
<COLGROUP align="char" char=".">
```

BUTTON

Although the **BUTTON** tag isn't completely new, HTML 4.0 takes its use into fresh territory. With HTML 3.2, **BUTTON** was mostly restricted for use with forms. The 4.0 specification, however, makes the **BUTTON** tag dynamic by letting you put script-triggering button controls anywhere on an HTML page. It's no longer necessary to define a form to contain the buttons.

The **BUTTON** element can be one of three types:

- **submit** (the default)
- **reset**
- **button**

Because you can put images within the **BUTTON** tag, using it rather than **TYPE=*submit*** with the **INPUT** form tag stretches the multimedia capabilities. Because HTML 4.0's implementation of **BUTTON** lets buttons appear anywhere in HTML pages, buttons can now also be used for event handling with JavaScript.

There are clear similarities between a **BUTTON** element whose type is **submit** and an **INPUT** element whose type is **submit**. Both of these elements enable a form to be submitted; however, the **BUTTON** element gives designers more sophisticated capacities of presentation. While **INPUT** elements appear as flat images, **BUTTON** elements contain relief that makes them actually look like buttons. The button created through the **BUTTON** element will also give an up and down motion when the user clicks on it. In the following example, the **INPUT** elements that create submit and reset are combined with **BUTTON** instances. The buttons obtain their images thanks to the **IMG** element (as usual, when using the **IMG** element, you should create alternate text to accompany the image):

```
<FORM action="http://mysite.org/addperson" method="post">
    <P>
    First name: <INPUT type="text" name="firstname"><BR>
    Last name: <INPUT type="text" name="lastname"><BR>
    email: <INPUT type="text" name="email"><BR>
```

```
<BUTTON name="submit" value="submit" type="submit">
    Send<IMG src="/icons/smile.gif" alt="smile"></BUTTON>
    <BUTTON name="reset" type="reset">
    Reset<IMG src="/icons/frown.gif" alt="frown"></BUTTON>
    </P>
</FORM>
```

*It is illegal to associate an image map with an **IMG** that appears as the contents of a **BUTTON** element.*

FIELDSET/LEGEND

The **FIELDSET** and **LEGEND** elements are usually found together. The **FIELDSET** element allows you to group labels and controls that share a common theme. The ability to group controls is one of HTML 4.0's accessibility features; when controls are grouped, they're easier for visual- and speech-oriented user agents to navigate. The **LEGEND** elements work with **FIELDSET** by assigning **FIELDSET** a caption. In cases where **FIELDSET** is rendered non-visually, the legend adds to **FIELDSET**'s accessibility.

The following example demonstrates how a form might be used to glean information about what people have read and are reading for a book club. Through the **LEGEND** and **FIELDSET** tags, each section contains controls for inputting the requested information.

```
<FORM action="..." method="post">
<P>
<FIELDSET>
<LEGEND>Personal Information</LEGEND>
Last Name: <INPUT name="personal_lastname" type="text" tabindex="1">
First Name: <INPUT name="personal_firstname" type="text" tabindex="2">
...more personal information...
</FIELDSET>
<FIELDSET>
<LEGEND>Reading History</LEGEND>
<INPUT name="history_reading"
       type="checkbox"
       value="Shakespeare "tabindex="30"> Shakespeare
<INPUT name="history_reading"
       type="checkbox"
       value="Dickens" tabindex="31"> Dickens
<INPUT name="history_reading"
       type="checkbox"
       value="Austen" tabindex="32"> Austen
```

```
...more reading history...
</FIELDSET>
<FIELDSET>
<LEGEND>Current Books In Progress </LEGEND>
Are you currently reading any books?
<INPUT name="current_books"
       type="text"
       value="Yes" tabindex="35">Yes
<INPUT name="current_books"
       type="text"
       value="No" tabindex="35">No
</FIELDSET>
</FORM>
```

Using JavaScript Style Sheets

Here's an example of the way a JavaScript Style Sheet could be used in creating bubble help. The finished product is shown in Figure 7.4. Chapter 13 also uses this example to demonstrate Netscape's layer model. In the following code, we excerpt the style sheet markup to show how JSSS can create bubble help in the same way Netscape's **LAYER** tag does.

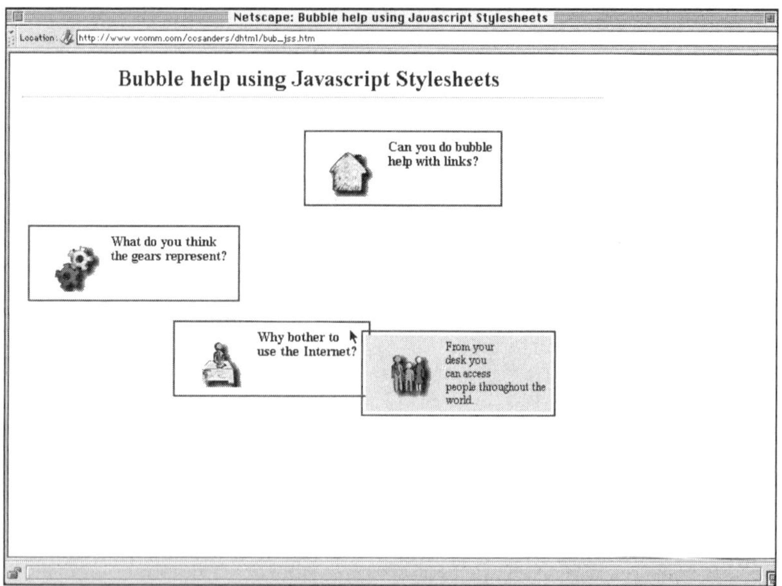

Figure 7.4

Bubble help script made with JavaScript Style Sheets.

```
<HTML>

 <!-- Copyright (C) 1997 by Christopher D. Brown of Austin, TX -->

 <HEAD>
  <TITLE> Bubble help using JavaScript Style Sheets </TITLE>
 </HEAD>

<!-- Styles -->

 <STYLE TYPE="text/javascript">
   with ( classes.hinner.all )
   {
    borderWidth=2;
    borderColor="blue";
    borderStyle="ridge";
    padding="2px";
    backgroundColor="#FFCCFF";
   }
   with ( classes.houter.all )
   {
    position="absolute";
    top=10;
    left=10;
    width=50;
    zIndex=2;
    visibility="hidden";
   }
   with ( classes.rinner.all )
   {
    borderWidth=2;
    borderColor="blue";
    borderStyle="ridge";
    padding="2px";
    backgroundColor="#FFFFFF";
   }
   with ( classes.gear.all )
   {
    position="absolute";
    top=180;
    left=20;
    width=300;
    zIndex=1;
   }
   with ( classes.desk.all )
   {
    position="absolute";
```

```
    top=280;
    left=180;
    width=300;
    zIndex=1;
   }
   with ( classes.up.all )
   {
    position="absolute";
    top=80;
    left=320;
    width=300;
    zIndex=1;
   }
// The CSS way
//   .hinner { border-width:2; border-color:blue; border-style:ridge;
//             padding:2px; background-color:rgb(255,204,255); }
//   .houter { position:absolute; top:10; left:10; width:50; z-index:2;
//             visibility:hidden; }
//   .rinner { border-width:2; border-color:blue; border-style:ridge;
//             padding:2px; background-color:rgb(255,255,255); }
//   .gear { position:absolute; top:180; left: 20; width:300; z-index:1; }
//   .desk { position:absolute; top:280; left:180; width:300; z-index:1; }
//   .up   { position:absolute; top: 80; left:320; width:300; z-index:1; }
 </STYLE>
```

The VBScript Way

The following is the bubble help example created with VBScript. Again, only the code related to scripting is included. Note the **if...then** that makes the code run for Internet Explorer, and the alert, **alert "VBScript without Internet Explorer ... no sale"** that will pop up for those not using IE as their Web browser.

```
<HTML>
<!-- Copyright (C) 1997 by Christopher D. Brown of Austin, TX -->

 <HEAD>
  <TITLE> Bubble Help Using VBScript </TITLE>
 </HEAD>

  <SCRIPT LANGUAGE="VBSCRIPT">
    if ( inStr( navigator.userAgent, "MSIE" ) > 0 ) then
        bIsNS = false
    else
        bIsNS = true
        alert "VBScript without Internet Explorer ... no sale"
    end if
```

```
sub HelpPos ( base, help )
    if ( base.posLeft > help.posWidth ) then
        help.posLeft = base.posLeft - help.posWidth + 10
    else
        help.posLeft = base.posLeft + base.posWidth - 10
    end if
    help.posTop = base.posTop + 10
    help.visibility = "visible"
end sub

sub HelpOnGear
    HelpPos document.all.gear.style, document.all.helpgear.style
end sub
sub HelpOffGear
    document.all.helpgear.style.visibility="hidden"
end sub

sub HelpOnDesk
    HelpPos document.all.desk.style, document.all.helpdesk.style
end sub
sub HelpOffDesk
    document.all.helpdesk.style.visibility="hidden"
end sub

sub HelpOnUp
    HelpPos document.all.up.style, document.all.helpup.style
end sub
sub HelpOffUp
    document.all.helpup.style.visibility="hidden"
end sub

</SCRIPT>
```

Netscape TrueDoc Fonts

Netscape claims that its dynamic fonts handle these forms:

```
<LINK REL="fontdef" SRC=fontfile.pfr>
  @fontdef url(fontfile.pfr);
  @font-face { src: url(fontfile.pfr);}
```

However, our experiments showed that this support is not very firmly established. The last form, **FONT-FACE**, is CSS1-compliant; it's only the first form, **LINK**, that we could get to work reliably.

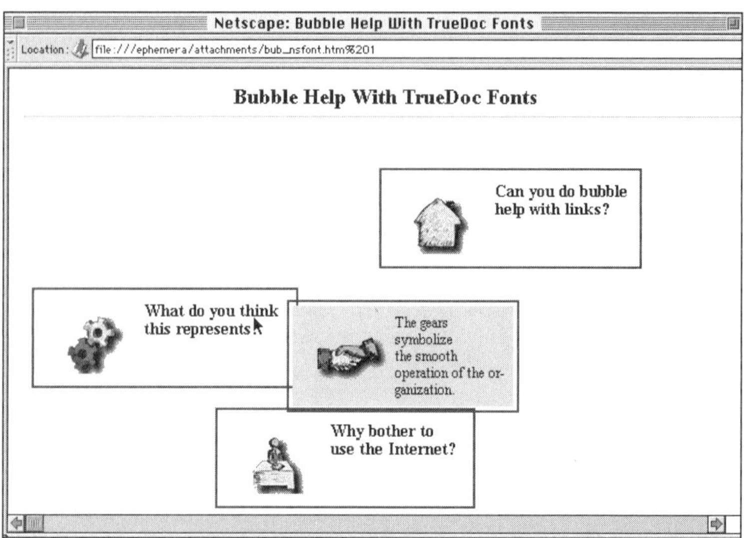

Figure 7.5

A Netscape TrueDoc Font example

In the following excerpt, we show the syntax that would be used to employ a font called Comic-Sans. Note the proprietary .pfr file type and the way that **FONT-FACE** sits between the **<H2>...</H2>** tags. The result is shown in Figure 7.5.

```
<HTML>

 <!-- Copyright (C) 1997 by Christopher D. Brown of Austin, TX -->

 <HEAD>
  <TITLE> Bubble Help With TrueDoc Fonts </TITLE>
  <LINK REL="fontdef" SRC="http://www.vcomm.com/ccsanders/dhtml/
    Comic_Sans_MS.pfr">
 </HEAD>

<!-- Styles -->

 <STYLE TYPE="text/css">
  <!--
   .hinner { border-width:2; border-color:blue; border-style:ridge;
             padding:2px; background-color:rgb(255,204,255); }
   .houter { position:absolute; top:10; left:10; width:50; z-index:2;
             visibility:hidden; }
   .rinner { border-width:2; border-color:blue; border-style:ridge;
             padding:2px; background-color:rgb(255,255,255); }
```

```
   .gear { position:absolute; top:180; left: 20; width:300; z-index:1; }
   .desk { position:absolute; top:280; left:180; width:300; z-index:1; }
   .up   { position:absolute; top: 80; left:320; width:300; z-index:1; }
  -->
 </STYLE>

<!-- Body not required -->
 <BODY BGCOLOR="#FFFFCC">

  <TABLE WIDTH="640"><TR><TD ALIGN="CENTER">
   <H2><FONT FACE="Comic Sans MS"> Bubble Help With TrueDoc Fonts
   <HR> </FONT> </H2>
  </TD></TR></TABLE>
```

PART 3

WORKING WITH MICROSOFT'S DHTML COMPONENTS

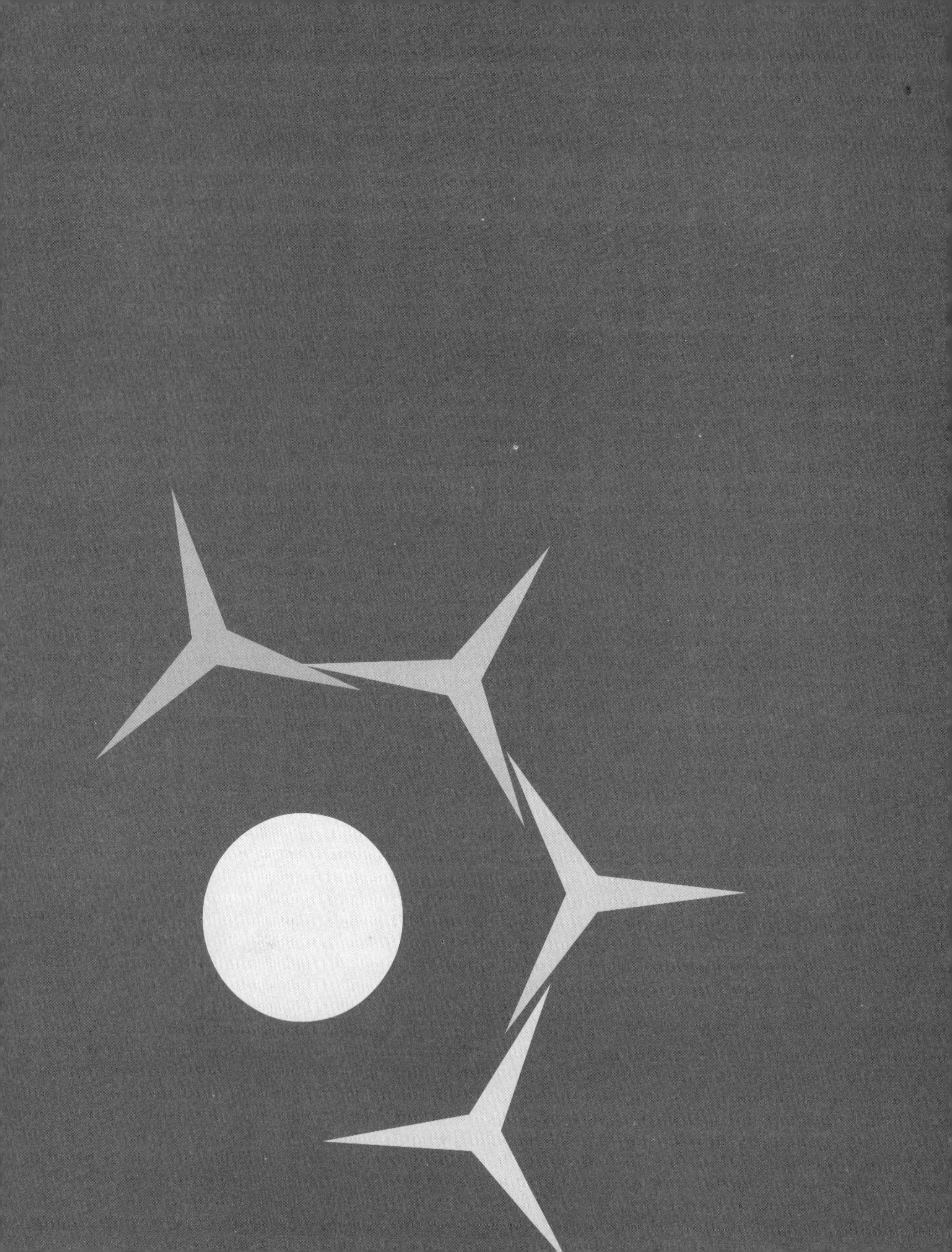

Chapter 8

Events And Dynamic HTML

In this chapter, we explore the Dynamic HTML event model, and learn about the different object-specific events.

Notes...

Chapter 8

In the previous chapter, you learned about the HTML 4.0 enhancements for Dynamic HTML. In this chapter, you will learn about the Dynamic HTML event model. The traditional HTML event model provided a limited number of events. The World Wide Web Consortium (W3C: **www.w3.org**), in association with companies including Microsoft and Netscape, fleshed out the Dynamic HTML event model to provide an extended set of events.

There are additional object events within the Dynamic HTML event model; for example, the **onbounce** and **onfinish** events associated with the marquee object and the **onload**, **onerror**, and **onabort** events associated with the image object. Events such as **onclick** and **ondblclick** are associated with a number of objects within the Document Object Model (DOM) hierarchy. The Dynamic HTML event model also supports event bubbling. If you do not associate an action with a button's **onclick** event, the **onclick** event will traverse the hierarchy until an association is found. If you do associate an action with the document object's **onclick** event, the browser executes the action. You can disable event bubbling if you associate an action with the button's event and you do not want the action to bubble up through the hierarchy to the document object. To disable event bubbling, set the event object's **cancelBubble** property to True, as shown in Listing 8.1; the default value is False.

Listing 8.1 Disabling event bubbling.

```
<script language = "VBScript" for="cb1" event="onclick()">
   Msgbox("You triggered the command button control's click event.")
   window.event.bubble = True
</script>
```

To associate an action with the event, choose either VBScript or JavaScript as the scripting language and use one of following three forms of syntax.

The first form of syntax:

```
<script language=scripting_language for=object event=event_handler>
...
</script>
```

For example:

```
<script language="JavaScript" for="Form1" event="onreset()">
alert ("You triggered the form's reset event.")
</script>
```

The second form of syntax:

```
<script language=scripting_language>
Sub object_event
...
End Sub
</script>
```

For example:

```
<script language="vbscript">
Sub Document_OnKeyDown
HelpText.innerHTML = "This is the help message.<br>Add your help text here."
End Sub
</script>
```

The third form of syntax:

```
<A event=event_handler language=scripting_language>
```

For example:

```
<A onmouseout="processmouseout" language="VBScript">
```

Only Internet Explorer supports VBScript. Both Internet Explorer and Netscape Navigator support JavaScript.

In this chapter, we cover the different object-specific events, including the event's syntax, return value (if applicable), and the action that triggers the event. We also include code that demonstrates the definition and use of the different events using both VBScript and JavaScript. We provide example code for most of the events, leaving the rest as an exercise for the reader.

Terms

Below is a list of some of the commonly used terms with respect to using DHTML and the event model to design Web sites. Understanding these terms helps you knowledgeably take the DHTML event model approach to building interactive Web sites.

- *Bubbling*—If no action is associated with the current object's event, the action will traverse the event hierarchy until an association is found.
- *Cancel bubbling*—If you cancel event bubbling, the action will not traverse the event hierarchy even if no action is associated with the current object's event.
- *Event model*—The event model defines the events associated with the hierarchy of objects defined within the DOM.
- *Form events*—The events associated with the form object; i.e., **onreset**, **onsubmit**.
- *Image events*—The events associated with the image object; i.e., **onabort**, **onerror**, **onload**.
- *Keyboard events*—The events associated with the keyboard object; i.e., **onkeypress**, **onhelp**, **onkeydown**.
- *Marquee events*—The events associated with the marquee object; i.e., **onbounce**, **onfinish**.
- *Mouse events*—The events associated with the mouse object; i.e., **onmouseover**, **onmouseout**, **onmouseup**.
- *Object-specific events*—The events associated with a specific DOM element; i.e., form, image, marquee, and so on.

- *Window events*—The events associated with the window object; i.e., **onload**, **onunload**.

The following sections describe events associated with the different objects.

Form Events

This section describes the events associated with the form object. For each event, this section shows the syntax, identifies the actions that trigger the events associated with the form object, and indicates the return value. In addition, this section shows VBScript and JavaScript examples of using the events.

onreset

- *Syntax*—**onreset**.
- *Returns*—No return value.
- *Event Occurrence*—To trigger the form object's **onreset** event, click the form's Reset button (**INPUT TYPE="RESET"**).
- *Example*—Listing 8.2 shows a VBScript example of the **onreset** event.

onsubmit

- *Syntax*—**onsubmit**.
- *Returns*—No return value.
- *Event Occurrence*—To trigger the form object's **onsubmit** event, click on the form's Submit button (**INPUT TYPE="SUBMIT"**).
- *Example*—Listing 8.2 shows a VBScript example of the **onsubmit** event; Listing 8.3 shows a JavaScript example of the **onsubmit** and **onreset** events.

Listing 8.2 Triggering the onsubmit and onreset events associated with the form object (VBScript).

```
<HTML>
<HEAD>
</HEAD>
<BODY TEXT="#000000" LINK="#0000ff" VLINK="#800080">

<FORM Name="Form1">
<TABLE CELLSPACING=0 BORDER=0 CELLPADDING=7 WIDTH=638>
<TR>
```

```
<TD WIDTH="10%" VALIGN="TOP">Name:</TD>
<TD WIDTH="90%" VALIGN="TOP"><INPUT TYPE="TEXT" MAXLENGTH="25" NAME="Fld1">
</TD>
</TR>
<TR>
<TD WIDTH="10%" VALIGN="TOP">Address1:</TD>
<TD WIDTH="90%" VALIGN="TOP"><INPUT TYPE="TEXT" MAXLENGTH="25" NAME="Fld2">
</TD>
</TR>
<TR>
<TD WIDTH="10%" VALIGN="TOP">Address2:</TD>
<TD WIDTH="90%" VALIGN="TOP"><INPUT TYPE="TEXT" MAXLENGTH="25" NAME="Fld3">
</TD>
</TR>
<TR>
<TD WIDTH="10%" VALIGN="TOP">City:</TD>
<TD WIDTH="90%" VALIGN="TOP"><INPUT TYPE="TEXT" MAXLENGTH="25" NAME="Fld4">
</TD>
</TR>
<TR>
<TD WIDTH="10%" VALIGN="TOP">State:</TD>
<TD WIDTH="90%" VALIGN="TOP"><INPUT TYPE="TEXT" MAXLENGTH="25" NAME="Fld5">
</TD>
</TR>
<TR>
<TD WIDTH="10%" VALIGN="TOP">Zip:</TD>
<TD WIDTH="90%" VALIGN="TOP"><INPUT TYPE="TEXT" MAXLENGTH="25" NAME="Fld6">
</TD>
</TR>
<TR>
<TD WIDTH="10%" VALIGN="TOP"><INPUT TYPE="SUBMIT"></TD>
<TD WIDTH="90%" VALIGN="TOP"><INPUT TYPE="RESET"></TD>
</TR>
</TABLE>
<P>
</FORM>

<SCRIPT LANGUAGE="VBSCRIPT">
Sub Form1_OnSubmit
   MsgBox ("You triggered the form's submit event.")
End Sub

Sub Form1_OnReset
   MsgBox ("You triggered the form's reset event.")
End Sub
</SCRIPT>

</BODY>
</HTML>
```

When you click Submit Query, Internet Explorer displays a message box, as shown in Figure 8.1.

When you click Reset, Internet Explorer displays a message box, as shown in Figure 8.2.

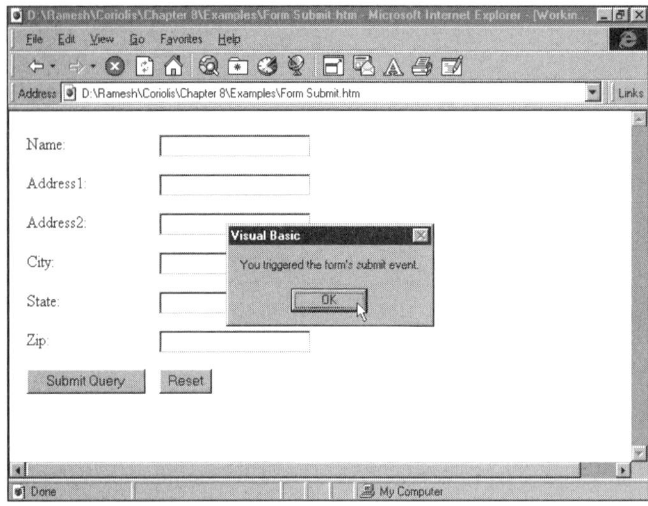

Figure 8.1

Invoking the form object's ***onsubmit*** *event.*

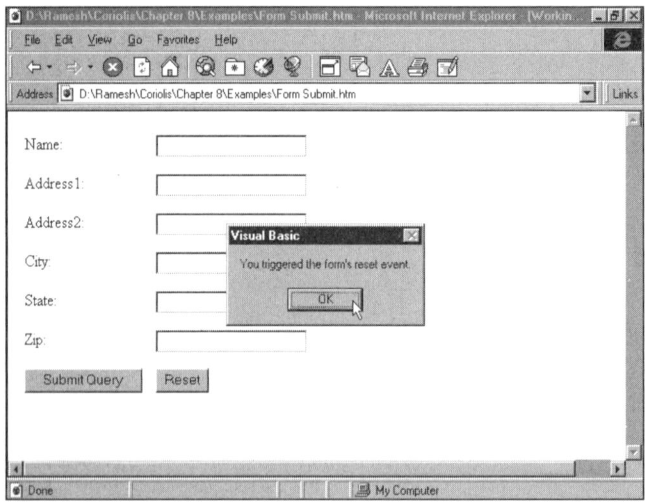

Figure 8.2

Invoking the form object's ***onreset*** *event.*

Listing 8.3 Triggering the onsubmit and onreset events associated with the form object (JavaScript).

```
<HTML>
<HEAD>
</HEAD>
<BODY TEXT="#000000" LINK="#0000ff" VLINK="#800080">

<FORM Name="Form1">
<TABLE CELLSPACING=0 BORDER=0 CELLPADDING=7 WIDTH=638>
<TR>
<TD WIDTH="10%" VALIGN="TOP">Name:</TD>
<TD WIDTH="90%" VALIGN="TOP"><INPUT TYPE="TEXT" MAXLENGTH="25" NAME="Fld1">
</TD>
</TR>
<TR>
<TD WIDTH="10%" VALIGN="TOP">Address1:</TD>
<TD WIDTH="90%" VALIGN="TOP"><INPUT TYPE="TEXT" MAXLENGTH="25" NAME="Fld2">
</TD>
</TR>
<TR>
<TD WIDTH="10%" VALIGN="TOP">Address2:</TD>
<TD WIDTH="90%" VALIGN="TOP"><INPUT TYPE="TEXT" MAXLENGTH="25" NAME="Fld3">
</TD>
</TR>
<TR>
<TD WIDTH="10%" VALIGN="TOP">City:</TD>
<TD WIDTH="90%" VALIGN="TOP"><INPUT TYPE="TEXT" MAXLENGTH="25" NAME="Fld4">
</TD>
</TR>
<TR>
<TD WIDTH="10%" VALIGN="TOP">State:</TD>
<TD WIDTH="90%" VALIGN="TOP"><INPUT TYPE="TEXT" MAXLENGTH="25" NAME="Fld5">
</TD>
</TR>
<TR>
<TD WIDTH="10%" VALIGN="TOP">Zip:</TD>
<TD WIDTH="90%" VALIGN="TOP"><INPUT TYPE="TEXT" MAXLENGTH="25" NAME="Fld6">
</TD>
</TR>
<TR>
<TD WIDTH="10%" VALIGN="TOP"><INPUT TYPE="SUBMIT"></TD>
<TD WIDTH="90%" VALIGN="TOP"><INPUT TYPE="RESET"></TD>
</TR>
</TABLE>
<P>
</FORM>
```

```
<script language = "JavaScript" for="Form1" event="onsubmit()">
   alert ("You triggered the form's submit event.")
</script>

<script language = "JavaScript" for="Form1" event="onreset()">
   alert ("You triggered the form's reset event.")
</script>

</BODY>
</HTML>
```

Keyboard Events

This section reviews the events associated with the keyboard object. For each event, this section shows the syntax, identifies the actions that trigger the events associated with the keyboard object, and indicates the return value. In addition, this section shows VBScript and JavaScript examples of using the events.

onhelp

- *Syntax*—**onhelp**.
- *Returns*—No return value.
- *Event Occurrence*—To trigger the **onhelp** event, press F1.
- *Example*—Listing 8.4 shows a VBScript example of the **onhelp** event associated with the document object; Listing 8.5 shows a JavaScript example. When you press F1, Internet Explorer displays the online help shown in Figure 8.3.

Listing 8.4 Triggering the onhelp event (VBScript).

```
<script language = "VBScript" for="document" event="onhelp()">
Msgbox("You pressed the F1 help key.")
</script>
```

Listing 8.5 Triggering the onhelp event (JavaScript).

```
<script language = "JavaScript" for="document" event="onhelp()">
   alert("You pressed the F1 help key. The document event handler will
   process the onhelp event.")
</script>
```

onkeydown

- *Syntax*—**onkeydown** (keycode as integer, shift as htmlshift).

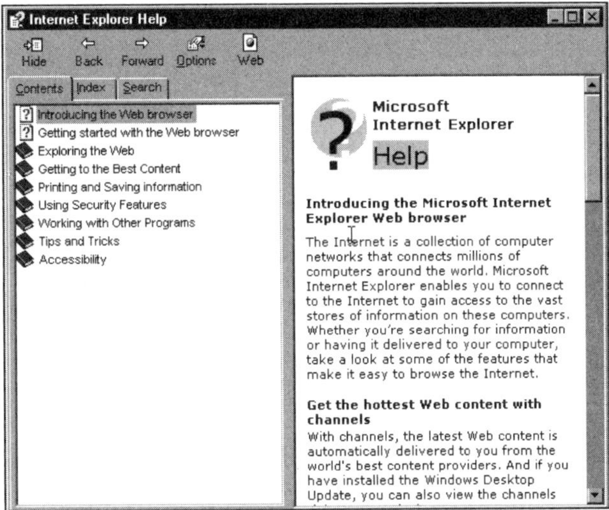

Figure 8.3

Invoking the online help for Internet Explorer.

  - *keycode*—A numeric ASCII keycode for key events.
  - *shift*—Indicates whether the user pressed the shift key at the time of the event.

- *Returns*—No return value.
- *Event Occurrence*—To trigger the **onkeydown** event, press a key.
- *Example*—Listing 8.6 shows a VBScript example of triggering the **onkeydown** event. Listing 8.7 shows a JavaScript example.

Listing 8.6 Triggering the onkeydown event (VBScript).

```
<html>
<HEAD><TITLE>Using the onkeydown event</TITLE></HEAD>
<body>
<H2>Press any key to view help</H2>
<hr>

<br>
<div id=HelpText></div>
<P>

<SCRIPT LANGUAGE="VBSCRIPT">
Sub Document_OnKeyDown
   HelpText.innerHTML = "This is the help message.<br>Add your help text here."
```

```
End Sub
</SCRIPT>

<br>
</body>
</html>
```

Listing 8.7 Triggering the onkeydown event (JavaScript).

```
<script language = "JavaScript" for="document" event="onkeydown()">
   alert ("You pressed a key down.")
</script>
```

onkeypress

- *Syntax*—**onkeypress** (keycode as integer).
- *Returns*—No return value.
- *Event Occurrence*—To trigger the **onkeypress** event, press a key.
- *Example*—Listing 8.8 shows a VBScript example of the **onkeypress** event associated with the document object; Listing 8.9 provides a JavaScript example.

Listing 8.8 Triggering the onkeypress event (VBScript).

```
<script language = "VBScript" for="document" event="onkeypress()">
   Msgbox("You pressed a key.")
</script>
```

Listing 8.9 Triggering the onkeypress event (JavaScript).

```
<script language = "JavaScript" for="document" event="onkeypress()">
   alert ("You pressed a key.")
</script>
```

onkeyup

- *Syntax*—**onkeyup** (keycode as integer, shift as htmlshift).
- *Returns*—No return value.
- *Event Occurrence*—To trigger the **onkeyup** event, press a key and then release.
- *Example*—See Listing 8.10 for an example of triggering the **onkeyup** event.

Listing 8.10 Triggering the onkeyup event.

```
<html>
<HEAD><TITLE>Using the onkeyup event</TITLE></HEAD>
<body>
<H2>Press any key to view help</H2>
<hr>

<br>
<div id=HelpText></div>
<P>

<SCRIPT LANGUAGE="VBSCRIPT">
Sub Document_OnKeyUp
   HelpText.innerHTML = "This is the help message.<br>Add your help text here."
End Sub
</SCRIPT>

<br>
</body>
</html>
```

Mouse Events

The following list describes the events associated with the mouse object. For each event, this section shows the syntax, identifies the actions that trigger the events associated with the mouse object, and indicates the return value. In addition, this section shows VBScript and JavaScript examples of using the events.

onmousedown

- *Syntax*—**onmousedown** (button as htmlbutton, shift as htmlshift, x as long, y as long).
  - *x*—The mouse's horizontal position with respect to the document's origin.
  - *y*—The mouse's vertical position with respect to the document's origin.
- *Returns*—No return value.
- *Event Occurrence*—To trigger the **onmousedown** event associated with an object, place the cursor over the object and hold down the left mouse button.

- *Example*—Listing 8.17 shows an example of triggering the **onmouse-down** and **onmouseup** events.

onmousemove

- *Syntax*—**onmousemove** (button as htmlbutton, shift as htmlshift, x as long, y as long).
- *Returns*—No return value.
- *Event Occurrence*—To trigger the **onmousemove** event associated with an object, move the cursor over the object.
- *Example*—Listing 8.11 shows a VBScript example of the **onmousemove** event associated with the document object. Listing 8.12 shows the JavaScript example.

Listing 8.11 Triggering the onmousemove event (VBScript).

```
<script language = "VBScript" for="document" event="onmousemove()">
   Msgbox("You moved the mouse over the document object.")
</script>
```

Listing 8.12 Triggering the onmousemove event (JavaScript).

```
<script language = "JavaScript" for="document" event="onmousemove()">
   alert("You moved the mouse over the document object.")
</script>
```

onmouseout

- *Syntax*—**onmouseout**.
- *Returns*—No return value.
- *Event Occurrence*—To trigger the **onmouseout** event associated with an object, move the cursor away from the object.
- *Example*—Listing 8.13 shows a VBScript example of the **onmouseout** event associated with the document object; Listing 8.14 shows a Java Script example.

Listing 8.13 Triggering the onmouseout event (VBScript).

```
<script language = "VBScript" for="document" event="onmouseout()">
   Msgbox("You moved the mouse away from the document object.")
</script>
```

Listing 8.14 Triggering the onmouseout event (JavaScript).

```
<script language = "JavaScript" for="document" event="onmouseout()">
   alert("You moved the mouse away from the document object.")
</script>
```

onmouseover

- *Syntax*—**onmouseover**.
- *Returns*—No return value.
- *Event Occurrence*—To trigger the **onmouseover** event associated with an object, move the cursor over the object.
- *Example*—Listing 8.15 shows a VBScript example of the **onmouseover** event associated with the document object; Listing 8.16 shows a Java Script example.

Listing 8.15 Triggering the onmouseover event (VBScript).

```
<script language = "VBScript" for="document" event="onmouseover()">
   Msgbox("You moved the mouse over the document object.")
</script>
```

Listing 8.16 Triggering the onmouseover event (JavaScript).

```
<script language = "JavaScript" for="document" event="onmouseover()">
   alert("You moved the mouse over the document object.")
</script>
```

onmouseup

- *Syntax*—**onmouseup** (button as htmlbutton, shift as htmlshift, x as long, y as long).
- *Returns*—No return value.
- *Event Occurrence*—To trigger the **onmouseup** event associated with an object, click and release the mouse on the object.
- *Example*—Listing 8.17 shows an example of triggering the **onmouse down** and **onmouseup** events. When you hold the mouse down on the Click Me! button, the browser will display the text "Mouse Down for the button fired." When you click on the button and release the mouse, the browser will display the text "Mouse Up for the button fired."

Listing 8.17 Triggering the onmousedown and onmouseup events.

```
<html>
<HEAD><TITLE>Mouse Events</TITLE></HEAD>
<BODY TOPMARGIN=0 LEFTMARGIN=40 BGCOLOR="#FFFFFF" LINK="#000066"
VLINK="#666666" TEXT="#000000">
<FONT FACE="verdana,arial,helvetica" SIZE=2>

<H2>Mouse Events</H2>
<hr>
<div id=ReplaceText></div>

<FORM>
<input type="button" value="Click me" onmousedown="ReplaceText.innerHTML = 'Mouse-
Down for the button fired!'" onmouseup="ReplaceText.innerHTML = 'Mouse Up for
the button fired!'">
</FORM>

</body>
</html>
```

onclick

- *Syntax*—**onclick**.
- *Returns*—No return value.
- *Event Occurrence*—To trigger the **onclick** event associated with an object, click the mouse on the object.
- *Example*—Listing 8.18 shows a VBScript example of the **onclick** event associated with the document object; Listing 8.19 provides a JavaScript example. When you click within the Internet Explorer window, you will see the message box shown in Figure 8.4. Listing 8.20 shows a VBScript example of an **onclick** event associated with the Click Me! command button.

Listing 8.18 Triggering the onclick event associated with the document object (VBScript).

```
<script language = "VBScript" for="document" event="onclick()">
   Msgbox("You clicked within the Internet Explorer window.")
</script>
```

Listing 8.19 Triggering the onclick event associated with the document object (JavaScript).

```
<script language = "JavaScript" for="document" event="onclick()">
   alert("You clicked within the Internet Explorer window.")
</script>
```

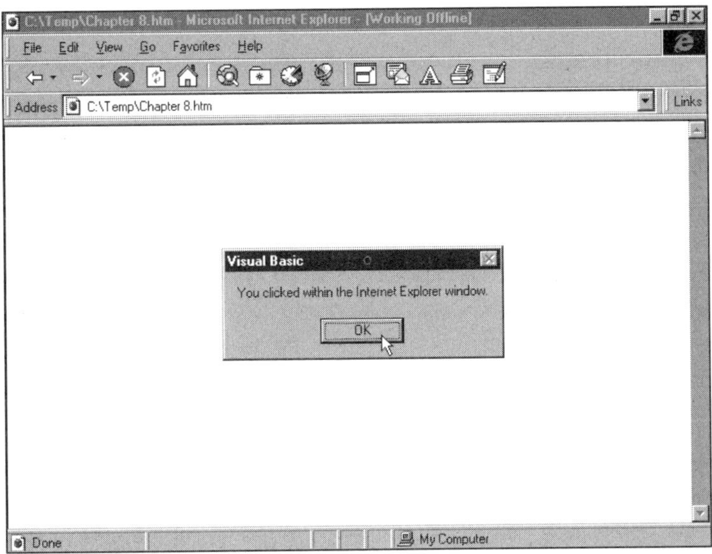

Figure 8.4

Invoking the click event associated with the Internet Explorer document object.

Listing 8.20 Triggering the onclick event associated with the command button (VBScript).

```
<p align="center"><input type="button" value="Click Me!" onclick="ClickMe()">
</p>

<script language="VBSCRIPT">

Sub ClickMe ()
   Msgbox("You clicked me!")
End Sub

</script>
```

ondblclick

- *Syntax*—**ondblclick**.
- *Returns*—No return value.
- *Event Occurrence*—To trigger the **ondblclick** event associated with an object, double click the mouse on the object.

- *Example*—Listing 8.21 shows a VBScript example of the **ondblclick** event associated with the document object; Listing 8.22 shows a JavaScript example. When you double-click within the Internet Explorer window, Internet Explorer displays the message box shown in Figure 8.5. Listing 8.23 provides a VBScript example of the **ondblclick** event associated with the Double Click Me! command button.

Listing 8.21 Triggering the ondblclick event associated with the document object (VBScript).

```
<script language = "VBScript" for="document" event="ondblclick()">
   Msgbox("You double clicked within the Internet Explorer window.")
</script>
```

Listing 8.22 Triggering the ondblclick event associated with the document object (JavaScript).

```
<script language = "JavaScript" for="document" event="ondblclick()">
   alert("You double clicked within the Internet Explorer window.")
</script>
```

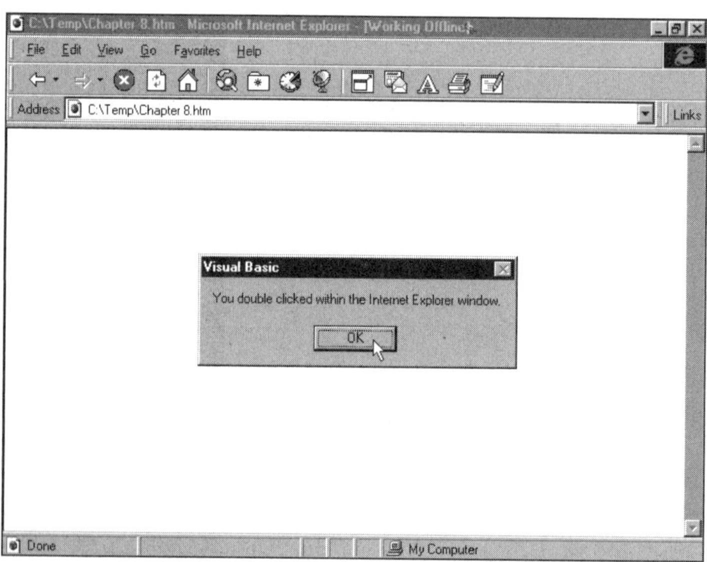

Figure 8.5

Invoking the double-click event associated with the Internet Explorer document object.

Listing 8.23 Triggering the ondblclick event associated with the command button (VBScript).

```
<p align="center"><input type="button" value="Double Click Me!"
    onclick="DoubleClickMe()"></p>

<script language="VBSCRIPT">

Sub DoubleClickMe ()
   Msgbox("You double clicked me!")
End Sub

</script>
```

Window Events

This section covers the events associated with the window object. For each event, this section shows the syntax, identifies the actions that trigger the events associated with the window object, and indicates the return value. In addition, this section shows VBScript and JavaScript examples of using the events.

onload

- *Syntax*—**onload**.
- *Returns*—No return value.
- *Event Occurrence*—To trigger the **onload** event associated with the Internet Explorer window object, open the Internet Explorer window.
- *Example*—Listing 8.24 shows a VBScript example of the **onload** event; Listing 8.25 shows a JavaScript example.

Listing 8.24 Triggering the onload event (VBScript).

```
<script language = "VBScript" for="window" event="onload()">
   Msgbox("Initializing variables ... ")
</script>
```

Listing 8.25 Triggering the onload event (JavaScript).

```
<script language = "JavaScript" for="window" event="onload()">
   alert("Initializing variables ... ")
</script>
```

onunload

- *Syntax*—**onunload**.
- *Returns*—No return value.
- *Event Occurrence*—To trigger the **onunload** event associated with the Internet Explorer window object, close or refresh the Internet Explorer window.
- *Example*—Listing 8.26 shows a VBScript example of the **onunload** event; Listing 8.27 shows a JavaScript example.

Listing 8.26 Triggering the onunload event (VBScript).

```
<script language = "VBScript" for="window" event="onunload()">
   Msgbox("Releasing resources... ")
</script>
```

Listing 8.27 Triggering the onunload event (JavaScript).

```
<script language = "JavaScript" for="window" event="onunload()">
   alert("Releasing resources... ")
</script>
```

Focus-Specific Events

This section describes the events associated with the focus on an object. For each event, this section shows the syntax, identifies the actions that trigger the events associated with the focus on an object, and indicates the return value. In addition, this section shows VBScript and JavaScript examples of using the events.

onblur

- *Syntax*—**onblur**.
- *Returns*—No return value.
- *Event Occurrence*—To trigger the **onblur** event associated with an object, move the focus away from the object. To move the focus away from the object, click or tab away from the object. An object will lose focus only if the focus is presently on the object.
- *Example*—Listing 8.28 shows a VBScript example of the **onblur** event; Listing 8.29 shows a JavaScript example.

Listing 8.28 Triggering the onblur event (VBScript).

```
<p align="center"><input type="button" value="Calculate" onblur="LostFocus()">
</p>

<script language="VBSCRIPT">

Sub LostFocus ()
     Msgbox("The Calculate button has lost focus.")
End Sub

</script>
```

Listing 8.29 Triggering the onblur event (JavaScript).

```
<p align="center"><input type="button" value="Calculate" onblur="LostFocus()">
</p>

<script language="JavaScript">

function LostFocus ()
{
     alert("The Calculate button has lost focus.")
}

</script>
```

onfocus

- *Syntax*—**onfocus**.
- *Returns*—No return value.
- *Event Occurrence*—To trigger the **onfocus** event associated with an object, set the focus on the object. To set the focus on an object, click or tab to the object.
- *Example*—Listing 8.30 shows a VBScript example of the **onfocus** event; Listing 8.31 shows a JavaScript example.

Listing 8.30 Triggering the onfocus event (VBScript).

```
<p align="center"><input type="button" value="Calculate" onfocus="GotFocus()">
</p>

<script language="VBSCRIPT">

Sub GotFocus ()
     Msgbox("Focus is on the Calculate button")
```

```
End Sub

</script>
```

Listing 8.31 Triggering the onfocus event (JavaScript).

```
<p align="center"><input type="button" value="Calculate" onfocus="GotFocus()">
</p>

<script language="JavaScript">

function GotFocus ()
{
     alert("Focus is on the Calculate button")
}

</script>
```

Marquee Events

This section reviews the events associated with the marquee object. As in the previous sections, this section shows the syntax, identifies the actions that trigger the events associated with the marquee object, and indicates the return value. In addition, this section shows VBScript and JavaScript examples of using the events.

onbounce

- *Syntax*—**onbounce** (side as string).
- *Returns*—no return value.
- *Event Occurrence*—When the marquee (with **behavior=alternate text**) hits an edge (**LEFT**, **RIGHT**, **TOP**, or **BOTTOM**), the marquee will trigger the **onbounce** event.
- *Example*—Listing 8.32 shows a VBScript example of the **onbounce** and **onfinish** events; Listing 8.33 shows a JavaScript example.

onfinish

- *Syntax*—**onfinish**.
- *Returns*—no return value.
- *Event Occurrence*—When the marquee's motion is complete, it will trigger the **onfinish** event.

- *Example*—Listing 8.32 shows a VBScript example of the **onbounce** and **onfinish** events; Listing 8.33 shows a JavaScript example.

Listing 8.32 Triggering the onbounce and onfinish events (VBScript).

```
<html>
<head>
<title>Marquee Events</title>
</head>

<body bgcolor="#FFFFFF">

<p><marquee behavior="alternate" loop="2" name="Marquee1"
onbounce="Bouncing()" onfinish="Complete()">Marquee Events</marquee></p>

<DIV ID="idMarquee_OnBounce" STYLE="position:relative; top:0; visibility:hidden;
left:50; height:25; width:300;">
 The marquee is still bouncing ... (the OnBounce event is fired)
</DIV>

<DIV ID="idMarquee_OnFinish" STYLE="position:relative; top:0; visibility:hidden;
left:50; height:25; width:300;">
 The marquee has stopped! (the OnFinish event is fired)
</DIV>

<script language="vbscript">
<!--
Sub Bouncing()
   idMarquee_OnBounce.style.visibility = "visible"
End Sub

Sub Complete()
   idMarquee_OnBounce.style.visibility = "hidden"
   idMarquee_OnFinish.style.visibility = "visible"
End Sub
</script>

</body>
</html>
```

Listing 8.33 Triggering the onbounce and onfinish events (JavaScript).

```
<html>
<head>
<title>Marquee Events</title>
</head>

<body bgcolor="#FFFFFF">
```

```
<p><marquee behavior="alternate" loop="2" name="Marquee1"
onbounce="Bouncing()" onfinish="Complete()">Marquee Events</marquee></p>

<DIV ID="idMarquee_OnBounce" STYLE="position:relative; top:0; visibility:hidden;
left:50; height:25; width:300;">
 The marquee is still bouncing ... (the OnBounce event is fired)
</DIV>

<DIV ID="idMarquee_OnFinish" STYLE="position:relative; top:0; visibility:hidden;
left:50; height:25; width:300;">
 The marquee has stopped! (the OnFinish event is fired)
</DIV>

<script language="javascript">
<!--
function Bouncing() {
   idMarquee_OnBounce.style.visibility = "visible"
}

function Complete() {
   idMarquee_OnBounce.style.visibility = "hidden"
   idMarquee_OnFinish.style.visibility = "visible"
}
</script>
</body>
</html>
```

Image Events

This section reviews the events associated with the image object. For each event, this section shows the syntax, identifies the actions that trigger the events, and indicates the return value. In addition, this section shows an example of using the events.

onabort

- *Syntax*—**onabort**.
- *Returns*—No return value.
- *Event Occurrence*—To trigger the **onabort** event, abort the image's download.
- *Example*—Listing 8.34 shows an example of the **onabort** event.

onerror

- *Syntax*—**onerror**.
- *Returns*—No return value.
- *Event Occurrence*—If there is an error loading the image within the browser, the image will trigger the **onerror** event.
- *Example*—Listing 8.34 shows an example of the **onerror** event.

onload

- *Syntax*—**onload**.
- *Returns*—No return value.
- *Event Occurrence*—When the browser loads the image, the image will trigger the **onload** event.
- *Example*—Listing 8.34 shows an example of the **onload** event.

Listing 8.34 Triggering the onabort, onerror, and onload events.

```
<html>
<head>
<title>Image Events</title>
</head>

<body bgcolor="#FFFFFF">

<p><img src="logosm.jpg" width="100"
height="100" onerror="this.src='help.gif';"
onload="alert('Image is loading')"
onabort="idImage_OnAbort.style.visibility = "visible""></p>

<div id="idImage_OnLoad" STYLE="position:relative; top:0; visibility:hidden;
left:50; height:25; width:100;">
 The image is loading...
</div>

<div id="idImage_OnAbort" STYLE="position:relative; top:0; visibility:hidden;
left:50; height:25; width:300;">
 The image loading was aborted.
</div>

</body>
</html>
```

In this example, the browser displays the logosm.jpg image when loading the page. To trap the image's **onerror** event, remove the logosm.jpg file from the directory, reload the page, and the browser processes the image's **onerror** event, displaying the help.gif image because that is the image associated with the **onerror** event. To trap the image's **onabort** event, click the Stop button within the browser's toolbar while the browser loads the image.

You may find it difficult to trap the ***onabort*** *event on a fast machine like a Pentium 233MHz because the browser processes the page very quickly.*

Other Events

This section discusses some other events. For each event, this section shows the syntax, identifies the actions that trigger the events, and indicates the return value. In addition, this section identifies the different objects these other events are associated with. VBScript and JavaScript examples are provided for the events.

onchange

- *Syntax*—**onchange**.
- *Returns*—No return value.
- *Event Occurrence*—When the object's contents change, the object will trigger the **onchange** event.
- *Objects*—**<INPUT TYPE=FILE>**, **<INPUT TYPE=RADIO>**, **<INPUT TYPE=CHECKBOX>**, **<INPUT TYPE=TEXT>**, **<TEXTAREA>**, **<SELECT>**
- *Example*—Listing 8.35 shows a VBScript example of the **onchange** event; Listing 8.36 shows a JavaScript example.

onselect

- *Syntax*—**onselect**.
- *Returns*—No return value.
- *Event Occurrence*—When a text element's text selection changes, the object will trigger the **onselect** event.

- *Objects*—**<INPUT TYPE=TEXT>**, **<INPUT TYPE=PASSWORD>**, **<TEXTAREA>**
- *Example*—Listing 8.35 shows a VBScript example of the **onselect** event; Listing 8.36 shows a JavaScript example.

Listing 8.35 Triggering the onchange and onselect events (VBScript).

```
<INPUT TYPE="TEXT" MAXLENGTH="25" NAME="Fld1" onchange="processchangeevent()"
 onselect="processselectevent()">

<script language="VBScript">

<!--

Sub processchangeevent()
   Msgbox("You triggered the onchange event.")
End Sub

Sub processselectevent()
   Msgbox("You triggered the onselect event.")
End Sub

//-->

</script>
```

Listing 8.36 Triggering the onchange and onselect events (JavaScript).

```
<INPUT TYPE="TEXT" MAXLENGTH="25" NAME="Fld1" onchange=processchangeevent()
 onselect=processselectevent()>

<script language="javascript">

<!--

function processchangeevent() {
   alert("You triggered the onchange event.");
}

function processselectevent() {
   alert("You triggered the onselect event.");
}

//-->

</script>
```

onscroll

- *Syntax*—**onscroll** (scrollparam as scrollobject).
- *Returns*—No return value.
- *Event Occurrence*—When you scroll the object, the object will trigger the **onscroll** event.
- *Example*—Listing 8.37 shows a VBScript example of the **onscroll** event; Listing 8.38 shows a JavaScript example.

Listing 8.37 Triggering the onscroll event (VBScript).

```
<TEXTAREA rows="10" cols="80" onscroll="processscrollevent()">
This is an example of using the TEXTAREA tag. The browser will display an
input text area of 10 rows and 80 columns.
</TEXTAREA>

<script language="VBScript">

<!--

Sub processscrollevent()
   Msgbox("You triggered the onscroll event.")
End Sub

//-->

</script>
```

Listing 8.38 Triggering the onscroll event (JavaScript).

```
<TEXTAREA rows="10" cols="80" onscroll=processscrollevent()>
This is an example of using the TEXTAREA tag. The browser will display an
input text area of 10 rows and 80 columns.
</TEXTAREA>

<script language="javascript">

<!--

function processscrollevent() {
   alert("You triggered the onscroll event.");
}

//-->

</script>
```

Additional Resources

For more information on DOM, visit **www.w3.org/DOM**.

For more information on the HTML 4.0 specification, visit **www.w3.org/TR/PR-html40**.

To view demos of the event model and other features of DHTML using Internet Explorer, visit the Microsoft Web site at **www.microsoft.com/ie/ie40/demos**.

To view demos of the event model and other features of DHTML using Netscape Navigator, visit the Netscape Web site at **search.netscape.com/comprod/products/communicator/beta_features.html**.

For more information on HTML, Netscape, JavaScript, and VBScript, refer to the following books from The Coriolis Group (**www.coriolis.com**):

- *The New Netscape and HTML Explorer*; ISBN: 1-883577-91-8
- *JavaScript and Netscape Wizardry*; ISBN: 1-883577-86-1
- *Web Developer's Guide to JavaScript and VBScript*; ISBN: 1-883577-97-7

Practical Guide To

Events And Dynamic HTML

- Using The Mouse And Form Events
- Using The **onclick** Event With The Image And Document Objects
- Displaying MicroHelp By Using The **onfocus** Event
- Using The **onload** And **onunload** Events With The Window Object

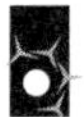

Using The Mouse And Form Events

This example demonstrates how to use the **onmouseover**, **onmouseout**, and **onload** events. You will design a home page for a consulting company XYZ Consultants Inc. The page will display the following hyperlinked menu:

- About Us
- Consulting Services
- Products
- Training

When you move your mouse over a menu item (**onmouseover** event), the color of the menu item will change from black to red. When you move your mouse away from the highlighted menu item (**onmouseout** event), the menu item's color reverts to black. The following outlines the steps you can use to create the XYZ Consultants' home page by using Notepad or WordPad.

To create the HTML file, you can also use graphical user interface (GUI) tools like FrontPage 98.

1. Since the page will display four menu items (About Us, Consulting Services, Products, and Training), define four anchor links by using the **<A>...</A>** HTML tags. Associate actions with each anchor link's **onmouseover** and **onmouseout** events. Listing 8.39 shows the code for the first menu item, About Us.

Listing 8.39 Displaying the first menu item, About Us.

```
<center><a href="http://xyz.com/aboutus.htm">
<span style="color: black"><font face="Arial, Helvetica" color="#000000"
onmouseover="this.style.color='#CC0000'" onmouseout="this.style.color='black'"
size="-1"><strong>About Us</strong></font></span></a></center>
```

As you can see from the code, the action you associate with the **onmouseover** event is **this.style.color='#CC0000'** and the action you associate with the **onmouseout** event is **onmouseout="this.style.color='black'"**.

2. Similarly, associate the color change actions with the **onmouseover** and **onmouseout** events for the remaining anchor links (the Consulting Services, Products, and Training menu items), as shown in Listing 8.40.

Listing 8.40 Displaying the remaining menu items.

```
<center><a href="http://xyz.com/consulting.htm">
<span style="color: black"><font face="Arial, Helvetica" color="#000000"
onmouseover="this.style.color='#CC0000'" onmouseout="this.style.color='black'"
size="-1"><strong>Consulting Services</strong></font></span></a></center>
<p>

<center><a href="http://xyz.com/products.htm">
<span style="color: black"><font face="Arial, Helvetica"
color="#000000" onmouseover="this.style.color='#CC0000'"
onmouseout="this.style.color='black'" size="-1"><strong>Products</strong>
</font></span></a></center>
<p>

<center><a href="http://xyz.com/training.htm">
<span style="color: black"><font face="Arial, Helvetica" color="#000000"
onmouseover="this.style.color='#CC0000'" onmouseout="this.style.color='black'"
size="-1"><strong>Training</strong></font></span></a></center>
```

3. Next, write a JavaScript function **transitionHead()** that displays the company's name with a transition effect when you load the page within your browser. To display the transition effect upon loading, associate the JavaScript function with the browser's **onload** event. Listing 8.41 shows that function's code and the function's association with the browser's **onload** event.

Listing 8.41 Declaring the JavaScript function, transitionHead().

```
<script language="javascript">
<!--
function transitionHead() {
   idHead.style.visibility = "hidden"
      idHeader.filters.item(0).apply()
      idHeader.filters.item(0).transition = 23
      idHead.style.visibility = "visible"
      idHeader.filters(0).play(1.000)
}
//-->
</script>

<BODY TEXT="#000000" LINK="#0000ff" VLINK="#800080" ONLOAD="transitionHead()">
```

4. To view the page, open the page within Internet Explorer (see Figure 8.6).

Listing 8.42 shows the complete code for the page.

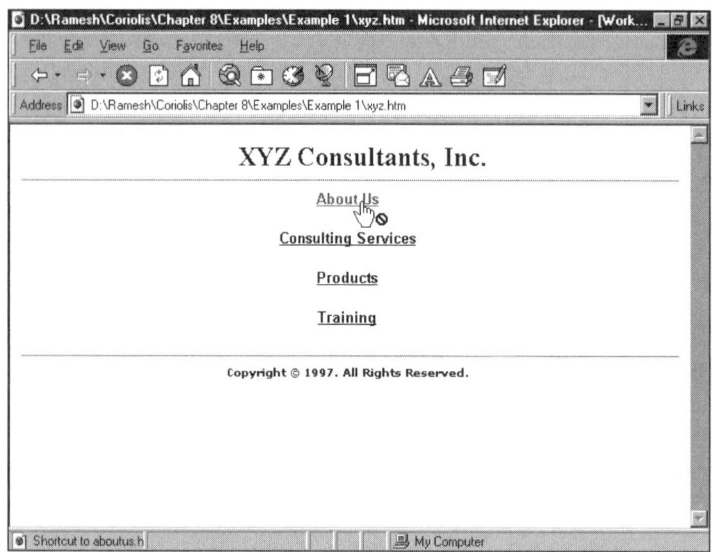

Figure 8.6

Home page for XYZ Consultants, Inc.

Listing 8.42 HTML code for XYZ Consultants, Inc.'s home page.

```
<HTML>
<HEAD>
</HEAD>

<script language="javascript">
<!--
function transitionHead() {
       idHead.style.visibility = "hidden"
       idHeader.filters.item(0).apply()
       idHeader.filters.item(0).transition = 23
       idHead.style.visibility = "visible"
       idHeader.filters(0).play(1.000)
}
//-->
</script>

<BODY TEXT="#000000" LINK="#0000ff" VLINK="#800080" ONLOAD="transitionHead()">

<DIV ID="idHeader" STYLE="position:relative; top:0; left:200; height:25;
width:300; filter:revealTrans(duration=3.0, transition=0);">
<H2 id="idHead" STYLE="position:relative; visibility:visible; margin-bottom:0;">
XYZ Consultants, Inc.</H2>
</DIV>
<hr>
```

```
<center><a href="http://xyz.com/aboutus.htm">
<span style="color: black"><font face="Arial, Helvetica" color="#000000"
onmouseover="this.style.color='#CC0000'" onmouseout="this.style.color='black'"
size="-1"><strong>About Us</strong></font></span></a></center>
<p>

<center><a href="http://xyz.com/consulting.htm">
<span style="color: black"><font face="Arial, Helvetica" color="#000000"
onmouseover="this.style.color='#CC0000'" onmouseout="this.style.color='black'"
size="-1"><strong>Consulting Services</strong></font></span></a></center>
<p>

<center><a href="http://xyz.com/products.htm">
<span style="color: black"><font face="Arial, Helvetica" color="#000000"
onmouseover="this.style.color='#CC0000'" onmouseout="this.style.color='black'"
size="-1"><strong>Products</strong></font></span></a></center>
<p>

<center><a href="http://xyz.com/training.htm">
<span style="color: black"><font face="Arial, Helvetica" color="#000000"
onmouseover="this.style.color='#CC0000'" onmouseout="this.style.color='black'"
size="-1"><strong>Training</strong></font></span></a></center>
<p>

<hr>

<span style="color: red"><font face="Verdana, Arial, Helvetica" color="#000000"
size="1"><strong><center>Copyright &copy; 1997. All Rights Reserved.
</center></strong></font></span>

</BODY>
</HTML>
```

Using The **onclick** Event With The Image And Document Objects

This example demonstrates how to use the **onclick** event with the image and document objects. We will design a page that displays a small image and the text headers "More information on Microsoft" and "More information on Microsoft Products" (see Figure 8.7).

To expand the image, click on it; the browser processes the image's **onclick** event. Figure 8.8 shows the resulting page. Click the hyperlink "More information on Microsoft," and the browser processes the document's **onclick** event displaying additional information on Microsoft (see Figure 8.9). Click the hyperlink "More information on Microsoft Products," and the browser processes the document's **onclick** event displaying additional information on Microsoft products (see Figure 8.10).

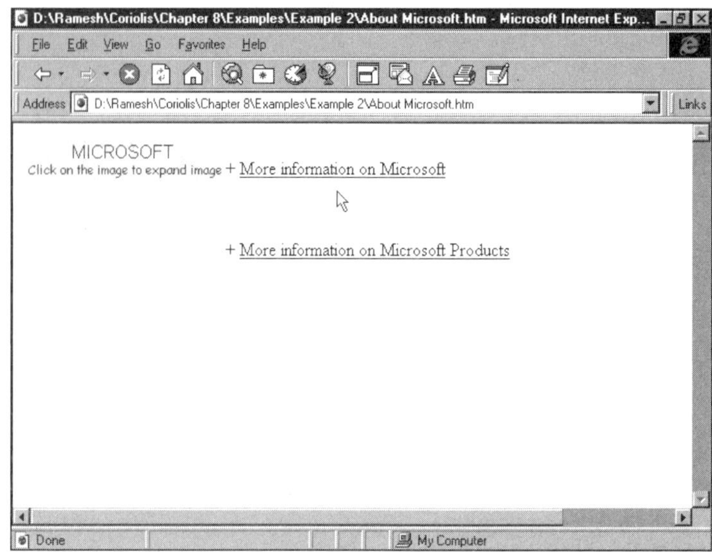

Figure 8.7

Learning about Microsoft.

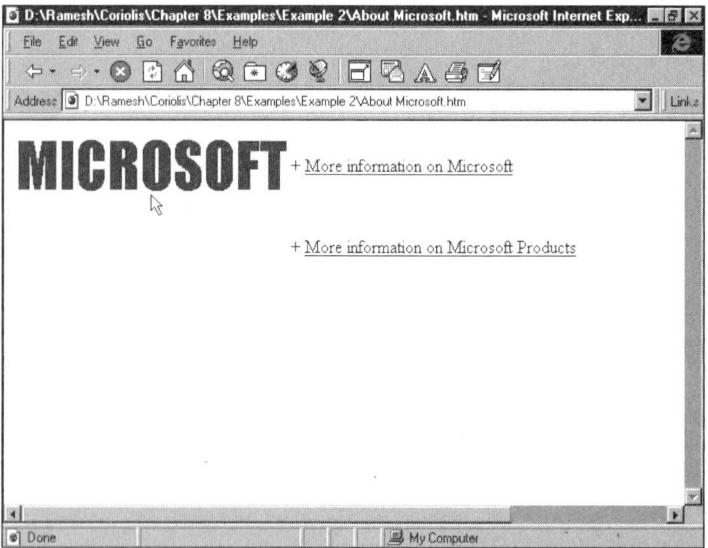

Figure 8.8

*Processing the image's **onclick** event.*

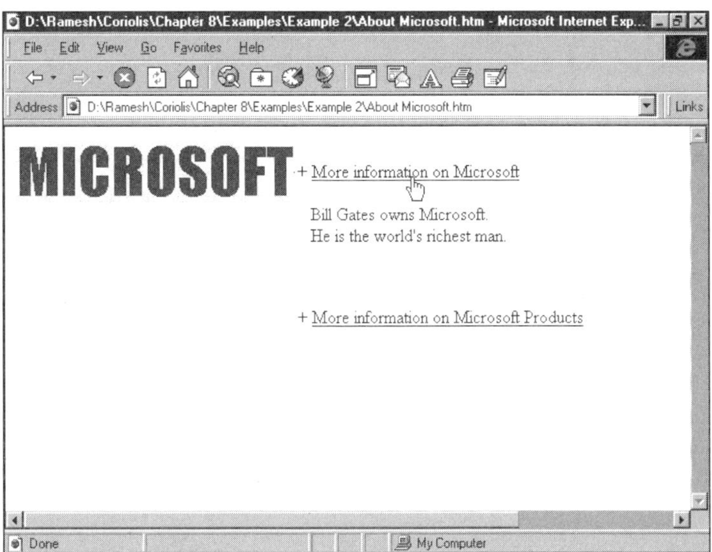

Figure 8.9

Displaying additional information on Microsoft.

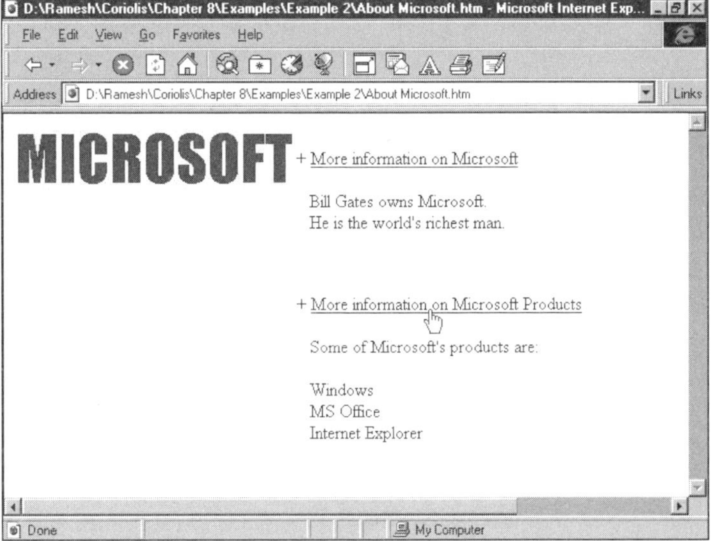

Figure 8.10

Displaying additional information on Microsoft products.

The following outlines the steps you can use to create the Microsoft page by using Notepad or WordPad.

1. When the browser loads the page, the browser should display a small image. When the user clicks on the image, the browser should display the enlarged image. This means you need to process the image's **onclick** event. Within the image's **onclick** event, specify the appropriate value for the enlarged image's source (**SRC**):

```
<img border=0 name=img1 src="microsoft_small.jpg" align="left" hspace="0"
 onclick="img1.src = 'microsoft_big.jpg';">
```

2. Next, display the text "More information on Microsoft" by using the **<DIV>...</DIV>** and **<SPAN>...</SPAN>** HTML tags. When the user clicks on the text, the browser displays additional information about Microsoft. Listing 8.43 shows the code.

Listing 8.43 Displaying additional information on Microsoft.

```
<div id=Out0 style="position:relative; left:0; top:+15px; width:90%;" >
<span id=Out1 class=Outline style="cursor: hand; ">+ </span>
<u id=Out1 class=Outline style="cursor: hand; ">
More information on Microsoft</u>

<div id=Out1details style="display:None; position:relative; left:12;">
<br>
Bill Gates owns Microsoft.<br>
He is the world's richest man.
</div>
```

3. Now, display the text "More information on Microsoft Products" by again using the **<DIV>...</DIV>** and **<SPAN>...</SPAN>** HTML tags. When the user clicks on the text, the browser displays additional information about Microsoft products. Listing 8.44 shows the code.

Listing 8.44 Displaying additional information on Microsoft products.

```
<div id=Out3 style="position:relative; left:0; top:+15px; width:90%;" >
<span id=Out4 class=Outline style="cursor: hand; ">+ </span>
<u id=Out4 class=Outline style="cursor: hand; ">
More information on Microsoft Products</u>

<div id=Out4details style="display:None; position:relative; left:12;">
<br>
```

```
Some of Microsoft's products are:<br>
<br>
Windows<br>
MS Office<br>
Internet Explorer<br>
</div>
```

4. Next, write a JavaScript function **clickHandler()** that will process the **onclick** events. When the user clicks on the hyperlink, the browser will process the document's **onclick** event and call the JavaScript function. Listing 8.45 shows the code for the JavaScript function **clickHandler** and the function's association with the document's **onclick** event.

Listing 8.45 Code for JavaScript function clickHandler.

```
<script language=JavaScript>
function clickHandler() {
  var targetId, srcElement, targetElement;
  srcElement = window.event.srcElement;
  if (srcElement.className == "Outline") {
     targetId = srcElement.id + "details";
     targetElement = document.all(targetId);
     if (targetElement.style.display == "none") {
        targetElement.style.display = "";
     } else {
        targetElement.style.display = "none";
     }
  }
}

document.onclick = clickHandler;
```

5. To view the page, open the page within Internet Explorer. Listing 8.46 shows the page's complete code.

Listing 8.46 The complete HTML code for the Microsoft page.

```
<HTML>
<HEAD>
</HEAD>
<BODY TEXT="#000000" LINK="#0000ff" VLINK="#800080">

<img border=0 name=img1 src="microsoft_small.jpg" align="left" hspace="0"
 onclick="img1.src = 'microsoft_big.jpg';">
<p>
<br>
<div id=Out0 style="position:relative; left:0; top:+15px; width:90%;" >
```

```
<span id=Out1 class=Outline style="cursor: hand; ">+ </span>
<u id=Out1 class=Outline style="cursor: hand; ">
More information on Microsoft</u>

<div id=Out1details style="display:None; position:relative; left:12;">
<br>
Bill Gates owns Microsoft.<br>
He is the world's richest man.
</div>
<br>
<br>

<div id=Out3 style="position:relative; left:0; top:+15px; width:90%;" >
<span id=Out4 class=Outline style="cursor: hand; ">+ </span>
<u id=Out4 class=Outline style="cursor: hand; ">
More information on Microsoft Products</u>

<div id=Out4details style="display:None; position:relative; left:12;">
<br>
Some of Microsoft's products are:<br>
<br>
Windows<br>
MS Office<br>
Internet Explorer<br>
</div>

<script language=JavaScript>
function clickHandler() {
  var targetId, srcElement, targetElement;
  srcElement = window.event.srcElement;
  if (srcElement.className == "Outline") {
     targetId = srcElement.id + "details";
     targetElement = document.all(targetId);
     if (targetElement.style.display == "none") {
        targetElement.style.display = "";
     } else {
        targetElement.style.display = "none";
     }
  }
}

document.onclick = clickHandler;

</script>

</BODY>
</HTML>
```

Displaying MicroHelp By Using The **onfocus** Event

This example demonstrates using the **onfocus** event to display MicroHelp. We will design a page that displays two input text fields (see Figure 8.11). When a user clicks within the first text field, the browser processes the text field's **onfocus** event and displays the MicroHelp for the text field "Enter Last Name." Figure 8.12 shows the resulting page. Click within the second text field, and the browser processes the text field's **onfocus** event and displays the microhelp for the text field "Enter First Name." Figure 8.13 shows the resulting page.

The following outlines the steps you can use to create the Microsoft page by using Notepad or WordPad.

1. To display MicroHelp for the text fields within the browser, you must designate a certain area within the browser. You can do so by using the **<DIV>...</DIV>** HTML tags, as shown here:

```
<div id=MicroHelp></div>
```

2. When the browser loads the page, it should display the two input text fields. When the user clicks within the first text field, the browser should display the MicroHelp for the first text field. Similarly, when the user clicks within the

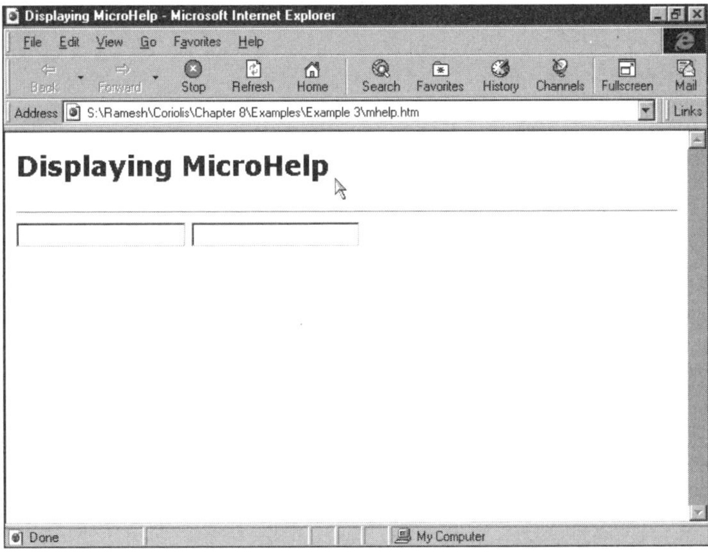

Figure 8.11

The two input text fields.

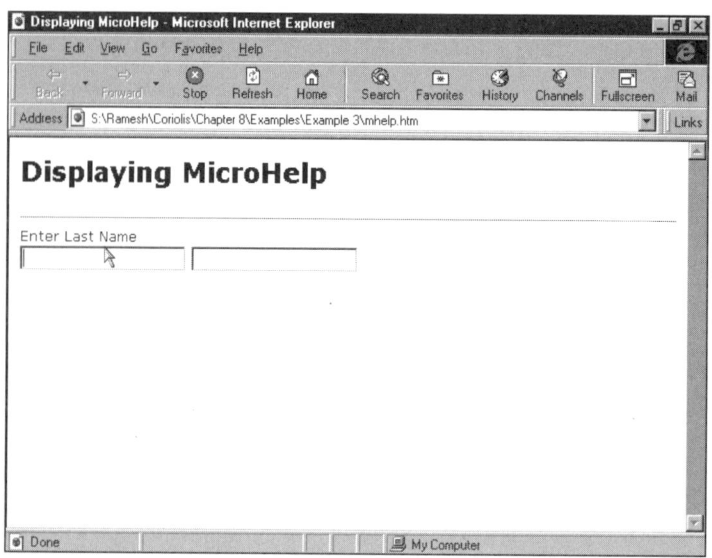

Figure 8.12

*Processing the first text field's **onfocus** event.*

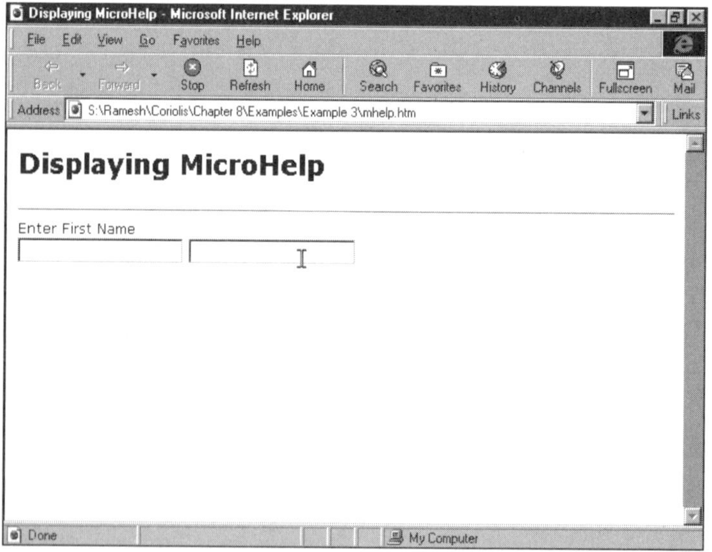

Figure 8.13

*Processing the second text field's **onfocus** event.*

second text field, the browser should display the MicroHelp for the second text field. This means you need to process both the text fields' **onfocus** events. Within the text fields' **onfocus** events, call the appropriate JavaScript function:

```
<INPUT TYPE="TEXT" MAXLENGTH="25" NAME="Fld1" onfocus=showmicrohelp1()>
<INPUT TYPE="TEXT" MAXLENGTH="25" NAME="Fld2" onfocus=showmicrohelp2()>
```

3. Define the two JavaScript functions, **showmicrohelp1()** and **showmicro help2()**, as shown in Listing 8.47. When the user clicks within the first input text field, the browser will process the text field's **onfocus** event and call the JavaScript function **showmicrohelp1()**. When the user clicks within the second input text field, the browser will process the text field's **onfocus** event and call the JavaScript function **showmicrohelp2()**.

Listing 8.47 Defining the two JavaScript functions.

```
<script language="javascript">

<!--

function showmicrohelp1() {
   MicroHelp.innerHTML = 'Enter Last Name'
}

function showmicrohelp2() {
   MicroHelp.innerHTML = 'Enter First Name'
}
//-->

</script>
```

4. To view the page, open the page within Internet Explorer. Listing 8.48 shows the page's complete code.

Listing 8.48 The complete HTML code.

```
<HTML>
<HEAD>
</HEAD>
<BODY TEXT="#000000" LINK="#0000ff" VLINK="#800080">

 <html>
 <HEAD><TITLE>Displaying MicroHelp</TITLE></HEAD>
 <BODY TOPMARGIN=0 LEFTMARGIN=40 BGCOLOR="#FFFFFF" LINK="#000066"
  VLINK="#666666" TEXT="#000000">
```

```
 <FONT FACE="verdana,arial,helvetica" SIZE=2>

 <H2>Displaying MicroHelp</H2>
 <hr>
 <div id=MicroHelp></div>

<INPUT TYPE="TEXT" MAXLENGTH="25" NAME="Fld1" onfocus=showmicrohelp1()>
<INPUT TYPE="TEXT" MAXLENGTH="25" NAME="Fld1" onfocus=showmicrohelp2()>

<script language="javascript">

<!--

function showmicrohelp1() {
   MicroHelp.innerHTML = 'Enter Last Name'
}

function showmicrohelp2() {
   MicroHelp.innerHTML = 'Enter First Name'
}
//-->

</script>

</BODY>
</HTML>
```

Using The **onload** And **onunload** Events With The Window Object

This example demonstrates using the **onload** and **onunload** events with the window object. We will design a page that displays a small image with a transition effect when the browser loads the page (see Figure 8.14). When the user clicks Refresh or closes the browser, the browser processes the **onunload** event and displays a message box, as shown in Figure 8.15.

The following outlines the steps you can use to create the Microsoft page by using Notepad or WordPad.

1. When the browser loads the page, the browser should display an image with a transition effect. This means you must define a display area for the image within the browser. To do so, use the **<DIV>...</DIV>** tags, as shown in Listing 8.49.

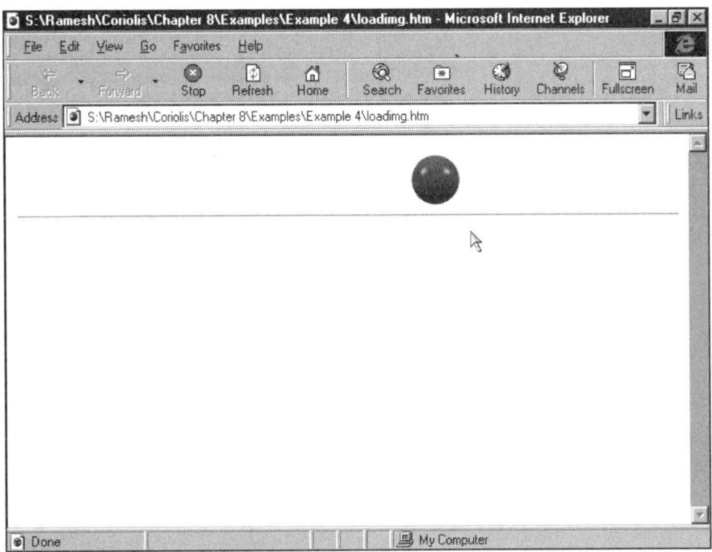

Figure 8.14

*Processing the window's **onload** event.*

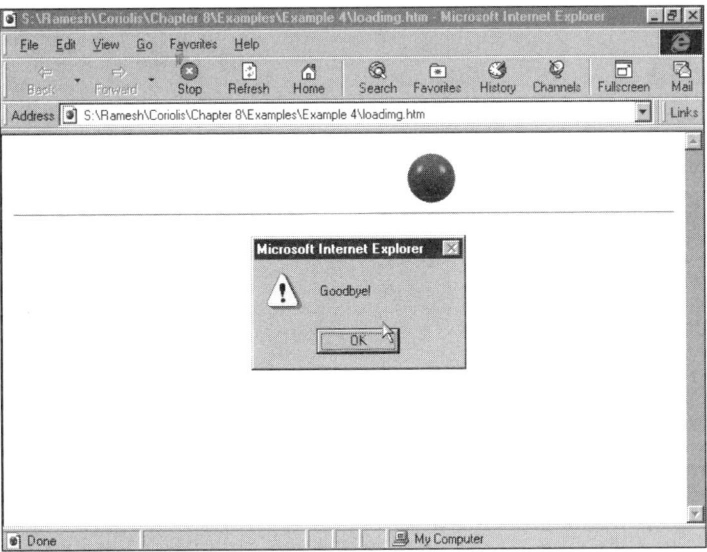

Figure 8.15

*Processing the window's **onunload** event.*

Listing 8.49 Specifying the image's display area within the browser.

```
<DIV ID="idHeader" STYLE="position:relative; top:0;
left:350; height:25; width:300; filter:revealTrans(duration=3.0,
   transition=0);">
  <H2 id="idHead" STYLE="position:relative; visibility:visible;
   margin-bottom:0;">
   <img border=0 name=img1 src="redball.gif" align="left" hspace="0"></H2>
</DIV>
```

2. Write two JavaScript functions: **transitionHead()** and **goodbye()**. When the browser loads the page, the browser processes the window object's **onload** event and calls the function **transitionHead()**, which then applies the transition effect to the image. When the user closes the browser window (or clicks the Refresh button within the browser's toolbar), the browser processes the window object's **onunload** event and calls the function **goodbye()**, which displays a message box. Listing 8.53 shows the code for the two JavaScript functions.

Listing 8.50 Code for the two JavaScript functions.

```
<script language="javascript">
<!--
function transitionHead() {
   idHead.style.visibility = "hidden"
   idHeader.filters.item(0).apply()
   idHeader.filters.item(0).transition = 35
   idHead.style.visibility = "visible"
   idHeader.filters(0).play(1.000)
}

function goodbye() {
   alert("Goodbye!");
}
```

3. Associate the functions **transitionHead()** and **goodbye()** with the window's **onload** and **onunload** events, respectively:

```
window.onload = transitionHead;
window.onunload = goodbye;
```

4. To view the page, open the page within Internet Explorer. Listing 8.51 shows the page's complete code.

Listing 8.51 The complete HTML code.

```
<HTML>
<HEAD>
</HEAD>
<BODY TEXT="#000000" LINK="#0000ff" VLINK="#800080">

<DIV ID="idHeader" STYLE="position:relative; top:0;
left:350; height:25; width:300; filter:revealTrans(duration=3.0,
transition=0);">
  <H2 id="idHead" STYLE="position:relative; visibility:visible;
   margin-bottom:0;">
   <img border=0 name=img1 src="redball.gif" align="left" hspace="0"></H2>
</DIV>
<hr>

<script language="javascript">
<!--
function transitionHead() {
   idHead.style.visibility = "hidden"
   idHeader.filters.item(0).apply()
   idHeader.filters.item(0).transition = 35
   idHead.style.visibility = "visible"
   idHeader.filters(0).play(1.000)
}

function goodbye() {
   alert("Goodbye!");
}

//-->

window.onload = transitionHead;
window.onunload = goodbye;

</script>

</BODY>
</HTML>
```

Chapter 9

Advanced HTML 4 And Object Model Techniques

In this chapter, you'll learn about the HTML 4 tags that interact with the Document Object Model.

Notes...

Chapter 9

In Chapter 8, you learned about the HTML 4 enhancements for DHTML. In this chapter, we discuss the HTML 4 tags that interact with the Document Object Model (DOM). The DHTML DOM includes an expanded and extended set of objects. All the objects are exposed, and you can control their behavior and appearance by using scripting languages such as VBScript and JavaScript. The objects offer an extended set of attributes and events. As a result, you can create dynamic and interactive Web pages. In addition, this chapter includes a table of HTML tags that identifies which ones work with both Netscape Navigator and Internet Explorer and which ones are proprietary.

Terms

This section explains some of the commonly used terms with respect to designing Web sites by using the DOM and HTML 4 tags. By learning these terms, you will better understand the approach to building interactive Web sites by using the DOM.

- *Element*—An element is a document object, such as **<A>**, **<IMG>**, **<LINK>**, and so on.
- *Collection*—A collection of elements on a page.
- *Exposed object*—An exposed object is one whose behavior and appearance can be manipulated by scripting languages such as VBScript and Java-

Script. An object is considered exposed if you can access and manipulate the object's properties, methods, and events.

Dynamic HTML Object Model

The Dynamic HTML object tree contains the following objects:

- *Document Object Model*—Per the W3C definition, the DOM is a platform- and language-neutral interface that lets programs and scripts dynamically access and update the document's structure, style, and content. The DOM provides a standard set of elements you can use to design your Web application's HTML documents.
- *Event*—The traditional HTML event model provided a limited number of events. The W3C (**www.w3.org**), in association with companies including Microsoft and Netscape, fleshed out the DHTML event model to provide an extended set of events. For more information on the DHTML event model, see Chapter 8.
- *History*—The history object contains a list of the sites the navigator object recently visited. You can retrieve the URL of a recently visited site from the history object and direct the navigator object to jump to the URL within your application's script.
- *Navigator*—The browser is the navigator object. By using the navigator object, you can determine the browser's characteristics. For example, you can determine the browser's name, version, and so on.
- *Visual*—To determine the user's viewing capabilities and preferences—such as system resolution, color depth, and so on—use the visual object.
- *Window*—The browser's window is the window object.

DOM Element Properties

Every element of the document object has properties you can configure by using scripting languages such as VBScript and JavaScript. In addition, some elements may have additional properties. Table 9.1 lists the properties common to all the elements of the document object.

Table 9.1 DOM element properties.

Property	Description
className	The class to which the given element belongs
document	The document containing the given element
id	The element's identifier
left	The element's left coordinate with respect to the window (type is long)
parentElement	The element containing the given element
style	A style object representing the element's style
tagName	The element's tag name
top	The element's top coordinate with respect to the window (type is long)

DOM Element Methods

In addition to the properties, every element of the document object supports methods you can use to manipulate the behavior of your page's elements. In addition, some elements may have additional methods. Table 9.2 lists the methods common to all the elements of the document object.

Table 9.2 Methods of the document object.

Element	Parameters	Return Type	Description
contains(elem as Element)	**elem**—The element	Boolean	Use the **contains()** method to determine if the given element is contained within the element's sub-tree.
getMember(atrb as String)	**atrb**—The attribute whose value you would like to retrieve	String	Use the **getMember()** method to retrieve the value of a given attribute.
removeMember (atrb as String)	**atrb**—The attribute you would like to remove	None	Use the **removeMember()** method to remove a given attribute.

(continued)

Table 9.2 Methods of the document object *(continued).*

Element	Parameters	Return Type	Description
scrollIntoView (st as Boolean)	**st**—A boolean indicating whether you would like to scroll the element into view	None	Use the **scrollIntoView()** method to scroll the current element into view.
setMember(atrb as String, vl as Variant)	**atrb**—The attribute whose value you would like to set; **vl**—The value you would like to set for the given attribute	None	Use the **setMember()** method to set a value for the given attribute

HTML 4 Tags

A number of HTML 4 tags interact with the DOM. Table 9.3 lists the tags that are not browser-independent.

Table 9.3 Non-cross-platform HTML 4 tags.

Tag	IE4	Netscape
ACRONYM	Y	N
BDO	N	N
BGSOUND	Y	N
BLINK	N	Y
BUTTON	Y	N
COL	Y	N
COLGROUP	Y	N
DEL	Y	N
DFN	Y	N

(continued)

Table 9.3 Non-cross-platform HTML 4 tags *(continued)*.

Tag	*IE4*	*Netscape*
FIELDSET	Y	N
IFRAME	Y	N
ILAYER	N	Y
INS	Y	N
KEYGEN	N	Y
LABEL	Y	N
LAYER	N	Y
LEGEND	Y	N
MARQUEE	Y	N
MULTICOL	N	Y
NOLAYER	N	Y
Q	Y	N
SERVER	N	Y
SPACER	N	Y
TFOOT	Y	N
THEAD	Y	N

The following is a list of some of the tags in Table 9.3, including syntax, attributes (if any), and examples. This section is not intended to be a complete reference, but rather for quick look-ups.

The **<ACRONYM>** Tag

To define an acronym, use the **<ACRONYM>** tag.

Syntax:

```
<ACRONYM> text </ACRONYM>
```

Example:

```
<ACRONYM> The Acronym tag is supported by IE </ACRONYM>
```

The <BGSOUND> Tag

To specify the background sound the browser will play when the browser opens the page, use the **<BGSOUND>** tag.

Syntax:

```
<BGSOUND SRC="URL" LOOP=n>
```

Attributes:

```
URL, n
```

Example:

```
<BGSOUND SRC="song.avi" LOOP="INFINITE">
```

The <BLINK> Tag

To highlight the text by blinking it on and off, use the **<BLINK>** tag.

Syntax:

```
<BLINK> text </BLINK>
```

Example:

```
<BLINK> The BLINK tag causes the text to blink! </BLINK>
```

The <BUTTON> Tag

To display a command button control, use the **<BUTTON>** tag.

Syntax:

```
<BUTTON attribute1=value attribute2=value … attributeN=value></BUTTON>
```

Attributes:

```
disabled, name, tabindex, type, value
```

Events:

```
onblur, onfocus
```

Example:

```
<BUTTON name="reset" value="reset" type="reset">
<BUTTON name="submit" value="submit" type="submit">
```

The <DEL> Tag

To convert the text to a strikethrough format font to indicate the text is marked for deletion, use the **<DEL>** tag.

Syntax:

```
<DEL> text </DEL>
```

Examples

```
<DEL> The DEL tag converts the text to a strikethrough format font to show
 that the text that has been deleted. </DEL>
```

The <DFN> Tag

To define the text that defines a term, use the **<DFN>** tag.

Syntax:

```
<DFN> text </DFN>
```

Example:

```
<DFN> The DFN tag shows the text in italics. </DFN>
```

The <DIV> And <SPAN> Tags

To display data in a structured manner within your Web page, use the **<DIV>** and **<SPAN>** tags.

Syntax:

```
<DIV attribute1=value attribute2=value … attributeN=value>
<SPAN attribute1=value attribute2=value … attributeN=value></SPAN>
```

Attributes:

```
align, class, dir, id, lang, style, title
```

Events:

```
onclick, ondblclick, onkeydown, onkeypress, onkeyup, onmousedown, onmousemove,
onmouseout, onmouseover, onmouseup
```

Example:

```
<DIV id="teacher" class="teacher">
<SPAN class="teacherlastname">Last name:</SPAN> Johnson,
<SPAN class="teacherfirstname">First name:</SPAN> Rudolph
</DIV>
```

The **<FIELDSET>** Tag

To group related controls together, use the **<FIELDSET>** tag.

Syntax:

```
<FIELDSET></FIELDSET>
```

Example:

```
<FIELDSET>
<INPUT name="credit_card"
type="checkbox"
value="visa" tabindex="20"> Visa</INPUT>
<INPUT name="credit_card"
type="checkbox"
value="mastercard" tabindex="21"> MasterCard</INPUT>
<INPUT name="credit_card"
type="checkbox"
value="AmericanExpress" tabindex="22"> American Express</INPUT>
<INPUT name="credit_card"
type="checkbox"
value="Discover" tabindex="23"> Discover</INPUT>
</FIELDSET>
```

To view the results, open the page within Internet Explorer and Netscape Navigator. As you can see in Figures 9.1 and 9.2, Internet Explorer supports the **<FIELDSET>... </FIELDSET>** tag but Netscape Navigator does not.

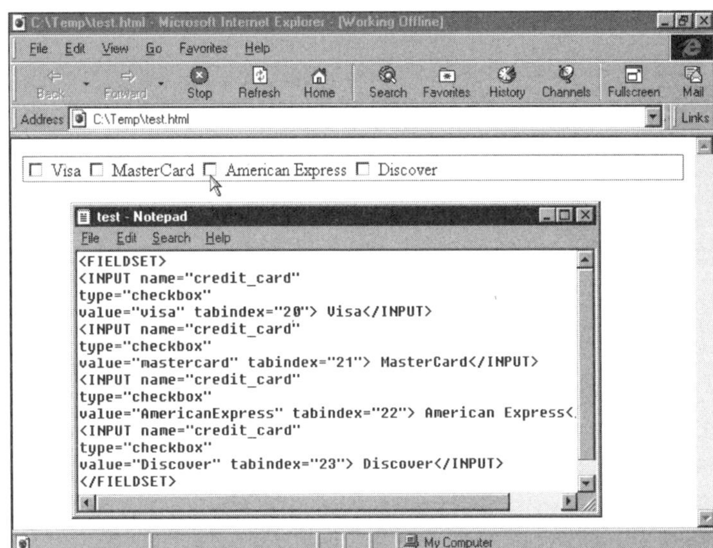

Figure 9.1

*Internet Explorer supports the **<FIELDSET>...</FIELDSET>** tags.*

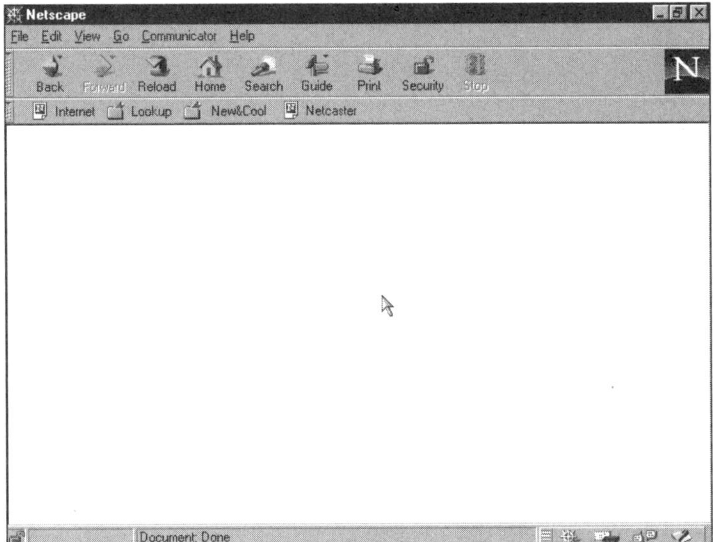

Figure 9.2

*Netscape Navigator does not support the **<FIELDSET>...</FIELDSET>** tags.*

The <ILAYER> Tag

To define an inner layer, use the **<ILAYER>** tag.

Syntax:

```
<ILAYER attribute1=value attribute2=value … attributeN=value></ILAYER>
```

Attributes:

```
id, left, top, pageX, pageY, src, z-index, above, below, width, height,
clip, visibility, bgcolor, background
```

Events:

```
onmouseover, onmouseout, onfocus, onblur, onload
```

Example:

```
<P>The ILAYER Tag helps to
<ILAYER TOP=20 LEFT=30>offset words</ILAYER>
from their original position.</P>
```

The <INS> Tag

To convert the text to an underline format font to indicate the text is marked for insertion, use the **<INS>** tag.

Syntax:

```
<INS> text </INS>
```

Example:

```
<INS> The INS tag converts the text to an underline format font to show that
 the text that has been inserted. </INS>
```

The <LABEL> Tag

To specify a label for a control-like element, use the **<LABEL>** tag.

Syntax:

```
<LABEL> text </LABEL>
```

Example:

```
<LABEL> Internet Explorer supports the label tag. </LABEL>
```

The <LAYER> Tag

To define a layer of text or graphics, use the **<LAYER>** tag.

Syntax:

```
<LAYER attribute1=value attribute2=value … attributeN=value></LAYER>
```

Attributes:

```
id, left, top, pageX, pageY, src, z-index, above, below, width, height,
clip, visibility, bgcolor, background
```

Events:

```
onmouseover, onmouseout, onfocus, onblur, onload
```

Example:

```
<layer name="Balloon">
<img ALIGN="left" ALT="It's a Party" src="One Green Balloon.GIF" width="92"
 height="164" border="00">
</layer>
```

The <LEGEND> Tag

To assign a caption to the fieldset, use the **<LEGEND>** tag.

Syntax:

```
<LEGEND attribute1=value attribute2=value … attributeN=value></LEGEND>
```

Attributes:

```
accesskey, align, class, dir, id, lang, style, title
```

Events:

```
onclick, ondblclick, onkeydown, onkeypress, onkeyup, onmousedown,
onmousemove, onmouseout, onmouseover, onmouseup
```

Example:

```
<FIELDSET>
<LEGEND align="top">Credit Card Type</LEGEND>
<INPUT name="credit_card"
type="checkbox"
value="visa" tabindex="20"> Visa</INPUT>
<INPUT name="credit_card"
type="checkbox"
value="mastercard" tabindex="21"> MasterCard</INPUT>
<INPUT name="credit_card"
type="checkbox"
value="AmericanExpress" tabindex="22"> American Express</INPUT>
<INPUT name="credit_card"
type="checkbox"
value="Discover" tabindex="23"> Discover</INPUT>
</FIELDSET>
```

The **<MARQUEE>** Tag

To display a marquee, use the **<MARQUEE>** tag.

Syntax:

```
<MARQUEE> text </MARQUEE>
```

Attributes:

```
align, behavior, bgcolor, direction, height, hspace, loop, scrollamount,
scrolldelay, width, vspace
```

Events:

```
onfinish, onbounce
```

Example:

```
<MARQUEE> Internet Explorer supports the marquee tag. </MARQUEE>
```

The **<MULTICOL>** Tag

To split the display into columns without using tables or frames, use the **<MULTICOL>** tag.

Syntax:

```
<MULTICOL COLS="columns" GUTTER="gutterWidth" WIDTH="colWidth"> text </MULTICOL>
```

Example:

```
<MULTICOL COLS="2" WIDTH="200">
<P>
The column tag is a good way to divide the HTML pages into columns.
<P>
This way you can avoid tables, if you like.
</P>
</MULTICOL>
```

The **<NOLAYER>** Tag

To display alternate text for browsers that do not support the **<LAYER>** tag, use the **<NOLAYER>** tag.

Syntax:

```
<NOLAYER> text </NOLAYER>
```

Example:

```
<NOLAYER> Browsers like Internet Explorer that do not support layers can see this
text. </NOLAYER>
```

The **<Q>** Tag

To display text within a short quote, use the **<Q>** tag.

Syntax:

```
<Q attribute1=value attribute2=value … attributeN=value></Q>
```

Attributes:

```
cite, class, dir, id, lang, style, title
```

Events:

```
onclick, ondblclick, onkeydown, onkeypress, onkeyup, onmousedown, onmousemove,
onmouseout, onmouseover, onmouseup
```

Example:

```
<Q>
The history object contains a list of the sites the navigator object recently
visited. You can retrieve the URL of a recently visited site from the history
object, and direct the navigator object to jump to the URL within your
application's script.
</Q>
```

The <SERVER> Tag

To specify the server-side scripting, use the **<SERVER>** tag.

Syntax:

```
<SERVER>...</SERVER>
```

Example:

```
<P>The Server Tag specifies Server Side Scritping. For example, this open will
 specify your IP Address <SERVER>write(request.ip);</SERVER>
<BR>
<P> For this example to run, you will need to have a Web Server that responds
 to a query with this page.
```

The <SPACER> Tag

To create an area of white space within the document, use the **<SPACER>** tag.

Syntax:

```
<SPACER>
```

Attributes:

```
type, size, width, height, align
```

Example:

```
<SPACER TYPE=VERTICAL SIZE=30>
```

The <TFOOT> Tag

To specify the table footer, use the **<TFOOT>** tag.

Syntax:

```
<TFOOT>…</TFOOT>
```

Attributes:

```
align, bgcolor, class, id, lang, language, style, title, valign
```

Events:

```
onclick, ondblclick, ondragstart, onhelp, onkeydown, onkeypress, onkeyup,
onmousedown, onmousemove, onmouseout, onmouseover, onmouseup, onselectstart
```

Example:

```
<TABLE><TBODY> <TR>Table Body</TR><TFOOT>Table Footer</TABLE>
```

The **<THEAD>** Tag

To specify the table header, use the **<THEAD>** tag.

Syntax:

```
<THEAD>
```

Attributes:

```
align, bgcolor, class, id, lang, language, style, title, valign
```

Events:

```
onclick, ondblclick, ondragstart, onhelp, onkeydown, onkeypress, onkeyup,
onmousedown, onmousemove, onmouseout, onmouseover, onmouseup, onselectstart
```

Example:

```
<TABLE><THEAD>Table Header<TBODY> <TR>Table Body</TR> </TABLE>
```

Additional Resources

For more information on DOM, visit **www.w3.org/DOM**.

For more information on the HTML 4 specification, visit **www.w3.org/TR/PR-html40**.

To view demos that show the DHTML model and its features by using Internet Explorer, visit the Microsoft site at **www.microsoft.com/ie/ie40/demos**.

To view demos that show the DHTML model and its features by using Netscape Navigator, visit the Netscape site at **search.netscape.com/comprod/products/communicator/beta_features.html**.

For more information on HTML, Netscape, JavaScript, and VBScript, refer to the following books from The Coriolis Group (**www.coriolis.com**):

- *HTML Style Sheets Design Guide* (ISBN: 1-57610-211-4)
- *JavaScript and Netscape Wizardry* (ISBN: 1-88357-786-1)
- *Web Developer's Guide to JavaScript and VBScript* (ISBN: 1-88357-797-7)
- *The New Netscape and HTML Explorer* (ISBN: 1-88357-791-8)

Practical Guide To

Advanced HTML 4 And Object Model Techniques

- Using The **<SCRIPT>**, **<DIV>**, **<TABLE>**, **<INPUT>**, And **<OBJECT>** Tags

Using The **<SCRIPT>**, **<DIV>**, **<TABLE>**, **<INPUT>**, And **<OBJECT>** Tags

In this example, you will use the Tabular Data Control (TDC) control within a Web page to read and display data from an ASCII-delimited data source, the nbateams.txt file. The example demonstrates the use of some of the HTML 4 tags that interact with the DOM. In particular, the example demonstrates the use of the following HTML tags:

- **<SCRIPT>**
- **<DIV>**
- **<TABLE>**
- **<INPUT>**
- **<OBJECT>**

The browser will read and display a single record at a time, and the user can use the navigational controls to navigate through the text file a single record at a time. You will use the **<DATASRC>** and **<DATAFLD>** tag attributes to bind the data control within the Web page to the data within the text file. The following steps demonstrate the use of the TDC control and the other HTML tags:

1. Create a comma-delimited ASCII file that includes a list of NBA teams. Listing 9.1 shows the text file:

Listing 9.1 The nbateams.txt data source.

```
"id","name"
"1","Chicago Bulls"
"2","Miami Heat"
"3","Atlanta Hawks"
"4","Indiana Pacers"
"5","Utah Jazz"
"6","Los Angeles Lakers"
"7","Los Angeles Clippers"
"8","Boston Celtics"
"9","Houston Rockets"
"10","Seattle Supersonics"
```

As you can see, the text file's first row contains header information, the file is comma delimited, and each field is specified within quotes.

2. To insert the TDC control within the page, type the following lines of code:

```
<object id="NBATeamList" classid="clsid:333C7BC4-460F-11D0-BC04-0080C7055A83"
 width="0" height="0">
  <param name="UseHeader" value="True">
  <param name="TextQualifier" value="&quot;">
  <param name="FieldDelim" value=",">
  <param name="DataURL" value="nbateams.txt">
</object>
```

The preceding lines of code demonstrate the use of the **<OBJECT>...</OBJECT>** tags and specifying values for the different attributes of the control. For example, the object's class id is a hexadecimal number uniquely identifying the object.

For this example, set the control's FieldDelim, TextQualitifer, DataURL, and UseHeader properties only. The FieldDelim property specifies the delimiter the data file includes. By default, the FieldDelim is a comma. The Text Qualifier property specifies the field qualifier. By default, the TextQualifier is " (open quote). The DataURL property specifies the data file's name. In this example, the data file's name is nbateams.txt residing within the same directory as the HTML file. Finally, the UseHeader property specifies if the ASCII delimited file includes headers within the first row. By default, the data control's UseHeader property is set to False. As shown within the code above, set the control's UseHeader property to True.

3. Add text fields within which the browser will display the data by using the **<TABLE>...</TABLE>** HTML tags, as shown in Listing 9.2. The text fields include the following labels:

   - Id
   - Name

   Specify values for the **<DATASRC>** and **<DATAFLD>** tag attributes of each text field. Use the **<DATASRC>** tag attribute to specify the data source file's name, #NBATeamList. Use the **<DATAFLD>** tag attribute to specify the data field's name for each text field. For the Id text field, the **<DATAFLD>** tag attribute is Id. For the Name text field, the **<DATAFLD>** tag attribute is Name, and so on.

Listing 9.2 Using the <TABLE>...</TABLE> and <DIV>...</DIV> tags.

```
<body>
<div align="center"><center>

<table border="1" width="53%">
  <tr>
```

```
    <td width="100%" colspan="2"><p align="center"><strong>NBA Teams</strong>
    </td>
  </tr>
  <tr>
    <td width="41%">Id</td>
    <td width="59%"><input type="text" datasrc="#NBATeamList" datafld="id"
     border="1" size="20"></td>
  </tr>
  <tr>
    <td width="41%">Name</td>
    <td width="59%"><input type="text" datasrc="#NBATeamList"
     datafld="Name" border="1" size="20"></td>
  </tr>
</table>
</center></div>
```

4. Add the navigational controls. The navigational controls include command button controls the user can access to move to the last, previous, next, and first record within the data set. To do so, add the following HTML code by using the **<INPUT>...</INPUT>** tags:

```
<p align="center"><input type="button" value="First" onclick="First()"> <input
type="button" value="Prior" onclick="Back()"> <input type="button"
value="Next"
onclick="Forward()"> <input type="button" value="Last" onclick="Last()"> </p>
```

5. As shown in Listing 9.3, use the **<SCRIPT>...</SCRIPT>** tags to add event-driven code to the click events of the command button controls. The events will use the record set object's four methods (**MoveFirst**, **MovePrevious**, **MoveNext**, and **MoveLast**).

Listing 9.3 Using the <SCRIPT>...</SCRIPT> tags.

```
<script language="VBSCRIPT">

Sub First ()
   If NBATeamList.Recordset.AbsolutePosition <> 1 Then
      NBATeamList.Recordset.MoveFirst()
   Else
      MsgBox ("Already at the first record")
   End If
End Sub

Sub Forward ()
   If NBATeamList.Recordset.AbsolutePosition <>
         NBATeamList.Recordset.RecordCount Then
      NBATeamList.Recordset.MoveNext()
   Else
```

```
      MsgBox ("Already at the last record")
   End If
End Sub

Sub Back ()
   If NBATeamList.Recordset.AbsolutePosition <> 1 Then
      NBATeamList.Recordset.MovePrevious()
   Else
      MsgBox ("Already at the first record")
   End If
End Sub

Sub Last ()
   If NBATeamList.Recordset.AbsolutePosition <>
          NBATeamList.Recordset.RecordCount Then
      NBATeamList.Recordset.MoveLast()
   Else
      MsgBox ("Already at the last record")
   End If
End Sub

</script>
```

6. To preview the page, open the page within Internet Explorer 4. Use the navigational controls to navigate through the list of NBA teams (see Figure 9.3).

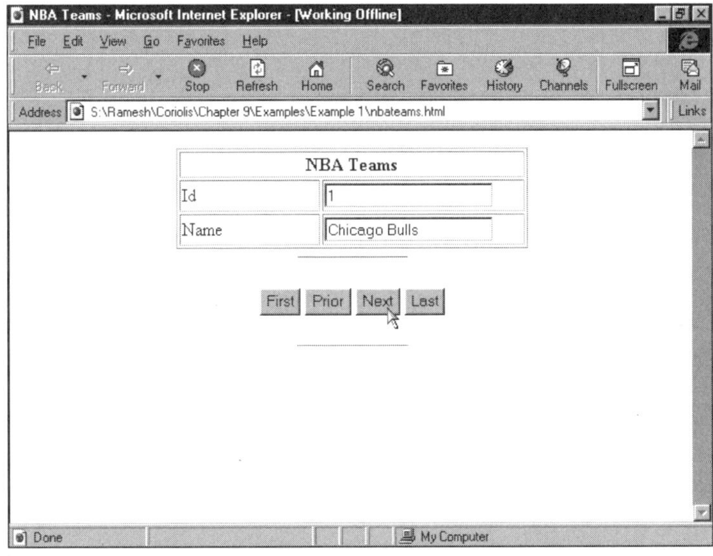

Figure 9.3

Displaying the NBA teams.

Chapter 10

Data Sources And Dynamic HTML

In this chapter, we explore data binding and Dynamic HTML, and how to implement data binding using Microsoft's data controls and Internet Explorer.

Notes...

Chapter 10

By using data binding, you can bind data controls within a Web page to a local data engine, which can often be very useful; however, only browsers based on the Dynamic HTML object model, such as Internet Explorer 4.0 and Netscape Navigator 4.0, support data binding. Adding a data control to your Web page's HTML is similar to adding any other ActiveX control; you use the **<OBJECT>...</OBJECT>** tag. To understand a data control and its behavior, you need to understand the control's interface, including properties, methods, and events. You can bind a data control to a variety of data sources, including ASCII-delimited files, Microsoft Excel, and any ODBC-compliant (Open Database Connectivity) relational database, such as Microsoft Access. As you will see, data binding is a very simple technique offering a number of advantages. If you have designed data-driven client/server applications using Microsoft Visual Basic, Microsoft Visual C++, or another language, you will find data binding with Dynamic HTML very easy to learn and use. In this chapter, you will learn about data binding and Dynamic HTML, and how to implement data binding using Microsoft's data controls and Internet Explorer. Netscape's approach to implementing data binding is—not surprisingly—different from Microsoft's approach. You will learn more about Netscape's use of layers for data binding in the next chapter.

Data Binding

In this section, you will learn about the disadvantages of building a data-driven Web site without using data binding. In addition, you will learn more about commonly used terms, such as data binding, data control, data source, recordset, ActiveX control, and ActiveX scripting.

Traditional Data-Driven HTML

The Web started as a medium for delivering static, noninteractive information; you could only view the data because it was read-only. The medium did not offer the user any way of changing or interacting with the data. With the introduction and implementation of technologies such as Common Gateway Interface (CGI), Microsoft's Internet Server Application Programming Interface (ISAPI), and Netscape's Server Application Programming Interface (NSAPI), you can now design Web sites to deliver data that you can change and with which you can interact. For example, you can retrieve a list of company employees from a database connected to your company's Web site. You can also change the employee data by using your browser to update the database. However, with the database residing on the server, every time you issue a **SELECT** or **UPDATE** statement, the browser sends the command across the network to the server, which executes the statement and returns the results to the browser. The browser then displays them by building a new page. As a result of all this activity, the server load and network traffic will increase, especially when a lot of users are logging onto the site. This could easily result in serious performance bottlenecks for data-driven Web sites.

Let's say you would like to sort the employee data displayed on a Web page by the name column. With a typical implementation scenario that does not use data binding, the browser sends the sort request to the server and the server returns the sorted data. If you use data binding, the Web site's performance benefits from a local data engine residing on the client machine. As a result, the client machine's *local* data engine processes the sort request and displays the results within the browser.

This configuration reduces the number of trips to the server and keeps the network traffic comparatively light; it also reduces the number of new pages the server creates. Functions such as sorting and filtering data are ideal for data binding. When you sort data, the end result is the same data rearranged by the sort column, so a trip to the server is not really necessary if a local data engine can store the data. As an example, let's say that thousands of users are connected to the Web site and about 100 of them at any given point want to sort the data the site displays by different columns. You can very well imagine the number of commands the server would need to process and the heavy load this would place on the server. You can use data binding to handle such situations, effectively reducing the server load.

HTML Using Data Binding

You can use data binding to reduce the number of trips to the server, effectively improving the network bandwidth and Web site performance. Using data binding, you can tie the list of employees (or the results the server returns) to a local data store against which the sort and filter requests are executed, thus reducing the number of trips to the server, the number of screen refreshes, and the number of new pages the browser displays. By using data binding and Dynamic HTML, you can bind all the elements within a Web page and manipulate them by using scripting languages such as VBScript, JavaScript, and JScript. The user can also edit the data within the Web page and you can write scripts to validate the data the user enters and to commit the changes to the database. In addition, you can bind the elements within a Web page to the data set's current record set.

As you will see later in the chapter, you must identify a data control to implement data binding. Internet Explorer 4 comes with two interesting data controls, the Advanced Data Connector (ADC) and Tabular Data Control (TDC). In this chapter, you will learn about the TDC and how you can use it to implement local, engine-based, data-driven Web sites. You can also write your own data controls to implement data binding, choosing from a variety of development tools, including Visual Basic, Visual C++, Visual J++, and so on.

You can find more information about data binding in the Microsoft Internet SDK's Dynamic HTML section. In addition, you can find examples of data binding at Microsoft's Internet Explorer Web site (**www.microsoft.com/ie/ie40/demos**). In particular, we recommend that you explore the Arcadia Bay data binding example, which is located at **www.microsoft.com/ie/ie40/demos/arcadia/default.htm**.

Terms

This section explains some of the common terms used when designing Web sites that apply data binding and Dynamic HTML, as well as some of the terms related to Microsoft's Internet model, the Active Platform. A better understanding of the terms will help you comprehend the methods for building data-driven Web sites using Dynamic HTML and data binding.

- *Active container*—Active containers are applications supporting ActiveX technology, such as Internet Explorer.
- *Active documents*—An "active" document is a non-HTML document that is HTML-aware and capable of integrating with and supporting ActiveX controls and ActiveX scripting. Examples include Microsoft Word 97 documents, Microsoft Excel 97 spreadsheets, and so on.
- *Active Platform*—The Active Platform is Microsoft's Internet model and includes a suite of technologies you can use to design ActiveX-based intranet and Internet applications.
- *ActiveX controls*—An ActiveX control is an OLE control optimized for size, speed, and use over the Internet.
- *ActiveX scripting*—ActiveX scripting allows you to add event-driven code to the controls within a Web page. As a result, the controls respond to different events as they occur.
- *BOF*—A recordset's BOF (beginning of file) property indicates that you are at the beginning of the recordset.
- *Data binding*—Data binding is tying a data control to a data source within a Web page or application.
- *Data control*—A data control is an ActiveX control you can use to bind a Web page to a data source. Binding the control to a data source lets you display data from the data source easily. In addition, you can take advantage of the data control's properties, methods, and events to provide an easy-to-use interface for users navigating through the data.
- *Data source*—Examples of data sources include ASCII-delimited files, Microsoft Excel spreadsheets, and ODBC-compliant databases such as Microsoft Access, Microsoft SQL Server, and the like.
- *EOF*—A recordset's EOF (end of file) property indicates that you are at the end of the recordset.
- *Recordset*—A recordset contains the result set obtained by executing a SQL request at the database server.

Data Control Interface

To understand how a data control works, you must understand the control's interface, which includes properties, methods, and events. The properties define the control's appearance, the methods define the control's behavior, and the events define the actions to which the control will respond.

Integrating Data Controls With Dynamic HTML

Internet Explorer 4 comes with a number of data controls, including ADC and TDC. You use the ADC control to access relational databases through ODBC; use the TDC control to bind your page elements to an ASCII-delimited file. You can also use the TDC control to sort and filter a data set residing on the client machine.

Integrating a data control within your Dynamic HTML code is very simple—you just use the **<OBJECT>** tag. You can choose from a number of different tools to integrate ActiveX controls with HTML code, such as Microsoft FrontPage or Microsoft Visual InterDev.

The following code shows an example of a data control's **<OBJECT>** tag declaration:

```
<OBJECT ID="employee" WIDTH=100 HEIGHT=51
    CLASSID="CLSID:333C7BC4-460F-11D0-BC04-0080C7055A83">
    <PARAM NAME="FieldDelim" VALUE=",">
    <PARAM NAME="DataURL" VALUE="employee.txt">
    <PARAM NAME="UseHeader" VALUE=TRUE>
</OBJECT>
```

The **ID** identifies the control's name. The **CLASSID** identifies a unique hexadecimal ID for the control that is registered with the system on which the control will reside. In addition, you can configure the control's behavior and appearance by specifying particular values for the control's parameters. In the previous example, employee.txt is an ASCII-delimited file specified as the data source by the **DataURL** parameter. A **TRUE** value for the **UseHeader** parameter indicates that the first row in the text file includes header names, not data. The field delimiter within the ASCII file, specified by the **FieldDelim** parameter, is a comma.

Data Binding And IE4

Internet Explorer 4 supports three new HTML tag attributes for implementing data binding: **DATASRC**, **DATAFLD**, and **DATAFORMATS**. Implementing data binding requires specifying the data source and the column within the data source whose data you want the application to read and display. The **DATASRC** attribute is used to specify the data source and **DATAFLD** is used to specify the column. Using the tag attributes **DATASRC** and **DATAFLD** together produces a complete data binding.

The following code shows an example of using the two tag attributes:

```
<SPAN DATASRC=#DSC1 DATAFLD=Employee_Name></SPAN>
```

You can use the **DATASRC** and **DATAFLD** tag attributes with the following HTML elements:

- **A**
- **APPLET**
- **BUTTON**
- **DIV**
- **FRAME**
- **IFRAME**
- **IMG**
- **INPUT-CHECKBOX**
- **INPUT-HIDDEN**
- **INPUT-RADIO**
- **INPUT-TEXT**
- **LABEL**
- **MARQUEE**
- **OBJECT**
- **PARAM**
- **SELECT**
- **SPAN**
- **TEXTAREA**

With the HTML ***<TABLE>*** *tag, you can use only the* ***DATASRC*** *attribute.*

The **DATAFORMATS** tag attribute specifies the format the browser is to use in displaying the data, using one of the following values:

- **Text**—To render plain text
- **HTML**—To render HTML text
- **None**—No format is specified, the browser determines the display settings

*You can use only the **DATAFORMATS** attribute with the **<SPAN>**, **<MARQUEE>**, and **<DIV>** HTML tags.*

Tabular Data Control's Properties

Table 10.1 lists TDC properties and descriptions. Understanding the control's properties allows you to more easily configure the control's appearance and behavior to meet your application's requirements.

Table 10.1 Tabular Data Control properties.

Property Name	Property Description
AppendData	Specifies whether the control will read and append data from the data source to the existing data.
CaseSensitive	Specifies whether the control will use a case-sensitive match.
CharSet	Specifies the character set the control will use.
CodeBase	Specifies the URL where the browser can download the control.
DataURL	Specifies the control's data source.
EscapeChar	Specifies the escape character the control will use.
FieldDelim	Specifies the delimiter within the ASCII data source. By default, the delimiter is a comma.
Filter	Specifies the column the control will use as a filter.
Height	Specifies the control's vertical size in pixels.
ID	Specifies the control's ID.

(continued)

Table 10.1 Tabular Data Control properties *(continued)*.

Property Name	Property Description
Language	Specifies the language the control will use.
Left	Specifies the number of pixels between the control and the left edge of the HTML layout containing the control.
ReadyState	Specifies the control's state.
RowDelim	Specifies the row delimiter within the data source.
Sort	Specifies the column by which the control will sort the data.
TextQualifier	Specifies the qualifier the control will use to identify the text representing each field within a row.
Top	Specifies the number of pixels between the control and the top edge of the HTML layout containing the control.
UseHeader	Specifies whether the data source's first row will contain headers. By default, the **UseHeader** property's value is False.
Width	Specifies the control's horizontal size in pixels.

SQL Design Tips And Techniques

An application's performance depends on the application's architecture and design. The performance of a data-driven application also depends on network traffic, server efficiency and capacity, and efficient use of SQL statements. This section outlines a few useful tips and techniques you should keep in mind when you design the SQL queries for your application.

Avoid Long-Running Transactions

If you do not commit or rollback a transaction immediately, your application's users will wait for a long time, affecting the application's overall response time. Commit or rollback the transactions immediately and do not display a message box requiring user input or response within a transaction.

Once your application obtains a connection to the database, set the database's auto-commit mode to False so you can use explicit commit or rollback statements.

Avoid Cursors

Cursors are suitable for row-by-row processing of data sets. However, SQL is a set-processing language. If you use a cursor to process a data set row-by-row, your application will not benefit from the set processing language's capabilities.

Use cursors only when absolutely needed.

Use Stored Procedures

Stored procedures are SQL procedures that reside and execute on the server. As a result, your application benefits from the server's processing power, and you can improve your application's overall performance and response time.

Be sure to use stored procedures for complex SQL statements that would otherwise take a long time to execute.

Write Efficient SQL Queries

Writing efficient SQL queries is both an art and a science. You can have the best processing server and still get terrible response time if the SQL query is not efficient. For example, the following **SELECT** clause will result in an expensive table scan if the table contains millions of records and you have not indexed the cost field:

```
SELECT * FROM  products
WHERE cost != 0
```

Searching through each and every record within a table is called a table scan.

To improve your application's response time, index the cost field and rewrite the above **SELECT** clause as follows:

```
SELECT * FROM  products
WHERE cost > 0
```

If your application doesn't need to display all the fields from the products table, you can rewrite the **SELECT** clause to return only those fields that arc required (this will also improve network transportation time):

```
SELECT name FROM products
WHERE cost > 0
```

Adopt Consistent Standards

Typically, corporations have internal design and implementation standards and it is important that you adhere to these standards for consistency and ease of maintenance. If your organization does not have such standards, adopt your primary vendor's suggested standards or create your own.

Always Document

Yes, we all know documentation is something that most of us do not enjoy. However, the importance of documenting your application's design and code cannot be stressed strongly enough. Documenting your application properly means that you and/or your employer will benefit from reduced maintenance costs in the long run.

Data Sources

As mentioned earlier, you can use a variety of data sources with data binding, including ASCII-delimited files, Excel spreadsheets, and any ODBC-compliant database, such as Microsoft Access and Sybase SQL Anywhere 5.0.

If you use an ASCII-delimited file as the data source, you must specify the character to be used as a delimiter separating the fields of a record. By default, the delimiter is a comma. In addition, you must specify whether the file's first row contains headers. The examples discussed later in this chapter explain using an ASCII-delimited file as a data source for your application's Web page.

Similarly, you can use an Excel spreadsheet as your Web page's data source. In this case, you must specify whether the spreadsheet's first row contains headers. If you use ODBC-compliant relational databases, your Web page can issue SQL commands that the database processes. If you are already familiar with programming in SQL and using the ODBC protocol, you will find implementing data binding very easy.

Using The ODBC Protocol

By using the ODBC protocol, you can focus on your application's business requirements and not have to worry about the database-specific function calls. With a client/server architecture using the ODBC communication protocol, the high-level application communicates with an ODBC driver manager which, in turn, communicates with the database-specific driver. For example, if your application's back-end database is Microsoft SQL Server, the ODBC driver manager communicates with the driver specific to Microsoft SQL Server. The ODBC driver manager translates the

SQL command into the database driver-specific function call. This means that you don't have to worry about the database-specific functions and can focus on your application's business logic and on formulating efficient SQL queries.

Using the ODBC protocol adds an additional communication layer, the ODBC driver-manager layer. Instead of the application communicating directly with the database drivers, it goes through the ODBC driver manager. Although this may create a performance delay, an application's speed and performance depend on the efficiency of the database drivers; choosing the right driver is critical to your application's performance. A number of vendors, including Microsoft, offer database drivers. You can use the **SQL_PASSTHROUGH** option to bypass the ODBC driver manager and have your application communicate directly with the database drivers to speed performance.

Per Microsoft's specification, there are three ODBC application programming interface (API) conformance levels: Core, Level 1, and Level 2. The Core API is the minimum level a database driver must conform to. Level 1 API includes a higher level of conformance, including the Core level. Level 2 API includes both Core and Level 1 API conformance.

Core API

The Core API supports the following functions:

- Establishing a connection with the database
- Preparing and executing transaction-based SQL statements after the application establishes a connection with the database
- Committing or rolling back transactions
- Retrieving the result set and error information from the data source
- Allocating and freeing memory for connections, statements, and environment
- Using variables to hold parameters for SQL statements
- Using variables to hold data from the result set

Level 1 API

The Level 1 API supports the Core API, as well as the following functions:

- Retrieving information about drivers and data sources

- Retrieving catalog information about database items
- Retrieving information about current option settings
- Setting options for statements and connections
- Sending part, or all, of result column value and/or parameter value
- Using driver-specific dialog boxes to connect to data sources

Level 2 API

In addition to supporting Core and Level 1 APIs, the Level 2 API supports the following functions:

- Using cursors
- Retrieving information about parameters for stored procedures
- Cataloging information from the system tables, native SQL statements the driver generates, and information about the connection to the data source
- Calling DLLs
- Assigning values to array parameters
- Using arrays with stored procedures

Additional Resources

For more information on ODBC, visit the following sites:

- ODBC FAQ—**www.roth.net/odbc/odbcfaq.htm**
- Win32 ODBC documentation and object description—**www.roth.net/odbc/**

For more information on Microsoft SQL Server, refer to *The Microsoft SQL Server Black Book* (ISBN: 1-57610-149-5), published by The Coriolis Group, whose Web site is at **www.coriolis.com**.

Practical Guide To

Data Sources And Dynamic HTML

- Using The TDC To Read And Display Data From An ASCII-Delimited Data Source
- Using FrontPage 98 With Data Binding
- Using The TDC To Read And Display Data
- Filtering Data Within The TDC
- Using The TDC To Sort Data By Column

Using The TDC To Read And Display Data From An ASCII-Delimited Data Source

In this example, you'll learn how to use the TDC control within a Web page to read and display data from an ASCII-delimited data source, the employee.txt file. When you install Internet Explorer 4, the setup utility also installs and registers the TDC control (tdc.ocx) with your system's registry. You will find the TDC control in the Windows\System directory.

The browser reads and displays a single record at a time and users can use the navigational controls to move through the text file a single record at a time. Use the **DATASRC** and **DATAFLD** tag attributes to bind the data control within the Web page to the text file data. The following steps demonstrate the use of the TDC control:

1. Create a comma-delimited ASCII file that includes your company's employee information, such as employee ID, name, title, social security number, phone number, and email address. The text file looks like this:

```
"id","name","title","social security
number","phone","e-mail address"
"1","Robert Benson","Manager","098-74-1234",
"904-555-1234","rbenson@mymail.com"
"2","Julia Rojas","Manager","123-45-1234",
"904-555-2345","jrojas@mymail.com"
"3","Cynthia Preston","Team Leader","654-12-6789",
"904-555-5432","cpreston@mymail.com"
"4","John DVos","Senior Programmer",
"555-67-1298","904-555-8765","jdvos@mymail.com"
"5","Martha Jenkins","Programmer","498-23-8765",
"904-555-1987","mjenkins@mymail.com"
```

   As you can see, the text file's first row contains header information, the file is comma-delimited, and each field falls within quotation marks.

2. Insert the TDC within the Web page using a tool, such as Microsoft FrontPage or Microsoft Visual InterDev, that provides a graphical, easy-to-use interface for inserting ActiveX controls and Java applets. To learn how to use FrontPage 98 to create the Web page, refer to the section "Using FrontPage 98 With Data Binding" later in the chapter.

   You can also use Notepad or WordPad to write HTML code. However, the process will be tedious and time-consuming, especially the important task of typing the control's unique ID correctly. Tools such as Microsoft FrontPage and Visual InterDev make these tasks easy for you.

If you want to use Notepad or WordPad to insert the control, use the following lines of code:

```
<object id="EmpList" classid=
"clsid:333C7BC4-460F-11D0-BC04-0080C7055A83"
width="0" height="0">
  <param name="UseHeader" value="True">
  <param name="TextQualifier" value="&quot;">
  <param name="FieldDelim" value=",">
  <param name="DataURL" value="employee.txt">
</object>
```

The object's width and height are immaterial because the browser hides the control by default; you can set the object's width and height to any reasonable numbers. The object's class ID is a hexadecimal number uniquely identifying the object. The class ID must be correct or the control and the example will not work properly.

3. Define the control's properties by specifying the parameters and the values for the parameters. Although the control has a number of properties you can set, you need to set only the control's **FieldDelim**, **TextQualifer**, **DataURL**, and **UseHeader** properties for this example. The **FieldDelim** property specifies the data file delimiter; by default, the **FieldDelim** is a comma. The **Text Qualifier** property specifies the field qualifier; by default, the **TextQualifier** is a single quotation mark ("). The **DataURL** property specifies the data file's name, in this example employee.txt, which should reside in the same directory as the HTML file. The **UseHeader** property specifies whether the ASCII-delimited file includes headers within the first row. By default, the data control's **UseHeader** property is set to False. As shown within the code above, you need to set the **UseHeader** property to True.

4. Add text fields to be displayed using the **<TABLE>...</TABLE>** HTML tag, as shown in Listing 10.1. The text fields you add include the following labels:

   - ID
   - Name
   - Title
   - Social Security Number

- Voice
- Email Address

5. Specify the **DATASRC** and **DATAFLD** tags for each text field. Use the **DATASRC** tag to specify the data source file's name, #EmpList. Use the **DATAFLD** tag to specify the data field's name for each text field.

   For the ID text field, the **DATAFLD** tag attribute is **Id**. For the Name text field, the **DATAFLD** tag attribute is **Name**, and so on. The tag attribute you specify must match the name in the ASCII file's header row, or the browser will not display the data and the example will not work.

Listing 10.1 Using the <TABLE>...</TABLE> tags to display text fields.

```
<body>
<div align="center"><center>

<table border="1" width="53%">
  <tr>
    <td width="100%" colspan="2"><p align="center">
<strong>Employee Data</strong></td>
  </tr>
  <tr>
    <td width="41%">Id</td>
    <td width="59%"><input type="text"
     datasrc="#EmpList" datafld="id" border="1"
     size="20"></td>
  </tr>
  <tr>
    <td width="41%">Name</td>
    <td width="59%"><input type="text"
     datasrc="#EmpList" datafld="Name" border="1"
     size="20"></td>
  </tr>
  <tr>
    <td width="41%">Title</td>
    <td width="59%"><input type="text"
     datasrc="#EmpList" datafld="title" border="1"
     size="20"></td>
  </tr>
  <tr>
    <td width="41%">Social Security Number</td>
    <td width="59%"><input type="text"
     datasrc="#EmpList" datafld="social
     security number"
    border="1" size="20"></td>
```

```
  </tr>
  <tr>
    <td width="41%">Phone</td>
    <td width="59%"><input type="text"
     datasrc="#EmpList" datafld="phone" border="1"
     size="20"></td>
  </tr>
  <tr>
    <td width="41%">E-mail address</td>
    <td width="59%"><input type="text"
     datasrc="#EmpList" datafld="e-mail address"
     border="1"
    size="20"></td>
  </tr>
</table>
</center></div>
```

6. Add the navigational controls, which include command button controls that can be used to move to the last, previous, next, and first record within the data set. To do this, add the following lines of HTML code:

   ```
   <p align="center"><input type="button" value="First" onclick="First()"> <input
   type="button" value="Prior" onclick="Back()"> <input type="button"
   value="Next"onclick="Forward()"> <input type="button" value="Last"
   onclick="Last()"> </p>
   ```

7. At this point, you need to use a scripting language such as VBScript or JavaScript to add event-driven code to the controls. Specifically, you want to add event-driven code to the click events of the command button controls. Listing 10.2 shows the event-driven code. As you can see, the events use the recordset object's four methods (**MoveFirst**, **MovePrevious**, **MoveNext**, **MoveLast**).

Listing 10.2 Adding VBScript-based, event-driven code.

```
<script language="VBSCRIPT">

Sub First ()
  If EmpList.Recordset.AbsolutePosition <> 1 Then
    EmpList.Recordset.MoveFirst()
  Else
    MsgBox ("Already at first employee")
  End If
End Sub

Sub Forward ()
  If EmpList.Recordset.AbsolutePosition <> EmpList.Recordset.RecordCount Then
    EmpList.Recordset.MoveNext()
```

```
  Else
    MsgBox ("Already at last employee")
  End If
End Sub

Sub Back ()
  If EmpList.Recordset.AbsolutePosition <> 1 then
    EmpList.Recordset.MovePrevious()
   else
    MsgBox ("Already at first employee")
  end if
End Sub

Sub Last ()
  If EmpList.Recordset.AbsolutePosition <> EmpList.Recordset.RecordCount Then
    EmpList.Recordset.MoveLast()
  Else
    MsgBox ("Already at last employee")
  End If
End Sub

</script>
```

If you use Microsoft FrontPage or Microsoft Visual InterDev, you can use the built-in Script Wizard to add event-driven code to the command button controls. The Script Wizard supports both JScript and VBScript. By default, the Script Wizard's scripting language is VBScript. You can also use the Microsoft Script Debugger to debug a script; however, you may not find it necessary to use Script Debugger for this simple example.

Microsoft Internet Explorer supports both VBScript and JavaScript (in the form of JScript). JScript is Microsoft's open implementation of JavaScript. On the other hand, Netscape Navigator supports only JavaScript. As a result, you can reach a wider audience if you use JavaScript as your Web application's scripting language. JavaScript's syntax is based on the C++ programming language, while VBScript is a subset of Visual Basic. If you are an experienced Visual Basic (or Visual Basic for Applications) programmer, you will find VBScript very easy to learn and use. The following VBScript commands are used to move through the data retrieved:

- **MoveFirst**—Navigates the program's control to the first record within the data set

- **MovePrevious**—Navigates the program's control to the previous record within the data set
- **MoveNext**—Navigates the program's control to the next record within the data set
- **MoveLast**—Navigates the program's control to the last record within the data set

The recordset object's BOF and EOF properties indicate whether the program's control is at the beginning or end of the data set, respectively.

At this point, the Web page, viewed by Internet Explorer 4, should look like Figure 10.1.

You can now use the command buttons to navigate through the data set one record at a time. As you can see, integrating the TDC with a Web page is simple and easy. If

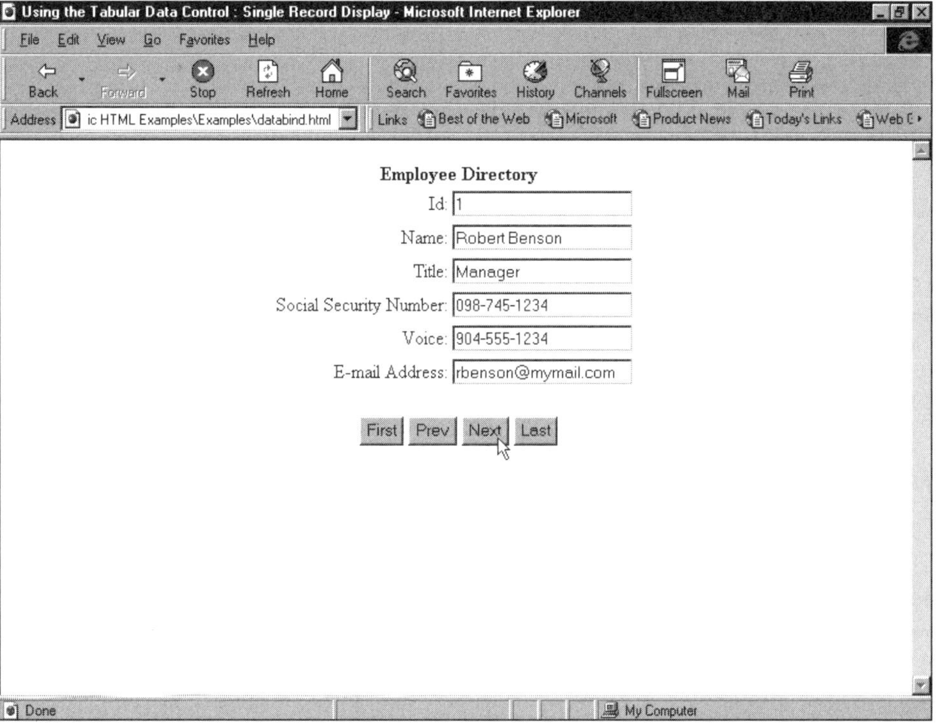

Figure 10.1

Displaying a single employee record at a time by using the TDC.

you are an experienced Visual Basic or Visual C++ programmer, you will notice the similarities between designing a data-driven client/server application using data controls with Visual Basic and Visual C++ and using data controls with ActiveX scripting within Web pages.

Using FrontPage 98 With Data Binding

This section outlines the steps you can use to create the Web page with data binding by using FrontPage 98.

1. Start FrontPage 98 Editor with a new HTML page.
2. Set the new HTML page's title to "Using the Tabular Data Control: Single Record Display" by selecting File|Page Properties|General. Set the title, then click OK.
3. Insert the Tabular Data Control by selecting Insert|Advanced|ActiveX Control. FrontPage 98 will display the ActiveX Control Properties dialog box, as shown in Figure 10.2.
4. You will see a list of all the ActiveX controls registered on your system in a dropdown list. Select Tabular Data Control and click on Properties. In the Edit Properties dialog box, set the following properties:

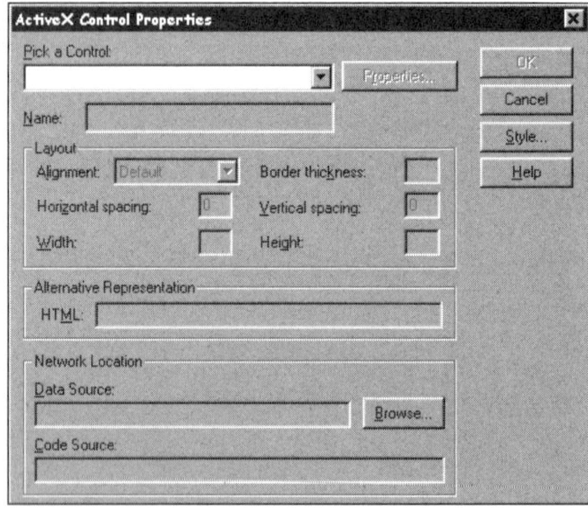

Figure 10.2

Setting the control's properties.

- UseHeader: True
- TextQualifier: "
- FieldDelim: ,
- DataURL: employee.txt

5. Click OK and FrontPage 98 returns you to the ActiveX Control Properties dialog box. Set the control's Name to EmpList and click OK to insert the control.
6. Insert a 2×7 table in the Web page to display the list of employees by selecting Insert Table from the Table menu. In the Insert Table dialog box, set the Rows Size to 7 and the Column box to 2. Choose Center in the Alignment Layout box. To create the table, click OK.
7. Merge the first row's columns by selecting the first row, then selecting Merge Cells from the Table menu. Set the table's heading to List of Employees and center the text.
8. Add the labels in the left column and the actual data in the right column. To add a text field, select Insert|Form Field|One-Line Text Box. Add the following properties to the dialog box: datasrc="#EmpList" and datafld="Id".
9. Add more properties by using HTML code. (The beta release of FrontPage 98 does not let you add more properties to the text box.) The HTML code for the text field looks like this:

   ```
   <input type="text" datasrc="#EmpList" datafld="id" border="1" size="20">
   ```

   Similarly, add the remaining fields—name, title, and so on.
10. Insert a Command button within the Web page by selecting Insert|Form Field|Push Button. Display the Push Button Properties dialog box by double-clicking on the Command button. Set the button's Value to First and click OK.
11. Add script to the Command button's clicked event. Select the Command button and right-click. From the popup menu, select Script. In the Script Wizard dialog box, select the First button's onclick event and type the following lines of code in the code window:

   ```
   Sub First_onclick()
       If EmpList.Recordset.AbsolutePosition <> 1 Then
           EmpList.Recordset.MoveFirst()
   ```

```
        Else
            MsgBox ("Already at first employee")
        End If
    End Sub
```

12. When you are finished, click OK. Add the other three Command buttons and event-driven code for the buttons' click events in the same way. To preview the Web page, open the page within Internet Explorer 4.0.

Using The TDC To Read And Display Data In A Tabular Format

In the previous example, you learned how to use the TDC to display data on your Web page from an ASCII-delimited file one record at a time. In this example, we will use the TDC to read and display data from the employee.txt file in a tabular format.

By using a tabular format, you can display multiple records on a Web page at the same time. To display data in tabular format, use the **<TABLE>...</TABLE>** HTML tag. You can use the **DATASRC** attribute with the **<TABLE>** tag, which will provide the data source the HTML table will use to read and display the data.

The following steps demonstrate using the TDC to display data in a tabular format:

1. Create a comma-delimited ASCII file, as shown earlier in Example 1.
2. Insert the TDC within the Web page by using a tool such as Microsoft Front-Page, also shown earlier.
3. Add the HTML code to display the data in a tabular format, as shown in Listing 10.3, using the **<TABLE>...</TABLE>** and **<SPAN>...</SPAN>** tags. Specify **#employee** for the HTML table's data source. The values you specify for the **DATAFLD** tag attribute must match the headers within the text file, or the data control and example will not work properly. The browser displays the data spanning 100 percent of the display area.

Listing 10.3 Displaying the list of employees in a tabular format.

```
<table  id=tabbind width=100% datasrc=#EmpList>
<thead>
  <th align=left> Id </th>
  <th align=left> Name </th>
  <th align=left> Title </th>
  <th align=left> Social Security </th>
```

```
  <th align=left> Voice </th>
  <th align=left> E-mail </th>
</thead>
<tbody>
  <tr>
  <td align=left> <span datafld="Id"> </span> </td>
  <td align=left> <span datafld="Name"> </span> </td>
  <td align=left> <span datafld="Title"> </span> </td>
  <td align=left> <span datafld="Social Security Number"> </span> </td>
  <td align=left> <span datafld="Phone"> </span> </td>
  <td align=left> <span datafld="E-mail Address"> </span> </td>
  </tr>
</tbody>
</table>
```

To view the results, open the tabbind.html file in Internet Explorer 4, as shown in Figure 10.3.

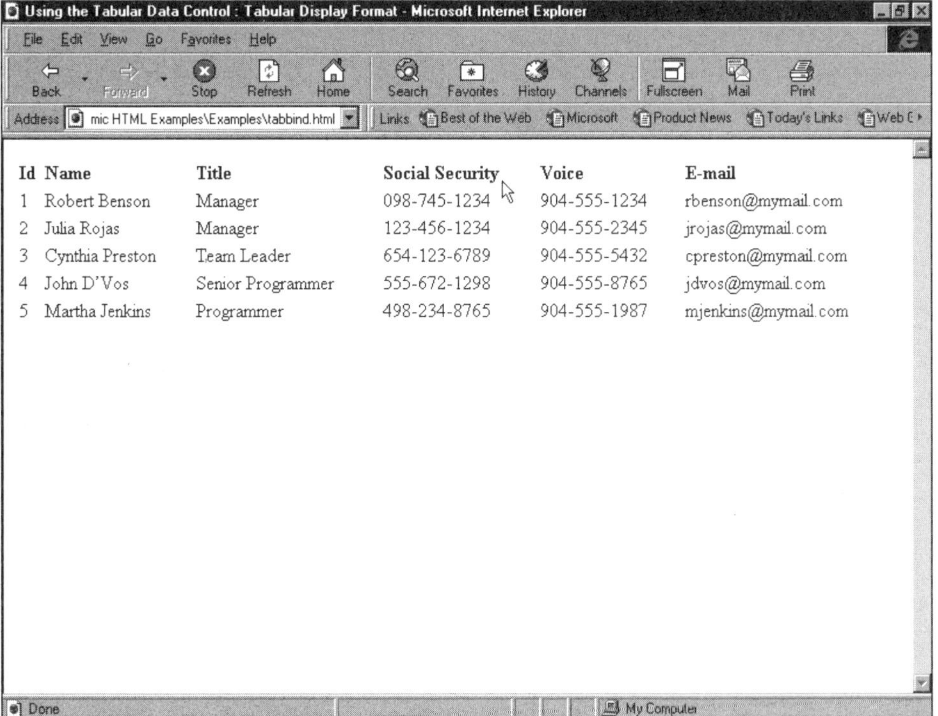

Id	Name	Title	Social Security	Voice	E-mail
1	Robert Benson	Manager	098-745-1234	904-555-1234	rbenson@mymail.com
2	Julia Rojas	Manager	123-456-1234	904-555-2345	jrojas@mymail.com
3	Cynthia Preston	Team Leader	654-123-6789	904-555-5432	cpreston@mymail.com
4	John D'Vos	Senior Programmer	555-672-1298	904-555-8765	jdvos@mymail.com
5	Martha Jenkins	Programmer	498-234-8765	904-555-1987	mjenkins@mymail.com

Figure 10.3

Displaying employee data in a tabular format using the TDC.

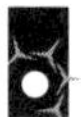

Filtering Data Within The TDC

To filter the data based on a certain criterion, specify a filter criterion within the data control's definition. For example, the following lines of code will display a list of managers only, as shown in Figure 10.4:

```
<param name="FilterColumn" value="Title">
<param name="FilterCriterion" value= "=">
<param name="FilterValue" value="Manager">
```

The **FilterColumn** parameter's value specifies the column the data control is to use in filtering the data. The **FilterCriterion** parameter's value specifies the filter operator. You can specify =, >, >=, <, <=, and so on as a filter operator. The **FilterValue** parameter's value specifies the value the data control will use to filter the data.

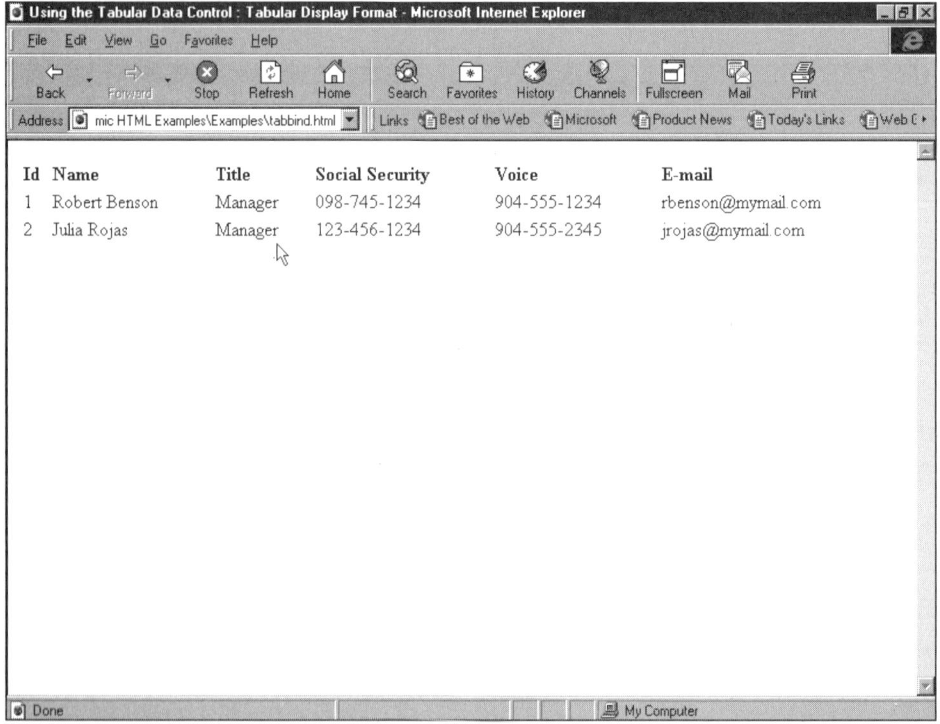

Figure 10.4

Displaying a list of managers only.

1. To filter the employee data set and display a list of only senior programmers within the organization, as shown in Figure 10.5, define the data control's parameters as follows:

```
<param name="FilterColumn"" value="Title">
<param name="FilterCriterion"" value="=">
<param name="FilterValue"" value="Senior Programmer">
```

2. Similarly, to display a list of only programmers, as shown in Figure 10.6, specify the values for the data control's parameters as follows:

```
<param name="FilterColumn" value= "Title">
<param name="FilterCriterion" value="=">
<param name="FilterValue" value="Programmer">
```

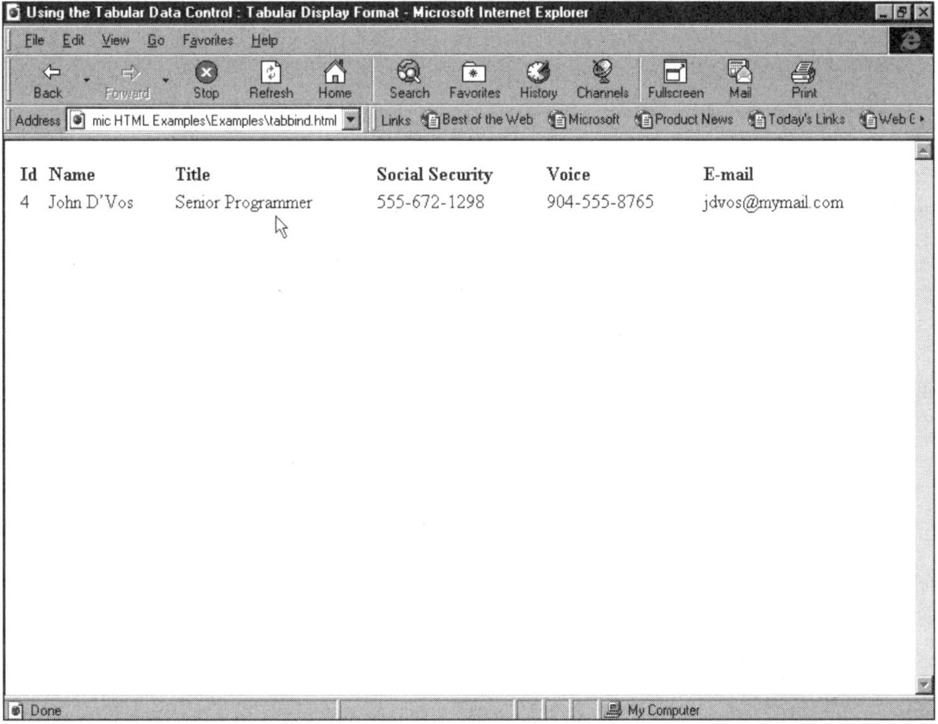

Figure 10.5

Displaying a list of senior programmers only.

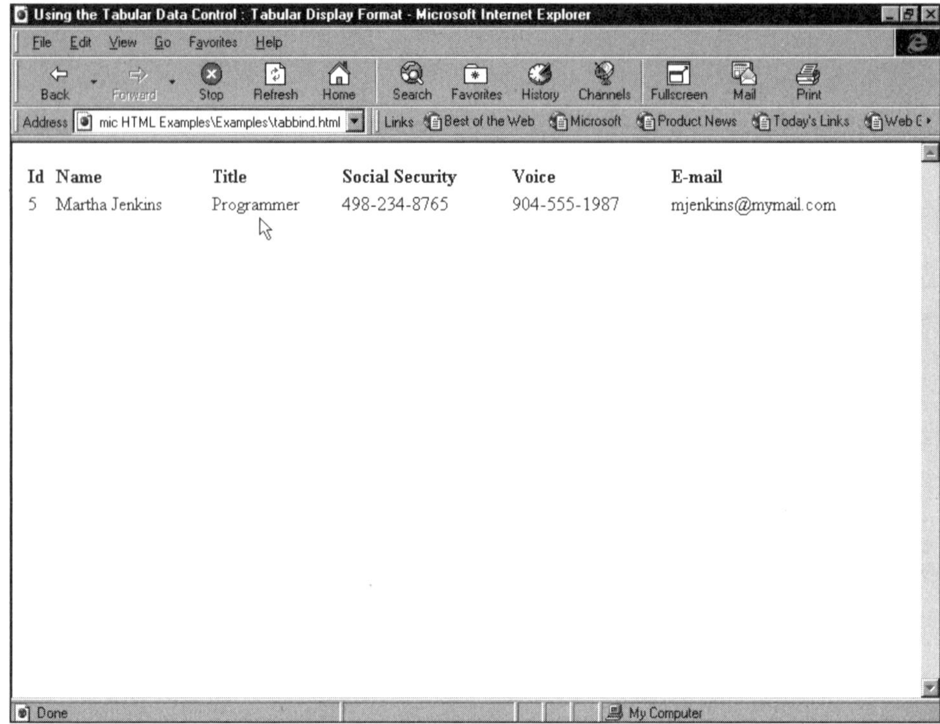

Figure 10.6

Displaying a list of programmers only.

Using The TDC To Sort Data By Column

The following example explains how to sort data by a particular column.

1. To sort the data by a particular column, specify the sort criteria within the data control's definition. For example, to display a list of employees sorted by the Title column, as shown in Figure 10.7, add the following line of code to the data control's parameter definitions:

```
<param name="SortColumn" value="Title">
```

2. To display a list of employees sorted by the Name column, as shown in Figure 10.8, use the following line of code within the control's parameter definitions:

```
<param name="SortColumn" value="Name">
```

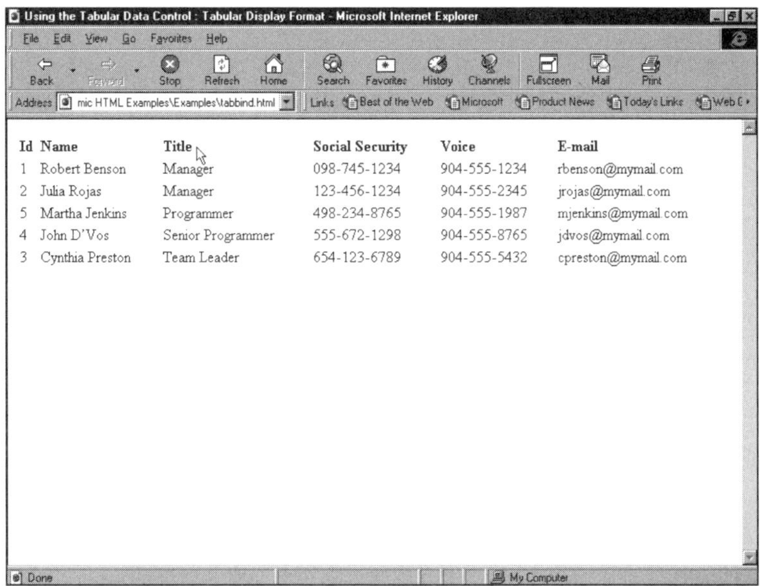

Id	Name	Title	Social Security	Voice	E-mail
1	Robert Benson	Manager	098-745-1234	904-555-1234	rbenson@mymail.com
2	Julia Rojas	Manager	123-456-1234	904-555-2345	jrojas@mymail.com
5	Martha Jenkins	Programmer	498-234-8765	904-555-1987	mjenkins@mymail.com
4	John D'Vos	Senior Programmer	555-672-1298	904-555-8765	jdvos@mymail.com
3	Cynthia Preston	Team Leader	654-123-6789	904-555-5432	cpreston@mymail.com

Figure 10.7

Sorting the employee data by title.

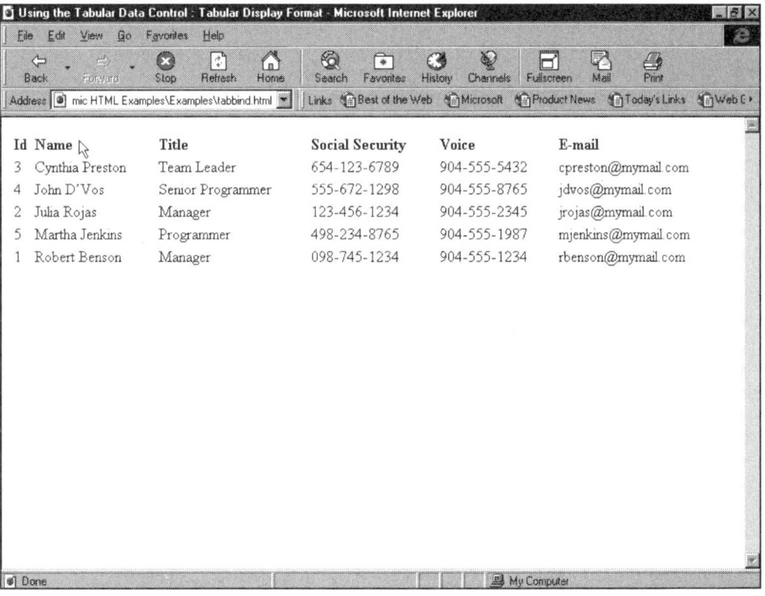

Id	Name	Title	Social Security	Voice	E-mail
3	Cynthia Preston	Team Leader	654-123-6789	904-555-5432	cpreston@mymail.com
4	John D'Vos	Senior Programmer	555-672-1298	904-555-8765	jdvos@mymail.com
2	Julia Rojas	Manager	123-456-1234	904-555-2345	jrojas@mymail.com
5	Martha Jenkins	Programmer	498-234-8765	904-555-1987	mjenkins@mymail.com
1	Robert Benson	Manager	098-745-1234	904-555-1234	rbenson@mymail.com

Figure 10.8

Sorting the employee data by name.

Chapter 11

Sound And DHTML

This chapter explores how to include sound on your pages. Implemented properly, sound can make your pages come to life.

Notes...

Chapter 11

Audio is the secret element that can destroy or define a site. It is an invisible weapon that can either make people linger comfortably at your site or rush to escape. By featuring well-designed audio that complements the site's graphics and textual information, you can exploit audio's subtleties to make a powerful, cohesive impression. When visitors react positively to Web information presented not only at the visual level, but also at the auditory level, their entire online experience is improved. However, if your site contains inappropriate or distracting sound, people are prone to rapidly click through your site and restlessly move on.

Although DHTML's audio implementation is still somewhat unseasoned, once its minor quirks are smoothed out, audio will be an even more formidable component in the mix of highly interactive multimedia that DHTML brings to the Web. Many of the new abilities that DHTML brings to Web design—particularly animation, advanced scripting, and graphical dimensions—have significant implications for Web audio. When coupled with these techniques, audio gains more power, and its implementation analogously requires a more refined skill. In cases where DHTML's potentially distracting and overwhelming design capabilities are poorly applied in conjunction with audio, it can be a disastrous experience. To help you avoid such dire situations, we provide insight into the considerations that implementing audio with DHTML demands in this chapter's Practical Guide. We also examine the creative process behind adding audio to a site.

As you think about creating audio for your Web sites, keep some of these ideas in mind. Music can be used effectively to reduce the feeling of entropy in the online experience. If your site can succeed at making a visitor feel less overwhelmed and anxious through the music you play, the visitor's positive reaction will extend to their perception of your site.

Considering Web Audio

As we devour Web content, we usually don't consider how the sound waves that occasionally emanate from the computer affect us physiologically. However, as an increasing number of Web sites—and push channels—add audio enhancements, this question takes on greater importance.

Music is simply organized sound, and, like repetitive patterns, its effects on the body and mind have been oft-proven. Certain rhythmic patterns—those that spill from shamans' drums in South America and Siberia, for example—have long been used to produce trance. Harmonic patterns can affect the mind and body as well; the Greeks believed that music written in certain modes, or tonalities, produced clear psychological results. This area of research continues to attract attention; recent discoveries have suggested that listening to the compositions of Mozart have a special ability to improve concentration and aid in the process of making the intuitive mental leaps that are so valuable when working on the computer. In his book *The Mozart Effect* (**www.themozarteffect.com**), author Don Campbell writes of research indicating that the complex patterns contained in Mozart's music prime the brain for complex neuronal activity, such as playing chess or doing math. According to Campbell, scientists suggest that, "listening to Mozart helps 'organize' the firing patterns of neurons in the cerebral cortex, especially strengthening creative right-brain processes associated with spatial-temporal reasoning." Listening to Mozart, they concluded, "acts as 'an exercise' for facilitating operations associated with higher brain functions."

The implications of this type of research for computer work, and for DHTML, with its novel possibilities for sensory evocation, are clear. As DHTML brings streaming content to the Web, and paves the way for channel delivery and WebTV, issues of how content's rhythm and flow affect the Web experience, as well as viewers' bodies and minds, are more crucial than ever. Although television has squelched the human imagination by cramming so much visual stimulation into the parameters of its box that its viewers have time only to react, not think, before the next idea or image spills across the screen, DHTML is still able to combine the best of both push and pull media. DHTML can impress site visitors with streaming multimedia content, while still allowing them to interactively direct the content and explore at their own pace. Through scripting, DHTML audio can react at an individual level, based on the user's navigational choices. DHTML's ability to map complex moving images with music truly boosts it into a new realm of interest, and pushes Web audio's potential to a higher level.

DHTML And Web Audio

Web audio has suffered from a strange litany of problems. Although the Web is seemingly optimized to become the richest forum the world has ever seen for the experiencing and exchange of audio, a statistic taken from BMI's MusicBot research (beginning in October 1997) indicates that, in 1997, only about 2 percent of Web sites contained audio or rich-media files. (For more information, visit **www.bmi.com.**)

In the past several years, millions of people have been underwhelmed, even irritated, by the sound they've encountered online. One of the reasons for these negative impressions is that many sites force the repetitive drone of a computer-generated MIDI file on their visitors, and insensitively fail to provide controls that allow people to stop the sound file from playing. Until recently, the most popular PC sound cards have also rendered MIDI files with poor sound, although in the late 1990s that hardware has improved significantly. However, the burden of understanding audio plug-ins, coupled with the need to perform MIME-type configuration, is still leaving both Web users and developers confused about how audio is to be used. Additionally, because many Web designers regard audio as an afterthought, or as the easiest expense to cut when the budget becomes tight, the quality of online audio is often mediocre.

Unfortunately, the 4.0 browser releases didn't solve Web audio problems. In Netscape's rush to release the 4.0 browser, it barely addressed the LiveConnect API and its LiveAudio component developed for Navigator 3.0, even though 4.0's capabilities are really primed to put audio in a more prominent position. Although Netscape still touts LiveConnect as the way to incorporate audio with Navigator, problems plague almost every DHTML Netscape site with LiveAudio that we have encountered in researching this book. Configuring MIME and helper applications to handle audio also continues to be a confusing process—one that keeps many people from experiencing audio.

Microsoft's DHTML provides an audio-related tag that Netscape doesn't: the **BGSOUND** tag, which simply adds background sound. However, Microsoft's most sophisticated DHTML audio capabilities are invoked through DirectX controls, which we examine in this chapter's Practical Guide, and profile extensively in Chapter 13.

Netscape's LiveConnect And LiveAudio

With the release of Navigator 3.0, Netscape created an API for multimedia creation called LiveConnect. LiveAudio is the part of the API that's used to add sound to Web sites. Through the LiveAudio plug-in module, you can place sounds on a Web site. LiveAudio lets you play audio files in the WAV, AIFF, AU, and MIDI formats.

LiveAudio is distributed with Netscape Navigator 3.x and 4.x, and can also be installed as a plug-in under Microsoft Internet Explorer 3.x. If your browser is using LiveAudio as your audio plug-in, it will appear in the plug-in menu (in Netscape, "About Plug-Ins" located under the Help menu).

The **EMBED** tag's audio controls appear according to the size that you specify in the tag's **WIDTH** and **HEIGHT** parameters. The following six views can be featured in the LiveAudio console:

- *Console*—Consists of a Play, Pause, Stop, and volume-control lever (see Figure 11.1).
- *SmallConsole*—Consists of a Play, Stop, and volume-control lever (when this view of the applet class begins, a sound will "autostart" by default). The SmallConsole's view has smaller buttons than the standard Console.
- *PlayButton*—The button that begins playing the sound.
- *PauseButton*—The button that pauses the sound while it is playing (without unloading it).

Figure 11.1

The LiveAudio control module.

- *StopButton*—The button that stops the sound from playing and unloads it.
- *VolumeLever*—The lever that adjusts the volume level for playback of the sound (and adjusts the system's volume level).

*If you have other plug-ins for playback of sound installed, you have no guarantee that LiveAudio will be the active plug-in. Whether it is active depends on the physical placement of the LiveAudio file, NPAUDIO.DLL, in the PLUGINS folder. In Netscape Navigator, the file has to be placed last, whereas in Microsoft Internet Explorer, it has to be placed first. Note that the physical placement cannot be seen in Windows' File Manager/Explorer; use the DOS command **DIR** to see it.*

JavaScript With LiveAudio And LiveConnect

By using a combination of LiveConnect, LiveAudio, and JavaScript, it's possible to:

- Defer the load of a sound file until the user clicks the "play" button
- Customize sound-control interfaces
- Have buttons "click" when users select them
- Make noises play according to what transpires on the page—moving over an image can make the image "say" what clicking it would produce

Microsoft's DirectAnimation/DirectSound Controls And DHTML Audio

As we've mentioned in several other chapters, Microsoft's vision for DHTML is intimately bound to the DirectX controls. Microsoft is pushing DirectSound 5.0 as the preeminent API for PC-based audio/multimedia/game development, which promises advanced audio functionality paired with widespread interoperability. (Direct- Sound will be part of Windows 98 and NT 5.0.) DirectSound can perform realtime mixing of multiple audio streams, giving exact control over volume, panning (left/right balance control), frequency shift, and other parameters. DirectSound's low-latency playback (about 20 milliseconds) optimizes it for games and DHTML content that needs to be highly synchronized.

DirectSound3D allows sounds to be located in any 3D space position and supports hardware that performs 3D audio positioning. When 3D hardware is not available, DirectSound3D can be accelerated in hardware or implemented in software.

DirectSound also permits both recording and playback capability within its single API.

It's through the DASound object and the Java **SoundBvr** behavior class that sound is implemented in DirectAnimation (DA). Through DirectAnimation, you can import sound formats, including WAV, MIDI, and MP2 files, and you can also synthesize sound from built-in synthesizer audio sources. DA features a mixer control that can be used to create and play multi-channel stereo sounds; sound files can be loaded into the mixer control, combined with other sound files, and then played on demand through scripts. The sound files that are mixed can even have different file format types.

DirectAnimation also has advanced capabilities such as sound spatialization, which is achieved by embedding sounds in 3D objects, then rendering them with either DAMicrophone or MicrophoneBvr. Watch for sound spatialization ability to become increasingly important as Microsoft expands its 3D horizons and targets DirectX controls for technology such as VRML (Virtual Reality Modeling Language).

There are two key DirectAnimation concepts that significantly pertain to DHTML:

- Continuous behaviors
- Events

Through DirectAnimation, these two concepts combine into *reactive behaviors*. Reactive behaviors vary continuously with time—they show their reaction to specific events by switching to new behaviors. When dynamic audio is combined with these behaviors, impressive multimedia/interactive content can be created. We feature an in-depth example of how DirectAnimation can be used with these behaviors and with audio in Chapter 13. See the CD-ROM that accompanies this book to view the corresponding creation of Silent Lucidity that takes advantage of DirectAnimation's full powers.

Web Audio Basics

In this section, we will examine the technical information needed to add audio to Web pages.

The Code For Sound

Here is the basic **EMBED** tag commonly used to add sound to pages:

```
<EMBED
SRC="http://mymusic.francesca.org/mymusic.mid"
```

```
LOOP=false
AUTOSTART=true
MASTERSOUND
NAME="buzz"
HIDDEN=true
VOLUME=100
WIDTH=0
HEIGHT=0 >
```

One of the most important attributes of DHTML is the scripting abilities it brings to content. Audio can technically be scripted through JavaScript, although this is one of the realms in which designers are not experiencing consistent success. The following example shows how the **<EMBED>** tag can be used with JavaScript to produce simple scripting functions:

```
<HTML>
<HEAD>
<TITLE>My Midi </TITLE>
<SCRIPT LANGUAGE="JavaScript">
function play_sound(sound_name) {
  if (navigator.appName == "Netscape") {
    eval('document.' +sound_name+ '.play(false)');
  }else{
        eval('document.'+sound_name+'.FileName=document.
        '+sound_name+'.FileName');
  }
}

</SCRIPT>

</HEAD>
<BODY BGCOLOR="#000000">
<BR>
<BR>
<EMBED SRC=" http://mymusic.francesca.org/mid" LOOP=false
AUTOSTART=true MASTERSOUND name="trio" HIDDEN=true VOLUME=100
WIDTH=0 HEIGHT=0 >

<A HREF="http://mymusic.francesca.org " onMouseOver="play_sound('trio');"">
<IMG SRC="http://mymusic.francesca.org/images/greenstone.gif" WIDTH=100
HEIGHT=76 BORDER=0></A>

</BODY>
</HTML>
```

MIDI

MIDI (Musical Instrument Digital Interface) is a protocol that emerged in the 1980s for the exchange of musical information between computers and electronic audio devices. MIDI allows electronic instruments such as synthesizers, audio hardware such as sequencers, and computers to "talk" to each other. Although MIDI is oft-maligned on the Web these days, and frequently passed over in favor of other sound formats, this phenomenon is partially because of inappropriate MIDI use and the poor sound quality that many sound cards have forced upon PC users over the years. MIDI has a huge advantage over other audio formats; specifically, audio files stored as MIDI data *aren't* huge, but extremely compact. Their streamlined state stems from the way they store information that's used to create audio. A MIDI file doesn't hold audio data, but rather simple binary information that indicates where and how musical notes are turned on and off, as well as specific controller information.

MIDI often confuses people because, although it is used to create audio, it's not an audio format like WAV or AU. Unlike those formats, MIDI files don't consist of sound, but rather information.

Although creating stereo-quality AIFF or WAV files to go with your latest DHTML masterpiece might be appealing, when you face the download time that DHTML can already force upon your users, using MIDI is often a better choice for Web audio.

However, MIDI must be implemented with extreme care and sensitivity if you don't want your site visitors to run away from the computer, holding their ears (or simply switch off their audio). MIDI preserves the exact interpretation that the performer gives, down to a millisecond break in phrasing. That's why it's such a wonderful method of transmitting real performances— that's also why listening to MIDI files generated by a computer to the persistent beat of a metronome can be so droningly intolerable. When you use MIDI on your site, keep in mind that although audio generated solely by a computer can work in certain situations, music performed by humans is usually much more interesting. Compare the human performances of Mozart piano sonatas at the Internet Piano Page (**www.geocities.com/Paris/3486/moz_fi.htm**) to the computer renditions of Bach's Goldberg Variations that are "untouched by human hands" at **www.unpronounceable.com/bach/index.html**.

To provide illumination about the sound quality between WAV, AIFF, AU, and MIDI files, the CD-ROM that accompanies this book contains an original composition titled "Madness" that's saved in this range of file formats. See Madness.wav, Madness.aif, Madness.au, and Madness.mid on the CD-ROM to compare the way audio first created as MIDI sounds in these different files. For additional information on MIDI, see the MIDI Home Page at **www.eeb.ele.tue.nl/midi/index.html**.

One of the reasons MIDI files often sound so tinny and ridiculous is because the pieces they are trying to reproduce simply aren't ideal for the MIDI format. For example, an Aretha Franklin song just isn't going to sound good in MIDI—vocal nuances and embellishments are meant to be sung by a human, not rendered by a computer. However, there's a great deal of piano music that sounds wonderful in MIDI, especially when it's performed by humans. Some New Age music also works well in MIDI, and don't forget that sometimes a MIDI drum track can provide an ideal amount of aural stimulation.

General MIDI

Prior to General MIDI's entry on the computer music scene in 1991, there was no guarantee that your MIDI files would play back with the correct instrument sound. If you created a drum track with your Yamaha Synthesizer, it might come out sounding like a cymbal crash on a Korg, for example. However, General MIDI (GM) addresses this consistency problem by standardizing "patch mapping," offering 128 standard sounds that sound (essentially) the same. Therefore, the piano tracks on this book's CD-ROM, assigned to General MIDI channel 1, Acoustic Grand Piano, play as an acoustic grand piano on any GM sound card. Despite GM's standardization, though, the quality level of playback still differs between sound cards. Companies such as Yamaha and Roland have even released extended GM formats, XG and GS, respectively, that add extra control over GM.

Third-Party Web Audio Extensions

In addition to Yamaha's and Roland's General MIDI extensions mentioned previously (whose benefits, of course, are not restricted to Web use), there are many other third-party developers that have enjoyed success with Web audio. Shockwave audio technology gained early prominence and was an innovator in streaming audio. (We discuss Shockwave audio in Chapter 17; see **www.macromedia.com** for more Shockwave information.) In addition to Shockwave, many people were introduced to early Web audio through RealAudio.

RealAudio

RealAudio is one of the Web's greatest audio success stories. Developed by long-time Microsoft employee Rob Glaser, Progressive Networks began broadcasting Web audio through RealAudio in the mid-1990s. Progressive Networks has branched far beyond its original audio focus; the RealAudio Player's successor, RealPlayer, now broadcasts not only audio, but streaming video, and is used by many Webcasting sites. Live Online (**www.liveconcerts.com**) is one such site; at Live Online, you can download Webcasts, online music recordings and live performances, and interviews with a bevy of performers from all musical genres. To consult the RealPlayer's official guide to audio broadcasts, travel to The Timecast Audio Guide at **timecast.timecast.com/audio/**.

RealPlayer servers traditionally have been relatively affordable; for more information about these products, see **www.real.com**.

Beatnik

Beatnik is a free system for creating and delivering high-quality interactive music and sound on Web pages. Beatnik works on Windows 95/NT (with DirectSound installed) and Power Macintosh. It can play Standard MIDI files (SMF) and also includes a General MIDI (GM) software synthesizer. The Beatnik Editor can import SMFs from any MIDI sequencer that can export them. You can also trigger individual MIDI notes or events from a simple HTML tag right in your Web page. Beatnik also offers custom sounds, so you're not limited to the GM sound set when you're creating content for people who have the Beatnik plug-in. Also, Beatnik guarantees playback fidelity across the Windows 95/NT and Macintosh PowerPC platforms.

The Beatnik player supports the MIDI, WAV, AIFF, Sound Designer II, MOD, and RMF (Rich Music Format) file formats.

Headspace also makes a Beatnik editor, which can be used to make RMF files. RMF is a hybrid file type that encapsulates MIDI and audio samples. It combines these samples with some interactive performance settings as well as encrypted copyright data. Composers and publishers can keep track of where their music is being used through Beatnik's ability to encode 40-bit encrypted copyright and licensing information into a file. This information can be easily displayed anywhere an RMF file plays. For more information on Beatnik, see **www.headspace.com/beatnik/index.html**.

Yamaha's MIDPLUG

MIDPLUG (**www.ysba.com/midplug_index.html**) is Yamaha's offering in the Soft Synthesizer category. MIDPLUG contains its own AWM2 (WaveTable) tone generator that operates at 22.1 kHz/16 bit within the plug-in module. Because of this tone generator, when MIDPLUG plays audio, it doesn't depend on QuickTime sounds or the sound board's sounds on the FM tone generator. In addition to fully implementing all 128 GM sounds, MIDPLUG offers eight drum sets and reverb.

QuickTime Music Architecture

The QuickTime Music Architecture (QTMA) is Apple's contribution to software-based MIDI synthesizers. QTMA lets you create sound libraries and custom software synthesizers, and makes Web audio relatively low-demand. For additional information, consult **quicktime.apple.com**.

Copyright Issues And Web Audio

Most mainstream music composers and publishers belong to either BMI (Broadcast Music Inc., **www.bmi.com**) or ASCAP (American Society of Composers, Authors, and Publishers, **www.ascap.com**), and the rights to their creative output are protected by these powerful entities.

If you illegally use copyrighted music or sound clips, online or offline, you can be fined as much as $100,000 per violation. There are still some gray areas regarding the use of copyrighted and licensed music online, but when in doubt, simply stay away from audio that you believe to be copyrighted. Any music that was copyrighted before 1929 is now in the public domain, and therefore available for free use. However, *performances* of music written before this date can still be copyrighted, so although you can use an audio clip of Gregorian chants at your Web site, you *can't* lift it from a CD without violating copyright. See BMI's Web Licensing FAQ (**www.bmi.com/licensing/webfaq.html**) for in-depth information on legal Web audio use.

The Web, coupled with digital performance technology such as synthesizers and electronic keyboards, provides an incredible forum for performing musicians and music aficionados. However, this is the very technology that the music industry most fears; global distribution of copyrighted music could seriously threaten the structure of today's music industry. In an attempt to gain some control over the global distribution of digital audio over the Net, BMI has launched a search tool called MusicBot. MusicBot exists to locate WAV, RAM, and MIDI audio files online, and see if their use is violating the copyrights held by the 200,000 composers that BMI represents. BMI has also created three new licenses to exert greater control over Web music; see **www.bmi.com** for additional information.

Crafting Stellar Audio For Your DHTML Sites

Composing the audio for a site can be one of the most creatively challenging tasks you'll face. When you undertake DHTML audio design, it's essential to have as much information about your audience as possible, including demographics and browser type. As always, you'll need to consider hardware and software (i.e., if you use MIDI, what percentage of your visitors will hear it through high-quality sound cards?). Here are some additional considerations:

- Will adding sound to the site distract viewers from the site content, or make viewers take longer to process it?
- Are the graphics the main focus of the page, and, if so, is the sound appropriately unobtrusive?
- How is the tempo, density, and volume of the audio affecting the Web page experience?
- Who will your visitors be? GenerationXers used to techno drones and edgy guitars, or elevator music consumers? Whether your site will have more female or male visitors might also affect the way you implement sound, as studies indicate that women perceive more through their ears than men.

There are a few technologies that you can use to feature streaming audio on your Web pages, including Shockwave and RealAudio. It's appropriate to use streaming audio when the sound files you want to play are relatively large. Compressing large audio files and sending them in streamed form is more efficient than forcing the browser to download them all at once.

Finding Digital Audio Files And Information On The Web

If you are not a musician, or don't have the technology to create audio files, you can still find a great deal of interesting, free audio online to add to your site. You're welcome to use any of the music we've included on the CD-ROM; the recording of J.S. Bach's Prelude in E Major (bach.mid) is the most soothing and widely applicable audio file on the disk. Baroque and classical compositions work especially well with MIDI, and most people visiting your sites won't be offended by them. You can search for free audio at sites such as the MIDI Farm at **www.midifarm.com**, or the Partners In Rhyme site at **www.partnersinrhyme.com**.

If you're interested in learning more about Web audio, electronic composition, sequencing software, and so on, investigate links such as the Electronic Music Foundation's Internet Resources page at **www.emf.org/sites_directory.html**, which contains hundreds of links to Internet sites specializing in a variety of musical interests, or the Shareware Directory at **www.sharewaredirectory.com/multimedia/auwav/index.shtml**, where you can find an extensive listing of shareware AU/WAV players and editors.

DHTML's Role In The Future Of Online Audio

As DHTML is integrated into technologies such as WebTV, Windows 98 and NT 5.0, and becomes a key component of Webcasts and channel content delivery, it will be interesting to see how its audio is used. Will designers approach it in much the same way as television audio? Or will an appropriate sensitivity be applied to the technology's new boundaries and thereby take audio endeavors into fresh innovation? As the relationship between computers and the mind continues to be studied, and the role played by rhythmic and harmonic patterns are more deeply understood, what kind of compositions will result from this knowledge? Will subliminal—or hyperspeed—content that's clandestinely buried in Web audio become a concern for those who open their ears to it?

DHTML's advanced multimedia capabilities give it great appeal for audio designers, and Microsoft's DirectX controls make DHTML even more alluring. Still, the most important element of Web audio is *quality*. Even if everyone visiting your audio-laden DHTML site has the choicest sound cards and the latest third-party General MIDI enhancements, it's of little use if the audio content that graces your site is not done well.

Practical Guide To

Implementing DHTML Audio

- Creating Web Page Audio With LiveAudio And The **EMBED** Tag
  - Embedding Your Sound File
  - Writing A Function That Plays Sound On Command
  - Deciding How You Want To Play The Sound
  - Using LiveAudio And JavaScript Functions
- Working With Direct-Animation/DirectSound
- Audio Design In Action: Composing Dynamic Audio For Natespace

Creating Web Page Audio With LiveAudio And The **EMBED** Tag

As we mentioned earlier in the chapter, it's possible to add audio to your Web pages by using the **EMBED** tag with the LiveAudio plug-in. Here are the essential steps used to add Web page audio through the **EMBED** tag:

1. Embed the sound file.
2. Write a function that will make sound play on command.
3. Decide how you want to play the sound.

Embedding Your Sound File

In the following section, we examine the details of the code that's used to add audio to a Web page with Netscape's LiveAudio plug-in and IE's equivalent sound player. Here is the basic code, followed by a detailed description:

```
<EMBED
SRC="mymusic.francesca.org/mymusic.mid"
LOOP=false
AUTOSTART=true
STARTTIME
ENDTIME
MASTERSOUND
NAME=""
HIDDEN=true
VOLUME=100
WIDTH=0
HEIGHT=0 >
```

- **EMBED**—The tag that tells the browser to embed an object, specifically, your audio file.
- **SRC**—This is where the source of your audio file goes. Because relative links don't work consistently in Netscape Navigator, use an absolute link.
- **LOOP**—Set to either **TRUE** or **FALSE**, depending on whether you want your audio file to play as a continuous loop. If you set the value to **TRUE**, you can make the sound play continuously until the stop button is clicked on the console or the user goes to another page. You can also use an **INTEGER** value, and repeat the sound the number of times indicated by the integer.

- **AUTOSTART**—Setting the value to **TRUE** allows the sound, music, or voice to begin playing automatically when the Web page is loaded. The default is **FALSE**.
- **STARTTIME**—Used to designate where in the sound file you would like playback to begin. If you want to begin the sound at 1 minute, 30 seconds, you would set the value to 01:30. **STARTTIME** works only on Windows 95, NT, and Macintosh.
- **ENDTIME**—Can be used to designate where in the sound file you would like playback to stop. If you want to stop the sound at 2.5 minutes, you would set the value to 02:30. Like **STARTTIME**, **ENDTIME** works only on Windows 95, NT, and Macintosh.
- **MASTERSOUND**—This attribute has to be used to group sounds together in a **NAME** group and must exist to control your sound through JavaScript. **MASTERSOUND** takes no value (it must merely be present in the **EMBED** tag), but tells LiveAudio which file is a genuine sound file and allows it to ignore any stub files.
- **NAME**—Through **NAME**, you can group controls together to make them control one sound. **NAME** must be used for **MASTERSOUND** to be included; they are both required for JavaScript to be applied to audio.
- **HIDDEN**—This attribute should be **TRUE**, or it should not be included in the **EMBED** tag. If it is specified as **TRUE**, no controls will load and the sound will act as a background sound. When **HIDDEN** isn't specified as true, browsers will display an audio control panel.
- **VOLUME**—Determines volume number from 1 to 100. The default volume level is the current system volume.
- **WIDTH**—This attribute, measured in pixels, is used to display the width of the console or console element. The **CONSOLE** and **SMALL CONSOLE** have a default of **WIDTH=144**. The **VOLUMELEVER** has the default **WIDTH=74**. A button has the default of **WIDTH=37**.
- **HEIGHT**—The height default for the console is **HEIGHT=60**. The **SMALLCONSOLE** has a default of **HEIGHT=15**. For the **VOLUMELEVER**, the default is **HEIGHT=20**. For a button, the default is

HEIGHT=22. Unless you set **WIDTH** and **HEIGHT** to zero, the browser will show a gray box as the audio loads, even if you've set the plug-in to **HIDDEN**.

If you want to have several controls over a single sound file, you would create code containing "stub" files like this:

```
<EMBED SRC="mymidi.mid" HEIGHT=22 WIDTH=37 CONTROLS=PLAYBUTTON NAME="MyConsole"
MASTERSOUND>
<EMBED SRC="stub1.mid" HEIGHT=22 WIDTH=37 CONTROLS=PAUSEBUTTON
NAME="MyConsole">
<EMBED SRC="stub2.mid" HEIGHT=22 WIDTH=37 CONTROLS=STOPBUTTON NAME="MyConsole">
<EMBED SRC="stub3.mid" HEIGHT=20 WIDTH=74 CONTROLS=VOLUMELEVER
NAME="MyConsole">
```

Writing A Function That Plays Sound On Command

After completing the code just listed, it's time to make the code that plays the sound file. The code that follows is numbered by line, with a line-by-line description following:

```
1: function play_sound(sound_name) {
2:    if (navigator.appName == "Netscape") {
3:       eval('document.' +sound_name+ '.play(false)');
4:    }else{
5:       eval('document.'+sound_name+'.FileName=document.'+sound_name+'.FileName');
6:    }
7: }
```

1. The name in this line should be the exact name that's specified in the **<EMBED>** tag. Here, **play_sound(sound_name)** defines the name of the function its parameter (the name of the sound file). The name should be the same name as specified in the **EMBED** tag.

2. Tells the browser, "If the visitor is using Netscape, perform Line 3."

3. Calls the **play()** method of the LiveAudio plug-in.

4. Tells the browser, "If the visitor is using any browser other than Netscape, perform Line 5."

5. This line assigns the file name of the specified sound to the **FileName** property of the specified sound. Although this might sound strange, it's a reliable way to make the sound play on IE.

These are some other sound file properties that may be useful:

```
document.sound_name.CurrentState    (0=stopped  1=paused  2=playing) - read only
document.sound_name.CurrentPosition (runtime counter)
document.sound_name.SelectionEnd    (length of audio)  - read only
document.sound_name.FileName        (URL of audio)
document.sound_name.FileName ="shout.mid"; (how to select an audio file)
document.sound_name.CurrentPosition = document.sound_name.SelectionEnd;  (how
  to stop)
```

Deciding How You Want To Play The Sound

The sound will play when the **play_sound()** function is called. There's a variety of ways to call the function: from a button, from the **onLoad** handler, or from any other event or function (e.g., the one that controls an animation). For example, if you want to make a button that plays a sound through an **onMouseOver** event handler, you can pass the name of the sound to the **play_sound** by the **onMouseOver**:

```
<A HREF="midilandia.html" onMouseOver="play_sound('mymusic');"">
<IMG SRC="../. /main/greenstone.gif" WIDTH=100 HEIGHT=76 BORDER=0></A>
```

For audio to work on your site, your HTTP Daemon must send out MID files with MIME type audio/x-midi, and WAV files with MIME type audio/x-wav.

Using LiveAudio And JavaScript Functions

LiveAudio can be used with the following major JavaScript controlling methods:

- **play({loop[TRUE, FALSE or an INT]}, '{url_to_sound}')**
- **pause()**
- **stop()**
- **StopAll()**
- **start_time({number of seconds})**
- **end_time({number of seconds})**
- **setvol({percentage number - without "%" sign})**
- **fade_to({volume percent to fade to, without the "%"})**
- **fade_from_to({volume % start fade}, {volume % end fade})**

- **start_at_beginning()**
- **stop_at_end()**

For these methods to be available to JavaScript, it's necessary to embed a LiveAudio console somewhere on your page, even if it's rendered invisibly.

The following JavaScript state indication methods don't control the LiveAudio plug-in; they do, however, provide information about the plug-in's current state:

- **GetVolume()**—Returns the current volume as a percentage
- **IsPaused()**—Returns **TRUE** if the sound is currently paused
- **IsReady()**—Returns **TRUE** if the plug-in instance has completed loading
- **IsPlaying()**—Returns **TRUE** if the sound is currently playing

Working With DirectAnimation/DirectSound

Microsoft's DirectAnimation takes audio control into a precise realm by generating sounds according to what's transpiring in animated content. It can produce synthetic sounds from basic sound seeds through parameterization and layering (or mixing), as DirectAnimation works on DASound objects (and Java **SoundBvr** objects). These operations can lead you to explore advanced sound techniques, such as sound layering and sound spatializiation. DirectAnimation's ability to make sounds unfold in reaction to animation pairs extremely well with DHTML; for example, when using DirectAnimation, you could hear the hoots of owls swooping around you as you walk through a deserted barn.

Through DAStatic's **ImportSound** and **ImportSoundAsync** functions, or with the Java **importSound** method, you can import sound from a file in WAV, MIDI, and MP2 formats. If you wanted to import and play a sound in JScript, for example, you could use the following code:

```
m = DAControl.PixelLibrary;
mySound = m.ImportSound("file://c:/dxmedia/media/sound/forest.mid").Sound;
DAControl.Sound = mySound.Loop();
```

DirectAnimation's current standard for audio format is an internal one, with a dynamic range of 16 bits and a sampling rate of 22,050 Hz. It's ideal to import audio files in this format, because DirectAnimation will convert the files to its internal standard, and this conversion which may result in degradation if the files are in different formats.

DirectAnimation lets you synthesize sound and perform feats such as mixing multiple sine waves. Because each sine wave can have different attributes, a mix of sine waves can produce a variety of interesting sounds. If you want to invoke a constant tone, use the DAStatics property and **SoundBvr** type **sinSynth**; to make complete silence, use the silence property and type. **SinSynth** by default produces a 1 Hz tone that is subaudible, so you need to increase the frequency. You could produce a tone with this JScript code:

```
sndMidC = m.sinSynth.Rate(440);
```

You could also create a tone through this Java code:

```
SoundBvr sndMidC = sinSynth.rate(toBvr(440));
```

When you want to use DirectAnimation to create sounds from other sounds, you can modify or mix sound parameters. In DirectAnimation, the following DASound class functions render animations that sound complex, but that don't have many operations:

- **Loop()**—By using the **Loop()** function, you can make a sound repeat continuously. When a sound whose composition changes with an event or user interaction is instructed to loop, it will loop on its individual parts, not on the composition.
- **GainAnim** and **Gain**—The **Gain** (volume) function scales the amplitude of the sound wave.
- **RateAnim** and **Rate**—This function alters the rate of sample playback. Audio that's in MIDI format undergoes a tempo change, whereas digital audio and synthesized sounds scale their frequency and change their pitch.
- **PhaseAnim** and **Phase**—The **PhaseAnim** and **Phase** functions make the point in the sound cycle where the sound starts shift; positive phase values start their sound later in the sound cycle, whereas negative values start their sound starts earlier.

See Chapter 13 for additional information and examples of DirectAnimation controls.

Audio Design In Action: Composing Dynamic Audio For Natespace

As you experience Natespace, which is on the CD-ROM as well as at **www.vcomm.com/nathan/exp/gallery/Default.htm**, you'll see references to several original pieces of music that were written specifically for Natespace, including:.

- walk1.mid
- walk2.mid
- walk3.mid
- cass.mid

In the JavaScript that follows, you'll see that MIDI files were scripted to add audio as visitors explore Natespace. Note the provisions made so that the script functions with both IE 4 and Navigator 4:

```
<script LANGUAGE="javascript">

    function playAudio( file, loop )
    {
        if ( bIsNS )
        {
            document.layers.music.document.open('text/html');
            document.layers.music.document.write('<EMBED SRC="'
            + file + '" HIDDEN="TRUE" LOOP="' + ((loop) ? 'TRUE' : 'FALSE') + '"
            AUTOSTART="TRUE">');
            document.layers.music.document.close();
        }
    }

    function stopAudio()
    {
        if ( bIsNS )
        {
            document.layers.music.document.open('text/html');
            document.layers.music.document.write('');
            document.layers.music.document.close();
        }
    }

    function DeltaMusicOn()
    {
        if ( !bIsNS )
            return;
        ++iCurMusic;
```

```
        strNewMusic = 'walk1.mid';
        if ( iCur == 10 )
            strNewMusic = 'cass.mid';
        else
        {
            switch ( iCurMusic )
            {
            case 1:
                strNewMusic = 'walk2.mid';
                break;
            case 2:
                strNewMusic = 'walk3.mid';
                break;
            default:
                iCurMusic = 0;
                break;
            }
        }
        if ( strCurMusic != strNewMusic )
        {
            strCurMusic = strNewMusic;
            playAudio( strCurMusic, true );
        }
        setTimeout( 'DeltaMusic();', iMusicDurSeconds * 1000 );
    }

    function DeltaMusic()
    {
        if ( !bIsNS )
            return;
//          if ( iCur != 10 )
//              stopAudio();
        setTimeout( 'DeltaMusicOn();', 1 * 1000 );
    }

    function WalkReally( iNext )
    {
        if ( bCloseUp )
            RestoreGallery();
        else
        {
            if ( bIsNS )
            {
                eval( strBase+'gal'+iCur+strStyle+'visibility="hidden"' );
                eval( strBase+'gal'+iNext+strStyle+'visibility="visible"' );
            }
            else if ( !bTransActive )
            {
```

```
                bTransActive = true;
                eval(
'document.all.gal'+iCur+'.style.filter="blendTrans(duration=1.00)"' );
                eval(
'document.all.gal'+iNext+'.style.filter="blendTrans(duration=1.00)"' );
                strTransOld = 'document.all.gal'+iCur;
                strTransNew = 'document.all.gal'+iNext;
                Seq("1").Play();
            }
            iCur = iNext;
        }
        if ( iCur == 10 || (iCur != 10 && strCurMusic == 'cass.mid') )
            DeltaMusic();
    }

    function Walk( iNext )
    {
//          if ( bArmed )
            WalkReally( iNext );
    }

    function StepBack()
    {
        if ( (i = iCur - 1) < 1 )
            i = iCurMax;
        WalkReally( i );
    }

    function StepForward()
    {
        if ( (i = iCur + 1) > iCurMax )
            i = 1;
        WalkReally( i );
    }

    function ReArm()
    {
        /* "Hide old layer" is the true to false transition */
        /* "Mouse out of new layer" is the false to true transition */
        bArmed = !bArmed;
    }

    function ShowPic( strUrl )
    {
        bCloseUp = true;
        eval( strBase+'gal'+iCur+strStyle+'visibility="hidden"' );
        eval( strBase+'closeup'+strStyle+'visibility="visible"' );
        if ( bIsNS )
        {
```

```
            document.layers.closeup.document.open('text/html');
            document.layers.closeup.document.write('<table border="0"
 cellpadding="0" cellspacing="0" WIDTH="432"><tr>');
            document.layers.closeup.document.write('<td><img src="sp1x1t.gif"
 border="0" width="1" height="288"></td>');
            document.layers.closeup.document.write('<td align="center"
valign="middle"><a HREF="javascript:RestoreGallery();">
<img SRC="'+strUrl+'" BORDER="0"></a></td>');
            document.layers.closeup.document.write('</tr></table>');
            document.layers.closeup.document.close();
        }
        else
            eval( strBase+'closeups.src="'+strUrl+'"' );
    }

    function RestoreGallery()
    {
        bCloseUp = false;
        eval( strBase+'closeup'+strStyle+'visibility="hidden"' );
        eval( strBase+'gal'+iCur+strStyle+'visibility="visible"' );
    }

    function seq_done()
    {
        bTransActive = false;
    }

    function ShowNewPic()
    {
        eval( strTransNew + '.filters(0).apply()' );
        eval( strTransNew + '.style.visibility = "visible"' );
        eval( strTransNew + '.filters(0).play()' );
    }

    function HideOldPic()
    {
        eval( strTransOld + '.filters(0).apply()' );
        eval( strTransOld + '.style.visibility = "hidden"' );
        eval( strTransOld + '.filters(0).play()' );
    }

    function StartItUp()
    {
        eval( strBase+'loading'+strStyle+'visibility="hidden"' );
        eval( strBase+'gal'+iCur+strStyle+'visibility="visible"' );
    }
```

```
    var bArmed = true;
    var bCloseUp = false;
    var iCur = 0;
    var iCurMax = 10;
    var strTransOld = "";
    var strTransNew = "";
    var bTransActive = false;
    var iCurMusic = 0
    var strCurMusic = ""
    var iMusicDurSeconds = 3 * 60

    bIsNS = (navigator.userAgent.indexOf ("MSIE") == -1);
    if ( bIsNS )
    {
        strBase = 'document.layers.';
        strStyle = '.';
    }
    else
    {
        strBase = 'document.all.';
        strStyle = '.style.';
    }

    DeltaMusic();

</script>
```

There is a certain trajectory that's followed in the process of creating audio for a site, whether it's an artistic showcase like Natespace or a pragmatic corporate site:

1. Meet with the site's creators—and/or those who are funding the audio development—to learn how they would like to use audio in the site. Jensen suggested several album titles featuring music that he thought would work well for the site, and we also discussed the sensation of navigating through virtual Natespace, and pondered the type of music that would enhance such navigation.

2. After numerous visits to Natespace, and time spent poring over its art, the compositional process began on a Yamaha Diskclavier, a piano with built-in MIDI capabilities. As we visited different parts of the site, we imagined the audio accompaniments that would most enhance the journey. Because the Diskclavier records in realtime, we were able to capture our exact compositional ideas while looking through the site (any keyboard or instrument that is capable of outputting MIDI data could be used to work in this way). For

example, it seemed that the initial entrance to Natespace, seen in Figure 11.2, required music that was evocative, yet not aggressive.

3. The room in which Jensen collected the series of paintings inspired by his recent marriage, however, required a different sort of compositional approach. The music inspired by the paintings shown in Figure 11.3 reflects both the hope and the somber undertones that the works contain.

4. We spent about 2 months composing and improvising roughly 30 audio tracks, 5 of which were ultimately selected for use at the space. After we decided which ones to use, we imported them into Opcode's Studio Vision Pro sequencing software to perform minor edits, such as the slips of the finger seen in Figure 11.4's notation, and corrected in Figure 11.5's.

*There are many types of sequencing software and sound editors that can perform these functions. See the Digital Audio Directory for a mega-list of almost every hardware and software company that's involved with digital audio at **www.westworld.com/~wizard/dad.html**, or consult Harmony Central's variety of topics at **www.harmony-central.com**.*

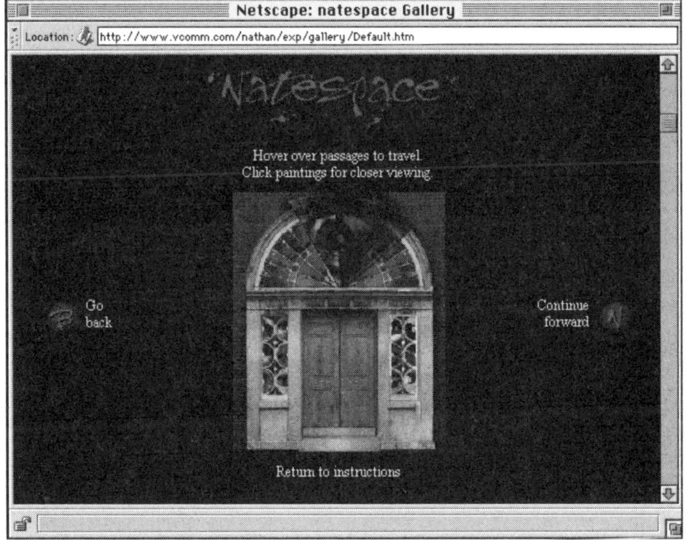

Figure 11.2

Natespace's front door led us to create the walk1.mid file found on the CD-ROM.

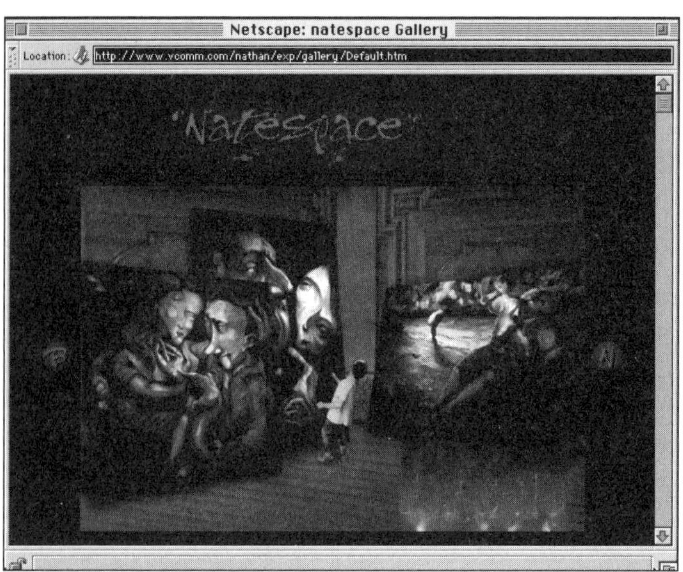

Figure 11.3

The music inspired by the paintings in this room has a significantly different flavor from the music that plays at Natespace's entrance.

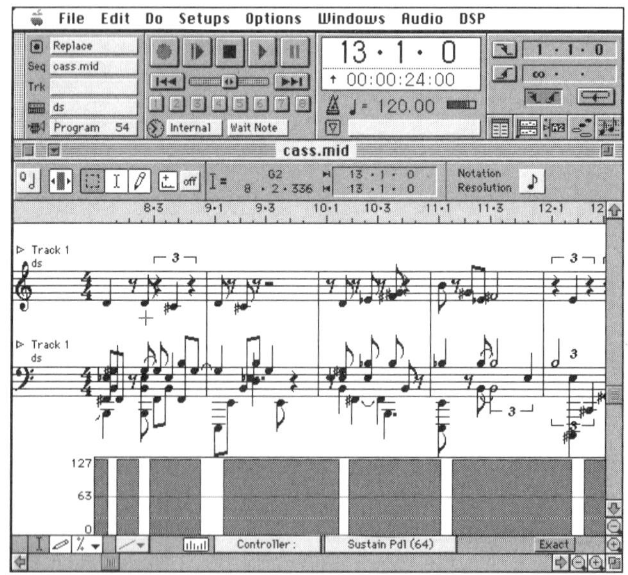

Figure 11.4

The notation showing the pre-edited version of cass.mid music for Natespace; the mistake is above the cross.

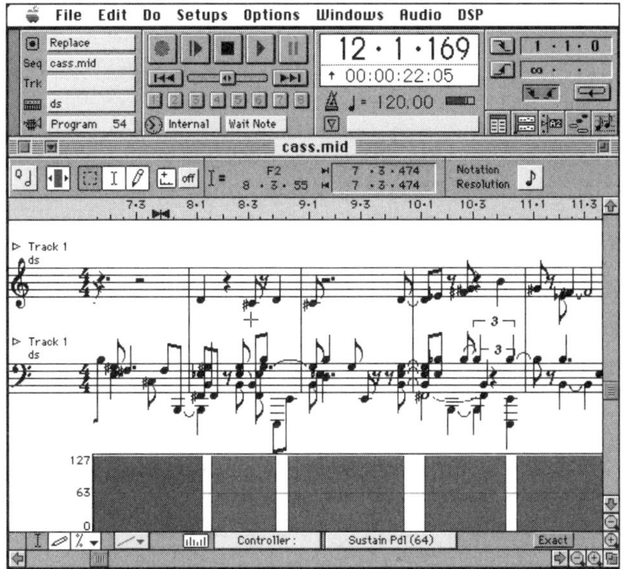

Figure 11.5

The notation showing the post-edited version of cass.mid music for Natespace; the note above the cross was removed in a matter of seconds.

5. Finally, we exported them as MIDI files, mapped them with General MIDI Channel 1 (Acoustic Grand Piano) to ensure conformity in playback, and uploaded them to Natespace's server.

Chapter 12

Graphics With DHTML

In this chapter, we examine the essential role that graphics play with Dynamic HTML content. We also demonstrate some of the most popular and effective DHTML graphics techniques.

Notes...

Chapter 12

Dynamic HTML thrusts Web designers into an entirely new realm of graphic possibilities. DHTML's abilities to make graphics more easily manipulated from the developer's end as well as more interactive from the user's end translates into stronger Web multimedia at both ends of the browser. The more exposed object model that forms the core of Microsoft's DHTML significantly extends HTML's ability to activate and maneuver graphics. In addition, the added precision that CSS and absolute/relative positioning bring to this latest incarnation of HTML gives Web developers increased control over expression through graphics.

Of course, these heady powers cannot be taken lightly. Considerate implementation of content must always be on a designer's mind, especially with the complications brought about by the proprietary battles currently being waged in Web territory. If you're concerned about reaching the broadest online audience, you won't be able to fully exploit all of DHTML's prowess until its support is more widespread, unless you're willing to create separate DHTML pages (which many developers are doing). The bulk of the Web's users are still using 3.0, or even 2.0, browsers, and it's therefore crucial to test your bleeding-edge dynamic content to see how it renders under such conditions. Cross-testing for both Netscape and Microsoft browsers is also essential; they've (tragically) never been further apart in the way they handle HTML.

CSS Positioning And Graphics

Both Netscape and Microsoft have included support for CSS positioning (CSS-P) in their 4.0 Web browsers, and it plays an important role in graphics within DHTML. CSS-P brings several distinct abilities to designers. For one, it lets you hide or display objects of your choice, producing rather stunning—and rapid—graphical effects. Through CSS-P, multiple HTML objects can be contained within the same physical space on the page, and you can choose to display a specific portion of an object. Although the effects achieved through CSS-P and Netscape's layers can look similar, you can apply CSS-P to practically any HTML element, whereas with layers, you must put tags around each element you want to position.

DHTML lets you choose either absolute or relative positions for your graphics, with new positioning properties of **POSITION**, **LEFT**, **TOP**, **OVERFLOW**, **CLIP**, **Z-INDEX**, **VISIBILITY**, **WIDTH**, and **HEIGHT**. *Absolute positioning* makes graphics appear in a fixed place no matter what other activity is happening on the page, whereas the way graphics appear with *relative positioning* depends on the previous elements' end points. We'll provide examples that make use of the powers of CSS-P in this chapter's Practical Guide; see Chapter 6 for additional information on CSS, or consult the CSS FAQ at **www.hwg.org/resources/faqs/cssFAQ.html**.

CSS And Image Filters

One of DHTML's new abilities—at least in Microsoft's implementation—is image filtering. Designers who have used graphics programs such as Photoshop are already acquainted with what image filtering can accomplish—you can blur images, create drop shadows, add a glowing outline to an image, make text appear backwards, and so on. Because image filters let you make designs with actual text, rather than relying on cumbersome text bitmaps, they can save significant download time. Additionally, they can work their magic effects after a Web page has already downloaded, so a site visitor can watch an image blur or fade without requiring input from the server. Keep in mind that these filters are currently part of Microsoft's DHTML, not the W3C's official HTML, so if it's essential that *all* your site's visitors can experience your graphic content, avoid these proprietary filters.

The following section explores Microsoft's use of filters and other graphical controls in more detail.

Microsoft ActiveX Multimedia Controls

ActiveX is the name that Microsoft has given to its distributed object technology. ActiveX controls (once called OLE controls) are small packages of executable code modules, all with a standard interface. This consistent interface conveniently travels between any container application that works with ActiveX (such as today's Microsoft products). Because ActiveX's customizable controls are treated as objects in Microsoft's DOM and because IE 4 exposes all objects to scripting languages, it's possible for scripts to access and affect the properties and methods of ActiveX objects.

The ActiveX multimedia controls that can be used to change the way a Web page appears are a subset of the ActiveX technology. Given that the ActiveX multimedia controls are bundled with IE 4 and exist in the Windows Registry as well, people experiencing the Web through ActiveX-friendly interfaces can experience the functionality of these multimedia controls without downloading the controls themselves. We'll step through some examples of how these multimedia controls work later in this chapter.

Even though ActiveX controls are so clearly created for use with Microsoft products, there are ways to use ActiveX with Netscape Navigator (through the NCompass plug-in, for example). However, because it's not possible to access any scripts when you use ActiveX with Navigator, the essence of DHTML doesn't really come through in such implementations. And although ActiveX tools do exist for the Macintosh, again, they're afflicted by Microsoft's proprietary ways, as a Macintosh browser requires a separate set of controls.

Because Microsoft's multimedia strategy—and version of DHTML—relies so heavily on ActiveX, we'll outline IE 4's ActiveX controls that have the most bearing on graphics with DHTML.

Visual Filter

You can use the visual filter control to apply special effects to Web page elements. Blurs, transparency, shadows, and waves are some of the distortions you can apply with this control, whose filters work in a similar way to filters in Adobe Photoshop. Some of the effects that can be invoked through the visual filter control include:

- *Chromakey*—Eliminates the specified color from the Web page object
- *Drop Shadow*—Puts a drop shadow behind the object
- *Flip Horizontal*—Creates a horizontal mirror image of the object

- *Flip Vertical*—Creates a vertical mirror image of the object
- *Grayscale*—Renders the object in grayscale mode
- *Invert*—Creates a negative image of the object
- *Lights*—Illuminates the object with a shining light
- *Mask*—Makes the object into a mask, underneath which content can be selectively displayed
- *Motion Blur*—Creates a blurring effect that resembles a drop shadow
- *Opacity*—Renders the object semitransparent
- *Shadow*—Adds a shadow based on the object's shape
- *Wave*—Puts a wave pattern over the image, thereby distorting it
- *Xray*—Makes an X-ray effect that's reminiscent of Photoshop's Find Edges filter

To add a visual filter control, use the **OBJECT** tag along with the visual filter's unique class ID:

```
<OBJECT ID=ExampleFilter CLASSID="CLSID:DA9E9D23-3661-11D0-BDC2-00A0C908DB96">
```

Each of the special effects also has a unique class ID that is set with a **PARAM** tag. Each effect is also numbered. For more information on effect settings, refer to Microsoft's documentation at **www.microsoft.com/workshop/prog/inetsdk/docs/**.

Structured Graphics Control

The structured graphics control is used to make drawings from scratch, in the form of basic geometric shapes such as lines, curves, and polygons. These graphics can be drawn directly on the Web page and affected by a script, so that they respond to user input or play as animations. The structured graphics control differs from the visual filter and transition controls in that it doesn't use HTML page elements as raw material. For that reason, when Web browsers other than IE 4 view the page, the structured graphics simply don't appear.

Again, the **OBJECT** tag is used for a structured graphic's syntax, in conjunction with the control's unique class ID. The height and width expressed in the **STYLE** attribute don't refer to the size of the object that the control draws, but rather to the expanse of Web page space that the control can use for drawing. Here's the syntax for the structured graphics control:

```
<OBJECT ID=myRect STYLE="height:50; width:50;"
CLASSID="CLSID:5FD6A143-372A-11D0-A521-0080C78FEE85">
```

Refer to Microsoft's documentation at the URL given previously for additional information about the structured graphics control's command set.

Transition Control

The effects that the transition control displays aren't too different from those of the visual filter. The affected object is added or removed from the layout in the same way, but the transition filter's effects display at a gradual rate, normally over the course of a few seconds.

The transition control is put into a Web page in a now-familiar manner: through the **OBJECT** tag in conjunction with the control's unique class ID. This would be the syntax used to apply a transition effect to a Web page object (called WebPage):

```
<DIV ID="WebPage" STYLE="position:Absolute">Exciting Web page!</div>
```

The **PARAM** tag specifies which transition effect is to be used:

```
<OBJECT ID=TransOne
CLASSID="CLSID:F0F70103-6A8F-11d0-BD28-00A0C908DB96">
<PARAM NAME="Transition" VALUE="0">
</OBJECT>
```

Additional ActiveX Multimedia Controls

In addition to the previously mentioned controls, IE 4 has several more multimedia controls that complement DHTML:

- *Sequencer*—Adds a master timing mechanism to Web page activities
- *Mixer*—Dynamically mixes and plays .wav audio files
- *Path*—Animates and repositions other Web page controls
- *Sprite*—Uses a sequence of image files to create animations

Shockwave And DHTML

Macromedia's Shockwave plug-in was a major addition to the Web when it debuted a few years ago. Interestingly, many of Shockwave's multimedia advances—streaming content, interactive graphics, and others—have now been duplicated in DHTML. But Shockwave's presence on Web pages is significantly more restricted than DHTML's; by avoiding the limitation of the **EMBED** area, DHTML allows designers to infuse an entire Web page with multimedia, not just a partitioned portion of a page.

As we're writing this, Shockwave Director is in the final stages of integrating its capabilities with DHTML (intelligently so, because DHTML is poised to threaten the entire plug-in paradigm). Because Shockwave Director currently runs as a "windowed" plug-in with Netscape Navigator 4.0 and an ActiveX control with Internet Explorer on Windows 95 and Windows NT 4, Director movies always rise to the top of the page, floating over other layers. It's also not possible to have a transparent background with the **EMBED** tag, so Shockwave Director movies currently play in an opaque rectangle. Upcoming Shockwave releases will eliminate such behaviors: Macromedia is releasing windowless versions of Shockwave plug-ins/ActiveX controls to address the z-order layering, and these new versions will respect transparency, as well.

By pairing with DHTML, Shockwave will be able to expand its capabilities beyond the box it's been kept in on Web pages. Because Shockwave can receive events from and send messages to JavaScript, it's primed for integration with DHTML. Unlike DHTML, which blatantly discriminates against pre-4.0 browsers and Windows 3.1 and Macintosh 68K users, Shockwave supports both Macintosh 68K and Windows 3.1. It also can be used with Navigator 2 and 3 and Internet Explorer 3. Shockwave, therefore, is an option for imbuing pages with DHTML-like dynamism that functions with older browsers.

Shockwave Strategy: DHTML Extension

Once Shockwave and DHTML become true partners, Shockwave Director will try to extend DHTML's ability through its famous interactivity, along with these features:

- Streaming control
- Transitions
- Ink effects
- Media cue points for synchronizing playback

- Tempo control
- Sound control

Shockwave DHTML Syntax

The **OBJECT** tag is perfectly suited to using Shockwave Director on a page (because **OBJECT** contains an **EMBED** tag, Navigator can deal with it as well). Because layers are open to any HTML element, it's easy to place a Shockwave movie within a layer; just use an **OBJECT** or **EMBED** tag within the **DIV** tag to specify the layer. Because the movie is treated—and acts—like any other element, you can now reposition it on the page or affect its visibility. Here's an example of the code you can use to invoke a Shockwave Director movie:

```
<DIV ID="layMov">
Layered movie:
<EMBED SRC="movie.dcr" HEIGHT=200 WIDTH=500 NAME="my Movie">
additional images and text can be included here
</DIV>
```

To call methods with Shockwave, you have to specify the **NAME** attribute in either the **OBJECT** or **EMBED** tag. Naming your Shockwave movie in this way lets you use JavaScript to call methods. For example, in Internet Explorer you can refer to the Shockwave movie in this way

```
myMovie.Stop();
```

whereas in Netscape Navigator, you use this type of code:

```
document.myMovie.Stop();
```

Although you can make the methods that you call in Shockwave movies function independently of a layer's action, it's not possible to make a movie override a layer's formatting.

An Interview With DHTML Designer Jeff Rule

Jeff Rule is a Web developer for the Discovery Channel who specializes in Internet Explorer 4.0 implementation. At his DHTML Demo site (**www.ruleweb.com/dhtml/**), he has created examples of DHTML content that showcase DHTML's powers for the Discovery folks. The last two projects in the Practical Guide profile Jeff's work.

You've been working with Web technology since its inception. How do the capabilities of DHTML affect your design?
I originally came out of a CD-ROM development background before getting into Web design. The static nature of early Web design was a real limitation to dynamic storytelling. With Dynamic HTML we finally have the tools to do this type of interactive storytelling in today's bandwidth, which is important, because viewers who have been raised on TV and CD-ROM have a higher expectation level than former generations. However, higher bandwidth development also means more work preparing more content for more immersive experiences. Rapid development tools, such as mBed Interactor and Macromedia's Dreamweaver, are needed to speed up production. Companies such as Macromedia must port tools such as Director, Authorware, and Flash to this new environment to give us the capabilities of Shockwave without the plug-ins.

What do you find to be some of DHTML's most useful implementations?
The new document object model that allows dynamic updating of Web pages is very compelling. Being able to change text or graphics on a page without loading a new page allows for more fluid and natural storytelling. DHTML gives us the ability to move from page-based static presentations to a continuous flow of information. Even when a new page must be loaded, Dynamic HTML offers a range of transitions and filters to ease the change. Animation is the feature I have found most compelling to this point. DHTML allows you to break out of the static positioning on the page and move the graphics around. Combined with animated GIFs or other animated objects, this allows for realistic character creation.

Do you have tips for creating DHTML content that works for both IE and Navigator?
Cross-platform development is difficult at this time. I recommend building separate pages that can take advantage of the best capabilities of each. By compromising, you dilute the power of this new technology. If possible, use JavaScript to load separate pages or, even better, use a server-side solution to separate browsers. I believe that the Internet Explorer document object model is more powerful and will be adopted in the future by the standards boards.

At your home page (www.ruleweb.com), you warn TV to look out for its audience; do you predict that DHTML's dynamism will attract more "watchers" to the Web?
I look for the Web to become more like CD-ROMs. Web sites will not be as page-based as they are today; the content will occur on one page with occasional transfers to new areas. These transfers will be smooth with transitions that feel natural, not like the abrupt changes you get on the Web today. This style will

translate better into a show-based format. Interactive TV proved technologically impossible; it was too much infrastructure to put in one place at one time. The Web will grow up, through increments in bandwidth, to become what we wanted Interactive TV to be. I think the convergence of TV and the Web is inevitable and will be accelerated by Microsoft's purchase of WebTV. I just hope that the Web doesn't become "millions of channels with nothing on."

Practical Guide To Graphics With DHTML

- Making A Browser Warning Exploiting Visibility: Do's Decahedron
- Creating Effective Transitions
- Animation
  - Appropriate Animation Use
  - Creating Animation
- A Gallery Of Layers
- Minimizing Link Lag With Client-Side Image Maps
- Unleashing A Spin Vector
- Making A Sequence/Fade

There are a few courtesies to observe when you're experimenting with the graphical powers of DHTML (and using Web site visitors as crash-test dummies). First, if you want your content to reach a broad audience, test it in both Navigator and Internet Explorer; also, test with pre-4.0 browsers to see how they display your content. When you have a download that takes more than 30 seconds on a 28.8Kbps modem (or is larger than 50K), it's also a good idea to add a download message, such as, "We appreciate your patience as our 75K file downloads. Once this file has downloaded, expect no more delays!" In addition, make a browser warning.

Making A Browser Warning

Let's take a moment to recognize those unfortunate souls who won't be able to see your DHTML content because of their pre-4.0 browsers. Letting them know—through a kind error message, sandwiched between **NOLAYER** tags—and redirecting them to the Netscape or Microsoft sites is the best way to handle the situation. For example:

```
<body bgcolor="000000" text="cccccc" link="cc0000" vlink="cc0000"
onLoad="openGrid();">
<nolayer>
<h1><center>Sorry, you'll need a 4.0 browser to experience this site!
</center></h1>
<font size="+3">This page experiments with Netscape 4.0 layering features.
Please obtain the latest copy of <a href="http://home.netscape.com">
Netscape</a>.</font>
</nolayer>
</body>
```

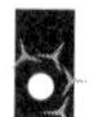

Exploiting Visibility: Do's Decahedron

At the Do's Decahedron site (see Figure 12.1), Antony Quintal of Fabric8 has put layers and **mouseOver** event handling to evocative use. By exploiting DHTML's ability to preload images, he's enhanced the experience of visiting the site. As you're visiting the opening page, pondering the fact that "the dodecahedron, a 12-faced 3D object of 'sacred' geometric shape, has been the fascination of philosophers, artists, musicians, and mathematicians alike," the images that we'll examine in a minute are preloading, through this code:

```
var pre1 = new Image();
pre1.src = "images/cube-large.gif";
var pre2 = new Image();
pre2.src = "images/octahedron-large.gif";
var pre3 = new Image();
pre3.src = "images/icosahedron-large.gif";
var pre4 = new Image();
pre4.src = "images/dodecahedron-large.gif";
```

When you enter the area where these shapes reside (see Figures 12.2 and 12.3), they are spinning, their red hue contrasted against the black background and the green grid underneath them. As you pass your mouse over each shape, a different quote about the shape (and Plato's belief about its essence) appears at the top of the page. Simultaneously, a much larger version of the shape appears to the left, rendered in a grayish-purple hue. The effect is instantaneous and engaging. As you can see from the code excerpt that follows, Antony has hidden the layers, and uses an **onMouseOver** to reveal the larger images. (See the original Do's Decahedron site, which also features a VRML version, at **www.fabric8.com/antony/index.html**.)

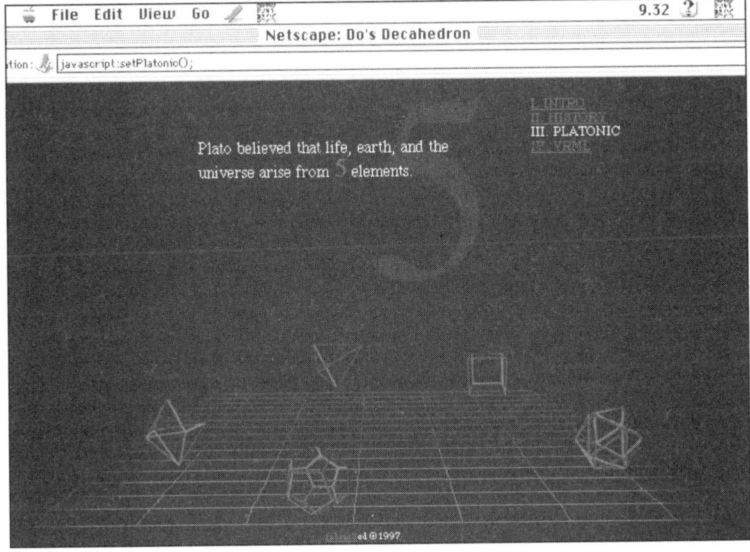

Figure 12.1

The grid for the primitives at Do's Decahedron.

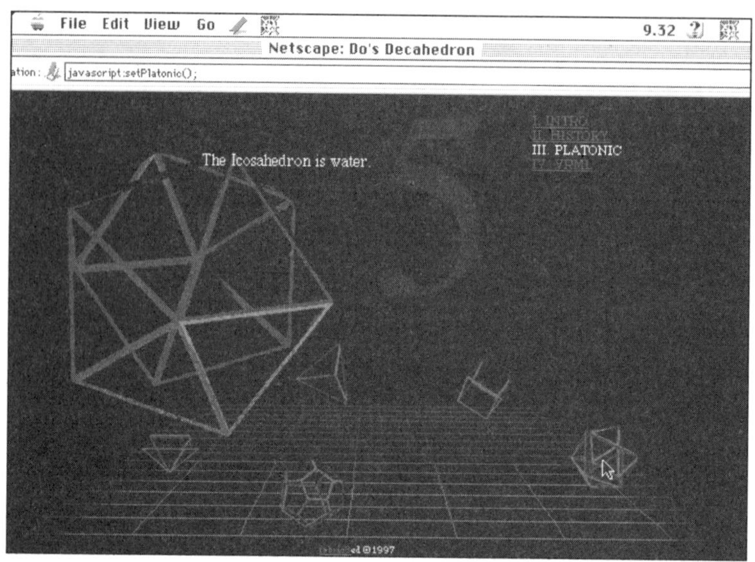

Figure 12.2

The icosahedron made visible at Do's Decahedron.

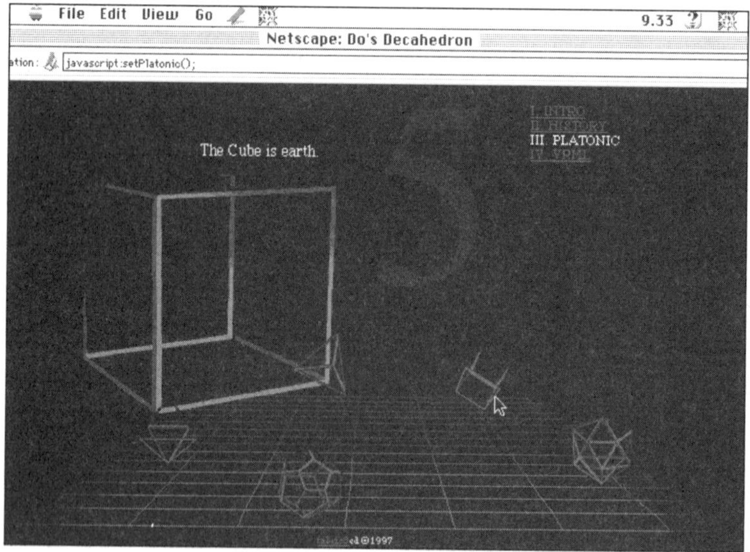

Figure 12.3

The cube made visible at Do's Decahedron.

```
<layer  name="platonic_text"
        top="12%"
        left="&{document.layers['solids'].left
document.layers['solids'].document.width/2;};"
        width="37%"
        visibility="hide">
        <p class="description">Plato believed that life, earth,
        and the universe arise from <span id="numbers"> 5</span>
        elements.</p>
</layer>
<layer  name="tetrahedron"
        top="50%"
        left="40%"
        width="65"
        height="65"
        visibility="hide"
        onMouseOver="revealSolid(this,'The Tetrahedron is fire.');"
        onMouseOut="hideSolid();">
        <img src="images/space.gif" width="65" height="65">
</layer>
<layer  name="cube"
        top="53%"
        left="60%"
        width="65"
        height="65"
        visibility="hide"
        onMouseOver="revealSolid(this,'The Cube is earth.');"
        onMouseOut="hideSolid();">
        <img src="images/space.gif" width="65" height="65">
</layer>
<layer  name="octahedron"
        top="64%"
        left="20%"
        width="65"
        height="65"
        visibility="hide"
        onMouseOver="revealSolid(this,'The Octahedron is air.');"
        onMouseOut="hideSolid();">
        <img src="images/space.gif" width="65" height="65">
</layer>
<layer  name="icosahedron"
        top="67%"
        left="75%"
        width="65"
        height="65"
        visibility="hide"
```

```
        onMouseOver="revealSolid(this,'The Icosahedron is water.');"
        onMouseOut="hideSolid();">
        <img src="images/space.gif" width="65" height="65">
</layer>
<layer  name="dodecahedron"
        top="75%"
        left="38%"
        width="65"
        height="65"
        visibility="hide"
        onMouseOver="revealSolid(this,'The Dodecahedron is heaven.');"
        onMouseOut="hideSolid();">
        <img src="images/space.gif" width="65" height="65">
</layer>
```

Creating Effective Transitions

One of the effects that DHTML can invoke, especially through Microsoft's ActiveX controls, is a sense of continuation between images and action. You can use these transitions to pack an extra effect as users enter and leave a page, as well as determine the time that the transition effects will take to unfold (usually several seconds). As a timesaving device, Table 12.1 is an official list of numbers that you can use to refer to the transition effect you desire.

Table 12.1 Transition effects.

Effect	Number
Box in	0
Box out	1
Circle in	2
Circle out	3
Wipe up	4
Wipe down	5
Wipe right	6
Wipe left	7
Vertical blinds	8

(continued)

Table 12.1 Transition effects *(continued)*.

Effect	Number
Horizontal blinds	9
Checkerboard across	10
Checkerboard down	11
Random dissolve	12
Split vertical in	13
Split vertical out	14
Split horizontal in	15
Split horizontal out	16
Strips left down	17
Strips left up	18
Strips right down	19
Strips right up	20
Random bars horizontal	21
Random bars vertical	22
Random	23

Here's how you would use these transitions for entering or exiting a page (placed between the **HEAD** tags) to create a circle in as you enter the page:

```
<META http-equiv="Page-Enter" content="RevealTrans (Duration=5, Transition=2)">
```

To create a circle out as you exit the page:

```
<META http-equiv="Page-Exit" content="RevealTrans (Duration=5, Transition=3)">
```

Animation

One of the most exciting things about DHTML is its ability to animate content. DHTML's animation abilities—in both Netscape and Microsoft's versions of the language—reduce the need to rely on animation technologies such as Java applets and Shockwave. Although animation looks complex and flashy, it's basically a matter of identifying which objects are to be animated, then putting the objects into action through a scripting language. The creative process of developing animated content that's truly worth viewing can actually be a much greater challenge than the act of setting animations into motion.

DHTML's ability to exert control over how animations appear gives designers greater graphical flexibility. The interactive nature of DHTML also allows users to affect the way that animations appear. With DHTML, animations can respond to user input in the same way as other objects on the page. Unlike the relatively rough type of animation that's created by animated GIFs, DHTML lets designers craft precise pathways of animated action by applying JavaScript or a similar scripting language. When you're using Microsoft's animation controls, you can also determine an animation's frame order, frames per second, etc.

Appropriate Animation Use

Just because DHTML endows designers with fresh animation abilities doesn't mean that animation should appear on every page. Animation is visually demanding for site visitors—when an animated image runs continuously within a viewer's peripheral vision, it's much more difficult for the viewer to concentrate on other content.

If you want your visitors to be able to read and remember information from the site, apply animation strategically and sparsely. These are some instances that would benefit from animated content:

- Indicating continuity in actions or transitions
- Pulling attention toward a specific space or object
- Showing how an image changes over time
- Emphasizing an object's 3D appearance
- Enriching the overall graphical presentation

Creating Animation

To create animation on a DHTML Web site, you can use JavaScript 1.2. The following example manipulates Netscape layers through an **animImage()** function and changes in the x, y variables:

```
//a JavaScript function to move the image
//
function animImage() {
        var image=document.layers["image"];
        if (image.left<0) {
                x=1;
                changeImage();
        }
        if (image.left>w-200) {
                x=-1;
                changeImage();
        }
        if (image.top<0) {
                y=1;
                changeImage();
        }
        if (image.top>h-200) {
                y=-1;
                changeImage();
        }
        image.moveBy(x,y);
        setTimeout("animImage()",10);
}
```

See the Fabric8 site examples on the CD-ROM for additional insight into animation.

A Gallery Of Layers

In this example, we look at a Web site that was originally created in HTML 3.0 and modified for DHTML. Nathan Jensen is a painter and muralist who crafted this viewing space, the illoviewer, to display his graphical works in a sequential setting. Although the HTML 3.0 version of the illoviewer looks superficially similar to the DHTML version, the important difference is in the amount of time that transpires as you experience the two versions. The HTML 3.0 illoviewer must query the server before it shows the next graphic (with a total of 19 graphics) and also before it can display the thumbnail graphic as a larger, more detailed picture; it therefore demands a significant amount of download time. With the DHTML version, implemented with layers and JavaScript, once the initial download is complete, the viewer can speed through the graphics almost instantaneously. The initial download itself demands less than a minute, so for those interested in viewing all 19 pictures, the time saved with the DHTML version is remarkable. Figures 12.4 through 12.6 show some of the different pictures that gallery visitors can click through using the illoviewer.

Figure 12.4

The illoviewer displays Nathan Jensen's paintings as JavaScripted, layered graphics.

Figure 12.5

Gallery visitors can click through the images much more quickly than in their previous HTML 3 version.

Figure 12.6

DHTML makes viewing Jensen's gallery a much more fluid experience.

The following code shows how JavaScript is used with layers in the illoviewer to produce a truly dynamic viewing experience. See the CD-ROM for the full code example:

```
<html>
<head>
  <title>experimental natespace(tm)</title>
</head>

 <body background="textur4.GIF" bgcolor="#330000" link="#330000"
  vlink="#330000" alink="#330000" topmargin="14" leftmargin="10" width="600">

  <LAYER id="illo" TOP="24" LEFT="142" WIDTH="315" ALIGN=CENTER ZINDEX="10"
   visibility="VISIBLE">

   <layer id="illopicture1"  top="156" left="172" width="73" height="73"
    visibility="HIDDEN"  zindex="30"><img src="sill3.GIF"  width="73"
    height="73" border="1"></layer>
   <layer id="illopicture2"  top="156" left="172" width="73" height="73"
    visibility="HIDDEN"  zindex="30"><img src="scom4.GIF"  width="73"
    height="73" border="1"></layer>
...
<layer id="illopicture19" top="156" left="172" width="73" height="73"
 visibility="HIDDEN" zindex="30"><img src="sill6.GIF" width="73" height="73"
 border="1"></layer>

   <table border="0" cellpadding="10" cellspacing="10">
    <tr>
```

```
   <td align="CENTER" valign="TOP" colspan="3"><img src="illview.GIF"
    width="148" height="33" border="0" alt="Illoviewer(tm)"></td>
  </tr>
  <tr>
   <td align="RIGHT" valign="MIDDLE"><a href="javascript:ShowPriorPic();">
   <img src="ibbut.GIF" width="37" height="37" border="0" alt="Back"></a></td>
   <td align="CENTER">
    <img src="sldtop.GIF" width="241" height="60" border="0"><br>
    <table border="0" cellpadding="1" cellspacing="1" width="100%">
     <tr>
      <td align="LEFT"><img src="sldleft.GIF" width="53" height="90"></td>
      <td align="RIGHT"><img src="sldrght.GIF" width="53" height="90"
       border="0"></td>
     </tr>
    </table>
    <img src="sldbot.GIF" width="241" height="60" border="0"><br>
    <a href="http://www.vcomm.com/nathan/main.htm"><img src="imbut.GIF"
     width="37" height="37" border="0" alt="Main"></a>
   </td>
   <td align="LEFT" valign="MIDDLE"><a href="javascript:{ShowNextPic();}">
   <img src="inbut.GIF" width="37" height="37" border="0" alt="Next"></a></td>
  </tr>
 </table>

</layer>

<layer top="390" left="10" ZINDEX="1">
 <table border="0" cellpadding="0" cellspacing="0"><tr><td nowrap>
  <font color="#FAEBD7" size="1"><b>
   <hr width="120" align="left" color="#FAEBD7">
   Graphical images, concept, and initial implementation Copyright (c) 1997
   by Nathan Jensen, All rights reserved<br>
   Dynamic HTML adaptation Copyright (c) 1997 by Christopher D. Brown, All
   rights reserved<br>
   The trademarks natespace<sup>tm</sup> and Illoviewer<sup>tm</sup> are
   the property of Nathan Jensen
  </b></font>
 </td></tr></table>
</layer>

<LAYER id="startup1" TOP="14" LEFT="290" ZINDEX="40" visibility="VISIBLE">
 <font color="#FAEBD7">Welcome to the</font>
</LAYER>
<LAYER id="startup2" TOP="84" LEFT="170" ZINDEX="40" visibility="VISIBLE">
 <table border="0" cellpadding="0" cellspacing="0"><tr>
 <td align="CENTER" nowrap>
  <font color="#FAEBD7">With this machine, you can peruse illustrations <br>
   created by <b>Nathan Jensen.</b></font>
```

```
  </td></tr></table>
 </LAYER>
 <LAYER id="startup3" TOP="218" LEFT="42" ZINDEX="40" visibility="VISIBLE">
  <font color="#FAEBD7">Prior picture</font>
 </LAYER>
 <LAYER id="startup4" TOP="218" LEFT="554" ZINDEX="40" visibility="VISIBLE">
  <font color="#FAEBD7">Next picture</font>
 </LAYER>
 <LAYER id="startup5" TOP="360" LEFT="270" ZINDEX="40" visibility="VISIBLE">
  <font color="#FAEBD7">Nathan's Home page</font>
 </LAYER>

</body>

<script language="javascript">

 var CurLayer=1;
 var NLayers=19;
 function ShowNextPic()
 {
    document.layers.startup1.visibility="hidden";
    document.layers.startup2.visibility="hidden";
    document.layers.startup3.visibility="hidden";
    document.layers.startup4.visibility="hidden";
    document.layers.startup5.visibility="hidden";
    document.layers.illo.visibility="visible";
    eval( 'document.layers.illo.layers.illopicture'
      +CurLayer+'.visibility="hidden"');
    if ( CurLayer >= NLayers )
       CurLayer = 1;
    else
       ++CurLayer;
    eval( 'document.layers.illo.layers.illopicture'
      +CurLayer+'.visibility="visible"');
 }
 function ShowPriorPic()
 {
    document.layers.startup1.visibility="hidden";
    document.layers.startup2.visibility="hidden";
    document.layers.startup3.visibility="hidden";
    document.layers.startup4.visibility="hidden";
    document.layers.startup5.visibility="hidden";
    document.layers.illo.visibility="visible";
    eval( 'document.layers.illo.layers.illopicture'
      +CurLayer+'.visibility="hidden"');
    if ( CurLayer < 2 )
       CurLayer = NLayers;
```

```
        else
          --CurLayer;
        eval( 'document.layers.illo.layers.illopicture'
          +CurLayer+'.visibility="visible"');
    }

</script>

</html>
```

Minimizing Link Lag With Client-Side Image Maps

Webreference.com's site is an excellent example of how using DHTML and JavaScript 1.2 can greatly increase a Web page's efficiency. If you were to use an image-swapping rollover with JavaScript 1.1 and the image object, the image rollover would require a total of 14 images and the browser would have to connect to the server to obtain each image. However, the speed and effect is greatly enhanced by JavaScript 1.2's capabilities and by simply creating two images—one of the highlighted style that shows when the mouse passes over the words and one of the normal text—you completely eliminate the server-client lag. Figures 12.7 and 12.8 show the two images that the site uses for the navigation map.

The first image serves as the default menu bar; the second image, positioned over the first, is rendered invisible. When the user's mouse passes over the first image's links, the corresponding part of the second image is clipped and becomes visible, and *voilà*, the rollover effect ensues (see Figure 12.9).

Figure 12.7

Webreference.com's plain menu bar.

Figure 12.8

Webreference.com's enhanced menu bar.

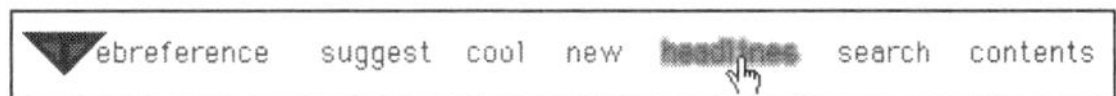

Figure 12.9

The fully sensitized menu.

The client-side image map is divided into links according to the measurements shown in Figure 12.10.

By adding the following JavaScript and **OnMouseOver/OnMouseOut** event handlers, the map responds to the user's mouse actions:

```
<DIV ID="elMenu">
     <DIV ID="elMenuUp">
       <IMG SRC="menu.gif" USEMAP="#mpMenu" WIDTH=468 HEIGHT=18 BORDER=0>
     </DIV>
     <DIV ID="elMenuOver">
       <SCRIPT LANGUAGE="JavaScript">document.write(secondIm)</SCRIPT>
     </DIV>
</DIV>
   .
   .
   .
<MAP NAME="mpMenu">
  <AREA SHAPE="RECT" COORDS="0,0 116,18" HREF="/"
   onMouseOver="mapOver(1,true)" onMouseOut="mapOver(1,false)">
  <AREA SHAPE="RECT" COORDS="117,0 181,18" HREF="/cgi-bin/suggest.cgi"
   onMouseOver="mapOver(2,true)" onMouseOut="mapOver(2,false)">
  <AREA SHAPE="RECT" COORDS="182,0 222,18" HREF="http://www.coolcentral.com"
   onMouseOver="mapOver(3,true)" onMouseOut="mapOver(3,false)">
  <AREA SHAPE="RECT" COORDS="223,0 263,18" HREF="/new/"
   onMouseOver="mapOver(4,true)" onMouseOut="mapOver(4,false)">
  <AREA SHAPE="RECT" COORDS="264,0 339,18" HREF="/headlines/"
   onMouseOver="mapOver(5,true)" onMouseOut="mapOver(5,false)">
  <AREA SHAPE="RECT" COORDS="340,0 397,18" HREF="/search.cgi"
   onMouseOver="mapOver(6,true)" onMouseOut="mapOver(6,false)">
  <AREA SHAPE="RECT" COORDS="398,0 468,18" HREF="/index2.html"
   onMouseOver="mapOver(7,true)" onMouseOut="mapOver(7,false)">
</MAP>
```

Unleashing A Spin Vector

This is the first example of Jeff Rule's work. The way Jeff has used the DirectAnimation ActiveX object with this spin vector example provides a lot of animation and rotation options in a compact download (see Figure 12.11). (To see it in action, go to **www.ruleweb.com/dhtml/Vector/vectorx.html**.)

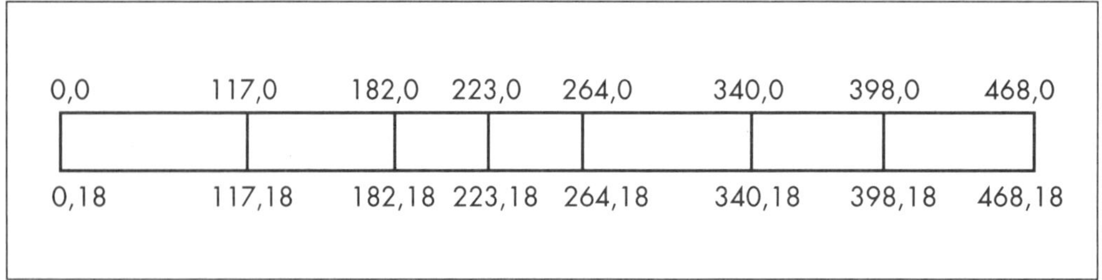

Figure 12.10

The measurements of the menu's links.

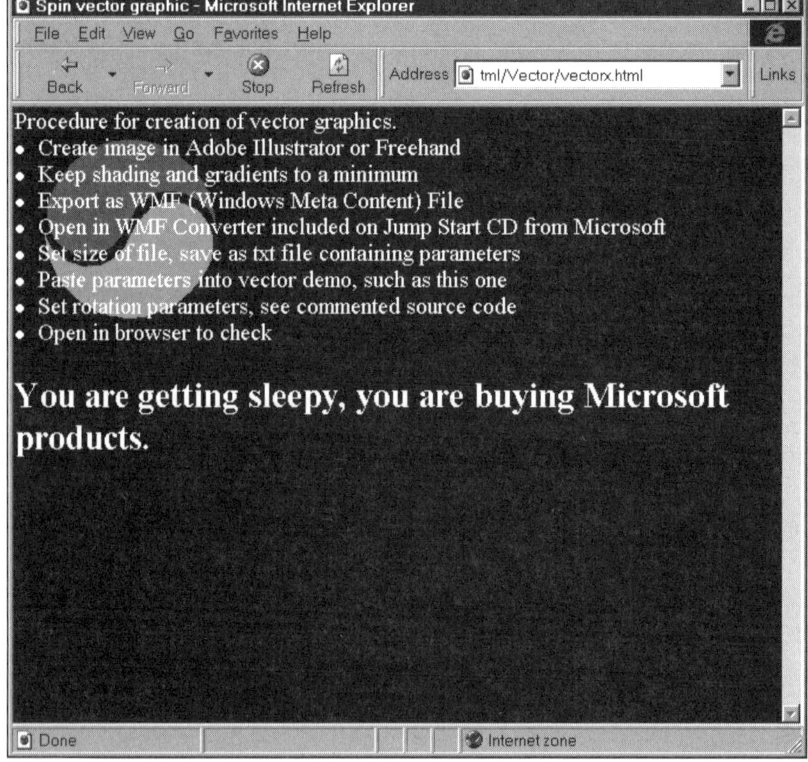

Figure 12.11

Jeff Rule's vector animation, using DirectAnimation ActiveX.

As you can see, this code example even gives you tips on creating vector animations in Internet Explorer 4.0:

```
<HTML>
<HEAD>
<TITLE>
Spin vector graphic
</TITLE>
<SCRIPT LANGUAGE="VBScript">

<!--
'Sets initial variables and letter starting positions

Sub Window_OnLoad()
        call SG1.Scale(0.50, 0.50, 0.50)
        call SG1.Rotate(0, 0, 0)

        RotateAll
end sub

'Sets rotation speed and behavior as well as creating loop
'The three numbers below control the rotation in the three axis
'The first # is the rotation around a horizontal axis
'The second # is around a vertical axis
'The third # is rotation clockwise
Sub RotateAll
        Call SG1.Rotate(0,0,-10)
        FILK = Window.SetTimeOut("Call RotateAll", 10, "VBScript")
End Sub
-->

</SCRIPT>

<style>
#style1 {
        visibility: show;
        position: absolute;
        top: 0;
        left: 0;
        z-index: 1;
}
</style>

</HEAD><BODY BGCOLOR="Black" TEXT="White">
<div id="style1">
Procedure for creation of vector graphics.<br>
<li>Create image in Adobe Illustrator or Freehand
```

```
<li>Keep shading and gradients to a minimum
<li>Export as WMF (Windows Meta Content) File
<li>Open in WMF Converter included on Jump Start CD from Microsoft
<li>Set size of file, save as txt file containing parameters
<li>Paste parameters into vector demo, such as this one
<li>Set rotation parameters, see commented source code
<li>Open in browser to check<br>
<h2>You are getting sleepy, you are buying Microsoft products.</h2>
</div>

<OBJECT id=SG1

STYLE="POSITION:ABSOLUTE; HEIGHT: 300; LEFT: -50; TOP: -50; WIDTH: 300;
ZINDEX: 0" CLASSID = "CLSID:369303C2-D7AC-11D0-89D5-00A0C90833E6">
<PARAM NAME="Line0001" VALUE="SetLineColor(0,0,0)">
<PARAM NAME="Line0002" VALUE="SetFillColor(255,0,0)">
<PARAM NAME="Line0003" VALUE="SetLineStyle(6)">
<PARAM NAME="Line0004" VALUE="Polygon(102,6,13,-1,7,-8,1,-23,-10,-31,-17,-36,
-24,-42,-35,-45,-44,-49,-54,-50,-62,-50,-70,-49,-78,-48,-88,-44,-97,-40,-105,
-35,-114,-27,-123,-21,-130,-15,-134,-8,-138,-1,-141,6,-143,14,-144,19,-145,25,
-145,40,-144,29,-147,21,-148,12,-149,3,-149,-5,-149,-13,-149,-21,-148,-29,
-147,-39,-144,-49,-142,-59,-138,-67,-134,-76,-129,-85,-124,-91,-119,-98,-113,
-105,-107,-111,-101,-116,-95,-121,-88,-126,-82,-131,-74,-134,-67,-138,-59,
-141,-51,-144,-42,-147,-34,-148,-25,-150,-15,-150,-7,-150,2,-150,10,-149,20,
-147,31,-145,40,-143,49,-140,56,-136,64,-133,71,-128,79,-123,87,-117,94,-112,
101,-106,107,-100,113,-95,117,-88,123,-81,127,-76,130,-70,133,-64,136,-59,137,
-50,139,-44,140,-37,140,-31,140,-23,139,-16,137,-9,134,-3,131,4,127,9,123,14,
118,19,112,23,105,26,99,29,91,31,83,32,75,32,67,31,58,29,50,26,42,22,35,18,28,
12,21)">
<PARAM NAME="Line0005" VALUE="SetFillColor(255,162,0)">
<PARAM NAME="Line0006" VALUE="Polygon(102,-7,-12,0,-
6,7,0,22,11,30,18,35,25,41,36,44,45,48,54,49,63,49,71,48,79,47,89,43,98,39,
106,34,115,26,124,20,130,14,135,7,139,0,142,-7,144,-15,145,-20,146,-26,146,
-41,145,-30,147,-22,149,-13,150,-4,150,4,150,12,150,20,149,28,148,38,145,48,
142,58,139,66,135,75,130,84,125,90,119,97,114,104,108,110,102,115,96,120,89,
125,83,130,75,133,68,137,60,140,52,143,43,146,35,147,26,149,16,149,8,150,-1,
149,-10,148,-20,146,-30,144,-39,142,-48,139,-55,135,-63,132,-70,127,-78,122,
-86,116,-93,111,-100,105,-106,99,-112,94,-116,87,-122,80,-126,75,-130,69,-132,
63,-135,58,-136,49,-138,43,-139,36,-139,30,-139,22,-138,15,-136,8,-133,2,-130,
-5,-126,-10,-122,-15,-117,-20,-111,-24,-105,-27,-98,-30,-90,-32,-83,-33,-74,
-33,-66,-32,-57,-30,-49,-27,-41,-23,-34,-19,-28,-13,-20)">
</OBJECT>

</BODY>
</HTML>
```

Making A Sequence/Fade

In this example, as with the previous example, the ActiveX objects are built into the browser and, therefore, don't require the user to download. The sepia-toned graphics of this example use absolute positioning in combination with VBScript to give the user an interestingly blended perspective of historical photographs. Note the transition effects that Jeff is using in the code. You can see the graphic shown in Figure 12.12 in action at **www.ruleweb.com/dhtml/Sequence/jeffsequencex.html**.

```
<HTML>
<HEAD>
<TITLE>Sequence</TITLE>
<SCRIPT LANGUAGE="VBSCRIPT">
<!--
```

Figure 12.12

A sequence/fade example.

```
Sub Window_onload()
	Call Seq("1").Play
End Sub

Sub Seq_OnInit()
	Call seq("1").at(1.000, "pic1_show", 1, 0.000, 1)
	Call seq("1").at(3.000, "pic2_show", 1, 0.000, 1)
	Call seq("1").at(6.000, "pic1_hide", 1, 0.000, 1)
	Call seq("1").at(8.000, "pic3_show", 1, 0.000, 1)
	Call seq("1").at(10.200, "pic2_hide", 1, 0.000, 1)
	Call seq("1").at(11.100, "pic3_hide", 1, 0.000, 1)

End Sub

Sub pic1_show()
	pic1.filters(0).apply()
	pic1.style.visibility = "visible"
	pic1.filters(0).play()
End Sub

Sub pic2_show()
	pic2.filters(0).apply()
	pic2.style.visibility = "visible"
	pic2.filters(0).play()
End Sub

Sub pic1_hide()
	pic1.filters(0).apply()
	pic1.style.visibility = "hidden"
	pic1.filters(0).play()
End Sub

Sub pic3_show()
	pic3.filters(0).apply()
	pic3.style.visibility = "visible"
	pic3.filters(0).play()
End Sub

Sub pic2_hide()
	pic2.filters(0).apply()
	pic2.style.visibility = "hidden"
	pic2.filters(0).play()
End Sub

Sub pic3_hide()
	pic3.filters(0).apply()
	pic3.style.visibility = "hidden"
	pic3.filters(0).play()
```

```
End Sub
-->

</SCRIPT>

<style>
#pic1 {
        position: absolute;
        top: 1;
        left: 1;
}

#pic2 {
        position: absolute;
        top: 150;
        left: 150;
}

#pic3 {
        position: absolute;
        top: 200;
        left: 300;
}
</style>

</HEAD>
<BODY topmargin="0" leftmargin="0" bgcolor="#FFFFFF">
<CENTER>

<IMG id="pic1" SRC="image2/1.jpg" WIDTH=300 HEIGHT=408 BORDER="0"
style="position: absolute; left: 100; top: 100; z-index: 1; visibility: hidden;
filter:blendTrans(duration=2.50)">

<IMG id="pic2" SRC="image2/2.jpg" WIDTH=300 HEIGHT=207 BORDER=0
style="position: absolute; left: 200; top: 150; z-index: 1; visibility: hidden;
filter:blendTrans(duration=1.4)">

<IMG id="pic3" SRC="image2/3.jpg" WIDTH=300 HEIGHT=238 BORDER=0
style="position: absolute; left: 350; top: 200; z-index: 1; visibility: hidden;
filter:revealTrans(duration=1.0,transition=5)">

<OBJECT ID="Seq" CLASSID="CLSID:B0A6BAE2-AAF0-11d0-A152-00A0C908DB96">
</OBJECT>

</CENTER>

</BODY>

</HTML>
```

Chapter 13

Arranging General Content

In this chapter, we explore the various methods of arranging your dynamic Web site. We examine some DHTML authoring tools and provide a hands-on approach to content arrangement.

Notes...

Chapter 13

Dynamic HTML is accompanied by new powers of precise control over object speed, motion, placement, and so on. When combined with Microsoft's DirectX tool set, DHTML's capabilities aggrandize, as we demonstrate through several examples in this chapter's Practical Guide. Although it's dangerously easy to exploit DHTML technology to make unpleasantly intense and overwhelming content, we've chosen examples—and included original audio and multimedia on the CD-ROM—that exemplify how DHTML can be sagely used to create effective Web content.

Using DHTML Authoring Tools

There are several authoring tools available for making DHTML content. The following sections explore a few of the offerings:

- *Dreamweaver*—You can produce DHTML content with Macromedia's Dreamweaver through its Beatnik plug-in, as well as an optimized version of the ever-popular BBEdit. See Macromedia's DHTML Zone at **www.dhtmlzone.com** for more information and a free beta download.

- *mBed Interactor*—mBed Interactor is a DHTML-upgraded version of the popular mBed Interactor graphics software. See **www.mbed.com** for additional information and a trial download.

- *ColdFusion*—ColdFusion Studio features two DHTML wizards for creating DHTML; it's also compatible with the HTML editor Homesite. Visual programming and database tools, as well as team development tools, are integrated into ColdFusion. See **www.coldfusion.com** for more information or to download.

Creating Clear Content

Despite what competitive computer industry pundits would have you believe, fast-paced content is not necessarily better or more effective. DHTML's animating abilities and rapid content delivery bring new considerations to Web use. Some factors that now need to be given more careful consideration through DHTML's increased sensitivity include:

- Considering how nondynamic users (and WebTV users) see your content
- Respecting the rhythm of the user experience
- Optimizing color for dynamic content
- Directing attention through dynamic paths
- Giving multimedia controls to the end user

Crafting Web content is increasingly demanding more skill from developers, a trend reflected by DHTML's more programming-oriented nature (especially when combined with DirectX). The Web itself contains thousands of references that can help you create effective, aesthetically pleasing content. See sites such as **www. developer.com** for design tips; projectcool has Microsoft DHTML developer resources at its site, along with a well-organized basic HTML tag reference (see **www.projectcool.com/developer/**). The increased use of scripting languages makes references such as Netscape's JavaScript documentation especially useful as well (**developer.netscape.com/library/documentation/communicator/jsguide/contents.htm**).

At **www.useit.com/alertbox/**, Jakob Nielsen writes a column called Alertbox. In the spring of 1997, he gave the following guidelines for writing for the Web, "Be succinct: write no more than 50 percent of the text you would have used in a hardcopy publication." In addition, he stated, "Write for scannability: don't require users to read long continuous blocks of text." Finally, "Use hypertext to split up long information into multiple pages."

These useful suggestions still apply to DHTML Web content. It's essential that you don't overwhelm visitors with excessively active DHTML, just because the technology now exists to do so. Here are some other sites that may aid you in your quest to create stellar DHTML:

- The HTML 4.0 validator—**validator.w3.org**
- The ultimate spatialized audio index—**www.dform.com/inquiry/spataudio.html**
- Pantone All About Color—**38.219.133.4/pantone/allaboutcolor/allaboutcolor.asp**
- Psychological color associations; this site evaluates colors' positive and negative associations—**www.nwnet.net/~sallyn/colors.html**

In the following sections, we examine some examples of sensitive and interesting DHTML programming. In the Practical Guide, we'll take a look at two new features in DHTML, the canvas mode and scriptlets.

An Interview With DHTML Designer Olivia Ongpin

At Fabric8 (**www.fabric8.com**), designer Olivia Ongpin adeptly demonstrates the panache that DHTML can add to a Web site. We've profiled Fabric8's work with layers in other chapters; in this chapter's Practical Guide, we take a look at Fabric8's recently developed online shopping arena and study the layout principles and techniques that the Fabric8 design applied to the site. We've also interviewed Ongpin about her DHTML experiences.

How have DHTML's capabilities affected your approach to Web design?
DHTML allows us to more effectively incorporate typography, complex layout, and layering in our design. Because it offers more elements, DHTML has the potential to enrich the graphical impact of a Web site. However, since the 4.0 browsers have so many more features than earlier ones, we were forced to build two versions of the I-Shoppe site (**www.fabric8.com/shoppe**)—quite tedious. So, our next goal for the site is to develop it in one "universal" version.

How did you decide what dynamic elements would be best used in Fabric8's DHTML I-Shoppe site?
Our long-term goal is to make Web sites that are like applications/environments unto themselves. It is important to us that the interface is engaging and enticing;

thus, features such as layering and JavaScript animations were a natural choice for the I-Shoppe site.

In addition, we wanted to use dynamic elements that would work in both Netscape and MSIE. Although both event models are extensive, the actual crossover is limited.

You've concentrated on Netscape DHTML content to this date; do you ever plan to feature Microsoft-specific DHTML content as well?
Actually, our latest sites are cross-browser. Because Netscape [Navigator] is our preferred browser, we optimize for it. However, we do test the sites in MSIE and modify our code to work under that browser.

Do you use authoring tools to create your DHTML?
We use authoring tools to some extent, but would like to use them more. For example, Macromedia's Dreamweaver is useful because much of the code is built-in, reducing the tedium of hand coding. Programs such as BBEdit and Homesite are also important for fine-tuning the code.

What advice do you have for designers starting out with Dynamic HTML?
I think that some designers are reluctant to learn DHTML because of the programming side of it. But, similar to HTML, once you're over the hurdle, programming DHTML can be just as creative as other types of design. DHTML pushes the limits of Web design and, as the creative environment develops, it will open up even more artistic possibilities.

Practical Guide To

Arranging General Content

- Netscape's Canvas Mode
- Using Scriptlets
- A Study In DHTML Layout: Fabric8's I-Shoppe
- Programming The Natespace Virtual Gallery
- Exploiting DirectX Controls Experimental Multimedia

Netscape's Canvas Mode

With the release of Navigator 4, Netscape offers developers the option of putting Web content inside a window minus the familiar borders, which offers increased space for content display. This option is called the "canvas mode," and is a feature of JavaScript 1.2. We've shown examples of the full-screen canvas mode through the book; Chapter 17's images from the Freefall Web site are a good example of how the canvas mode can be used.

In order to make the canvas mode appear within a page, use the following Java Script call:

```
window.open("my_page.html",
       "canvas_window","titlebar=no,left=0,top=0,outerWidth=screen_width,
       outerHeight=screen_height,alwaysRaised=yes")
```

To maintain proper security when you invoke the canvas mode, your JavaScript must be signed for security. For more information on signed JavaScripts, and signing tools, go to **developer.netscape.com/library/documentation/communicator/jssec/index.htm**.

Using Scriptlets

Scriptlets are being touted by Microsoft as a replacement for Java applets on Web pages. Scriptlets, which are nothing more than an HTML file containing a body and some script code, are essentially HTML files that can be nested inside other HTML pages. In this relationship, the Web page serves as the "container" and the scriptlet occupies a specific area of the page, as specified by the **<OBJECT>** tag. Scriptlets can accomplish many of the same multimedia effects as Java applets and Shockwave.

Scriptlets are HTML text, don't need to be registered or compiled, and can be easily reused and distributed. They can, however, only be used with Internet Explorer 4 and beyond, so whether you decide to use scriptlets depends on if you want visitors surfing with Netscape Navigator to be able to see your page content. In order to maintain security, scriptlets will only download to your computer if the server's zone isn't set to "high."

The body of a scriptlet represents the user interface. This body can be changed dynamically, and can be defined either on-the-fly or at the time of coding. It's necessary to include some scripting code within the source code of the scriptlet, in order to produce its multimedia effects. If you were to use the JScript public_description object to define a scriptlet's public interface, you could write the following code:

```
<script language="JScript">
public_description = new CreateScriptlet();
```

CreateScriplet would be the placeholder for the actual routine, and its content could be written like this:

```
function CreateScriptlet () {
  this.put_Text = put_Text;
  this.get_Text = get_Text;
  this.event_OnExpand = "";
```

You can also define a scriptlet's public interface by using the default interface description, which is a special naming convention. To do so, you would use the prefix "public" to make a symbol available from outside the scriptlet:

```
function public_get_Text
Subpublic_put_Text
Sub public_Expand
' events do not have to be declared
```

For additional information on scriplets, see the following pages at the Microsoft site: **www.microsoft.com/sitebuilder/featured/scriptlet.asp** and **www.microsoft.com/workshop/prog/ie4/scriptlet/faq-f.htm**.

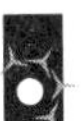

A Study In DHTML Layout: Fabric8's I-Shoppe

In the following section, we take a look at some of the ways DHTML has been used to craft the layout of Fabric8's excellent I-Shoppe online store. This store, nicknamed "a holiday site for hi-tech hipsters," entered the online realm for the 1997-1998 holiday season. In the following sections, we examine some of the layout techniques that the Fabric8 ensemble of designers incorporated to make the I-Shoppe site an effective and aesthetically rewarding online shopping experience.

As seen in Figure 13.1, when you initially enter the I-Shoppe site, you can choose between an "experimental DHTML" version and a "universal version." This opening page also gives the visitor the chance to go directly to the I-Shoppe Wishlist, where people post their holiday wish lists to provide friends and family with shopping tips (and convenient suggestions from the I-Shoppe site).

The tiny red lights (which are hard to see in Figure 13.1) demonstrate an effective use of dynamism at the I-Shoppe site, even before the DHTML kicks in. As they blink on and off, they add a subtle, although not distracting, sense of rhythm to the page.

Figure 13.1

The opening appearance of Fabric8's I-Shoppe site.

The lights blink as part of an inventive use of a table and the corresponding table row (**<TR>...</TR>**) and table data (**<TD>.../TD>**) tags, as seen in the following code fragment:

```
<tr align=center valign=middle>
      <td> </td>
      <td> </td>
      <td><img src="images/blink5.gif" width="8" height="8" border=0></td>
      <td> </td>
      <td> </td>
      <td> </td>
      <td><img src="images/blink2.gif" width="8" height="8" border=0></td>
      <td> </td>
      <td> </td>
      <td> </td>
      <td> </td>
      <td> </td>
</tr>
```

Through their varied color scheme, the shadows and multiple shadings of color used in the I-Shoppe logo, also seen in Figure 13.1, add an impression of movement, even though the logo itself remains static.

Figure 13.2 shows the I-Shoppe's main navigational center. When you enter the page shown in Figure 13.2, Java launches; the combination of Java and DHTML that's used on the ensuing I-Shoppe pages is what makes the site so heavily interactive. The head seen in Figure 13.2 is animated to jauntily travel around the page. Figure 13.3 shows another stop on the head's range of motion.

As you can see, the I-Shoppe has a menu bar that allows visitors to order products directly from the page that shows the item for sale. The site's system for placing orders relies heavily on Java, as demonstrated in the following code:

```
<script language="JavaScript">
<!--
//  all code is Copyright (C) 1996, 97, 98 fabric8
//  please don't just copy our code, improve it!
//  send suggestions to olivia ongpin, ooo@fabric8.com
//  cross browser code adapted from dreamweaver and netscape
//  ******************************************************
//  limited tech support on these scripts w/ every fabric8 purchase :)
//
var isDescription = isDetails = isZoom = isOrder = false;
var netscape = (document.layers) ? 1 : 0;
var range = "";
var styleObj = "";
if (!netscape) {
   range = ".all";
   styleObj = ".style";
}
var mac = (navigator.appVersion.indexOf("Mac") != -1) ? 1 : 0;
var isOrder = false;
var arrLayers = new Array();
function registerLayers(myLayers) { arrLayers = myLayers; }
function Product(productID, name, price, hasColor, hasFabric, hasSize) {
   this.productID = productID;
   this.name = name;
   this.price = price;
   this.hasColor = hasColor;
   this.hasFabric = hasFabric;
   this.hasSize = hasSize;
   this.visited = false;
   return this;
}
var shoppe = new Array();
<!-- xssi -->
shoppe[1] = new Product("F80100", "$ound Buys",14,0,0,0);
shoppe[2] = new Product("IC0100", "Incase Cell Phone Case",26,1,0,1);
shoppe[3] = new Product("F80200", "fabric8 Gift Certificate",25,0,0,0);
shoppe[4] = new Product("WB0100", "Wishbone Inflatable Pillows",24,1,0,0);
```

Figure 13.2

The I-Shoppe site's main navigational hub.

Figure 13.3

DHTML is used to animate this head so that it sometimes looks directly at you.

```
shoppe[5] = new Product("LM0100", "Lily Millinery Dollop Toppy Hat",55, 0,1,1);
shoppe[6] = new Product("PS0100", "Penelope Starr Zip Jacket",90,0,0,1);
shoppe[7] = new Product("PD0100", "Phobos & Deimos Salvation
   Sweater",140,0,0,1);
shoppe[8] = new Product("LA0100", "Labyrinth Astarte Coat",240,0,0,1);
shoppe[9] = new Product("SG0100", "Sui Generis Squats",60,1,0,1);
shoppe[10] = new Product("MA0100", "Manifesto Retro Plaid Shirt",60,0,0,1);
shoppe[11] = new Product("PS0200", "Penelope Starr Patrice Blouse",68,1,0,1);
shoppe[12] = new Product("PS0300", "Penelope Starr Charlotte Blouse",72,1,0,1);
shoppe[13] = new Product("KW0100", "Kweejibo Touchie Feelie Shirt",74,0,1,1);
shoppe[14] = new Product("MA0200", "Manifesto Flannel Man Shirt",94,0,0,1);
shoppe[15] = new Product("KW0200", "Kweejibo Triptych Shirt",94,0,0,1);
shoppe[16] = new Product("MA0300", "Manifesto Opaque Dress",120,0,0,1);
shoppe[17] = new Product("AJ0100", "American Junkies Cabbie Hat",20,1,0,1);
shoppe[18] = new Product("AJ0200", "American Junkies Player Wallet",10,0,0,0);
shoppe[19] = new Product("AJ0300", "American Junkies Basketball
   Jersey",40,1,0,1);
shoppe[20] = new Product("KS0100", "Kingsize Record Bag",78,0,1,0);
shoppe[21] = new Product("LU0100", "Luminations Yayo! Lamp",55,0,1,0);
shoppe[22] = new Product("F80101", "Future Primitive",14,0,0,0);
shoppe[23] = new Product("F80102", "Terbo Ted",14,0,0,0);
shoppe[24] = new Product("F80103", "Thievery Corporation",14,0,0,0);
shoppe[25] = new Product("F80104", "Audio Alchemy 2",14,0,0,0);
<!- end xssi ->

function Order(product,quantity,size,color,fabric) {
   this.product = product;
   this.quantity = quantity;
   this.size = size;
   this.color = color;
   this.fabric = fabric;
   return this;
}
var cart = new Array;
function orderIt(form, productID) {
   var strProduct = "", strMessage = "";
   var index,quantity,size,color,fabric,subtotal;
   var incomplete = false;
   if (!versionCheck()) incomplete = true;
   if (form == null) {
      // is this ugly or what? looking for a better solution.
      // please email us. thanks!
      var strHref = window.fraStage.location.href;
      if (strHref.indexOf("home") != -1) {
         alert("Please select an item in our catalogue.\n\nThen press this
               button, silly\n\n\t 8)");
         incomplete = true;
      }
      if (!incomplete) form = (netscape) ?
```

```
window.fraStage.document.layers.lyrOrder.document.forms[0] :
window.fraStage.document.forms[0];
      isOrder = (netscape) ? (window.fraStage.document.layers.lyrOrder.
      visibility == "visible") : (window.fraStage.document.all.lyrOrder.
      style.visibility == "visible");
      if (!incomplete && !isOrder) {
         strLayer = (netscape) ? "window.fraStage.document.layers" :
         "window.fraStage.document.all";
         for (var i = 0; i < arrLayers.length; i++) eval(strLayer + "." +
         arrLayers[i] + styleObj + ".visibility = 'hidden'");
         eval(strLayer + ".lyrOrder" + styleObj + ".visibility = 'visible'");
         isOrder = true;
      }
      productID = strHref.substring(strHref.indexOf("_") + 1,
      strHref.indexOf("_") + 7);
   }
   if (!incomplete) index = searchProducts(productID);
   if (!incomplete && index >= shoppe.length) {
      alert("This item was not found in our catalogue.\n\nWe suspect foul
            play\n\nPlease alert the authorities");
      incomplete = true;
   }
   if (!incomplete && productID.indexOf("F80100") != -1) {
      incomplete = isComplete(form, "cd");
      if (!incomplete) index = searchProducts(returnSelection(form.cd));
   }
   if (!incomplete && productID.indexOf("IC") != -1) {
      if(!incomplete && returnSelection(form.size) == null) {
         alert("\nPlease select a cell phone model.");
         incomplete = true;
      }
   }
   if (!incomplete && shoppe[index].hasFabric) incomplete = isComplete(form,
       "fabric");
   if (!incomplete && shoppe[index].hasSize) incomplete = isComplete(form,
       "size");
   if (!incomplete && shoppe[index].hasColor) incomplete = isComplete(form,
       "color");
   if (!incomplete && form.quantity.value == "") {
      alert ("Please enter a quantity");
      incomplete = true;
   }
   if (!incomplete) {
      strProduct = shoppe[index].name;
      quantity = parseInt(form.quantity.value);
      size = (shoppe[index].hasSize) ? returnSelection(form.size) : null;
      color = (shoppe[index].hasColor) ? returnSelection(form.color) : null;
      fabric = (shoppe[index].hasFabric) ? returnSelection(form.fabric) : null;
```

```
      cart[cart.length] = new Order(shoppe[index], quantity, size, color,
        fabric);
      subtotal = quantity * parseInt(shoppe[index].price);
      strMessage = "\n\"" + strProduct + "\" has been added to your gift
        collection.\n\nQuantity:\t\t" + quantity;
      if (size != null) strMessage += "\nSize:\t\t" + size;
      if (color != null) strMessage += "\nColor:\t\t" + color;
      if (fabric != null) strMessage += "\nFabric:\t\t" + fabric;
      strMessage += "\nPrice:\t\t" + "US$" + subtotal + ".00";
      strMessage += "\n\nTo submit your order, select \"checkout\".";
      alert(strMessage);
   }
}
function searchProducts(productID) {
   for (var i = 1; i < shoppe.length; i++) if (shoppe[i].productID ==
        productID) break;
   return i;
}
function isComplete(form, strElement) {
   var incomplete = false;
   if(returnSelection(form[strElement]) == null) {
      alert("\nPlease select a " + strElement + ".");
      incomplete = true;
   }
   return incomplete;
}
function deleteOrder(i) {
   if(confirm("Are you sure you want to delete this " + cart[i].product.name
      + "?")) {
      cart[i] = null;
      createNewCart();
      window.fraStage.location.href="dyn_checkout.html";
   }
}
```

The I-Shoppe also exploits DHTML for interactive effects. Note how "checkout" swells through the use of the **MouseOver** event in Figure 13.3.

Figure 13.4 shows an example of how DHTML is used to let visitors evaluate I-Shoppe products from different perspectives. The page for the Yayo! Lamp by Lumniations, like many of the other I-Shoppe pages, includes a selection called "More Pics and Tricks." When More Pics and Tricks is selected, an alternate view of the Yayo! lamp pops up. The use of DHTML here allows the new page to load instantly, because the images used in More Pics and Tricks have been preloaded. Figure 13.5 shows the More Pics and Tricks showcase for the Yayo! lamp.

Figure 13.4

The initial appearance of the Yayo! Lamp by Luminations page.

Programming The Natespace Virtual Gallery

In the subsequent section, we take a step-by-step overview of how key components of the Natespace code were written to make Natespace viewable for both browsers, and examine its use of Netscape's layer model and Microsoft's DirectAnimation. We also explain how the sound, rendered as MIDI, is scripted to function with the content.

We have used Natespace, artist Nathan Jensen's virtual gallery, as an example in several other chapters, particularly 11 and 17. For that reason, and because we include the Natespace virtual gallery in its entirety on the CD-ROM, we won't reproduce Natespace's images here.

1. Upon entering Natespace, you encounter a warning message about the large download. In addition to transitioning from the "loading" display to the initial display, the **StartItUp** function starts the Natespace music at the appropriate time, i.e., after the layers are loaded:

Figure 13.5

Yayo! Lamp's display when More Pics and Tricks is selected.

```
<body onload="StartItUp();">

<script LANGUAGE="javascript">
    function StartItUp()
    {
        eval( strBase+'loading'+strStyle+'visibility="hidden"' );
        eval( strBase+'gal'+iCur+strStyle+'visibility="visible"' );
        if ( bIsNS )
            DeltaMusic();
    }
</script>
```

2. This layer, which reconciles differences between the Microsoft and Netscape models, is set to invisible once the whole page has loaded:

```
<div id="loading" class="cssload">
<layer>
<div class="rinner">
 <table border="1" bgcolor="#000000" cellpadding="0"
    cellspacing="0" WIDTH="432"><tr>
     <td><img src="sp1x1t.gif" border="0" width="1" height="288"></td>
```

```
      <td align="center" valign="middle"><H2>Loading ...</h2>
       Estimated 3 minutes with a 28.8 Modem </td>
     </tr></table>
</div>
</layer>
</div>
```

3. The music layer not only reconciles the Microsoft and Netscape layer differences, it also addresses radically different audio approaches. Netscape seems to require that all sounds are embedded and allowed to load before our LiveConnect workaround will function. By using Microsoft's DAViewer to implement DirectAnimation, we also create Microsoft audio:

```
<div id="music" class="cssload" visibility="hidden">
<layer>
<div class="rinner">
 <EMBED SRC="walk1.mid" HIDDEN="TRUE" AUTOSTART="FALSE">
 <EMBED SRC="walk2.mid" HIDDEN="TRUE" AUTOSTART="FALSE">
 <EMBED SRC="walk3.mid" HIDDEN="TRUE" AUTOSTART="FALSE">
 <EMBED SRC="cass.mid"  HIDDEN="TRUE" AUTOSTART="FALSE">
 <OBJECT ID="DAViewer"
  CLASSID="CLSID:B6FFC24C-7E13-11D0-9B47-00C04FC2F51D">
 </OBJECT>
</div>
</layer>
</div>
```

4. Variations of the code lines below are used for each room of the gallery:

```
<div id="gall" class="csshall">
   <layer>
   <div class="rinner" align="center">
    <img SRC="gal1.jpg" WIDTH="396" HEIGHT="288"
     USEMAP="#map1" ISMAP BORDER="0"><p>
    <map NAME="map1">
     <area HREF="javascript:ShowPic('pai1.gif');" SHAPE="polygon"
      COORDS="31,146 55,146 55,90 31,84 31,146">
     <area HREF="javascript:ShowPic('pai2.gif');" SHAPE="polygon"
      COORDS="68,106 97,110 97,142 68,142 68,106">
     <area HREF="javascript:ShowPic('pai3.gif');" SHAPE="polygon"
      COORDS="97,184 131,184 189,89 182,78 121,96 97,184">
     <area HREF="javascript:ShowPic('pai4.gif');" SHAPE="polygon"
      COORDS="201,133 221,138 221,93 203,99 201,133">
     <area HREF="javascript:Walk(2);" onmouseover="Walk(2)"
      SHAPE="polygon"
      COORDS="137,184 191,95 191,200 141,208 137,184">
     <area HREF="javascript:Walk(10);" onmouseover="Walk(10)"
```

```
        SHAPE="rect" COORDS="257,1 350,227">
      </map>
    </div>
    </layer>
</div>
```

5. In the body itself, the Seq object is added to support the crossfade effects:

```
<object ID="Seq"
 CLASSID="CLSID:B0A6BAE2-AAF0-11d0-A152-00A0C908DB96">
 </object>
 </body>
 <script LANGUAGE="javascript">
```

6. The **playAudio** function illustrates the brute force workaround for Netscape—blast a new **EMBED** into the layer with appropriate parameterization. Were LiveConnect more reliably available, something like the DirectAnimation **SwitchTo** would be used:

```
function playAudio( iFile )
{
    if ( bIsNS )
    {
        document.layers.music.document.open('text/html');
        document.layers.music.document.write
        ('<EMBED SRC="' + rgstrMusic[iFile] +
         '" HIDDEN="TRUE" LOOP="TRUE" AUTOSTART="TRUE">');
        document.layers.music.document.close();
    }
    else
        behMusic.SwitchTo( rgMusic[iFile] );
}
```

7. Stopping audio is a matter of playing silence:

```
function stopAudio()
{
    if ( bIsNS )
    {
        document.layers.music.document.open('text/html');
        document.layers.music.document.write('');
        document.layers.music.document.close();
    }
    else
        behMusic.SwitchTo( dav.Silence );
}
```

8. **DeltaMusic()** and **DeltaMusicOn()** control how songs are automatically cycled with silence separating them. As you can see in the following code, the special song that's scripted to play in gallery 10 makes things a little messy:

```
function DeltaMusicOn()
{
    if ( iCurMusic != iNewMusic )
    {
        iCurMusic = iNewMusic;
        playAudio( iCurMusic );
    }
    setTimeout( 'DeltaMusic();', iMusicDurSeconds * 1000 );
}
function DeltaMusic()
{
    if ( iCur == iSpecialSong )
        iNewMusic = nSongs;
    else
    {
        switch ( iNewMusic = iCurMusic + 1 )
        {
        case 1:
        case 2:
            break;
        default:
            iNewMusic = 0;
            break;
        }
    }
    if ( iCurMusic != iNewMusic )
        stopAudio();
    setTimeout( 'DeltaMusicOn();', 2 * 1000 );
}
```

9. Turning layers on and off is, of course, old hat to us now. Support for the **CloseUp** layer, Netscape/Microsoft object models, and Microsoft's transition effects are all demonstrated:

```
function Walk( iNext )

   if ( bCloseUp )
       RestoreGallery();
   else
   {
       if ( bIsNS )
       {
```

```
            eval( strBase+'gal'+iCur+strStyle+'visibility="hidden"' );
            eval( strBase+'gal'+iNext+strStyle+'visibility="visible"' );
        }
        else if ( !bTransActive )
        {
            bTransActive = true;
            eval(
          'document.all.gal'+iCur+'.style.filter="blendTrans(duration=1.00)"'
);
             eval(
          'document.all.gal'+iNext+'.style.filter="blendTrans(duration=1.00)"'
);
             strTransOld = 'document.all.gal'+iCur;
             strTransNew = 'document.all.gal'+iNext;
             Seq("1").Play();
         }
         iCur = iNext;
    }
    if ( iCur == iSpecialSong || (iCur != iSpecialSong && iCurMusic == nSongs)
)
        DeltaMusic();
}
function StepBack()
{
    if ( (i = iCur - 1) < 1 )
        i = iCurMax;
    Walk( i );
}
function StepForward()
{
    if ( (i = iCur + 1) > iCurMax )
        i = 1;
    Walk( i );
}
function ShowPic( strUrl )
{
    bCloseUp = true;
    eval( strBase+'gal'+iCur+strStyle+'visibility="hidden"' );
    eval( strBase+'closeup'+strStyle+'visibility="visible"' );
    strLayer = '<table border="0" bgcolor="#000000" cellpadding="0" ' +
        'cellspacing="0" WIDTH="432"><tr>' +
        ' <td><img src="sp1x1t.gif" border="0" width="1" height="288"></td>' +
        ' <td align="center" valign="middle"><a ' +
        ' HREF="javascript:RestoreGallery();"><img SRC="' + strUrl +
        '" BORDER="0"></a></td>' +
        '</tr></table>';
```

```
    if ( bIsNS )
    {
        document.layers.closeup.document.open('text/html');
        document.layers.closeup.document.write( strLayer );
        document.layers.closeup.document.close();
    }
    else
        document.all.closeup.innerHTML = strLayer;
}
function RestoreGallery()
{
    bCloseUp = false;
    eval( strBase+'closeup'+strStyle+'visibility="hidden"' );
    eval( strBase+'gal'+iCur+strStyle+'visibility="visible"' );
}
function seq_done()
{
    bTransActive = false;
}
function ShowNewPic()
{
    eval( strTransNew + '.filters(0).apply()' );
    eval( strTransNew + '.style.visibility = "visible"' );
    eval( strTransNew + '.filters(0).play()' );
}
function HideOldPic()
{
    eval( strTransOld + '.filters(0).apply()' );
    eval( strTransOld + '.style.visibility = "hidden"' );
    eval( strTransOld + '.filters(0).play()' );
}
```

10. Finally, here is the script that runs as the page loads. Nothing eventful happens here until the setup for DirectAnimation sounds:

```
var bCloseUp = false;
var iCur = 0;
var iCurMax = 10;
var strTransOld = "";
var strTransNew = "";
var bTransActive = false;
var iMusicDurSeconds = 5 * 60;
var iSpecialSong = 10;
var nSongs = 3;
var iCurMusic = Math.floor( (nSongs - 0.02) * Math.random() );
var rgstrMusic = new Array( 'walk1.mid',
```

```
    'walk2.mid', 'walk3.mid', 'cass.mid' );
var rgMusic = new Array();

bIsNS = (navigator.userAgent.indexOf ("MSIE") == -1);
if ( bIsNS )
{
    strBase = 'document.layers.';
    strStyle = '.';
}
else
{
    strBase = 'document.all.';
    strStyle = '.style.';
```

11. There are several approaches that are viable for use with DirectAnimation sounds. For example, it's possible to string all of the sounds together and switch them with an application-triggered event. Using modifiable behaviors makes it easier to show Netscape and Microsoft techniques side by side:

```
dav = DAViewer.PixelLibrary;
rgMusic[0] = dav.ImportSound( rgstrMusic[0] ).Sound.Loop();
rgMusic[1] = dav.ImportSoundAsync ( rgstrMusic[1], dav.Silence ).Sound.Loop();
rgMusic[2] = dav.ImportSoundAsync( rgstrMusic[2], dav.Silence ).Sound.Loop();
rgMusic[3] = dav.ImportSoundAsync( rgstrMusic[3], dav.Silence ).Sound.Loop();
behMusic = dav.ModifiableBehavior( rgMusic[iCurMusic] );
DAViewer.Sound = behMusic;
DAViewer.Start();
DeltaMusic();
}
 </script>
```

12. This bit of VBScript could have been rewritten in JavaScript; here, it is Microsoft-only and potentially quirky:

```
 <script LANGUAGE="vbscript">
    Sub Seq_OnInit()
        Call seq("1").at(0.500, "ShowNewPic", 1, 0.000, 1)
        Call seq("1").at(1.000, "HideOldPic", 1, 0.000, 1)
        Call seq("1").at(2.000, "seq_done", 1, 0.000, 1)
    End Sub
 </script>
</html>
```

Exploiting DirectX Controls For Experimental Multimedia

We've created a multimedia setting of one of C.C. Sanders' musical compositions, Silent Lucidity, to demonstrate how Microsoft's powerful and seductive DirectX Controls can push Web content into the next circle of artistic possibility. With such strongly developed authoring tools, there is little question that Microsoft's DHTML/DirectX strategy will become ubiquitous not only in the online realm, but across Microsoft's global product line (including in its new favorite product, content).

The virtual multimedia version of Silent Lucidity was created by C.C. Sanders, Christopher D. Brown, and Virigina Brown, using a Yamaha Diskclavier, a Roland synthesizer, a Turtle Beach board, a Studio 4 MIDI controller, and Opcode's Studio Vision Pro sequencing software, as well as Cakewalk sequencing software. The original MIDI was played by C.C. Sanders on the Yamaha Diskclavier, an acoustic upright piano with MIDI capabilities, and lightly edited through Studio Vision Pro and Cakewalk.

Figures 13.6 through 13.9 show the sequence of images that unfold to meld with Silent Lucidity's music (invoked through DirectAnimation controls). The images used for the setting of Silent Lucidity, shown in Figures 13.6 through 13.9 as well as on the

Figure 13.6

The mandala moves in a DirectAnimation path across the background of swirls.

Figure 13.7

DirectX is used to position the mandala in a new place on its continuing path.

CD-ROM, were scanned from everyday items as varied as scarves and checkbook covers, then organized through the storyboard process to complement the piece's lyric.

Silent Lucidity intentionally unfolds in a slow and evocative manner. Although DirectX controls could easily permit a barrage of extremely intense, fast-paced images to accompany the piece, we decided to highlight the more hypnotic side of DirectX's capabilities, and therefore created a setting that would allow the viewer to experience the work's music, words, and images at a deliberately relaxed pace. DirectX's ability to control the way that multimedia unfolds at a precise level was extremely valuable in this piece, because the lyrics needed to be timed by the second to correspond to the music. In order to make each line of the lyric, organized in a text array, emerge on the screen with the correct bar of music, we took timings from the MIDI file and matched them to the corresponding code (see this book's CD-ROM for the full code). When the verse ends and the chorus begins, DirectX is used to make the background image change in exact synchronization with the music's progression, as depicted in Figure 13.9.

This level of exact multimedia control is what makes DirectX so appealing for Web developers. Netscape's development tools for audio and multimedia on this advanced level simply pale compared to Microsoft's, especially considering Microsoft's strategy

Figure 13.8

DirectX is used to make the mandala perform a 3D rotation.

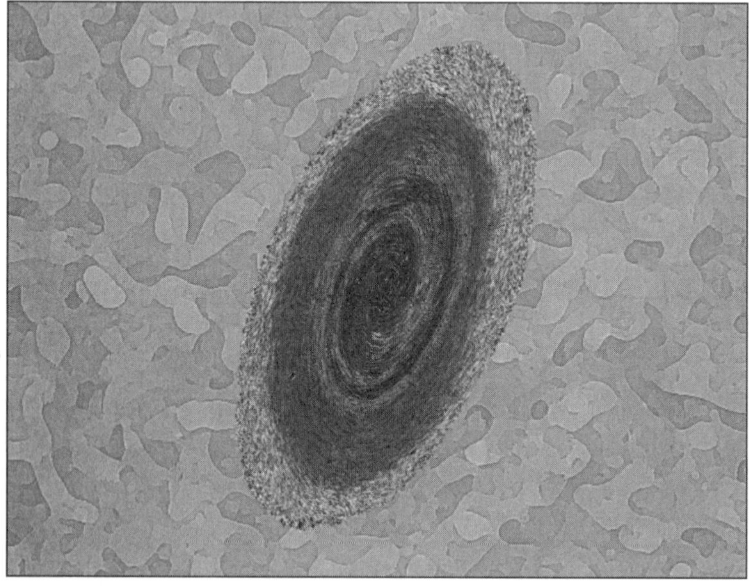

Figure 13.9

The circular whorl of color that the mandala becomes when it flips over.

to apply these DirectX controls across applications such as Memphis/Windows 98 and Windows NT 5.0. Although we wanted to write a Netscape-friendly version of Silent Lucidity that would accomplish the same multimedia feats, Netscape's DHTML offerings of JavaScript and layers simply weren't up to the task. As this instance exemplifies, Microsoft's strong effort to make a ubiquitous environment for both content creation and consumption will be difficult for Netscape to defeat, especially as technologies such as DirectX-influenced DHTML and WebTV merge in upcoming months.

As is mentioned in the CD-ROM's notes, the music for Silent Lucidity went through several modulations before reaching its final key, the dolorous F minor, in which it's played on the CD-ROM. Color theories were also invoked to make the marriage of the audio, text, and imagery as effective as possible. Because multimedia settings such as Silent Lucidity combine sound, imagery, and color in a way that promotes synesthesia—the cross-experiencing of the senses—ideas about synesthesia that have been used by artists and musicians such as Wassily Kandinsky and Richard Wagner were also applied here. For additional insight into synesthesia (or synaesthesia) and its fascinating implications for digital multimedia, see the International Synaesthesia Association Index site at **nevis.stir.ac.uk/~ldg/ISA/ISAIndex.html** or MIT's Synesthetic Experience site at **web.mit.edu/synesthesia/www/synesthesia.html**.

The following code contains comments indicating how the DirectAnimation effects were achieved:

```
<OBJECT ID="DAControl"
  STYLE="position:absolute; left:0; top:0;width:780;height:560;"
  CLASSID="CLSID:B6FFC24C-7E13-11D0-9B47-00C04FC2F51D">
</OBJECT>

 <script LANGUAGE="javascript">

// Returns normalized 3D vector
  function Normalize( vec3 )
  {
    return vec3.DivAnim( m.Sqrt( m.Add( m.Mul( vec3.X, vec3.X ),
      m.Add( m.Mul( vec3.Y, vec3.Y ), m.Mul( vec3.Z, vec3.Z ) ) ) ) );
  }

  m = DAControl.MeterLibrary;

// Constants
  period = 7.5; // time to complete the loop in secs
  radius = 0.09; // trajectory loop
```

```
  yingImg = m.ImportImage( "yingying.gif" );

// A 3D version of image of equal dimensions
  squareGeo = m.ImportGeometry( "square.wrl" );
  imgBbox = yingImg.BoundingBox;
  yingGeo = squareGeo.Transform( m.Scale3Anim
  ( imgBbox.Max.X, imgBbox.Max.Y, m.DANumber( 1 ) ) )
      .Texture( yingImg.MapToUnitSquare() );

// Angle that repeatedly spans circle in period time
  eval = m.SlowInSlowOut( 0, 2*Math.PI, period, 0 ).RepeatForever();

// 3D point that repeatedly travels around circle in period time
  pos = m.Point3SphericalAnim( eval, m.DANumber( 0 ), m.DANumber( radius ) ).
    transform( m.Compose3( m.Translate3( 0, radius / 3, 0 ),
      m.Rotate3( m.XVector3, Math.PI/8 ) ) );

// Find orientation parameters along tangent to trajectory
  direction = Normalize( m.DerivativePoint3( pos ) );
  normal = m.CrossVector3( m.XVector3, direction );
  angle = m.Acos( m.DotVector3( m.XVector3, direction ) );

// Get the ying to travel along trajectory with proper orientation
  flyingYingGeo = yingGeo.Transform( m.Compose3(
    m.Translate3Point( pos ), m.Rotate3Anim( normal, angle ) ) );

// Render ying with a camera and ambient light
  camera = m.PerspectiveCamera( radius+0.03, radius+0.01 );
  finalImg = m.UnionGeometry( flyingYingGeo, m.AmbientLight ).render( camera );
  DAControl.Image = finalImg;

// Construct sound that pans with horizontal and gains with depth
  slSnd = m.ImportSound( "sl.mid" ).Sound;
  panFac = m.Div( pos.X, m.DANumber( radius ) );
  gainFac = m.Abs( m.Div( pos.Z, m.DANumber( radius ) ) );
  finalSnd = slSnd.Loop().GainAnim( gainFac ).PanAnim( panFac );
  DAControl.Sound = finalSnd;

// Start the animation
  DAControl.Start()

</SCRIPT>

<DIV ID="Text"
</DIV>
</FONT>
</BODY>
</HTML>
```

PART 4

NETSCAPE'S LAYER APPROACH

Chapter 14

Netscape's Layer Model

*In this chapter, we take an in-depth look at Netscape's **LAYER** tag and provide a hands-on discussion of its use.*

Notes...

Chapter 14

Layers are a key component in Netscape's version of Dynamic HTML. They are a proprietary Netscape offering primed to work with JavaScript and implemented through the **LAYER** tag. Netscape's layer technology is designed to let you place images—or text—in a precisely indicated location; these layers can move dynamically around the page.

Although Netscape Navigator and Microsoft Internet Explorer both support layer-like blocks of page content that can be positioned, Netscape believes that the complex potential for layer use merits its own tag, and has, therefore, created a specific **LAYER** tag. However, the **LAYER** tag appears nowhere in Microsoft's version of Dynamic HTML.

Although Microsoft's version of Dynamic HTML can layer page content, it doesn't do so through a specific layer tag or even a single tag; instead, Microsoftian DHTML relies on cascading style sheets and tags, such as **DIV** and **SPAN,** for its version of layers. Because the W3C rejected Netscape's **LAYER** tag as a standard, Netscape has been forced to include support for style sheets in its version of Dynamic HTML as well; therefore, Netscape Navigator 4.0 gives developers two options for dynamically positioning layers:

1. By defining a style that has a position property
2. Through the **LAYER** tag

In this chapter, we focus on the complexities of the **LAYER** tag.

The **LAYER** Tag—W3C Reject

Although the **LAYER** tag has been officially rejected by the W3C, Netscape continues to support it and uses it prominently at **www.netscape.com**. The company will supposedly conform to the HTML 4.0 standard that's ultimately adopted, but until that adoption process is complete, it's still important for developers to understand layers. Because the dual implementations of DHTML promote unnecessary complexity and are destined to merge into something less disparate, we've included examples of code in this chapter that will allow you to create layers while still making your Web content viable for Microsoft products.

Why did the W3C reject the **LAYER** tag? Because fundamentally it defies the separation of content and style that the W3C is attempting to re-establish. By literally combining style and content, Netscape's use of the **LAYER** tag disregards SGML's division of the two. Netscape continues to support the **LAYER** tag, but the W3C's reaction to the **LAYER** tag's implementation essentially forced Netscape to change tactics and incorporate support for the W3C's proposed standard as well.

Netscape's **LAYER** Model: A Technical Description

Layers manifested through the **LAYER** tag are an essential part of Netscape's Dynamic HTML implementation. By pairing the precise design control of layers with JavaScript's heady multimedia possibilities, Netscape's DHTML formula arms designers with significant creative power and enhanced control over how Web pages appear. Netscape's layer-oriented version of DHTML is so reliant on JavaScript, though, that its code can be more awkward than corresponding Microsoft or W3C versions. Still, the possibilities for truly dynamic Web page content have definitely been expanded through the **LAYER** tag, especially because Netscape was first to release a browser that enabled dynamic layer movement with Navigator 4.0.

Layers can be conceived of as a blank canvas on which you can paint—or carve, scan, or import—the visual content that appears across a Web page. Developers who are familiar with the way layers work in Adobe Photoshop will recognize parallels between Adobe's and Netscape's layers; as with Photoshop, Netscape's layers let you stack content to create customized graphics effects.

Everything that is included inside a **LAYER** tag is part of that layer. Because you can position layers in precise locations and in carefully scripted succession, the ways in which they can be placed under, over, or beside each other provide excellent opportunities to shape Web page images and actions. Through the click of a mouse, layers can appear to unstack themselves, peeling away like the skin of an onion. They can be transparent or opaque, can expand and contract, and can be nested. Exploiting the capability for layers to be positioned along the z-axis also lets you project the illusion of three-dimensional Web pages.

The **LAYER** tag can include multiple layers of content on a single page, with all of the layers treated as objects. Layers can hold content, such as active URLs and multimedia files. These layers can overlap, become animated, visually interact with each other, create a timed succession of events or images, and respond instantly to end-user input. These types of dynamic action require the combination of layers with a scripting language such as JavaScript.

It's possible to draw any HTML element onto a layer.

Because the browser is not forced to return to the server to obtain layered dynamic content, layers are highly efficient as well as extremely responsive to interactivity. Layers permit Web page animation that doesn't require applets or animated GIFs; in addition, layers generally have smaller file sizes than applets or animated GIFs. In fact, one of layers' biggest advantages is that content created with them is impressively small in file size. For example, a 10K layer might be able to accomplish the same thing as a 50K animated GIF.

It's no coincidence that like 3D languages such as VRML (Virtual Reality Modeling Language), DHTML's use of layers, and the z-axis, lead the Web toward a greater feeling of dimensionality. The Web is indubitably becoming a place where the idea of *space* is more essential. Although there's still a (low-bandwidth) place for pages with only text, hyperlinks, and no visual stimulation beyond a gray background, technology such as layers provides a foundation for Web pages to contain compelling content that extends into three dimensions.

At the metalevel, layers are a step toward blending HTML with the 3D reality of tomorrow's Web space. Because layers are treated as objects, Netscape's use of the **LAYER** tag also reflects the trend of increasingly object-oriented HTML.

LAYER Tag Uses

Here are some of the **LAYER** tag's most important uses:

- Improving layout control

- Customizing background images and colors
- Nesting layers
- Hiding/Emphasizing Web page content

Improving Layout Control

Netscape's implementation of layers is designed to give Web developers extremely precise control over content positioning. Through layers, images can animate to a user's mouse movements, pile on top of each other, or fly out from corners of the screen at speeds that make viewers dizzy. Because layers have a stacking order, you can accurately control how layers appear on top of one another and overlap layers so that they reveal content according to your detailed wishes. Layers are particularly useful for emphasizing—or hiding—content based on user selection.

Layers permit an impressive level of control over the way HTML elements are positioned. In previous versions of Navigator, the browser arranged HTML objects in a sequential manner rather than in a way that relied on specific coordinates. The layer model, however, allows you to specify more detailed spatial location. Layers have **LEFT** and **TOP** attributes; mapping the coordinates of these two attributes determines exactly where on a page's x- and y-axes a layer will be executed.

For example, a layer that contains several lines of bold text underneath a transparent picture of daisies can be charted to appear at coordinates 10,40. Having determined the exact page location at which this layer will appear, you can then position other HTML layers relative to the first layer. A layer that contains an image of the sun can be tagged with the layer's **ABOVE** attribute and hover at the specified distance above the daisy, while a patch of grass can appear below the daisy—thanks to the **BELOW** attribute.

Customizing Background Images And Colors

Layers provide stellar opportunities for customizing a Web page's background colors and images. Where earlier versions of Navigator delegated background images and colors to a document's background or to tables within a document, layers bring background images and colors into a prominent role.

The precision that characterizes layer use makes it possible to render a page's sections in multiple types of background colors and patterns. Background images and colors for layers are specified in the same way as they are for the body of an HTML document. Intriguing visual effects can grace a page through a variety of layer manipulations, including overlapping multiple layers and applying transparency to the layers. When a layer is transparent, the color of the layer underneath it shows through.

Nesting Layers

Layers can also be nested inside each other when you want to give Web pages an impression of depth or stacked content. Similar to the way that HTML tables can be used within table cells, nested layers (minus the JavaScript) can be used as a layout method for documents that need to appear in a hierarchy. These nested layers can include URLs for a variety of sites, movies, scripted action, and so on.

Hiding/Emphasizing Web Page Content

Layers bring new control over the way that Web content can be emphasized in the foreground or pushed invisibly into the background. It's possible to create layers that are transparent; every pixel that a layer contains, can, in fact, appear as either transparent or solid. Making pixels transparent means that the content of underlying layers will be visible through the layer above.

As with the **BODY** tag, you can specify background images and colors for layers; if you specify a background color, the entire layer becomes opaque. Tiled background images can be used very effectively with layers; the tiles can include transparent pixels, resulting in intriguing, even psychedelic, effects.

LAYER Tag Disadvantages

Netscape's implementation of the **LAYER** tag has a few problems beyond its proprietary status. One is that whereas Microsoft's document object model (DOM) allows you to automatically resize layers and reflow page content, Navigator's DOM allows only partial updating of a page without requiring a reload.

Additionally, Netscape's layers fundamentally maintain the same size, even if their content changes. Resizing can be accomplished through scripting, but using a scripting language can get messy when the new content's size is unknown. The success of Netscape's **LAYER** tag is also heavily dependent on the scripting power it gains from JavaScript.

Although the **LAYER** tag might be useful for Netscape-oriented developers to learn and use, it seems unlikely that it will ever make it into the W3C's HTML standard. Why, then, does Netscape continue to include the **LAYER** tag in its documentation and content examples? Perhaps because XML, the language that will succeed HTML for certain applications, will make it possible to define new tags, and Netscape could therefore make the **LAYER** tag a component of their XML strategy.

Understanding The LAYER Tag

Layers take their name from the proprietary Netscape **LAYER** tag. Here's a first look at the **LAYER** tag's code:

```
<!-- default units for TOP, LEFT, and WIDTH is pixels -->
<LAYER ID=layer1 TOP=30pt LEFT=10pt
BGCOLOR="#CC00EE" WIDTH=100>
<H1>Layer 1</H1>
<P>Fascinating layer content goes here<P>
<IMG SRC=clouds.gif align=right>
<P>Layer 1 content.</P>
</LAYER>
<LAYER ID=layer2 TOP=100 LEFT=200 BGCOLOR=blue WIDTH=100>
<P>Layer 2 content</P>
</LAYER>
<LAYER ID=layer3 TOP=170 LEFT=250 BGCOLOR="#2222FF">
<H1>Layer 3 content </H1>
<P>Observe this fascinating DHTML content.</P>
</LAYER>
```

Positioning With The LAYER Tag

As mentioned earlier, layers can be placed under, over, and beside each other, and can be either opaque or transparent. There are two ways in which layer content can be positioned:

- Absolute positioning
- Relative positioning

Absolute Positioning

The **LAYER** tag and its **POSITION** attribute are used for absolute positioning of content. When an element is positioned absolutely, it always remains constant in its named position. By using inline JavaScript, a layer's absolute position can be animated, and layers can assume positions that are relative to one another. Absolutely positioned layers are considered to be "out-of-line," because they can appear anywhere in an HTML document and don't occupy space in the document flow. Layers defined as styles can have absolutely positioned layers as long as you specify that the position property is absolute. For instance:

```
<LAYER ID=firstlayer TOP=100 LEFT=150>
<P>Put firstlayer content here</P>
</LAYER>
<STYLE type="text/css">
<!--
#layer1 {position:absolute; top:100px; left:150px;}
-->
</STYLE>
```

Relative Positioning And The ***ILAYER*** *Tag*

Relative positioning makes elements flow, moving them in a way determined by the other changes that occur on the page. Relative positioning uses containers to create boundaries for movable items; for example, it's essential to keep an item you want to flow within the container in which you want it to flow.

Layers with relative positions are called *inflow layers* and are actually both inflow and inline because they share line space with other HTML elements. You can make an inflow layer appear on a separate line by wrapping the layer in the **DIV** tag or inserting a break before the layer. Layers with relative positions use the **LEFT** and **TOP** attributes/properties to specify the offset of the layer's top-left corner (from the current document position).

The **ILAYER** tag is used to create an inflow layer. Layers that are defined as styles can make an inflow layer by specifying a relative position property:

```
<ILAYER ID=secondlayer>
 <P>Put secondlayer content here</P>
</ILAYER>
<STYLE type="text/css">
<!--
#secondlayer{position:relative; }
-->
</STYLE>
```

LAYER Tag Attributes

The **LAYER** tag's attributes determine various characteristics of how the layer will appear. A **LAYER** tag's attributes control its:

- Position

- Size
- Color
- Transparency
- Background image

Detailed coverage of the **LAYER** tag syntax used to control these attributes follows.

The **LAYER** Tag And Styles

Netscape has been persuaded to recognize the value of using the **LAYER** tag with styles to create stylized layers. For example, you can use the following code to apply a color-laden style class to a layer:

```
<STYLE TYPE="text/css">
<!--
all.style4 {
color:red;
border-width:40px; border-color:blue;
border-style:ridge;
padding:10%;
}
-->
</STYLE>
<BODY BGCOLOR=green>
<LAYER ID=layer4 TOP=200 LEFT=125 BGCOLOR=white
CLASS=style4>
<H1>Layer 4 </H1>
<P>A color-laden layer! <P>
</LAYER>
</BODY>
```

Documents can contain layers that are defined as styles as well as layers that are defined with the **LAYER** tag (which can make use of styles). Documents that contain more than one absolutely positioned layer have difficulty sharing styles, though, because each layer needs its own specific value for **TOP** and **LEFT** to indicate its position. Because you can define a named style for each layer, individually named styles can be highly effective for defining layers. (Keep in mind that a named style and a style with a unique ID are the same.)

The following code demonstrates how you can use the **STYLE** tag to define styles for two layers. In this example, the layer named "firstlayer" is positioned 40 pixels from the top of the page and 15 pixels from the left, whereas the "secondlayer" is positioned 70 pixels from the top and 175 pixels from the left:

```
<STYLE TYPE="text/css">
<!--
#firstlayer {position:absolute;
top:40px; left:15px;
background-color:#000000;
border-width:1; border-color:#000000;
width:200px;
}
#secondlayer{position:absolute;
top:70px; left:175px;
background-color:green;
width:200px;
border-width:2px; border-color:yellow; }
-->
</STYLE>
```

If you want to indicate that the element is a positioned layer, you can use the **STYLE** attribute directly in an element, as the following markup shows:

```
<DIV STYLE="position:absolute; top:125px; left:175px;
border-width:2px; border-color:yellow;
background-color:#000000">
<H1>Layer</H1>
<P>Aren't layers interesting?</P>
</DIV>
```

Although the **LAYER** tag and the **CSS** tag use the same positioning properties, the two tags differ in the way that they respond to default situations. **LAYER** tags are intended for implementing highly specific positioning. When no top or left coordinates are specified, layers will default to a position below the document's top-left corner (specifically, in a spot that's seven pixels below and seven pixels to the right of the top-left corner). CSS properties, however, will default to static and auto when their positions aren't specified, so unlike the **LAYER** tag's default position, the elements of CSS properties are still displayed normally on the page.

Despite the creation of the **LAYER** tag, Netscape is also striving to successfully include CSS and, unlike Explorer, Navigator supports absolute positioning with CSS as well as with the **LAYER** tag. It's through its support of the **DIV** tag that Navigator can use CSS absolute positioning; this tag makes content self-contained so that it can be manipulated like a layer (displayed, hidden, positioned, etc.).

Choosing Between CSS And **LAYER**

Which positioning technique should you use, **LAYER** or CSS? Because Microsoft and Netscape have agreed that they'll both support whatever standard the W3C adopts, this choice seems to be a temporary burden. CSS is what has garnered the W3C's endorsement, so if you're concerned about creating content that works in all browsers, CSS would be the more pragmatic choice.

CSS Vs. **LAYER**: A Comparative Example

One of the **LAYER** tag's drawbacks is that it can require extra work for the developer. For example, if you want to position an image—and only an image—CSS lets you do so with a single declarative rule. The **LAYER** tag, on the other hand, requires you to both recognize the image and assign it a position by wrapping it in a layer. For example:

```
<LAYER TOP=20 LEFT=20 NAME="firstlayer">
<IMG SRC="fish.gif" NAME="fish">
</LAYER>
```

To move the image, you have to move the layer that contains it:

```
document.layers["firstlayer"].top = 100
document.layers["firstlayer"].left = 100
```

If you want to change the source, you have to use the image:

```
document.images["fish"].src = "fish.gif"
```

CSS's method of positioning the element is much more direct; rather than defining a separate object to be manipulated, the object itself is affected:

```
<IMG SRC="fish.gif" NAME="fish" STYLE="position: absolute; top: 20px;
left: 20px">
document.images["fish"].style.top = "100px"
document.images["fish"].style.top = "100px"
document.images["fish"].src = "fish.gif"
```

The Key Combination: Layers And JavaScript

Pairing JavaScript with the **LAYER** tag has ensured that scripting page content is easier than ever. All of a layer's properties are accessible through JavaScript. Because page content that animates through **LAYER** operates within the page itself and doesn't need to be refreshed by the server, the page's hot content can move smoothly and efficiently.

Whether a layer is visible makes no difference to JavaScript's ability to recognize it. Using JavaScript lets you dynamically change a layer's visibility, causing it to hide and then reappear on the page. In Navigator 4, JavaScript has the ability to dynamically control layers' position, visibility, and z-order (stacking order). It's through the layer object and layer array attributes that all of a document's layers are enumerated.

When you use JavaScript to dynamically change a page's layers, resizing the browser will cause the layers to reset to their original state. So simply resize the browser if you want the layers to return to the way they initially appeared.

This is the syntax through which JavaScript accesses a particular property in a layer:

```
document.layers.layername.propertyname
```

If you want to affect the visibility of **SomeLayer()**, you can use the script:

```
<SCRIPT LANGUAGE="JavaScript"> function hideSomeLayer()
{document.layers.SomeLayer.visibility ="hidden"; }
</SCRIPT>
```

JavaScript can also be used to change layer content or create new positioned blocks of content on the fly. When you want to modify positioned blocks of HTML content, you can use JavaScript to do so, no matter how the blocks are defined. Even when layers are defined as styles, JavaScript can still be used to manipulate them.

Inside The **LAYER** Tag Syntax

The following is the syntax for **LAYER** tag use:

```
&ltLAYER
NAME="layerName"
LEFT=xPosition (number of pixels or percentage of window/parent layer)
TOP=yPosition (number of pixels or percentage of window/parent layer)
Z-INDEX=layerZ (positive integer)
WIDTH=layerWidth (number of pixels or percentage of window/parent layer)
HEIGHT=layerHeight (number of pixels or percentage of window/parent layer)
CLIP="x1_offset, y1_offset, x2_offset, y2_offset "(number of pixels or
  percentage of window/parent layer)
ABOVE="layerName"
BELOW="layerName"
```

```
VISIBILITY= SHOW | HIDE | INHERIT
BGCOLOR="rgbColor" (name of a standard color or a hexidecimal RGB value)
BACKGROUND="imageURL" (URL of a background image) SRC="URL"
```

LAYER

The **<LAYER>** tag starts a layer and the **</LAYER>** tag ends the layer. All of the content that falls between the opening and closing **LAYER** tags is treated as a single layer of content. This content can be altered in a variety of ways; for example, through scripted instructions that make layers bounce around the page.

When you surround Web page content with **LAYER**, it partitions documents into sections, similarly to the way that the **DIV** tag creates page segments with CSS. By using JavaScript in conjunction with the **LAYER** tag's positioning abilities, you can dynamically change the status of a layer's visibility, making layers hide and reappear at will.

NAME="layerName"

The **NAME** tag is a layer's ID tag; these layer names are required to begin with an alphabetic character. HTML and external scripting languages, such as JavaScript, refer to the layer's name to identify the layer. Therefore, each layer name that you assign must be unique. The **NAME** attribute is optional, and all layers are unnamed by default.

LEFT=xPosition TOP=yPosition

You indicate a layer's pixel position or relative position in terms of horizontal/vertical orientation through the **LEFT** and **TOP** attributes. **LEFT** defines a layer's x (horizontal) location on the page, whereas **TOP** defines a layer's y (vertical) location on the page. For example, this layer will appear 30 pixels from the left and 90 pixels from the top of the parent layer:

```
<LAYER LEFT=30 TOP=90>
</LAYER>
```

The **LEFT** and **TOP** attributes' orientation originates in the parent layer/document's upper-left corner, and the attributes express the orientation in terms of the horizontal and vertical positions of the layer's top-left corner. The coordinates of this location increase downward and to the right. A 32-bit, signed integer is limited by values within the range of [-2147483648, 2147483647] for the **LEFT** and **TOP** attributes.

Both **LEFT** and **TOP** attributes are optional. When the **LAYER** tag is encountered, the HTML that follows will resume at whatever x,y location the page's content occupied before the **LAYER** tag was encountered.

A layer's position can be either absolute (and expressed in pixels), or relative (and expressed in percentages). Absolute positioning makes a layer appear at a specific place on a page; relative positioning makes the layer flow onto the page as an inline image would, following whatever is slated to precede it.

WIDTH=layerWidth

You control how the **LAYER** tag's contents will be wrapped through the **WIDTH** attribute. When an element such as an image extends beyond the width specified and can't be wrapped, the **WIDTH** attribute will make the contents of the layer have a larger actual width than the layer's specified value. The **WIDTH** is specified in terms of pixels and a 32-bit, signed integer must fall in the range [-2147483648, 2147483647]. The **WIDTH** attribute is optional: When there's no specified **WIDTH**, the layer contents wrap at the right boundary of the enclosing block.

HEIGHT=layerHeight

HEIGHT determines a child layer's reference length; these attribute values are specified through percentages.

CLIP="x1_offset, y1_offset, x2_offset, y2_offset" or CLIP="x2_offset, y2_offset"

The **CLIP** attribute defines the clipping rectangle, which indicates the part of a layer that is seen. The clip's coordinate system originates in the left and top of the layer space. Because any content that falls outside this rectangle is drawn transparently, it doesn't visually register.

There are four numbers, in pixels, that are used to specify the **CLIP** attribute:

- x1_offset
- y1_offset
- x2_offset
- y2_offset

The **CLIP** attributes' x1 and y1 offsets specify the upper-left corner of the displayed region relative to the layer's **LEFT** and **TOP** position values. The x2 and y2 offsets specify the lower-right corner. Therefore, the numbers that are specified from left to right in the attribute are:

- The horizontal left value
- The vertical top value
- The horizontal right value
- The vertical bottom value

For a 32-bit, signed integer or as a percentage, the numbers have to fall within the range [-2147483648, 2147483647].

When the **CLIP** attribute is eliminated, the x2_offset and y2_offset make everything appear visible (or unclipped) within the layer. In cases where the x1_offset and y1_offset aren't included, they both default to the (0,0) coordinates expressed by the layer's **LEFT** and **TOP** attributes.

Z-INDEX/ABOVE/BELOW

You indicate how layers are to be stacked through the **Z-INDEX**, **ABOVE**, and **BELOW** attributes. Using these attributes allows you to put new layers over layers that already exist or to override the default behavior. It's possible to employ only one of the **Z-INDEX**, **ABOVE**, and **BELOW** attributes at a time to affect a layer.

A layer's z-order is specified through the **Z-INDEX** attribute in terms of a positive integer:

```
Z-INDEX=layerZ
```

A browser stacks the layerZ values with higher-numbered layers above those with lower ones.

The **ABOVE** and **BELOW** attributes are added to affect the placement of specific layers. The layers referred to by **ABOVE** and **BELOW** need to have been previously created and named.

When you want to indicate the **NAME** attribute of the layer that exists immediately above a newly made layer, use the **ABOVE** attribute:

```
ABOVE="layerName"
```

To refer to the **NAME** attribute of the layer that will fall immediately underneath a newly created layer, use the **BELOW** attribute in a parallel manner:

```
BELOW="layerName"
```

Don't attempt to make forward references to other layers with ***Z-INDEX, ABOVE,*** *and* ***BELOW*** *attributes. Doing so will form the page according to the default settings for layer creation, and make the page appear as if there were no* ***BELOW*** *or* ***ABOVE*** *attributes included.*

VISIBILITY=SHOW/HIDE/INHERIT

The **VISIBILITY** attribute determines whether the layer is initially displayed. Although the **SHOW** attribute doesn't appear in Navigator 4's preview release, it will eventually be used to tell the browser that the layer should be drawn. **HIDE** instructs the browser to hide the layer, whereas **INHERIT** indicates that a layer should share the same level of visibility as its parent layer. **VISIBILITY=INHERIT** is the default, and the attribute is optional.

To dynamically change a layer's hidden state, you can employ a scripting language such as JavaScript.

BGCOLOR="*rgbColor*" BACKGROUND="*imageURL*"

BGCOLOR and **BACKGROUND** determine the way that a layer's background appears. To evoke a standard color or an RGB value, use **BGCOLOR**. When you want to call up the URL of a background image, use **BACKGROUND**. Both **BGCOLOR** and **BACKGROUND** are attributes of the **BODY** tag, and their background images may contain transparent pixels.

By default, a layer is transparent; therefore, when neither attribute is included in a lower layer, the bottom layer's attributes show up in the area where the background pattern or color would otherwise appear.

SRC=*URL*

The **SRC** property brings external content into a layer. **SRC=***URL* indicates which Web address the layer should link to; all of the content that **SRC=***URL* refers to is brought into the layer.

NOLAYER

Use **NOLAYER** to ensure that Navigator ignores the HTML that falls between the **<NOLAYER>** and **</NOLAYER>** tags. Using this tag is crucial when you're creating content that will be viewed by a variety of browsers, including older ones that don't support the **LAYER** tag.

JavaScript Extensions Used With The **LAYER** Tag

There are four types of JavaScript extensions that work in conjunction with the **LAYER** tag:

- Layer Objects
- Layer Object Properties
- Layer Object Methods
- Layers Array

Layer Objects

Layer objects are associated with the sections of an HTML document contained within the **LAYER** tags. Layer objects are created automatically; their properties are associated with whatever corresponding properties appear between the **LAYER** tags.

All JavaScript objects allow a layer object's properties and methods to be accessed in the following ways:

- layerName.propertyName
- layerName.methodName(parameters)

It's possible to modify select layer properties directly, by assignment. If you want to hide a visible layer, for instance, you can use:

```
SomeLayer.visibility = "hide"
```

Layer Object Properties

The following list describes the various layer object properties:

- **name**—The name that a layer takes, assigned by the **NAME** attribute. Cannot be modified.
- **left**—Indicates (in pixels) the horizontal position of a layer's left edge. This position is relative to the enclosing layer's origin. Can be modified.
- **top**—Indicates (in pixels) the vertical position of a layer's top edge, relative to the enclosing layer's origin. Can be modified.

- **visibility**—Can make a layer invisible, visible, or be inherited. Can be modified.
- **clip.left**, **clip.top**, **clip.right**, **clip.bottom**, **clip.width**, and **clip.height**—These properties define the clipping rectangle, which specifies which part of a layer is visible. Can be modified.
- **siblingAbove**—In z-order, the sibling layer above the one being referenced. If the referenced layer is the one on top, this property is void. Cannot be modified.
- **siblingBelow**—In z-order, the sibling layer below the one being referenced. If the referenced layer is the one on the bottom, this property is void. Cannot be modified.
- **parentLayer**—This property is the layer object that corresponds to the enclosing layer environment. It's null if it is the root layer. Cannot be modified.
- **layers**—This associative array property numerates all child layer objects by both name and index. It's null if no child layers exist. Cannot be modified.

Layer Object Methods

The following list describes the various layer object methods:

- **moveBy(*x, y*)**—Changes a layer's position by applying the specified deltas, measured in pixels.
- **moveTo(*x, y*)**—Translates a layer so its upper-left corner is (x,y).
- **resizeTo(*width, height*)** and **resizeBy(*delta width, delta height*)**—These two object methods change the lower-right corner coordinates of a layer's clipping rectangle.
- **moveAbove(*layer*)**—Stacks a layer above the specified layer.
- **moveBelow(*layer*)**—Stacks a layer below the specified layer.

Layers Array

You can reference a layer in JavaScript through the layers array, which has an entry for each object that has been created. To access these objects, invoke the layer's name as specified by the **NAME** attribute or use a non-negative integer index. In cases where a non-negative integer index is used, an array's elements will appear in z-order from back to front (zero will be the bottom-most layer and higher layers will be indexed by consecutive integers).

These examples of syntax are all viable and valid ways to access layer objects:

- **document.layerName**
- **document.layers[index]**
- **document.layers["layerName"]**

Because a layer's z property doesn't necessarily enumerate layers with integers that are both unique and consecutive, a layer's array index is not the same as its z property.

Ensuring Browser Backward Compatibility With The **NOLAYER** Tag

One of the problems with using cutting-edge technology such as DHTML is that not all site visitors are prepared to encounter the content that it brings. People surfing with pre-4.0 versions of Navigator or Internet Explorer simply won't be able to experience layers. However, you can ensure that the HTML you code is still compatible with their browsers by using the **NOLAYER** tag.

When a browser that doesn't support the **LAYER** tag comes across content that's contained within the **NOLAYER** tag, it will automatically display it. This content can appear in the same source page as the DHTML data; when a layer-friendly browser such as Navigator 4 encounters the **NOLAYER** tag, it simply ignores it. Therefore, users who can't see layers can still experience the content of the DHTML page, whereas those who can see layers won't have to bother with the content within the **NOLAYER** tag. This tag works in a similar way to the **NOFRAMES** tag that makes nonframe browsers able to display content intended for frames.

Final Thoughts About The **LAYER** Tag

Although Netscape had agreed not to promote the **LAYER** tag, at the time of this writing it had launched a redesigned, highly dynamic home page that made prominent (and dizzyingly active) use of the tag. See Netscape's home page at **www.netscape.com** or its developers section at **developer.netscape.com** for illumination about its current position on—and use of—the **LAYER** tag. C|Net columnist Rafe Needleman has often provided good analyses of Netscape's battle to beat Microsoft in the Web game, as well as Netscape's layer strategy, in columns such as "Netscape Pulls A Fast One": **www.cnet.com/Content/Voices/Needleman/092297/index.html.**

Although Netscape's development of the **LAYER** tag was an exciting advance for Web design, the W3C's failure to embrace it doomed the future of the proprietary tag. (Unsurprisingly, Microsoft's PR machine has also undermined the **LAYER** tag's reputation through a truckload of negative press.) The W3C's official version of HTML 4.0 will contain elements of the work that Netscape accomplished through **LAYER** tag implementation—such as the flexibility of the clipping model—but the official specification will clearly separate style from content, something that the **LAYER** tag doesn't do.

Considering Layers And Push

Before we delve into the wide possibilities of layer use, a few words about layers and push content:

With the new push power that layers and DHTML unleash, it's essential to be aware of how to create content that makes good use of the new technologies. A caveat: If you're interested in designing valuable Web content, the point is *not* to see how many frenetically morphing images you can squeeze into a page. Although creating page content that fully exploits the speed and dynamic action that DHTML and **LAYER** tags can produce may be an interesting experiment, it's not ideal for site visitors. Instead, the goal is to create compelling, meaningful content that shows respect for the end-user experience. Resist the temptation to overpower your visitors with scattered or pointless dynamic content—a faster stream of images does not ensure that users will process information more quickly or effectively. Be sensitive to the power of this technology; users are more willing to spend time at a site that gives them information at a speed that makes them both comfortable and interested.

Many content providers are now turning to television's effective, but arguably numbing, push delivery as a model for Web content. The Web's incredibly innovative content model is still in a fledgling state, however, and although the way that television delivers its content is not without its benefits, forcing TV-like assumptions on Web users doesn't take into account the Web's fresh potential. Feeding push to Web users obligates them to have a passive relationship to information rather than the active one the Web's structure offers. The feedback loop and opportunities for global interactivity that the Web provides are unparalleled in human history; the **LAYER** tag and accompanying technologies take the potential one step further. So code with creativity, intelligence, and sensitivity!

Practical Guide To

Netscape's Layer Model

- Creating Animation With The **LAYER** Tag
- Making Layers Move (After A Web Page Has Loaded)
    - Using The **moveTo()** And **offset()** Methods
    - Using Event Handlers
    - Defining New Functions
- Resizing Layers With The **CLIP** Attribute
- Nesting Layers
- Creating Condition-Specific Content
- Using The **LAYER** Tag For Bubble Help
- Using The **NOLAYER** Tag

In this section, we examine ways that layers can be used. For additional examples, see Netscape's page of layer examples at **developer.netscape.com/library/examples/dhtml.html**.

Creating Animation With The **LAYER** Tag

One of the **LAYER** tag's most important characteristics is its ability to create intense, relatively low-demand animation on Web pages. It brings a new level of control over the rhythm at which images shift across a Web page. By using the **LAYER** tag, you can make a graphic *slide* rather than jump across the page; using the **setTimeout()** method within a recursive function determines the speed at which layers will shift in front of users' eyes. For example:

```
function moveMyLayer()
The code for the layer(s) that you want to move goes here
function layer_timeout()
moveMyLayer();
setTimeout("layer_timeout()",80);
layer_timeout();
```

For additional information on animation, see Chapter 12, as well as the Fabric8 examples on the CD-ROM.

Making Layers Move (After A Web Page Has Loaded)

One of the most gripping—even startling—capabilities of layers is the way in which they can rapidly shift or jump across a page. Users who are accustomed to seeing Web page action that's tethered to the generally lethargic pace of the Internet are often surprised at the speed at which layers can shift across a page. Although you can move a layer by repeatedly changing its **LEFT** and **TOP** properties, there are several different techniques that you can also use to dynamically move a layer after the page that contains it has already been drawn, including:

- The **moveTo()** method
- The **offset()** method

*Using The **moveTo()** And **offset()** Methods*

Using JavaScript's **moveTo()** function shifts a layer to an exact left/top coordinate. The following code would move the layer 75 pixels to the left of the window and 30 from the top:

```
myLayer.moveTo(75, 30);
```

You can achieve a similar effect by using the **offset()** method, but rather than moving the layer to an exact position, it offsets the layer by the specified values. The following code would shift a layer 40 pixels over and 20 down from its position:

```
myLayer.offset(40, 20);
```

Using Event Handlers

If you want to display a layer that "explodes" when the user passes the mouse over it, you can include several hidden layers on the page. Using the **onMouseOver()** and **onMouseOut()** event handlers in tandem with the layer will ensure that when the selected area is passed over with the mouse, the layers will shift and the targeted layer will "blow up."

For more information on event handlers, refer to Chapter 9, or see Netscape's reference on JavaScript 1.2's event handlers at **developer.netscape.com/library/technote/index.html?content=javascript/eventhandler/eventhandler.htm**.

Defining New Functions

Although JavaScript lets you use the **moveTo()** function, this function doesn't permit you to slowly slide an element from one coordinate to another. To do this, as well as other more sophisticated layer manipulations, it's necessary to define your own functions. For example, to slide a layer, you could first define a function called **slideLayer**, then specify information such as the beginning and ending coordinates, the number of steps to move, and the time that should elapse between the steps and, therefore, control the speed of the slide.

The following code has several variables:

- **lyr**—Defines the document that you want to slide
- **xsft** and **ysft**—Indicate the amount that the left/top layer values should shift

- **sfttime**—Indicates how much delay time should fall between increments (in milliseconds)
- **xstop**—Indicates the x-value at which the slide will finish.

*The line beginning with **setTimeout** is wrapped for readability purposes, but it must appear as a single line to work properly.*

```
<script language="JavaScript">
function slideLayer(lyr,xsft,ysft,sfttime,xstop) {
 lyr.top += ysft
 lyr.left += xsft
 if (((xsft > 0) && (lyr.left < xstop)) ||
     ((xsft < 0) && (lyr.left > xstop))) {

setTimeout('slideLayer(document.layers["'+lyr.name+'"],'+xsft+',
           '+ysft+','+sfttime+','+xstop+')',sfttime)
     }
}
</script>
```

If you want to slide a layer to the left, you would use negative **xsft** values, whereas positive **ysft** values would move layers down. Additionally, positive **xsft** values would shift the layer to the right, whereas negative **ysft** values would move it up.

Resizing Layers With The **CLIP** Attribute

Layers are extremely handy for designing pulldown menus; by resetting a layer's **clip.bottom** property you can make the menu scroll open rather than suddenly appear. You determine which part of the layer is to be changed through the layer object's **clip** property and **resize()** method.

With a pulldown menu, for instance, you can define a layer so that it displays a full list of menu choices. However, by defining the layer's **CLIP** attribute so that only the menu's title appears when the page loads, you can hide the rest of the menu's content until the user clicks on the menu title. Clicking the title alters the layer's clipping, rendering the entire menu visible. Clicking one of the menu items resets the menu layer's **clip** property to its original value.

Nesting Layers

Layers can be nested without requiring the aid of JavaScript. For example, if you want to create a scene that shows a blue sky containing an airplane, a hawk, and a white cloud, you can use a background rectangle, rendered in a single shade of blue, and images of the other items:

```
<!-- Define a layer with a background to serve as the "sky"-->
<LAYER NAME="SKY" BACKGROUND="LIGHT BLUE" CLIP=500,200>
<LAYER TOP=100 LEFT=100>
<IMG SRC="hawk.gif">
</LAYER>
<LAYER TOP=200 LEFT=200>
<IMG SRC="airplane.gif">
</LAYER>
<LAYER TOP=300 LEFT=300>=>
<IMG SRC="cloud.gif">
</LAYER>
</LAYER>
```

Because the images of the hawk, airplane, and cloud occupy positions that are relative to the sky—which acts as the parent layer—moving the sky layer to a different place on the page will ensure that the other images move as well. Changing the individual coordinates of the images wouldn't be necessary, as the space they occupy is defined according to where the sky parent layer appears.

Creating Condition-Specific Content

By using conditional comments, you can make layers behave according to whether conditions within a page are fulfilled. They act as an "if/then" response; for example, if a browser supports layers, then a slew of layered animation could appear.

Conditional comments, a Netscape-only option, appear directly after the opening comment markup. Their syntax consists of an ampersand, followed by a set of brackets containing the test condition, followed by a semicolon. The following example uses a conditional comment to ensure that the code will run only if the **navigator. platform** property is equal to the string "win95":

```
<!--&{navigator.platform == "win95"};
  <SCRIPT>
    ... // JavaScript code goes here
  </SCRIPT>
-->
```

If the condition turns out to be true, the browser ignores the comment markup, and the comment content integrates with the page. If the condition is false, however, the comment will simply remain as a comment.

Browsers such as Internet Explorer that don't support conditional comments will regard them as normal comments.

Using The **LAYER** Tag For Bubble Help

One of the most exciting things about the **LAYER** tag is its ability to feature—or hide—layers of your choice. When you initially load a page that has HTML layers with their **VISIBILITY** set to **HIDE**, the **HIDDEN** property determines which of the layers will be visible or invisible. Although Netscape is also promising a **SHOW** property, it was not implemented at the time of this writing. When **SHOW** *is* functional, it will be used with JavaScript events to make content suddenly appear—in the middle of a page, for instance.

As you'll see in the following example, **HIDDEN** can be used to formulate dynamic content with the **LAYER** tag when used in conjunction with JavaScript. It's also feasible to use **HIDDEN** without scripting action; you can hide content such as text entries if you use **HIDDEN** without JavaScript.

Combining several hidden layers can unleash a stream of dramatic content on your viewers. By making layers materialize and disappear as a mouse passes over them, they can reveal content that isn't initially visible. Take the example of a Web site quiz in which users check boxes to indicate their quiz answers. If they pass the mouse over a spot on the page that's triggered to reveal the correct answer, hidden layer content can then be revealed indicating whether they selected the right one. An animation that indicates whether the user answered the quiz question successfully could be set off at this point. All of this content can unfold without requiring the page to reload or refresh, making it take place at an impressively lag-free speed.

Layers can be put to excellent use for creating didactic content that appears suddenly, including popup menus or bubble help. The following code example demonstrates the latter.

As you can see in the code that follows, this document contains layers that, with a little help from JavaScript, respond when the mouse travels across them. This response is achieved by combining layers with **OnMouseOver()** and **OnMouseOut()**. Figures 14.1 and 14.2 show a sequence of pop-up bubbles that appears almost instantaneously when triggered by the mouse's movements. When the mouse travels over the layer, **OnMouseOver()** and **OnMouseOut()** trigger the bubble to appear and disappear (see Figure 14.3).

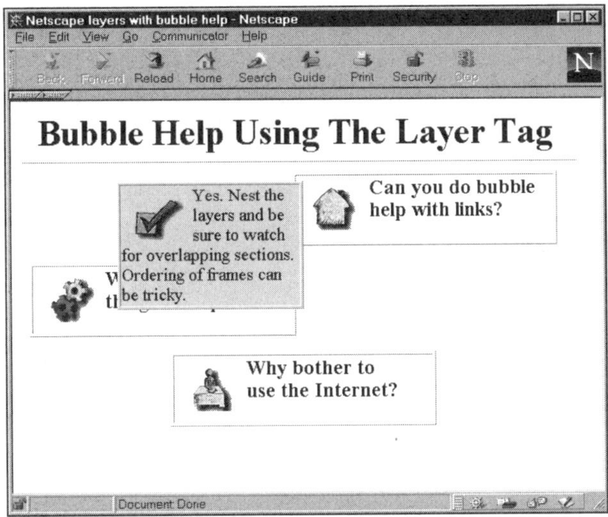

Figure 14.1

The bubbles appear and disappear by making the layers first invisible, then visible.

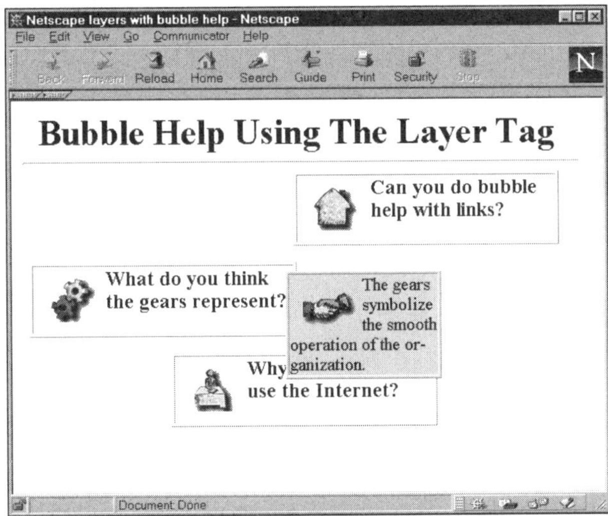

Figure 14.2

The layers can overlap, as shown in the bottom three images on this screen.

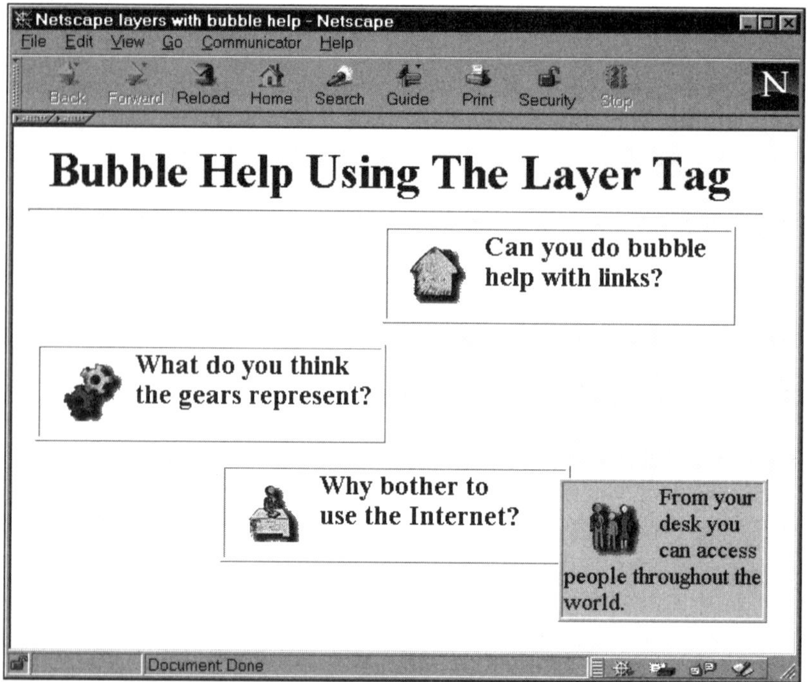

Figure 14.3

The instantaneous appearance and disappearance of the bubbles make the page dynamic and responsive with no server-side lag.

```
<HTML>
 <!-- Copyright (C) 1997 by Christopher D. Brown of Austin, TX -->
 <HEAD>
  <TITLE> Netscape layers with bubble help </TITLE>
 </HEAD>

<!-- Body not required -->
 <BODY BGCOLOR="#FFFFCC">

  <TABLE WIDTH="640"><TR><TD ALIGN="CENTER">
   <H1> Bubble Help Using The Layer Tag <HR> </H1>
  </TD></TR></TABLE>

<!-- The objects that use bubble help -->

  <LAYER TOP="180" LEFT="20" WIDTH="300" ZINDEX=1 BGCOLOR="#FFFFFF"
    ONMOUSEOVER="HelpOnGear();" ONMOUSEOUT="HelpOffGear();">
   <TABLE WIDTH="100%" BORDER="1"><TR><TD NOWRAP VALIGN="TOP">
    <H3>
```

```
    <IMG SRC="igear.gif" BORDER="0" HEIGHT="60" WIDTH="75" ALIGN="LEFT">
    What do you think <BR>
    the gears represent?
   </H3>
  </TD></TR></TABLE>
 </LAYER>

 <LAYER TOP="280" LEFT="180" WIDTH="300" ZINDEX="1" BGCOLOR="#FFFFFF"
   ONMOUSEOVER="HelpOnDesk();" ONMOUSEOUT="HelpOffDesk();">
  <TABLE WIDTH="100%" BORDER="1"><TR><TD NOWRAP VALIGN="TOP">
   <H3>
    <IMG SRC="idesk.gif" BORDER="0" HEIGHT="60" WIDTH="75" ALIGN="LEFT">
    Why bother to<BR>
    use the Internet?
   </H3>
  </TD></TR></TABLE>
 </LAYER>

 <LAYER TOP="80" LEFT="320" WIDTH="300" ZINDEX="1" BGCOLOR="#FFFFFF"
   ONMOUSEOVER="HelpOnUp();" ONMOUSEOUT="HelpOffUp();">
  <TABLE WIDTH="100%" BORDER="1"><TR><TD NOWRAP VALIGN="TOP">
   <H3>
    <IMG SRC="iup.gif" BORDER="0" HEIGHT="60" WIDTH="75" ALIGN="LEFT">
    Can you do bubble<BR>
    help with links?
   </H3>
  </TD></TR></TABLE>
 </LAYER>

<!-- Functions are required to reference layers within the correct scope -->

 <SCRIPT>
   function HelpOnGear() {document.layers.helpgear.visibility="visible";}
   function HelpOffGear(){document.layers.helpgear.visibility="hidden";}
   function HelpOnDesk() {document.layers.helpdesk.visibility="visible";}
   function HelpOffDesk(){document.layers.helpdesk.visibility="hidden";}
   function HelpOnUp()   {document.layers.helpup.visibility="visible";}
   function HelpOffUp()  {document.layers.helpup.visibility="hidden";}
 </SCRIPT>

<!-- Bubble help objects -->

 <LAYER ID="helpgear" TOP="190" LEFT="310" WIDTH="50" HEIGHT="50"
   VISIBILITY="HIDDEN" BGCOLOR="#FFCCFF" ZINDEX="3">
   <TABLE WIDTH="100%" BORDER="1"><TR><TD NOWRAP VALIGN="TOP">
    <IMG SRC="ihands.gif"  BORDER="0" HEIGHT="60" WIDTH="75" ALIGN="LEFT">
    The gears<BR>
```

```
      symbolize<BR>
      the smooth<BR>
      operation of the or-<BR>
      ganization.
     </TD></TR></TABLE>
    </LAYER>

    <LAYER ID="helpdesk" TOP="290" LEFT="470" WIDTH="50" HEIGHT="50"
     VISIBILITY="HIDDEN" BGCOLOR="#FFCCFF" ZINDEX="3">
     <TABLE WIDTH="100%" BORDER="1"><TR><TD NOWRAP VALIGN="TOP">
      <IMG SRC="ipeople.gif"  BORDER="0" HEIGHT="60" WIDTH="75" ALIGN="LEFT">
      From your<BR>
      desk you<BR>
      can access<BR>
      people throughout the<BR>
      world.
     </TD></TR></TABLE>
    </LAYER>

    <LAYER ID="helpup" TOP="90" LEFT="120" WIDTH="50" HEIGHT="50"
     VISIBILITY="HIDDEN" BGCOLOR="#FFCCFF" ZINDEX="3">
     <TABLE WIDTH="100%" BORDER="1"><TR><TD NOWRAP VALIGN="TOP">
      <IMG SRC="icheck.gif"  BORDER="0" HEIGHT="60" WIDTH="75" ALIGN="LEFT">
       Yes.  Nest the <BR>
       layers and be <BR>
       sure to watch <BR>
       for overlapping sections. <BR>
       Ordering of frames can <BR>
       be tricky.
     </TD></TR></TABLE>
    </LAYER>

  </BODY>
</HTML>
```

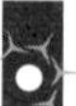 Using The **NOLAYER** Tag

As we explained earlier in the chapter, the **NOLAYER** tag is used to ensure that browsers can still view DHTML content even if they can't process the **LAYER** tag. For example, you can use the **NOLAYER** tag to provide an alternative to an animated logo you've included in a DHTML page. Layer-capable browsers will show a dynamic animated logo. However, browsers that are unequipped to handle the **LAYER** tag will display only the static logo indicated by the **IMG** tag. Using the **NOLAYER** tag in this instance tells a browser such as Navigator 4 that the image tag should be ignored, eliminating the static logo from the page.

```
<LAYER
SRC="animated-logo.html"></LAYER>
<NOLAYER>
<IMG
SRC="logo.gif">
</NOLAYER>
```

Chapter 15

Handling Events Using Layers

In this chapter, you will learn how to capture and handle events when using layers.

Notes...

Chapter 15

Chapter 14 explored changes to content layout and structure necessitated by the use of layers and explained how to arrange such information to support the broadest possible audience. In this chapter, you will learn how to capture and handle events when using layers and, thereby, how to achieve the most dynamic and useful forms of Web pages' behavior.

The Event Model

The traditional HTML event model included a limited number of events. The DHTML event model was developed by the World Wide Web Consortium (W3C), in association with companies including Microsoft and Netscape. The DHTML event model includes additional object events. For example, the **onload**, **onerror**, and **onabort** events are associated with the image object. The marquee object supports the **onbounce** and **onfinish** events. Similarly, the layer object supports a number of events, including **onblur**, **onfocus**, **onload**, **onmouseover**, and **onmouseout**. In this chapter, you'll learn more about these events and how you can use them with layers to create dynamic Web pages. The chapter includes three examples that demonstrate the use of the **onblur**, **onfocus**, **onload**, **onmouseover**, and **onmouseout** events with the **<LAYER>...</LAYER>** tags. To learn more about the DHTML event model, see Chapter 8. Note, however, that only Netscape Navigator supports the **<LAYER>...</LAYER>** (and the **<ILAYER>...</ILAYER>**) tags. As a result, the Web pages you design by using layers will not work with Internet Explorer.

Terms

This section explains some of the terms commonly used with respect to designing Web sites by using layers. By gaining an understanding of these terms, you will better understand the approach to designing dynamic Web sites by using techniques such as layering.

- *Absolute positioning and layering*—By using Netscape's DHTML specification that includes absolute positioning and layering, you can define the exact location of the elements that will appear within the Web pages you design. In addition, you can layer text over text, text over images, images over text, and so on. As a result, you gain better control over the look and feel of your Web pages.
- ***<LAYER>...</LAYER>***—By using the **<LAYER>...</LAYER>** tag pair, you can define a layer with absolute position.
- ***<ILAYER>...</ILAYER>***—By using the **<ILAYER>...</ILAYER>** tag pair, you can define a layer with relative position.
- *Event model*—The event model defines the events associated with the hierarchy of objects within the DOM.
- *Object-specific events*—These are the events associated with a specific DOM element, e.g., form, image, layer, and so on.

Layering

By using layering, you can define a layer or block of text and graphics. By using content positioning, you can define the layer's exact location within the Web page. Within the DHTML object model, a layer represents an object. Like any other object, the layer object's interface includes properties, methods, and events. By using the JavaScript scripting language, you can control the layer's appearance and behavior. You can implement a number of variations, including the following:

- Overlap one layer over another
- Hide and show the layer (use the **VISIBILITY** attribute)
- Move the layer from one location to another
- Rotate or animate the layer
- Change the layer's color and font dynamically

Content positioning and layering provides greater control over your Web page's elements. As a result, you can design compelling Web pages that are more dynamic in nature.

<LAYER> And **<ILAYER>** Tags

Only Netscape Navigator 4 supports the **<LAYER>...</LAYER>** and **<ILAYER>... </ILAYER>** tag pairs. Like any other HTML object, you can configure a layer's appearance and behavior by manipulating the **<LAYER>** (or **<ILAYER>**) tag's attributes. Table 15.1 shows a list of these attributes. Table 15.2 lists the **<LAYER>** (or **<ILAYER>**) tag's events.

*A layer with a relative position is an inflow layer (**<ILAYER>** tag). Use the **TOP** and **LEFT** attributes to specify the offset of the layer's top-left corner from the current position within the document.*

Table 15.1 <LAYER> (or <ILAYER>) tag's attributes.

Attribute	Description
ABOVE	Specifies the layer that will be above the new layer
BACKGROUND	Specifies the URL that will contain the new layer's background image
BELOW	Specifies the layer that will be below the new layer
BGCOLOR	Specifies the new layer's background color
CLIP	Specifies the new layer's visible area
HEIGHT	Specifies the new layer's height; you can specify the height as an integer value or as a percentage of the layer that will enclose the new layer
ID	Specifies the new layer's name
LEFT	Specifies the horizontal position of the new layer's top-left corner with respect to the parent layer, or the HTML document
PAGEX	Specifies the horizontal position of the new layer's top-left corner, in pixels, with respect to the HTML document

(continued)

Table 15.1 <LAYER> (or <ILAYER>) tag's attributes *(continued)*.

Attribute	Description
PAGEY	Specifies the vertical position of the new layer's top-left corner, in pixels, with respect to the HTML document
SRC	Specifies the external HTML file that contains data the new layer will display
TOP	Specifies the vertical position of the new layer's top-left corner with respect to the parent layer, or the HTML document
VISIBILITY	Specifies if the browser will show or hide the new layer
WIDTH	Specifies the new layer's width. You can specify the width as an integer value. You can also specify the width as a percentage of the layer that will enclose the new layer.
Z-INDEX	Specifies the layers' stacking order

Table 15.2 <LAYER> (or <ILAYER>) tag's events.

Events	Description
onblur	Triggered when the new layer loses keyboard focus
onfocus	Triggered when the new layer gets keyboard focus
onload	Triggered when the browser loads the layer
onmouseout	Triggered when you move your mouse away from the layer
onmouseover	Triggered when you move your mouse over the layer

Additional Resources

For more information about Netscape and Netscape One Technologies, visit the following sites:

- Netscape One Technologies and Netscape Developer Home—**developer.netscape.com/one/index.html**
- Demos of dynamic Web sites using the DHTML specification and Netscape Navigator—**search.netscape.com/comprod/products/communicator/beta_features.html**

For more information on Netscape, HTML 4, JavaScript, and VBScript, refer to the following books from The Coriolis Group (**www.coriolis.com**):

- *Web Design & Development Black Book,* ISBN: 1-57610-162-2
- *JavaScript and Netscape Wizardry,* ISBN: 1-88357-786-1
- *Web Developer's Guide to JavaScript and VBScript,* ISBN: 1-88357-797-7
- *HTML 4 Programmer's Reference,* ISBN: 1-56604-730-7
- *HTML Publishing on the Internet, Second Edition,* ISBN: 1-56604-625-4

Practical Guide To

Handling Events Using Layers

- Using The **<LAYER>... </LAYER>** Tags With The **on mouseover** And **onmouseout** Events
- Using The **<LAYER>... </LAYER>** Tags With The DHTML Event Model
- Using The **<LAYER>... </LAYER>** Tags With The **onload**, **onfocus**, And **onblur** Events

Using The **<LAYER>...</LAYER>** Tags With The **onmouseover** And **onmouseout** Events

This example demonstrates the use of the **<LAYER>...</LAYER>** tag pair and the **onmouseover** and **onmouseout** events. In addition, the example demonstrates how you can implement animation by using layers. To view the page, use Netscape Navigator to open the page from the directory where you saved it. Three images of Coriolis books (*Developing Databases for the Web and Intranets, Developing Real-World Intranets,* and *Cutting Edge Java Game Programming*) slide up and across the Navigator window, as shown in Figure 15.1.

Move your mouse over any of the book images, and Navigator, in turn, displays more information about the book. For example, move your mouse over the image for the book *Developing Real-World Intranets,* and Navigator, in turn, displays the book's description, as shown in Figure 15.2. Move your mouse over the image for the book *Developing Databases for the Web and Intranets,* and Navigator, in turn, displays the book's description.

Move your mouse away from the book's image, and Navigator displays the original instruction text, as shown in Figure 15.3.

Figure 15.1

Layers slide up and across the Netscape Navigator window.

Figure 15.2

Navigator displaying additional information on Developing Real-World Intranets.

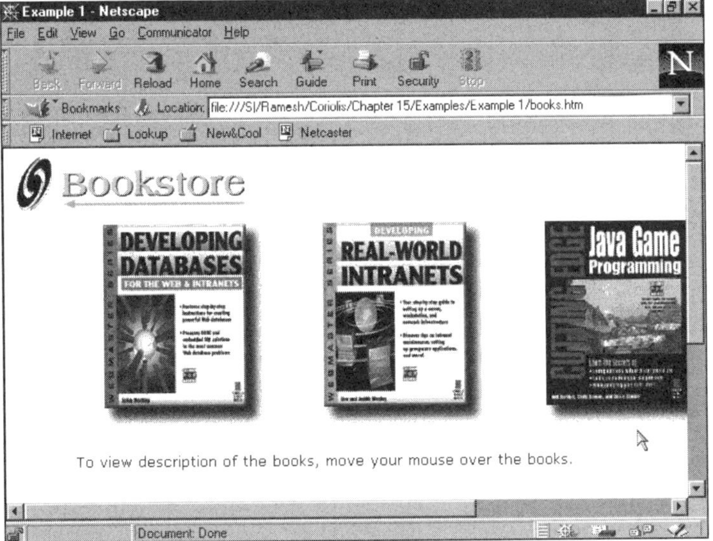

Figure 15.3

Navigator displaying the instruction text.

1. Before writing the HTML code, give some thought to the page's design. Because you will use layers to implement the page, determine what constitutes a layer for the example. Each book's image constitutes a layer. This means you will need three layers for the three images. In addition, each message text needs a layer—another three—as well as the page that provides a description for each book. That is a total of seven layers.

2. Listing 15.1 shows the code for declaring layers for the three book images. Specify values for each layer's **TOP**, **LEFT**, **WIDTH**, and **HEIGHT** attributes. In addition, set each layer's **VISIBILITY** attribute to **HIDE**, and specify the image file's name. By specifying a value for each layer's **ALT** attribute, browsers that do not support layers (e.g., Internet Explorer) will display the alternate text. Also, specify the functions as shown in the code that the browser will call when the **onmouseover** and **onmouseout** events are triggered.

Listing 15.1 Declaring layers for the three book images.

```
<layer name="lyr_image1" top="375" left="-50" visibility="hide"
 onmouseover="show_text(1)" onmouseout="show_text(0)">
        <img src="devdbwi.gif" width="160" height="200" border="0"
         alt="Developing Databases for the Web & Intranets" >
</layer>

<layer name="lyr_image2" top="50" left="-150" visibility="hide"
 onmouseover="show_text(2)" onmouseout="show_text(0)">
        <img src="wdgintra.gif" width="160" height="200" border="0"
         alt="Developing Real-World Intranets" >
</layer>

<layer name="lyr_image3" top="375" left="350" visibility="hide"
 onmouseover="show_text(3)" onmouseout="show_text(0)">
        <img src="jgdevw.gif" width="160" height="200" border="0"
         alt="Cutting-Edge Java Game Programming" >
</layer>
```

3. Listing 15.2 shows the code for declaring a layer for the message text. Specify values for the layer's **TOP**, **LEFT**, and **WIDTH** attributes as shown in the code. In addition, set the layer's **VISIBILITY** attribute to **HIDE**.

Listing 15.2 Declaring a layer for the message text.

```
<layer name="lyr_instruction" top="270" left="10%" width="700"
 visibility="hide" >
<p><font size="2" face="Verdana">To view description of the
    books, move your mouse over the books.<br>
</layer>
```

Similarly, the code for declaring layers for the books' descriptions is shown in Listing 15.3.

Listing 15.3 Declaring layers for the three books.

```
<layer name="lyr_text1" top="275" left="10%" width="700"
 visibility="hide">
<p><font size="2" face="Verdana"><strong>Developing Databases for
the Web &amp; Intranets</strong><br>
Your Step-by-Step Guide to Creating Powerful Web Databases<br>
by John Rodley <br>
<br>
Written by bestselling author John Rodley, Developing
Databases for the Web and Intranets covers both intranet and
commercial Web development. Readers will learn how to design
secure databases (using ODBC and SQL examples) that work smoothly
over the Web and corporate intranets. Readers will also learn how
to use CGI, HTML, script languages, and Web programming tools
such as Java applets. No other book provides coverage of all
these topics in a single, comprehensive volume. </font></p>
</layer>

<layer name="lyr_text2" top="275" left="10%" width="700"
 visibility="hide">
<p><font size="2" face="Verdana"><strong>Developing Real-World Intranets
</strong><br>
Your Hands-On Guide to Implementing Intraprise-Wide Systems<br>
by Dan and Judith Wesley <br>
<br>
Developing Real-World Intranets shows how companies can save thousands of
dollars, while doing away with unnecessary paper-based manuals
and communications tools. The authors explore details that you need to know
before creating an intranet for your business: design strategies, database
integration, security, maintenance, application software selection, and
connectivity issues. Emerging technologies and trends in intranet development
are also discussed. Based on Internet technology, intranets are the hottest
new information-sharing tool for companies. </font></p>
</layer>

<layer name="lyr_text3" top="275" left="10%" width="700"
 visibility="hide">
<p><font size="2" face="Verdana"><strong>Cutting-Edge Java Game Programming
</strong><br>
Everything You Need to Create Interactive Internet Games with Java<br>
by Neil Bartlett, Chris Stranc, and Steve Simkin <br>
<br>
Cutting-Edge Java Game Programming teaches readers to use Java to create
multi-player World Wide Web games, and how to create several different types
of games for the World Wide Web, including action games with realistic
```

```
movement and collision detection. Games are the next killer app for the
Internet and Cutting-Edge Java Game Programming shows you how to write them.
Packed with advanced Java programming, it clearly and concisely presents all
you need to excel in this entertainment revolution. Included are two free
complete game development frameworks: one for single-player games and one
for multiplayer networked games.  </font></p>
</layer>
```

4. Again, specify values for each layer's **TOP**, **LEFT**, and **WIDTH** attributes as shown in the code. In addition, set each layer's **VISIBILITY** attribute to **HIDE**. To implement the animation and display text when the user moves the mouse over and away from the book's images, write event-driven code by using JavaScript. Specify counters for each layer's movement across the screen. In addition, save a reference to each layer by indexing into the layers array of the document object, as shown in Listing 15.4.

Listing 15.4 Saving references and establishing counters.

```
lyr1_step1 = 25;
lyr1       = document.layers["lyr_image1"];

lyr2       = document.layers["lyr_image2"];
lyr2_step1 = 50;
lyr2_step2 = 50;

lyr3_step1 = 25;
lyr3       = document.layers["lyr_image3"];

lyr4       = document.layers["lyr_instruction"];
lyr5       = document.layers["lyr_text1"];
lyr6       = document.layers["lyr_text2"];
lyr7       = document.layers["lyr_text3"];
```

5. Define a function **start_slide1** that will slide the first layer (lyr1) up the screen. Listing 15.5 shows the code. Within the function, set the layer's **VISIBILITY** attribute to show. Then, if lyr1's counter is greater than zero, move the layer to the given x and y location within the screen, and decrement the layer's counter by 1. If the layer's counter is still greater than zero, set the timeout to 20 seconds. After 20 seconds, the browser calls the function **start_slide1**, slides the layer up again, and decrements the layer's counter by 1. As a result, you see the image moving up the screen. The above steps repeat until the layer's counter reaches 0. Then, the browser calls the function **start_slide2**.

Listing 15.5 The JavaScript function start_slide1.

```
function start_slide1()
{
   lyr1.visibility="show";
        if(lyr1_step1>0)
   {
             lyr1.moveBy(1,-lyr1_step1);
                  lyr1_step1--;
      if(lyr1_step1 > 0)
      {
         setTimeout("start_slide1()",20);
      }
      else
      {
         start_slide2();
      }
   }
}
```

6. Define another function, **start_slide2**, that will slide the second layer (lyr2) across the screen. Within the function **start_slide2**, move the layer to the given x and y location within the screen as shown in Listing 15.6. In addition, set the layer's **VISIBILITY** attribute to **SHOW**, and set the timeout to 30 seconds. When the timer expires, the browser calls the function **move_slide2**. Within the function **move_slide2**, the browser moves the layer to the given x and y location within the screen. Decrement the layer's counters as shown in Listing 15.6. Then, if the layer's step1 counter is greater than 3, set the timer to 20 seconds, or else call the function **start_slide3**. When the timer expires, the browser calls the function **move_slide2** again. As a result, you see the image moving across the screen.

Listing 15.6 The JavaScript functions start_slide2 and move_slide2.

```
function start_slide2()
{
   lyr2.moveBy(-600,0);
        lyr2.visibility="show";
        setTimeout("move_slide2()",30);
}

function move_slide2()
{
   lyr2.moveBy(lyr2_step2,0);
   lyr2_step1-=2;
        lyr2_step2-=1;
```

```
        if(lyr2_step1 > 3)
        {
           setTimeout("move_slide2()",20);
        }
        else
        {
           start_slide3();
        }
}
```

7. Define another function **start_slide3** that will slide the third layer (lyr3) up the screen. Listing 15.7 shows the code. This function is similar to the function **start_slide1**. Within the function, set the layer's visibility attribute to show. Then, if lyr3's counter is greater than 0, move the layer to the given x and y location within the screen, and decrement the layer's counter by 1. If the layer's counter is still greater than zero, set the timeout to 20 seconds. After 20 seconds, the browser calls the function **start_slide1** again. The browser, in turn, slides the layer up again, and decrements the layer's counter by 1. These steps repeat until the layer's counter reaches zero. Then, the browser calls the function **show_text**.

Listing 15.7 The JavaScript function start_slide3.

```
function start_slide3()
{
   lyr3.visibility="show";
         if(lyr3_step1>0)
   {
         lyr3.moveBy(1,-lyr3_step1);
                lyr3_step1--;
      if(lyr3_step1 > 0)
      {
         setTimeout("start_slide3()",20);
      }
      else
      {
         show_text(0);
      }
   }
}
```

8. Define the function **show_text** that will hide or show the appropriate layer based on the user's mouse movement. Listing 15.8 shows the code.

Listing 15.8 The JavaScript function show_text.

```
function show_text(layer_no)
{
   if (layer_no == 0)
   {
      lyr4.visibility="show";
      lyr5.visibility="hide";
      lyr6.visibility="hide";
      lyr7.visibility="hide";
   }
   else if (layer_no == 1)
   {
      lyr4.visibility="hide";
      lyr5.visibility="show";
      lyr6.visibility="hide";
      lyr7.visibility="hide";
   }
   else if (layer_no == 2)
   {
      lyr4.visibility="hide";
      lyr5.visibility="hide";
      lyr6.visibility="show";
      lyr7.visibility="hide";
   }
   else if (layer_no == 3) {
      lyr4.visibility="hide";
      lyr5.visibility="hide";
      lyr6.visibility="hide";
      lyr7.visibility="show";
   }
}
```

Because Internet Explorer does not support the **<LAYER>** tag, the example will not work within the browser. Internet Explorer displays an error message, as shown in Figure 15.4. Listing 15.9 shows the page's complete code.

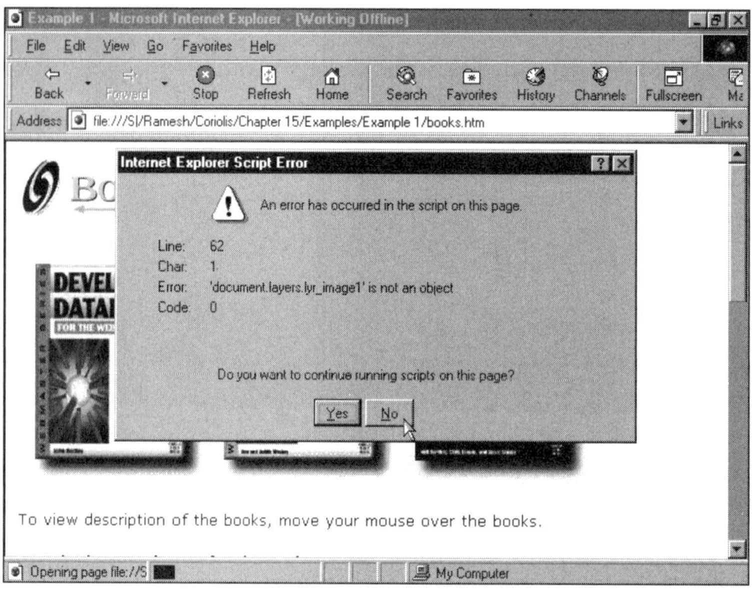

Figure 15.4

Viewing the page within Internet Explorer.

Listing 15.9 Using the <LAYER> tag with the onmouseover and onmouseout events.

```
<html>
<head>
<title>Example 1</title>
</head>

<body bgcolor="#FFFFFF" onload="start_slide1()">

<p><img src="bookstoretitle.gif" width="245" height="50"></p>

<layer name="lyr_image1" top="375" left="-50" visibility="hide"
 onmouseover="show_text(1)" onmouseout="show_text(0)">
       <img src="devdbwi.gif" width="160" height="200" border="0"
        alt="Developing Databases for the Web & Intranets" >
</layer>

<layer name="lyr_image2" top="50" left="-150" visibility="hide"
 onmouseover="show_text(2)" onmouseout="show_text(0)">
       <img src="wdgintra.gif" width="160" height="200" border="0"
        alt="Developing Real-World Intranets" >
</layer>
```

```
<layer name="lyr_image3" top="375" left="350" visibility="hide"
 onmouseover="show_text(3)" onmouseout="show_text(0)">
       <img src="jgdevw.gif" width="160" height="200" border="0"
        alt="Cutting-Edge Java Game Programming" >
</layer>

<layer name="lyr_instruction" top="270" left="10%" width="700"
 visibility="hide">
<p><font size="2" face="Verdana">To view description of the books, move
   your mouse over the books.<br>
</layer>

<layer name="lyr_text1" top="275" left="10%" width="700" visibility="hide">
<p><font size="2" face="Verdana"><strong>Developing Databases for
the Web &amp; Intranets</strong><br>
Your Step-by-Step Guide to Creating Powerful Web Databases<br>
by John Rodley <br>
<br>
Written by bestselling author John Rodley, Developing
Databases for the Web and Intranets covers both intranet and
commercial Web development. Readers will learn how to design
secure databases (using ODBC and SQL examples) that work smoothly
over the Web and corporate intranets. Readers will also learn how
to use CGI, HTML, script languages, and Web programming tools
such as Java applets. No other book provides coverage of all
these topics in a single, comprehensive volume. </font></p>
</layer>

<layer name="lyr_text2" top="275" left="10%" width="700" visibility="hide">
<p><font size="2" face="Verdana"><strong>Developing Real-World Intranets
</strong><br>
Your Hands-On Guide to Implementing Intraprise-Wide Systems<br>
by Dan and Judith Wesley <br>
<br>
Developing Real-World Intranets shows how companies can save thousands of
dollars, while doing away with unnecessary paper-based manuals and
communications tools. The authors explore details that you need to know
before creating an intranet for your business: design strategies, database
integration, security, maintenance, application software selection, and
connectivity issues. Emerging technologies and trends in intranet development
are also discussed. Based on Internet technology, intranets are the hottest
new information-sharing tool for companies. </font></p>
</layer>

<layer name="lyr_text3" top="275" left="10%" width="700" visibility="hide">
<p><font size="2" face="Verdana"><strong>Cutting-Edge Java Game Programming
</strong><br>
```

```
Everything You Need to Create Interactive Internet Games with Java<br>
by Neil Bartlett, Chris Stranc, and Steve Simkin <br>
<br>
Cutting-Edge Java Game Programming teaches readers to use Java to create
multi-player World Wide Web games, and how to create several different types
of games for the World Wide Web, including action games with realistic
movement and collision detection. Games are the next killer app for the
Internet and Cutting-Edge Java Game Programming shows you how to write them.
Packed with advanced Java programming, it clearly and concisely presents all
you need to excel in this entertainment revolution. Included are two free
complete game development frameworks: one for single-player games and one
for multiplayer networked games.  </font></p>
</layer>

<script language="JavaScript">

lyr1_step1 = 25;
lyr1       = document.layers["lyr_image1"];

lyr2       = document.layers["lyr_image2"];
lyr2_step1 = 50;
lyr2_step2 = 50;

lyr3_step1 = 25;
lyr3       = document.layers["lyr_image3"];

lyr4       = document.layers["lyr_instruction"];
lyr5       = document.layers["lyr_text1"];
lyr6       = document.layers["lyr_text2"];
lyr7       = document.layers["lyr_text3"];

function start_slide1()
{
   lyr1.visibility="show";
   if(lyr1_step1>0)
{
      lyr1.moveBy(1,-lyr1_step1);
      lyr1_step1--;
      if(lyr1_step1 > 0)
      {
         setTimeout("start_slide1()",20);
      }
      else
      {
         start_slide2();
      }
    }
}
```

```
function start_slide2()
{
   lyr2.moveBy(-600,0);
   lyr2.visibility="show";
   setTimeout("move_slide2()",30);
}

function move_slide2()
{
   lyr2.moveBy(lyr2_step2,0);
   lyr2_step1-=2;
   lyr2_step2-=1;

   if(lyr2_step1 > 3)
   {
      setTimeout("move_slide2()",20);
    }
    else
    {
      start_slide3();
    }
}

function start_slide3()
{
    lyr3.visibility="show";
    if(lyr3_step1>0)
    {
       lyr3.moveBy(1,-lyr3_step1);
       lyr3_step1--;
       if(lyr3_step1 > 0)
       {
       setTimeout("start_slide3()",20);
       }
       else
       {
          show_text(0);
       }
    }
}

function show_text(layer_no)
{
   if (layer_no == 0)
   {
     lyr4.visibility="show";
     lyr5.visibility="hide";
```

```
      lyr6.visibility="hide";
      lyr7.visibility="hide";
    }
    else if (layer_no == 1)
    {
      lyr4.visibility="hide";
      lyr5.visibility="show";
      lyr6.visibility="hide";
      lyr7.visibility="hide";
   }
   else if (layer_no == 2)
   {
      lyr4.visibility="hide";
      lyr5.visibility="hide";
      lyr6.visibility="show";
      lyr7.visibility="hide";
   }
   else if (layer_no == 3) {
      lyr4.visibility="hide";
      lyr5.visibility="hide";
      lyr6.visibility="hide";
      lyr7.visibility="show";
    }
}

</script>

</body>
</html>
```

 Using The **<LAYER>...</LAYER>** Tags With The DHTML Event Model

This example demonstrates the use of the **<LAYER>...</LAYER>** tag pair and the event model's **mousemove**, **mouseup**, and **mousedown** events. By using these events, the example demonstrates how you can apply drag-and-drop functionality to layers.

Load the page from your local directory within Netscape Navigator. The three blocks shown in Figure 15.5 will display. The task is to drag and drop the blocks to construct a rectangle. Move your mouse over the blocks, and you will notice the cursor's shape changes to a hand. You can now move the blocks to construct the rectangle.

1. As in the previous example, give some thought to the page's design before writing the HTML code. Because you will use layers to implement the page, determine what constitutes a layer for the example. Each block constitutes a layer. Because there are three blocks, declare three layers, one for each block.

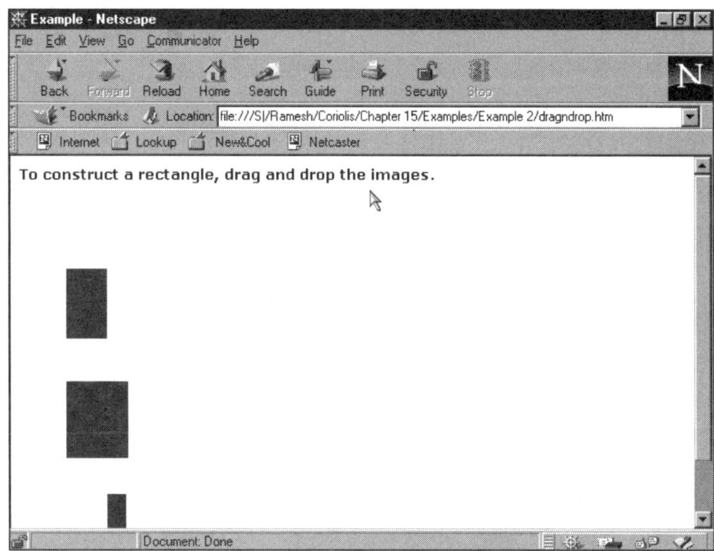

Figure 15.5

Navigator displaying the three blocks.

Specify values for each layer's anchor, image, width, height, border, and alternate text attributes as shown in Listing 15.10.

Listing 15.10 Declaring layers for the three blocks.

```
<layer name="layer_img1" top="100" left="50">
   <a href="#"><img src="block_a.gif" width="37" height="62" border="0"
   alt="Block A"></a>
</layer>

<layer name="layer_img2"  top="200" left="50">
   <a href="#"><img src="block_b.gif" width="56" height="68" border="0"
   alt="Block B"></a>
</layer>

<layer name="layer_img3"  top="300" left="50">
   <a href="#"><img src="block_c.gif" width="110" height="82" border="0"
   alt="Block C"></a>
</layer>
```

2. Declare JavaScript functions that the browser will execute based on the events triggered. The three functions **stop_drag**, **start_drag**, and **continue_drag** process the events. On the **mousedown** event, the function **start_drag** grabs

the **mousemove** events. On the **mousemove** event, the function **continue_drag** executes the dragging of the image.

To implement dragging, the function **continue_drag** uses the **moveBy** method. In addition, the function **continue_drag** saves the image's new x and y coordinates as the current coordinates. On the **mouseup** event, the function **stop_drag** clears the **onmousemove** events and stops the drag.

3. Define a function **start** that calls another function **initialize** for the three layers, as shown in Listing 15.11. When you load the page within Navigator, Navigator calls the function **start**. The function **initialize** performs initialization by specifying the layer capturing the event, obtaining a handle to the parent object of the layers, specifying the starting position, and defining the events the browser will handle.

Listing 15.11 The JavaScript functions to process the events.

```
<script>
function start()
{
   myDrag = new initialize(1);
   myDrag2= new initialize(2);
   myDrag3= new initialize(3);
}

function initialize(layer_no)
{
   if (layer_no == 1)
   {
      // specified the layer capturing the event
      this.layer=window.document.layers["layer_img1"];
   }

   if (layer_no == 2)
   {
      // specified the layer capturing the event
      this.layer=window.document.layers["layer_img2"];
   }

   if (layer_no == 3)
   {
      // specified the layer capturing the event
      this.layer=window.document.layers["layer_img3"];
   }

   // handle to the object
   this.layer.document.parent0=this;
```

```
    // specified the old position
    this.oldX=0;
    this.oldY=0;

    // define the events to handle
    this.layer.document.captureEvents(Event.MOUSEUP|Event.MOUSEDOWN);
    this.layer.document.onmousedown=start_drag;
    this.layer.document.onmouseup  =stop_drag;
}

// On mouseup event, clear the mouseMove events
function stop_drag(e)
{
    this.onmousemove=null;
    this.releaseEvents(Event.MOUSEMOVE);
    return false;
}

// On mousedown event, grab the mouseMove events
function start_drag(e)
{
    this.parent0.layer.zIndex=10
    this.captureEvents(Event.MOUSEMOVE);
    this.onmousemove=continue_drag;
    this.parent0.oldX= e.pageX;
    this.parent0.oldY= e.pageY;
    return false;
}

// On mousemove event, move the layers
function continue_drag(e)
{
    this.parent0.layer.moveBy(e.pageX - this.parent0.oldX, e.pageY -
    this.parent0.oldY);
    this.parent0.oldX = e.pageX;
    this.parent0.oldY = e.pageY;
}
</script>
```

As in the previous example, this will not work within Internet Explorer. Listing 15.12 shows the page's complete code.

Listing 15.12 Using the <LAYER>...</LAYER> tag with the DHTML event model.

```
<HTML>
<TITLE>Example
</TITLE>
```

```
<HEAD>
</HEAD>
<BODY onLoad="start()">
<p><font size="2" face="Verdana">
<strong>To construct a rectangle, drag and drop the images.</strong>
<p>

<layer name="layer_img1" top="100" left="50">
   <a href="#"><img src="block_a.gif" width="37" height="62"
   border="0" alt="Block A"></a>
</layer>

<layer name="layer_img2"  top="200" left="50">
   <a href="#"><img src="block_b.gif" width="56" height="68"
   border="0" alt="Block B"></a>
</layer>

<layer name="layer_img3"  top="300" left="50">
   <a href="#"><img src="block_c.gif" width="110" height="82"
   border="0" alt="Block C"></a>
</layer>

</BODY>

<script>
function start()
{
   myDrag = new initialize(1);
   myDrag2= new initialize(2);
   myDrag3= new initialize(3);
}

function initialize(layer_no)
{
   if (layer_no == 1)
   {
      // specified the layer capturing the event
      this.layer=window.document.layers["layer_img1"];
   }

   if (layer_no == 2)
   {
      // specified the layer capturing the event
      this.layer=window.document.layers["layer_img2"];
   }

   if (layer_no == 3)
   {
```

```
        // specified the layer capturing the event
        this.layer=window.document.layers["layer_img3"];
    }

    // handle to the object
    this.layer.document.parent0=this;

    // specified the old position
    this.oldX=0;
    this.oldY=0;

    // define the events to handle
    this.layer.document.captureEvents(Event.MOUSEUP|Event.MOUSEDOWN);
    this.layer.document.onmousedown=start_drag;
    this.layer.document.onmouseup  =stop_drag;
}

// On mouseup event, clear the mouseMove events
function stop_drag(e)
{
    this.onmousemove=null;
    this.releaseEvents(Event.MOUSEMOVE);
    return false;
}

// On mousedown event, grab the mouseMove events
function start_drag(e)
{
    this.parent0.layer.zIndex=10
    this.captureEvents(Event.MOUSEMOVE);
    this.onmousemove=continue_drag;
    this.parent0.oldX= e.pageX;
    this.parent0.oldY= e.pageY;
    return false;
}

// On mousemove event, move the layers
function continue_drag(e)
{
    this.parent0.layer.moveBy(e.pageX - this.parent0.oldX, e.pageY -
        this.parent0.oldY);
    this.parent0.oldX = e.pageX;
    this.parent0.oldY = e.pageY;
}
</script>

</HTML>
```

Using The **<LAYER>...</LAYER>** Tags With The **onload**, **onfocus**, And **onblur** Events

This example demonstrates the use of the **<LAYER>...</LAYER>** tag pair, and the **onload**, **onfocus**, and **onblur** events. Load the page from your local directory using Navigator. The page is shown in Figure 15.6.

When you load the page within Navigator, Navigator displays the text "We welcome your suggestions." Click your mouse within the Suggestions input text area, and the input text area gets focus, and the text "The best suggestion gets a free T-shirt!!!" will display, as shown in Figure 15.7. Click your mouse outside the Suggestions input text area and the input text area loses focus, reverting to the text "We welcome your suggestions."

1. Again, before writing the HTML code, determine what constitutes a layer for the example. The input text area constitutes a layer. In addition, the message bar constitutes a layer. Because the page will display two different messages, design two layers for the two messages. You can also design the page's title as a layer. That is a total of four layers.
2. Declare a layer for the page's title and specify values for the layer's **TOP** and **LEFT** attributes, as shown in Listing 15.13.

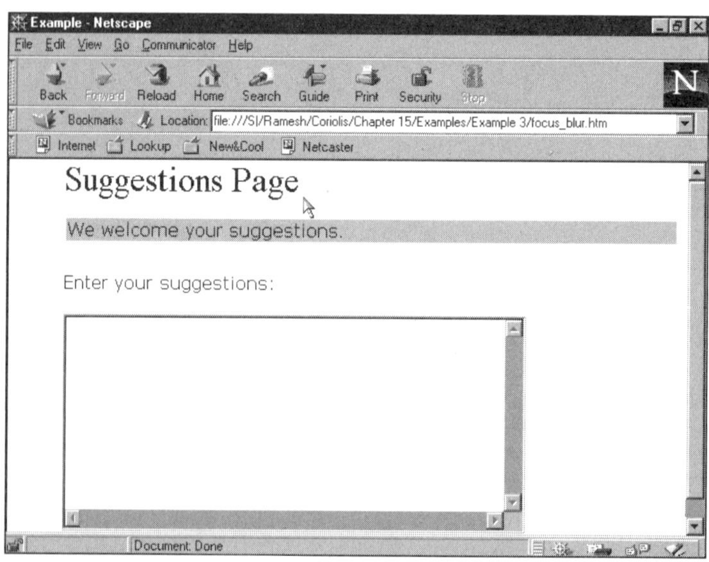

Figure 15.6

Navigator displaying the Suggestions Page.

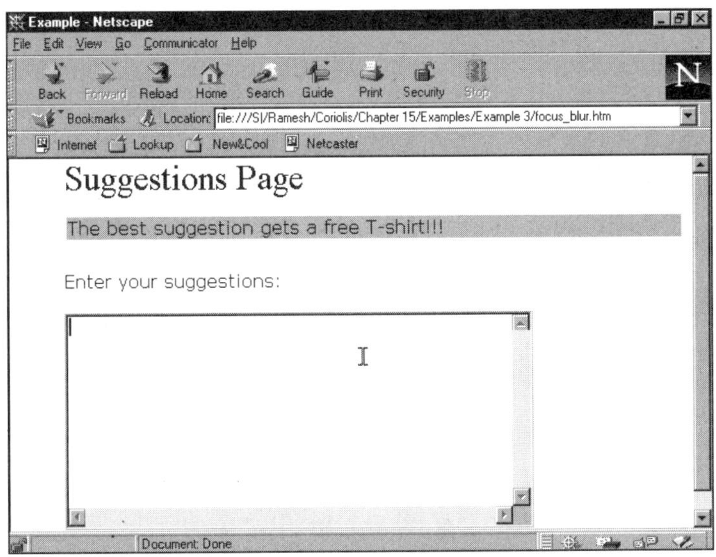

Figure 15.7

When you click within the input text area, the message bar displays a different message.

Listing 15.13 Declaring a layer for the page's title.

```
<layer name="title" top="0" left="50">
<font color="#000080" size="6">Suggestions Page</font>
</layer>
```

3. Declare the two layers for the two messages and specify values for each layer's **TOP** and **LEFT** attributes, as shown in Listing 15.14.
4. Set each layer's **VISIBILITY** attribute to **HIDE**. Use the **<TABLE>...</TABLE>** tags to display the message bar within each layer.

Listing 15.14 Declaring layers for the two messages.

```
<layer name="lyr_clear" top="50" left="50" visibility="hide">
<table border="0" width="100%" bgcolor="#C0C0C0">
    <tr>
        <td width="100%"><font face="Verdana">We welcome your
         suggestions.</font></td>
    </tr>
</table>
</layer>
```

```
<layer name="lyr_instruction" top="50" left="50" visibility="hide">
<table border="0" width="100%" bgcolor="#C0C0C0">
    <tr>
        <td width="100%"><font face="Verdana">The best suggestion gets a
         free T-shirt!!!</font></td>
    </tr>
</table>
</layer>
```

5. Before you declare the remaining layer, define the two JavaScript functions **show_help** and **no_help**, as shown in Listing 15.15. This is because the remaining layer's declaration will reference the two JavaScript functions. The function **show_help** displays the context-sensitive message layer (the layer that displays the text "The best suggestion gets a free T-shirt!!!") and hides the welcome message layer (the layer that displays the text "We welcome your suggestions."). The function **no_help** does the opposite of **show_help**, that is, the function **no_help** displays the welcome message layer and hides the context-sensitive message layer.

Listing 15.15 The JavaScript functions show_help and no_help.

```
<script>
lyr1 = document.layers["lyr_clear"];
lyr2 = document.layers["lyr_instruction"];

function show_help()
{
  lyr1. visibility="hide";
  lyr2.visibility="show";
}

function no_help()
{
  lyr1.visibility="show";
  lyr2.visibility="hide";
}
```

6. Declare a layer for the input text area, specify values for the layer's top and left attributes, and specify the JavaScript functions for the layer's three events: **onfocus**, **onblur**, and **onload**, as shown in Listing 15.16. Use the **<TEXTAREA> ...</TEXTAREA>** tags to display the input text area.

Listing 15.16 Declaring a layer for the input text area.

```
<layer name="lyr_form" top="100" left="50" onfocus="show_help()" onblur="no_help
()" onload="no_help()">
   <form name="test">
     <p>
        <font face="Verdana">Enter your suggestions: </font><p>
        <textarea name="suggestion" rows="10" cols="50"></textarea>
     </p>
   </form>
</layer>
```

As in the previous examples, this example will not work within Internet Explorer. Listing 15.17 shows the page's complete code.

Listing 15.17 Using the <LAYER>...</LAYER> tags with the onload, onblur, and onfocus events.

```
<html>

<head>
<title>Example </title>
</head>

<body bgcolor="#FFFFFF">

<layer name="title" top="0" left="50">
<font color="#000080" size="6">Suggestions Page</font>
</layer>

<layer name="lyr_clear" top="50" left="50" visibility="hide">
<table border="0" width="100%" bgcolor="#C0C0C0">
   <tr>
      <td width="100%"><font face="Verdana">We welcome your
          suggestions.</font></td>
   </tr>
</table>
</layer>

<layer name="lyr_instruction" top="50" left="50" visibility="hide">
<table border="0" width="100%" bgcolor="#C0C0C0">
    <tr>
      <td width="100%"><font face="Verdana">The best suggestion gets a
          free T-shirt!!!</font></td>
    </tr>
</table>
</layer>
```

```
<script>
lyr1 = document.layers["lyr_clear"];
lyr2 = document.layers["lyr_instruction"];

function show_help()
{
   lyr1.visibility="hide";
   lyr2.visibility="show";
}

function no_help()
{
   lyr1.visibility="show";
   lyr2.visibility="hide";
}
</script>

<layer name="lyr_form" top="100" left="50" onfocus="show_help()"
onblur="no_help()" onload="no_help()">
   <form name="test">
     <p>
       <font face="Verdana">Enter your suggestions: </font><p>
       <textarea name="suggestion" rows="10" cols="50"></textarea>
     </p>
   </form>
</layer>

</body>
</html>
```

Chapter 16

Data Sources And Layers

In this chapter, we explore data binding and Dynamic HTML, as well as how to implement data binding using layers and Netscape Navigator.

Notes...

Chapter 16

In Chapter 10, you learned how to implement data binding using Microsoft technology: Internet Explorer 4, the Advanced Data Connector (ADC), and the Tabular Data Control (TDC). Only browsers based on the Dynamic HTML object model (Internet Explorer 4 and Netscape Navigator/Communicator 4) will support data binding. In this chapter, you will learn about Netscape's approach to implementing data binding. As you will see, Netscape's approach is different from Microsoft's.

Dynamic HTML Model

Although Microsoft Internet Explorer's market share continues to grow, Netscape commands a very strong share of the browser market; both industry giants are obviously interested in increasing their share of the market. Like Microsoft's Internet Explorer 4, Netscape's Navigator 4 is a major release that supports the Dynamic HTML model among other important features. However, Netscape's specification for dynamic HTML is different from Microsoft's Dynamic HTML, even though both companies worked with the World Wide Web Consortium (W3C) in developing their specifications. Whereas Microsoft's model relies primarily on its ActiveX technology, Netscape's model includes layering, Cascading Style Sheets, and downloadable fonts.

Netscape distributes Navigator 4 as part of its Communicator 4 suite, which includes the following programs:

- *Navigator*—You can use Netscape Navigator to access information on the Internet and over an intranet. Netscape Navigator allows you to access information from a variety of datasources, including legacy applications and corporate databases. The Microsoft counterpart to Navigator is Internet Explorer.
- *Messenger*—Netscape Messenger is an email program that allows you to create rich, HTML-aware email. In addition, you can embed images in your email documents and filter and organize the incoming messages into folders. For security, you can encrypt and decrypt your Messenger email. The Microsoft counterpart to Messenger is Outlook Express.
- *Collabra*—Netscape Collabra allows you to conduct online discussion groups on the Internet and over your organization's intranet. The Microsoft counterpart is NetMeeting.
- *Composer*—Netscape Composer helps you create, edit, and publish WYSIWYG online documents very easily. The Microsoft counterpart to Composer is FrontPage Express.
- *Conference*—Netscape Conference enables you to conduct online audio and video conferencing. Conference also supports such features as chat, whiteboard, and file transfer. The Microsoft counterpart to Conference is NetMeeting.
- *Netcaster*—Netscape Netcaster allows you to subscribe to information and schedule automatic delivery of the information to your desktop. You can configure Netcaster to view the latest and greatest information offline, thus reducing online time and charges. The Microsoft counterpart to Netcaster is its Active Desktop components.

*To download Netscape Navigator or to get more information about the different editions of Netscape Navigator and Netscape Communicator, visit Netscape's Web site at **www.netscape.com/download/index.html**.*

Learning By Example

The best way to learn about the kind of dynamic Web sites you can design using Netscape Navigator and Netscape's dynamic HTML specification is by looking at a few Web sites that have already put this technology to work. You will find a number of Web sites powered by Netscape's dynamic HTML specification, starting with Netscape's home page (see Figure 16.1) at **home.netscape.com**, which uses layering to display the information.

Dynamic HTML Demos At Netscape's Web Site

The Web site at **search.netscape.com/comprod/products/communicator/beta_features.html** includes hyperlinks to a number of demos you can view using Navigator 4 to gain a better understanding of Netscape's dynamic HTML features and capabilities. We recommend you start by choosing the appropriate screen resolution and clicking over to the Stella Chelsea demo for an excellent example of dynamic HTML positioning and layering (see Figure 16.2).

Navigator will load the demo, as shown in Figure 16.3.

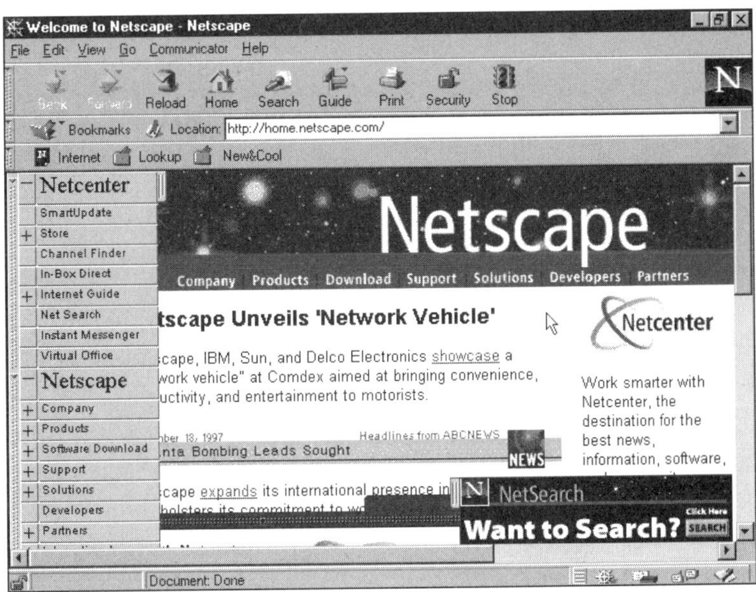

Figure 16.1

Netscape's home page uses layers to display information.

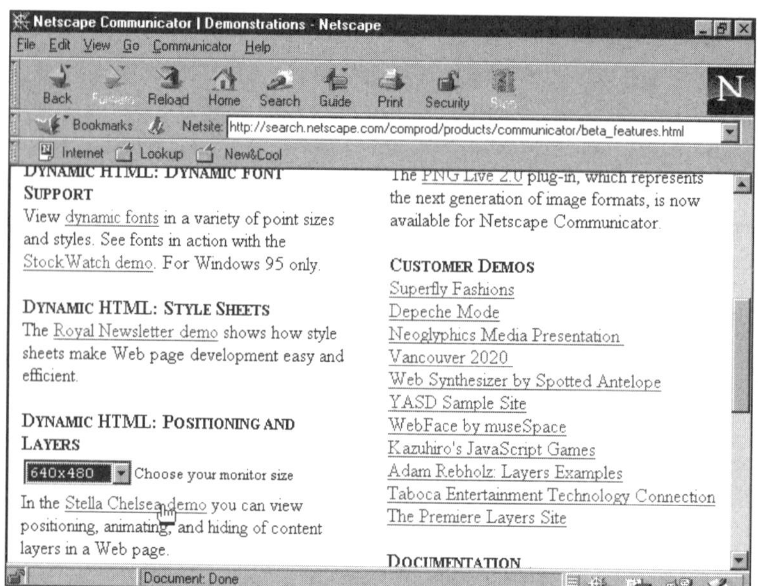

Figure 16.2

Getting ready to view the Stella Chelsea demo.

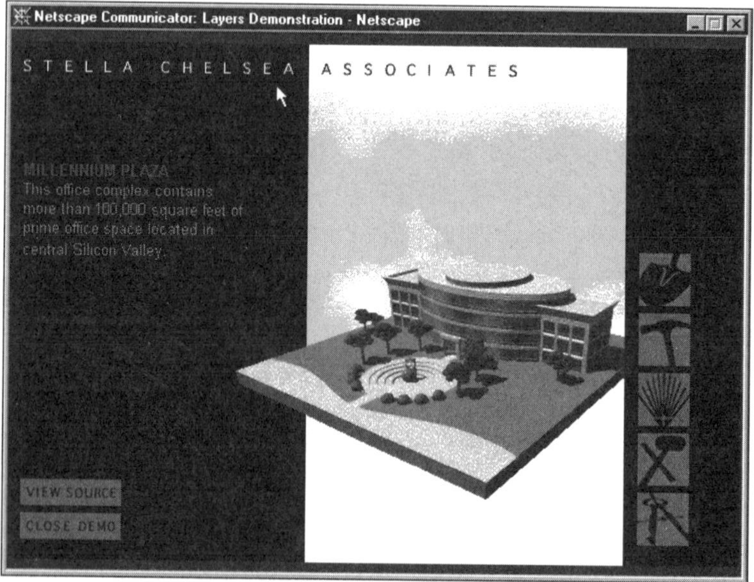

Figure 16.3

Running the Stella Chelsea demo.

On the right-hand side of your screen you will see a column of five different icons. Move your mouse over the first icon and Navigator will display the text for Groundwork on your screen's left-hand side. Next, move your mouse over the second icon; Navigator will display the text for Building Contractor on the left-hand side your screen, as shown in Figure 16.4. As you can see, the information on the left-hand side of your screen changes dynamically as you move your mouse to different locations on the right-hand side. The Stella Chelsea demo uses dynamic HTML layering and positioning. To view the page's source code, click View|Source.

To view another demo that demonstrates dynamic HTML layering, click over to Adam Rebholz: Layers Examples. You might also want to spend few moments viewing other dynamic HTML demos, including the following:

- The Royal Newsletter, which demonstrates dynamic HTML style sheets
- The StockWatch, which illustrates the use of dynamic fonts
- The Vacation Planner, which shows how you can drag and drop HTML objects

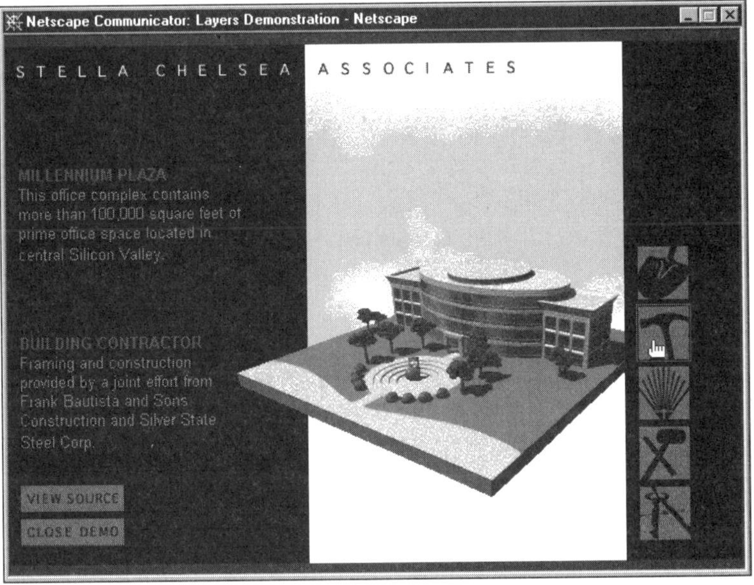

Figure 16.4

Navigator displays information about the Building Contractor.

Two Different Worlds

Netscape's dynamic HTML specification differs from Microsoft's and as a result, the dynamic and data-driven sites developed using Microsoft's technology, the Dynamic HTML model, and Internet Explorer will not work with Netscape Navigator, and vice-versa. For example, load the Example1.html file you created in Chapter 10 using Netscape Navigator. Figure 16.5 shows the results.

The difference in the results is because Netscape Navigator and Microsoft Internet Explorer are designed using different technologies; Internet Explorer is based on Microsoft's COM and ActiveX technology and Netscape uses plug-in technology. Internet Explorer is an ActiveX container supporting a suite of ActiveX technologies, including ActiveX controls, Active documents, ActiveX scripting, and so on. For example, Internet Explorer includes full support for controls such as the Advanced Data Connector (ADC) and Tabular Data Control (TDC). In addition, you can view Microsoft Word and Excel documents (Active documents) within Internet Explorer; with Netscape Navigator you must use a plug-in to view Word and Excel documents.

Netscape Navigator does not include built-in support for ActiveX technology. To view Active content using Netscape Navigator, you must use a third-party plug-in,

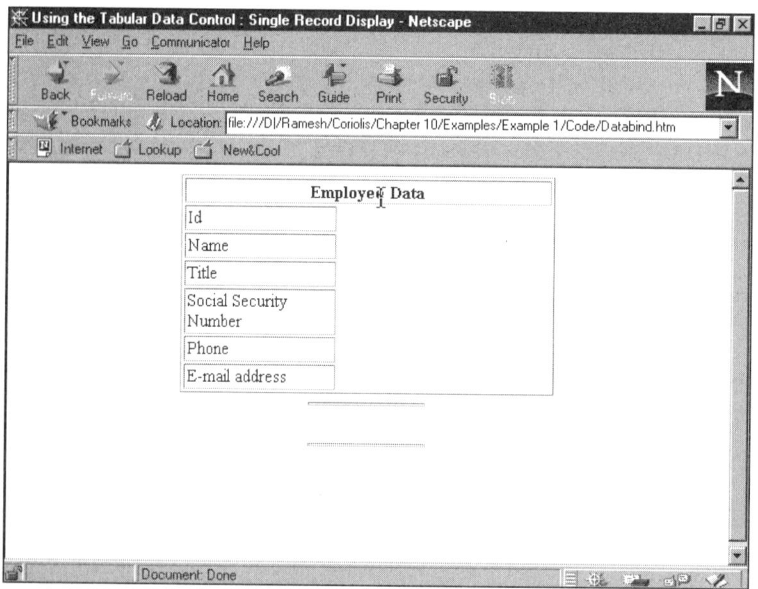

Figure 16.5

Using Netscape Navigator with Microsoft's Tabular Data Control.

such as NCompassLabs' ScriptActive. Bear in mind, however, that the ScriptActive plug-in will not work with every ActiveX control (see Figure 16.5). This means that you need to choose the technology for designing your Web site judiciously. Your choice should depend primarily on your target audience and the hardware and software your audience uses. For example, if you design an intranet site for a corporation that already has significant investment in Microsoft technology, it makes sense to design the site based on Microsoft's ActiveX. Assuming everyone within the corporation will be using the same technology to view and interact with the site, you can be sure the Active site you design will work without any major problems. This lets you take advantage of ActiveX controls; Microsoft's Dynamic HTML specification; and other Microsoft technologies, such as Active documents, ActiveX scripting, Active server, Active Server Components, and so on. On the other hand, Netscape Navigator currently supports the widest possible target clients, including Windows, Macintosh, and Unix. So, if you're not sure about the client platform of your target audience, consider using Netscape technology.

Terms

This section explains some of the common terms used when designing Web sites with Netscape's dynamic HTML specification. An understanding of these terms helps you to understand better how to design dynamic Web sites:

- *Absolute positioning and layering*—Netscape's dynamic HTML specification includes absolute positioning and layering, which you use to define the exact location of the elements that appear in your Web pages. You can layer text over text, text over images, images over text, and so on, which gives you better control over the Web pages' look and feel.
- *Downloadable fonts*—Prior to downloadable fonts, you could design a Web site using a particular font, but your users might get a different look altogether because their system didn't support that font. Using the dynamic HTML downloadable font feature, you can configure your Web site to download the required fonts onto the user's system at runtime, and all your visitors will see the site as you designed it.
- *Plug-ins*—Plug-ins are external helper applications that add new functionality to the basic programs such as Netscape Communicator and Netscape Navigator. The ScriptActive plug-in we mentioned earlier is an example of this kind of application. There are also audio or video plug-ins that you can use with Netscape Navigator to play audio or video.

- *Style sheets*—Style sheets are essentially Web page templates that allow you to simplify and expedite Web page design.
- *JavaScript*—JavaScript is Netscape's scripting language for writing event-driven code for your HTML pages. JavaScript works with both Netscape Navigator and Microsoft Internet Explorer, unlike VBScript, which works only with Microsoft Internet Explorer.
- *JScript*—Microsoft's implementation of JavaScript.
- *Visual JavaScript*—Netscape's GUI tool for writing JavaScript-based HTML pages. You can download Visual JavaScript's Preview Release from Netscape's Web site at **www.netsape.com**.

Additional Resources

For more information about Netscape and Netscape One Technologies, visit the following sites:

- Netscape Developer Home—**developer.netscape.com/index.html**
- Netscape One Technologies—**developer.netscape.com/one/index.html**

For more information about the W3C, visit the Consortium's Web site at **www.w3.org**. Founded in 1994, the W3C's mission is to develop common protocols for the evolution of the World Wide Web.

For more information on Netscape Navigator, refer to these books from The Coriolis Group (**www.coriolis.com**):

- *The New Netscape and HTML Explorer* (ISBN: 1-883577-91-8)
- *JavaScript and Netscape Wizardry* (ISBN: 1-883577-86-1)
- *Web Developer's Guide to JavaScript and VBScript* (ISBN: 1-883577-97-7)

Traditional HTML Development

Before the advent of dynamic HTML, designing a Web page involved displaying information (text and graphics) sequentially. For example, a Web page displays text or graphics in the title, the body, and the footer, in that order. However, this gave you little or no control over the exact placement of the information within the Web page. For example, using the traditional HTML document model, you could not display your company logo at a particular location within the Web page identified by the Web page's x and y coordinates. Listing 16.1 shows an example of HTML code.

Listing 16.1 Displaying text and graphics.

```
<html>
<head>
<title></title>
<style>
<!--
BODY {
margin-top: 30;
margin-left: 10;
}
UL, OL, DIR, MENU, DIV, DT, DD, ADDRESS, BLOCKQUOTE, PRE, BR, P, LI
{
color: 003366;
font-size: 18pt;
font-weight: regular;
font-family: "Comic Sans MS", "Arial";
}
h1
{
color:003366;
font-size: 40pt;
font-weight: regular;
font-family: "Comic Sans MS", "Arial";
margin-top: -30pt;
}
h2
{
color: 003366;
font-size: 18pt;
font-weight: regular;
font-family: "Comic Sans MS", "Arial";
}
-->
</style>
</head>
<body background="Balloon Party Invitation Bkgrd.jpg" leftmargin=10
topmargin=30>
<img ALIGN="left" ALT="It's a Party" src="One Green Balloon.GIF" width="92"
height="164" border="00">
<center><h1>It's a Party and<br>You're Invited</h1></center>
<img ALIGN="right" ALT="It's a Party" src="One Green Balloon.GIF" width="92"
height="164" border="00">
<br><br><br><br><br>
```

```
<h2>Day:</h2>
<br>
<h2>Time:</h2>
<br>
<h2>Place:</h2>
</body>
</html>
```

As shown in Figure 16.6, you can use Netscape Navigator to view the Web page you created.

If you have Outlook Express, you will find the HTML files and JPEG images for the nonlayers version of the balloon party invitation Web page in the \Program Files\Common Files\Microsoft Shared\Stationery directory on your system.

As you can see, after displaying the background color, the browser first displays the image One Green Balloon.gif. Next, the browser displays the text "It's a Party and You're Invited," followed by the One Green Balloon.gif again. Finally, the browser displays the text "Day, Time, and Place." As shown in the preceding code, you can

Figure 16.6

Using Netscape Navigator to view the nonlayers version of the balloon party invitation Web page.

specify the width and height of the text and graphics the browser is to display, but not their exact location within the Web page.

By using the dynamic HTML absolute positioning and layering technique, you can specify the exact x,y location within the Web page at which the browser is to display the text and graphics. Being able to specify the precise location of text or images gives you tighter control over your Web page's layout and look and feel. In addition, the layering technique lets you define layers (or blocks) of text and graphics, allowing you to overlap one layer of text or graphics over another. The next section discusses the absolute positioning and layering technique in more detail.

Absolute Positioning And Layering

Layering allows you to define a layer or block of text and graphics; content positioning allows you to define the layer's exact location within a Web page. In the dynamic HTML object model, a layer represents an object and, like any other object, the layer object's interface includes properties, methods, and events. Using JavaScript, you can control the layer's appearance and behavior, including the following:

- Moving a layer from one location to another
- Overlapping layers
- Rotating or animating a layer
- Hiding and showing a layer
- Changing a layer's color and font dynamically

As you can see, content positioning and layering give you greater control over your Web page's elements, which means you can design dynamic, more compelling Web pages.

Using The **<LAYER>** Tag

To define a layer with absolute position, use the **<LAYER>...</LAYER>** tags. To define a layer with relative position, use the **<ILAYER>...</ILAYER>** tags. As with any other HTML object, you can configure a layer's appearance and behavior by manipulating the **<LAYER>** (or **<ILAYER>**) tag's attributes.

You can define an inflow layer (a layer with a relative position) using the ***<ILAYER>*** *tag. Use the* ***TOP*** *and* ***LEFT*** *attributes to specify the offset of the layer's top-left corner from the current position within the document. At this time, only Netscape Navigator 4 supports the use of* ***<LAYER>*** *and* ***<ILAYER>*** *tags.*

Table 16.1 shows a list of the **<LAYER>** and **<ILAYER>** tags' attributes and Table 16.2 lists the **<LAYER>** and **<ILAYER>** tags' events.

Table 16.1 <LAYER> and <ILAYER> tags' attributes.

Attribute	Description
ID	Specifies the new layer's name.
LEFT	Specifies the horizontal position of the new layer's top-left corner with respect to the parent layer or the HTML document.
TOP	Specifies the vertical position of the new layer's top-left corner with respect to the parent layer or the HTML document.
PAGEX	Specifies the horizontal position of the new layer's top-left corner, in pixels, with respect to the HTML document.
PAGEY	Specifies the vertical position of the new layer's top-left corner, in pixels, with respect to the HTML document.
SRC	Specifies the external HTML file that contains the data the new layer will display.
Z-INDEX	Specifies the layers' stacking order.
ABOVE	Specifies the layer that will be above the new layer.
BELOW	Specifies the layer that will be below the new layer.
WIDTH	Specifies the new layer's width. You can specify the width as an integer value or as a percentage of the layer that will enclose the new layer.
HEIGHT	Specifies the new layer's height. You can specify the height as an integer value or as a percentage of the layer that will enclose the new layer.
CLIP	Specifies the new layer's visible area.
VISIBILITY	Specifies if the browser will show or hide the new layer.
BGCOLOR	Specifies the background color for the new layer.
BACKGROUND	Specifies the URL that will contain the background image for the new layer.

Table 16.2 <LAYER> and <ILAYER> tags' events.

Events	Description
OnMouseOver	The **OnMouseOver** event will be triggered if you move your mouse over the layer.
OnMouseOut	The **OnMouseOut** event will be triggered if you move your mouse away from the layer.
OnFocus	The **OnFocus** event will be triggered if the new layer gets focus.
OnBlur	The **OnBlur** event will be triggered if the new layer loses focus.
OnLoad	The **OnLoad** event will be triggered when the browser loads the layer.

Listing 16.2 illustrates the use of the **<LAYER>** tag, showing the balloon party page designed using layers. As shown within the code, you declare three new layers: Balloon, Message, and Balloon2. First, Netscape Navigator will display the balloon layer that includes the One Green Balloon.gif image, then the Message layer with the text "It's a Party and You're Invited." Next, Netscape Navigator will display the Balloon2 layer that includes the One Green Balloon.gif image. Finally, the browser displays the text "Day, Time, and Place."

Listing 16.2 Using the <LAYER> tag.

```
<html>
<head>
<title></title>
<style>
<!--
BODY {
margin-top: 30;
margin-left: 10;
}
UL, OL, DIR, MENU, DIV, DT, DD, ADDRESS, BLOCKQUOTE, PRE, BR, P, LI
{
color: 003366;
font-size: 18pt;
font-weight: regular;
font-family: "Comic Sans MS", "Arial";
}
h1
{
```

```
color:003366;
font-size: 40pt;
font-weight: regular;
font-family: "Comic Sans MS", "Arial";
margin-top: -30pt;
}
h2
{
color: 003366;
font-size: 18pt;
font-weight: regular;
font-family: "Comic Sans MS", "Arial";
}
-->
</style>
</head>

<body background="Balloon Party Invitation Bkgrd.jpg" leftmargin=10
topmargin=30>

<layer name="Balloon">
<img ALIGN="left" ALT="It's a Party" src="One Green Balloon.GIF" width="92"
height="164" border="00">
</layer>

<layer name="Message">
<center><h1>It's a Party and You're Invited</h1></center>
</layer>

<layer name="Balloon2">
<img ALIGN="right" ALT="It's a Party" src="One Green Balloon.GIF" width="92"
height="164" border="00">
</layer>

<br><br><br><br><br>
<h2>Day:</h2>
<br>
<h2>Time:</h2>
<br>
<h2>Place:</h2>
</body>
</html>
```

The page viewed with Netscape Navigator is shown in Figure 16.7.

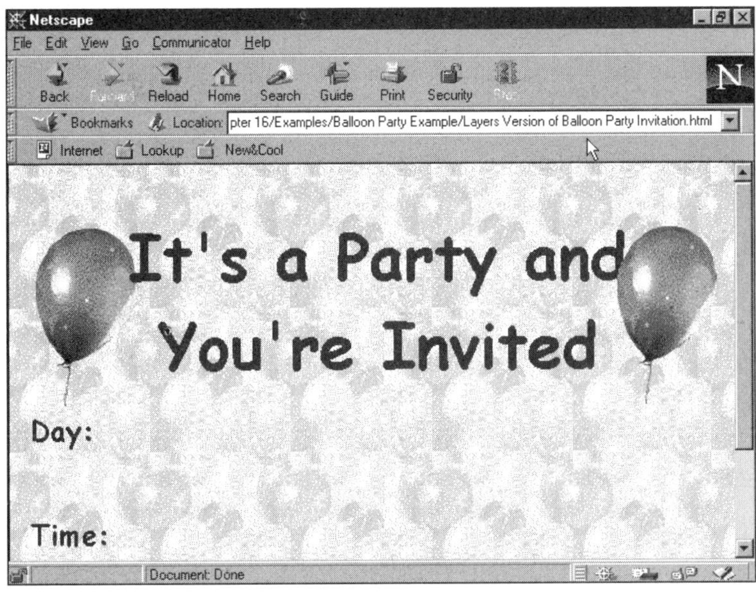

Figure 16.7

Using Netscape Navigator to view the layers version of the balloon party invitation Web page.

Practical Guide To

Data Sources And Layers

- Using Layers To Display An Employee Directory
- Using A Separate HTML File To Display The Employee Directory

Using Layers To Display An Employee Directory

In Chapter 10, you learned how to use Microsoft's Tabular Data Control (TDC) to read and display data from an ASCII-delimited data source, the employee.txt file. In this example, we will use layers to display the employee information within a Web page in Netscape Navigator 4. We will use JavaScript to write event-driven code for the page.

*You can use the Netscape JavaScript debugger to debug the Web page's JavaScript code. Download the debugger from Netscape's Web site at **www.netscape.com/download/index.html**.*

There are a number of ways to create the Web page; the easiest and recommended way is by using graphical user interface (GUI) tools. Netscape's Visual JavaScript is one such tool; you can download the GUI tool from Netscape's Web site at **www.netscape.com/download/index.html**. However, you should be aware that the tool is not yet complete; it has extremely slow response times and does not yet support adding dynamic HTML components—including layers, downloadable fonts, and Cascading Style Sheets—interactively. We fervently hope that Netscape will fix these problems before Visual JavaScript's final release. At this point, a better option is to write the HTML code using editors such as Notepad and WordPad.

If you use a GUI tool such as Netscape's Visual JavaScript, you can create your Web page's interface interactively, and then add the dynamic HTML component manually by using editors such as Notepad and WordPad.

Within the Web page, you will display a dropdown list of current employees, from which a user can choose a particular employee and see employee information such as title, Social Security number, phone number, and email address. Table 16.3 shows the sample employee data.

Table 16.3 Employee data.

Id	Name	Title	SS#	Voice	Email
1	Robert Benson	Manager	098-75-1234	904-555-1234	rbenson@mymail.com
2	Julia Rojas	Manager	123-45-1234	904-555-2345	jrojas@mymail.com

(continued)

Table 16.3 Employee data *(continued).*

Id	Name	Title	SS#	Voice	Email
3	Cynthia Preston	Team Leader	654-12-6789	904-555-5432	cpreston@mymail.com
4	John Dvos	Sr. Programmer	555-67-1298	904-555-8765	jdvos@mymail.com
5	Martha Jenkins	Programmer	498-23-8765	904-555-1987	mjenkins@mymail.com

Before writing the HTML code, give some thought to the page's overall design. Because you are using layers to implement the page, it is important to determine what will constitute each layer. In this example, each employee's information constitutes an individual layer. You will also design a top layer that includes the dropdown list of current employees. Our example shows five employees; therefore, you will have five layers, plus the page's top layer containing the dropdown list.

1. To declare the top layer, use the **<ILAYER>** tag and set the following parameters:

   - **NAME=toplayer**
   - **LEFT=10**
   - **BGCOLOR=#FFFFFF**

   A dropdown list is displayed within this layer, as shown in Listing 16.3.

Listing 16.3 Declaring the top layer.

```
<ILAYER NAME="toplayer" LEFT=10 BGCOLOR="#FFFFFF">

<H3>Choose an employee from the drop-down list box :</H3>
    <FORM>
                <SELECT name=employeeDropDown onChange=
                        "showEmployee(this.selectedIndex); return false;">
                        <OPTION>Robert Benson
                        <OPTION>Julie Rojas
                        <OPTION>Cynthia Preston
                        <OPTION>John Dvos
                        <OPTION>Martha Jenkins
                </SELECT>
    </FORM>
</LAYER>
```

As you can see from the code, you call the function **showEmployee** within the dropdown list **onChange** event. The **showEmployee** is a JavaScript function you write to display the selected employee.

2. Declare a layer for each employee, and set the following parameters for each employee layer:

   - **NAME=employee*N***, where *N* is the employee number
   - **LEFT**=**10**
   - **WIDTH**=**400**
   - **BGCOLOR**=(a different hexadecimal number for each employee layer)

3. Include employee information within each employee layer. The code for the layer declaration for Robert Benson is:

```
<LAYER name="employee0" LEFT=10 width=400 BGCOLOR="#DDDDDD">
        <H1>Robert Benson</H1>

        <H2><P>Manager</H2></P>
        <P>Social Security Number : 098-75-1234</P>
        <P>Voice                  : 904-555-1234</P>
        <P>Email                  : rbenson@mymail.com</P>
</LAYER>
```

4. In the same way, declare layers for Julia Rojas, Cynthia Preston, John Dvos, and Martha Jenkins. As you can see, the layer declaration for Robert Benson does not include the **VISIBILITY** parameter; by default, a layer's **VISIBILITY** value is set to **SHOW**. As a result, when you first load the page Netscape Navigator displays the layer for Robert Benson. The layer declarations for other employees do include the **VISIBILITY** parameter with the parameter's value set to **HIDE**. This means that when you first load the page the browser will not display the layers for any of the other employees. For example, the layer declaration for Julia Rojas is:

```
<LAYER name="employee1" LEFT=10 width=400 BGCOLOR="#FFDDDD" visibility="hide">
        <H1>Julia Rojas</H1>

        <H2><P>Manager</H2></P>
        <P>Social Security Number : 123-45-1234</P>
        <P>Voice                  : 904-555-2345</P>
        <P>Email                  : jrojas@mymail.com</P>
</LAYER>
```

5. Add the JavaScript event-driven code. Without this code, the browser will not display the employee information when a user selects an employee from the dropdown list box. You need to define two JavaScript functions: **hideAll-Employees** and **showEmployee**. The **hideAllEmployees** function hides all employee layers; the browser calls this function before displaying information about a particular employee selected from the dropdown list. The **show-Employee** function displays the selected employee's layer; to hide and show an employee layer, use the layer's **VISIBILITY** attribute. To direct the browser to hide a layer, set the layer's **VISIBILITY** attribute to **HIDE**. To direct the browser to show a layer, set the layer's **VISIBILITY** attribute to **SHOW**. As shown in the code below, you reference a layer by using the document object:

```
<SCRIPT>

// This function will hide all layers
function hideAllEmployees() {
    for (i=0;i<=4;i++) {
           document.layers["employee" + i].visibility = "hide";
         }
}

// This function will display information about the selected employee
function showEmployee(n) {
         hideAllEmployees();
         document.layers["employee" + n].visibility = "show";
}

</SCRIPT>
```

6. Complete the code by adding the page's title, background image, and so on. Listing 16.4 shows the complete code.

Listing 16.4 Using layers to display XYZ Corporation's employee directory.

```
<HTML>
<HEAD>
<TITLE>Employee Directory</TITLE>
</HEAD>
<BODY background="Ivy.gif">

<SCRIPT>

// This function will hide all layers
function hideAllEmployees() {
```

```
    for (i=0;i<=4;i++) {
          document.layers["employee" + i].visibility = "hide";
        }
}

// This function will display information about the selected employee
function showEmployee(n) {
        hideAllEmployees();
        document.layers["employee" + n].visibility = "show";
}

</SCRIPT>

<H1 align="center">XYZ Corporation Employee Directory</H1>

<ILAYER NAME="toplayer" LEFT=10 BGCOLOR="#FFFFFF">

<H3>Choose an employee from the drop-down list box :</H3>
    <FORM>
                <SELECT name=employeeDropDown onChange=
                        "showEmployee(this.selectedIndex); return false;">
                        <OPTION>Robert Benson
                        <OPTION>Julie Rojas
                        <OPTION>Cynthia Preston
                        <OPTION>John Dvos
                        <OPTION>Martha Jenkins
                </SELECT>
    </FORM>
</LAYER>

<LAYER name="employee0" LEFT=10 width=400 BGCOLOR="#DDDDDD">
        <H1>Robert Benson</H1>

        <H2><P>Manager</H2></P>
        <P>Social Security Number : 098-75-1234</P>
        <P>Voice                  : 904-555-1234</P>
        <P>Email                  : rbenson@mymail.com</P>
</LAYER>

<LAYER name="employee1" LEFT=10 width=400 BGCOLOR="#FFDDDD" visibility="hide">
        <H1>Julia Rojas</H1>

        <H2><P>Manager</H2></P>
        <P>Social Security Number : 123-45-1234</P>
        <P>Voice                  : 904-555-2345</P>
        <P>Email                 : jrojas@mymail.com</P>
</LAYER>
```

```
<LAYER name="employee2" LEFT=10 width=400 BGCOLOR="#AAFFDD" visibility="hide">
        <H1>Cynthia Preston</H1>

        <H2><P>Team Leader</H2></P>
        <P>Social Security Number : 654-12-6789</P>
        <P>Voice                  : 904-555-5432</P>
        <P>Email                  : cpreston@mymail.com</P>
</LAYER>

<LAYER name="employee3" LEFT=10 width=400 BGCOLOR="#DDFFDD" visibility="hide">
        <H1>John Dvos</H1>

        <H2><P>Senior Programmer</H2></P>
        <P>Social Security Number : 555-67-1298</P>
        <P>Voice                  : 904-555-8765</P>
        <P>Email                  : jdvos@mymail.com</P>
</LAYER>

<LAYER name="employee4" LEFT=10 width=400 BGCOLOR="#DDDDFF" visibility="hide">
        <H1>Martha Jenkins</H1>

        <H2><P>Programmer</H2></P>
        <P>Social Security Number : 498-23-8765</P>
        <P>Voice                  : 904-555-1987</P>
        <P>Email                  : mjenkins@mymail.com</P>
</LAYER>

</BODY>
</HTML>
```

7. Use Netscape Navigator 4 to view the page; it will look like Figure 16.8.

Using A Separate HTML File To Display The Employee Directory

In the previous example, we used layers to display XYZ Corporation's employee directory, designing a layer for each employee's information. In addition, we used JavaScript event-driven code to show and hide the appropriate layers. In this example, we will again use layers to display the company's employee directory, but we will create an HTML file that contains the employee information for each employee. We use the layer's **SRC** attribute to include the employee HTML files within the main HTML file. Like the previous example, you use JavaScript event-driven code to show and hide the appropriate layers and use a dropdown list to display current employees.

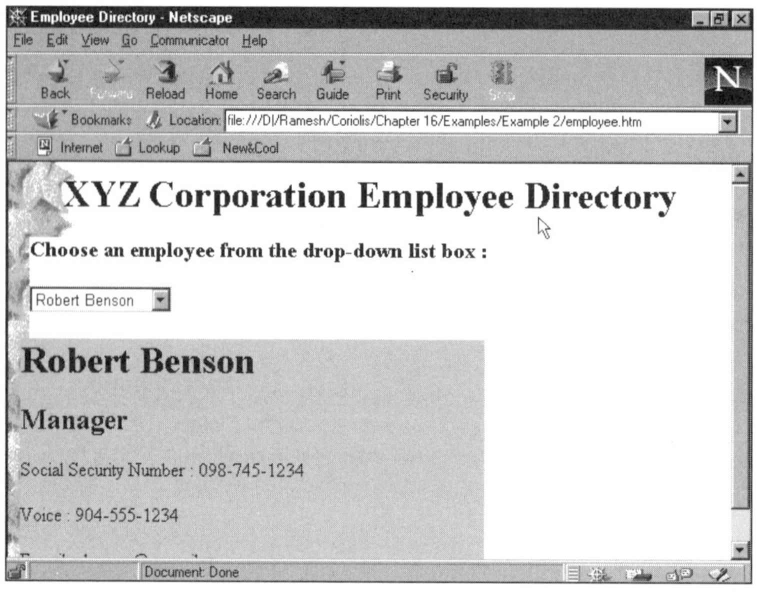

Figure 16.8

Using Netscape Navigator to view the layers version of the employee directory.

As in the previous example, each employee's information constitutes an individual layer and you design a top layer that includes the dropdown list that displays current employees. This example uses the same five employees, so you will have five layers plus the Web page's top layer containing the dropdown list.

1. To declare the top layer, you will use the **<ILAYER>** tag. Set the following parameters for the top layer:
   - **NAME=toplayer**
   - **LEFT=10**
   - **BGCOLOR=#FFFFFF**
2. Within the layer, display a dropdown list; this involves declaring the top layer as we did in the earlier example (see Listing 16.3). Again, you call the **showEmployee** function within the dropdown list box's **onChange** event. The **showEmployee** is a JavaScript function you write to display the selected employee.

3. Declare a layer for each employee, setting the following parameters for each employee layer:

    - **NAME=employee*N***, where *N* is the employee number
    - **LEFT=10**
    - **WIDTH=400**
    - **BGCOLOR=**(a different hexadecimal number for each employee layer)
    - **SRC=**(the employee's HTML file)

    The following bit of code shows the layer declaration for Robert Benson:

```
<LAYER name="employee0" LEFT=10 width=400 BGCOLOR="#DDDDDD" src="rbenson.htm">
</LAYER>
```

    As you can see, the employee0 layer's **SRC** attribute refers to the rbenson.htm file, which includes information about Robert Benson such as title, Social Security number, phone number, and email address. Here is the rbenson.htm file's code:

```
<H1>Robert Benson</H1>

        <H2><P>Manager</H2></P>
        <P>Social Security Number : 098-75-1234</P>
        <P>Voice                  : 904-555-1234</P>
        <P>Email                  : rbenson@mymail.com</P>
```

4. Repeat this process to declare layers for Julia Rojas, Cynthia Preston, John Dvos, and Martha Jenkins, and create four additional HTML files: jrojas.htm, cpreston.htm, jdvos.htm, and mjenkins.htm.

    As you saw earlier, the layer declaration for Robert Benson does not include the **VISIBILITY** parameter. The layer declarations for other employees will include the **VISIBILITY=HIDE** parameter. As a result, when you first load the page within Netscape Navigator, it will display the layer for Robert Benson, but will hide the layers for the other employees.

5. Define two JavaScript functions: **hideAllEmployees**, and **showEmployee**. The **hideAllEmployees** function will hide all employee layers. The browser will call the **hideAllEmployees** function before displaying the information about the

employee the user selected from the dropdown list box. The **showEmployee** function will display the selected employee's layer. As shown in Listing 16.5, you will reference a layer by using the **document** object.

Listing 16.5 JavaScript code to hide and show layers.

```
<SCRIPT>

// This function will hide all layers
function hideAllEmployees() {
   for (i=0;i<=4;i++) {
           document.layers["employee" + i].visibility = "hide";
        }
}

// This function will display information about the selected employee
function showEmployee(n) {
        hideAllEmployees();
        document.layers["employee" + n].visibility = "show";
}

</SCRIPT>
```

6. Complete the code by adding the page's title, background image, and so on. Listing 16.6 shows the complete code.

Listing 16.6 Using layers with the SRC attribute to display XYZ Corporation's employee directory.

```
<HTML>
<HEAD>
<TITLE>Employee Directory</TITLE>
</HEAD>
<BODY background="Ivy.gif">

<SCRIPT>

// This function will hide all layers
function hideAllEmployees() {
   for (i=0;i<=4;i++) {
           document.layers["employee" + i].visibility = "hide";
        }
}

// This function will display information about the selected employee
function showEmployee(n) {
        hideAllEmployees();
        document.layers["employee" + n].visibility = "show";
}
```

```
</SCRIPT>

<H1 align="center">XYZ Corporation Employee Directory</H1>

<ILAYER NAME="toplayer" LEFT=10 BGCOLOR="#FFFFFF">

<H3>Choose an employee from the drop-down list box :</H3>
  <FORM>
    <SELECT name=employeeDropDown onChange=
            "showEmployee(this.selectedIndex); return false;">
                <OPTION>Robert Benson
                <OPTION>Julie Rojas
                <OPTION>Cynthia Preston
                <OPTION>John Dvos
                <OPTION>Martha Jenkins
    </SELECT>
  </FORM>
</LAYER>

<LAYER name="employee0" LEFT=10 width=400 BGCOLOR="#DDDDDD" src="rbenson.htm">
</LAYER>

<LAYER name="employee1" LEFT=10 width=400 BGCOLOR="#FFDDDD" src="jrojas.htm"
 visibility="hide" >
</LAYER>

<LAYER name="employee2" LEFT=10 width=400 BGCOLOR="#AAFFDD" src="cpreston.htm"
 visibility="hide">
</LAYER>

<LAYER name="employee3" LEFT=10 width=400 BGCOLOR="#DDFFDD" src="jdvos.htm"
 visibility="hide">
</LAYER>

<LAYER name="employee4" LEFT=10 width=400 BGCOLOR="#DDDDFF" src="mjenkins.htm"
 visibility="hide">
</LAYER>

</BODY>
</HTML>
```

Listings 16.7 through 16.11 show the HTML files for the five employees.

Listing 16.7 rbenson.htm.

```
<H1>Robert Benson</H1>

<H2><P>Manager</H2></P>
<P>Social Security Number : 098-75-1234</P>
```

```
<P>Voice                      : 904-555-1234</P>
<P>Email                      : rbenson@mymail.com</P>
```

Listing 16.8 jrojas.htm.

```
<H1>Julia Rojas</H1>

<H2><P>Manager</H2></P>
<P>Social Security Number : 123-45-1234</P>
<P>Voice                  : 904-555-2345</P>
<P>Email                  : jrojas@mymail.com</P>
```

Listing 16.9 cpreston.htm.

```
<H1>Cynthia Preston</H1>

<H2><P>Team Leader</H2></P>
<P>Social Security Number : 654-12-6789</P>
<P>Voice                  : 904-555-5432</P>
<P>Email                  : cpreston@mymail.com</P>
```

Listing 16.10 jdvos.htm.

```
<H1>John Dvos</H1>

<H2><P>Senior Programmer</H2></P>
<P>Social Security Number : 555-67-1298</P>
<P>Voice                  : 904-555-8765</P>
<P>Email                  : jdvos@mymail.com</P>
```

Listing 16.11 mjenkins.htm.

```
<H1>Martha Jenkins</H1>

<H2><P>Programmer</H2></P>
<P>Social Security Number : 498-23-8765</P>
<P>Voice                  : 904-555-1987</P>
<P>Email                  : mjenkins@mymail.com</P>
```

Since Internet Explorer's Dynamic HTML object model does not support layers, Internet Explorer will display an error message (see Figure 16.9) when you load the layers version of employee.htm file.

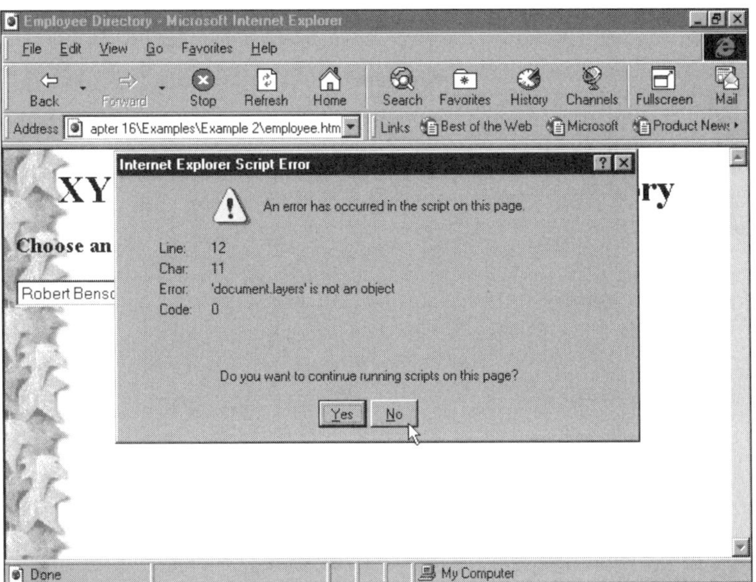

Figure 16.9

Using Internet Explorer to view the layers version of the employee directory.

Chapter 17

Sound And Graphics Within Layer Environments

In this chapter, we explore how to incorporate layered sound and graphics into DHTML pages. In addition, we provide detailed examples of how to best achieve control over these features.

Notes...

Chapter 17

Netscape's **LAYER** tag gives Web developers significant control over how graphics appear, where they're positioned, and the way in which they move around a page. Because the **LAYER** tag functions as a generic container, a variety of graphics and media—such as audio—can be put inside a layer. In combination with JavaScript, layers work to bring the essential capabilities of multimedia creation to DHTML.

The <LAYER> Tag, Graphics, And JavaScript

As we detailed in Chapter 13, a layer begins with the **<LAYER>** tag and ends with the **</LAYER>** tag; there is also an **ILAYER** tag that creates an inline layer. Whereas the **LAYER** tag makes a layer's position relative to the base document, the **ILAYER** tag creates an inline layer with a position that's relative to the text that contains the **ILAYER** tag, similarly to the way an inline image is handled.

Content that is sandwiched between **LAYER** tags can be maneuvered as a single unit of content and can be moved and affected in a variety of ways. Because it's possible to specify a layer's position and content inside the **LAYER** tag in the body of the page, it's not necessary to predefine the layer before indicating its specific content.

LAYER tags are designed specifically for positioning and they're crafted to handle sophisticated graphics. **LAYER** and **ILAYER** tags can be treated basically like **FRAME** tags—frames that may be positioned, re-positioned, hidden, and displayed.

When you're trying to decide what image formats to use within layers, remember that GIF works best for non-photographic, cartoon-like images that consist of only a few colors. JPEG is preferred for more complex images, including photographs and graphics with intense patterns.

Absolutely Positioned Layers

Layers can be absolutely positioned, i.e., made to occupy a pixel-specific location on a Web page. Here's an example of a layer that would be positioned 35 pixels from a document's x coordinate (the document's left side) and 60 pixels from the document's y coordinate (the document's top):

```
<layer left="35" top="60">
The layer text goes here
</layer>
```

In addition to the x and y coordinates, you can also take layers into the third dimension by specifying a z coordinate. The **Z-INDEX** parameter can be used to specify layer order for absolute positioning. To position layers in this way, assign each layer a number, beginning with 1 for the top layer. For instance:

```
<layer name="FocusLayer" z-index="1" left="35" top="60">
FocusLayer will appear in front of all the other layers
</layer>
```

Relatively Positioned Layers

Layers can also be positioned relatively for 3D stacking by using the **ABOVE** and **BELOW** parameters and specifying the name of the corresponding layer. For example:

```
<layer name="LayerBack" below="LayerMiddle" left="35" top="60">
The LayerBack layer will always appear below the LayerMiddle layer.
</layer>
```

Layers occupying relative positions are called *inflow layers*, and they appear in the place where they naturally fall in the flow of the document. Inflow layers can be created through the **<ILAYER>...</ILAYER>** tags. To make an inflow layer appear on a separate line, either insert a break before the layer or wrap the layer in the **<DIV>** tag. When working with layers defined as styles, specify the **position** property as **relative** to make an inflow layer, like this:

```
<ILAYER ID=InflowLayer>
<P>InflowLayer content goes here</P>
```

```
</ILAYER>
<STYLE type="text/css">
<!--
#InflowLayer {position:relative; }
-->
```

When you don't specify top or left coordinates, layers default to a position seven pixels below and seven pixels to the right of a document's top left corner.

Layers And External Content

When you want to include external content, such as an external image or sound file, you can insert it through the **SRC** property; both **LAYER** and **ILAYER** allow a layer's content to be stored in an external file. This is the code used to access external content through the **SRC** property:

```
<LAYER SRC="url"></LAYER>
<ILAYER SRC="url"></ILAYER>
```

The ability to change an image's source in tandem with moving the image extends your graphic possibilities. When using Internet graphics, keep in mind that if the image source changes too quickly (or too often), it's possible that the actual image may not be able to download across the Net's wires at a speed that matches that of the animation. For this reason, if you have a script that changes the source of an image in a moving layer, make sure that the image has fully loaded before you try to alter or move it.

Preloading Images With Layers

It's always a good idea to preload images whenever possible, especially since DHTML pages can require an initially larger download than HTML 3.2 pages. Preloaded images will be in the browser cache and ready to flow when they're summoned—through an animation, for instance.

You can preload—or "prefetch"—an image by embedding it in a layer. Preloading works well with DHTML because when a layer loads, it loads all its content, including both visible and invisible images.

Suppressing Icons While Images Are Loading

When a Web page opens, by default it displays a placeholder icon for every image in the page that is in the process of loading. You may sometimes encounter a situation—

such as an animation sequence—that requires multiple images. If you would prefer that the viewer didn't see placeholder icons while the real images are loading, you can use the **IMG** tag's new attribute, **SUPPRESS**, to suppress the display of placeholder icons.

The **SUPPRESS** attribute can be set for the **IMG** tag to either true or false (the default value is false). When **SUPPRESS** is set to **true**, neither the placeholder icon nor the frame that appears during image loading will be displayed, and tool tips will also be disabled for that image.

When **SUPPRESS** is set to **false**, you'll always see the placeholder icon and frame during loading, even in instances when the images are transparent and would not otherwise be displayed. When **SUPPRESS** is **false**, tool tips will be active.

Animating Layers

One of the most outstanding features of layers is the way that they can be animated; these powers of animation finally make HTML a feasible method for authoring CD-ROM-like multimedia and interactive content.

The layers animation feature basically functions as cell-based animation; you select a single image that you want to animate across the larger stage. Many animations, particularly those of the looping variety, simply repeat an action over and over again. JavaScript provides the fuel for the layers' actions.

setInterval()

To repeatedly call a function at a given interval, use the JavaScript **setInterval()** function. For instance, you could use this code to make the **ContinueGrowth()** function swell every 30 seconds, with arguments of 10, 30, 50, and 70:

```
setInterval(ContinueGrowth, 30, 10, 30, 50, 70);
```

Use the **setInterval()** function to activate the repeated, unconditional invocation of a function; use the **setTimeout()** function to conditionally re-invoke a function.

setTimeout()

JavaScript's **setTimeout()** function enables you to call another function after a given amount of time. There are two forms that the **setTimeout()** function employs:

```
setTimeout("executable code here", delay)
setTimeout(function, delay, args...)
```

To invoke **GoStellarContent("Content1", "Content2")** after five seconds, you can use either of the following statements:

```
setTimeout("GoStellarContent('Content1, 'Content2)", 3)
setTimeout(GoStellarContent, 3, "Content1", "Content2");
```

You can use **setTimeout()** to alter a layer's clipping area. For example, if you want to repeatedly make a layer's clipping area 10 pixels wider and 10 pixels higher until the layer reaches a width of 500 pixels, you can do so in this way:

```
function expand(layer)
{

    if (layer.clip.right < 500) {

    layer.resizeBy(10, 10);

    setTimeout(expand, 10, layer);

  }

 return false;

}
```

See the Freefall site profile in this chapter's Practical Guide for specific examples of **setTimeout** use.

Sound Within Layer Environments

We covered the full use of audio files—with and without layers—in Chapter 11 and expanded upon Microsoft's DirectX/DHTML sound tools in Chapter 13. Just for review, the code that's used for adding audio to layers with JavaScript follows:

```
<EMBED
SRC="http://www.excellentaudio.org"
LOOP=true|false
AUTOSTART=true|false
MASTERSOUND
CONTROL=CONSOLE|SMALLCONSOLE|PLAYBUTTON|PAUSEBUTTON|STOPBUTTON|VOLUMELEVER
NAME="audio"
HIDDEN=true|false
VOLUME=100
WIDTH=0
HEIGHT=0 >
```

HIDDEN=true will make your audio file play as a background sound, and none of the console buttons indicated in the **CONTROL** attribute will appear in the browser. However, consider including a console; users will appreciate the ability to control the page's audio.

***MASTERSOUND** must be present for the audio to be controlled through JavaScript.*

Using Streaming Audio

It's appropriate to use streaming audio when the sound files you want to play are relatively large; compressing large audio files and sending them in streamed form is more efficient than forcing the browser to download them all at once.

There are a few technologies that you can use to feature streaming audio on your Web pages, including Shockwave and RealAudio. The **OBJECT** tag can be used to embed these media types into layered pages; see Chapter 11 for additional information.

Practical Guide To

Using Sound And Graphics Within Layer Environments

- Creating Animated Layers
- Producing Dynamic Surrealism
  - Adding A Background Manager
  - The Freefall Dude's Layer Code
  - Adding Spin Within A Layer
  - Using **setTimeout** To Make The Freefall Dude Fly
  - Using **setTimeout** To Bounce The Freefall Dude
  - Rotating The Freefall Dude
  - Layer Animation
  - Adding LiveAudio To Freefall
- Mixing Layers
- Designing Dynamic Animation
- Making A Virtual Gallery Dynamic And Cross-Platform Compatible

In this section, we peruse some of the Web's most intriguing DHTML sites featuring sound and graphics created through the **LAYER** tag. The Freefall Web Design site and Natespace both show how audio is being used with layer environments. We'll also take a look at a simple yet creative implementation of layers, the Mix-A-Pol.

Please Be Aware That This Book Breaks Code

Please note that, as in other chapters, the book's formatting requires the example lines of code to be broken in certain places. For instance, the following code should be written as a single line in your markup, but is broken into several sections in our code examples:

```
var d0 = ""; var d1 = ""; var d2 = ""; var d3 = "";
          var d4 = ""; var d5 = ""; var d6 = ""; var d7 = "";
          var d8 = ""; var d9 = ""; var d10 = "";
```

Creating Animated Layers

Animated layers are a key component of the Taboca Artwork site's Layer Station, created by designer Marcio Galli. The site, located at **www.taboca.com/layer/**, opens with the letters of a welcome message flying in from afar, as shown in Figure 17.1.

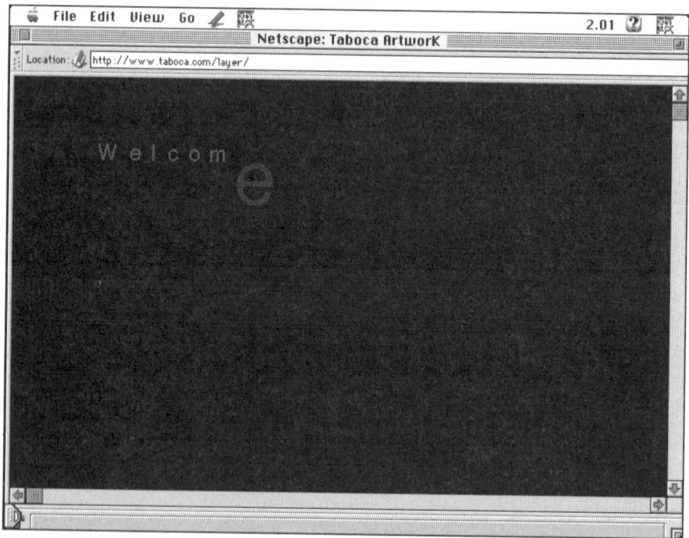

Figure 17.1

The welcoming letters from Taboca Artwork's Layer Station.

Then the fragments of an image designating the Layer Station begin to materialize, as shown in Figure 17.2.

Eventually, a train speeds into view, making excellent use of vertical compression and vanishing perspective (see Figure 17.3).

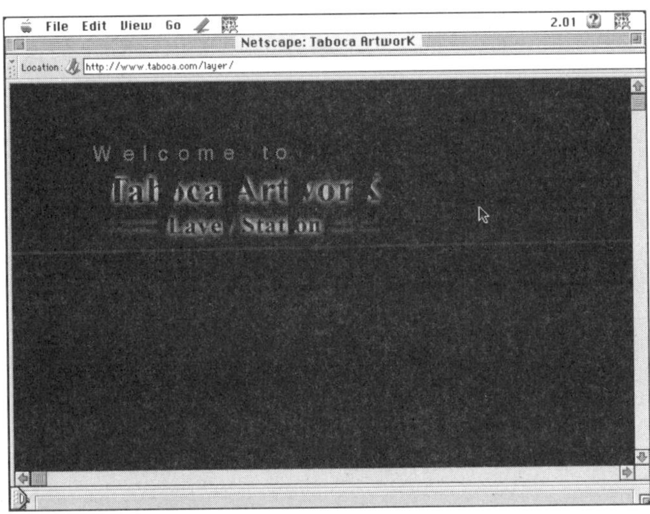

Figure 17.2

The Taboca Artwork's Layer Station image begins to form.

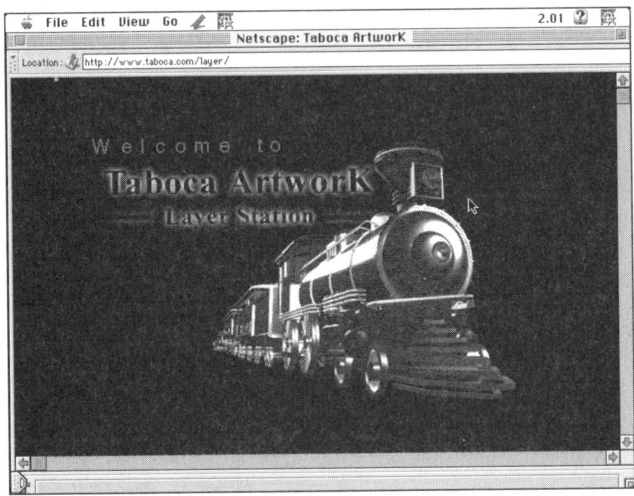

Figure 17.3

Watch the train speed toward you.

Here is the code indicating the layers that are used in this chain of events. Note how Galli achieves maximum dramatic effect by extensively using the hide/show layer visibility:

```
<layer name="mask" visibility="show" top=60 left="50%">
<img src="layermask.gif">
</layer>
<layer name="black" visibility="show" top=0 left=0 width=1500 height=120
bgcolor="#000000">
</layer>
<layer name="black2" visibility="show" top=475 left=0 width=1500 height=700
bgcolor="#000000">
</layer>
<layer name="bp01" visibility="hide" top=20 left=350>
        <layer name="bro2" top=0 left=200><img src="minibro6.jpg" width=80
         height=120 border=0>
        </layer>
</layer>
<layer name="bp02" visibility="hide" top=20 left=-150>
        <layer name="bro1" top=0 left=100><img src="minibro6.jpg" width=180
         height=220 border=0>
        </layer>
</layer>
<layer name="1" visibility="hide" left="50%" top="20">
<img src="tr0.gif" border=0>
        <layer name="al0" visibility="hide" left=96 top=41>

        </layer>
        <layer name="al1" visibility="hide" left=96 top=41>
        <img src="rod02.gif" border=0>
        </layer>
        <layer name="al2" visibility="hide" left=96 top=41>
        <img src="rod03.gif" border=0>
        </layer>
        <layer name="al3" visibility="hide" left=96 top=41>
        <img src="rod04.gif" border=0>
        </layer>
        <layer name="minirod" visibility="hide" left=199 top=52>
        <img src="minirod02.gif" border=0>
        </layer>

        <layer name="sensor01" visibility="show" top=5 left=5>
        <a href="" onclick="settext(2);return false;"><img border=0
         src="transp.gif" width=170 height=60></a>
        </layer>
```

```
        <layer name="sensor02" visibility="show" top=5 left=200>
        <a href="" onclick="settext(3);return false;"><img border=0
         src="transp.gif" width=90 height=60></a>
        </layer>

        <layer name="sensor03" visibility="show" top=5 left=320>
        <a href="" onclick="settext(4);return false;"><img border=0
         src="transp.gif" width=170 height=60></a>
        </layer>

        <layer name="sensor04" visibility="show" top=5 left=520>
        <a href="" onclick="settext(5);return false;"><img src="transp.gif"
         border=0 width=90 height=60></a>
        </layer>
</layer>
<layer name="bp03" visibility="hide" top=60 left=-600>
        <layer name="brol" top=0 left=300><img src="minibro6.jpg" border=0>
        </layer>
</layer>

<layer name="buga" width=250 height=300>
</layer>
```

When you enter more deeply into the Layer Station, the train metaphor continues with an image of a train speeding by (and cleverly backing up, using multiple images to make it appear that the train actually is propelling itself backward). The train's animation is thrust into counterpoint with other animated images flying around the page, specifically, empty Netscape Navigator browser windows. Galli achieves an intriguing effect by juxtaposing the images of the train with those of the browser, which are tweaked to give the blurred illusion of speed (see Figure 17.4). Figure 17.5 is the actual image that's used for the animation—note how the browser's softened edges give it the appearance of speed. Clicking on the train's different cars makes old layers fade and new ones appear.

Listing 17.1 shows the JavaScript that's used to create the Layer Station's animation. Note how Galli uses several of the techniques we reviewed in the first half of this chapter, including image clipping and **setTimeout**.

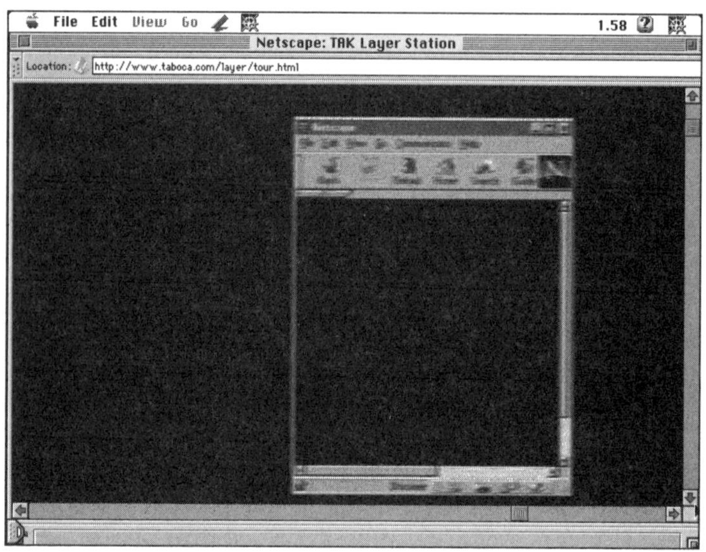

Figure 17.4

This blurred Netscape image imparts the feeling of speed when the layers cross each other.

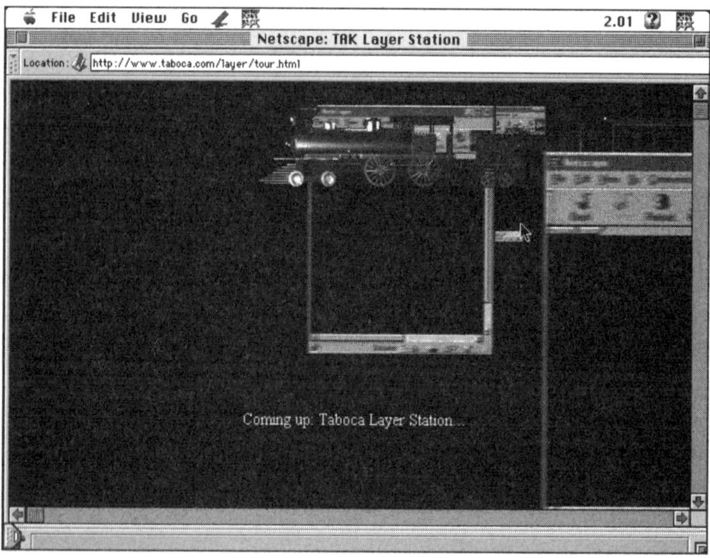

Figure 17.5

The train graphics and the blurred Netscape Navigator interface dynamically speed toward each other.

Listing 17.1 Layer Station's animation.

```
<script>

        plan1=document.layers["bp01"];
        plan2=document.layers["bp02"];
        plan3=document.layers["bp03"];

        a=document.layers["1"];
        step=50;
        step2=50;
        tp=0;           // the locomotive sprite step
        stepointer=-30; // the presentarion step mode
        moveto=1;
        target=0;

        function start() {

                plan1.moveBy(-600,0);
                plan2.moveBy(-600,0);
                plan3.moveBy(-600,0);

                // centering the layers...
                for(u=0;u<=5;u++) {
                        document.layers["content"+u].moveBy
                            (-document.layers["content"+u].clip.width/2,0);
                }
                document.layers["mask"].moveBy
                    (-document.layers["mask"].clip.width/2,0);

                // setting visibility for them...
                for(u=0;u<=5;u++) {
                        document.layers["content"+u].visibility="show";
                }

                plan1.visibility="show";
                plan2.visibility="show";
                plan3.visibility="show";

                a.moveBy(320,0);
                a.visibility="show";

                setTimeout("movetrain()",30);

        }

        function TIP_centerlayers_hor(basename,number) {
                document.layers[basename+number].moveBy
                    (-document.layers[basename+number].clip.width/2,0);
        }
```

```
function movetrain() {
        a.moveBy(-step,0);
        plan1.moveBy(step2,0);
        plan2.moveBy(step2*2,0);
        plan3.moveBy(step2*3,0);
        step2-=1;
        step-=2;
        if(step>3) {
                setTimeout("movetrain()",30);
        } else {
                navigation_pointer();
        }
}


function navigation_pointer() {
        a.document.layers[tp].visibility="show";
        if(tp!=0) a.document.layers[0].visibility="hide";
        if(tp!=1) a.document.layers[1].visibility="hide";
        if(tp!=2) a.document.layers[2].visibility="hide";
        if(tp!=3) a.document.layers[3].visibility="hide";
        if(tp==0||tp==1) {
                a.document.layers[4].visibility="show";
        } else {
                a.document.layers[4].visibility="hide";
        }
        if(moveto==0) tp++;
        if(moveto==1) tp--;
        if(tp<0) tp=3;
        if(tp>3) tp=0;

        if(moveto==1) stepointer++;
        a.moveBy(6,0);
        if(stepointer==target) {
                set_content();
        } else {
                setTimeout('navigation_pointer()',30);
        }
}

function set_content() {

        //setTimeout("move_content()",15);
        settext(1);

}
```

```
        // runtime
        animdelay=23;
        indexcontent=0;
        var movelay1;
        var movelay2;

        // we have 4 texts...
        function settext(number) {
         document.layers["mask"].visibility="show";
                if(indexcontent!=number) {
                        document.layers["content"+number].top=480;
                        movelay1=document.layers["content"+indexcontent];
                        movelay2=document.layers["content"+number];
                        animate();
                        indexcontent=number;
                }
        }
        function move_content() {
                movelay1.moveBy(0,-animdelay);
                movelay2.moveBy(0,-animdelay);
                animdelay--;
                if(animdelay>0) {
                        setTimeout("move_content()",20);
                }
                else {
                        document.layers["mask"].visibility="hide";
                }
        }

        function animate() {
                animdelay=24;
                setTimeout("move_content()",20);
        }

</script>
```

Producing Dynamic Surrealism

The Dali-esque shapes and stones of the Freefall Web Design Studio site were created by Jeff Rouyer, who explains that he "painted all the images in Photoshop 4.0 using extensive masking, airbrushing, and overlapping transparent layers." His self-defined "gothic surrealism" is paired with Netscape's DHTML for a most creative Web site, full of hidden content and unexpected animation.

Rouyer's site exists in canvas mode (see Figure 17.6), a Navigator option that renders the page in a window devoid of any distractions. In fact, the only two choices

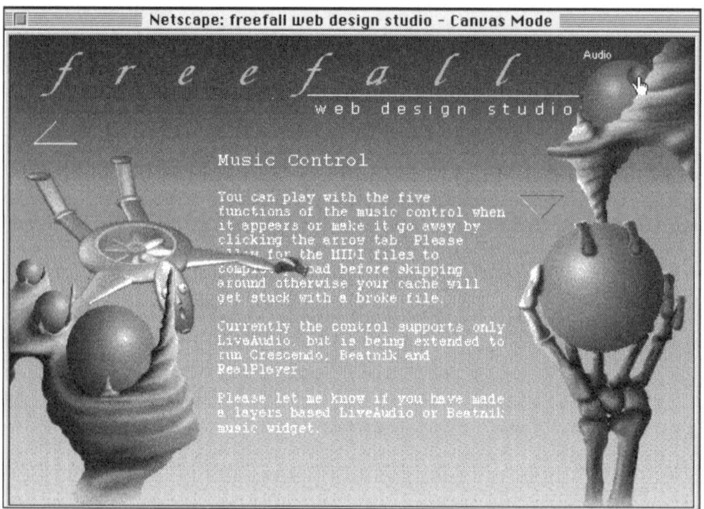

Figure 17.6

The Freefall site's canvas mode: Note the absence of navigation buttons or other distractions.

contained in the canvas mode's toolbar are Close and Quit, quite a far cry from the option-happy 4.0 browser toolbars.

The text that explains the site's content is also stored in layers and can be manipulated in an interesting way: Clicking near the top of the text results in the text inching up the page, whereas clicking near the bottom of the text makes the text layer reveal words at the bottom of the screen. This intuitive control eliminates the need for navigation buttons, which is good, because the canvas mode doesn't offer any.

Adding A Background Manager

Rouyer has written a background manager to automatically match your computer's background to known resolutions. When you enter the site, this code determines what you will see:

```
var screen_height = screen.height;
        var screen_width = screen.width;
        var canvas_height = window.innerHeight;
        var canvas_width = window.innerWidth;
        var background_img = "";

        if (screen_height >= 864) {
                background_img = "images/sunrise870.gif";
        }
```

```
        else if (screen_height >= 768) {
                background_img = "images/sunrise768.gif";
        }
        else if (screen_height >= 624) {
                background_img = "images/sunrise624.gif";
        }
        else if (screen_height >= 600) {
                background_img = "images/sunrise600.gif";
        }
        else if (screen_height >= 480) {
                background_img = "images/sunrise480.gif";
        }
        else {
                background_img = "images/sunrise600.gif";
        }
```

The Freefall Dude's Layer Code

Site visitors are greeted by the "freefall dude" character (shown in Figure 17.6), which Rouyer says was inspired by "my ceiling fan and a moment of vertigo." This character, which has a constantly spinning propeller in the middle of his back, moves in a variety of ways around the site. This is the layer code used to create the freefall dude. Note the layer within a layer in the section that contains the propeller layer:

```
<LAYER ID="dude_lyr" LEFT="-300" TOP=&{canvas_height/4}; Z-INDEX="3"
 VISIBILITY="SHOW" WIDTH="300" HEIGHT="174">
        <IMG NAME="dude_img" SRC="images/dude_se.gif" WIDTH="300" HEIGHT="174"
         BORDER="0" USEMAP="#dude_map">
        <LAYER ID="propeller_lyr" LEFT="115" TOP="60" VISIBILITY="SHOW"
         WIDTH="39" HEIGHT="33">
           <IMG NAME="propeller_img" SRC="images/blank.gif" WIDTH="69"
            HEIGHT="33" BORDER="0">
        </LAYER>
</LAYER>
```

Adding Spin Within A Layer

In order to make the freefall dude character's propeller spin at a skittish rate, Rouyer uses a recursive **setTimeout** loop with an image replacement function to cycle through three images:

```
var rotation = 1;

        function propControl() {
                if (rotation == 3) {
                        rotation = 1;
```

```
		} else {
			rotation++;
		}
		document.dude_lyr.document.propeller_lyr.document.
		   propeller_img.src = eval("propeller" + rotation + ".src");
		setTimeout("propControl()", 30);
	}
```

Using **setTimeout** To Make The Freefall Dude Fly

To make the freefall dude fly (see Figure 17.7), Rouyer relies on a recursive **setTimeout** loop with pixel boundaries. Once the dude hits these boundaries, his layer is repositioned off screen and continues to fly from the opposite side. Here is the code that achieves this effect:

```
var move_x = 0;
	var move_y = 0;
	var timer4 = null;

	function flyDude() {
		var dude = document.dude_lyr;
		clearTimeout(timer4);
		oss_dir = false;
		dude.moveBy(move_x, move_y);
		if ((dude.top+174) < 0) {
			dude.moveTo(document.dude_lyr.left, canvas_height);
		} else if (document.dude_lyr.top > canvas_height) {
			dude.moveTo(document.dude_lyr.left, -174);
		}
		if ((dude.left+300) < 0) {
			dude.moveTo(canvas_width, document.dude_lyr.top);
		} else if (document.dude_lyr.left > canvas_width) {
			dude.moveTo(-300, document.dude_lyr.top);
		}
		timer4 = setTimeout("flyDude()", 2);
	}
```

Using **setTimeout** To Bounce The Freefall Dude

In addition to spinning and flying, the freefall dude also bounces; again, the recursive **setTimeout** loop is involved. This loop moves the layer up and down, and is dependent on the state of a toggle—**oss_dir**:

```
var ossilate = 1;
	var timer2 = null;
	var oss_dir = true;
```

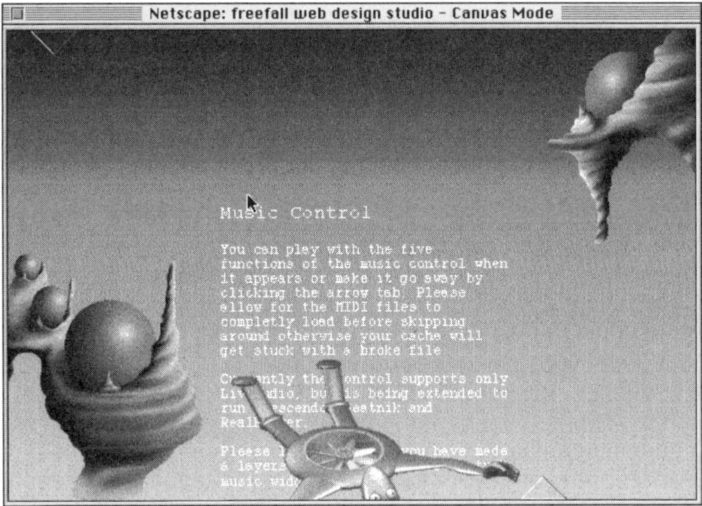

Figure 17.7

The freefall dude moves.

```
function osscilateDude() {
        if (oss_dir == true) {
                if (ossilate >= 1 && ossilate <=3) {
                        document.dude_lyr.moveBy(0,-1);
                        ossilate++;
                }
                else if (ossilate >= 4 && ossilate <=6) {
                        document.dude_lyr.moveBy(0,1);
                        ossilate++;
                } else {
                        ossilate = 1;
                }
                timer2 = setTimeout("osscilateDude()", 120);
        }
}
```

Rotating The Freefall Dude

The dude also rotates in different directions, thanks to the following code, which contains a series of array sequences:

```
var dude_switch = false;
var old_direction = "east";
```

```
        move_south = new Array("west","north","east","sw","w","sw",
          "w","nw","n","se","e");
        move_west = new Array("north","east","south","nw","n","nw",
          "n","ne","e","sw","s");
        move_north = new Array("east","south","west","ne","e","ne",
          "e","se","s","nw","w");
        move_east = new Array("south","west","north","se","s","se",
          "s","sw","w","ne","n");
        var d0 = ""; var d1 = ""; var d2 = "";
var d3 = "";     var d4 = ""; var d5 = ""; var d6 = "";
var d7 = ""; var d8 = ""; var d9 = "";   var d10 = "";

        function rotateDude(new_direction) {
                if (dude_switch == true) {
                        d0 = eval("move_" + old_direction + "[0]");
                        d1 = eval("move_" + old_direction + "[1]");
                        d2 = eval("move_" + old_direction + "[2]");
                        d3 = eval("move_" + old_direction + "[3]");
                        d4 = eval("move_" + old_direction + "[4]");
                        d5 = eval("move_" + old_direction + "[5]");
                        d6 = eval("move_" + old_direction + "[6]");
                        d7 = eval("move_" + old_direction + "[7]");
                        d8 = eval("move_" + old_direction + "[8]");
                        d9 = eval("move_" + old_direction + "[9]");
                        d10 = eval("move_" + old_direction + "[10]");
                        if (new_direction == d0) {
                                setTimeout("document.dude_lyr.document.dude
                                 _img.src =eval ('dude_' + d3 + '.src')", 100);
                                setTimeout("document.dude_lyr.document.dude
                                 _img.src = eval('dude_' + d4 + '.src')", 300);
                        }
                        else if (new_direction == d1) {
                                setTimeout("document.dude_lyr.document.dude
                                 _img.src = eval('dude_' + d5 + '.src')", 100);
                                setTimeout("document.dude_lyr.document.dude
                                 _img.src = eval('dude_' + d6 + '.src')", 300);
                                setTimeout("document.dude_lyr.document.dude
                                 _img.src = eval('dude_' + d7 + '.src')", 500);
                                setTimeout("document.dude_lyr.document.dude
                                 _img.src = eval('dude_' + d8 + '.src')", 700);
                        }
                        else if (new_direction == d2) {
                                setTimeout("document.dude_lyr.document.dude
                                 _img.src = eval('dude_' + d9 + '.src')", 100);
                                setTimeout("document.dude_lyr.document.dude
                                 _img.src = eval('dude_' + d10 + '.src')", 300);
                        }
```

```
                if (new_direction != "center" || new_direction != "up"
                    || new_direction != "down") {
                        old_direction = new_direction;
                }
        }
}

function centerDude() {
        clearTimeout(timer4);
        document.dude_lyr.moveTo(-40, canvas_height/4);
        rotateDude("east");
        oss_dir = true;
        osscilateDude();
}
```

Layer Animation

After you've initially been exposed to the freefall dude, a layer emerges from the top of the Web site that displays the phrase "Freeform Web Design Studio." One of the subtleties of this site is that the layer containing the Freeform information not only slides down gracefully, but also recoils at a pleasing pace when you click on a small triangle near the layer, as shown in Figure 17.8.

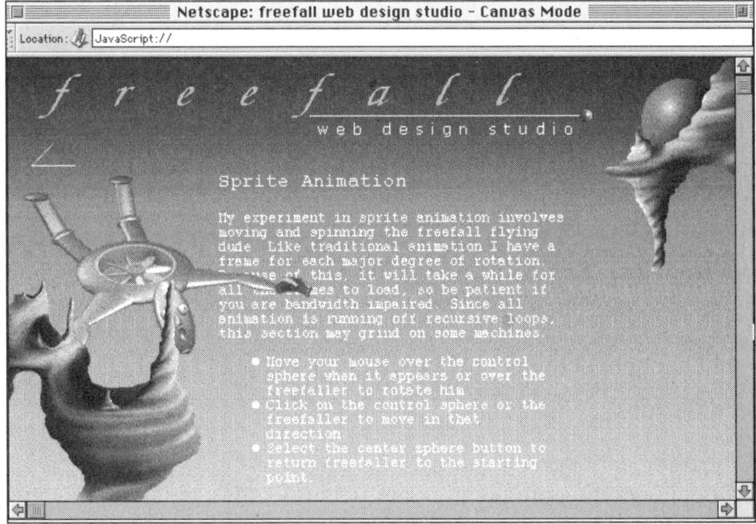

Figure 17.8

Notice the small triangle under the Freefall logo; clicking that triangle smoothly raises the logo layer.

The dropping and raising of the Freefall logo employs a recursive **setTimeout** loop that animates the layer's movement until a certain pixel distance is met:

```
        var logoTab = false;

        function moveLogo() {
                var tab1 = document.freefall_lyr.document.tab1_img;
                var logo = document.freefall_lyr;
                var text = document.content_lyr;
                if (logoTab == false) {
                        if (logo.top < 10) {
                                logo.moveBy(0,10);
                                setTimeout("moveLogo()", 2);
                        } else {
                                logoTab = true;
                                tab1.src = uparrow.src;
                        }
                        if (text.top < 95) {
                                text.top = 95;
                        }
                }
                else if (logoTab == true) {
                        if (logo.top > -60) {
                                logo.moveBy(0,-10);
                                setTimeout("moveLogo()", 2);
                        } else {
                                logoTab = false;
                                tab1.src = dnarrow.src;
                        }
                }
        }
```

Adding LiveAudio To Freefall

The Freefall site also contains audio, housed in a 2D data array that all the control functions can use:

```
musicData = new Array();
        musicData[0] = "levis.mid";
        musicData[1] = "bladerun.mid";
        musicData[2] = "jarre.mid";
        musicData[3] = "countdown.mid";
        musicData[4] = "majortom.mid";
```

The audio that plays at the site (see Figure 17.9) is handled by the music manager, which also tests to make sure that the user's browser has the LiveAudio plug-in (notice the alert in the last lines of this code that appears to viewers without the plug-in):

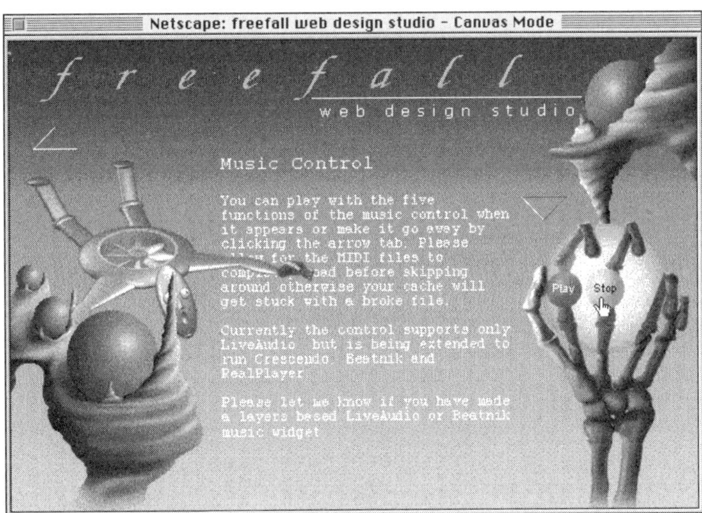

Figure 17.9

The audio plays as the skeleton hand appears.

```
function audioEnabled(plug_in) {
            for (var i = 0; i < navigator.plugins.length; i++) {
                  if (navigator.plugins[i].name.toLowerCase() ==
                     plug_in.toLowerCase()) {
                        for (var j = 0;
                           j < navigator.plugins[i].length; j++) {
                              if (navigator.plugins[i][j]
                                 .enabledPlugin) {
                                     return true
                              }
                        }
                        return false
                  }
            }
            return false
      }

      var track = 1;
      var music = null;
      lastImage = "stop";

      function musicToggle(arg1, arg2) {
            if (arg1 != lastImage) {
              document.skeleton_lyr.document.audio
              _lyr.document.images[arg1 + "_img"].src = eval(arg2 + ".src");
            }
      }
```

```
        function musicControl(cmd) {
                document.skeleton_lyr.document.audio
                 _lyr.document.images[cmd + "_img"].src = eval(cmd + "_dn.src");
                document.skeleton_lyr.document.audio
                 _lyr.document.images[lastImage + "_img"].src = blank.src;
                lastImage = cmd;
                if (audioEnabled("LiveAudio")) {
                        if (cmd == "play") {
                              music.play(false, "music/" + musicData[track-1]);
                        }
                        else if (cmd == "stop") {
                              music.stop();
                        }
                        else if (cmd == "pause") {
                              music.pause();
                        }
                        else if (cmd == "next") {
                              if (track == (musicData.length)) {
                                        track = 1;
                              } else {
                                        track++;
                              }
                              setTimeout("musicControl('play')", 750);
                        }
                        else if (cmd == "prev") {
                                if (track == 1) {
                                        track = musicData.length;
                                } else {
                                        track--;
                                }
                                setTimeout("musicControl('play')", 750);
                        }
                } else {
                        alert("I could not find the required LiveAudio plugin");
                }
        }

</SCRIPT>

</HEAD>
```

The music is invoked by the user's mouse actions; Rouyer also uses a table in conjunction with the audio:

```
<LAYER ID="audio_lyr" LEFT="18" TOP="25" VISIBILITY="SHOW" WIDTH="106"
   HEIGHT="105">
<TABLE BORDER="0" CELLPADDING="0" CELLSPACING="0">
```

```
<TR>
<TD></TD>
<TD><A HREF="JavaScript://" onClick="musicControl('next');
 return false";
 onMouseOver="musicToggle('next','next_up')";
 onMouseOut="musicToggle('next',
 'blank')">
<IMG NAME="next_img" SRC="images/blank.gif" WIDTH="37" HEIGHT="34"
 BORDER="0"></A></TD>
<TD></TD>
</TR>

<TR>
<TD><A HREF="JavaScript://" onClick="musicControl('play'); return false";
 onMouseOver="musicToggle('play','play_up')";
 onMouseOut="musicToggle('play', 'blank')">
<IMG NAME="play_img" SRC="images/blank.gif" WIDTH="35" HEIGHT="37"
 BORDER="0"></A></TD><TD><A HREF="JavaScript://"
 onClick="musicControl('stop');
 return false"; onMouseOver="musicToggle('stop','stop_up')";
 onMouseOut="musicToggle('stop', 'blank')">
<IMG NAME="stop_img" SRC="images/blank.gif" WIDTH="37" HEIGHT="37"
 BORDER="0"></A></TD><TD>
<A HREF="JavaScript://" onClick="musicControl('pause'); return false";
 onMouseOver="musicToggle('pause','pause_up')";
 onMouseOut="musicToggle('pause','blank')">
<IMG NAME="pause_img" SRC="images/blank.gif" WIDTH="34" HEIGHT="37"
 BORDER="0"></A></TD>
</TR>

<TR>
<TD></TD>
<TD><A HREF="JavaScript://" onClick="musicControl('prev'); return false";
 onMouseOver="musicToggle('prev','prev_up')";
 onMouseOut="musicToggle('prev','blank')">
<IMG NAME="prev_img" SRC="images/blank.gif" WIDTH="37" HEIGHT="34"
 BORDER="0"></A></TD>
<TD></TD>
</TR>

</TABLE>
```

Immediately preceding the final **</BODY>** tag, the following code is included to embed the audio's source:

```
<EMBED SRC="music/levis.mid" AUTOSTART="FALSE" HIDDEN="TRUE" VOLUME="90"
 NAME="musicSource" MASTERSOUND>
```

```
</BODY>

</HTML>
```

At the Freefall site, Rouyer generously offers templates of his design for anyone interested in learning more about the intricacies of DHTML. Find them and additional stimulating content at **www2.bw.edu/~cgrant/lab/layers/layers.htm**.

Mixing Layers

Dave April provides visitors with a highly entertaining, postmodern perspective on the politician genus with his Mix-A-Pol Web creation. Mix-A-Pol features a composite face made from six different images, as shown in Figure 17.10.

By clicking on an image such as the nose, the n layer will switch, cleverly swapping parts of politicians' faces. Notice in the following code how April has positioned the six layers (see Figure 17.11), naming their different values according to the first letter in their names (i.e., head is the h layer, eye is the e layer, etc.). Note the form within a layer that uses the button input type to let users determine which image is visible by clicking on the image:

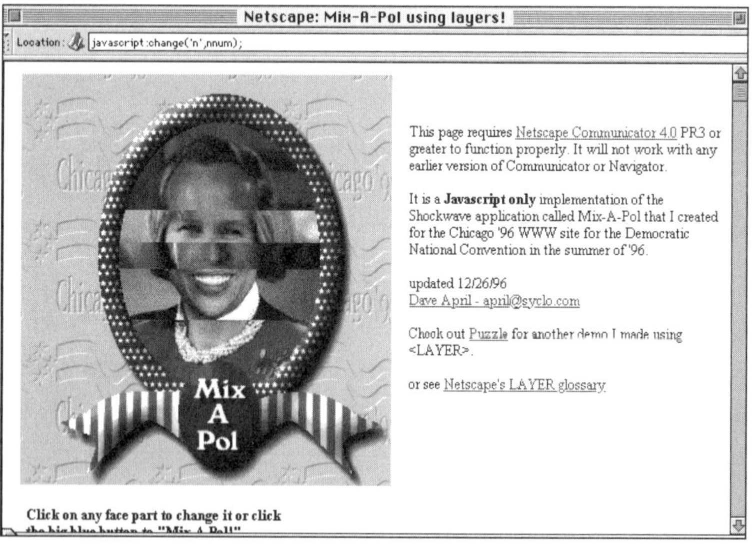

Figure 17.10

The Mix-A-Pol combines politicians' facial features in six different layers.

Figure 17.11

Another combination of six layers for Mix-A-Pol.

```
<layer name="h" left=100 top=50><img name="i_h" border=0 src="h1.jpeg"></layer>
<layer name="e" left=100 top=123><img name="i_e" border=0 src="e2.jpeg"></layer>
<layer name="n" left=100 top=150><img name="i_n" border=0 src="n3.jpeg"></layer>
<layer name="m" left=100 top=172><img name="i_m" border=0 src="m4.jpeg"></layer>
<layer name="b" left=100 top=214><img name="i_b" border=0 src="b5.jpeg"></layer>

<!--
<layer name="label" visibility=hide left=55 top=20><img border=0 src="l1.gif">
</layer>
-->

<layer name="border" left=15 top=10><img usemap="#theMap" border=0
src="border.gif"></layer>

<layer name="formLayer" left=20 top=370>
<!--
<form name="form0">
<input type="button" onclick="change('h',hnum);" value=" Head ">
<input type="button" onclick="change('e',enum);" value=" Eyes ">
<input type="button" onclick="change('n',nnum);" value=" Nose ">
<input type="button" onclick="change('m',mnum);" value=" Mouth ">
<input type="button" onclick="change('b',bnum);" value=" Body ">
<br><input type="button" onclick="mix();" value="      Mix-A-Pol     ">
<br><input name="fld" size=10>
```

```
</form>
-->
<b>Click on any face part to change it or click
<br>the big blue button to "Mix-A-Pol!"</b>
</layer>
```

Here are two fragments of the JavaScript that April used to ensure that the Mix-A-Pol's layers change in the desired sequence. You can see how April has named the various JPEG images and created JavaScript functions to cause them to change according to user input. Refer to the CD-ROM for this example's complete JavaScript.

```
function loadFaces() {
  for (x=1; x<=6; x++) {
    eval('img_h'+x+'= new Image();');
    eval('img_e'+x+'= new Image();');
    eval('img_n'+x+'= new Image();');
    eval('img_m'+x+'= new Image();');
    eval('img_b'+x+'= new Image();');
    eval('lbl'+x+'= new Image();');
    eval('img_h'+x+'.src=\"h'+x+'.jpeg\";');
    eval('img_e'+x+'.src=\"e'+x+'.jpeg\";');
    eval('img_n'+x+'.src=\"n'+x+'.jpeg\";');
    eval('img_m'+x+'.src=\"m'+x+'.jpeg\";');
    eval('img_b'+x+'.src=\"b'+x+'.jpeg\";');
    //eval('lbl'+x+'.src=l'+x+'.gif;');
  }
}
...
function change(name,theNum) {
  num=theNum + 1;
  if (num > max) { num=1; }
  imgName = name + num;
  if (name == "h") { change2(name,hnum,"head","hnum") }
  if (name == "e") { change2(name,enum,"eyes","enum") }
  if (name == "n") { change2(name,nnum,"nose","nnum") }
  if (name == "m") { change2(name,mnum,"mouth","mnum") }
  if (name == "b") { change2(name,bnum,"body","bnum") }
}
```

To see Mix-A-Pol in action, visit the site at **www.xnet.com/~april/mix/**.

Designing Dynamic Animation

Fabric8's Olivia Ongpin has used Macromedia's Dreamweaver to build a highly dynamic site featuring the wares of independent fashion designers, artists, and musicians in San Francisco. Here we take a look at Fabric8's online magazine for October 1997.

When it launches, the page performs a server-side "browser sniff" and warns non-Netscape 4 users that they'll need Netscape 4 to fully experience the Fabric8 site:

```
<tr>
        <td valign=top><font face="arial, helvetica">
        <font size="+2">This fabric8 page uses frames and JavaScript, viewable
         on Netscape 2.0 or higher. However, you can view the home page by
        <a href="fabric8_nondyn.html">clicking here</a>. To see fabric8 in all
         its glory, we suggest that you download the latest version of
        <a href="http://home.netscape.com/">Netscape</a>. Thank you.</font>
</td>
</tr>
```

The initial image layer that Fabric8 unleashes on Navigator 4 users is the female form shown in Figure 17.12, the "Benday" layer. After duplicating itself across the page several times, the figure unclones itself—through becoming nonvisible—so that the viewer ultimately sees only a single layer of the female form. In the opening sequence, the Fabric8 logo, "layerLogo," also slides across the page, as seen in Figures 17.13 and 17.14.

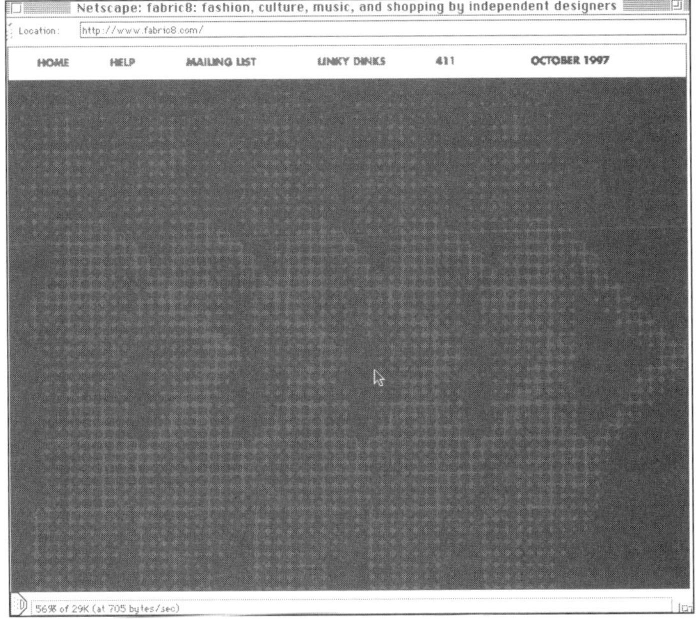

Figure 17.12

Fabric8's initial layer positioned across the screen.

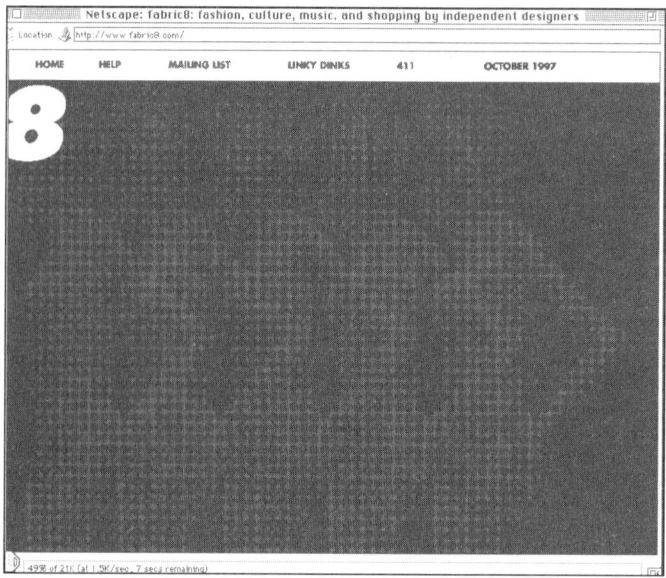

Figure 17.13

The first position of the Fabric8 logo animation, which uses layers.

Figure 17.14

The second stage of the Fabric8 logo animation.

Figure 17.15

The fully loaded Fabric8 Web site.

A backlit male mannequin also appears on the left side of the page, as shown in Figure 17.15. All of these images are layers with locations determined through absolute positioning:

```
<div id="layerBenday" style="position:absolute; left:390; top:0; width:319;
 height:840; z-index:2;">
  <img src="images/benday_off.gif" width="319" height="840">
</div>
<div id="layerBenday3" style="position:absolute; left:275; top:0; width:319;
 height:840; z-index:2;">
  <img src="images/benday_off.gif" width="319" height="840">
</div>
<div id="layerBenday2" style="position:absolute; left:160; top:0; width:319;
 height:840; z-index:2;">
  <img src="images/benday_off.gif" width="319" height="840">
</div>
<div id="layerBenday1" style="position:absolute; left:45; top:0; width:319;
 height:840; z-index:2;">
  <img src="images/benday_off.gif" width="319" height="840">
</div>
```

```
<div id="layerLogo" style="position:absolute; left:-190px; top:3; width:185;
 height:81; z-index:100;">
  <img src="images/fabric8_logo.gif" name="logo" height="87" width="185">
</div>
<div id="layerBenday0" style="position:absolute; left:-60; top:0; width:319;
 height:840; z-index:2;">
  <img src="images/benday_off.gif" width="319" height="840" onload="init()">
</div>
<div id="layerMannequin" style="position:absolute; left:7; top:15; width:119;
 height:339; z-index:3; visibility: hidden">
  <img src="images/mannequin.gif" name="mannequin" width="150" height="322">
</div>
<div id="layerLight" style="position:absolute; left:-20; top:-15; width:220;
 height:274; z-index:1; visibility: hidden">
  <img src="images/light.gif" height="274" width="220">
</div>
```

As you can see in Figure 17.16, when you run your mouse over the page's sections, such as "Revolution," the **onMouseOver** rollover and rolloff makes the Benday image swivel and the selected section name switch layers so that it appears with more intense colors:

Figure 17.16

MouseOver *sensitivity changes the "Revolution" image as well as the pose of the Benday female form.*

```
<p class="section"><a href="revolution/index.html"
onMouseOver=
"rollover('revolution','fabric8_type_revolution_on.gif','made in the ghetto');
 return true"
        onMouseOut="rolloff('revolution','fabric8_type_revolution_off.gif')">
<imgsrc="images/fabric8_type_revolution_off.gif" name="revolution"
 alt="revolution" border="0" vspace="0" hspace="0" width="143" height="25">
</a></p>
  <p class="motto">GEAR FOR THE NEW MILLENNIUM</p>
  <p class="description">the streets are stirring; their words whisper change.
    stay tuned and support the revolution network as it chronicles the days
    until high noon.</p>
```

Making A Virtual Gallery Dynamic And Cross-Platform Compatible

Natespace, a virtual gallery, was originally created by the artist Nathan Jensen in a way that required the server to load the next image whenever you rounded a corner. However, the DHTML layers incorporated into Natespace by Christopher D. Brown radically alter the end-user experience. Rather than having to wait for the download before you can peruse the art, the layer environment loads completely when you first enter the site, so that navigating through the virtual gallery's rich and trippy hallways becomes a fluid experience, as shown in Figures 17.17 through 17.19.

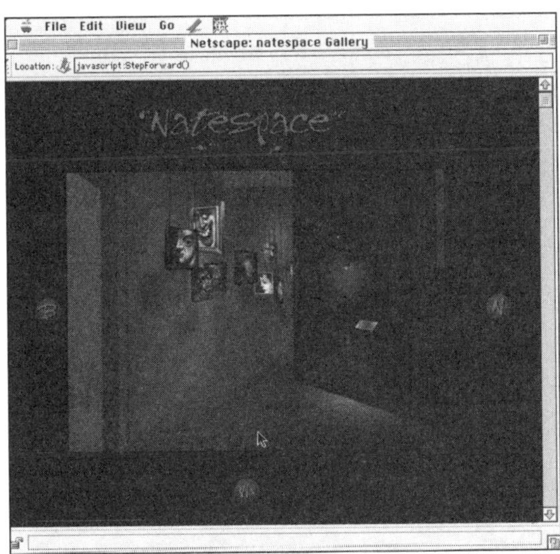

Figure 17.17

A dynamically navigable room in the Natespace Gallery.

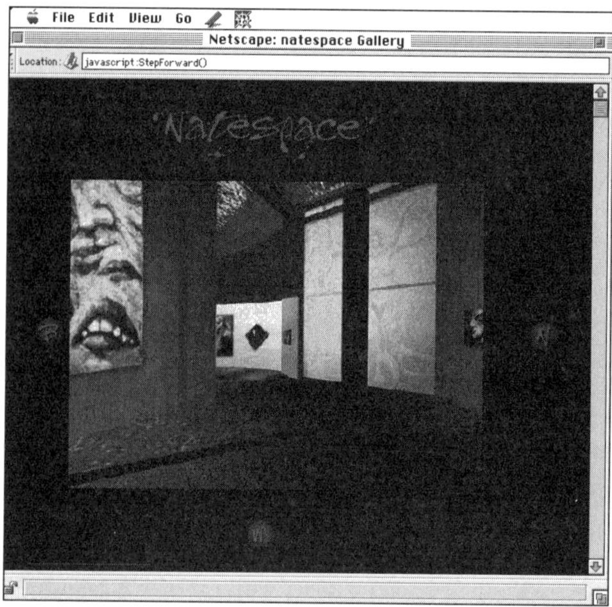

Figure 17.18

The use of ***MouseOver*** *sensitivity lets you swiftly navigate Natespace's artistic corridors just by moving your mouse. Clicking your mouse over a painting will show an enlarged version of the selected canvas.*

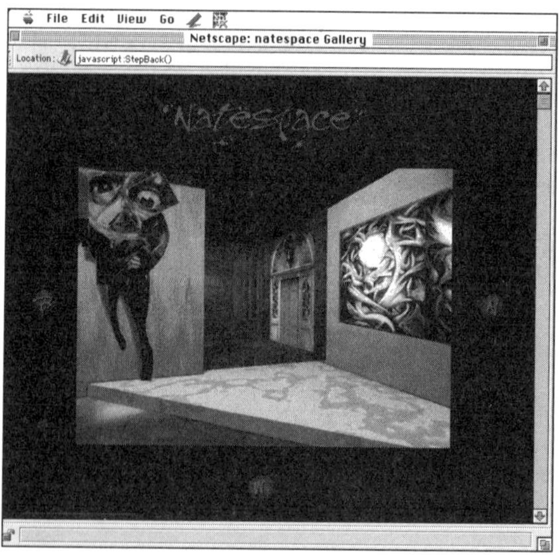

Figure 17.19

Natespace is entered and exited through this door.

The following code demonstrates how Brown used DHTML to take Natespace into a dynamic realm. Although Natespace contains layers, Brown's blending of JavaScript, CSS, VBScript, and layers allows it to work for IE 4.0 as well as Netscape Navigator. Note the use of the **BGSOUND** tag, which, although IE-specific, can be used to add a MIDI file to Natespace. Chapter 11 contains a detailed overview of how JavaScript was also used to script Natespace's audio.

```
<!-- Styles -->

 <STYLE TYPE="text/css">
  <!--
   .rinner      { border-width:0; border-color:blue; border-style:ridge;
                  padding:2px; }
   .cinner      { border-width:0; border-color:blue; border-style:ridge;
                  padding:2px; }
   .csscloseup { position:absolute; top: 90; left: 60; height:288; width:432;
                  z-index:30; visibility:hidden; }
   .csshall     { position:absolute; top: 90; left: 60; height:288; width:432;
                  z-index:30; visibility:hidden; }
   .cssload     { position:absolute; top:  0; left: 60; height: 55; width:432;
                  z-index:30; visibility:visible; }
   .csstop      { position:absolute; top: 20; left: 60; height: 55; width:432;
                  z-index:20; visibility:visible; }
   .cssleft     { position:absolute; top: 90; left: 20; height:288; width: 40;
                  z-index:20; visibility:visible; }
   .cssright    { position:absolute; top: 90; left: 492; height:288; width: 40;
                  z-index:20; visibility:visible; }
   .cssmain     { position:absolute; top:400; left: 60; height: 37; width:432;
                  z-index:20; visibility:visible; }
   .csscredit   { position:absolute; top:440; left: 20; height: 80; width:472;
                  z-index:30; visibility:visible; }
  -->
 </STYLE>


 <BODY BGCOLOR="#330000" TEXT="#FAEBD7" LINK="#FAEBD7" VLINK="#FAEBD7"
  ALINK="#FAEBD7">

   <BGSOUND src="gallery.mid" LOOP="-1">

   <DIV id="loading" class="cssload">
   <layer>
   <DIV class="rinner">
    <table width="100%"><tr><td align="center" valign="middle"nowrap>
    <font size="4"><b> Giant Download       
```

```
  Please Wait </b></font></td></tr></table>
</DIV>
</layer>
</DIV>

<DIV id="gal0" class="csshall" ONMOUSEOUT="ReArm();">
<layer ONMOUSEOUT="ReArm();">
<DIV class="rinner" align="center">
 <table cellpadding="0" cellspacing="0" border="0" width="432">
  <tr>
   <td rowspan="3" align="left" valign="middle" width="75" nowrap>
     Go <br> back </td>
   <td align="center" valign="top" width="282" nowrap>
    Hover over passages to travel. <br>
    Click paintings for closer viewing.
   </td>
   <td rowspan="3" align="right" valign="middle" width="75" nowrap>
     Continue <br> forward </td>
  </tr>
  <tr>
   <td align="center"><a href="javascript:Walk(1)" onmouseover="Walk(1);">
   <IMG SRC="frtdoor.jpg" width="181" height="216" BORDER="0"
    ALT="Doorway to gallery" vspace="10" hspace="4"></a></td>
  </tr>
  <tr>
   <td align="center" valign="bottom" nowrap> Return to instructions </td>
  </tr>
 </table>
</DIV>
</layer>
</DIV>

<DIV id="gal1" class="csshall" ONMOUSEOUT="ReArm();">
<layer ONMOUSEOUT="ReArm();">
<DIV class="rinner" align="center">
 <IMG SRC="gal1.jpg" WIDTH="396" HEIGHT="288" USEMAP="#map1"
  ISMAP BORDER="0" ALT="ART when really understood is the province
  of every human being."><P>
 <MAP NAME="map1">
  <AREA HREF="javascript:ShowPic('pai1.GIF');" SHAPE="polygon"
   COORDS="31,146 55,146 55,90 31,84 31,146">
  <AREA HREF="javascript:ShowPic('pai2.GIF');" SHAPE="polygon"
   COORDS="68,106 97,110 97,142 68,142 68,106">
  <AREA HREF="javascript:ShowPic('pai3.GIF');" SHAPE="polygon"
   COORDS="97,184 131,184 189,89 182,78 121,96 97,184">
  <AREA HREF="javascript:ShowPic('pai4.GIF');" SHAPE="polygon"
   COORDS="201,133 221,138 221,93 203,99 201,133">
  <AREA HREF="javascript:Walk(2);" onmouseover="Walk(2)" SHAPE="polygon"
```

```
   COORDS="137,184 191,95 191,200 141,208 137,184">
  <AREA HREF="javascript:Walk(10);" onmouseover="Walk(10)" SHAPE="rect"
   COORDS="257,1 350,227">
 </MAP>
</DIV>
</layer>
</DIV>
```

PART 5

THE REALITIES OF IMPLEMENTING DHTML

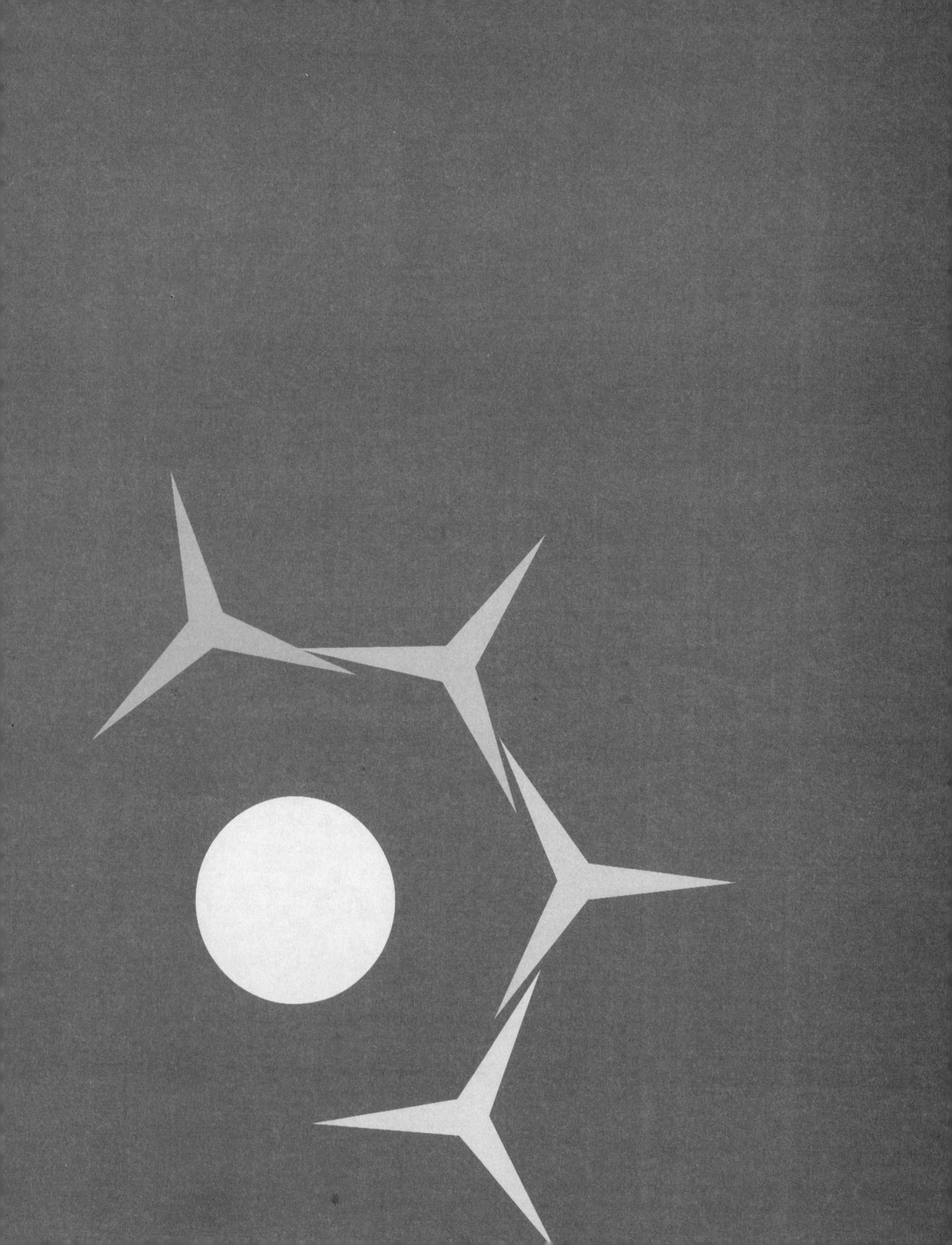

Chapter 18

Creating DHTML That Looks Good In Any Environment

In this chapter, we discuss how to incorporate Dynamic HTML into your Web pages so they can display successfully in both Internet Explorer and Netscape Navigator.

Notes...

Chapter 18

Parts 3 and 4 of this book have outlined in detail how to create dynamic Web pages using both Microsoft's Dynamic HTML and Netscape's layers methods. But as we've said before, many of the techniques are proprietary and will work only with Internet Explorer 4.0 or Netscape Navigator 4.0. The realities of the Web world are that your pages will be viewed with both browsers. If you use one technique at the expense of the other, you will be alienating at least half of your viewers, and that can't be good.

Should you wait until 1999, when a standard is created, to create your dynamic Web pages? If we believed that, we wouldn't have written this book. We do suggest that you not create an entire site that revolves around DHTML any time soon, because the specification will change over and over again in the coming months. Instead, use DHTML to create bleeding-edge sections of your site to practice using the technology in a realistic environment and to show your visitors that you're keeping up with the times. Even though these special sections will be mainly for demonstration purposes, you'll still want them to be viewable by as many people as possible.

This chapter discusses ways that you can create dynamic Web pages that can be displayed successfully by both Internet Explorer 4 and Netscape Navigator 4. Because we have already discussed the hows and specifics of many of the techniques behind these methods, we don't want to tell you how all over again. This chapter will show you how to combine them to create dynamic pages that both browsers can access.

Real-world implementations always speak louder than words, so the bulk of this chapter will be devoted to showing how three different Web sites have used combined techniques to create interesting, attractive, and fun sites that look good in both browsers.

Combining Disparate DHTML Techniques

The techniques you can use to create cross-browser-compatible pages are derived from these three different DHTML components:

- Style sheets
- DOM
- Scripting

As we've shown throughout the book, Microsoft and Netscape have their individual proprietary ideas about how each of these components should be created and implemented in Web pages. In many cases, it is possible to include both vendors' methods in the same Web page; in others, one method works with both browsers. We'll examine each of these components and how you can include them in your multibrowser-compatible dynamic pages.

Style Sheets

As we described in Chapter 6, Cascading Style Sheets are the industry standard, and a DOM that meets the W3C's standards must support style sheets. Microsoft's DHTML allows HTML elements tied to style-sheet rules to be altered via scripting. Netscape's layers technology works with CSS but works even better with Netscape's own JavaScript Style Sheets. In addition, Netscape doesn't support dynamic changes to a Web page via scripting and style sheets. So how do you accommodate both of these methods? Simple: You use redundant style sheets and scripts. Creating identical CSS and JSS rules is not too difficult since the methods are the same even if the syntax isn't. You then write separate scripts for both the Microsoft and Netscape methods to modify pages dynamically. Writing redundant style rules and scripts may take a while, but the end results will be well worth it.

DOMs

Both Microsoft's and Netscape's Document Object Models provide access to Web page elements for scripts. But while Microsoft's DOM encompasses all of HTML's elements, Netscape's is limited to only some of them. This means that a script that uses objects supported by the Microsoft DOM but not by the Netscape DOM will work correctly only when the page is viewed with Internet Explorer. The only way to deal with this particular difference in DOMs is to create a reference variable that can be set when the page is loaded to use the syntax for whichever browser is being used to view the page. The variable looks something like this:

```
if (navigator.appName == "Netscape") {
     layerRef="document.layers";
     styleRef="";
} else {
     layerRef="document.all";
     styleRef=".style";
}
```

Scripting

A DOM that is W3C-standard is not restricted to any single scripting language but can be used with any language. The two most prevalent Web scripting languages are JavaScript and VBScript—JavaScript is Netscape's creation and JScript is Microsoft's adaptation of this scripting language. Only Microsoft supports VBScript. Common sense tells you that JavaScript is the language of choice for pages that work with both browsers. To create compatible scripts, don't write scripts that pass any events to parent event handlers, known in Microsoft terminology as "event bubbling," because the passing order is different in each browser.

In addition to the HTML 4.0 events that Netscape supports, Microsoft has its own set of proprietary events. Use only those events in your scripts that are HTML 4.0-standard and avoid problems with Netscape not recognizing Microsoft's proprietary events.

Differences In A Nutshell

The easiest way to gather from each DHTML method the components you can use to create multibrowser-compatible pages is by skipping any components that are proprietary and that currently work with only one browser.

Microsoft's proprietary DHTML components include:

- Data binding
- VBScript

- Direct animation controls
- OpenType fonts

Netscape's proprietary DHTML components include:

- The **<LAYER>** tag
- JavaScript Style Sheets
- Bitstream fonts

Practical Guide To

Creating DHTML That Looks Good In Any Environment

- The DHTML Zone
- The "Duoh!" Site
- Virtual Pig

Now that we've given you a brief rundown on what techniques you can combine to create cross-browser-compatible dynamic Web pages, it's time to take a look at three different sites that incorporate such pages. We've included several screen shots of each, taken with each browser, and the source code for two of them. The source speaks the loudest. Take some time to read through the code and see how the designers created their sites.

The DHTML Zone

The DHTML Zone is a site sponsored and created by Macromedia. It seems that Macromedia has decided to involve itself very deeply in the development of DHTML, and rightly so since its primary products focus on multimedia development. The home page of the DHTML Zone includes a dynamic menu that flies in as the page loads. Amazingly, it works with both Internet Explorer 4.0 and Navigator 4.0 on a PC. Figure 18.1 shows two different stages of the flying menu as seen through Internet Explorer. Figure 18.2 shows the same page when viewed with Navigator.

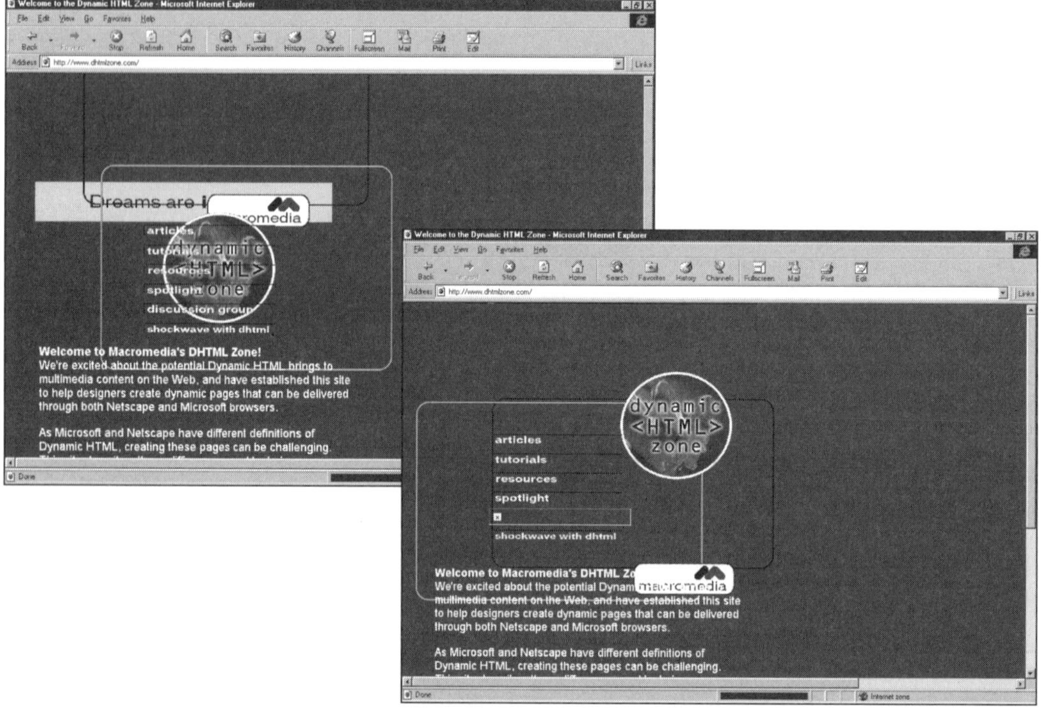

Figure 18.1

The DHTML Zone home page menu fly-in as seen with Internet Explorer.

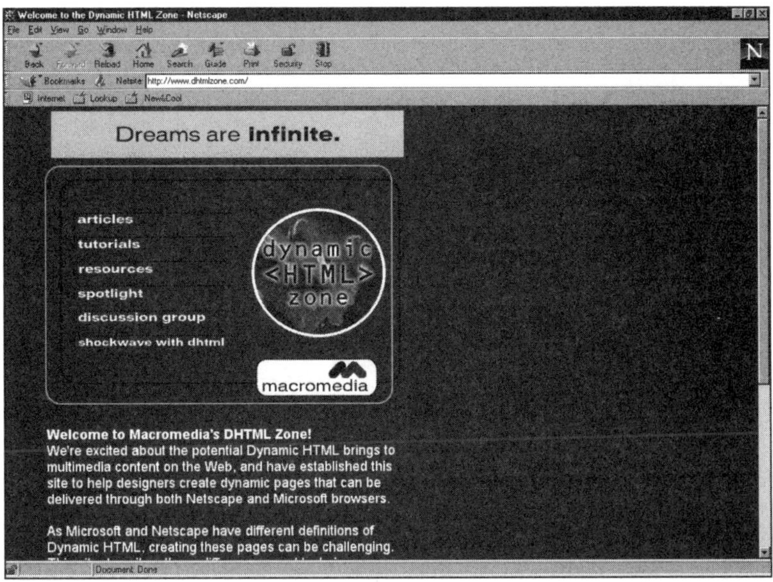

Figure 18.2

The complete DHTML Zone home page as seen with Navigator.

Once the menu has been loaded, menu buttons cause a different picture to appear in the orange circle when a mouse runs over the button. Figures 18.3 and 18.4 show this effect as seen by Internet Explorer and Navigator, respectively.

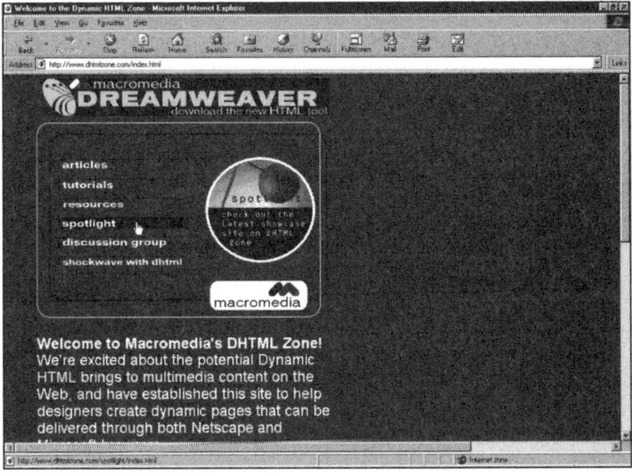

Figure 18.3

*The DHTML Zone menu buttons cause a different image to appear in response to an **onMouseOver**, as seen with Internet Explorer.*

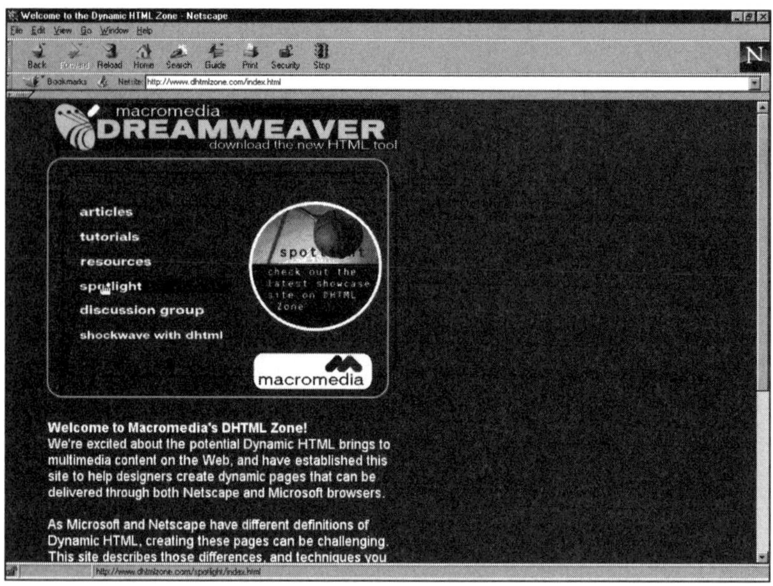

Figure 18.4

*The DHTML Zone menu buttons cause a different image to appear in response to an **onMouseOver**, as seen with Navigator.*

Listing 18.1 shows the code behind this creative page.

Listing 18.1 The style sheets, scripts, and HTML behind the DHTML Zone home page.

```
<html>
<head>
<title>Welcome to the Dynamic HTML Zone</title>
</head>

<style>

body {
  background: #990000;
  text: #FFFFFF;
  link: #99CCFF;
  vlink: #FFFFCC;
}

#adbanner {
  position: absolute;
  top: 3;
  left: 60;
}
```

```
#blacksquare {
  position: absolute;
  top: 90;
  left: 70;
  visibility: hidden;
}

#bluesquare {
  position: absolute;
  top: 70;
  left: 45;
  visibility: hidden;
}

#logo {
  position: absolute;
  top: 325;
  left: 330;
  visibility: hidden;
}

#circle {
  position: absolute;
  top: 130;
  left: 325;
  visibility: hidden;
}

#thelinks{
  position: absolute;
  top: 130;
  left: 85;
  visibility: hidden;
}

#loading{
  position: absolute;
  top: 200;
  left: 200;
}

#text{
  position:absolute;
  top:410;
  left: 50;
}
```

```
#preload{
  position:absolute;
  visibility: hidden;
}

</style>


<script language = JavaScript 1.1>


master = new Array();     // names of each animation layer
dx = new Array();         // horizontal speed of each layer
dy = new Array();         // vertical speed of each layer

var max_jump = 10;        // maximum distance of animation step
var steps = 20;           // total number of animation frames
var delay = 1;            // pause between animation frames


function initSpeeds() {
  for (var ctr = 0; ctr < master.length; ctr++) {
    dx[ctr] = Math.ceil(Math.random() * max_jump);
    if (Math.random() > .5) {
      dx[ctr] *= -1;
    }
    dy[ctr] = Math.ceil(Math.random() * max_jump);
    if (Math.random() > .5) {
      dy[ctr] *= -1;
    }
  }
}

function MSinitPositions() {
  for (var ctr = 0; ctr < master.length; ctr++) {
    document.all.tags("div")[ctr].style.posLeft += (-steps *
dx[ctr]);
    document.all.tags("div")[ctr].style.posTop += (-steps *
dy[ctr]);
    document.all.tags("div")[ctr].style.visibility = "visible";
  }
  loading.style.visibility = "hidden";
}

function NSinitPositions() {
  for (var ctr = 0; ctr < master.length; ctr++) {
    eval("document." + master[ctr] + ".left += (-steps *
```

```
dx[ctr])");
    eval("document." + master[ctr] + ".top += (-steps *
dy[ctr])");
    eval("document." + master[ctr] + ".visibility = 'visible'");
  }
  document.loading.visibility = "hidden";
}

function MSfixPositions() {
    for (var ctr = 0; ctr < master.length; ctr++) {
      document.all.tags("div")[ctr].style.posLeft += dx[ctr]
      document.all.tags("div")[ctr].style.posTop += dy[ctr]
    }

    if (steps > 1) {
      steps--;
      setTimeout("MSfixPositions()", delay);
    }
}

function NSfixPositions() {
    for (var ctr = 0; ctr < master.length; ctr++) {
    eval("document." + master[ctr] + ".left += dx[ctr]");
    eval("document." + master[ctr] + ".top +=  dy[ctr]");
    }

    if (steps > 1) {
      steps--;
      setTimeout("NSfixPositions()", delay);
    }
}

function runAnimation() {
  initSpeeds();
  if (window.navigator.userAgent.indexOf("MSIE") > 0) {
    MSinitPositions();
    MSfixPositions();
  } else {
     NSinitPositions();
     NSfixPositions();
  }
}

//MM hiliteImg() courtesy of www.coolnote.com
function MS_hiliteImg()  {
  srcImgArray = new Array;  //used for reset
  for (var i=0; i < (MM_hiliteImg.arguments.length-1); i+=2) {
    theObj = MM_hiliteImg.arguments[i];
```

```
    srcImgArray[i] = theObj;
    newImgFile = MM_hiliteImg.arguments[i+1];
    srcImgArray[i+1] = eval('document.'+theObj+'.src');
    eval('document.'+theObj+'.src = "'+newImgFile+'"');
  }
  document.MM_hiliteImgSrcs = srcImgArray; //used for reset
}

function NS_hiliteImg()  {
  document.oldObjectSrc = document.circle.document.images[0].src;
  document.circle.document.images[0].src =
MM_hiliteImg.arguments[1];
  document.oldImgRef =
document.thelinks.document.images[NS_hiliteImg.arguments[2]].name.toString();
  document.oldImgFile =
document.thelinks.document.images[NS_hiliteImg.arguments[2]].src;

document.thelinks.document.images[NS_hiliteImg.arguments[2]].src
= NS_hiliteImg.arguments[3];
}

//MM_hiliteImgRestore() courtesy of www.coolnote.com
function MS_hiliteImgRestore()  {
  if (document.MM_hiliteImgSrcs != null) {
    scrImgArray = document.MM_hiliteImgSrcs;
    for (var i=0; i < (scrImgArray.length-1); i+=2) {
      theObj = scrImgArray[i];
      srcImgFile = scrImgArray[i+1];
      eval('document.'  +  theObj  +  '.src = "'  +  srcImgFile
+  '"');
    }
  }
}

function NS_hiliteImgRestore()  {
  document.circle.document.images[0].src = document.oldObjectSrc;
  document.thelinks.document.images[document.oldImgRef].src =
document.oldImgFile;
}

MM_hiliteImg = new Function();
MM_hiliteImgRestore = new Function();

if (window.navigator.userAgent.indexOf("MSIE") > 0) {
  MM_hiliteImg = MS_hiliteImg;
  MM_hiliteImgRestore = MS_hiliteImgRestore;
```

```
} else {
  MM_hiliteImg = NS_hiliteImg;
  MM_hiliteImgRestore = NS_hiliteImgRestore;
}

//store each layer's name in a master array
master[0] = "blacksquare";
master[1] = "bluesquare";
master[2] = "logo";
master[3] = "thelinks";
master[4] = "circle";
master[5] = "adbanner";

</script>


<body onload = "runAnimation()">

<!-- adbanner-->
<div id = adbanner>
<!--begin mm adshow code-->
<a target="mm_window"
href="http://www.macromedia.com/software/dreamweaver/">
<img src="images/ads/dreamdownload.gif"
height="60" width="468" alt="click here to download macromedia
dreamweaver"></a>
<!--end mm adshow code-->
</div>

<!--the moving layers...each layer is positioned via the doc's
style sheet-->
<div  id = blacksquare><img src="images/blacksquare.gif"
width="461" height="277"></div>
<div  id = bluesquare><img src="images/bluesquare.gif"
width="480" height="321"></div>
<div  id = logo><a href="http://www.macromedia.com/"><img
src="images/logo.gif" width="165" height="54" border="0"
alt="Click here to go to Macromedia.com"></a></div>

<div id = circle>
<img src="images/dhtml_c.gif" name="dhtml_circle" width="183"
height="170" border="0" alt="Welcome to the Dynamic HTML Zone!">
</div>

<div id = thelinks>
<table cellspacing = 0 cellpadding = 0>
<tr><td>
```

```
<A HREF="articles/index.html"
onMouseOver="MM_hiliteImg
     ('dhtml_circle','images/article_c.gif','articles','images/
     article0.gif')"
onMouseOut="MM_hiliteImgRestore()">
<img src="images/article1.gif" name="articles" width="227"
height="26" border="0" alt=""></a>
</td></tr>
<tr><td>
<A HREF="tutorials/index.html"
onMouseOver="MM_hiliteImg
     ('dhtml_circle','images/tutorial_c.gif','tutorial','images/
     tutorial0.gif')"
onMouseOut="MM_hiliteImgRestore()">
<img src="images/tutorial1.gif" name="tutorial" width="227"
height="26" border="0" alt=""></a>
</td></tr>
<tr><td>
<A HREF="resources/index.html"
onMouseOver="MM_hiliteImg('dhtml_circle','images/
     resource_c.gif','resource','images/resource0.gif')"
onMouseOut="MM_hiliteImgRestore()">
<img src="images/resource1.gif" name="resource" width="227"
height="26" border="0" alt=""></a>
</td></tr>
<tr><td>
<A HREF="spotlight/index.html"
onMouseOver="MM_hiliteImg('dhtml_circle','images/
     spotlight_c.gif','spotlight','images/spotlight0.gif')"
onMouseOut="MM_hiliteImgRestore()">
<img src="images/spotlight1.gif" name="spotlight" width="227"
height="26" border="0" alt=""></a>
</td></tr>
<tr><td>
<A HREF="discussion/index.html"
onMouseOver="MM_hiliteImg('dhtml_circle','images/
     discuss_c.gif','discuss','images/discuss0.gif')"
onMouseOut="MM_hiliteImgRestore()">
<img src="images/discuss1.gif" name="discuss" width="227"
height="26" border="0" alt=""></a>
</td></tr>
<tr><td>
<A HREF="swdhtml/index.html"
onMouseOver="MM_hiliteImg('dhtml_circle','images/
     shockwave_c.gif','shockwave','images/shockwave0.gif')"
onMouseOut="MM_hiliteImgRestore()">
<img src="images/shockwave1.gif" name="shockwave" width="227"
```

```
height="26" border="0" alt=""></a>
</td></tr>
</table>
</div>


<!--this layer is only visible while the rest of the doc is
loading-->
<div id = loading>
<font color = #ffffff size = +2>
<font face="arial, helvetica, *">l o a d i n g . . .</font>
</font>
</div>

<!--this layer preloads the layover images-->
<div id = preload>
<img src="images/article_c.gif" align="" width="183"
height="170" border="0" alt="Articles">
<img src="images/article0.gif" align="" width="227" height="26"
border="0" alt="Articles">
<img src="images/discuss_c.gif" align="" width="183"
height="170" border="0" alt="Discussion Group">
<img src="images/discuss0.gif" align="" width="227"
height="26" border="0" alt="Discussion Group">
<img src="images/resource_c.gif" align="" width="183"
height="170" border="0" alt="Resources">
<img src="images/resource0.gif" align="" width="227"
height="26" border="0" alt="Resources">
<img src="images/shockwave_c.gif" align="" width="183"
height="170" border="0" alt="Shockwave in Dynamic HTML">
<img src="images/shockwave0.gif" align="" width="227"
height="26" border="0" alt="Shockwave in Dynamic HTML">
<img src="images/spotlight_c.gif" align="" width="183"
height="170" border="0" alt="Spotlight">
<img src="images/spotlight0.gif" align="" width="227"
height="26" border="0" alt="Spotlight">
<img src="images/tutorial_c.gif" align="" width="183"
height="170" border="0" alt="Tutorials">
<img src="images/tutorial0.gif" align="" width="227"
height="26" border="0" alt="Tutorials">

</div>

<div id = text>

<table width="500">
<tr>
<td  valign="top">
```

```
<font size="4"><font color="#ffffff" face="arial, helvetica, *">
<b>Welcome to Macromedia's DHTML Zone!</b><br>
We're excited about the potential Dynamic HTML brings to
multimedia content on the Web, and have established this site to
help designers create dynamic pages that can be delivered
through both Netscape and Microsoft browsers.

<p>

As Microsoft and Netscape have different definitions of Dynamic
HTML, creating these pages can be challenging. This site
describes those differences, and techniques you can use to get
your content to display successfully. Today, Shockwave
participates as a full-fledged element of Dynamic HTML,
and runs across older and newer browsers seamlessly. It's all in our
<a href="swdhtml/index.html"><font color="#99ccff">
Shockwave with DHTML</font></a> area.

<p>

We're also busily working on a new visual web site authoring tool
that will support Dynamic HTML called
<a target="mm_window" href="http://www.macromedia.com/
software/dreamweaver/">
<font color="#99ccff">Dreamweaver</font></a>, and are interested
in any <a href="discussion/index.html">
<font color="#99ccff">suggestions</font></a>
you have or <a href="discussion/index.html">
<font color="#99ccff">obstacles</font></a>
you run into as you begin creating DHTML pages.
<a target="mm_window" href="http://www.macromedia.com/
software/dreamweaver/"><font color="#99ccff">
Download a beta copy of Dreamweaver today!</font></a>

<p>

</font>
</td>
</tr>
</table>
<p>

<center>

<br>

<hr width=500 align=left noshade>

<code>
```

```
<a href="index.html" target="_top">
<font color="#99ccff">home</font></a> |
<a href="articles/index.html" target="_top">
<font color="#99ccff">articles</font></a> |
<a href="resources/index.html" target="_top">
<font color="#99ccff">resources</font></a> |
<a href="tutorials/index.html" target="_top">
<font color="#99ccff">tutorials</font></a> |
<a href="spotlight/index.html" target="_top">
<font color="#99ccff">spotlight</font></a> |<br>
<a href="discussion/index.html" target="_top">
<font color="#99ccff">discussion group</font></a> |
<a href="swdhtml/index.html" target="_top">
<font color="#99ccff">shockwave with dhtml</font></a> |
<a href="http://www.macromedia.com/" target="_top">
<font color="#99ccff">macromedia</font></a>

<p>
<font size=2><a
href="http://www.macromedia.com/help/copyright.html">
<font color="#99ccff">Copyright</font></a> &#169;1997
Macromedia&#174; Inc. All rights reserved.
<a href="http://www.macromedia.com/help/copyright.html">
<font color="#99ccff">Disclaimer</font></a>.
<br><a href="mailto:dhtmlzone@macromedia.com">
<font color="#99ccff">dhtmlzone@macromedia.com</font></a>
</code>
</font>
</center>
<!--end footer-->

</div>

</body>
</html>
```

To see the DHTML Zone dynamic page in action visit the site at **www.dhtmlzone.com**.

The Duoh! Site

The Duoh! site, a sample cross-browser-compatible site recommended on the Macromedia DHTML Zone site, utilizes a fly-in menu similar to the DHTML Zone's menu. Figure 18.5 shows Internet Explorer 4's view of this site while Figure 18.6 shows Navigator 4's view.

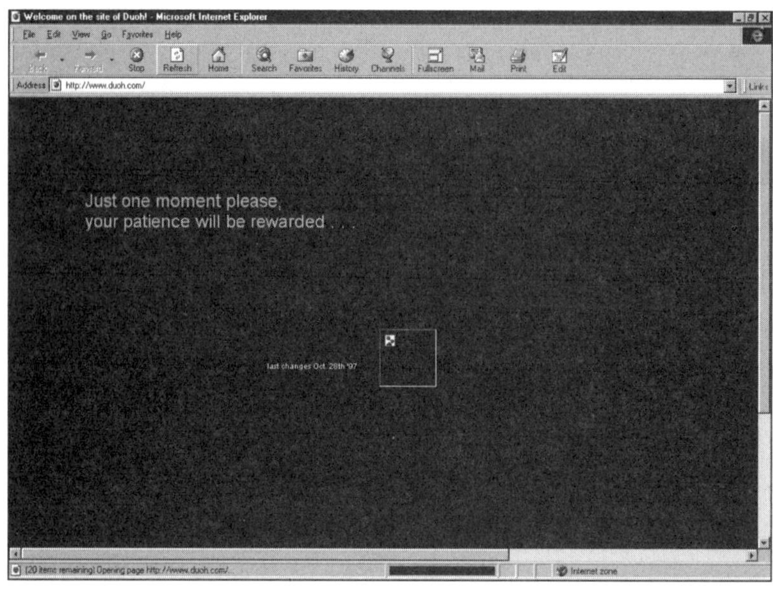

Figure 18.5

The start of the Duoh! home page menu fly-in as seen with Internet Explorer.

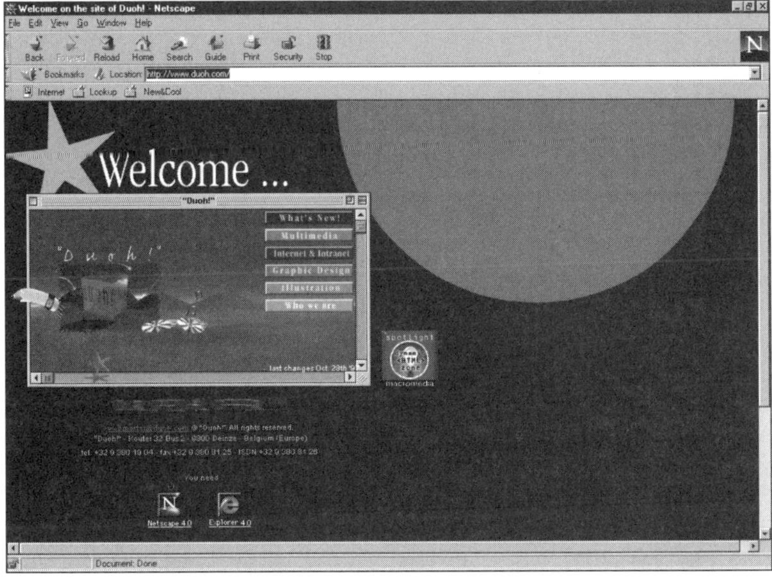

Figure 18.6

And the complete Duoh! home page menu fly-in as seen with Navigator.

As on the DHTML Zone site, running a mouse over the menu buttons in the Duoh! site causes a different image to appear. Figures 18.7 and 18.8 show this effect as seen by Internet Explorer and Navigator, respectively.

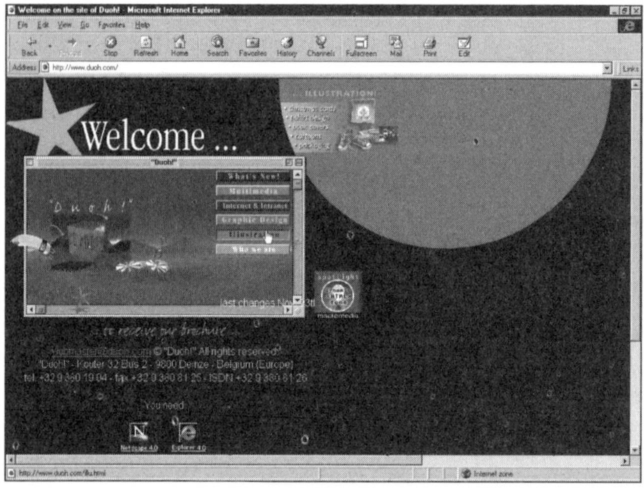

Figure 18.7

The Duoh! menu buttons cause a different image to appear in response to an ***onmouseOver****, as seen with Internet Explorer.*

Figure 18.8

The Duoh! menu buttons cause a different image to appear in response to an ***onmouseOver****, as seen with Navigator.*

Listing 18.2 shows the code behind this wonderful page.

Listing 18.2 The scripts and HTML behind the Duoh! home page.

```
<html>
<head>
<title>Welcome on the site of Duoh!</title>

<SCRIPT>
<!------------------------------------------------------
var version = 0;
bName = navigator.appName;
bVer = parseInt(navigator.appVersion);

if ((bName == "Netscape" || bName =="Microsoft Internet
Explorer")
  && bVer >= 4) version = 4;
if (version == 4)
               {
                //load this page
               }
else {
                //load page for older browsers
        location.href="old/index2.html";
        }
//-->
</SCRIPT>


</head>

<style>

body {
  background: #090851;
  text: #FFFFFF;
  link: #99ccff;
  alink: #00BB00;
  vlink: #FF0000;
}

#star {
  position: absolute;
  top: -5;
  left: -10;
  visibility: hidden;
}
```

```
#circle2 {
  position: absolute;
  top: 0;
  left: 440;
  visibility: hidden;
}

#text{
  position:absolute;
  top:375;
  left: 19;
  visibility: hidden;
}

#welcome {
  position: absolute;
  top: 58;
  left: 120;
  visibility: hidden;
}

#landscape {
  position: absolute;
  top: 140;
  left: 30;
  visibility: hidden;
}

#window {
  position: absolute;
  top: 120;
  left: 27;
  visibility: hidden;
}

#logo {
  position: absolute;
  top: 188;
  left: 70;
  visibility: hidden;
}

#potlood {
  position: absolute;
  top: 238;
  left: 2;
  visibility: hidden;
}
```

```
#cdroms {
  position: absolute;
  top: 245;
  left: 180;
  visibility: hidden;
}

#circle {
  position: absolute;
  top: 0;
  left: 440;
  visibility: hidden;
}


#thelinks{
  position: absolute;
  top: 142;
  left: 343;
  visibility: hidden;
}

#loading{
  position: absolute;
  top: 120;
  left: 100;
}

#preload{
  position:absolute;
  visibility: hidden;
}

#update{
  position:absolute;
  top:337;
  left: 350;
}

#award{
  position:absolute;
  top:300;
  left:500;
}

#stat{
  position:absolute;
```

```
  top:800;
  left: 10;
}

</style>


<script language = JavaScript 1.1>


master = new Array();     // names of each animation layer
dx = new Array();         // horizontal speed of each layer
dy = new Array();         // vertical speed of each layer

var max_jump = 10;        // maximum distance of animation step
var steps = 20;           // total number of animation frames
var delay = 1;            // pause between animation frames


function initSpeeds() {
  for (var ctr = 0; ctr < master.length; ctr++) {
    dx[ctr] = Math.ceil(Math.random() * max_jump);
    if (Math.random() > .5) {
      dx[ctr] *= -1;
    }
    dy[ctr] = Math.ceil(Math.random() * max_jump);
    if (Math.random() > .5) {
      dy[ctr] *= -1;
    }
  }
}

function MSinitPositions() {
  for (var ctr = 0; ctr < master.length; ctr++) {
    document.all.tags("div")[ctr].style.posLeft += (-steps *
dx[ctr]);
    document.all.tags("div")[ctr].style.posTop += (-steps *
dy[ctr]);
    document.all.tags("div")[ctr].style.visibility = "visible";
  }
  loading.style.visibility = "hidden";
}

function NSinitPositions() {
  for (var ctr = 0; ctr < master.length; ctr++) {
    eval("document." + master[ctr] + ".left += (-steps *
dx[ctr])");
    eval("document." + master[ctr] + ".top += (-steps *
```

```
dy[ctr])");
    eval("document." + master[ctr] + ".visibility = 'visible'");
  }
  document.loading.visibility = "hidden";
}

function MSfixPositions() {
    for (var ctr = 0; ctr < master.length; ctr++) {
      document.all.tags("div")[ctr].style.posLeft += dx[ctr]
      document.all.tags("div")[ctr].style.posTop += dy[ctr]
    }

    if (steps > 1) {
      steps--;
      setTimeout("MSfixPositions()", delay);
    }
}

function NSfixPositions() {
    for (var ctr = 0; ctr < master.length; ctr++) {
    eval("document." + master[ctr] + ".left += dx[ctr]");
    eval("document." + master[ctr] + ".top +=  dy[ctr]");
    }

    if (steps > 1) {
      steps--;
      setTimeout("NSfixPositions()", delay);
    }
}

function runAnimation() {
  initSpeeds();
  if (window.navigator.userAgent.indexOf("MSIE") > 0) {
    MSinitPositions();
    MSfixPositions();
  } else {
     NSinitPositions();
     NSfixPositions();
  }
}

//MM_hiliteImg() courtesy of www.coolnote.com
function MS_hiliteImg()  {
  srcImgArray = new Array;  //used for reset
  for (var i=0; i < (MM_hiliteImg.arguments.length-1); i+=2) {
    theObj = MM_hiliteImg.arguments[i];
    srcImgArray[i] = theObj;
```

```
    newImgFile = MM_hiliteImg.arguments[i+1];
    srcImgArray[i+1] = eval('document.'+theObj+'.src');
    eval('document.'+theObj+'.src = "'+newImgFile+'"');
  }
  document.MM_hiliteImgSrcs = srcImgArray; //used for reset
}

function NS_hiliteImg()  {
  document.oldObjectSrc = document.circle.document.images[0].src;
  document.circle.document.images[0].src =
MM_hiliteImg.arguments[1];
  document.oldImgRef =
document.thelinks.document.images[NS_hiliteImg.arguments[2]].name.toString();
  document.oldImgFile =
document.thelinks.document.images[NS_hiliteImg.arguments[2]].src;

document.thelinks.document.images[NS_hiliteImg.arguments[2]].src
= NS_hiliteImg.arguments[3];
}

//MM_hiliteImgRestore()
function MS_hiliteImgRestore()  {
  if (document.MM_hiliteImgSrcs != null) {
    scrImgArray = document.MM_hiliteImgSrcs;
    for (var i=0; i < (scrImgArray.length-1); i+=2) {
      theObj = scrImgArray[i];
      srcImgFile = scrImgArray[i+1];
      eval('document.'  +  theObj  +  '.src = "'  +  srcImgFile
+  '"');
    }
  }
}

function NS_hiliteImgRestore()  {
  document.circle.document.images[0].src = document.oldObjectSrc;
  document.thelinks.document.images[document.oldImgRef].src =
document.oldImgFile;
}

MM_hiliteImg = new Function();
MM_hiliteImgRestore = new Function();

if (window.navigator.userAgent.indexOf("MSIE") > 0) {
  MM_hiliteImg = MS_hiliteImg;
  MM_hiliteImgRestore = MS_hiliteImgRestore;
} else {
  MM_hiliteImg = NS_hiliteImg;
  MM_hiliteImgRestore = NS_hiliteImgRestore;
}
```

```
//store each layer's name in a master array
master[0]="circle2";
master[1]="star";
master[2]="text";
master[3]="landscape";
master[4]="thelinks";
master[5]="circle";
master[6]="window";
master[7]="logo";
master[8]="welcome";
master[9]="potlood";
master[10]="cdroms";


</script>


<body onload="runAnimation()"TEXT="#99ccff" LINK="#88DD33"
VLINK="#84DC08" ALINK="#090851" BGCOLOR="#090851">
<script language="JavaScript">
        <!--
        document.write("<img
src=\"http://www.nedstat.nl/
cgi-bin/referstat.gif?name=macline&refer=
"+escape(document.referrer)+"\"
width=1 height=1 alt=\"\">");
        // -->
        </script>

<!--the moving layers...each layer is positioned via the doc's
style sheet-->
<div id="circle2"><IMG SRC="images/circle2.gif" WIDTH="534"
HEIGHT="266" BORDER="0"></div>
<div id="star"><IMG SRC="images/star.gif" WIDTH="162"
HEIGHT="161"></div>
<div id="text">
<TABLE WIDTH=480><TR><TD><center>
<A HREF="infoform.html">
<IMG SRC="images/infoanim.gif" ALT="receive more info"
WIDTH="255" HEIGHT="30" BORDER="0"></A>
<BR>
<a href="mailto:webmaster@duoh.com" target="_top">
<font size=1 COLOR="#FF3700" face="arial, helvetica,
*">webmaster@duoh.com</font></a>
<font size=1 color="#99ccff" face="arial, helvetica, *">&#169;
"Duoh!" All rights reserved.<BR>
"Duoh!" - Kouter 32 Bus 2 - 9800 Deinze - Belgium (Europe)<BR>
```

```
tel. +32 9 380 19 04 - fax +32 9 380 81 25 - ISDN +32 9 380 81
26</font>
<BR><BR>
<font size=1 color="#99ccff" face="arial, helvetica, *">You
need<BR><BR>

<A HREF="http://www.netscape.com">
<IMG SRC="images/netscape.gif" WIDTH="57" HEIGHT="45" BORDER="0"
HSPACE="10"></A>

<A HREF="http://www.microsoft.com/ie">
<IMG SRC="images/explorer.gif" WIDTH="57" HEIGHT="45" BORDER="0"
HSPACE="10"></A>
<BR><BR>
(final versions only!!! No beta or preview releases!!!) to view
our pages</font>
</CENTER>
</TD></TR></TABLE><BR><BR>

</div>
<div id="welcome"><IMG SRC="images/welcome.gif" WIDTH="260"
HEIGHT="57"></div>
<div id="circle"><img src="images/dhtml_c.gif"
name="dhtml_circle" width="198"
height="120" border="0" alt="Welcome on the site of Duoh!"></div>
<div id="landscape"><IMG SRC="images/landscape.gif" WIDTH="454"
HEIGHT="217"></div>
<div id="window"><IMG SRC="images/window.gif" WIDTH="460"
HEIGHT="254"></div>
<div id="logo"><IMG SRC="images/icon.gif" WIDTH="137"
HEIGHT="114"></div>
<div id="potlood"><IMG SRC="images/potlood.gif" WIDTH="81"
HEIGHT="51"></div>
<div id="cdroms"><IMG SRC="images/cdroms.gif" WIDTH="95"
HEIGHT="58"></div>

<div id="thelinks">
<table cellspacing="0" cellpadding="0" WIDTH="118" HEIGHT="89">
<tr><td>
<A HREF="new.html"
onMouseOver="MM_hiliteImg('dhtml_circle','images/new_c.gif',
'whatsnew','images/new0.gif')"
onMouseOut="MM_hiliteImgRestore()">
<IMG SRC="images/new1.gif" name="whatsnew" WIDTH="118"
HEIGHT="17" BORDER="0"></a>
</td></tr>
<tr><td>
<A HREF="multi.html"
```

```
onMouseOver="MM_hiliteImg('dhtml_circle','images/multi_c.gif',
'multimedia','images/multi0.gif')"
onMouseOut="MM_hiliteImgRestore()">
<IMG SRC="images/multi1.gif" name="multimedia" WIDTH="118"
HEIGHT="17" BORDER="0"></a>
</td></tr>
<tr><td>
<A HREF="web.html"
onMouseOver="MM_hiliteImg('dhtml_circle','images/web_c.gif',
'webdesign','images/web0.gif')"
onMouseOut="MM_hiliteImgRestore()">
<IMG SRC="images/web1.gif" name="webdesign" WIDTH="118"
HEIGHT="17" BORDER="0"></a>
</td></tr>
<tr><td>
<A HREF="graph.html"
onMouseOver="MM_hiliteImg('dhtml_circle','images/graph_c.gif',
'graphicdesign','images/graph0.gif')"
onMouseOut="MM_hiliteImgRestore()">
<IMG SRC="images/graph1.gif" name="graphicdesign" WIDTH="118"
HEIGHT="17" BORDER="0"></a>
</td></tr>
<tr><td>
<A HREF="illu.html"
onMouseOver="MM_hiliteImg('dhtml_circle','images/illu_c.gif',
'illustration','images/illu0.gif')"
onMouseOut="MM_hiliteImgRestore()">
<IMG SRC="images/illu1.gif" name="illustration" WIDTH="118"
HEIGHT="17" BORDER="0"></a>
</td></tr>
<tr><td>
<A HREF="who.html"
onMouseOver="MM_hiliteImg('dhtml_circle','images/who_c.gif',
'whoweare','images/who0.gif')"
onMouseOut="MM_hiliteImgRestore()">
<IMG SRC="images/who1.gif" name="whoweare" WIDTH="118"
HEIGHT="17" BORDER="0"></a>
</td></tr>
</table>
</div>

<!--this layer is only visible while the rest of the doc is
loading-->
<div id="loading">
<font color = #99ccff size = +2>
<font face="arial, helvetica, *">Just one moment please,<BR>
your patience will be rewarded . . .</font>
</font>
</div>
```

```
<!--this layer preloads the layover images-->
<div id="preload">
<img src="images/new_c.gif" width="198" height="120" border="0"
alt="What's New">
<img src="images/new0.gif" width="118" height="17" border="0"
alt="What's New">
<img src="images/multi_c.gif" width="118" height="17" border="0"
alt="Multimedia">
<img src="images/multi0.gif" width="118" height="17" border="0"
alt="Multimedia">
<img src="images/web_c.gif" width="118" height="17" border="0"
alt="Webdesign">
<img src="images/web0.gif" width="198" height="120" border="0"
alt="Webdesign">
<img src="images/graph_c.gif" width="183" height="170" border="0"
alt="Graphic Design">
<img src="images/graph0.gif" width="227" height="26" border="0"
alt="Graphic Design">
<img src="images/illu_c.gif" width="183" height="170" border="0"
alt="Illustration">
<img src="images/illu0.gif" width="227" height="26" border="0"
alt="Illustration">
<img src="images/who_c.gif" width="183" height="170" border="0"
alt="Who we are">
<img src="images/who0.gif" width="227" height="26" border="0"
alt="Who we are">

</div>

<div id="update">
<font size=1 COLOR="#FFFFFF" face="arial, helvetica, *">last
changes Oct. 28th '97</font>
</div>

<div id="award">
<A HREF="http://www.dhtmlzone.com/spotlight/">
<IMG SRC="images/spotlight_award.gif" ALT="Award DHTML zone
Macromedia" WIDTH="75" HEIGHT="75" BORDER="0"></A>
</div>


<div id="stat">
<img src="http://www.xs4all.be/cgi-bin/Count.cgi?dd=C&df=duohl"
height=22 width=70>
<a href="http://www.nedstat.nl/cgi-bin/viewstat?name=macline">
<img src="http://www.nedstat.nl/cgi-bin/nedstat.gif?name=macline"
 border=0 alt="" width=3 height=3 hspace=2></a>
```

```
</div>
</body>
</html>
```

To see the dynamic Duoh! page, point your browser at **www.duoh.com**.

Virtual Pig

Ever wanted to be a pig farmer? At the Pig Pen dynamic site you can own, feed, play with, and groom your very own virtual pig. This site works just fine with both Internet Explorer and Navigator and is tons of fun. If you neglect your pig it sends you email; ours is currently at death's door because we've been so busy writing this chapter. The source code behind the site was nearly 20 pages long, so we couldn't include it here. However, we thought you'd like to get a taste (so to speak) of the pigs—as viewed through both browsers, of course. Figure 18.9 shows Internet Explorer's rendition

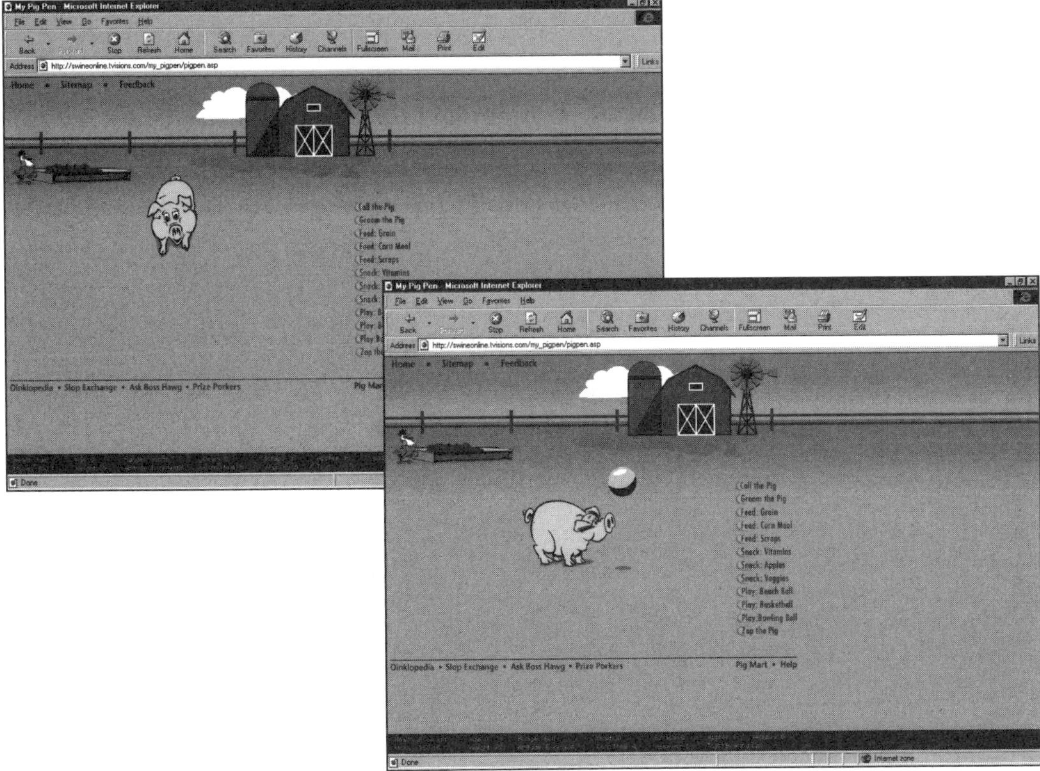

Figure 18.9

The Pig Pen as seen with Internet Explorer.

of the pig, while Figure 18.10 shows Netscape's version. Watch closely as we groom, play with, call, and even zap our cute porker friend.

To adopt your own pig visit the Pig Pen site at **swineonline.tvisions.com**.

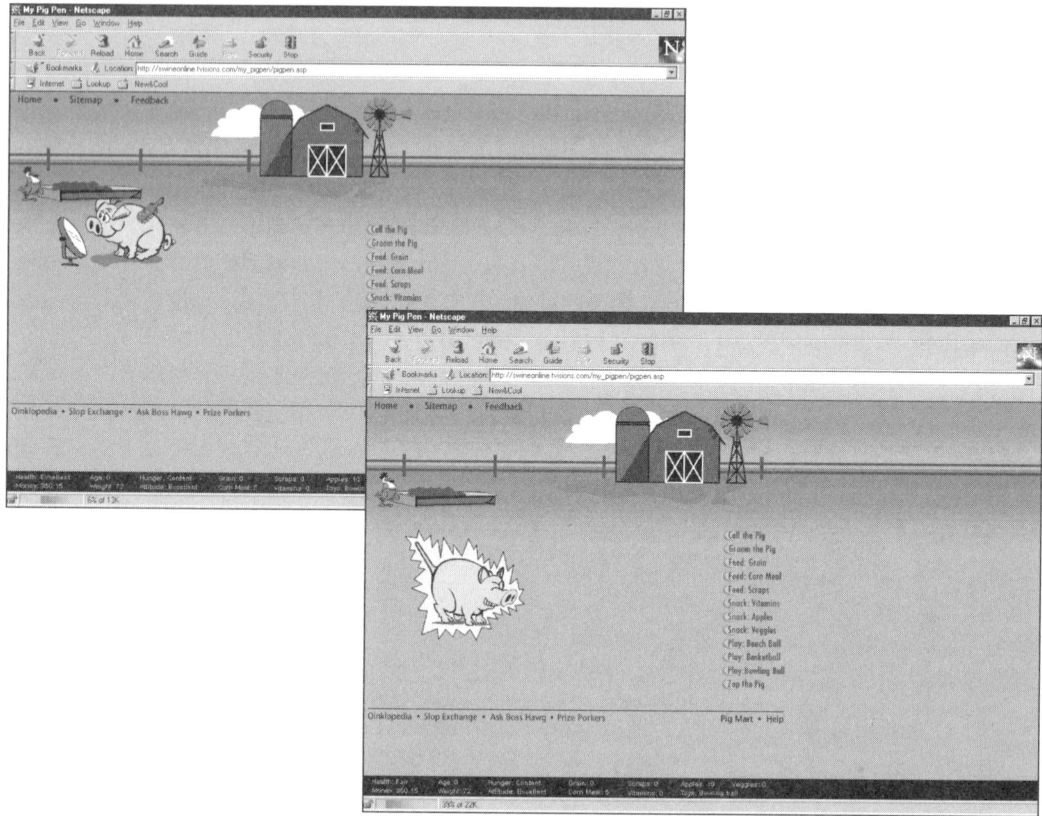

Figure 18.10

The Pig Pen as seen with Navigator.

Chapter 19

DHTML At Work In The Web World

In this chapter, we explore some Web sites that have implemented Dynamic HTML. In addition, we show you the code behind these cutting-edge sites.

Notes...

Chapter 19

Although theories and examples are all well and good, seeing a technology work IRL (in real life) is the best proof of what it can really do. Because dynamic Web pages are a relatively young technology (in Web years, anyway) the proof, as they say, is in the pudding. Throughout the book we've discussed the techniques, tips, and tricks that will help you implement DHTML in your Web pages. In Chapter 18, we proved—by showing you successful real-world examples—it is possible to create dynamic Web pages that look good when viewed with both Internet Explorer and Netscape Navigator.

In this chapter, we'd like to take you on a tour of six of the most innovative, fun, and interesting dynamic sites we could find, not counting the three wonderful cross-platform-compatible sites we showed you in the last chapter. For each site, we'll show you a series of screenshots that illustrate what kind of dynamic content the site has to offer. In addition, we've included the code behind the sites so you can answer the ever-elusive question, "How'd they do that?" To be fair, we've chosen three sites that work exclusively with Internet Explorer and make use of Dynamic HTML techniques, and three that work exclusively with Netscape Navigator and make use of layers techniques. Since the pages of this book are as static as the first Web pages, we suggest you take the time to visit these sites IRL to see them in their full dynamic glory.

Pack a lunch and jump on the bus, the tour is about to begin.

Practical Guide To

DHTML At Work In The Web World

- First Stop: IE's Dynamic HTML
  - The Wrox Press Jigsaw Puzzle
  - Seer Media's Home Page
  - Microsoft's Best Of The Web
- Next Stop: Netscape's Layers
  - Premier Advertising
  - Taboca Art
  - Space Fire
- Join The Ranks Of DHTML Designers

First Stop: IE's Dynamic HTML

This first stop on our tour of sites takes us to three interesting and entertaining sites that implement the very best parts of the Microsoft's Dynamic HTML, including on-screen drag-and-drop functions, advanced event handing, and data-binding.

The Wrox Press Jigsaw Puzzle

As part of the resources for its *Instant Dynamic HTML Programmer's Reference*, Wrox Press has created a series of DHTML examples and tutorials available online. We chose the Jigsaw puzzle because it's fun, functional, and shows how to create elements on a Web page that you can drag and drop.

When you first arrive at the Jigsaw puzzle site (**rapid.wrox.co.uk/books/0685/Jigsaw/Jigsaw.htm**), you're presented with a series of puzzle pieces and a blank grid, as shown in Figure 19.1.

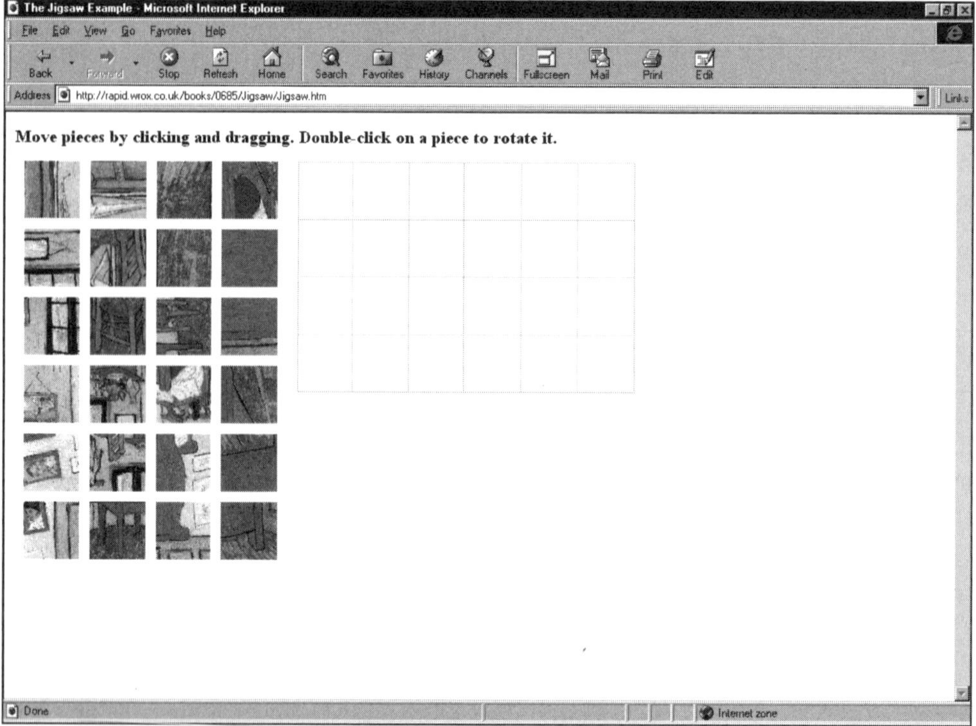

Figure 19.1

The Wrox Press Dynamic HTML Jigsaw puzzle incorporates drag-and-drop technology into a Web page.

Your job is to put the pieces together correctly to form a complete picture. But there's a catch: The pieces aren't necessarily right-side-up. To rotate a piece, simply click on it; then it's just a matter of dragging the pieces to the correct portion of the grid. Figure 19.2 shows our progress after about 10 minutes attempting to solve the puzzle.

After a while the puzzle starts to come together. It helps if you're a fan of Van Gogh and recognize the painting, but it's not a prerequisite. After all, we finally managed to solve the puzzle, as shown in Figure 19.3.

It's obvious that drag-and-drop techniques can be used for more than just games, but this was a great way of demonstrating this particular application of Dynamic HTML.

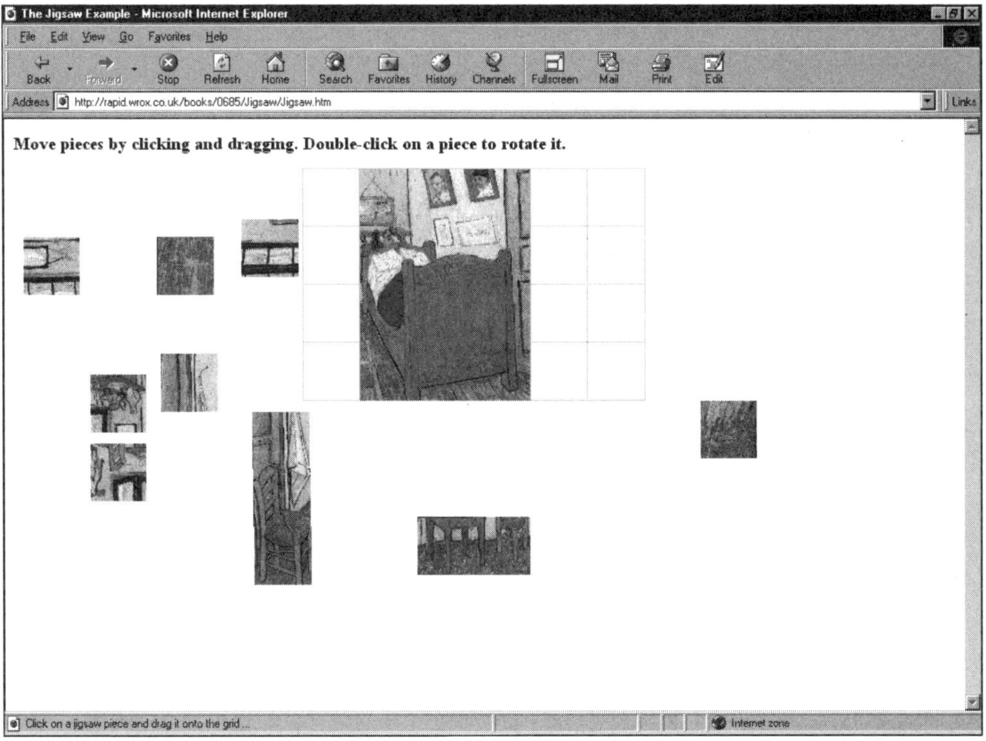

Figure 19.2

The Jigsaw puzzle pieces can be rotated and then dragged across the screen and placed in the grid.

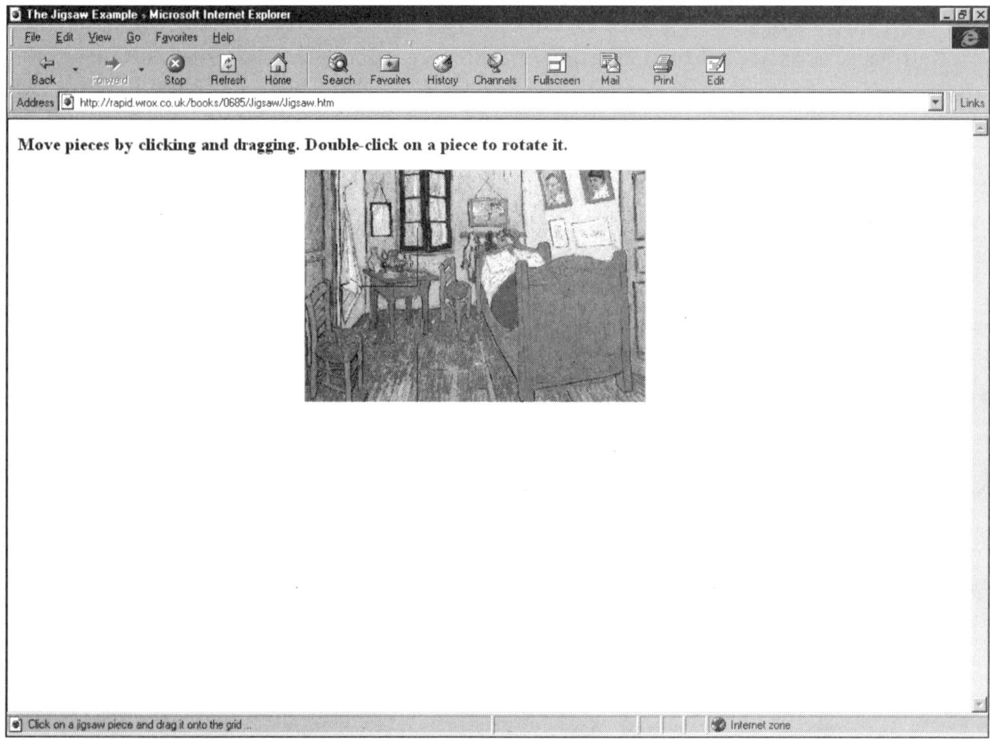

Figure 19.3

The solved Jigsaw puzzle.

Listing 19.1 shows the code behind this creative puzzle.

Listing 19.1 The Wrox Jigsaw puzzle.

```
<!DOCTYPE HTML PUBLIC "-//IETF//DTD HTML//EN">
<HTML>
<HEAD><TITLE>The Jigsaw Example</TITLE></HEAD>

<BODY>

<H3> Move pieces by clicking and dragging. Double-click on a piece to rotate
it.</H3>

<IMG ID="Grid" SRC="jig1.gif" STYLE="position:absolute; top=50; left=310;
width=356; height=237">
<IMG ID="P1" SRC="gogh11.gif" STYLE="position:absolute; top=50; left=20;
width=59; height=59">
<IMG ID="P2" SRC="gogh22.gif" STYLE="position:absolute; top=120; left=20;
width=59; height=59">
```

```
<IMG ID="P3" SRC="gogh33.gif" STYLE="position:absolute; top=190; left=20;
width=59; height=59">
<IMG ID="P4" SRC="gogh41.gif" STYLE="position:absolute; top=260; left=20;
width=59; height=59">
<IMG ID="P5" SRC="gogh54.gif" STYLE="position:absolute; top=330; left=20;
width=59; height=59">
<IMG ID="P6" SRC="gogh61.gif" STYLE="position:absolute; top=400; left=20;
width=59; height=59">
<IMG ID="P7" SRC="gogh72.gif" STYLE="position:absolute; top=50; left=90;
width=59; height=59">
<IMG ID="P8" SRC="gogh83.gif" STYLE="position:absolute; top=120; left=90;
width=59; height=59">
<IMG ID="P9" SRC="gogh91.gif" STYLE="position:absolute; top=190; left=90;
width=59; height=59">
<IMG ID="P10" SRC="gogh103.gif" STYLE="position:absolute; top=260; left=90;
width=59; height=59">
<IMG ID="P11" SRC="gogh113.gif" STYLE="position:absolute; top=330; left=90;
width=59; height=59">
<IMG ID="P12" SRC="gogh121.gif" STYLE="position:absolute; top=400; left=90;
width=59; height=59">
<IMG ID="P13" SRC="gogh133.gif" STYLE="position:absolute; top=50; left=160;
width=59; height=59">
<IMG ID="P14" SRC="gogh141.gif" STYLE="position:absolute; top=120; left=160;
width=59; height=59">
<IMG ID="P15" SRC="gogh154.gif" STYLE="position:absolute; top=190; left=160;
width=59; height=59">
<IMG ID="P16" SRC="gogh163.gif" STYLE="position:absolute; top=260; left=160;
width=59; height=59">
<IMG ID="P17" SRC="gogh172.gif" STYLE="position:absolute; top=330; left=160;
width=59; height=59">
<IMG ID="P18" SRC="gogh182.gif" STYLE="position:absolute; top=400; left=160;
width=59; height=59">
<IMG ID="P19" SRC="gogh193.gif" STYLE="position:absolute; top=50; left=230;
width=59; height=59">
<IMG ID="P20" SRC="gogh204.gif" STYLE="position:absolute; top=120; left=230;
width=59; height=59">
<IMG ID="P21" SRC="gogh212.gif" STYLE="position:absolute; top=190; left=230;
width=59; height=59">
<IMG ID="P22" SRC="gogh223.gif" STYLE="position:absolute; top=260; left=230;
width=59; height=59">
<IMG ID="P23" SRC="gogh233.gif" STYLE="position:absolute; top=330; left=230;
width=59; height=59">
<IMG ID="P24" SRC="gogh241.gif" STYLE="position:absolute; top=400; left=230;
width=59; height=59">

</BODY>
```

```
<SCRIPT LANGUAGE=JavaScript>

var strImgDragging = null;        // the global 'piece being moved' variable

function mouseDownEvent()         // set the jigsaw piece to be moved
{
  strID = event.srcElement.id;
  if (strID.indexOf("P") != -1)   // if this is a jigsaw piece
  {
    strImgDragging = strID        // save the ID in a global variable
    // bring the piece to the top of the z-order
    document.all[strImgDragging].style.zIndex = 1

    window.status = "Drag this piece onto the grid and release the mouse to
                     position it ..."
  }
  else
    strImgDragging = null;        // set global variable to null
}


function mouseMoveEvent()    // move the jigsaw piece
{
  if (strImgDragging != null)
  {
    // move the image to the new position
    // assume the mouse pointer is in middle of image
    document.all[strImgDragging].style.pixelLeft = event.x - 30;
    document.all[strImgDragging].style.pixelTop = event.y - 30;
  }

  // prevent event being handled elsewhere and the default action
  event.cancelBubble = true;
  event.returnValue = false;
}


function mouseUpEvent()     // place the jigsaw piece on the grid
{
  if (strImgDragging != null)
  {
    // stop dragging, and position the piece in line with grid.
    posLeft = Math.floor((document.all[strImgDragging]
    .style.pixelLeft - 280) / 59);
    posTop = Math.floor((document.all[strImgDragging]
    .style.pixelTop - 20) / 59);
    if (posLeft >= 0 && posTop >= 0)
    {
```

```
      document.all[strImgDragging].style.pixelLeft = (posLeft * 59) + 311;
      document.all[strImgDragging].style.pixelTop = (posTop * 59) + 51;
    }

    // return the piece to the lower z-order position
    document.all[strImgDragging].style.zIndex = 0;

    // reset the global 'dragging' variable
    strImgDragging = null;
    window.status = "Click on a jigsaw piece and drag it onto the grid ..."

    // prevent event being handled elsewhere and the default action
    event.cancelBubble = true;
    event.returnValue = false;
  }
}

function dblClickEvent()          // rotate the jigsaw piece
{
  objImage = event.srcElement;    // get a reference to the image
  strImageID = objImage.id;       // get the ID of the image

  // if it's a jigsaw piece then rotate it
  if (strImageID.indexOf("P") != -1)
  {
    strSrc=objImage.src   // get the image file name

    // extract just the image number as a string
    intStart = strSrc.indexOf("\gogh");
    if (intStart != -1)
      strSrc = strSrc.substring(intStart + 4);
    intEnd = strSrc.indexOf(".");
    if (intEnd != -1)
      strSrc = strSrc.substring(0, intEnd);

    //split into image and attitude numbers
    strImgNum = strSrc.substring(0, strSrc.length -1);
    strAttNum = strSrc.substring(strSrc.length - 1, strSrc.length);

    // calculate the new image attitude number
    intAttNum = strAttNum.valueOf();
    intAttNum ++;
    if (intAttNum > 4) intAttNum = 1;
    strAttNum = intAttNum.toString();

    // create and assign the new image name
    objImage.src = "gogh" + strImgNum + strAttNum + ".gif";
```

```
  }
  // prevent event being handled elsewhere and the default action
  event.cancelBubble = true;
  event.returnValue = false;
}

document.ondblclick=dblClickEvent;
document.onmousedown=mouseDownEvent;
document.onmousemove=mouseMoveEvent;
document.onmouseup=mouseUpEvent;
</SCRIPT>
</HTML>
```

Seer Media's Home Page

Seer Media is a Web design firm that has created several different Dynamic HTML demos to show prospective clients what they can do. Its gallery page (**www.seer-media.com/index.html**), shown in Figure 19.4, uses event handling to highlight each demonstration when an input device passes over it.

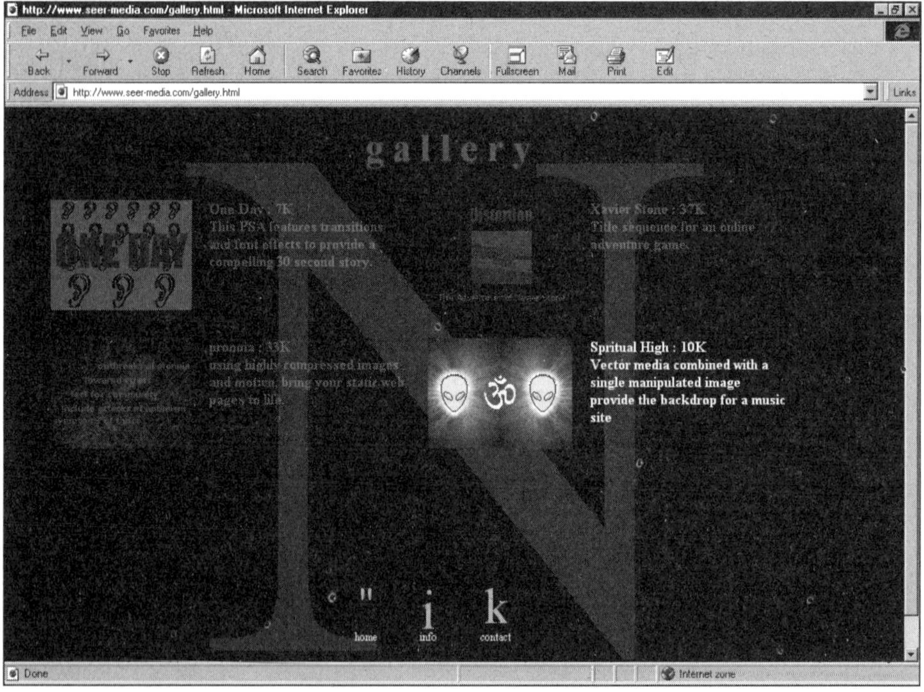

Figure 19.4

*The Seer Media Gallery page uses **onMouseOver** events to highlight sections of the page.*

The code behind the page is fairly straightforward, as DHTML goes; it includes a Java applet for the event handling and is shown in Listing 19.2.

Listing 19.2 The Seer Media DHTML Gallery page.

```
<HTML>
<HEAD>
<SCRIPT LANGUAGE="JScript">

function init() {
      document.body.insertAdjacentHTML("AfterBegin", distort.bop());
}
</SCRIPT>

</HEAD>
<BODY onload="init()" topmargin=0 leftmargin=0 BGCOLOR=black>
<APPLET name=distort code=distort width=0 height=0>
<PARAM NAME="key" VALUE="0^z8^z9-Fz+a.XDDBwzEz,VL">
<PARAM NAME="lock" VALUE="17KKz5qdl1=K@rLz4hl">
</APPLET>
</BODY>
</HTML>
```

Once you select a DHTML demo from the Java-based gallery page, it's all dynamic. Figure 19.5 shows one stage of the "pronoia" demonstration.

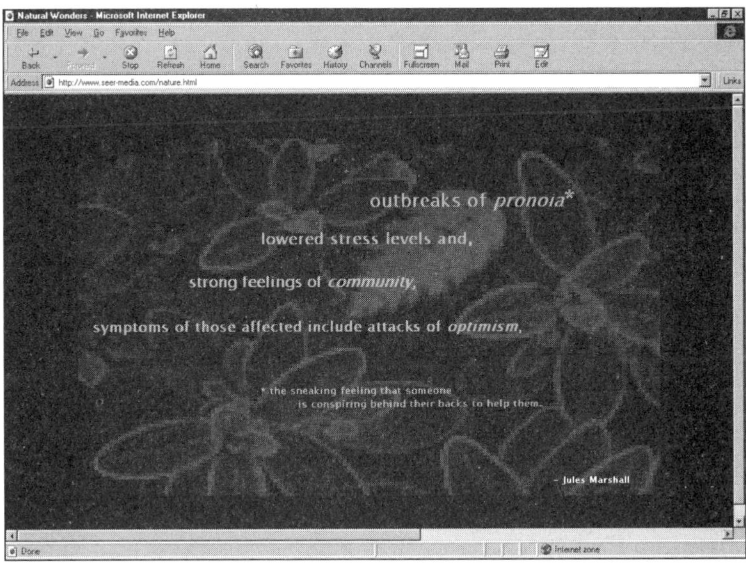

Figure 19.5

The Seer Media "pronoia" DHTML demo.

The code that makes this demo work is a bit involved, but surprisingly short and sweet, as shown in Listing 19.3.

Listing 19.3 The Seer Media pronoia demo.

```
<HTML>
<HEAD>
      <TITLE> Natural Wonders</TITLE>

<SCRIPT LANGUAGE="JScript">
      var tcnt;
      var txt;
      var sun;

function start() {
      tcnt=0;
      txt=0;
      sun=0;
      sunset.filters(0).Apply();
      sunset.style.visibility = 'visible';
      sun=1;
      sunset.filters(0).Play();
}

function transsun() {
      if (sun==0) {
            sunset.filters(0).Apply();
            sunset.style.visibility = 'visible';
            sun=1;
            sunset.filters(0).Play();}
      else {
            sunset.filters(0).Apply();
            sunset.style.visibility = 'hidden';
            sun=0;
            sunset.filters(0).Play();}
}

function transittxt() {
      if (txt==0) {
            thetext.filters(0).Apply();
            thetext.style.visibility = 'visible';
            txt=1;
            thetext.filters(0).Play();}
      else {
            thetext.filters(0).Apply();
            thetext.style.visibility = 'hidden';
            txt=0;
            thetext.filters(0).Play();}
```

```
}
</SCRIPT>

<SCRIPT FOR="sunset" EVENT="onfilterchange" language="Jscript">
      if (sun==1)      {
            leaves.style.visibility = 'visible';
            window.setTimeout("transittxt();");}
                  else {
            window.setTimeout("transsun();");}
</SCRIPT>


<SCRIPT FOR="thetext" EVENT="onfilterchange" language="JScript">
            window.setTimeout("transsun();",200);
</SCRIPT>

</HEAD>

<BODY BGCOLOR=black leftmargin=0 topmargin=0 onload="start();">

<IMG ID=leaves SRC=image/yellowleaf.jpg style="position:absolute; top:10%;
left:10%; width:80%; height:80%; visibility:hidden; filter:alpha(opacity=40)">

<IMG ID=sunset SRC=image/sunset.jpg style="position:absolute; top:10%;
left:10%; width:80%; height:80%; filter:blendTrans(duration=3);
visibility:hidden;">

<DIV ID=thetext STYLE="position:absolute; width:100%; height:100%; top:0;
top:0; visibility:hidden; filter:blendTrans(duration=3.0)">
    <SPAN style="position:absolute; top:50%; left:12%; font-weight: bold;
    font-family:Lucida Sans Unicode; font-size:14pt; color:silver">
    symptoms of those affected include attacks of <i>optimism</i>,</SPAN>
    <SPAN style="position:absolute; top:40%; left:25%; font-weight: bold;
    font-family:Lucida Sans Unicode; font-size:15pt; color:silver">
    strong feelings of <i>community</i>,</SPAN>
    <SPAN style="position:absolute; top:30%; left:35%; font-weight: bold;
    font-family:Lucida Sans Unicode; font-size:16pt; color:silver">
    lowered stress levels and,</SPAN>
    <SPAN style="position:absolute; top:20%; left:50%; font-weight: bold;
     font-family:Lucida Sans Unicode; font-size:18pt; color:silver">
    outbreaks of <i>pronoia</i><FONT COLOR=ORANGE SIZE=+3>
    *</FONT></SPAN>

    <SPAN style="position:absolute; top:65%; left:35%; font-weight: bold;
    font-family:Lucida Sans Unicode; font-size:10pt; color:orange">
    <B>*</B> the sneaking feeling that someone</SPAN>
    <SPAN style="position:absolute; top:68%; left:40%; font-weight: bold;
    font-family:Lucida Sans Unicode; font-size:10pt; color:orange">
    is conspiring behind their backs to help them.</SPAN>
```

```
    <SPAN style="position:absolute; top:85%; left:75%; font-weight: bold;
    font-family:Lucida Sans Unicode; font-size:9pt; color:white">
    - Jules Marshall</SPAN>
</DIV>

</BODY>
</HTML>
```

Microsoft's Best Of The Web

It's no surprise that Microsoft has its own gallery of DHTML pages. Our favorite site is the Best of the Web (**home.microsoft.com/exploring/exploring.asp**), which incorporates its proprietary data-binding technique to create a listing of Web sites organized by topic that changes with the click of a button and without a return to the Web server (you must use IE 4 for it to render properly). Figure 19.6 shows two different versions of the same page, each with a different set of data behind it.

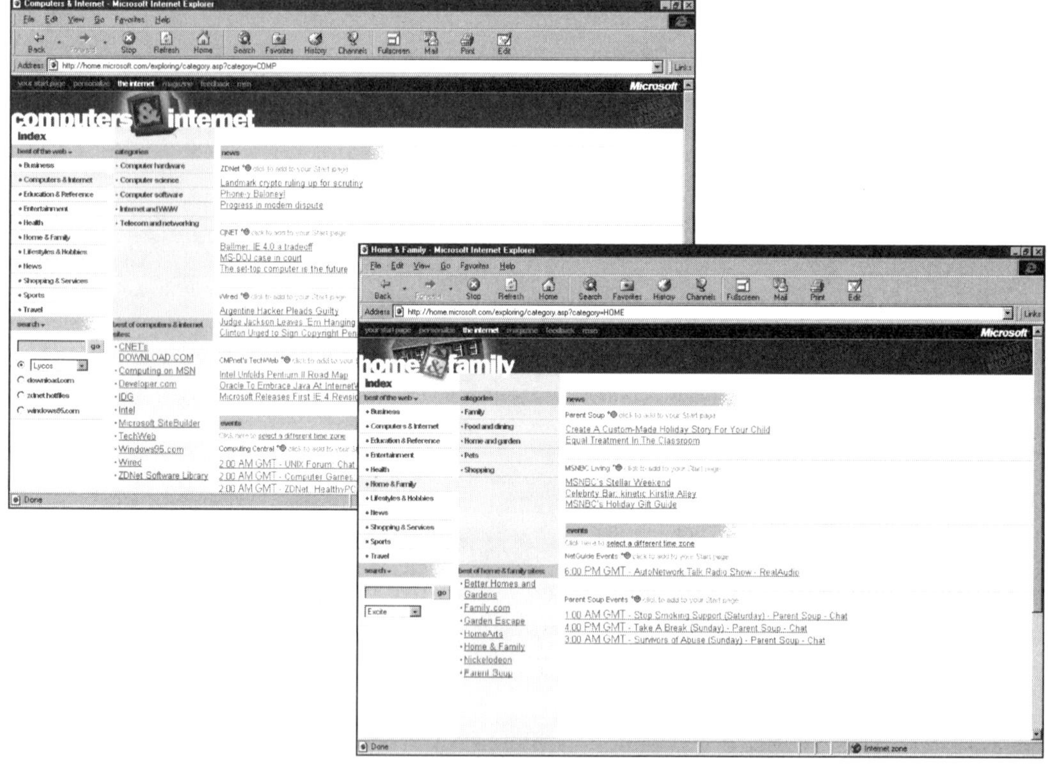

Figure 19.6

Microsoft's Best of the Web uses data binding to easily reorganize and refresh the information on a page without requesting each iteration from the Web server.

Listing 19.4 shows the DHTML and HTML that makes the Microsoft site tick.

Listing 19.4 Microsoft's Best of the Web site.

```
<HTML>
<script language="javascript">
function setFilter()  {
        var passed = this.location.hash;
        catdata = head_frame.catdata;
            weekdsc = body_frame.weekdata;
        //usdsc = body_frame.usdata;
        //intdsc = body_frame.intdata;

            if(location.hash != "")  {
                passed = passed.substring(1, passed.length);
                catdata.FilterValue=this.location.hash.substring
                         (1,this.location.hash.length);
                weekdsc.FilterValue=this.location.hash.substring
                         (1,this.location.hash.length);
                //usdsc.FilterValue=this.location.hash.substring
                          (1,this.location.hash.length);
                //intdsc.FilterValue=this.location.hash.substring
                          (1,this.location.hash.length);
            }

            else  {
                catdata.FilterValue="business";
                weekdsc.FilterValue="business";
                //usdsc.FilterValue="business";
                //intdsc.FilterValue="business";
            }

        catdata.Reset();
        weekdsc.Reset();
        //usdsc.Reset();
        //intdsc.Reset();
}

window.onload = setFilter;
</script>
<HEAD>
  <TITLE>Best of the Web</TITLE>
</HEAD>
<FRAMESET ROWS="45%,55%" frameborder=0>
  <FRAME SRC="header.htm" NAME="head_frame" SCROLLING=YES NORESIZE>
    <FRAME SRC="body.htm" NAME="body_frame" SCROLLING=YES NORESIZE>
  </FRAMESET>
</FRAMESET>
</HTML>
```

Next Stop: Netscape's Layers

The next three sites show how Netscape's layer technology can be used to create fun, interesting, and interactive Web sites.

Premier Advertising

Our first Netscape Navigator-compatible dynamic site is the work of Premier Advertising. This site (**www.premierecomm.com**) combines layers with a window controlled by JavaScript to include transitions, window movement, and event handling. Figures 19.7 through 19.9 show three stages in the appearance of the site's home page. The small window actually floats around the screen.

Once the entire home page is loaded, the site takes advantage of event handling to bring up a different graphic each time an input device rolls over a menu item, as shown in Figure 19.10.

The creator of the code behind this great site was kind enough to provide many comments throughout the code, so those learning from it will know what piece of script controls what. Listing 19.5 shows the code in its entirety.

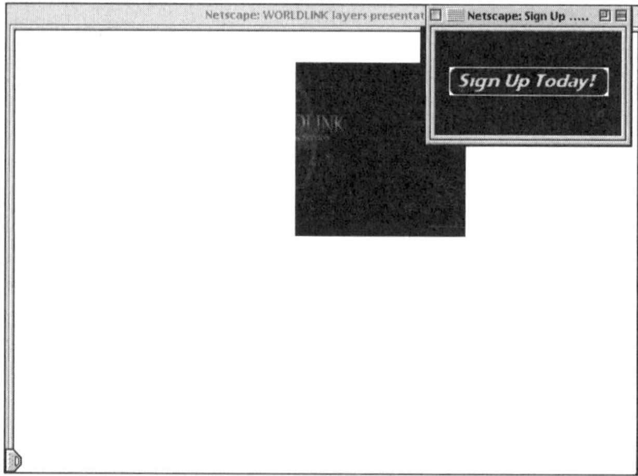

Figure 19.7

The home page starts to appear.

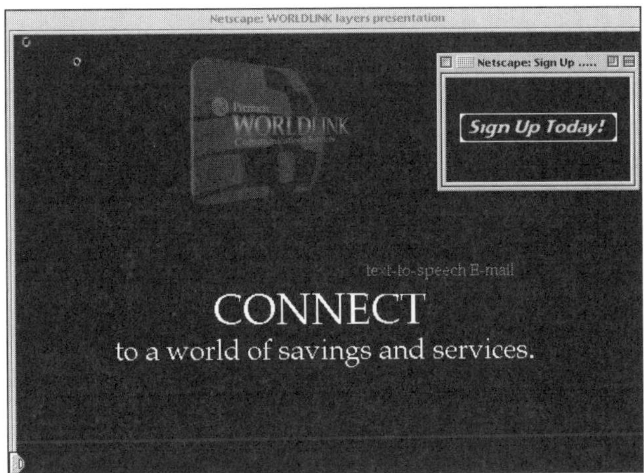

Figure 19.8

Premier Advertising's home page comes into view with a bang...

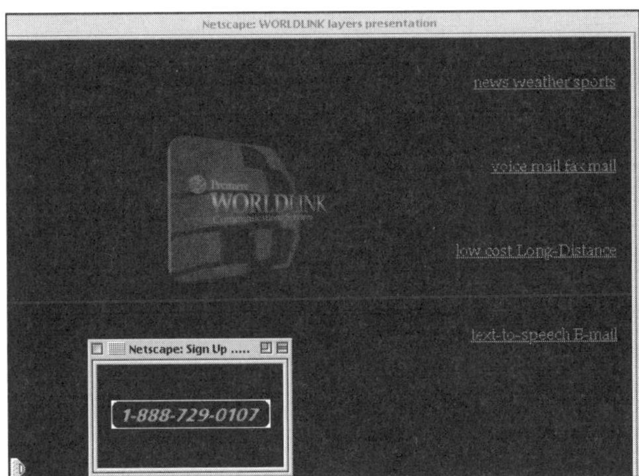

Figure 19.9

...and a floating window.

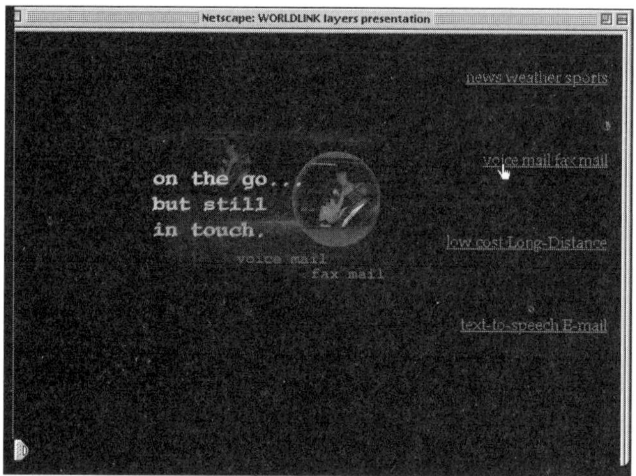

Figure 19.10

Event handling causes a new graphic to appear when the pointer moves over a menu item.

Listing 19.5 The Premier Advertising home page.

```
<HTML>
<HEAD>
 <TITLE>WORLDLINK layers presentation</TITLE>
<!--Author:  David S. Cohen, Webmaster - Premiere Technologies, Inc.
     dave@tc.net-->

  <SCRIPT LANGUAGE="JavaScript">

<!--
var cardSpot = 440;
var someB = 5
var hotSpot = 120;
var faxStart = 640;
var emailStart = 640;
var ephoneStart = 640;
var ttsStart = 640;

//pre-load images ---------------------------

cardclick = new Image();
cardclick.src = "cardclick.gif";
oldcard = new Image();
oldcard.src = "oldcard.gif";
email = new Image();
email.src = "ttsemail.gif";
ncontent = new Image();
```

```
ncontent.src = "news.gif";
ldcontent = new Image();
ldcontent.src = "ldcall.gif";
vfcontent = new Image();
vfcontent.src = "voice.gif";
daline = new Image();
daline.src = "bg/glowline.gif";
dbline = new Image();
dbline.src = "bg/underline.gif";

//functions ---------------------------------


function lastMove(){
      document.layers["words"].visibility="hide";
      if (hotSpot > 20) {
            hotSpot -=10;
            document.layers["playfour"].offset(0,10);
            setTimeout("lastMove()",200);
            }
      else {
            document.location.href='testmenu.html';
            }
      }

function doItDone(){
      setTimeout('document.layers["fader1"].visibility="show"',40);

      }



function growCard(someBit){
      cornerLeft = 221 - someBit;
      cornerRight = 221 + someBit;
      cornerTop = 105 - someBit;
      cornerBottom = 105 + someBit;
      document.layers["playfour"].clip.left = cornerLeft;
      document.layers["playfour"].clip.right = cornerRight;
      document.layers["playfour"].clip.top = cornerTop;
      document.layers["playfour"].clip.bottom = cornerBottom;
      }

function cardShower(){
      document.layers["playfour"].visibility="show";
      setTimeout('document.layers["words"].visibility="show"',1400);
      if (someB < 400){
            growCard(someB);
```

```
            someB = someB + 8;
            setTimeout("cardShower()",100);
            }
      else {
      document.bgColor=000000;
      document.layers["layone"].visibility = "HIDE";
      document.layers["fax"].visibility="hide";
      setTimeout('document.layers["words1"].visibility="show"',1400);
      setTimeout('document.layers["words2"].visibility="show";document.layers
           ["words1"].visibility="hide"',2400);
      setTimeout('document.layers["words3"].visibility="show";document.layers
           ["words2"].visibility="hide"',3400);
      setTimeout('document.layers["words4"].visibility="show";document.layers
           ["words3"].visibility="hide"',4400);
      setTimeout('lastMove();document.layers["words4"].visibility="hide"',7400);

      }
      }

function cardShow(){
      window.open('pong.html','newWing',
        'menubar=no,resizable=no,width=185,height=28,
         titlebar=no,left=400,top=-100,alwaysRaised=yes');
      setTimeout('cardShower(); document.layers["connectword"].
         visibility = "HIDE"; document.layers["layone"].visibility =
         "HIDE"',1000);

      }

function moveCard(){
      document.layers["layone"].left = cardSpot;
      document.layers["layone"].top = cardSpot;
      }

function ephoneMove(){
      if (ephoneStart > 0) {
            ephoneStart -=20;
            document.layers["ephone"].offset(0,25);
            document.layers["ephoneword"].offset(0,-20);
            setTimeout("ephoneMove()",100);
            }
      else {
            document.layers["ephone"].visibility="hide";
            document.layers["ephoneword"].visibility="hide";
            document.layers["canword"].visibility="show";
            }
      }
```

```
function emailMove(){
      if (emailStart > 0) {
            emailStart -=15;
            document.layers["email"].offset(0,-20);
            document.layers["emailword"].offset(-25,0);
            setTimeout("emailMove()",100);
            }
      else {
            document.layers["email"].visibility="hide";
            document.layers["emailword"].visibility="hide";
            document.layers["ephone"].visibility="show";
            document.layers["ephoneword"].visibility="show";
            ephoneMove();
            }
      }

function faxMove(){
      if (faxStart > 0) {
            faxStart -=15;
            document.layers["fax"].offset(-25,0);
            document.layers["faxword"].offset(25,0);
            setTimeout("faxMove()",150);
            }
      else {
            document.layers["fax"].visibility="hide";
            document.layers["faxword"].visibility="hide";
            document.layers["email"].visibility="show";
            document.layers["emailword"].visibility="show";
            emailMove();
            }
      }


function doItNow(){
      if (navigator.appVersion.substring(0,3) == '4.0'){
            document.layers["fax"].visibility="show";
            document.layers["faxword"].visibility="show";
            faxMove();
            }
      else {
      document.location = 'http://www.worldlinkservices.com';
      }
      }

//Done hiding from non-Navigator 2.0 browsers. -->
```

```
</script>



</HEAD>
<BODY bgcolor=ffffff text=000000 onLoad="setTimeout('doItNow()',200)">

<!-----------------------layone (cloudman) layer---------------->
<LAYER NAME="layone"  LEFT=100 TOP=10 >
       <!--<IMG SRC="images/abounce.gif" border=0>-->
       <br>
       <br>
       <br>
       <br>
       <br>
       <br>
       <img src="images/cloudman.jpg" border=0>
</LAYER>
<!-----------------------end layone (cloudman) layer---------------->

<!-----------------------------fax layer----------->
<LAYER NAME="fax" LEFT=640 TOP=25 clip="125,100" visibility="hide"  >
      <LAYER NAME="faxanim" LEFT=8 TOP=9 clip="125,100"   >
       <IMG SRC="fax.gif" border=0>
      </LAYER>
      <LAYER NAME="ovalmask"  clip="125,100"   >
       <IMG SRC="oval.gif" border=0>
      </LAYER>
</layer>
<!-------------------------------end fax layer---------->
<!-----------------------------faxword layer----------->
<LAYER NAME="faxword" LEFT=-475 TOP=155 clip="480,100" visibility="hide"  >
      <font size=6>
      Missing opportunities?
      </font>
</layer>
<!-------------------------------end faxword layer---------->


<!-----------------------------email layer----------->
<LAYER NAME="email" LEFT=50 TOP=500  visibility="hide"  >
      <img src="email.gif" border=0>
</layer>
<!-------------------------------end email layer---------->
<!-------------------------------emailword layer---------->
<LAYER NAME="emailword" LEFT=645 TOP=125 clip="850,100" visibility="hide"  >
      <font size=7>
      <nobr>How's that project moving?</nobr>
      </font>
```

```
</layer>
<!---------------------------------end emailword layer---------->


<!------------------------------ephone layer------------>
<LAYER NAME="ephone" LEFT=500 TOP=-100 clip="125,100" visibility="hide"  >
      <LAYER NAME="ephoneanim" LEFT=8 TOP=9 clip="125,100"   >
       <IMG SRC="phone.gif" border=0>
      </LAYER>
      <LAYER NAME="ovalphone"  clip="125,100"   >
       <IMG SRC="oval2.gif" border=0>
      </LAYER>
</layer>
<!---------------------------------end ephone layer---------->
<!------------------------------ephoneword layer------------>
<LAYER NAME="ephoneword" LEFT=10 TOP=500 clip="650,135" visibility="hide"  >
      <font size=7>
      <nobr>&quot;We wanted your input,<br>
       but you were out of reach.&quot;</nobr>
      </font>
</layer>
<!---------------------------------end ephoneword layer---------->


<!------------------------------canword layer------------>
<LAYER NAME="canword" LEFT=0 TOP=15 clip="650,400" visibility="hide"  >
 <p align=center>
      <a href="#" onClick="self.document.layers['canword'].visibility='hide';
      self.document.layers['connectword'].visibility='show'; cardShow();
            return false"><font size=6 >
      What can you do      when <br>
      you're out of the loop?
      </font></a>
  </p>
</layer>
<!---------------------------------end canword layer---------->


<!------------------------------connectword layer------------>
<LAYER NAME="connectword" LEFT=0 TOP=35 clip="650,400" visibility="hide"  >
 <p align=center>
      <a href="" onClick="cardShow(); return false">
      <font size=7 color=000000>
      CONNECT
      </font>
  </p>
</layer>
<!---------------------------------end connectword layer---------->
```

```
<!-------------------------------playfour layer---------->
<LAYER NAME="playfour" LEFT=150 TOP=10  visibility="hide" bgcolor=000000 >
      <a href="http://www.worldlinkservices.com/cardframe.html"
onClick="window.opener.document.location.href=
            'http://www.worldlinkservices.com/cardframe.html'; window.close();
             return false"
      onMouseOver="wlcard.src=cardclick.src; return true"
      onMouseOut="wlcard.src=oldcard.src; return true">
            <img name="wlcard" src="oldcard.gif" border=0></a>
</LAYER>
<!-------------------------------end playfour layer---------->

<!-------------------------------words layer---------->
<LAYER NAME="words" LEFT=0 TOP=250 clip="650,400"  visibility="hide"  >
       <p align=center>
      <font size=7 color=ffffff>
      CONNECT
      </font><br><font size=6 color=ffffff>
      to a world of savings and services.</font></p>
</LAYER>
<!-------------------------------end words layer---------->

<!-------------------------------words1 layer---------->
<LAYER NAME="words1" LEFT=350 TOP=225 clip="300,180" visibility="hide"  >
      <font color=9999aa size=4>text-to-speech E-mail</font>
      <br>
      <IMG  SRC="bg/underline.gif" border=0>
</LAYER>
<!-------------------------------end words1 layer---------->

<!-------------------------------words2 layer---------->
<LAYER NAME="words2" LEFT=200 TOP=185 clip="500,180" visibility="hide"  >
      <font color=9999aa size=4>
      low cost Long-Distance
      <br><IMG SRC="bg/underline.gif" border=0>
</LAYER>
<!-------------------------------end words2 layer---------->

<!-------------------------------words3 layer---------->
<LAYER NAME="words3" LEFT=400 TOP=125 clip="300,180" visibility="hide"  >
      <font color=9999aa size=4>
      voice mail fax mail
      <br><IMG SRC="bg/underline.gif" border=0>
      </font>
</LAYER>
<!-------------------------------end words3 layer---------->
```

```
<!--------------------------------words4 layer---------->
<LAYER NAME="words4" LEFT=375 TOP=80 clip="500,180" visibility="hide"  >
      <font color=9999aa size=4>
      news weather sports
      <br><IMG SRC="bg/underline.gif" border=0>
      </font>
</LAYER>
<!--------------------------------end words4 layer---------->
<!--------------------------------tts layer---------->
<LAYER NAME="tts" LEFT=12 TOP=50 clip="1270,1270" visibility="hide" >
      <img src="ttsemail.gif">
</LAYER>
<!--------------------------------end tts layer---------->
</BODY>
</HTML>
```

Taboca Art

The Taboca Web site (**www.taboca.com/layer/**) is quite a site to behold. Animation abounds and it's fun to surf the site's pages, which extensively use layers to make text and graphics zoom, fade, slide, and more. This site is truly a tribute to the amazing effects that can be created using layers and a bit of scripting. The home page, shown in Figures 19.11 through 19.13, uses several different animation techniques to fly-in text and graphics.

Listing 19.6 shows the HTML and scripting that are used to create this active page.

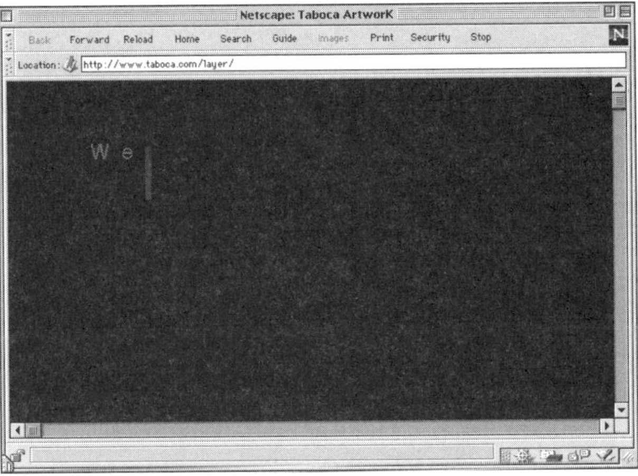

Figure 19.11

The Taboca Art home page uses layers to create animation.

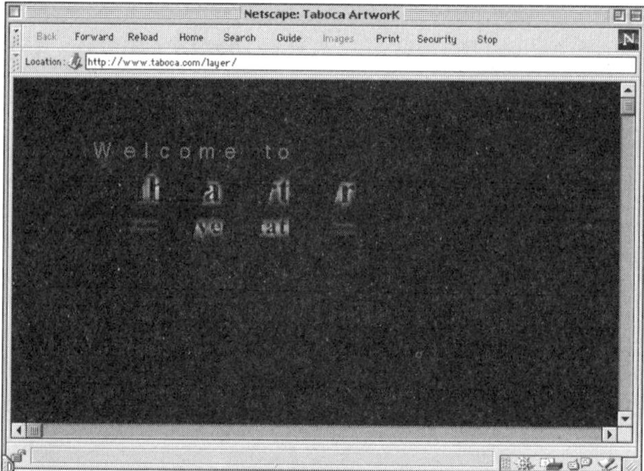

Figure 19.12

The page is starting to take shape.

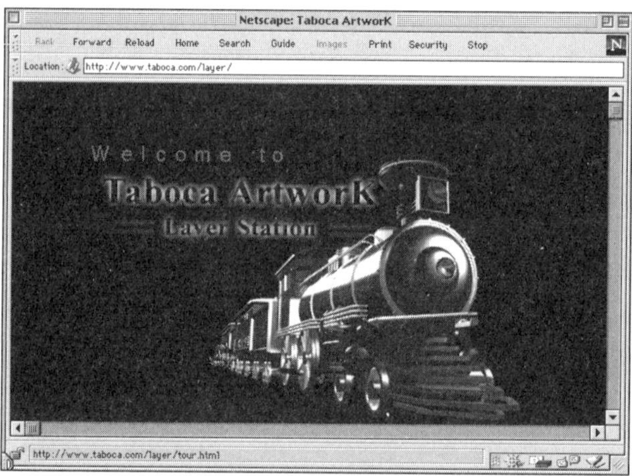

Figure 19.13

Pulling into the Layer Station.

Listing 19.6 The Taboca home page.

```
<HTML>

<HEAD>
<META NAME = "Producer"  CONTENT ="taboca producers(taboca@taboca.com)">
<TITLE>Taboca ArtworK</TITLE>

</HEAD>
```

```
<BODY BGCOLOR="#000000" LINK="#2D5D96" text="#ddaaff"
   onload="javascript:start()">

<embed src="ts2.wav" width=0 height=0 hidden autostart=true play=auto>
</embed>

<layer name="tittle" visibility="hide" top=80 left=80>
<img src="tstittle.jpg">
</layer>
<layer name="factory_mask" top=80 left=80 visibility="hide">
<img src="fmask.gif">
</layer>

<layer name="tp1" left=360 top=165 visibility="hide">
<img name="trim" src="t5.gif" width=10 height=09>
</layer>
<layer name="tp2" left=360 top=165 visibility="hide">
<img name="trim" src="t5.gif" width=20 height=17>
</layer>
<layer name="tp3" left=360 top=165 visibility="hide">
<img name="trim" src="t5.gif" width=40 height=35>
</layer>
<layer name="tp4" left=360 top=165 visibility="hide">
<img name="trim" src="t5.gif" width=80 height=70>
</layer>
<layer name="tp5" left=360 top=165 visibility="hide">
<img name="trim" src="t5.gif" width=160 height=140>
</layer>
<layer name="tp6" left=360 top=165 visibility="hide">
<a href="tour.html"><img border=0 name="trim" src="t5.gif" width=320 height=279>
      </a>
</layer>


<layer name="a01" visilibity="hide">
<font Face="sans-serif" Color="#000000" point-size="200">
W
</font>
</layer>
<layer name="a02" visibility="hide">
<font Face="sans-serif" Color="#200000" point-size="150">
W
</font>
</layer>
<layer name="a03" visibility="hide">
<font Face="sans-serif" Color="#400000" point-size="100">
W
</font>
```

```
</layer>
<layer name="a04" visibility="hide">
<font Face="sans-serif" Color="#800000" point-size="70">
W
</font>
</layer>
<layer name="a05" visibility="hide">
<font Face="sans-serif" Color="#BB0000" point-size="40">
W
</font>
</layer>
<layer name="a06" visibility="hide">
<font Face="sans-serif" Color="#ff0000" point-size="20">
W
</font>
</layer>

<layer name="a11" visilibity="hide">
<font  Face="sans-serif" Color="#000000" point-size="200">
e
</font>
</layer>
<layer name="a12" visibility="hide">
<font Face="sans-serif" Color="#200000" point-size="150">
e
</font>
</layer>
<layer name="a13" visibility="hide">
<font Face="sans-serif" Color="#400000" point-size="100">
e
</font>
</layer>
<layer name="a14" visibility="hide">
<font Face="sans-serif" Color="#800000" point-size="70">
e
</font>
</layer>
<layer name="a15" visibility="hide">
<font Face="sans-serif" Color="#BB0000" point-size="40">
e
</font>
</layer>
<layer name="a16" visibility="hide">
<font Face="sans-serif" Color="#ff0000" point-size="20">
e
</font>
</layer>
```

```
<layer name="a21" visilibity="hide">
<font Face="sans-serif" Color="#000000" point-size="200">
1
</font>
</layer>
<layer name="a22" visibility="hide">
<font Face="sans-serif" Color="#200000" point-size="150">
1
</font>
</layer>
<layer name="a23" visibility="hide">
<font Face="sans-serif" Color="#400000" point-size="100">
1
</font>
</layer>
<layer name="a24" visibility="hide">
<font Face="sans-serif" Color="#800000" point-size="70">
1
</font>
</layer>
<layer name="a25" visibility="hide">
<font Face="sans-serif" Color="#BB0000" point-size="40">
1
</font>
</layer>
<layer name="a26" visibility="hide">
<font Face="sans-serif" Color="#ff0000" point-size="20">
1
</font>
</layer>

<layer name="a31" visilibity="hide">
<font Face="sans-serif" Color="#000000" point-size="200">
c
</font>
</layer>
<layer name="a32" visibility="hide">
<font Face="sans-serif" Color="#200000" point-size="150">
c
</font>
</layer>
<layer name="a33" visibility="hide">
<font Face="sans-serif" Color="#400000" point-size="100">
c
</font>
</layer>
<layer name="a34" visibility="hide">
<font Face="sans-serif" Color="#800000" point-size="70">
```

```
c
</font>
</layer>
<layer name="a35" visibility="hide">
<font Face="sans-serif" Color="#BB0000" point-size="40">
c
</font>
</layer>
<layer name="a36" visibility="hide">
<font Face="sans-serif" Color="#ff0000" point-size="20">
c
</font>
</layer>

<layer name="a41" visilibity="hide">
<font Face="sans-serif" Color="#000000" point-size="200">
o
</font>
</layer>
<layer name="a42" visibility="hide">
<font Face="sans-serif" Color="#200000" point-size="150">
o
</font>
</layer>
<layer name="a43" visibility="hide">
<font Face="sans-serif" Color="#400000" point-size="100">
o
</font>
</layer>
<layer name="a44" visibility="hide">
<font Face="sans-serif" Color="#800000" point-size="70">
o
</font>
</layer>
<layer name="a45" visibility="hide">
<font Face="sans-serif" Color="#BB0000" point-size="40">
o
</font>
</layer>
<layer name="a46" visibility="hide">
<font Face="sans-serif" Color="#ff0000" point-size="20">
o
</font>
</layer>

<layer name="a51" visilibity="hide">
<font Face="sans-serif" Color="#000000" point-size="200">
```

```
m
</font>
</layer>
<layer name="a52" visibility="hide">
<font Face="sans-serif" Color="#200000" point-size="150">
m
</font>
</layer>
<layer name="a53" visibility="hide">
<font Face="sans-serif" Color="#400000" point-size="100">
m
</font>
</layer>
<layer name="a54" visibility="hide">
<font Face="sans-serif" Color="#800000" point-size="70">
m
</font>
</layer>
<layer name="a55" visibility="hide">
<font Face="sans-serif" Color="#BB0000" point-size="40">
m
</font>
</layer>
<layer name="a56" visibility="hide">
<font Face="sans-serif" Color="#ff0000" point-size="20">
m
</font>
</layer>

<layer name="a61" visilibity="hide">
<font Face="sans-serif" Color="#000000" point-size="200">
m
</font>
</layer>
<layer name="a62" visibility="hide">
<font Face="sans-serif" Color="#200000" point-size="150">
e
</font>
</layer>
<layer name="a63" visibility="hide">
<font Face="sans-serif" Color="#400000" point-size="100">
e
</font>
</layer>
<layer name="a64" visibility="hide">
<font Face="sans-serif" Color="#800000" point-size="70">
e
</font>
```

```
</layer>
<layer name="a65" visibility="hide">
<font Face="sans-serif" Color="#BB0000" point-size="40">
e
</font>
</layer>
<layer name="a66" visibility="hide">
<font Face="sans-serif" Color="#ff0000" point-size="20">
e
</font>
</layer>


<layer name="a71" visilibity="hide">
<font Face="sans-serif" Color="#000000" point-size="200">
t
</font>
</layer>
<layer name="a72" visibility="hide">
<font Face="sans-serif" Color="#200000" point-size="150">
t
</font>
</layer>
<layer name="a73" visibility="hide">
<font Face="sans-serif" Color="#400000" point-size="100">
t
</font>
</layer>
<layer name="a74" visibility="hide">
<font Face="sans-serif" Color="#800000" point-size="70">
t
</font>
</layer>
<layer name="a75" visibility="hide">
<font Face="sans-serif" Color="#BB0000" point-size="40">
t
</font>
</layer>
<layer name="a76" visibility="hide">
<font Face="sans-serif" Color="#ff0000" point-size="20">
t
</font>
</layer>


<layer name="a81" visilibity="hide">
<font Face="sans-serif" Color="#000000" point-size="200">
```

```
o
</font>
</layer>
<layer name="a82" visibility="hide">
<font Face="sans-serif" Color="#200000" point-size="150">
o
</font>
</layer>
<layer name="a83" visibility="hide">
<font Face="sans-serif" Color="#400000" point-size="100">
o
</font>
</layer>
<layer name="a84" visibility="hide">
<font Face="sans-serif" Color="#800000" point-size="70">
o
</font>
</layer>
<layer name="a85" visibility="hide">
<font Face="sans-serif" Color="#BB0000" point-size="40">
o
</font>
</layer>
<layer name="a86" visibility="hide">
<font Face="sans-serif" Color="#ff0000" point-size="20">
o
</font>
</layer>


<script>

        state=1;
        group=0;
        ztime=25;

        function start() {

                lx=60;
                for(g=0;g<9;g++) {
                        if(g==0) lx+=20;
                        if(g==1) lx+=30;
                        if(g==2) lx+=20;
                        if(g==3) lx+=15;
                        if(g==4) lx+=20;
                        if(g==5) lx+=20;
                        if(g==6) lx+=25;
                        if(g==7) lx+=40;
```

```
                if(g==8) lx+=12;
                for(s=1;s<7;s++) {
                        document.layers["a"+g+""+s].left=lx;
                        document.layers["a"+g+""+s].top=60;
                }
        }
        setTimeout("statezoomer()",ztime);
}


function statezoomer() {
        document.layers["a"+group+""+state].visibility="hide";
        state++;
        document.layers["a"+group+""+state].visibility="show";
        // basic counter
        if(state==6) {
                group++;
                state=1;
        }
        if(group!=9) {
                setTimeout("statezoomer()",ztime);
        }
        else {
                document.layers["factory_mask"].visibility="show";
                document.layers["tittle"].visibility="show";
                // state here is deprecated
                state=0;
                setTimeout("movelayer()",20);
        }
}


function movelayer() {
        document.layers["factory_mask"].moveBy(0,-8);
        state++;
        if(state<40) {
                setTimeout("movelayer()",20);
        }
        else {
                start2();
        }
}

i=1;
st=1;
```

```
        function start2() {
                document.layers["tp6"].moveBy(-160,-110);
                document.layers["tp5"].moveBy(-160,-10);
                document.layers["tp4"].moveBy(-160,50);
                document.layers["tp3"].moveBy(-160,79);
                document.layers["tp2"].moveBy(-160,93);
                document.layers["tp1"].moveBy(-160,93);
                setTimeout("stepmove()",50);
        }

        function stepmove() {
                document.layers["tp"+st].visibility="show";
                if(st<6) {
                        st++;
                        setTimeout("stepmove()",50);
                }
                else {
                        setTimeout("bstart()",6000);
                }
        }

        function bstart() {
                window.location="tour.html";
        }

</script>

<BR>

</BODY>

</HTML>
```

Once the Taboca home page is finished loading, click on the train and you are treated to yet another wonderful flurry of animation as windows fly across the screen (Figure 19.14) and a train pulls onto the screen.

Once the train is on the screen, you can click on any one of the cars or the engine and see a new batch of information and hyperlinks scroll up to replace the current display, as shown in Figure 19.15.

To see the HTML and scripting behind this part of the Taboca site, check out Listing 19.7.

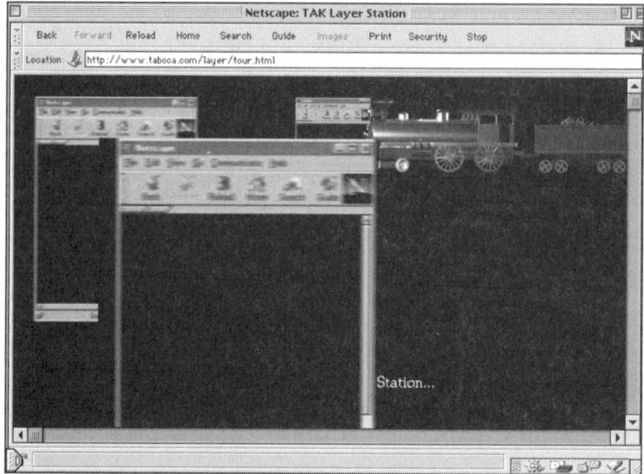

Figure 19.14

Watch as windows fly from one side of the screen to the other.

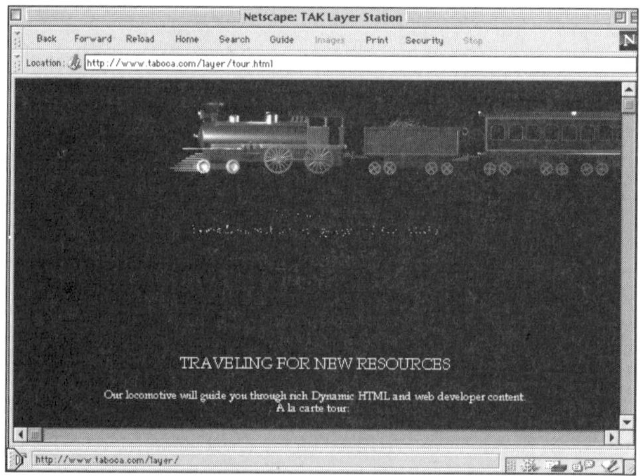

Figure 19.15

Click on a train car to watch the text scroll.

Listing 19.7 The Taboca DHTML Train page.

```
<HTML>
<HEAD>
<META NAME = "Producer"  CONTENT = "mgalli@taboca.com">
<META NAME = "LEGAL" CONTENT="TERMS OF USE -  ILLUSIONARY PROGRAM. THIS SOURCE
CODE IS PROVIDED IN AN 'AS-IS' FORM WITHOUT WARRANTY OF ANY KIND. THE TABOCA
ILLUSIONARY PROGRAM IS MANAGED  AND MAINTAINED BY TABOCA ARTWORK. TABOCA
```

```
ARTWORK RESERVES THE RIGHT TO CHANGE  DOCUMENT OR  SOFTWARE CONTENT AT
ANY TIME. THIS SOURCE CODE IS PROVIDED FOR LEARNING OF DYNAMIC HTML AND WEB
SPECIAL EFFECTS AS A COMPONENT OF THE  ILLUSIONARY PROGRAM. IT CANNOT BE USED
FOR ANY COMMERCIAL PURPOSES WITHOUT EXPRESS AUTHORIZATION OF TABOCA ARTWORK">

<TITLE>TAK Layer Station</TITLE>
</HEAD>

<BODY BGCOLOR="#000000" ONLOAD="start()">

<layer name="content0" visibility="hide" width=500 top=290 left="50%">
<font color="#ffffff" point-size="14pt" >
<center>
Coming up: Taboca Layer Station...
</font>
</layer>

<layer name="content1" visibility="hide" width=500 top=480 left="50%">
<font color="#ffffff" point-size="16pt"><center>
WELCOME TO TABOCA LAYER STATION<BR>
<font point-size="11pt">
Now you are on the Taboca ArtworK World of cool demonstrations
on Dynamic HTML - the Illusionary Program. Welcome to the Taboca Layer Station!
Click on each locomotive wagon and choose what you want to see!
</font>
</layer>

<layer name="content2" visibility="hide" width=500 top=480 left="50%">
<font color="#ffff10" point-size="14pt" >
<center><font point-size="16pt">TABOCA ARTWORK
<font point-size="11pt">aka Taboca Interactive is the innovative business mask
 for Marcio Galli. Taboca ArtworK goal is to produce innovative technology for
 the next web. We just want to spread happyness, lot of work and incredible
 content. Currently Taboca ArtworK can be requested to produce web oriented
 content, as promoting applications, environments, web desktops, or IT business
 consulting.
<br><br>
<a href="http://taboca.com">Visit TAS - our web site</a><br>
<a href="mailto:contact@taboca.com">Contact us!</a>
</font>
</layer>

<layer name="content3" visibility="hide" width=500 top=480 left="50%">
<font color="#ffffff" point-size="14pt" >
<center><font point-size="16pt">LAYER STATION - RESOURCES<BR>
<font point-size="12pt">Now, learn about these cool technologies and get
connected with the developer side of DHTML, layers and javascript world!<br>
<a href="http://taboca.com/illusionary"> The Illusionary DHTML Special
```

```
Edition</a>
<br><br>
<a href="http://www.taboca.com/illusionary">
<img border=0 src="http://taboca.com/illusionary/program-adv/mark_icon2.jpg">
</a>
</br>
<center><font point-size="10pt">Taboca Layer Station (C) Copyright 1997,
 Marcio Galli<br>
</font>
</layer>

<layer name="content4" visibility="hide" width=500 top=480 left="50%">
<font color="#ffffff" point-size="14pt" >
<font point-size="16pt"><center>
TRAVELING FOR NEW RESOURCES<br>
<br><font point-size="11pt">Our locomotive will guide you through rich Dynamic
 HTML and web developer content.<br>
A la carte tour: <br><br>
<a href="http://taboca.com/ETC">Taboca ArtworK Entertainment Technology
Connection</a><br>
<a href="http://developer.netscape.com">Netscape Communications Developer
Channel</a><br>
<a href="http://www.macromedia.com">Macromedia DHTML Zone</a>
</font>
</layer>
<layer name="content5" visibility="hide" width=500 top=480 left="50%">
<font color="#ffffff" point-size="14pt" >
<font point-size="16pt"><center>
CREDITS and THANKS<br>
<br><font point-size="11pt">To the incredible
<a href="http://www.intermidia.icmsc.sc.usp.br/~taboca/painel">
Computer Science Team</a> of city of Sao Carlos - Brazil<br>
the <a href="http://www.intermidia.icmsc.sc.usp.br">Intermidia Research Lab</a>
 - at University of Sao Paulo<br>
for <a href="http://taboca.com">Taboca ArtworK</a><br>
for Netscape Communications Developer Relations folks</br>
</font>
</layer>

<layer name="mask" visibility="show" top=60 left="50%">
<img src="layermask.gif">
</layer>
<layer name="black" visibility="show" top=0 left=0 width=1500 height=120
bgcolor="#000000">
</layer>
<layer name="black2" visibility="show" top=475 left=0 width=1500 height=700
bgcolor="#000000">
</layer>
```

```
<layer name="bp01" visibility="hide" top=20 left=350>
        <layer name="bro2" top=0 left=200><img src="minibro6.jpg" width=80
         height=120 border=0>
        </layer>
</layer>
<layer name="bp02" visibility="hide" top=20 left=-150>
        <layer name="bro1" top=0 left=100><img src="minibro6.jpg" width=180
         height=220 border=0>
        </layer>
</layer>
<layer name="1" visibility="hide" left="50%" top="20">
<img src="tr0.gif" border=0>
        <layer mame="al0" visibility="hide" left=96 top=41>

        </layer>
        <layer name="al1" visibility="hide" left=96 top=41>
        <img src="rod02.gif" border=0>
        </layer>
        <layer name="al2" visibility="hide" left=96 top=41>
        <img src="rod03.gif" border=0>
        </layer>
        <layer name="al3" visibility="hide" left=96 top=41>
        <img src="rod04.gif" border=0>
        </layer>
        <layer name="minirod" visibility="hide" left=199 top=52>
        <img src="minirod02.gif" border=0>
        </layer>

           <layer name="sensor01" visibility="show" top=5 left=5>
           <a href="" onclick="settext(2);return false;"><img border=0
            src="transp.gif" width=170 height=60></a>
           </layer>

           <layer name="sensor02" visibility="show" top=5 left=200>
           <a href="" onclick="settext(3);return false;">
              <img border=0 src="transp.gif" width=90 height=60></a>
           </layer>

           <layer name="sensor03" visibility="show" top=5 left=320>
           <a href="" onclick="settext(4);return false;">
              <img border=0 src="transp.gif" width=170 height=60></a>
           </layer>

           <layer name="sensor04" visibility="show" top=5 left=520>
           <a href="" onclick="settext(5);return false;">
              <img src="transp.gif" border=0 width=90 height=60></a>
           </layer>
```

```
</layer>
<layer name="bp03" visibility="hide" top=60 left=-600>
        <layer name="bro1" top=0 left=300><img src="minibro6.jpg" border=0>
        </layer>
</layer>

<layer name="buga" width=250 height=300>
</layer>

<script>

        plan1=document.layers["bp01"];
        plan2=document.layers["bp02"];
        plan3=document.layers["bp03"];

        a=document.layers["l"];
        step=50;
        step2=50;
        tp=0;           // the locomotive sprite step
        stepointer=-30; // the presentarion step mode
        moveto=1;
        target=0;

        function start() {


                plan1.moveBy(-600,0);
                plan2.moveBy(-600,0);
                plan3.moveBy(-600,0);

            // centering the layers...
            for(u=0;u<=5;u++) {
                  document.layers["content"+u].
                      moveBy(-document.layers["content"+u].clip.width/2,0);
            }
                document.layers["mask"].moveBy(-document.layers["mask"].
               clip.width/2,0);

            // setting visibility for them...
            for(u=0;u<=5;u++) {
                  document.layers["content"+u].visibility="show";
            }

            plan1.visibility="show";
                plan2.visibility="show";
                plan3.visibility="show";

                a.moveBy(320,0);
                a.visibility="show";
```

```
        setTimeout("movetrain()",30);

  }

function TIP_centerlayers_hor(basename,number) {
     document.layers[basename+number].moveBy(-document.layers
              [basename+number].clip.width/2,0);
}

  function movetrain() {
        a.moveBy(-step,0);
        plan1.moveBy(step2,0);
        plan2.moveBy(step2*2,0);
        plan3.moveBy(step2*3,0);
        step2-=1;
        step-=2;
        if(step>3) {
                setTimeout("movetrain()",30);
        } else {
                navigation_pointer();
        }
  }


  function navigation_pointer() {
        a.document.layers[tp].visibility="show";
        if(tp!=0) a.document.layers[0].visibility="hide";
        if(tp!=1) a.document.layers[1].visibility="hide";
        if(tp!=2) a.document.layers[2].visibility="hide";
        if(tp!=3) a.document.layers[3].visibility="hide";
        if(tp==0||tp==1) {
                a.document.layers[4].visibility="show";
        } else {
                a.document.layers[4].visibility="hide";
        }
        if(moveto==0) tp++;
        if(moveto==1) tp--;
        if(tp<0) tp=3;
        if(tp>3) tp=0;

        if(moveto==1) stepointer++;
        a.moveBy(6,0);
        if(stepointer==target) {
                set_content();
        } else {
                setTimeout('navigation_pointer()',30);
        }
  }
```

```
    function set_content() {

          //setTimeout("move_content()",15);
          settext(1);

     }

   // runtime
   animdelay=23;
   indexcontent=0;
   var movelay1;
   var movelay2;

   // we have 4 texts...
   function settext(number) {
document.layers["mask"].visibility="show";
          if(indexcontent!=number) {
                document.layers["content"+number].top=480;
                movelay1=document.layers["content"+indexcontent];
                movelay2=document.layers["content"+number];
                animate();
                indexcontent=number;
          }
   }
   function move_content() {
          movelay1.moveBy(0,-animdelay);
          movelay2.moveBy(0,-animdelay);
          animdelay--;
          if(animdelay>0) {
                setTimeout("move_content()",20);
          }
          else {
                document.layers["mask"].visibility="hide";
          }
   }



   function animate() {
          animdelay=24;
          setTimeout("move_content()",20);
   }

</script>

</BODY>
</HTML>
```

Space Fire

Our final stop on this tour of great dynamic Web sites is a game (**www1.nisiq.net/~jimmeans/harrier2/**) that turns your browser into a dragon-hunting expedition. Space Fire was created using dynamic techniques and relies heavily on layers and scripting. Moving your mouse moves the man on the screen, and a click of the mouse button shoots a fireball at offending trees or dragons. Keep track of your score on the right-hand side. This game is great fun, and we'll admit that we were sidetracked for a while playing it. Figures 19.16 and 19.17 show four different shots of the game action. As you can imagine, the source behind this game was rather lengthy, a whopping 30 pages worth, so you'll have to click inside the game frame and select View Source from your browser window to view this masterpiece in dynamic content.

Figure 19.16

The Space Fire site uses dynamic techniques, especially layers and scripting, to create a Web-based dragon hunting game.

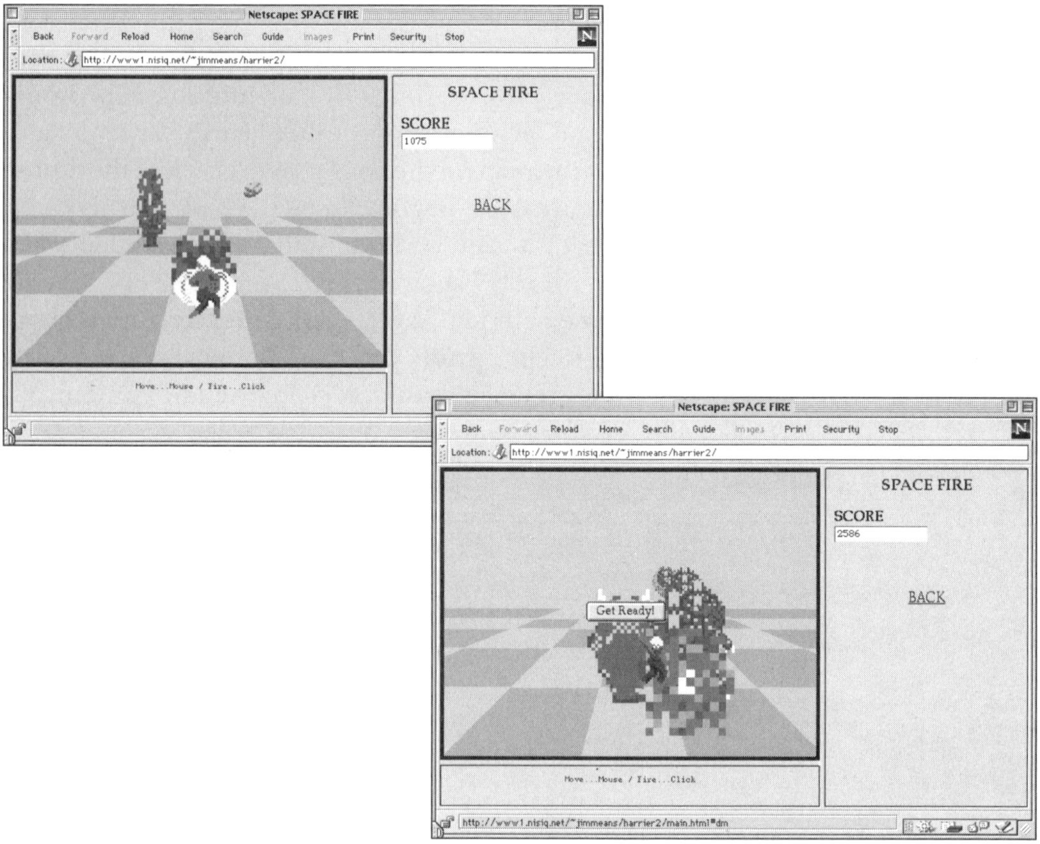

Figure 19.17

The DHTML gives an arcade-style look to this online game. You can vanquish dragons and obliterate offending shrubs, all within your Web browser.

Join The Ranks Of DHTML Designers

We hope that these sites have interested and inspired you. This book has given you the tools you need to begin creating dynamic Web sites, and we hope this short tour has shown you that the possibilities are endless. With the building blocks in hand, go forth and create. We'd love to see what you've created, so once you've gotten your dynamic pages up and running send us email at **dhtml@lanw.com** and share them with us. Until then, happy coding.

PART 6

RESOURCES

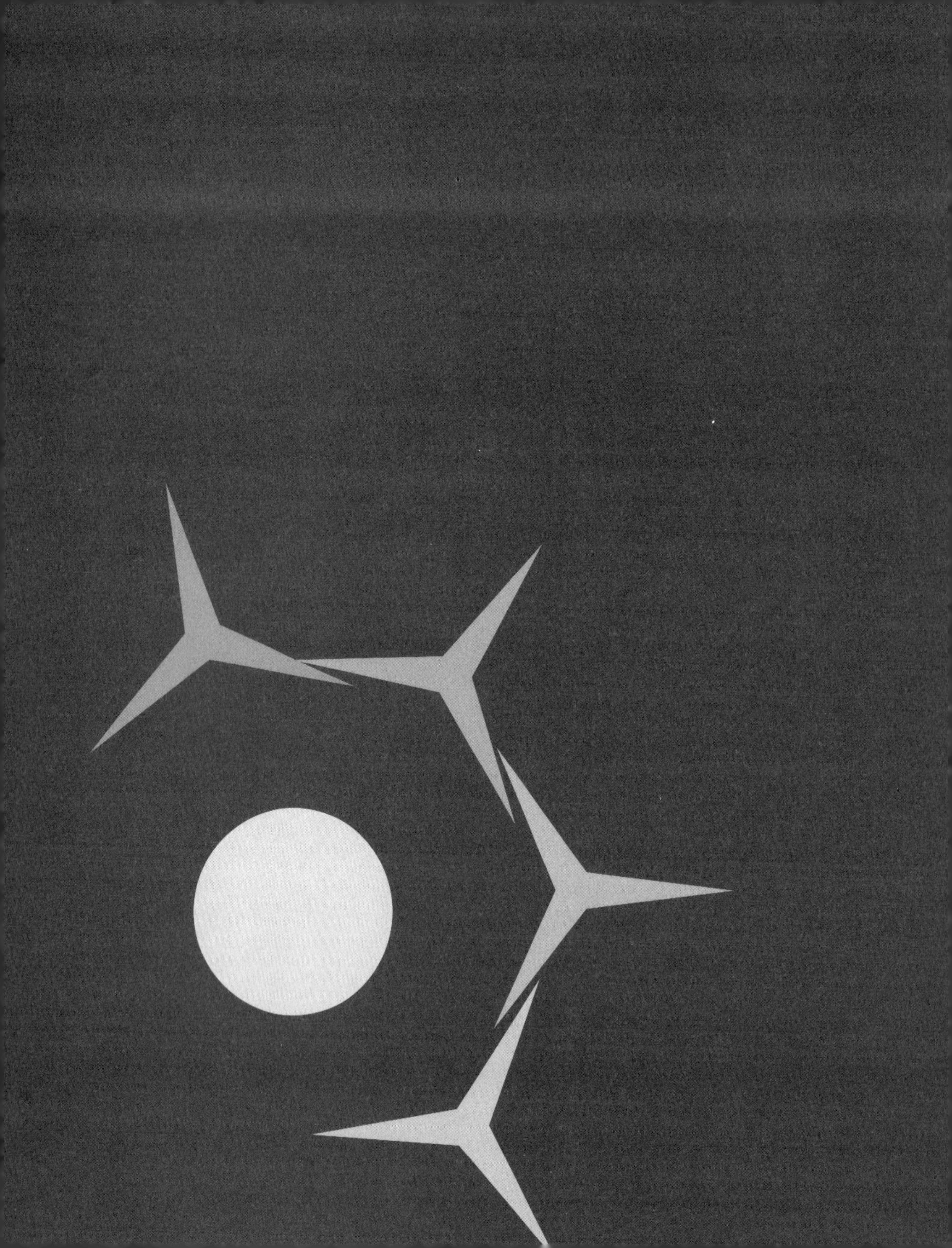

Appendix A

Glossary

Notes...

Appendix A

A

absolute positioning—A method for specifying a Web page element's exact location on a Web page relative to other elements and the bounds of the page itself.

Active Channels—A proprietary IE 4 push technology that provides a mechanism for dynamic Web data delivery to users without requiring an HTTP request from the user. Users subscribe to selected data channels and receive up-to-date information—created by developers using the Channel Data Format (CDF) technology—as it becomes available (pushed to the client) instead of only when the user requests the information (pulled by the client).

active container—An application that can download and utilize ActiveX components, such as Internet Explorer.

Active Desktop—The desktop model in IE 4 that uses HTML as the language for the desktop GUI. The Active Desktop combines an HTML background layer with the Windows 95 icon layer. This allows previously constructed shell-integration tools to be combined with other Web-based tools included under the icon layer using the z-ordering method.

active documents—A non-HTTP document that is Web-aware and capable of integrating with and supporting ActiveX controls and ActiveX scripting. Examples include Microsoft Word 97 documents and Microsoft Excel 97 spreadsheets.

Active Platform—The Microsoft platform development model that includes a suite of technologies used to design ActiveX-based intranet and Internet applications.

Active Server—Microsoft's Web server solution that combines HTML, scripting, and ActiveX controls to create Web pages on-the-fly.

ActiveX—A Microsoft technology that's actually a revamped version of OLE (Object Linking and Embedding). ActiveX lets developers use small software components to build larger software components.

ActiveX controls—An OLE control optimized for size, speed, and use over the Internet. ActiveX controls are miniature applications that, once installed on a user's computer, can be utilized by any Active application, including non-Web applications.

ActiveX scripting—A scripting technique that allows users to add event-driven code to the ActiveX controls within a Web page. This causes the controls to respond to different events as they occur.

ADC (Advanced Data Connector)—An IE 4 data control that is used to access relational ODBC-compliant databases.

AIFF (Audio IFF)—An audio file format by Apple that stores high-quality sampled audio information.

API (Application Programming Interface)—A set of functions or methods used to access some functionality within any given application.

ASCII (American Standard Code for Information Interchange)—An encoding method that translates letters, numbers, and symbols into digital form.

AU—The file extension for an audio file.

B

Beatnik—A system used to create and deliver high-quality interactive music and sound on Web pages.

bitmap—A graphic image that is depicted as an array of binary values. Bitmapped images are typically converted from some other graphics format.

BOF (Beginning of File)—A property that marks the beginning of a recordset.

boolean—An expression with two possible values: true or false.

C

cancel bubbling—A command that forces an action forced by an event to not traverse the event hierarchy, even if no action is associated with the current object's event.

canvas mode—A Navigator option that removes all navigation controls from the browser window. This renders the Web page content in a window, devoid of distraction, with a kiosk look-and-feel, and allows Web developers to include their own intra-document navigation unaffected by built-in browser navigation.

CDF (Channel Definition Format)—A file format, based on XML, used for publishing Web channel content.

CGI (Common Gateway Interface)—Programs and scripts that control how Web browsers communicate with Web servers and how they can request services from them. CGI is also the format and syntax used when information is passed from browsers to servers in the form of document-based queries or forms in HTML.

Collabra—The portion of the Netscape Communicator package that allows users to conduct online discussion groups over the Internet or their organization's intranet.

collection—A collection of elements.

Composer—The WYSIWYG editor included with the Netscape Communicator package that allows users to create, edit, and publish Web documents.

conditional compilation—Lets developers write scripts targeted to specific client platforms and browsers.

Conference—The portion of the Netscape Communicator package that enables users to conduct online audio and video conferencing; it also supports such features as chat, whiteboarding, and file transfer.

CSS1 (Cascading Style Sheets Level 1)—The current specification for providing style information for Web documents. CSS1 can be used with scripting to create dynamic Web pages.

D

DAControl—Direct Animation control, a Microsoft object for animating Web content.

DASound object—A Microsoft object that represents a synthesized or recorded sound, or a combination of the two. These objects have four functions: gain, rate, phase, and pan.

data binding—A unique feature of Microsoft's Dynamic HTML that allows users to bind individual elements in Web document to data from another source, such as a database or a text file.

data control—An ActiveX control used to bind a Web page to a data source.

database—A collection of information arranged and stored so that data can be accessed quickly and accurately.

declaration—One of the three parts of an SGML document; specifies which characters and delimiters are legal to use within a particular document.

DHTML (Dynamic HTML)—A term used by some vendors to describe the combination of HTML, style sheets, and scripts that allows documents to be animated.

digital signatures—Data added to the end of a message that identifies and authenticates the sender and the message.

DirectAnimation—Microsoft's sound system that produces synthetic sounds from basic sound seeds through parameterization and layering (or mixing).

DirectSound 5.0—Microsoft's API for PC-based audio/multimedia/game development.

DirectX—A Microsoft technology that provides Web developers with tools for interactive entertainment and Internet publishing.

document events—The events associated with the document object; i.e., **onselectionchange** and **onzoom**.

document instance—One of the three parts of an SGML document. The document instance is the actual document that contains the content and markup to be rendered by an SGML system. Many SGML documents may reference the same declaration and DTD.

document object—The conceptual root of the document tree that represents the entirety of an HTML or XML document.

DOM (Document Object Model)—Defined by the W3C as a platform- and language-neutral interface that allows programs and scripts to access and update the content, structure, and style of documents dynamically.

downloadable fonts—A Dynamic HTML feature that allows Web authors to configure their Web site to download any required font(s) onto a user's system at runtime.

DTD (Document Type Definition)—One of the three parts of an SGML document. An SGML DTD is a list of rules to which an SGML document must conform, including information about what markup is valid in the document and the document's structure.

dynamic fonts—Netscape's method of embedding fonts within an HTML document. This allows font information to be sent with the document as it is transferred from the server to the user's computer.

Dynamic HTML—Microsoft's specification for designing dynamic, data-driven Web pages.

E

electronic commerce—The sale of goods and services and the exchange of money over the Internet.

Element—A document object (such as **<A>**, **<IMG>**, **<LINK>**, etc.).

element nodes—An object that represents the element itself, as well as any contained nodes.

elements—The parts of a Web page as delineated by markup, such as section headings, images, lists, and paragraphs.

EOF (End of File)—A property that indicates that the user is at the end of a recordset.

EscapeChar—Specifies an escape character.

event bubbling—A process that permits objects to handle events or let events *bubble up* to the parent object.

event model—A description that defines the events associated with the hierarchy of objects defined within the DOM.

exposed object—An object whose behavior and appearance can be manipulated by scripting languages, such as VBScript and JavaScript. An object is considered exposed if you can access and manipulate the object's properties, methods, and events.

F

firewall—A barrier—made of software and/or hardware—between two networks, permitting only authorized communication to pass.

font definition file—A text file downloaded to a user's computer with a Web page that contains the description of and information about a font used in the Web page. This allows the Web page to be displayed using the fonts intended by the developer, even if the fonts are not stored locally on the user's computer. Font definition files are a Netscape proprietary technology and only function within Navigator 4 running a Windows OS.

form events—The events associated with the form object (**onreset**, **onsubmit**, and so on).

Full Event Model—Part of the Microsoft DOM that specifies a new variety of events that are recognized by the browser and can be tied to scripts; this causes the scripts to execute when a specific event occurs.

G

GIF (Graphics Interface Format)—A graphics format used in Web documents to encode images into bits so that a computer can "read" the GIF file and display the picture on a computer screen. GIFs only support 256 colors, which compresses the file and makes it easier to transfer across phone lines.

GM (General MIDI)—An audio format that ensures consistent sounds in MIDI files.

Gopher—A service that provides text-only information over the Internet, most suited to large documents with little or no formatting or images.

GUI (graphical user interface)—A computer interface that uses graphics, windows, and a trackball or mouse as the method of interaction with the computer.

H

hexadecimal color notation—The standard Web method for representing RGB color values using six letters or numbers.

HTTP (Hypertext Transfer Protocol)—The World Wide Web protocol that allows for the transfer of HTML documents over the Internet or intranets.

HyperCard—A technology released by Apple in 1987 that utilizes the Macintosh graphical user interface to create a virtual stack of cards on the computer screen.

hyperlinks—Links created within hypertext documents that allow users to link to other resources on the Web or within the same Web document.

hypertext—A way of organizing and describing data so that it allows for inter- and intra-document linking via marked text.

I

image events—The events associated with the image object (**onabort**, **onerror**, **onload**, and so on).

inflow layers—Layers with relative positions that appear in the place where they naturally fall in the flow of the document.

inline frames—Frames that permit the inclusion of compound documents.

instance hierarchy—A description, in a hierarchical order, of the actual elements present in an HTML page.

intranet—An internal, private network that uses the same protocols and standards as the Internet.

ISDN (Integrated Services Digital Network)—A form of digital communication that has a bandwidth of 128Kbps.

ISO-Latin-1 character set—A term that defines the character and numeric entities for non-Roman and special ASCII characters, along with the metacharacters used to bracket HTML markup itself.

J

Java—A programming language, developed by Sun Microsystems, used for the Web and intranet applications and applets.

Java SoundBvr—A behavior class used to condition delivery of audio information within a Java application or applet.

JavaScript—Netscape's scripting language for writing event-driven code for your HTML pages.

JScript—Microsoft's implementation of JavaScript.

JSS (JavaScript Style Sheets)—Sometimes called JavaScript-Accessible Style Sheets (JASS); Netscape's CSS1 alternative.

K

keyboard events—The events associated with the keyboard object (**onkeypress**, **onhelp**, **onkeydown**, and so on).

keycode—A numeric ASCII keycode for key events.

L

layer—A block of HTML that can be hidden, displayed, moved, and manipulated.

layer objects—A JavaScript extension that works with the **<LAYER>** tag. Layer objects are associated with the sections of an HTML document contained within the **<LAYER>** tags. Layer objects are created automatically; their properties are associated with whatever corresponding properties appear between the **<LAYER>** tags.

LiveAudio—The part of the LiveConnect API that's used to add sound to Web sites through the LiveAudio plug-in module.

LiveConnect—Netscape's API for multimedia creation.

M

Marquee events—The events associated with the marquee object (**onbounce**, **onfinish**, and so on).

Messenger—The email program within Netscape Communicator that provides for the creation of rich, HTML-aware email. Messenger supports HTML and embedded images in email documents, and filters and organizes incoming messages into folders, as well as email encryption and decryption.

MIDI (Musical Instrument Digital Interface)—A protocol that emerged in the 1980s for the exchange of information between computers and electronic audio devices.

MIDPLUG—Yamaha's offering in the Soft Synthesizer category. MIDPLUG contains its own AWM2 (WaveTable) tone generator that operates at 22.1 kHz/16 bit within the plug-in module.

MIME type—Any of a collection of predefined document types used by electronic mail software and HTTP-based services to identify the documents that are transported across a TCP/IP network.

MOD—The file extension used for a sampled music file format from Commodore Amiga. It is made up of digitized sound samples that are arranged in a particular pattern to create songs.

mouse events—The events associated with the mouse object (**onmouseover**, **onmouseout**, **onmouseup**, and so on).

moveAbove(layer)—The layer method that stacks a layer above the specified layer.

moveBelow(layer)—The layer method that stacks a layer below the specified layer.

moveBy(x, y)—The layer method that changes a layer's position by applying the specified deltas, measured in pixels.

moveTo(x, y)—The layer method that translates a layer so its upper-left corner is (x,y).

MP2 (MPEG-2)—A variation of the MPEG audio and video file format. It is used to enhance broadcast quality video.

N

Netcaster—Netscape's Webcasting solution that allows users to subscribe to information and schedule automatic delivery of the information to your desktop. Netcaster can be configured to view the latest and greatest information offline, reducing online time and charges.

node—The name for Web page objects, such as a document, element, or attribute.

O

object element—An element that allows objects, such as video, images, sound, specialized applications, mathematics, and others, to be wholly contained within an HTML document.

object-specific events—The events associated with a specific DOM element (form, image, marquee, and so on).

ODBC (Open Database Connectivity)—A Microsoft standard, used to access various database systems.

OLE (Object Linking and Embedding)—An object system and protocol that allows data or links from one Windows application to be embedded in another.

ONE (Open Network Environment)—A unifier for Netscape's crossware strategy.

OpenType Fonts—Netscape's Web font solution that allows Web developers to embed fonts within Web pages and have them display correctly on the user's machine, even if the user does not have the fonts installed on their system.

operating system—A software program that controls the operations on a computer system.

P

parsing engine—An application that reads an entire Web document, breaks it down into its component parts, such as tags and text, and then formats the content for display on the screen, based on the tags and text. A parser is an integral part of a Web browser.

Path Control—A control that lets Web authors move objects around a Web page using splines, geometric primitives, text outlines, or shapes. This control lets Web authors determine speed of motion, looping, forward or reverse playback, and bouncing behavior.

PFR (Portable Font Resource)—A compact data type that stores the characters from the fonts used by Web developers in their documents.

PI node (processing instruction)—Refers to a set of special processing instructions to be associated with an element within the DOM representation of a Dynamic HTML document. This provides a general purpose mechanism to associate programmatic handling for document components within a DHTML environment.

placeholder icon—An icon displayed by a Web page to signify images in a page that are in the process of loading.

plug-ins—External helper applications that add new functionality to the basic programs, such as Netscape Communicator and Netscape Navigator.

Q

QTMA (QuickTime Music Architecture)—Apple's contribution to software-based MIDI synthesizers. QTMA lets you create sound libraries, as well as custom software synthesizers. It makes Web audio relatively low-demand.

QuickTime—A standard created by Apple, used to combine full-motion video and digital sound with applications.

R

rapid development tools—Any of a class of software development tools designed to facilitate rapid production and testing of proposed implementations, also known as prototypes.

RealAudio—A sound technology, created by Progressive Networks, that provides streaming voice narration.

RealPlayer—RealAudio Player's successor.

recordset—The result set obtained by the execution of an SQL request at the database server.

reference—The base type for named entities, including parameter entities, but not numeric character entities.

relational databases—A database that supports the definition of relationships between items stored in it.

relative positioning—The mechanism that makes elements flow, moving them in a way determined by the other changes that occur on the page.

rich media files—Any of a number of multimedia file formats (.avi, .mov, .dvi, and so on) that provide synchronized delivery of one or more streams of audio and visual information.

RMF (Rich Music Format)—A hybrid file type that encapsulates MIDI and audio samples.

S

scriptlet—A Microsoft proprietary technology. Scriptlets are script components that can be combined and reused to create dynamic Web pages.

scripts—Non-compiled Web programs that are stored within a Web page and executed on the client side after the page has been downloaded.

sepia-toned—The term that describes photographs rendered in tones of brown and white instead of black and white.

Sequencer Control—A mechanism that lets Web authors make complex sequences of action through scripting, ActiveX controls, or DHTML elements.

SGML (Standard Generalized Markup Language)—An ISO standard text-based language that defines, specifies, and creates documents.

singleton tag—A tag that stands alone and requires no closing tag.

SMF (Standard MIDI files)—The format used for MIDI files.

SOM (Scripting Object Model)—In Internet Explorer, the SOM lets site designers use their scripting language of choice to control page objects.

Sound spatialization—Achieved by embedding sounds in 3D objects, then rendering them with either DAMicrophone or MicrophoneBvr.

Sprite Control—A control that gives Web authors control over playback speed, forward/reverse playback, and user on a frame-by-frame basis with still and animated images.

SQL (Structured Query Language)—A query language created specifically to search database records.

static document—A non-dynamic Web page that uses traditional HTML markup to display text. Static documents cannot be changed based on user input but are replaced by other static documents via requests to the server.

stored procedure—SQL procedures that reside and execute on the server.

Structured Graphics Control—A control that lets Web authors put lightweight vector graphics that can be scaled or rotated in three dimensions in their Web page. Solid colors, patterns, bitmap textures, or gradient fills can be applied to these graphics.

style sheet—A collection of rules that govern how HTML elements should be displayed by a browser. Style sheets are essentially Web page templates that allow you to simplify and expedite Web page design.

Stylesheet Object Model—An object model designed to allow Web authors to create, modify, and associate CSS style sheets on-the-fly within a Web document.

syntax—The "grammar" rules of HTML.

T

T3 lines—A communication line that carries a digital signal at 44.736Mbps.

TDC (Tabular Data Control)—An IE 4 control that is used to bind page elements to an ASCII-delimited file.

text node—Objects that contain just plain text, without markup and entities.

text object—Objects that contain the non-markup portion of a document.

typography—The process of making and laying out typewritten materials to print.

U

Unix—An interactive time-sharing operating system developed in 1969 by a hacker to play games. This system developed into the most widely used industrial-strength operating system in the world and ultimately supported the birth of the Internet.

URL (Uniform Resource Locator)—The World Wide Web addressing mechanism used to define what protocols to use, the domain name of the resource's Web server, the communication port address, and the directory path used to find the named Web file or resource.

V

VBScript (Visual Basic Scripting Edition)—A subset of Microsoft's Visual Basic language. VBScript is used as an interpreter in Web browsers and other applications that use OLE (Object Linking and Embedding) automation servers, ActiveX controls, and Java applets.

vector graphics—Images that are represented as lines and points.

Visual Basic—Microsoft's version of the Basic programming language, used to develop Windows applications.

Visual C++—Microsoft's proprietary object-oriented programming environment.

visual data stream—A form of streaming input data for rendering within a Web browser that supports double buffering to permit display of data that has already been received (from the head of the buffer), even while new data is still arriving (at the tail of the buffer).

visual filter—An IE 4 ActiveX control that is used to apply special effects to Web page elements.

Visual JavaScript—Netscape's GUI tool for writing JavaScript-based HTML pages.

visual objects—Sometimes called CA-visual objects because it is a client/server development system created by Computer Associates to develop Windows applications.

W

W3C (World Wide Web Consortium)—A consortium based in Cambridge, Mass. that develops the standards for the World Wide Web.

WAV—Microsoft Window's sound format.

Webcasting—A term that describes the automatic delivery of materials to users. Usually a user must first subscribe to this information.

WebTV—An Internet technology that runs from a set-top box connected to your TV.

Window events—The events associated with the window object(**onload**, **onunload**, and so on).

Windows DNA—A technology that facilitates the act of building applications. It seeks to make an easier, more casual task through DHTML's on-the-fly assembly.

WMF (Windows Meta File)—A file encoded using the Windows encoding scheme.

WYSIWYG (What You See Is What You Get)—A term that describes an authoring tool or text editor that attempts to display the on-screen text the same way it will appear in the Web page.

X

XML(Extensible Markup Language)—A simplified version of SGML, intended for general use on the Web.

Appendix B

Online Resources

Notes...

Appendix B

DHTML is truly a moving target and new information about DHTML and scripting will surface day after day—if not hour after hour—in the coming months. Although we've put together what we believe to be the comprehensive guide to creating dynamic Web sites with DHTML, we're very aware of the fact that it is easier to update information on the Web than it is to revise a printed book. For that reason, we've scoured the Web to find the best collection of online DHTML- and scripting-related resources. These sites will provide you with the most current information available and keep you informed of new developments in the ever-changing world of DHTML.

To make life easier for you, we've also included these resources on this book's CD-ROM as a page of active hyperlinks, so you can just point and click to visit them. The same resources page is mirrored on the Web site for this book and can be found at **www.lanw.com/books/dhtml/**.

Due to the volatile nature of the Web, we can't guarantee that these resources will be around forever or that they won't change location. We will keep the Web site version of this resource list updated and make notes next to changed or new links. If you find that one of these links is broken or changed, or discover any other useful resources, please drop us a note at **dhtml@lanw.com**.

Dynamic HTML Sites

- Dynamic HTML in Microsoft Internet Explorer (Microsoft)—**www.microsoft.com/workshop/author/dhtml/**
- Dynamic HTML in Netscape Communicator (Netscape)—**developer.netscape.com/library/documentation/communicator/dynhtml/index.htm**
- Dynamic HTML Sites (Yahoo)—**www.yahoo.com/Computers_and_Internet/Information_and_Documentation/Data_Formats/HTML/Dynamic_HTML/**
- Dynamic HTML Zone (Macromedia)—**www.dhtmlzone.com**
- Index Dynamic HTML—**www.all-links.com/dynamic/**
- Inside Dynamic HTML (Microsoft Press)—**www.insideDHTML.com**
- Sitebuilder—**www.sitebuilder.com**
- WebCoder—**www.webcoder.com**

JavaScript Sites

- Ask the JavaScript Pro (Inquiry)—**www.inquiry.com/techtips/js_pro/**
- Danny Goodman's JavaScript Pages—**www.dannyg.com/javascript/index.html**
- Hotsyte JavaScript—**www.serve.com/hotsyte/**
- JavaScript Authoring Guide (Netscape)—**home.netscape.com/eng/mozilla/Gold/handbook/javascript/index.html**
- JavaScript Documentation (Netscape)—**developer.netscape.com/library/documentation/javascript.html**
- JavaScript Resource Center (Live Software)—**www.livesoftware.com/jrc/index.html**
- JavaScript Sites (Yahoo)—**www.yahoo.com/Computers_and_Internet/Programming_Languages/JavaScript/**

- JavaScript Tip of the Week—**webreference.com/javascript/**
- JavaScript World—**www.jsworld.com**
- JavaScripts—**www.javascripts.com**
- JavaWorld's JavaScript—**www.javaworld.com/common/jw.nuts.toc.html**
- Sitebuilder—**www.sitebuilder.com**
- Verifying Form Input with JavaScript—**gmccomb.com/valid.htm**
- WebCoder—**www.webcoder.com**

VBScript Sites

- Scribe—**www.km-cd.com/scribe/**
- VBScript Information (Microsoft)—**www.microsoft.com/vbscript/**
- VBScript Sites (Yahoo)—**www.yahoo.com/Computers_and_Internet/Programming_Languages/Visual_Basic/VBScript/**
- VBScript Tutorial (Microsoft)—**www.microsoft.com/vbscript/us/vbstutor/vbstutor.htm**
- VBScripts—**www.vbscripts.com**

Appendix C

HTML Tags

Notes...

Appendix C

Even though we, as seasoned Webmasters, use HTML tags all the time, we can't always remember which attributes are used with which tags; especially because the DTDs are in a constant state of flux. Because DHTML is directly tied to HTML, we thought it might be nice for you to have an HTML reference handy so you don't have to waste your time looking up tags and their associated attributes in other resources. This appendix is that type of reference.

Table C.1 has been drawn from the most current version of the HTML 4.0 specification. However, because HTML is constantly changing, always check the World Wide Web Consortium's (W3C) Web page at **www.w3.org** for the most current HTML tags and attributes. To make this reference easy to use, we've created an HTML tag table that lists the tags in alphabetical order with their names, attributes, and a special note to mark deprecated tags.

Table C.1 The HTML 4.0 tag table.

Tag	Tag Name	Attributes	Note
<!-- . . . -->	Comments	None	
<!DOCTYPE>	Document Type	HTML PUBLIC="*version name*"	
<A> . . . </A>	Anchor	ACCESSKEY="*text*"	

(continued)

Table C.1 The HTML 4.0 tag table *(continued)*.

Tag	Tag Name	Attributes	Note
		CHARSET="*text*"	
		CLASS="*text*"	
		COORDS="X1, Y1, X2, Y2, *and so on.*"	
		DIR=(LTR | RTL)	
		HREF="*URL*"	
		ID="*name*"	
		LANG="*name*"	
		NAME="*text*"	
		REL="*text*"	
		REV="*text*"	
		SHAPE=(RECT | CIRCLE | POLY | DEFAULT)	
		STYLE="*text*"	
		TABINDEX=*number*	
		TARGET="*window*"	
		TITLE="*text*"	
<ABBR> . . . </ABBR>	Abbreviation	CLASS="*text*"	
		DIR=(LTR | RTL)	
		ID="*name*"	
		LANG="*name*"	
		STYLE="*text*"	
		TITLE="*text*"	

(continued)

Table C.1 The HTML 4.0 tag table *(continued)*.

Tag	Tag Name	Attributes	Note
<ADDRESS> . . . </ADDRESS>	Address	CLASS="*text*"	
		DIR=(LTR | RTL)	
		ID="*name*"	
		LANG="*name*"	
		STYLE="*text*"	
		TITLE="*text*"	
<APPLET> . . . </APPLET>		Applet	
		ALIGN=(LEFT | RIGHT | TOP | MIDDLE | BOTTOM)	Deprecated
		ALT="*text*"	
		ARCHIVE="*text*"	
		CLASS="*text*"	
		CODE="*URL*"	
		CODEBASE="*URL*"	
		DIR=(LTR | RTL)	
		HEIGHT=*number*	
		ID="*name*"	
		HSPACE=*number*	
		LANG="*name*"	
		NAME="*text*"	
		OBJECT="*text*"	
		STYLE="*text*"	
		TITLE="*text*"	

(continued)

Table C.1 The HTML 4.0 tag table *(continued).*

Tag	Tag Name	Attributes	Note
		VSPACE=*number*	
		WIDTH=(*number*|"%")	
<AREA>	Image Map Hot Spot	ACCESSKEY="*character*"	
		ALT="*text*"	
		CLASS="*text*"	
		COORDS="X1, Y1, X2, Y2, *and so on.*"	
		DIR=(LTR|RTL)	
		HREF="*URL*"	
		ID="*name*"	
		LANG="*name*"	
		NOHREF	
		SHAPE=(RECT: left-x, top-y, right-x, bottom-y |CIRCLE: center-x, center-y, radius |POLY: x1, y1, x2, y2, . . . , x*N*, y*N* |DEFAULT)	
		STYLE="*text*"	
		TABINDEX=*number*	
		TARGET="*window*"	
		TITLE="*text*"	
<B> . . . </B>	Bold Text	CLASS="*text*"	
		DIR=(LTR|RTL)	
		ID="*name*"	

(continued)

Table C.1 The HTML 4.0 tag table *(continued)*.

Tag	Tag Name	Attributes	Note
		LANG="*name*"	
		STYLE="*text*"	
		TITLE="*text*"	
<BASE>	Relative Addressing Base	CLASS="*text*"	
		DIR=(LTR | RTL)	
		HREF="*URL*"	
		ID="*name*"	
		LANG="*name*"	
		STYLE="*text*"	
		TARGET="*window*"	
		TITLE="*text*"	
<BASEFONT>	Base Font	CLASS="*text*"	Deprecated
		COLOR=(#*RRGGBB* | *colorname*)	
		DIR=(LTR | RTL)	
		FACE="*name*"	
		ID="*name*"	
		LANG="*name*"	
		SIZE=*number*	
		STYLE="*text*"	
		TITLE="*text*"	
<BDO> . . . </BDO>	Bi-Directional Algorithm	DIR=(LTR | RTL)	
		LANG="*language-code*"	

(continued)

Table C.1 The HTML 4.0 tag table *(continued)*.

Tag	Tag Name	Attributes	Note
<BIG> . . . </BIG>	Big Text	CLASS="*text*"	
		DIR=(LTR | RTL)	
		ID="*name*"	
		LANG="*name*"	
		STYLE="*text*"	
		TITLE="*text*"	
<BLOCKQUOTE> . . . </BLOCKQUOTE>	Blockquote	CITE="*text*"	
		CLASS="*text*"	
		DIR=(LTR | RTL)	
		ID="*name*"	
		LANG="*name*"	
		STYLE="*text*"	
		TITLE="*text*"	
<BODY> . . . </BODY>	Document Body	ALINK=(#*RRGGBB* | *colorname*)	
		BACKGROUND="*URL*"	
		BGCOLOR=(#*RRGGBB* | *colorname*)	
		CLASS="*text*"	
		DIR=(LTR | RTL)	
		ID="*name*"	
		LANG="*name*"	
		LINK=(#*RRGGBB* | *colorname*)	
		STYLE="*text*"	

(continued)

Table C.1 The HTML 4.0 tag table *(continued).*

Tag	Tag Name	Attributes	Note
		TEXT=(#*RRGGBB* | *colorname*)	
		TITLE="*text*"	
		VLINK=(#*RRGGBB* | *colorname*)	
 	Line Break	CLASS="*text*"	
		CLEAR=(LEFT | ALL | RIGHT | NONE)	
		DIR=(LTR | RTL)	
		ID="*name*"	
		LANG="*name*"	
		STYLE="*text*"	
		TITLE="*text*"	
<BUTTON> . . . </BUTTON>	Form Button	CLASS="*text*"	
		DIR=(LTR | RTL)	
		DISABLED	
		ID="*name*"	
		LANG="*name*"	
		NAME="*name*"	
		STYLE="*text*"	
		TABINDEX=*number*	
		TITLE="*text*"	
		TYPE=(BUTTON | SUBMIT | RESET)	
		VALUE="*value*"	
<CAPTION> . . . </CAPTION>	Table Caption	ALIGN=(LEFT | RIGHT | TOP | BOTTOM)	

(continued)

Table C.1 The HTML 4.0 tag table *(continued)*.

Tag	Tag Name	Attributes	Note
		CLASS="*text*"	
		DIR=(LTR | RTL)	
		ID="*name*"	
		LANG="*name*"	
		STYLE="*text*"	
		TITLE="*text*"	
<CENTER> . . . </CENTER>	Centered Text	CLASS="*text*"	Deprecated
		DIR=(LTR | RTL)	
		ID="*name*"	
		LANG="*name*"	
		STYLE="*text*"	
		TITLE="*text*"	
<CITE> . . . </CITE>	Citation Markup	CLASS="*text*"	
		DIR=(LTR | RTL)	
		ID="*name*"	
		LANG="*name*"	
		STYLE="*text*"	
		TITLE="*text*"	
<CODE> . . . </CODE>	Program Code Text	CLASS="*text*"	
		DIR=(LTR | RTL)	
		ID="*name*"	
		LANG="*name*"	

(continued)

Table C.1 The HTML 4.0 tag table *(continued)*.

Tag	Tag Name	Attributes	Note
		STYLE="*text*"	
		TITLE="*text*"	
<COL>	Table Column	ALIGN=(LEFT | RIGHT | CENTER | JUSTIFY | CHAR)	
		CHAR="*text*"	
		CHAROFF=*number*	
		CLASS="*text*"	
		DIR=(LTR | RTL)	
		ID="*name*"	
		LANG="*name*"	
		SPAN=*number*	
		STYLE="*text*"	
		TITLE="*text*"	
		VALIGN=TOP | MIDDLE | BOTTOM | BASELINE	
		WIDTH=*number*	
<COLGROUP>	Table Column Group	ALIGN=(LEFT | RIGHT | CENTER | JUSTIFY | CHAR)	
		CHAR="*text*"	
		CHAROFF=*number*	
		CLASS="*text*"	
		DIR=(LTR | RTL)	
		ID="*name*"	
		LANG="*name*"	

(continued)

Table C.1 The HTML 4.0 tag table *(continued)*.

Tag	Tag Name	Attributes	Note
		SPAN=*number*	
		STYLE="*text*"	
		TITLE="*text*"	
		VALIGN=(TOP | MIDDLE | BOTTOM | BASELINE)	
		WIDTH=*number*	
<DD>	Definition Description	CLASS="*text*"	
		DIR=(LTR | RTL)	
		ID="*name*"	
		LANG="*name*"	
		STYLE="*text*"	
		TITLE="*text*"	
<DEL> . . . </DEL>	Deleted Text	CITE="*URL*"	
		CLASS="*text*"	
		DATETIME=*YYYY-MM-DDThh:mm:ssTZD*	
		DIR=(LTR | RTL)	
		ID="*name*"	
		LANG="*name*"	
		STYLE="*text*"	
		TITLE="*text*"	
<DFN> . . . </DFN>	Definition of a Term	CLASS="*text*"	

(continued)

Table C.1 The HTML 4.0 tag table *(continued).*

Tag	Tag Name	Attributes	Note
		DIR=(LTR | RTL)	
		ID="*name*"	
		LANG="*name*"	
		STYLE="*text*"	
		TITLE="*text*"	
<DIR> . . . </DIR>	Directory List	CLASS="*text*"	Deprecated
		DIR=(LTR | RTL)	
		ID="*name*"	
		LANG="*name*"	
		STYLE="*text*"	
		TITLE="*text*"	
<DIV> . . . </DIV>	Logical Division	ALIGN=(LEFT | CENTER | RIGHT | JUSTIFY)	
		CLASS="*text*"	
		DIR=(LTR | RTL)	
		ID="*name*"	
		LANG="*name*"	
		STYLE="*text*"	
		TITLE="*text*"	
<DL> . . . </DL>	Definition List	CLASS="*text*"	
		COMPACT	
		DIR=(LTR | RTL)	

(continued)

Table C.1 The HTML 4.0 tag table *(continued).*

Tag	Tag Name	Attributes	Note
		ID="*name*"	
		LANG="*name*"	
		STYLE="*text*"	
		TITLE="*text*"	
<DT>	Definition Term	CLASS="*text*"	
		DIR=(LTR|RTL)	
		ID="*name*"	
		LANG="*name*"	
		STYLE="*text*"	
		TITLE="*text*"	
<EM> . . . </EM>	Emphasis	CLASS="*text*"	
		DIR=(LTR|RTL)	
		ID="*name*"	
		LANG="*name*"	
		STYLE="*text*"	
		TITLE="*text*"	
<FIELDSET> . . . </FIELDSET>	Set of Fields	CLASS="*text*"	
		DIR=(LTR|RTL)	
		ID="*name*"	
		LANG="*name*"	
		STYLE="*text*"	
		TITLE="*text*"	

(continued)

Table C.1 The HTML 4.0 tag table *(continued)*.

Tag	Tag Name	Attributes	Note
<FONT> . . . </FONT>	Font Appearance	CLASS="*text*"	Deprecated
		COLOR=(#*RRGGBB* | *colorname*)	
		DIR=(LTR | RTL)	
		FACE="*name*[, *name2*[, *name3*]]"	
		ID="*name*"	
		LANG="*name*"	
		SIZE=*number*	
		STYLE="*text*"	
		TITLE="*text*"	
<FORM> . . . </FORM>	User Input Form	ACCEPT="*Internet media type*"	
		ACCEPT-CHARSET="*text*"	
		ACTION="*URL*"	
		CLASS="*text*"	
		DIR=(LTR | RTL)	
		ENCTYPE="*Internet media type*"	
		ID="*name*"	
		LANG="*name*"	
		METHOD=(GET | POST)	
		STYLE="*text*"	
		TARGET="*window*"	
		TITLE="*text*"	
<FRAME> . . . </FRAME>	Frame Definition	CLASS="*text*"	

(continued)

Table C.1 The HTML 4.0 tag table *(continued)*.

Tag	Tag Name	Attributes	Note
		DIR=(LTR | RTL)	
		FRAMEBORDER=(1 | 0)	
		ID="*name*"	
		LANG="*name*"	
		MARGINHEIGHT=(*number* | %)	
		MARGINWIDTH=(*number* | %)	
		NAME="*text*"	
		NORESIZE	
		SCROLLING=(yes | no | auto)	
		SRC="*URL*"	
		STYLE="*text*"	
		TITLE="*text*"	
<FRAMESET> . . . </FRAMESET>	Frame Group Definition	CLASS="*text*"	
		COLS=(*col-widths* | % | *)	
		DIR=(LTR | RTL)	
		ID="*name*"	
		LANG="*name*"	
		ROWS=(*row-height* | % | *)	
		STYLE="*text*"	
		TITLE="*text*"	
<H*> . . . </H*>	Heading Level	ALIGN=(LEFT | CENTER | RIGHT | JUSTIFY)	

(continued)

Table C.1 The HTML 4.0 tag table *(continued)*.

Tag	Tag Name	Attributes	Note
		CLASS="*text*"	
		DIR=(LTR | RTL)	
		ID="*name*"	
		LANG="*name*"	
		STYLE="*text*"	
		TITLE="*text*"	
<HEAD> . . . </HEAD>	Document Head Block	CLASS="*text*"	
		DIR=(LTR | RTL)	
		ID="*name*"	
		LANG="*name*"	
		PROFILE="*URL*"	
		STYLE="*text*"	
		TITLE="*text*"	
<HR>	Horizontal Rule	ALIGN=(LEFT | CENTER | RIGHT)	
		CLASS="*text*"	
		DIR=(LTR | RTL)	
		ID="*name*"	
		LANG="*name*"	
		NOSHADE	
		SIZE=*number*	
		STYLE="*text*"	
		TITLE="*text*"	

(continued)

Table C.1 The HTML 4.0 tag table *(continued)*.

Tag	Tag Name	Attributes	Note
		WIDTH=(*number*|%)	
<HTML> . . . </HTML>	HTML Document	CLASS="*text*"	
		DIR=(LTR|RTL)	
		ID="*name*"	
		LANG="*name*"	
		STYLE="*text*"	
		TITLE="*text*"	
		VERSION="*URL*"	
<I> . . . </I>	Italic Text	CLASS="*text*"	
		DIR=(LTR|RTL)	
		ID="*name*"	
		LANG="*name*"	
		STYLE="*text*"	
		TITLE="*text*"	
<IFRAME> . . . </IFRAME>	Inline Frame	ALIGN=(LEFT|CENTER|RIGHT|TOP|MIDDLE|BOTTOM)	
		CLASS="*text*"	
		DIR=(LTR|RTL)	
		FRAMEBORDER=(1|0)	
		HEIGHT=(*number*|%)	
		ID="*name*"	
		LANG="*name*"	

(continued)

Table C.1 The HTML 4.0 tag table *(continued)*.

Tag	Tag Name	Attributes	Note
		MARGINHEIGHT=(*number*|%)	
		MARGINWIDTH=(*number*|%)	
		NAME="*text*"	
		SCROLLING=(yes|no)	
		SRC="*URL*"	
		STYLE="*text*"	
		TITLE="*text*"	
		WIDTH=(*number*|%)	
<IMG>	Inline Image	ALIGN=(LEFT|RIGHT|TOP|MIDDLE|BOTTOM)	
		ALT="*text*"	
		BORDER=*number*	
		CLASS="*text*"	
		DIR=(LTR|RTL)	
		HEIGHT=*pixels*	
		HSPACE=*number*	
		ID="*name*"	
		ISMAP	
		LANG="*name*"	
		SRC="*URL*"	
		STYLE="*text*"	
		TITLE="*text*"	

(continued)

Table C.1 The HTML 4.0 tag table *(continued)*.

Tag	Tag Name	Attributes	Note
		USEMAP=*map-name*	
		VSPACE=*number*	
		WIDTH=*pixels*	
<INPUT>	Input Object	ACCEPT="*Internet media type*"	
		ALIGN=(LEFT | CENTER | RIGHT | JUSTIFY)	
		ALT="*text*"	
		CHECKED	
		CLASS="*text*"	
		DIR=(LTR | RTL)	
		DISABLED	
		ID="*name*"	
		LANG="*name*"	
		MAXLENGTH=*number*	
		NAME="*text*"	
		READONLY	
		SIZE=(*width* | [*width, height*])	
		SRC="*URL*"	
		STYLE="*text*"	
		TABINDEX=*number*	
		TITLE="*text*"	

(continued)

Table C.1 The HTML 4.0 tag table *(continued)*.

Tag	Tag Name	Attributes	Note
		TYPE=(TEXT | PASSWORD | CHECKBOXRADIO | SUBMIT | RESET | FILE | HIDDEN | IMAGE | BUTTON)	
		USEMAP="*text*"	
		VALUE=*value*	
<INS> . . . </INS>	Inserted Text	CITE="*URL*"	
		CLASS="*text*"	
		DIR=(LTR | RTL)	
		ID="*name*"	
		LANG="*name*"	
		STYLE="*text*"	
		TITLE="*text*"	
<ISINDEX>	Single Line Input	CLASS="*text*"	Deprecated
		DIR=(LTR | RTL)	
		ID="*name*"	
		LANG="*name*"	
		PROMPT="*text*"	
		STYLE="*text*"	
		TITLE="*text*"	
<KBD> . . . </KBD>	Keyboard Text	CLASS="*text*"	
		DIR=(LTR | RTL)	
		ID="*name*"	

(continued)

Table C.1 The HTML 4.0 tag table *(continued)*.

Tag	Tag Name	Attributes	Note
		LANG="*name*"	
		STYLE="*text*"	
		TITLE="*text*"	
<LABEL> . . . </LABEL>	Control Label	ACCESSKEY="*text*"	
		CLASS="*text*"	
		DIR=(LTR | RTL)	
		DISABLED	
		FOR="*text*"	
		ID="*name*"	
		LANG="*name*"	
		STYLE="*text*"	
		TABINDEX=*number*	
		TITLE="*text*"	
<LEGEND> . . . </LEGEND>	Fieldset Caption	ACCESSKEY="*text*"	
		ALIGN=(LEFT | RIGHT | TOP | BOTTOM)	
		CLASS="*text*"	
		DIR=(LTR | RTL)	
		ID="*name*"	
		LANG="*name*"	
		STYLE="*text*"	
		TITLE="*text*"	

(continued)

Table C.1 The HTML 4.0 tag table *(continued)*.

Tag	Tag Name	Attributes	Note
<LI>	List Item	CLASS="*text*"	
		DIR=(LTR | RTL)	
		ID="*name*"	
		LANG="*name*"	
		STYLE="*text*"	
		TITLE="*text*"	
		TYPE=(DISC | SQUARE | CIRCLE) or (1 | a | A | i | I)	
		VALUE=*number*	
<LINK>	Link	CLASS="*text*"	
		DIR=(LTR | RTL)	
		HREF="*URL*"	
		ID="*name*"	
		LANG="*name*"	
		MEDIA=(SCREEN | PRINT | PROJECTION | BRAILLE | SPEECH | ALL)	
		REL="*text*"	
		REV="*text*"	
		STYLE="*text*"	
		TARGET="*window*"	
		TITLE="*text*"	
		TYPE="*text*"	

(continued)

Table C.1 The HTML 4.0 tag table *(continued)*.

Tag	Tag Name	Attributes	Note
<MAP> . . . </MAP>	Client-Side Image Map	CLASS="*text*"	
		DIR=(LTR | RTL)	
		ID="*name*"	
		LANG="*name*"	
		NAME="*text*"	
		STYLE="*text*"	
		TITLE="*text*"	
<MENU> . . . </MENU>	Menu List	CLASS="*text*"	Deprecated
		COMPACT	
		DIR=(LTR | RTL)	
		ID="*name*"	
		LANG="*name*"	
		STYLE="*text*"	
		TITLE="*text*"	
<META>	Meta-Information	CONTENT="*text*"	
		HTTP-EQUIV="*text*"	
		NAME="*text*"	
		SCHEME="*schemename*"	
<NOFRAMES> . . . </NOFRAMES>	Frames Alternative	CLASS="*text*"	
		DIR=(LTR | RTL)	
		ID="*name*"	
		LANG="*name*"	

(continued)

Table C.1 The HTML 4.0 tag table *(continued).*

Tag	Tag Name	Attributes	Note
		STYLE="*text*"	
		TITLE="*text*"	
<NOSCRIPT> . . . </NOSCRIPT>	No Script	CLASS="*text*"	
		DIR=(LTR | RTL)	
		ID="*name*"	
		LANG="*name*"	
		STYLE="*text*"	
		TITLE="*text*"	
		TYPE="*scripting language*"	
<OBJECT> . . . </OBJECT>	Object Embedding	ALIGN= (BASELINE CENTER | LEFT | MIDDE RIGHT | TEXT BOTTOM | TEXT MIDDLE | TEXTTOP)	
		BORDER=*number*	
		CLASS="*text*"	
		CLASSID="*URL*"	
		CODEBASE="*URL*"	
		CODETYPE="*codetype*"	
		DATA="*URL*"	
		DECLARE	

(continued)

Table C.1 The HTML 4.0 tag table *(continued)*.

Tag	Tag Name	Attributes	Note
		DIR=(LTR|RTL)	
		HEIGHT=*number*	
		HSPACE=*n*	
		ID="*name*"	
		LANG="*name*"	
		NAME="*URL*"	
		SHAPES	
		STANDBY="*message*"	
		TABINDEX=*number*	
		TYPE="*type*"	
		USEMAP="*URL*"	
		VSPACE=*number*	
		WIDTH=*number*	
		STYLE="*text*"	
		TITLE="*text*"	
<OL> . . . </OL>	Ordered List	CLASS="*text*"	
		COMPACT	
		DIR=(LTR|RTL)	
		ID="*name*"	
		LANG="*name*"	
		START="*value*"	
		STYLE="*text*"	

(continued)

Table C.1 The HTML 4.0 tag table *(continued)*.

Tag	Tag Name	Attributes	Note
		TITLE="*text*"	
		TYPE=(1 | a | A | i | I)	
<OPTION>	Selectable Item	CLASS="*text*"	
		DIR=(LTR | RTL)	
		DISABLED	
		ID="*name*"	
		LANG="*name*"	
		SELECTED	
		STYLE="*text*"	
		TITLE="*text*"	
		VALUE="*text*"	
<P> . . . </P>	Paragraph	ALIGN=(LEFT | CENTER | RIGHT | JUSTIFY)	
		CLASS="*text*"	
		DIR=(LTR | RTL)	
		ID="*name*"	
		LANG="*name*"	
		STYLE="*text*"	
		TITLE="*text*"	
<PARAM>	Object Parameters	CLASS="*text*"	
		DIR=(LTR | RTL)	
		ID="*name*"	

(continued)

Table C.1 The HTML 4.0 tag table *(continued)*.

Tag	Tag Name	Attributes	Note
		LANG="*name*"	
		NAME="*text*"	
		STYLE="*text*"	
		TITLE="*text*"	
		TYPE=*type*	
		VALUE=(*number* | *text*)	
		VALUETYPE=(DATA | REF | OBJECT)	
<PRE> . . . </PRE>	Preformatted Text	CLASS="*text*"	
		DIR=(LTR | RTL)	
		ID="*name*"	
		LANG="*name*"	
		STYLE="*text*"	
		TITLE="*text*"	
		WIDTH=*number*	
<Q> . . . </Q>	Quotation Markup	CITE="*text*"	
		CLASS="*text*"	
		DIR=(LTR | RTL)	
		ID="*name*"	
		LANG="*name*"	
		STYLE="*text*"	
		TITLE="*text*"	
<S> . . . </S>	Strike Through	CLASS="*text*"	Deprecated

(continued)

Table C.1 The HTML 4.0 tag table *(continued).*

Tag	Tag Name	Attributes	Note
		DIR=(LTR | RTL)	
		ID="*name*"	
		LANG="*name*"	
		STYLE="*text*"	
		TITLE="*text*"	
<SAMP> . . . </SAMP>	Sample Output	CLASS="*text*"	
		DIR=(LTR | RTL)	
		ID="*name*"	
		LANG="*name*"	
		STYLE="*text*"	
		TITLE="*text*"	
<SCRIPT> . . . </SCRIPT>	Inline Script	CLASS="*text*"	
		DIR=(LTR | RTL)	
		ID="*name*"	
		LANG="*name*"	
		LANGUAGE="*scripting language*"	
		SRC="*URL*"	
		STYLE="*text*"	
		TITLE="*text*"	
		TYPE="*scripting language*"	
<SELECT> . . . </SELECT>	Select Input Object	DISABLED	

(continued)

Table C.1 The HTML 4.0 tag table *(continued)*.

Tag	Tag Name	Attributes	Note
		MULTIPLE	
		NAME="*text*"	
		SIZE=*number*	
		TABINDEX=*number*	
<SMALL> . . . </SMALL>	Small Text	CLASS="*text*"	
		DIR=(LTR I RTL)	
		ID="*name*"	
		LANG="*name*"	
		STYLE="*text*"	
		TITLE="*text*"	
<SPAN> . . . </SPAN>	Localized Style Formatting	ALIGN=(LEFT I CENTER I RIGHT I JUSTIFY)	
		STYLE="*text*"	
<STRIKE> . . . </STRIKE>	Strike Through	CLASS="*text*"	Deprecated
		DIR=(LTR I RTL)	
		ID="*name*"	
		LANG="*name*"	
		STYLE="*text*"	
		TITLE="*text*"	
<STRONG> . . . </STRONG>	Strong Emphasis	CLASS="*text*"	
		DIR=(LTR I RTL)	
		ID="*name*"	

(continued)

Table C.1 The HTML 4.0 tag table *(continued)*.

Tag	Tag Name	Attributes	Note
		LANG="*name*"	
		STYLE="*text*"	
		TITLE="*text*"	
<STYLE> . . . </STYLE>	Style Information	MEDIA= (SCREEN | PRINT | PROJECTION | BRAILLE | SPEECH | ALL)	
		TYPE="*text*"	
_{. . .}	Subscript	CLASS="*text*"	
		DIR=(LTR | RTL)	
		ID="*name*"	
		LANG="*name*"	
		STYLE="*text*"	
		TITLE="*text*"	
^{. . .}	Superscript	CLASS="*text*"	
		DIR=(LTR | RTL)	
		ID="*name*"	
		LANG="*name*"	
		STYLE="*text*"	
		TITLE="*text*"	
<TABLE> . . . </TABLE>	Table	ALIGN=(LEFT | RIGHT | CENTER)	
		BGCOLOR="*color*"	
		BORDER=*number*	

(continued)

Table C.1 The HTML 4.0 tag table *(continued)*.

Tag	Tag Name	Attributes	Note
		CELLPADDING=*number*	
		CELLSPACING=*number*	
		CLASS="*text*"	
		COLS=*number*	
		DIR=(LTR | RTL)	
		FRAME=(VOID | ABOVE | BELOW | HSIDES | LHS | RHS | VSIDES | BOX | BORDER)	
		ID="*name*"	
		LANG="*name*"	
		RULES=(NONE | GROUPS | ROWS | COLS | ALL)	
		STYLE="*text*"	
		TITLE="*text*"	
		WIDTH=(*pixels* | %)	
<TBODY> . . . </TBODY>	Table Body	CLASS="*text*"	
		DIR=(LTR | RTL)	
		ID="*name*"	
		LANG="*name*"	
		STYLE="*text*"	
		TITLE="*text*"	
<TD> . . . </TD>	Table Cell	ALIGN=(LEFT | RIGHT | CENTER | JUSTIFY | CHAR)	
		AXES="*text*"	

(continued)

Table C.1 The HTML 4.0 tag table *(continued).*

Tag	Tag Name	Attributes	Note
		AXIS="*text*"	
		BGCOLOR="*color*"	
		CHAR="*text*"	
		CHAROFF=*number*	
		CLASS="*text*"	
		COLSPAN=*number*	
		DIR=(LTR | RTL)	
		ID="*name*"	
		LANG="*name*"	
		NOWRAP	
		ROWSPAN=*number*	
		STYLE="*text*"	
		TITLE="*text*"	
		VALIGN=(TOP | MIDDLE | BOTTOM | BASELINE)	
<TEXTAREA> . . . </TEXTAREA>	Text Input Area	CLASS="*text*"	
		COLS=*number*	
		DIR=(LTR | RTL)	
		DISABLED	
		ID="*name*"	
		LANG="*name*"	
		NAME="*text*"	

(continued)

Table C.1 The HTML 4.0 tag table *(continued).*

Tag	Tag Name	Attributes	Note
		READONLY	
		ROWS=*number*	
		STYLE="*text*"	
		TABINDEX=*number*	
		TITLE="*text*"	
<TFOOT> . . . </TFOOT>	Table Footer	CLASS="*text*"	
		DIR=(LTR | RTL)	
		ID="*name*"	
		LANG="*name*"	
		STYLE="*text*"	
		TITLE="*text*"	
<TH> . . . </TH>	Table Header	ALIGN=(LEFT | RIGHT | CENTER | JUSTIFY | CHAR)	
		AXES="*text*"	
		AXIS="*text*"	
		BGCOLOR="*color*"	
		CHAR="*text*"	
		CHAROFF=*number*	
		CLASS="*text*"	
		COLSPAN=*number*	
		DIR=(LTR | RTL)	
		ID="*name*"	

(continued)

Table C.1 The HTML 4.0 tag table *(continued).*

Tag	Tag Name	Attributes	Note
		LANG="*name*"	
		NOWRAP	
		ROWSPAN=*number*	
		STYLE="*text*"	
		TITLE="*text*"	
		VALIGN=(TOP | MIDDLE | BOTTOM | BASELINE)	
<THEAD> . . . </THEAD>	Table Header	CLASS="*text*"	
		DIR=(LTR | RTL)	
		ID="*name*"	
		LANG="*name*"	
		STYLE="*text*"	
		TITLE="*text*"	
<TITLE> . . . </TITLE>	Document Title	None	
<TR> . . . </TR>	Table Row	ALIGN=(LEFT | RIGHT | CENTER | JUSTIFY | CHAR)	
		BGCOLOR=*color*	
		CHAR="*text*"	
		CHAROFF=*number*	
		CLASS="*text*"	
		DIR=(LTR | RTL)	
		ID="*name*"	
		LANG="*name*"	

(continued)

Table C.1 The HTML 4.0 tag table *(continued)*.

Tag	Tag Name	Attributes	Note
		STYLE="*text*"	
		TITLE="*text*"	
		VALIGN=(TOP | MIDDLE | BOTTOM | BASELINE)	
<TT> . . . </TT>	Teletype Text	CLASS="*text*"	
		DIR=(LTR | RTL)	
		ID="*name*"	
		LANG="*name*"	
		STYLE="*text*"	
		TITLE="*text*"	
<U> . . . </U>	Underlined Text	CLASS="*text*"	Deprecated
		DIR=(LTR | RTL)	
		ID="*name*"	
		LANG="*name*"	
		STYLE="*text*"	
		TITLE="*text*"	
<UL> . . . </UL>	Unordered List	CLASS="*text*"	
		COMPACT	
		DIR=(LTR | RTL)	
		ID="*name*"	
		LANG="*name*"	
		STYLE="*text*"	

(continued)

Table C.1 The HTML 4.0 tag table *(continued).*

Tag	Tag Name	Attributes	Note
		TITLE="*text*"	
		TYPE=(DISC | SQUARE | CIRCLE)	
<VAR> . . . </VAR>	Variable Text	CLASS="*text*"	
		DIR=(LTR | RTL)	
		ID="*name*"	
		LANG="*name*"	
		STYLE="*text*"	
		TITLE="*text*"	

Appendix D

HTML And Related Specifications

Notes...

Appendix D

The heart of any Web-based technology is its specification. In theory, a specification describes how the technology works and its implementation specifics. The idea is that all the vendors and users working with a technology will use the same specification and cross-platform, cross-operating system, and cross-browser integration will be achieved. However, there is no rule that says there can only be one specification governing any technology. True, there can only be one "official" specification, but that doesn't stop vendors such as Microsoft and Netscape from creating their own specifications that outline their proprietary means to technology ends.

Throughout the book we've tossed Web resources galore at you and we know it can sometimes be difficult to sift through the barrage of information to get to the nitty-gritty and the important stuff. This appendix is dedicated to the core HTML, DHTML, and scripting resources—the specifications that govern them. We wish we could point you to one official specification for each, but one quick look at this book's content shows that to be impossible. Instead, we'll point you to the specification for HTML, DHTML, and scripting from the "big three"—the World Wide Web Consortium, Microsoft, and Netscape. Although we're sure the Web addresses of these heavy hitters are engraved in your brain by now, we thought we'd save you some search time and take you right to where you need to be. These specifications are bound to change on a regular basis, so we suggest you visit them every few weeks to see what new developments are afoot.

HTML Specifications

- Official (W3C) HTML 3.2 Reference Specification—**www.w3.org/TR/REC-html32.html**
- Official (W3C) HTML 4.0 Reference Proposed Recommendation—**www.w3.org/TR/PR-html40/**
- Microsoft's Internet Explorer DTD—**www.microsoft.com/workshop/author/newhtml/default.htm**
- Netscape's HTML Tag Reference—**developer.netscape.com/library/documentation/htmlguid/index.htm**

Dynamic HTML Specifications

- W3C's Document Object Model Specification—**www.w3.org/TR/WD-DOM**
- Microsoft's Dynamic HTML Reference—**www.microsoft.com/msdn/sdk/inetsdk/help/dhtml/references/dhtmlrefs.htm**
- Netscape's Dynamic HTML in Communicator Reference—**developer.netscape.com/library/documentation/communicator/dynhtml/index.htm**

Scripting Specifications

- Microsoft's Online VBScript Reference—**www.microsoft.com/vbscript/us/vbslang/vbstoc.htm**
- Microsoft's Online JScript Reference—**www.microsoft.com/JScript/us/Jslang/Jstoc.htm**
- ECMA 262 JavaScript Language Specification (in PDF format)—**developer. netscape.com/library/javascript/e262-pdf.pdf**
- Netscape's JavaScript Reference—**developer.netscape.com/library/documentation/communicator/jsref/index.htm**

Index

C

D

E

F

G

H

I

J

K

L

M

N

O

P

Q

R

S

T

U

V

Z

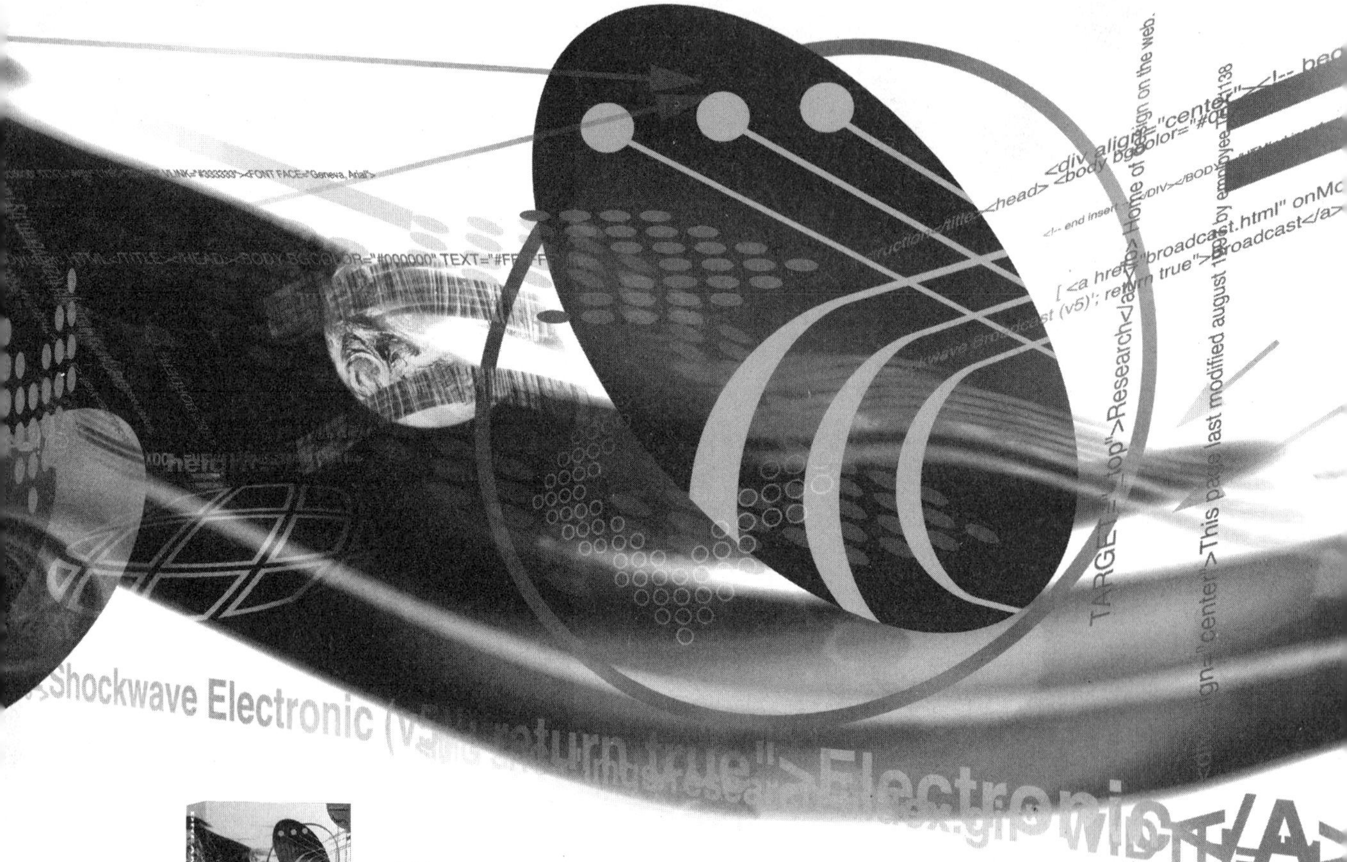